The Mythology of
Christianity

David Vaticus

Table of Contents

Preface – Why I am Writing This Book

I grew up fully indoctrinated in the Roman Catholic Church. I studied elementary Latin starting in the 2nd grade; and I was an altar boy throughout my grade school years. Like most people, I became what my parents were, and I believed what they believed – much as a child believes in Santa Claus and the Easter Bunny – because I was told what to believe and I wanted to do so. But over time, I could no longer accept what I had been taught by people who themselves had been deceived. Why? Like most people who undergo a change in their views, there were multiple influences that convinced me…. These forces can be conveniently categorized as logic, history, and science.

Logic – Our ability to think for ourselves. I have always strived to understand and corroborate information for myself, and to question and doubt what I have been told, observing human nature. I never accepted that a Catholic pope spoke with infallibility (on matters of faith and morals, or anything else), nor did I accept that this mortal man spoke directly to a divine God on behalf of all people. I asked as a child, why are most Irish Catholic? (Note: that has changed dramatically over the past 60 years). And why are most Indians Hindu (except the ones in the Islamic region)? Because people inherit their religion. Because of indoctrination over time… because of fear of dishonoring one's parents, or fear of being different, or because of inertia (it is just easier to go with the flow), etc.

But I did not go with the flow. I asked in a Catholic parochial school, why? Example: we were told that a mortal sin condemns one's soul to Hell, and the priest told us that if we knew it was Friday and we ate meat on Friday anyway (thus, it was done with deliberate intent), it was a mortal sin.[1] Wow! Condemned to Hell forever for that? If we failed to receive the sacrament of Holy Communion during the Easter season, it was a mortal sin! If we knowingly failed to fast before taking communion, it was a mortal sin.[2] Forty years later, there were few meatless Fridays, and not much fasting before communion (the fasting rules had changed from midnight the night before to 3 hours prior, then to one hour prior). All those souls condemned to Hell for eternity would not be condemned today![3] That was highly concerning!

Prior to the age of six, I eagerly accepted the belief in Santa Claus because I saw no reason not to, and because it was a pleasant belief. It gave me hope to feel that a benevolent being I didn't really know was watching me and would bring me presents. And it wasn't as if there were serious consequences when I was 'bad'. I always got presents, and so I assumed Santa was forgiving. Later, at the age of five, I began attending a parochial elementary school. Like most children, I asked how Santa got all over the world in one night. How did Santa obtain access to a locked house with no chimney? I was told to have faith in Santa; he does magical things! It defied logic, but at that age, I just wasn't sure. And adults, in their zeal to support this universal deception, provided different explanations and attributed god-like powers to Santa. But I still had my doubts. The story was not holding up even to the logic of a child. But there was a lot of pressure on me to believe because my siblings were younger.

My parents would become angry when I questioned the theology of Santa. I had to watch movies that spoke well of Santa (e.g., Miracle on 34th Street). They encouraged me to stay up and watch the late-night news on Christmas Eve, when the weatherman showed Santa's sleigh itinerary. All adults assured me that Santa was real, and my doubts were false. So even as my faith in Santa waned, I was afraid not to believe somewhat because everyone else said that they believed, and I didn't want to be the difficult child. And so, I half-believed.

Then one day, a week after I had just turned 7, an older girl down the street declared that there was no Santa. She basically said that there was a grand conspiracy among parents to create the illusion of Santa. I was crushed! I asked my parents. Had they declared emphatically that the girl had been wrong, I would have accepted that (for a while), as I really wanted her to be wrong; after all, I loved the concept of the benevolent gift-giver. But my parents acquiesced and said there was no Santa, and that I had to keep it to myself; it wasn't fair to my siblings to disavow their belief system (or so I was told).

Looking back on it, I can now see the clear parallel of Santa to Christianity. At times, the theology can seem almost a big conspiracy of delusion where doubters are ostracized (they used to be tortured and then burned at the stake) and the support groups all rush to tell you that you are wrong to be doubtful.... Why everyone knows that there is one true god, and his name is Jesus. (Note: a billion Muslims and a billion Hindus do not agree; can two billion people be wrong?). News flash: truth is not determined by majority rule. Look at all the different religions today; each one convinced that they are right, and all the others are false.

> *"Science is slowly whittling away at religious beliefs; but it's historians who gravely wound organized religion"*
> *– Anonymous*

History – What might be harder to evade is the historian. Of all the civilizations that existed in the first century CE, the one that documented everything was the Roman Empire. And as history continues to reveal time and again, it is unlikely that many of the events written in the New Testament could have occurred, as a matter of recorded history. I refer to various false narratives, for example, that the writers of the gospels used as a backstory to their tales. This occurred when the Gospel of Matthew declared that Herod had issued a decree to kill newborn babes, or the Gospel of Luke pretended that everyone in the Roman empire had to return to their home of birth for a census, or even that Jesus of Nazareth carried an entire cross shaped as a small 't'.

Based on my many discussions with both Catholic and Protestant clergy, it is my opinion that Christian clerics are either ignorant (don't know their own religious history) or simply feel comfortable not sharing some information with their constituents about the past, or at least ignoring it. Honestly, it is probably a combination of the two. And this isn't limited to Christianity, but Christianity is what I am most familiar with. Unlike many Christians, I have actually read most of the Old Testament and all of the New Testament, and more than once. I have taken Christian theology courses. And I am an amateur historian (by way of two college degrees). So here are some facts that I found to be illuminating:

- It is most likely that Jesus of Nazareth was born in Nazareth, not Bethlehem. Some of the story of his birth was contrived because it had been foretold in the Hebrew scriptures that the Jewish Messiah would be born in Bethlehem.
- Prior to the Internet, most Christians were taught that the gospels were written by the original apostles: Matthew, Mark, Luke and John. Some said that they referred to "evangelists" who were early Christian leaders. In any case, these "gospels" were written by unknown authors between 70 and 150 ACE, but not by the eye-witnessing apostles, or even by their immediate successors. And by the way, Mark and Luke were not among the twelve apostles! The truth is, <u>no one who ever met Jesus left us a written document</u>, and <u>no one who wrote about Jesus ever met him</u>. Sort of like me writing an account of General Custer's Last Stand 150 years after the event. Without reading or hearing eyewitness accounts, do you think my account of the Battle of the Little Bighorn would be remotely accurate? The truth is, the gospels were written by unknown authors with unknown motivations, and then they were copied, translated, re-copied by hand multiple times, and sometimes changed. But have you ever heard a Catholic priest or a Protestant minister recite the gospel in church? He generally starts with, "The gospel according to (fill in name). But it simply isn't true.
- The New Testament at least presents a generally joyous story... about a loving God. But the Old Testament is rife with the ranting of a vengeful God who is to be feared. The vengeful God, Yahweh, had people killed, raped and murdered... yes, if you actually read the Old Testament, it condones murder, rape and slavery; and it condemns homosexuality (which the New Testament does not). Indeed, isn't it interesting that the Ten Commandants left out such obvious sins as rape, molestation, enslavement, and torture. Why? Because it was written by zealous Hebrew 'holy men' (exact identities unknown) from the 7th to 2nd century BCE who merely wrote down the stories that had been handed down from person-to-person to them; and slavery, molestation and torture was just fine for slaves; you just couldn't kill someone's slave, or steal one away from his master – without paying financial compensation.
- In the early 4th century, the Roman Emperor, Constantine, was engaged in a civil war. He needed to expand his army. Early Christians refused to participate in warfare, but the sun-worshipping Emperor Constantine said he dreamed of a spear with cross bars; and it became his symbol. It was the conjoined first two Greek letters in 'Christos', Rho (P) and Chi (X). So, the Christians agreed to bear arms and support Constantine. After the death of Constantine, the Christians decided that the cross-like symbol (called the Labarum Cross) was meant to resemble the cross upon which Jesus of Nazareth died. Even today, we think of the Christian cross as modeled on the cross used for Roman crucifixion; but archaeologists have shown that the Romans, who crucified in mass numbers, primarily used a capital 'T', not a little 't'. Even common sense suggests that the T is easier to construct and use. But as we moved into the Dark Ages (450 to 1492 CE), most people were illiterate and thus unfamiliar with their history; and in their zeal, they chose the 't' as their symbol, or more likely, the Catholic Church chose the 't' for them.
- Some of the early Christians (circa 50 - 300 CE) believed that Jesus of Nazareth was divine; most did not. Emperor Constantine wanted societal stability. He called forth the Christian Council of Nicea in 325 AD. They voted. The side that believed Jesus to

be divine won out; the others were called heretics. And Constantine enforced the decision because he wanted unity in his empire. Although Constantine was a pagan, he was not baptized a Christian until he was dying (and there is no evidence that this baptism actually occurred). Constantine realized that he could control his empire through religion. Indeed, many rulers throughout history have realized that fact and used it to their advantage.

- Catholicism would evolve into a worldly focus with its beautiful, ornate buildings and its riches. But is that what Jesus of Nazareth was about? Look how the Vatican has become a monument to powerful religious men. Unfortunately, many of the popes were very evil men. Their immoral exploits have been well documented, as well as their temporal ownership of the Papal States in Italy, which lasted for well over 1,000 years. Not all Catholics realize that the Pope was the virtual emperor of the Papal States from 754 until 1870, when the Italians finally deposed Pope Pius IX – by force. That wasn't really that long ago.

Science – The dialogue between science and religion is complex and multifaceted. Science provides a framework for understanding the natural world through evidence and observation. Christianity has been jousting with science for two thousand years; and little by little, science is overwhelming the archaic beliefs put forth by some Christians. For example, it took nearly 200 years for the Catholic Church to surrender its stubborn position that the sun revolved around the Earth. Later, after 100+ years of railing against evolution, most Christian sects (not all) today accept the validity of that concept. But every so often, Christian apologists trot out various constructs to obfuscate their true positions, saying that evolution was part of the Intelligent Design or that Adam and Eve could have been just two hominids on the evolutionary path. When dealing with non-fact-based wishes, devoid of any supporting evidence, Christian apologists love to dodge.

The Age of Enlightenment and the Modern Era were especially hard on Judeo-Christianity. A few centuries after they came to grips with the world not being flat and the Earth revolving around the sun, Darwinism disproved Adam and Eve and their state of perfection. Before the Christian apologists could catch their collective breaths, archaeology suggested that there was no great flood, no enslavement in Egypt, no walls of Jericho knocked down, and the age of the Earth was 4.5 billion years, not 4.5 thousand years.

Science certainly refutes the existence of divine deities and all the mysteries attributed to them; but science cannot disprove deities, as no one can disprove a negative. Religious beliefs remain based on faith, not evidence.

****

Most of us are certainly aware that religion brings solace and comfort, especially to those who have had major challenges and difficulties in their lives. We believe in our religion because we want to believe in an afterlife (even though there is no evidence that there is an afterlife). It is tough to accept that this is all there is, and our time on this Earth is ephemeral. So, some people cling desperately to their religion because they can accept their status in this life only in the hope of a better situation in the next one. Unfortunately, adherence to organized religion might be a terrible price to pay for solace and comfort. Thus, organized religion fires up the overzealous among us, and it justifies excess (just look at the Catholic / Protestant inquisitions and witch hunts). Organized religions have been known to keep mankind in bondage to superstition and fantasy. The hallmark of organized religion has been its arrogant surety about God and the afterlife – and yet there is no proof, or even a slight indication that they could be right. In many ways, organized religion has been used as a tool to control humanity.

Believers may be wasting much of their finite resources (time, energy, and money) on organized religions, worshipping non-existent deities, and supporting their clergies. If those resources instead were harnessed to solving the world's problems, the condition of our planet and that of all the people and animals that dwell on it would greatly improve.

We humans do not have all the answers. Unfortunately, organized religion motivates humans to think that they <u>do</u> have all the answers, through faith in their God (of course, people don't agree on which god). But the foundation of faith is not using one's intellect, but rather, it is accepting the tenets of beliefs handed down by one's ancestors, just as a child is imbued with belief in Santa Claus, which he willingly accepts. Faith is not using the intellect we were born with. Faith is what you have when you lack facts and certainty.

Many of us tire of organized religion's preoccupation with inconsistent beliefs, irrational guidance, and the absolute surety that they are right. The future of mankind is anchored in our ability to think critically for ourselves and to solve problems bereft of folklore and divine guidance, which is not coming. The human race will move forward after we unshackle ourselves from the tyranny of organized religion.

****

In writing this book, it is not my intent to disparage anyone for his or her beliefs. I deeply support everyone's right to practice their religion as they see fit, as long as it doesn't infringe on the rights of others. What I am trying to do is to apply reason with logic, history, and science to the Judeo-Christian belief system. When I use the term, ignorance, or its derivative, ignorant, I am referring to simply a lack of knowledge, unfamiliarity, or lack of awareness. The 'willfully ignorant' are those who should know better due to their modern education, but who choose to either remain unaware or who want others to believe they are. Finally, by "superstitious" I am referring irrational beliefs and views with are inconsistent with the known science of our modern age.

****

Throughout this book, I have tried to reference verses of the Old and New Testaments in order to highlight concerns. These biblical verses come from the King James version of the Bible, which I had received as a wedding present many years ago, and which I actually read.

Finally, while I do provide some limited global information on religion, it is important to state upfront that my focus is on Judeo-Christianity and especially its effects on the people and their institutions in the United States of America.

[1] Until 1966, Roman Catholics could not eat meat on Fridays. Then they could. Later, in 1983 the RCC reconstructed prohibition of meat on Fridays, but only for Fridays that occur during the Lent period (from Ash Wednesday to Easter).

[2] Prior to March 19, 1957 the Eucharist fast began at midnight. Pope Pius XII changed the Church law to 3 hours of fasting in 1957; and Pope Paul VI changed it to 1 hour on Nov 21, 1964.

[3] It should be noted that not all Catholic clergy believe that violating a Church law, intentional or not, is a mortal sin. But as a child, I was taught by a priest who said it was a mortal sin.

Chapter 1 – Lack of Evidence for a Divinely Made Universe

"Blind faith is an ironic gift to return to the creator of human intelligence!"
– Anonymous

Creationism, Watchmaker Analogy, and Intelligent Design

In 1650, Archbishop James Ussher, the "primate" of the Church of Ireland, finished his painstaking study of the Old Testament and concluded that the world had been created in October 4004 BCE. After his chronology was appended to a new edition of the King James Bible, his calculations went unquestioned for generations.[4] But in 1811, 12-year-old Mary Anning discovered a fossilized skeleton of a 17-foot ichthyosaurus (a crocodile-like creature which lived more than 112 million years ago) on a limestone cliff in Dorset, England. The finding of a previously unknown, apparently extinct sea reptile made headlines worldwide;[5] and it shocked the conservative Christian society to whom the notion of animal extinction was a blasphemy. "Why would an all-perfect, all-powerful God have blotted out some of his creations?"[5] Why indeed!

Soon thereafter, other skeletal remains were discovered around the world. The discoveries in the 19th century of animal skeletons from the Jurassic and Cretaceous periods challenged long-held theological assumptions about nature and humankind's place in it. Evidence had been accruing for years that the Earth was far older than proponents of the Old Testament believed. In the late 18th century, James Hutton, a Scottish farmer and naturalist known as the founder of modern geology, espoused the view that Earth's landscapes, like mountains and oceans, formed over a long period of time through gradual processes.[6] The much greater age of the Earth was one of the first revolutionary concepts to emerge from the new science of geology.

By 1842, Charles Darwin (1809 – 1882), a British naturalist and biologist, had outlined his theory of natural selection, which holds that species better adapted to their environment are more likely to survive and pass beneficial characteristics on to their descendants. Then, after an acquaintance, British naturalist Alfred Russel Wallace, independently reached the same conclusion,[7] Darwin was then encouraged to publish On the Origin of Species in 1859 regarding the theory of evolution.[8] [9]

Sir Isaac Newton (1642 – 1726)[10], an English physicist and astronomer, Rene Descartes (1596 – 1650)[11], a French scientist and mathematician, and other leaders of the Enlightenment Age upheld the view "that the physical laws that had been discovered revealed the mechanical perfection of the workings of the universe to be akin to a watch, wherein the watchmaker is God."[12] [13] This is a teleological argument[14] which postulates that the appearance of a design and complexity in nature implies a designer; and an intelligent design implies an intelligent designer, which, prior to the mid-19th century, was accepted to be a creator deity. This argument played a central role in natural theology, supporting arguments for the existence of God. Newton stated that "like a watchmaker, [he believed] God was forced to intervene in the universe and tinker with the mechanism from time to time to ensure that it continued operating in good working order."[15] However, in the mid-18th century, evolution would explain that complexity can be derived from simplicity.

The concept of a deity watchmaker seemed a plausible argument at the time, although not everyone eagerly accepted it. For example, Voltaire (1694-1778), the pen name of François-Marie Arouet, argued that the teleological argument advanced by Newton could indicate the existence of a powerful, but not necessarily all-powerful or all-knowing intelligence. The Scottish philosopher and historian, David Hume (1711-1776), criticized the idea of God as a designer. He stated that the world was: "... only the first rude essay of some infant deity, who afterward abandoned it, ashamed of his performance."[16]

Still, the concept continued to gain traction, and William Paley[17] (1743 – 1805) presented his view of the watchmaker analogy in his book, Natural Theology, in 1802.[18] William Paley popularized the idea that the same complexity and utility evident in the design and functioning of a watch can also be discerned in the natural world.[19]

Half a century later, in 1859, Charles Darwin published his manuscript regarding natural selection. This book was based on his studies of various animals he had encountered on his travels throughout the world, including the Galapagos Islands. He posited the theory that all living creatures that exist today, including human beings, had evolved over a period of millions of years from primitive life forms, through a process of minute changes over time which he referred to as natural selection.

William Paley was not the first to compare God to a watchmaker, but he did so in a very logical, nuanced way.[20] The watchmaker analogy has had several generations of supporters and critics. Michael Behe (b. 1952), was an American biochemist and an advocate of the pseudoscientific intelligent design, and he helped launch the modern intelligent design movement.[21] With his 1996 book, Darwin's Black Box, he embraced Paley's watchmaker, while contending that the argument for design was scientific, not religious. Richard Dawkins (b. 1941), a British Evolutionary Biologist, satirized the analogy for the title of his 1986 book, The Blind Watchmaker, which attacked the Fundamentalist view that complex life needed a religious explanation."[22]

The intelligent design movement is a neo-creationist religious campaign to promote and support the pseudo-scientific idea of intelligent design. It appears to be based on a "fundamental misunderstanding of natural selection."[23] It is just the latest incarnation of creationism; and it advocates the belief that a supernatural being was involved in the evolution of life on Earth. More insidious than creationism, the view of Intelligent design is that it is possible to infer from empirical evidence that "certain features of the universe and of living things are best explained by an intelligent cause, not an undirected process such as natural selection."[24] Supporters of intelligent design often confuse the complexity of the universe with its design.

The proponents of intelligent design espouse the notion that society has endured negative cultural consequences from adopting materialism; that science is the cause of this decay because it seeks only natural explanations; and that it doesn't include the intervention of a divine deity. Those that promote intelligence design believe that evolution implies "that humans have no spiritual nature, no moral purpose, and no intrinsic meaning"; and they seek "a science in consonant with Christian and theistic convictions."[25] The National Academy of Sciences issued a policy statement saying, "Creationism, intelligent design, and other claims of supernatural intervention in the origin of life or of species are <u>not</u> science, because they are not testable by the methods of science.[26]

In the 1960s, US creationists reignited their dispute over the concepts of evolution and natural selection. This resulted in renewed interest in the watchmaker argument, and it sparked renewed efforts to teach creationism in public schools. Since 1987, the U S Supreme Court has ruled that teaching creationism in American public schools was unconstitutional. However, opponents of evolution began re-challenging science education using their concept of "intelligent design", which had been carefully stripped of all religious references. Unlike traditional Judeo-Christian-based creationism, which claims that God created the Earth in six days, proponents of intelligent design say the workings of this planet are too complex to be ascribed to evolution, and there must have been a deity directing the overall plan.[27] What is humorous to many Humanists is that the intelligent design argument tries to account for the complexity of our universe by adding more complexity, which is a god!

Richard Dawkins has argued that a watchmaker's creation of the watch implies that the watchmaker must be more complex than the watch. Since the concept of design is top-down, someone or something more complex must be designing something less complex. Following this line of thought demands that the watch was designed by a more complex watchmaker, and the watchmaker must have been created by a more complex being than himself. So, who designed the designer? Dawkins argues that (a) this line of reasoning continues ad infinitum, and (b) it does not explain anything. On the other hand, evolution takes a bottom-up approach;[28] and it explains how more complexity can arise gradually by building on or combining lesser complexities.

In October 2004, the Textbook Review Committee of the Dover Area School District (PA) recommended a new commercial text to replace the outdated biology book. When discussed at the Dover school board meeting, the chairperson of the board's curriculum committee complained that the proposed replacement book was "laced with Darwinism" and he wanted a more suitable textbook that would include biblical theories of creation. When asked whether this might offend those of other faiths, the chairperson replied, "This country wasn't founded on Muslim beliefs or evolution. This country was founded on Christianity, and our students should be taught as such." A week later, the same committee chairperson reportedly pleaded: "Two thousand years ago, someone died on a cross. Can't someone take a stand for him?" And he added: "Nowhere in the Constitution does it call for a separation of church and state."[29]

In 2005, eleven parents of students in Dover, PA, sued their School District regarding "intelligent design" in the public school system. Coincidentally, this occurred exactly eighty years after the Scopes "monkey trial" in Dayton, Tennessee. In December 2005, the judge's ruling concluded that "intelligent design is not science," and permanently barred the School Board from requiring teachers to disparage the scientific theory of evolution, and from requiring Intelligent Design to be taught as an alternative theory.[30]

It would seem that the Committee chairperson cited above might need to return to school himself and learn that the USA was not founded on Christianity (see Chapter 8). Moreover, the concept of the "separation of church and state" is enshrined in the very first freedom guaranteed by the First Amendment: "Congress shall make no law respecting an establishment of religion."[31] This incident is just a recent incarnation of yet more biblical creationism, which is considered an argument from ignorance.[32] It is yet another attempt to sneak religion, cloaked in the guise of science, into the public schools.

In 2005, the Kansas Board of Education approved new public-school science standards written to cast doubt on the theory of evolution. It ruled that science classes in public schools should include the teaching of intelligent design. The Board also revised the definition of science to remove its previous limitation to the search for natural explanations of phenomena.[33] A Kansas Board of Education member declared at the beginning of the hearings, "Evolution has been proven false *[it has not]*. Intelligent design is science-based and strong in facts. *[It is not]*." At their conclusion, she proclaimed that evolution is "an unproven, often disproven" theory *[totally untrue]*.[34] Any victory of those advocating intelligent design was short-lived. In 2007, Kansas reversed its decision, and on February 13, 2007, the Kansas Board of Education voted to reject the amended science standards enacted two years earlier. The definition of science was once again returned to "the search for natural explanations for what is observed in the universe."[35]

"Intelligent design" creationism is not supported by scientific evidence or by the scientific community. In addition, the pressure to downplay evolution or to emphasize non-scientific alternatives in public schools seriously compromises science education. Per a statement made in 2008 by the Central Conference of American Rabbis, regarding creationism in school textbooks: "... These students' lack of knowledge about evolution will seriously undermine their understanding of the world and the natural laws governing it..."[36]

Evolution

Having reviewed the creationist / intelligent design view, let's now focus on what the theory of evolution is, and what it means. In biology, evolution is the change in the characteristics of a species over many generations and relies primarily on the process of natural selection. It is based on the idea that all species are related and gradually change over time. There is tremendous genetic diversity within almost all species, including humans.[37] Evolution relies on there being enough genetic variation in a population, which affects the observable physical characteristics (referred to as its phenotype) of an organism.[38] Variation simply refers to differences in genetic makeup among the individuals in a species, and generally, several types of variation will be present. It is key that this is present as it enables hereditary changes to happen, especially beneficial ones. Without some version of a species possessing something in a particular realm, it is hard to pass on a major evolutionary change. Darwin proposed natural selection primarily to account for the adaptive organization of living beings; natural selection promotes or maintains adaptation.[39]

It is important here to acknowledge that religious people support a wide spectrum of beliefs. While some conservative, Fundamentalist Christians tend to believe in some form of creationism, many do not. Moreover, among Christians, there are many who accept evolutionary science while maintaining many of their own interpretations of biblical Scripture. And the number of Christians who accept evolution continues to grow.

Now, let's address the word, *theory*. Evolution is a "scientific theory" that refers to a comprehensive explanation of some aspect of nature and is accompanied by vast evidence.[40] In science, an observed phenomenon is elevated to the status of a general theory only after exhaustive study of objective data and extensive testing of the idea. On the other hand, evolution is also a "scientific fact" which refers to an observation, measurement, or other form of evidence that is expected to recur in the same way under similar circumstances.[41]

Scientists also use the term "fact" to refer to a scientific explanation that has been tested and confirmed so many times that there is no longer a compelling reason to keep testing it or looking for additional examples.[42] In that respect, the past and continuing occurrence of evolution remain a scientific fact. For readers who are wondering, theories cannot become laws because each serves a different purpose. Laws are generalizations that describe phenomena, whereas theories explain phenomena.[43]

One of the most useful properties of scientific theories is that they can be used to make predictions about natural events or phenomena that have not yet been observed. As one example, the evolutionary biologists who discovered a Tiktaalik fossil[44] had predicted that they would find fossils that were intermediate between fish and limbed terrestrial animals in sediments that were about 375 million years old.[45] Their follow-up discovery confirmed the prediction made on the basis of evolutionary theory.

Evolution by natural selection is the process by which traits that enhance survival and reproduction become more common in successive generations of a population. It embodies three principles:[46]

- *Phenotypic Variation* – such that variation exists within populations of organisms with respect to morphology, physiology, and behavior
- *Differential Fitness* – whereby different traits confer different rates of survival and reproduction
- *Heritability of Fitness* – thus, consequently, these traits can be passed from generation to generation

According to famed biologist, Richard Dawkins, the theory of evolution presents a solid argument against the belief that there is an all-knowing, all-powerful supernatural deity who created the universe and deals directly with the personal lives of humans.[47] In his book, The God Delusion, Dawkins argues that life was the result of complex biological processes, and what some creationists don't understand is that evolution proceeds via very tiny increments, with each step forward taken with perfectly reasonable probability.[48] The process happens constantly, just incredibly slowly for complex organisms, and somewhat faster for less complex ones. Thus, evolution occurs over many, many generations through minute, incremental changes within species populations.

Every individual has multiple small mutations. Some are beneficial, some are not; many don't matter. But over time, these mutations advance natural selection. Scientists' analyses of DNA have enabled humanity to better understand the mechanics of how evolution occurs. Our DNA has so much in common with the "lower life forms." Indeed, we share almost 98% of our DNA with chimpanzees.[49] DNA has confirmed that all organisms are related to one another. And millions of organisms' fossils have been recovered, providing evidence of how life forms evolved over time.[50] The resistance to and non-acceptance of evolutionary biology is most often rooted in concerns that such views will undermine one's religious foundations. Thus, it is the religious belief system that has to adjust, not science.

Variation of genes is what enables natural selection and evolution. Indeed, evolution has even affected skin pigmentation. For example, melanin dictates skin color and the changes that happen to it. In particular, this is a response to the environment and especially the sun as one's body slowly begins to switch skin color to battle the sun's ultraviolet rays. In Africa, it was important for humans to have dark skin to protect against the UV rays, which caused skin cancer. But in Europe and parts of Asia, it was important for humans to develop lighter skin to let in some UV rays and produce vitamin D. Melanin also dictates hair thickness as well as our eye color!

We should also acknowledge that the currently evolved human body is about adaptation of many genetic compromises which interacted to promote survivability, not perfection. That is why many human features seem inefficient, from our poor eyesight (relative to the eagle), our poor hearing (relative to a bat's exceptional auditory system), to the narrow (relative to a human baby's head) human birth canal. Unlike other ape mammals, humans evolved bigger brains, which gave babies bigger heads; and it appears that our standing up and walking on two legs contributed to women's narrow birth canals. Indeed, evolution of the human birth canal appears to have been "characterized by complex trade-off dynamics among multiple biological, environmental, and sociocultural factors."[51] All living things on Earth share common ancestors, as all mammals share a high percentage of genes. Existing patterns of biodiversity have been shaped by repeated formations of new species (speciation), changes within species (anagenesis), and loss of species (extinction) throughout the evolutionary history of life on Earth.[52] What occurred was a gradual process where populations within a species gradually diverged over time, eventually becoming distinct enough to be considered a new species. This was just as true with humans and their ancestors. No animal gives birth to another species of animal. Thus, there wasn't a single, distinct "first" of any species. So, there was never a first man and a first woman. And, no, humans are not descended from monkeys, nor any other primate living today. We do share a common ancestor with chimpanzees – a primate which lived approximately 8 to 6 million years ago.[53]

Humans split from other primates 8-10 million years ago. Indeed, modern homo sapiens (humans) evolved through multiple hominin lineages, beginning with the original *Hominini,* the closest related ancestor we as humans have to today's apes.[54] This lineage continued with Ardipithecus (the first bipedal humans, when our ancestors first walked on two legs),[55] Australopithecus (who was the first to begin using stone tools to create things),[56] Homo habilis (thought to be an evolved set of the Australopithecus, also referred to as the earliest known version of the caveman)[57], Homo erectus (the first version of humans to use fire and to cook),[58] and the sixth and final ancestor to the modern human was *H. heidelbergensis.*[59] Finally, *Cro-Magnon / **Homo Sapiens*** (modern humans) arrived.

Cro-Magnon Man and Homo Sapiens are both classified as members of the same species, Homo sapiens; but they lived in generally different time periods. Cro-Magnons lived during the Upper Paleolithic period, approximately 45,000 to 10,000 years ago, while Homo Sapiens are the modern humans that exist today.[60] When Cro-Magnons arrived in Europe about 40,000 BCE, they encountered the Neanderthals, who turned out to be compatible for mating. Today, millions of people of European descent have some Neanderthal genes.

Our Natural World

The Big Bang Theory is scientists' leading view regarding how the universe began. This theory states that the universe started with an infinitely hot and dense, single point that inflated and stretched — first at unimaginable speeds, and then at a more measurable rate — over the next 13.7 billion years to the still-expanding cosmos that we know today.[61] By expanding rapidly, it led to the formation of galaxies, stars, and planets. The Earth was created when elements were made by helium stars, and clusters of matter from its nebula cloud grew large enough to maintain its own gravitational pull. Eventually, it took the shape our current terrestrial planet, remaining relatively small and rocky.[62]

Naturalism relates the scientific method to philosophy by affirming that all beings and events in the universe are natural. Consequently, all knowledge of the universe falls within the wheelhouse of scientific investigation.[63] As Professor Jerry Coyne said so succinctly, "Religion and science are simply not compatible."[64] It has been said that if you don't believe in ghosts, magic, or a celestial divinity, then you are probably a naturalist. You might be a person who is swayed by evidence-based, empirical concepts. Your belief in science as reliable and objective probably surpasses uncorroborated revelations, conspiratory beliefs, religious authorities, or holy texts. Critical thinking may be your special power. The natural world is what we can see and know exists. As naturalists, we recognize that we are fully committed participants in the natural order, and as such, we must play by nature's rules.

What makes the Earth habitable? Is it the right distance from the sun? Is it protected from harmful solar radiation by its magnetic field? Is it kept warm by an insulating atmosphere? And does it have the right chemical ingredients for life, including water and carbon? Out of all the planets, moons, asteroids, and comets in our solar system, only Earth has liquid water on the surface and is capable of supporting life, at least as far as we know. That's because our planet sits in the "habitable zone" of our solar system. It's far enough from the Sun so that all our water doesn't boil away, but close enough so that it doesn't freeze. That said, there are many planets well beyond our solar system that have similar attributes for life. We know that life on other planets is probable, and sentient life elsewhere is plausible.

Many people believe that the Earth is fine-tuned for animal and human life. But this is an epic misunderstanding. It may appear that all animal life forms were designed for the environment in which they thrive, but that is an illusion. Similar to water-filled puddles on a road surface, the amount and shape of the water in the puddle were not designed for each exact hole; of course, the water was shaped by the holes, just as animal life on Earth (including humans) was shaped by their environments. The diversity of life is the result of the combination of the genetic variation of a given population and the principle of natural selection, which is based on the environment.

Our natural world is based on observable facts, while religion is based on faith and spiritual concepts. With the inventions of the telescope and microscope, humans began to discover the real truths about where we are and what we are made of. As we investigate the natural world, our methods include observations and experiments, not opinions. All components of our world – plants and animals, ecosystems and societies, galaxies and the cosmos can be observed and studied scientifically.

Humanist Point-of-View

While creationist claims struggle under scientific scrutiny, an alternative worldview, humanism, offers a perspective grounded in reason and evidence. Humanism is a rational, non-religious approach which is bereft of theism or other supernatural beliefs. Its intellectual framework is based on naturalism; and it includes the conviction that the universe or nature is all that exists or is real. For some, humanism serves some of the psychological and social functions of a religion, but without belief in deities, transcendental entities, miracles, life after death, and the supernatural. Humanists seek to understand the universe by using science and its methods of critical inquiry, logical reasoning, empirical evidence, and skeptical evaluation of conjectures and conclusions to obtain reliable knowledge. Humanists affirm that humans have the freedom to give meaning, value, and purpose to their lives by their own independent thought, free inquiry, and responsible, creative activity.[65] According to Dr. Marian Sherman, "Humanism seeks the fullest development of human beings."[66] Humanists tend to approach life from the perspective of science and reason.

Anthropologists estimate that humans have worshiped at least 18,000 different gods, goddesses, or objects since our species began.[67] Religious beliefs have been part of the human experience throughout history, from prehistoric to modern times. Prior to our understanding of our natural world, it was used to explain what had been unexplainable. But that crutch has been taken away, as we no longer need it.

Humanists base their worldview on reason and science. Science offers well-evidenced theories that clash with literal interpretations of the Bible. In the choice between science and faith, science usually is triumphant because it provides tangible, testable answers. So, humanists confront the fears, hopes, and superstitions of the religious with rationality, logic, and empirical evidence. Humanists reject the claim that the Bible is the word of God. They realize the book was written solely by humans in an ignorant and cruel age; and because the writers of the Bible lived in such a prejudiced era of superstition, humanists are cognizant that it contains many errors and harmful teachings[68]. On the other hand, some Christian believers use the circular argument[69] that the Bible is the word of God because the Bible says it is. But one cannot use the Bible to validate the Bible!

Thousands of religious and political leaders promote the Bible. In most communities, an opposing view is rarely heard. The massive and incessant promotion of the Bible significantly influences the beliefs of millions. A Gallup poll showed that over 30% of Americans believe that the Bible is the word of God and its teachings should be taken literally. Gallup identified an additional 25% of Americans who consider the Bible as inspired by God, but think some verses should be interpreted symbolically, rather than literally.[70] Gallup says many other people, while having doubts about whether the entire Bible is the word of God, still consider the book to be a source of moral truths and regard its teachings as deserving of great respect. Of course, most people who believe that the Bible reveals moral truths have never actually read the entire Bible. If they did so, they might learn that the Bible has only a limited understanding of ethics.

The claim of the Bible that supernatural beings intervene in our world is opposed by the scientific principle of natural laws, which operate in a uniform and unvarying fashion. The Bible present narratives of a talking snake **[Genesis 3:4-5]**, a talking donkey **[Numbers 22:28]**, a man living in the belly of a fish for 3 days and 3 nights **[Jonah 1:17]**, iron floating **[2 Kings 6:5-6]**, the sun standing still **[Joshua 10:13]**, and a very young virgin woman impregnated by a deity **[Matthew 1:20]** – to mention just some of the biblical myths. Throughout our recorded history, primitive people have been susceptible to the belief that supernatural beings intervene in our world. But without any evidence, these claims do not merit belief or respect. They misdirect human energies needed to solve society's problems, by indulging in these supernatural myths by trying "to obtain the assistance of the benevolent supernatural beings or thwart the influence of malicious one."[71]

Indeed, it was the false interpretations of the Bible and the resultant false religious teachings that caused Christians to believe that plagues were caused by the anger of their God, not sourced from their filthy living conditions. Adherents of the Bible promoted demonic activity as the key cause of disease. St. Augustine wrote in the 4th century: "All diseases of Christians are to be ascribed to these demons."[72] Even in the 16th century, Martin Luther, the founder of Protestant Lutheranism, attributed his own illness to "devil's spells," and he stated, "Satan produces all the maladies which afflict mankind..."[73] Religious leaders taught that plagues could be averted by seeking supernatural assistance. And of course, that assistance could be acquired by providing gifts to the churches, monasteries, shrines, and buying indulgences from the local priest or bishop. If that didn't work, one could persecute the Jews and kill witches, since they were seen as agents of Satan.[74] Unfortunately, plague frequency and severity didn't lessen until hygiene improved, which was promoted by science, not by Christian churches. And that refocus on our use of our resources to reduce misery and improve lives has been seen in many other endeavors as well.

In the United States, political opinions, whether at the national, state, or local level, are often influenced by biblical teachings. Biblical believers obtain inspiration for their views on everything from women's rights to immunizations to capital punishment. When well-meaning, but misguided people view the Bible as the inspired word of a just God and attempt to reflect their biblical views in current society's laws, then they follow a highly flawed approach that could undermine our past achievements in jurisprudence and fairness.

Humanists view the Bible as actually having been written by fallible humans. When people who view the Bible as the word of an omniscient God attempt to have society's laws and social practices reflect biblical teachings, then serious error and harm could occur.[75] Humanists' concerns with the Bible center on its contradictions, cruelties, and inaccuracies regarding our physical world and history, and its false teachings inconsistent with the laws of the natural world. Our world operates under natural laws that cannot be altered or suspended by religious belief, ritual, or entreaties for supernatural assistance. Humanism is a way to live an ethical and fulfilling life without religion.[76]

What if Earth Had a Divine Creator

The ideology of Judeo-Christianity is that the primary reason why the universe was created was to provide a home for humans. But the reality of the size and age of the universe at 13.8 billion years of age is quite different. Indeed, the universe has over two trillion observable galaxies; indeed, the observable universe is approximately 93 billion light-years in diameter[77] with approximately 100 billion stars in our own Milky Way galaxy.[78] So, given these early 21st century facts (and our information grows daily), if a benevolent, loving deity had created the Earth for humans, then:

- Why would our God have waited more than 9.2 billion years after creating the universe to create our planet?
- And once He constructed our Earth planet, why would our Creator wait 4.5 billion years to create human beings?
- And once humans existed, why would our Benevolent Guardian wait approximately 247,000 years before contacting them?
- Why did our Invisible Divine Benefactor wait another 2,200 years after the initial contact before spreading his 'Word'?
- And why create such a massively large universe to place such a relatively small number of humans on one little, obscure planet?

The universe existed for almost 10 billion years before life began on Earth, as a result of a chemical accident. The story of life on Earth is deeply intertwined with the evolution of photosynthesis, a process that transformed the planet's environment and paved the way for complex life.[79] Mainstream scientists tend to agree that the elements required to create amino acids – the building blocks of both proteins and DNA – first came together in the water. From these amino acids, the most primitive life forms developed. For a long time, single-celled lifeforms, such as bacteria, were the only life forms that could be found on the planet. They gradually developed into more complex lifeforms, which emerged out of the water and onto land. Single-cell life evolved for approximately two billion years before multicellular life arose.[80] Then it took another billion years or so for evolution to produce a wide variety of multi-celled animal life. This is exactly what you would expect in a godless universe. However, this is not at all consistent with a god-created world, if indeed there were a deity who intervened in our daily lives.

Would a Heavenly Divinity have covered 71% of the Earth's surface with water? And 96.5% of that was salt water (the salinity of the oceans is 3.5% or 35 parts per thousand), which is poisonous to humans and most animals.[81] Of the limited freshwater essential to life, 68.7% of it is trapped in icecaps and glaciers, with only about 30% (of the 2.5 %) being fresh groundwater. And less than 3 % of our fresh water can be found in surplus water of lakes, rivers, and swamps. What possible purpose would a Charitable Creator have to crowd its human and animal creations to less than 29% of the planet's surface? With only a very small fraction of fresh water (2.5% x 30.1% x 31%) or .23% of all water available to be consumed by its creations (animals and plants)? [82] That is less than one-fourth of one percent of the world's water.

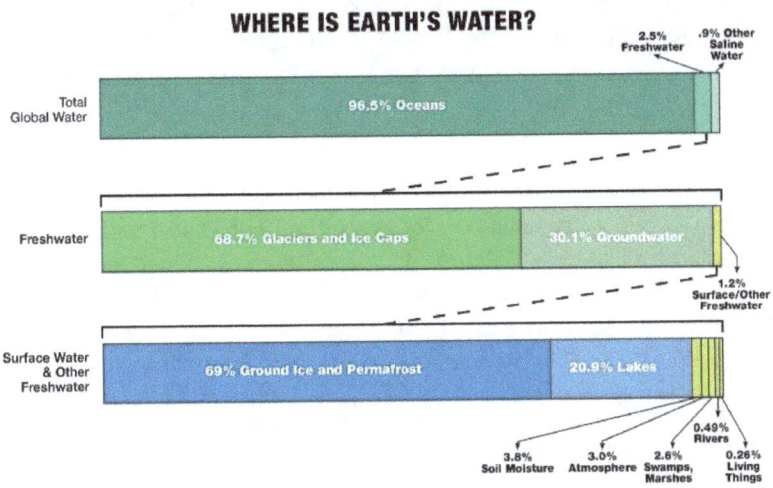

As depicted in the illustration on below[83], of the limited land mass (less than 30% of the total surface of the Earth), only **76%** of that land is considered habitable. That is because 10% of all land is considered ice tundra, which is so cold that no animals can survive there long-term, and because 14% of the land is considered barren as it is covered with sand and salt flats. And should the entire ice tundra ever melt, then the world as we know it would end. Together, the Antarctic and Greenland ice sheets hold enough water to raise the sea level by roughly 65 meters (more than 210 feet).[84] Thus, we have only **22%** of the planet's surface (.29 x .76) that is currently habitable by humans and by land animals of all types.

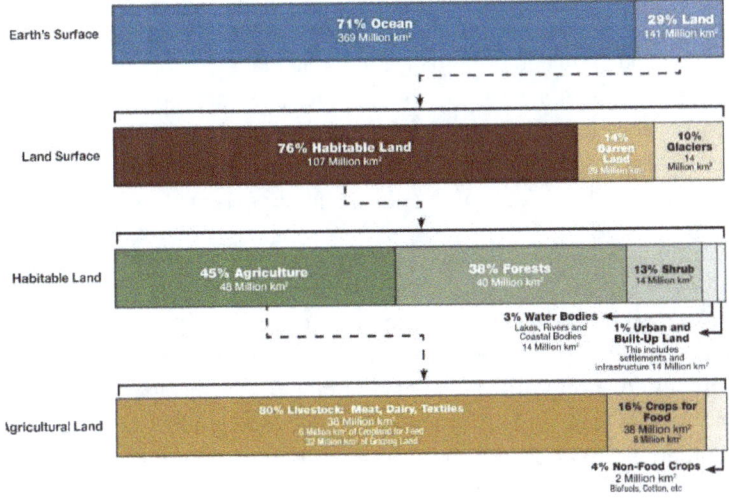

Almost half of the arable land is used for agriculture and 38% is forested.[85] That forested land is critical to the habitats of the land animals, as they provide a home to nearly half of all species; and the forests pump out the oxygen we need to live and absorb the carbon dioxide we exhale. They keep the Earth cool and prevent erosion, and thus flooding.[86] But except for some indigenous people, our modern human population cannot live in the forests without destroying them.

We live on 1% of the habitable land for our urban world and infrastructure; that is less than ¼ of 1% of the Earth's surface. Our freshwater lakes and rivers take up another 3%, and that leaves us with 45% of the habitable land for agricultural use. That sliver of land (under 10% of the Earth's surface) is further divided into grazing land for animals, growing feed, dairy, and a variety of textiles. That leaves us with 4% of all agricultural land for non-food crops (e.g., cotton) and 16% for food crops. That means that our Celestial Protector allocated humanity only 1.5% (.29 x .73 X .45 x .16) of the Earth's surface for the growing of its food.

If the Heavenly Inventor crafted the Earth through His own powers and handiwork, why is 80% of the planet's surface (above and below sea level) of volcanic origin?[87] Speaking of natural calamities such as volcanoes, why is there no place on Earth completely free from the potential devastation of earthquakes, hurricanes, tornadoes, tsunamis, mudslides, floods, avalanches, droughts, continual climate change, and other geologic hazards? And if he loves us so much, why would this supernatural being inflict on us horrible microbial diseases that cause so much suffering for both humans and for animals? Would a loving divinity have enabled birth defects which so severely limit the movements, actions, and happiness of those who are afflicted with them? And their families? And why create a world in which children and animals starve to death, drown in floods, or perish in anguish from parasites or animal/plant poisons? There is so much unnecessary suffering in the world, which our Loving Deity supposedly created and continues to allow.

This world is not what you would expect if a deity created it, and if that deity intervenes in our lives. The universe is just too vast and laden with billions of stars, planets, and other phenomena which are unrelated to humans for us to believe that it was all made just for us. Indeed, based on the available data, the current scientific estimate is that there are between 5 billion and 10 billion potentially habitable planets in our galaxy. This conclusion was reached via extrapolation by a team of cosmology researchers at Penn State University in August 2019.[88] They looked at numerous factors such as size, orbit times, and distance to the nearest star of planets discovered so far and extrapolated from that. While it is a large number, it is only 1% to 2.5% of the planets in our galaxy.[89]

So, upon reflection, what if the Earth was created through a natural cosmic process that took billions of years of effort? If that were the case (and I believe it is), we just might just see an imperfect world exactly like the one in which we now live; and indeed, this is the type of world we should expect. According to Stephen Hawking, it was the law of gravity rather than the intervention of a divine being that set the universe in motion. He wrote, "…because there is a law such as gravity, the universe can and will create itself from nothing. Spontaneous creation is the reason there is something rather than nothing, why the universe exists, [and] why we exist…"[90]

Science vs. Christianity

Judeo-Christianity has demonstrated repeatedly that it has a very limited understanding of cosmology[91]. In fact, you might say cosmology is Christianity's greatest failure. For most of its existence at least up to the Age of Enlightenment (18th century), Christianity taught that the Earth was the center of the universe and humans had been given exclusive domination over it. The Christian faithful could not have been more wrong!

Christians want to see the "hand of God" in the creation of the universe. Yet, it is extraordinarily early in our discoveries about the universe in which we dwell. We don't even know what we don't know. What we do know is that the universe is expanding at an accelerating rate, and the Andromeda galaxy is headed straight toward our Milky Way galaxy on a collision course that will cause massive destruction and end our planet among countless others. The result will be nothingness in approximately 4 billion years.[92]

After battling with Copernicus[93] and Galileo[94] regarding the heliocentric theory that the sun revolved around the Earth, initially the Catholic Church (and later Protestant denominations) could simply not accept evolution, the concept of natural selection, and random mutation (they are often affected by environmental factors) combined to transform species. The Catholic Church, along with many Protestant Churches, was deeply invested in the prevailing Adam and Eve fable. Nor can some Christian denominations and some Orthodox Jews accept the fact that planet Earth is approximately 4.6 billion years old (give or take 10 million), not six thousand years old, as determined from counting backwards from the stories found in the Pentateuch (Jewish Torah).

The Enlightenment of the 18th century introduced a seismic shift in Western thought. Empiricism, secularism, and rationalism, abetted by human reason, catalyzed unprecedented technological advancements which revolutionized societies. But the Churches, both Roman Catholic and Protestant, resisted the paradigm-shifting influence of the Enlightenment. Indeed, Enlightenment thinkers like Voltaire and Rousseau championed not just science, but individual liberties. [95]

So, when confronted by the realities of science, believers in the early 20th century declared, 'Well, who says when in that evolutionary process, Adam and Eve were born?' (Plus, having other members of the species around helped explain how their only surviving child, Cain, found a wife.) So, evolution was shoe-horned into "God's plan" as an 'Intelligent Design',[96] a sort of retrospective evidentialism[97], where anything can be force-fitted into a pre-determined belief. Fortunately, in the 21st century, Catholicism and many other Christian denominations are now accepting the reality of evolution, although some Christian sects are still desperately clinging to the archaic concept of original sin.

God of the Gaps

"God of the gaps" is a theological concept that emerged in the 19th century and revolves around the idea that gaps in scientific understanding are regarded as indications of the existence of God.[98] [99] Some believers point to areas where science falls short in explaining natural phenomena as opportunities to insert the presence of a deity. This view suggests that these gaps represent moments of divine intervention or influence. To the credit of many theists and most theologians, this old-fashioned concept is no longer taken too seriously.[100]

The God of the gaps is a fallacious argument for several reasons. First, similar to Bronze Age mankind, who couldn't explain lightning and decided that the gods (or more specifically, Zeus) did it, we are asked to accept that anything we cannot currently explain occurs through the magical hand of a deity. Only two centuries ago, we couldn't fully explain the origin of man; now we better understand the process of evolution; and we are increasing in knowledge daily. Science doesn't have all the answers, and it probably never will, but it is quickly acquiring many of them. A temporary gap in human knowledge doesn't automatically point to a deity. Believing that is a logical fallacy.

Second, gaps in knowledge are what drive science. As our knowledge advances, does that push out the deity and further weaken the argument for the existence of a god? Critics contend that such an approach can undermine religious beliefs by suggesting that God only operates in the unexplained areas of our understanding.[101] Moreover, it violates several fundamental principles of causal analysis and explanation in both science and theology. This thought was ratified by Dietrich Bonhoeffer, a German Christian theologian, who wrote the following while in a Nazi prison: "How wrong it is to use God as a stopgap for the incompleteness of our knowledge. If, in fact, the frontiers of knowledge are being pushed further back (and that is bound to be the case), then God is being pushed back with them and is therefore continually in retreat. We are to find God in what we know, not in what we don't know."[102] Eventually, scientific understanding closes the gap, making the appeal to divine explanation irrelevant.

British biologist, author, and atheist, Richard Dawkins, criticized the God-of-the-gaps argument with this scathing comment: "Creationists eagerly seek a gap in present-day knowledge or understanding. If an apparent gap is found, it is assumed that God, by default, must fill it. What worries thoughtful theologians such as Bonhoeffer is that gaps shrink as science advances, and God is threatened with eventually having nothing to do and nowhere to hide.[103]

Third, this argument has a built-in confirmation bias, since it involves interpreting ambiguous evidence (or rather, no evidence) to support an existing hypothesis. This type of reasoning does not provide an appropriate foundation for religious faith.

Charles Alfred Coulson (1910–1974), mathematics professor at Oxford University as well as a Methodist church leader, famously put the concept in perspective when he wrote: "There is no 'God of the gaps' to take over at those strategic places where science fails; and the reason is that gaps of this sort have the unpreventable habit of shrinking.[104] He followed that with the statement, "Either God is in the whole of Nature, with no gaps, or He's not there at all."[105]

Lack of Evidence and Irrationality

"Extraordinary claims require extraordinary evidence"
– Carl Sagan, Astronomer, 1979.

This aphorism from Carl Sagan is a rewording of the LaPlace principle, "The weight of evidence for an extraordinary claim must be proportioned to its strangeness."[106] This statement sits at the heart of the scientific method, and it is a model for critical thinking, rational thought, and healthy skepticism. It is the logic that has been used for the last four decades to challenge proponents of the paranormal, ghosts, UFOs, and spiritual miracles. Even if some evidence is accepted, weak evidence is not enough. For those who truly seek the truth, doubt is a crucial ingredient for all new discoveries.

Humans are pattern-seeking primates;[107] and we sometimes try to connect patterns even when they do not exist. Through trial and error, we have learned throughout human history how to do things, based on what we expect in given circumstances. We observed the patterns of some migrating animal species to trap them; and we determined the feeding habits of fish, and how to catch them. Theoretically, we observe, make hypotheses, and then discern if those hypotheses hold true. Even the Big Bang theory rests on concrete evidence.

Religion was our species' original attempts to explain the unexplainable, given our limited understanding of the natural world. Our ancestors learned the patterns of their world, and then they formed conclusions; and those conclusions were often inaccurate. Unfortunately, some of our ancestors decided that evil spirits caused disease. Earthquakes, volcanoes and floods were viewed as divine punishments for some activities or actions. Even in recent history, many Christians thought AIDS was a punishment from God for 'allowing' homosexuality to exist in society.[108] Unfortunately, when we don't fully understand things, we sometimes manufacture a 'plausible solution', and then over time, humans tend to accept their own invented beliefs as true. Furthermore, when we cannot get strong evidence to support our hypotheses, then junk evidence is often acceptable. And if we accept nonsense as evidence, that is because it is usually ancillary to the unfettered beliefs which we are already advancing. If we have no valid theories, that might propel us toward conspiracy theories. After all, humans are uncomfortable in an information void. Historically, prior to the Age of Reason, if humans didn't understand something, they enshrined it as 'magic', 'witchcraft', or other sorcery. Today, when we don't understand something, some of the more unenlightened among us declare that it must be the work of God.

One excellent example of religious leaders trying to thwart a scientific invention because of their own superstitions can be seen in the story of Ben Franklin and his lightning rod. In the mid-1700s, Mr. Franklin experimented with static electricity, and he came up with the idea of a lightning rod, which he tested and produced in 1752. This occurred after he heard about a bad storm in Italy in which lightning struck a building in which gunpowder was stored, and the resulting fire killed many people. He did not patent his invention, nor ask anyone for money. However, some local religious leaders objected that Franklin was attempting to interfere with "one of God's most effective methods of punishing sinners."[109] Franklin's response: "Surely the thunder of Heaven is no more supernatural than the rain, hail, or sunshine of Heaven, against the inconvenience of which we guard by roofs and shades without scruple." Indeed, when Boston was hit by a rare earthquake, one of its religious leaders blamed Mr. Franklin and his heretical lightning rod. Ironically, the tallest buildings in most cities and towns were churches; and they were the ones targeted by lightning most often, and people were sometimes killed. But Franklin's invention worked well; it saved lives and property (and many churches); and it caught on despite the decades-long opposition from the superstitious religious leaders, as the controversy continued into the 1780s.[110]

Why 30 CE?

The Earth has held millions of species since the Paleozoic Era (541-252 million years ago)[111] of the Phanerozoic[112] Eon – when many of the phyla[113] of animals began to appear in fossils to be discovered 541 million years later. Over those eons of time, there were innumerable deaths of species. Indeed, according to most scientific estimates, over 99% of all species that ever lived on Earth are now extinct. In many cases, it has been a cruel, pitiless annihilation. To what end? For the Intelligent Designer to finally create a species of humans to be the chosen ones? Was that Intelligent Design?

It is still a matter of debate when our homo sapiens 'modern man' species[114] started; but most scientists believe it was 300,000 to 225,000 years ago. So, for argument's sake, let us say it was 250,000 years ago. But God waited 248,000 more years before He revealed Himself in Roman-occupied, late Iron Age, Palestine. After waiting nearly a quarter-million years, he couldn't wait 2,000 more years for the TV cameras and the recordings! Had God done that, He could present a straightforward, unambiguous message with clarity, rather than have flawed men who never met Him create His god image. And what of all the people who died in those 248,000 years, without hearing about "the good news"? Over 118 billion people have been born on planet Earth, of which 8+ billion are still alive.[115] Over 9.4 billion people had lived and died prior to Jesus Christ's preaching.[116] [117] And what of all the other people on Earth (outside Europe and the Middle East) who lived and died in the next fifteen hundred years? And for that matter, there are people in the world today who know little of Christianity. Had such events occurred in the age of modern media, then we might have clearer theological documentation.

Why would a celestial deity confine his teachings to a relatively obscure town in Galilee (Nazareth) in an overlooked province (Judea) in an age of general illiteracy and superstition? The location was wrong, and the timing seemed way off any reasonable mark. After approximately 248,000 years of human history, Jesus finally shows up. So, if the goal was to get the word out to the entire human race, then the timing appears much too late. On the other hand, if the goal was to communicate the information from God to the people via rapid and accurate communications with text, audio, and video, then the timing seems almost two millennia too early.

One of the biggest concerns with the "good news" brought by Jesus is that his message, as written down by men, was less than articulate. Had it been clear and unambiguous, as you might expect from a deity, then we would not have all the misunderstandings, the discrepancies, the heresies, and the false information that have resulted in 40,000 different Christian sects today, each proclaiming to be the true religion. God could have solved this dilemma if only he had chosen a better venue at a better time and provided a clearer message, which He does not appear to have done.

Miracles

Many faiths hold accounts of miracles – events that seem to violate natural laws. These are extraordinary and astonishing happenings that tend to be attributed to the presence and action of an ultimate or divine power.[118] While science cannot disprove a miracle, it does prioritize the search for natural explanations for unusual phenomena. New Testament accounts of the advent, birth, life, passion, and resurrection of Christ include many miracles. David Hume (1711-1776), a British empiricist and a skeptic, defined a miracle as "a violation of the laws of nature."[119] It was Mr. Hume whose criticism that led him to a denial of causality, did not dismiss miracles because they were inconsistent with causal law; but he insisted on the probability factor and thus on the importance of assessing historical evidence.[120] In the view of those favoring Rationalist enlightenment, a belief in miracles, although remaining an essential element of faith to Christians, appeared as sheer superstition.

There is, of course, one central argument against miracles – that they violate natural law. In 1764, Voltaire wrote a particularly lucid rationale against miracles:

> "A miracle is the violation of mathematical, divine, immutable, eternal laws. By the very exposition itself, a miracle is a contradiction in terms: a law cannot at the same time be immutable and violated." [121]

In the centuries since Hume wrote about the violation of 'laws of nature' or Voltaire wrote that a miracle was a violation of 'eternal laws', we have learned much from the study of human perception, especially the cognitive biases that distort our picture of reality. As Bart Ehrmann explained, "People are routinely deceived by others, can be self-deceived by themselves, and they misperceive how the world works. When someone tells us of a miracle they witnessed, or of a miracle someone told them about, it is far more likely that they "either deceive or be deceived, or that the fact, which he relates, should really not have happened."[122]

While generally, miracles are immensely improbable, people have embraced them for millennia, seeing in them proof of a supernatural world that resists scientific explanation. Lawrence Shapiro's The Miracle Myth[123] reviews some attempts to justify belief in the supernatural, underscoring the fallacies that such attempts commit. People need to sharpen their critical thinking to become less susceptible to tales of myths and miracles.[124] Biblical miracles tend to be a perfect match for the definition of hearsay, which is defined by the Oxford dictionary as "information received from other people that one cannot adequately substantiate; rumor." The writers of these "biblical miracles" did not witness them (not even one); they wrote what others told them or what they read elsewhere, often many decades, or longer, after the events in question.

The Case Against Miracles[125] is a new anthology that explains why there isn't enough objective evidence to believe in them. Along the way, the book presents a major defense of Scottish philosopher, David Hume, and his ground-breaking arguments against miracles. We need to accept that biblical miracles are not testimonials, because they were written long after the miracle event supposedly occurred, by men who were not observers of the miracle(s).

The theologian, Rudolph Bultmann (1884-1976), tried to 'de-mythologize' the teaching of Jesus by stripping away the miraculous. He went so far as to say:

> "It is impossible to use electric light and the wireless and to avail ourselves of modern medical and surgical discoveries, and at the same time to believe in the New Testament world of spirits and miracles."[126]

Arguments against miracles come from the natural world. Often, what once seemed miraculous gains understanding through scientific investigation. In the past century, advances in medicine, physics, and psychology provided natural explanations for many events previously considered miraculous. Unfortunately, there is no evidence of any miracles in either the Old Testament or the New Testament occurring. Not one eyewitness report. There were many hearsay examples from writers who were not witnesses. So, without any evidence and hearsay reporting, can we say that miracles occurred? There is just no logical justification to believe in them.

Epicurus

Epicurus of Samos was an ancient Greek philosopher (341 – 270 BCE) whose philosophies on empiricism, materialism, and atomism were based on a deist belief system. Deism postulates that God exists, or in the case of ancient Greece, the gods exist, but they do not involve themselves with worldly affairs. There were four fundamental truths in Epicureanism[127]:

- There are no divine beings that can threaten us.
- There is no afterlife.
- What we actually need is easy to obtain.
- What makes us suffer is easy to endure.

Epicurus believed in an empirical, evidence-based view of "the gods." He espoused the doctrine of reliance upon physics and the other sciences, instead of religion, which offer a consistent, unambiguous explanation regarding how the world works. Since he didn't believe that any gods would intervene to help humanity, he posited that humans should depend on the sciences, which they could empirically observe and test. He famously put forth a quote regarding God based on his logic.[128] This quote appears to be from Chapter 10 of David Hume's <u>Dialogues Concerning Natural Religion</u>, which was published in 1779.

- Is God willing to prevent evil, but not able? Then he is not omnipotent.
- Is he able, but not willing? Then he is malevolent.
- Is he both able and willing? Then whence cometh evil?
- Is he neither able nor willing? Then why call him God?"

Epicurus is <u>not</u> known for wanting to disprove the existence of gods, but he did want to make his readers rethink the nature of deities. In many ways, Epicurus is presenting a straw-man argument, but it is a good one. Epicurus is critiquing the Platonian view of a world that contained perfect forms. But the world of Epicurus, much like our world, is an imperfect world. And there is no indication, much less actual evidence, that we have any omnipotent, omniprescient gods watching over us.

Burden of Proof

Let me just assert upfront that the burden of proof goes with the person or persons who suggest an extraordinary claim, such as the existence of a deity, any deity! When making such a claim, there is a requirement for evidence. I am not making a claim that there is no god. Not only is it nearly impossible to prove a negative, but I simply claim that I see no evidence of any deity, and the suggested 'evidence' that I have encountered has huge holes. And so, I reject the existence of a deity much like I rejected the reality of Santa Claus when I was a child.

But as a former indoctrinated Christian, I do recognize that many believers, not just Christians, have self-deluded themselves. They use what atheist blogger, Luke Muehlhauser, refers to as the double standard of "special thinking." Most people use common sense to solve most of their issues, but they find and use a different logic to justify their religious ideas. They don't believe in Zeus or Thor, but they believe in other supernatural concepts, just as far-fetched. When confronted, they move into what is possible, not what is probably, and certainly not verifiable. They suggest that any number of miracles are possible, even if the suspension of natural laws of physics or biology must occur.

Most of us believed in Santa Claus as young children; but then as we matured, we learned and accepted that Santa was a myth. There remain many 'believers' today who just cannot draw from that experience and extrapolate that other myths in their lives are not true either. Additionally, believers cannot claim that just because science cannot yet explain a given phenomenon, that their religion can explain it. There are many things that science couldn't explain in the past that it can now; obviously, there is much yet to learn. But the power of the scientific method, the mathematical and experimental techniques used in the construction and testing of a scientific hypothesis, has established standards for evidence and repeated proofs; religion doesn't do that.

Faith vs. Reason

Faith and reason both serve as sources of authority upon which beliefs can rest. Reason is not simply the rules of logic or the wisdom of an authority; but it is generally presupposed that some demonstration can be made. It involves a rational conclusion, and only then can an authoritative claim be made. Whereas faith involves a claim that is not demonstrable by reason. Thus, religious faith involves a belief that makes some kind of reference to a transcendent source.[129] Religious faith can be dichotomized into evidence-sensitive and evidence-insensitive. The former views faith as closely coordinated with demonstrable truths, and it includes evidence garnered from other believers; the latter is more an act of the will of the religious believer alone.[130] Unfortunately, there is no evidence for any of the assertions made in the Bible. No one who wrote the tales was an eyewitness; nor did any writers interview eyewitnesses. The source of all writings in both the Old and New Testaments came from the oral tradition. Thus, out of necessity, the Judeo-Christian faiths accept doctrines or beliefs without any empirical evidence.

"Faith consists in believing what reason cannot."
– Voltaire

Christianity, similar to most religions, makes claims about the existence of a deity, the nature of that deity, and how it interacts with the world. To understand those claims, one can use reason or faith, but together, they are incompatible. The more reason and evidence that one garners, then the less room there is for faith, since faith is not needed. The truth is the truth, and faith cannot contradict reason. As John W. Loftus explained, "Christians reject the faiths of other religions precisely because they are faith-based."[131] But when asked to take a critical look at their own religion or sect, they have difficulty seeing that it has the same faith-based foundations, bereft of reason or evidence.

In his book regarding Faith vs. Fact, Professor Jerry Coyne irrefutably demonstrates the grave harm to individuals and to our planet in mistaking faith for fact while making the most important decisions about the world we live in.[132] Religion has obstructed and undermined the reality of evolution, vaccinations, stem-cell research, homosexuality, and global warming, and many other important areas of understanding. Faith is not a virtue; nor is it a path for truth; it generates certainty, but not knowledge, and that can be a very dangerous thing.

> *"The Party told you to reject the evidence of your eyes and ears. It was their final, most essential command."*
> – George Orwell, 1984

Christianity Debunked

By History

Many of the Old Testament's claims expose it as historically inaccurate. Just because a place exists doesn't validate the reliability and authority of the story. Mount Olympus exists in Greece, but few if any believe that the Greek gods of legend resided there. Here are just some examples of those inaccuracies.

- There never appears to have been a worldwide flood. Egypt's civilization predates the biblical flood, and no flood interrupted it.[133]
- There is no archaeological evidence for slavery in Egypt, or for the Exodus, or for the destruction of the pharaoh's army. Indeed, several renowned Israeli and Egyptian archaeologists have emphatically stated that it is unlikely that Israelites ever went to Egypt at all. (See Chapter 2)
- There is no historical or archaeological record of a Jewish queen named Ester on the Persian throne.[134]
- In the book of Daniel, Belshazzar was not the son of Nebuchadnezzar and was never king; and Darius the Mede did not exist; it was Cyrus of Persia who conquered Babylon and released the Israelites. (See Chapter 2.)

The New Testament's false claims include the following, among many others (all discussed in Chapter 3):

- The Gospel of Matthew contrived the massacre of the innocents
- The Gospel of Luke falsely attested that Roman Emperor Augustus (or his Judean governor) ordered a census throughout the Roman world.
- The Gospel of Mark first contrived the story of Barabbas, which is not historical.

- All three of the synoptic authors reported that the sky over Judaea (or the whole world) is "darkened for three hours (from 3 to 6 PM). Such reporting was, at best, poetic license.
- There is no evidence at all that hundreds of graves in Jerusalem were opened, and multitudes of 'dead saints' (zombies) did rise from the dead.[135]

By Science

Some Christians think that the Bible contains accurate scientific facts. Unfortunately, the Bible runs rampant with statements that are scientifically false. Here are a few of them:

- **Leviticus 11:** Insects do not have four feet; nor does any animal that flies; rabbits do not chew their cud.
- **Deuteronomy 14:18:** Bats are not birds
- **Isaiah 11:12:** The Earth is not flat
- **Psalms 75:3:** The Earth has no pillars
- **Psalms 135:7:** Wind is not held in storehouses

Some Christians will claim that these verses are allegorical and are not to be taken literally. But many Christians take it quite literally; and why don't all Christians take all the verses from this imperfect, non-inspired Bible allegorically? The following are some of the ways that the sciences have exposed some false pretensions.[136]

Astronomy

The Copernican astronomical revolution, as defended later by Galileo, exposed that we do not live in a geocentric universe[137]; that is, under most geocentric models, our sun, moon, stars, and planets all orbit Earth. The biblical writers did not understand the basic fact that the Earth revolves around the Sun. And we exist on a spiral arm in one galaxy of billions in the universe. The Catholic Church inquisitors threatened Galileo, but the truth remained the truth.

Biology

It took almost a century, but even the Catholic Church came to embrace evolution (even if Catholicism cannot give up the concept of original sin). Christian Fundamentalists still denounce it, even though many are slowly converting to acceptance. With the truth of evolution, we no longer need a divine Creator, for there is nothing left to explain by means of the supernatural hypothesis. Evolution completely undercuts the Genesis' account of our origin. As Pierre-Simon Marquis de Laplace[138] (1749 – 1827) first informed us in response to a question from Napoleon regarding the supposed creator of the universe, "there is no need of that god-hypothesis."[139]

Archaeology

This scientific endeavor has debunked many stories in the Bible. Archaeologists have discovered several ancient Mesopotamian texts that predate the ones in the Bible, and they tell similar unconvincing stories of the origins of the universe. Archeology can find no evidence for the Exodus of the Israelites out of Egypt. The Walls of Jericho fell due to an Earthquake long before the Israelites showed up; there is no evidence of Sodom and

Gomorrah or a Tower of Babel; there was no great flood that covered the world; and King David's empire did not approach the size described in the Tanakh. Additionally, there is no evidence that the Ark of the Covenant ever existed, and if it did, it most likely had no special powers.

Philology

The science of philology is a branch of knowledge that dates manuscripts based on grammar, structure, vocabulary, and dialect. Lorenzo Valla (c.1406-1457) used it to show in 1440 that the newly discovered "Donation of Constantine"[140] the decree was a forgery. In this forged decree, the Emperor Constantine transferred authority over Rome and the western part of the Roman Empire and all its spiritual and temporal power to St. Sylvester (314 – 335), bishop of Rome, and to his successors. The consensus view is that the Donation was written in the 750s or 760s by a cleric of the Lateran in Rome, possibly with the knowledge of the pope. Lorenzo Valla demonstrated that the Latin used in the document was not that of the 4th century. Indeed, from the science of philology, we've learned there are many forgeries in the canonized Bible (e.g., 2nd Isaiah, Pastoral Epistles, II Peter, and so on).

Religion asserts and believes; Science searches and proves!
– [unknown author]

Chapter Summary

There is no evidence whatsoever that a divine deity, omnipotent, omniprescient, or otherwise, created us, our world, or the universe. However, there is indisputable evidence that our world formed from natural causes, and we humans and other animals evolved as a result. If there were a celestial being who created and watches over us, then there is no reason not to fully reveal Himself or Herself to us. He or She has not yet chosen to do so. Thus, we must accept that the concept of a benevolent celestial god is in fact a man-made construct. The last 400 years of science and discovery should demonstrate that the notion of a divine deity is not rational.

Our imperfect world appears exactly like it was created through a natural cosmic process, which would take several billion years of evolution. It doesn't offer nearly enough arable land to support our expanding human population; it provides way too much poisonous salt water which humans cannot consume; and it is beset with natural devastation such as earthquakes, hurricanes, tornadoes, tsunamis, floods, and climate changes, with a wide range of microbial diseases. This does not appear to be a world that a benevolent deity would have created for humans made in His or Her image. And of course, there is just no evidence of God's involvement, one way or the other. There is also a limited rationale for the poor timing in providing a divine appearance by voice to the Israelite people in approximately 1200 BCE, and appearing again in 30 CE as Jesus, when humans have been on the planet for at least the past quarter million years!

The Bible is laden with false prophecies, mistranslations, contradictions, historical inaccuracies, and other discrepancies. It offers many mistaken beliefs about our natural world and cosmology. Given its many errors, there is no reason to believe it is a reliable guide for spiritual and ethical issues. It is clearly not 'inerrant'; it was written by uneducated men, and it does not appear to be inspired by any god. Some parts of the Bible have been thoroughly debunked by history and by science.

---

[4] Gerard Helferich, "Impossible Monsters and Dinosaurs at the Dinner Table: Fossils Versus Faith," Sep 20, 2024;
Wall Street Journal; https://www.wsj.com/arts-culture/books/impossible-monsters-and-dinosaurs-at-the-dinner-table-fossils-versus-faith-1787ba99

[5] Ibid.

[6] "James Hutton: The Founder of Modern Geology," American Museum of Natural History, https://www.amnh.org/learn-teach/curriculum-collections/earth-inside-and-out/james-hutton

[7] "Who was Alfred Russel Wallace?" American Museum of Natural History, https://www.nhm.ac.uk/discover/who-was-alfred-russel-wallace.html

[8] "Charles Darwin," National Geographic; https://education.nationalgeographic.org/resource/charles-darwin/

[9] "Charles Darwin," Encyclopedia Britannica; https://www.britannica.com/biography/Charles-Darwin

[10] "Isaac Newton," Encyclopedia Britannica; https://www.britannica.com/biography/Isaac-Newton/Career

[11] "Rene Descartes' 'Proofs of God's Existence,' "Thought Co.; https://www.thoughtco.com/descartes-3-proofs-of-gods-existence-2670585

[12] Stephen Hicks, Ph.D., Philosopher, "The Watch and Watchmaker analogy for the existence of a god"; https://www.stephenhicks.org/2016/10/01/the-watch-and-watchmaker-analogy-for-the-existence-of-a-god/

[13] The Spiritual Life; https://slife.org/watchmaker-analogy/

[14] "Teleological Arguments for God's Existence," Stanford Encyclopedia of Philosophy; Apr 5, 2023; https://plato.stanford.edu/entries/teleological-arguments/

[15] The Spiritual Life; Ibid.

[16] "The existence of God—The Design Argument," Bitesize; https://www.bbc.co.uk/bitesize/guides/zv2fgwx/revision

[17] From "William Paley," Encyclopedia Britannica; https://www.britannica.com/biography/William-Paley. William Paley was an English Anglican cleric and Christian apologist. His manuscript strongly influenced Charles Darwin.

[18] William Paley, Natural Theology: or, Evidences of the Existence and Attributes of the Deity; p.1; London: J Faulder.

[19] "William Paley," Britannica; https://www.britannica.com/biography/William-Paley

[20] Adam Shapiro, "A Failed Metaphor for Intelligent Design," The Atlantic; February 12, 2015; https://finance.yahoo.com/news/failed-metaphor-intelligent-design-151042564.html

[21] Michael J. Behe, Darwin's Black Box; Nov 1996; Free Press; https://michaelbehe.com/books/darwins-black-box/

[22] Richard Dawkins, "The Blind Watchmaker: Why The Evidence Of Evolution Reveals A Universe Without Design"; SuperSummary; https://www.supersummary.com/the-blind-watchmaker-why-the-evidence-of-evolution-reveals-a-universe-without-design/summary/

[23] "Intelligent Design Movement," Britannica; https://www.britannica.com/topic/intelligent-design

[24] "Intelligent Design," New World Encyclopedia; https://www.newworldencyclopedia.org/entry/Intelligent_design

[25] Barbara Carroll Forrest, "How Intelligent Design Creationism Is Wedging Its Way into the Cultural and Academic Mainstream"; The Secular Web; Seattle, WA: Center for the Renewal of Science and Culture; January 1, 2001; Retrieved 2014-05-29. https://infidels.org/library/modern/barbara-forrest-wedge/

[26] National Academy of Science; Science, Evolution and Creationism; the National Academies Press, Washington D.C.; 2008; https://nap.nationalacademies.org/read/11876/chapter/1

[27] Susan Goldenberg, "Creationists defeated in Kansas school vote on science teaching," The Guardian; 15 Feb 2007;
https://www.theguardian.com/science/2007/feb/15/schoolsworldwide.religion

[28] Daniel Miessler, "The Power of Bottom-up (Evolution) vs. Top-down (Design)," Daniel Miessler; Oct 2016; https://danielmiessler.com/p/power-bottom-evolution-vs-top-design/

[29] Kitzmiller v. Dover Area School District; Casetext: Smarter Legal Research; p.54;
https://casetext.com/case/kitzmiller-v-dover-area-school-district-5

[30] Powell, Michael, "Judge Rules Against 'Intelligent Design'"; The Washington Post. (December 21, 2005); https://www.washingtonpost.com/archive/politics/2005/12/21/judge-rules-against-intelligent-design/4b2d6c66-543f-4273-86de-19307c584ae6/

[31] David Callaway, "What Is Separation of Church and State?" Freedom Forum;
https://www.freedomforum.org/separation-of-church-and-state/

[32] Throughout this book, I used the term "ignorance' not pejoratively, but to signify only a lack of knowledge.

[33] John Hanna, "Kansas Vote a Victory for "Intelligent Design," The Associated Press;
https://www.heraldtribune.com/story/news/2005/11/09/kansas-vote-a-victory-for-intelligent-design/28445080007/

[34] Jack Krebs, "Kansas Evolution Hearings - Summary of the Background to the Kansas 'Science Hearings' of May, 2005," The Talk Origins Archive;
https://www.talkorigins.org/faqs/kansas/evolutionhearings.html

[35] "Kansas Evolution Hearings – Result," LiquiSearch;
https://www.liquisearch.com/kansas_evolution_hearings/result

[36] "On Creationism in School Textbooks," from the Central Conference of American Rabbis; National Center for Science Education; Oct 1, 2008; https://ncse.ngo/central-conference-american-rabbis

[37] "Evolution: Fact and Theory," National Center for Science Education; July 2020;
https://ncse.ngo/evolution-fact-and-theory

[38] "What is Evolution," Your Genome; https://www.yourgenome.org/theme/what-is-evolution/

[39] "Evolution," Encyclopedia Britannica; https://www.britannica.com/science/evolution-scientific-theory/Modern-conceptions

[40] "Science and Religion," National Academies;
https://www.nationalacademies.org/evolution/science-and-religion

[41] "Definitions of Fact, Theory, and Law in Scientific Work," National Center for Science Education; March 16, 2016; https://ncse.ngo/definitions-fact-theory-and-law-scientific-work

[42] "Science and Religion," Ibid.

[43] "Theory vs. Law: Basics of the Scientific Method," MasterClass; June 2021;
https://www.masterclass.com/articles/theory-vs-law-basics-of-the-scientific-method

[44] "Tiktaalik roseae," Britannica; Tiktaalik is a monospecific genus of extinct sarcopterygian (lobe-finned fish) from the Late Devonian Period, about 350 - 375 Mya (million years ago);
https://www.britannica.com/animal/Tiktaalik-roseae

[45] "Science and Religion," Ibid.

[46] Richard C. Lewontin, (November 1970). "The Units of Selection" (PDF). Annual Review of Ecology and Systematics. ISSN 0066-4162. JSTOR 2096764. Archived (PDF) from the original on 6 February 2015.

[47] "The God Delusion Summary - Key Insights & Analysis," Instaread;
https://instaread.co/insights/religion-philosophy/the-god-delusion-book/o1unljvghz

[48] A book review of The God Delusion by Richard Dawkins; Modern Reformation;
https://www.modernreformation.org/resources/articles/the-god-delusion-by-richard-dawkins

[49] "What animal do we share 98% of our DNA with?" EnviroLiteracy (ELC); March 10, 2025;
https://enviroliteracy.org/animals/what-animal-do-we-share-98-of-our-dna-with/

[50] 'What Does It Mean to be Human - FAQs," Smithsonian Museum of Natural History;
https://humanorigins.si.edu/education/frequently-asked-questions

51 Philipp Mitteroecker, PhD, and Barbara Fischer, PhD, The American Journal of Obstetrics and Gynecology; Volume 230, Issue 3, Supplement, 2024; https://www.ajog.org/article/S0002-9378(22)00733-5/fulltext

52 Douglas J. The Fruit of the Tree of Life: Insights into Evolution and Ecology. p. 33; New York: Oxford University Press. ISBN 978-0-19-517234-8. LCCN 2003058012.

53 "What Does it Mean to be Human – Introduction to Human Evolution," Smithsonian Museum of Natural History; https://humanorigins.si.edu/education/introduction-human-evolution

54 The Hominin form a taxonomic tribe of the subfamily, Homininae. "Hominin," Britannica; https://www.britannica.com/topic/hominin

55 "Ardipithecus ramidus," Smithsonian National Museum of Natural History; https://humanorigins.si.edu/evidence/human-fossils/species/ardipithecus-ramidus

56 "Australopithecus afarensis," Smithsonian National Museum of Natural History; https://humanorigins.si.edu/evidence/human-fossils/species/australopithecus-afarensis

57 "Homo habilis," Smithsonian National Museum of Natural History; https://humanorigins.si.edu/evidence/human-fossils/species/homo-habilis

58 "Homo erectus," Smithsonian National Museum of Natural History; https://humanorigins.si.edu/evidence/human-fossils/species/homo-erectus

59 "Homo heidelbergensis," Smithsonian National Museum of Natural History; https://humanorigins.si.edu/evidence/human-fossils/species/homo-heidelbergensis

60 "Cro-Magnon Man vs. Homo Sapiens," This vs. That; https://thisvsthat.io/cro-magnon-man-vs-homo-sapiens

61 Elizabeth Howell and Andrew May, "What is the Big Bang Theory," Space.com; updated July 26, 2023; https://www.space.com/25126-big-bang-theory.html

62 "Formation of the Earth," National Geographic; https://education.nationalgeographic.org/resource/formation-earth/

63 "Naturalism," Encyclopedia Britannica; https://www.britannica.com/topic/naturalism-philosophy

64 Jerry A. Coyne, Faith Versus Fact: Why Science and Religion Are Incompatible – May 19, 2015; Penguin Books; ISBN: 978-0670026531

65 Steven Schafersman, "Definition of Humanism," American Humanist Association; https://americanhumanist.org/what-is-humanism/definition-of-humanism/

66 Marian Sherman, "What Makes Atheists Tick?" Toronto Star Weekly; Sep, 1965

67 Gary Wenk Ph.D., "Why Do Humans Keep Inventing Gods to Worship?" Psychology Today; https://www.psychologytoday.com/us/blog/your-brain-food/202107/why-do-humans-keep-inventing-gods-worship

68 Joseph C. Sommer, "Some Reasons Why Humanists Reject The Bible," American Humanist Association; https://americanhumanist.org/what-is-humanism/reasons-humanists-reject-bible/

69 A circular argument, also called circular reasoning, is a fallacy in which the reasoner begins with what he or she is trying to end with.

70 George Gallop, Jr. & Jim Castelli, The People's Religion: American Faith in the 90's (New York: MacMillan, 1989), pp. 60-61.

71 Joseph C. Sommer, "Some Reasons Why Humanists Reject The Bible," American Humanist Association; https://americanhumanist.org/what-is-humanism/reasons-humanists-reject-bible/

72 Andrew D. White, A History of the Warfare of Science with Theology in Christendom, Vol II (New York: D Appleton and Co., 1910), p. 27

73 Andrew D. White, Ibid., p. 45

74 Andrew D. White, Ibid., p. 72-75

75 Sommer, Ibid.

76 "What is Humanism," Humanists International, Inc.; https://humanists.international/support

77 "Observable Universe." Britannica; https://www.britannica.com/topic/observable-universe

78 "The Milky Way Galaxy," Imagine the Universe; https://imagine.gsfc.nasa.gov/science/objects/milkyway1.html#:~:text=It%20is%20very%20difficult%20to,is%20about%20100%2C000%20light%20years.

79 Joshua Shavit, "Scientists discover how life on Earth began 1.75 billion years ago," Brighter Side of News; https://www.msn.com/en-us/news/technology/scientists-discover-how-life-on-earth-began-1-75-billion-years-ago/

80 "Precambrian Eon: (4,550-543 mya)," PBS – Evolution; https://www.pbs.org/wgbh/evolution/change/deeptime/archaean.html

81 "The distribution of water on, in, and above the Earth," USGS; https://www.usgs.gov/media/images/distribution-water-and-above-earth

82 USBS; Ibid.

83 The data for this illustration was provided by Our World in Data, a scientific online publication that focuses on large global problems such as poverty, disease, hunger, climate change, war, existential risks, and inequality. It is affiliated with the University of Oxford. The illustration can be found in "Land Use," Wikipedia; https://en.wikipedia.org/wiki/Land_use

84 Michon Scott, "Where will sea level rise most from ice sheet melt?" National Snow and Ice Data Center

a part of CIRES at the University of Colorado Boulder; Jun 5, 2023; https://nsidc.org/learn/ask-scientist/where-will-sea-level-rise-most-ice-sheet-melt

85 "Half of the world's habitable land is used for agriculture." Our World in Data; https://ourworldindata.org/global-land-for-agriculture

86 Russell McLendon, "20 Reasons Why Forests Are Important," TreeHugger; October 16, 2024; https://www.treehugger.com/reasons-why-forests-are-important-4868826

87 "How much of the Earth is volcanic?" USGS; https://www.usgs.gov/faqs/how-much-earth-volcanic

88 "Occurrence Rates of Planets Orbiting FGK Stars" The Astronomical Journal; https://iopscience.iop.org/article/10.3847/1538-3881/ab31ab

89 SETI Institute, "How many habitable planets are out there?" Phys Org; Oct 29, 2020; https://phys.org/news/2020-10-habitable-planets.html#:~:text=Thanks%20to%20new%20research%20using%20data%20from,likely%20within%2030%20light%2Dyears%20of%20our%20Sun.

90 Nancy Atkinson, "Hawking: God Not Needed for Universe to be Created," Universe Today; https://www.universetoday.com/72605/hawking-god-not-needed-for-universe-to-be-created/

91 Cosmology is a branch of astronomy that involves the origin and evolution of the universe, from the Big Bang to today and the future. NASA defines cosmology as "the scientific study of the large-scale properties of the universe as a whole."

92 "The Andromeda and Milky Way collision, explained," Astronomy; Dec 1, 2023; https://www.astronomy.com/science/the-andromeda-and-milky-way-collision-explained/

93 Copernicus published his heliocentric theory in the 16th century. After initialing accepting it, the Catholic Church banned his "Des Revolutionibus" for more than 200 years (from 1616 till 1835); but that was in response to substantial Protestant opposition to his heliocentric theory

94 Galileo supported the writings of Copernicus and proposed that the Earth rotated around the sun; the Catholic Church's Inquisition found him guilty in 1616 and sentenced him to jail.

95 "The Influence of Religion on Technological Advancement in Europe," International Journal of Science and Society; Volume 5, Issue 4, 2003; https://ijsoc.goacademica.com/index.php/ijsoc/article/view/815

96 The Intelligent Design theory claims that some sort of supernatural designer was involved in the creation of life of Earth. If differs from Creationism because it divorces the creationist ideas from their roots in Scripture. v

97 "Evidentialism", Internet Encyclopedia of Philosophy; https://iep.utm.edu/evidentialism/; Evidentialism it is a thesis about what it takes for one to believe justifiably, or reasonably, in the sense thought to be necessary for knowledge.

98 "God of the Gaps," Encyclopedia.com; https://www.encyclopedia.com/education/encyclopedias-almanacs-transcripts-and-maps/god-gaps

99 "God of the gaps," Rational Wiki; https://rationalwiki.org/wiki/God_of_the_gaps

100 Kyle Butt, "The 'God of the Gaps' Argument: A Refutation," Apologetics Press; Issue 44 #2; https://apologeticspress.org/the-god-of-the-gaps-arguement-a-refutation/

[101] "God of the Gaps," Encyclopedia.com; https://www.encyclopedia.com/education/encyclopedias-almanacs-transcripts-and-maps/god-gaps

[102] Dietrich Bonhoeffer, 29 May 1944, pages 310–312, Letters and Papers from Prison, edited by Eberhard Bethge, translated by Reginald H. Fuller, Touchstone, ISBN 0-684-83827-3, 1997; Munich: Christian Kaiser Verlag, 1970

[103]Richard Dawkins, The God Delusion. Bantam Press. pp. 151–161. (2006); ISBN 978-0-593-05548-9.

[104] Charles Alfred Coulson, Science and Christian Belief; p. 20; Oxford University Press, Fontana Books; 1958.

[105] Ibid., p. 35

[106] Itamar Shatz, "The Sagan Standard: Extraordinary Claims Require Extraordinary Evidence," Effectiviology; https://effectiviology.com/sagan-standard-extraordinary-claims-require-extraordinary-evidence/

[107] Thomas Cotteril, "Humans Are Pattern Seeking Primates Hunting for Habit," Thomas Cotteril; https://thomascotterill.ca/2013/03/30/humans-are-pattern-seeking-primates-hunting-for-habits/

[108] Rich Barlow, "How the AIDS Crisis Became a Moral Debate," Boston University Today; Dec 2015; https://www.bu.edu/articles/2015/anthony-petro-after-the-wrath-of-god/

[109] "Why some religious leaders denounced Benjamin Franklin's lightning rod," The Big Think; https://bigthink.com/the-past/benjamin-franklin-lightning-rod/

[110] 'Kathy Loves Physis,' "The History of the Lightning Rod: How the Lightning Rod was Invented and Terrified and Offended People," You Tube Video; Oct 9, 2017; https://bigthink.com/the-past/benjamin-franklin-lightning-rod/

[111] "Paleozoic," USGS; https://www.usgs.gov/youth-and-education-in-science/paleozoic

[112] "Phanerozoic Eon", Britannica; https://www.britannica.com/science/Phanerozoic-Eon. Phanerozoic literally means "period of well-displayed life". The Phanerozoic is the current and the latest of the four geologic eons in the Earth's geologic time scale, covering the time period from 541 million years ago to the present.

[113] In biology, it is a taxonomic rank above Class.

[114]Brian Handwerk, "An Evolutionary Timeline of Homo Sapiens," Smithsonian Magazine; Feb 2, 2021; https://www.smithsonianmag.com/science-nature/essential-timeline-understanding-evolution-homo-sapiens-180976807/

[115] Toshiko Kaneda and Carl Haub, "How many people have ever lived?" YouTube; Nov 2022; https://www.prb.org/articles/how-many-people-have-ever-lived-on-earth/

[116] "Worldwide Population Throughout Human History," World Atlas; https://www.worldatlas.com/articles/worldwide-population-throughout-human-history.html

[117] "How Many People Have Ever Lived on Earth?" PRB; https://www.prb.org/articles/how-many-people-have-ever-lived-on-earth/

[118] "Miracle," Britannica; https://www.britannica.com/topic/miracle

[119] "Miracles," Stanford Encyclopedia of Philosophy; revised May 2, 2024; https://plato.stanford.edu/entries/miracles/

[120] "Miracle," Britannica; Ibid.

[121] "Miracles" Stanford Encyclopedia of Philosophy; Ibid.

[122] Michael Shermer, "On Miracles and Truth," printed in "The Case Against Miracles," The Ehrmann Blog; Dec 22, 2019: https://ehrmanblog.org/the-case-against-miracles/

[123] Lawrence Shapiro, The Miracle Myth, Why Belief in the Resurrection and the Supernatural Is Unjustified, Columbia University Press,; 2016

[124] "Miracle Myth," Apple Books Review; https://books.apple.com/us/book/the-miracle-myth/id1133008602

[125] John Loftus, editor, The Case Against Miracles; June 29, 2022; Hypatia Press; ISBN:978-1-83919008-7

[126] Mark Pickering and Peter Saunders, "Can we believe the Bible's miracles?" Be Thinking.Org; https://www.bethinking.org/are-miracles-possible/miracles

[127] Donald L. Wasson, "Epicurus," World History Encyclopedia; Sep 7, 2016; https://www.worldhistory.org/Epicurus/

[128] "Epicurus > Quotes," Goodreads; https://www.goodreads.com/quotes/8199-is-god-willing-to-prevent-evil-but-not-able-then

[129] "Faith: Historical Perspectives," Internet Encyclopedia of Philosophy; https://iep.utm.edu/faith-re/#:~:text=This%20article%20traces%20the

[130] "Faith: Historical Perspectives," Ibid.

[131] John W. Loftus, "Faith and Reason are Mutually Exclusive Opposites," Debunking Christianity; https://www.debunking-christianity.com/2012/03/faith-and-reason-are-mutually-exclusive.html

[132] Jerry A. Coyne, Faith vs. Fact: Why Science and Religion Are Incompatible; Penguin Random House; May 17, 2016 | ISBN 9780143108269

[133] Andrew D. White, A History of the Warfare of Science with Theology in Christendom, Vol I (New York: D. Appleton and Co., 1910). p. 257

[134] Stephen L. Harris, Understanding the Bible, 2nd ed (Palto Alto and London: Mayfield Publishing, 1985), p. 178

[135] Robert Ingersoll, The Christian Religion, Vol VI, p. 84;

[136] John W. Loftus, "Top Seven Ways Christianity is Debunked by Science", Debunking Christianity; Aug 8, 2020; https://www.debunking-christianity.com/2010/08/top-seven-ways-christianity-is-debunked.html

[137] From "Geocentric model," Britannica; https://www.britannica.com/science/geocentric-model

[138] Pierre-Simon Laplace was a prominent French mathematical physicist and astronomer of the 19th century, who made crucial contributions in the arena of planetary motion by applying Sir Isaac Newton's theory of gravitation to the entire solar system. His work on celestial mechanics is considered revolutionary "Pierre-Simon Laplace," Famous Scientists; https://www.famousscientists.org/pierre-simon-laplace/

[139] Byron Jennings, "There is No Need for God as a Hypothesis." Quantum Diaries; https://www.quantumdiaries.org/2011/09/16/there-is-no-need-for-god-as-a-hypothesis/

[140] "Donation of Constantine," Encyclopedia Britannica; https://www.britannica.com/topic/Donation-of-Constantine

Chapter 2 – The Old Testament (Tanakh)

Drawing on a rich tradition of religious storytelling that spanned centuries, the Old Testament (OT) was written down[141] over many centuries by over 40 authors. The Old Testament, aka the Tanakh, comprises over 75% of the Christian Bible. The Tanakh, an acronym derived from the names of its three divisions: Torah (Instruction, or Law, also called the Pentateuch), Nevi'im (Prophets), and Ketuvim (Writings).[142]

Judaism is characterized by a belief in one transcendent God who revealed himself to the Hebrew prophets and by a religious life in accordance with Scriptures and rabbinic traditions.[143] For Christians, the OT set the stage for the coming messiah who was to fulfill Jewish prophesies and redeem all believers.

Israel's Pre-Monotheism

Judaism is known for being one of the oldest religions to believe in one God. We tend to assume that it has always been that way. But the truth is that while the Old Testament not only hints that monotheism was not initially the prevailing system of belief among the ancient Israelites,[144] but archaeological records prove it. Indeed, the Bible is rife with references to deities other than Yahweh, such as El, Baal, and Asherah. There is both scriptural and archaeological evidence of polytheistic worship in Israel.[145]

Although the Old Testament narratives depict Yahweh as "the sole creator god, lord of the universe, and god of the Israelites," initially, he seems to have been Canaanite in origin and subordinate to the supreme god, El (Elyon)."[146] Indeed, it appears that YHWH was incorporated into the Canaanite polytheistic pantheon of gods as the son of El or Elyon. YHWH received Israel as his inheritance, and his consort was Asherah (but over time the Israelites edited her out).[147] Representing the biblical pronunciation of "YHWH," the name is composed from the sequence of consonants Yod, Heh, Waw, and Heh; together, they are known as the tetragrammaton.[148]

Many religions trace their beliefs back to precursor religions, as monotheistic religions often evolve from polytheistic ones. Indeed, the Old Testament implies that other gods exist. **Psalm 82** implies that God has power over other gods, and he has the power to demote them. **Psalm 82** presents the god El presiding in a divine assembly, at which Yahweh stands up and makes his accusation against the other gods. Here, the text shows the older religious framework that the passage is denouncing. God then announces that he has decided to demote the other gods, turning them into mere mortals.

- **Psalm 82:1:** "God standeth in the congregation of the mighty; He judgeth among the gods"...
- **Psalm 82:5-7:** "They know not; neither will they understand; they walk about in darkness; all the foundations of the earth are out of course. I have said, 'Ye are gods, and all of you are children of the most high. But ye will die like men, and fall like one of the princes.' "

It appears that the pre-Judaism Hebrews were pantheistic, but monotheism remains the defining feature in their switch to Judaism.[149] It was during the Iron Age period of the 11th century BCE that the Israelites moved toward Yahwism as the primary religion. They focused on the exclusive worship of Yahweh, who assumed the characteristics of El,[150] the supreme god of the Canaanite religion.[151] Indeed, over time, the existence of other gods was denied, and Yahweh became the sole divinity to be worshipped. Monotheism in ancient Israel seems to have developed over the span of time from approximately the 10th century BCE to the Babylonian Exile (6th century BCE).[152] Indeed, the exclusive worship of Yahweh is said to have begun at the earliest with Elijah in the 9th century; but more probably, it likely occurred with the prophet, Hosea[153] (from about 750 to 722 B.C.E.).[154]

According to American biblical researcher, D. M. Murdoch, "even after the fifth century (BCE), Jews in general continued to revere deities other than Yahweh, including syncretizing him with the gods Zeus, Dionysus, and others. It has been surmised that the Jews were not completely monotheistic until the time of the Maccabees (2nd century BCE)."[155]

There are several theories regarding how Yahweh worked his way through the pantheon of gods in Canaan to become the sole God of the Israelites. Today, one of the most prominent views of historians is that he was perceived as a warrior god at a time when Israel was in great peril from its enemies. The warrior leaders and their retinues called upon Yahweh, the warrior god, to aid them. When dealing with how Yahweh became the sole deity to the Israelites, Yahweh as a war god seems to make the most sense to those historians who have researched how the formation of Israel and the central cult in Jerusalem emerged through war.[156]

During the Babylonian captivity in the 6th and 5th centuries BCE, some exiled Judahites in Babylon refined pre-existing ideas about Yahwism, such as the nature of divine election (that they were the chosen people), Jewish religious laws, and various covenants with their god. Their ideas flourished to become the dominant view in the Jewish community in the following centuries.[157] The characteristics of Yahweh were codified following the Babylonian Captivity of the 6th century BCE, and the Hebrew Scriptures were eventually finalized during the Second Temple Period (c. 515 BCE-70 CE).[158]

Organization of the Old Testament

The Tanakh consists of three parts: the Torah, Nevi'im, and Ketuvim.[159] The Christian version can be organized into four major sections: (1) the Pentateuch, (2) the Historical Books, (3) the Wisdom Books, and (4) the Prophetic Books—subdivided into the Major and Minor Prophets.

1. <u>Pentateuch</u> (Torah): The Pentateuch is the first five books, which correspond to the Jewish Torah. This includes: Genesis, Exodus, Leviticus, Numbers, and Deuteronomy.
2. <u>Historical Books</u> (Nevi'im): Tell the history of the Israelites
3. <u>Wisdom Books (Ketuvim/Writings)</u>: Deal with questions of good and evil
4. <u>Prophetic Books (Nevi'im)</u>: Warn of the consequences of turning away from God. This includes Joshua, Samuel, Kings, Isaiah, Jeremiah/Lamentations, Ezekiel, and the Twelve (Hosea to Malachi).

Instead of being compiled in a chronological order, the Old Testament books are categorized into literary sections (e.g., the law, history, poetry, and prophecy). There is a series of differences among the Jewish, Orthodox Christians, Roman Catholics, and Protestant Bible versions:[160]

- The foundational texts can differ
- The total number of biblical books can differ: only 24 books for the Jewish Bible, but 46 books for the Roman Catholic Bible, 39 books for the Protestant Bible, and 53 books for the Orthodox Christian Bible
- The arrangement of the categories of the books differs
- The titles of some of the books differ
- The categorization of some books differs

Similarly to the New Testament, the division of chapters and verses was added much later than the original writing, to help readers refer to specific passages. The formatting of the Old Testament moves logically from higher subdivisions to smaller ones: Books –> Chapters –> Verses.

Most of the Old Testament was written in classical Hebrew. However, some sections were also written in Aramaic. For comparison purposes, the New Testament texts were written in koine (common) Greek. The Tanakh, or Old Testament, was put to written text primarily from 600 to 200 BCE.[161] Its compilation was a gradual process with successive writings from verbal stories. The Old Testament is sometimes contradicted by archaeological discoveries, and is sometimes full of revealing anachronisms,[162] as it is untethered to actual historical and scientific facts. It is in many ways an allegorical tale, and as such, it does not qualify as history.

The Jewish Tanakh ends with the books of Chronicles (1 & 2), which follow the exiled Jews back to the city of Jerusalem to rebuild. But the Christian Bible(s) rearranges the traditional order of the Bible and places the Prophetic books at the end. This is because the Christians have manufactured a connection with the predicted messiah of the Jews from **Isaiah 7:14** (regarding a virgin who would bear a son named Immanuel) and **Malachi 3:1** (which cites a "messenger of the Covenant"), which Christians wanted to believe referred to the coming of Jesus.[163] But what it really says is: "Behold. I will send my messenger, and he shall prepare the way before me..." Not exactly a detailed prediction. But similar to many of the prophecies in the Tanakh, such ambiguity enabled Christian enthusiasts to read into its fulfillment.

There are seven books in the Catholic Bible - Baruch, Judith, 1 and 2 Maccabees, Sirach, Tobit, and Wisdom - which are not included in the Protestant version of the Old Testament, nor the Jewish Tanakh. Roman Catholics refer to these seven books as the Deuterocanonical books (meaning second canon); whereas Protestants call them Apocrypha (meaning hidden).[164]

Strange Passages

The Old Testament (OT) is the result of multiple stories handed down over generations until they were finally written down. That said, the scribes who penned the stories apparently did so from rote memory, and they did not appear to adjust them due to logic. I am not referring to a comparison to the general knowledge and logic of 21st-century man, but rather to common sense. The OT is laden with exaggerations, historical mistakes, anachronisms, and contradictions. And it does not appear to be inspired by any deity; nor should it be perceived as a reliable source of truth. Indeed, there is so much misinformation in the Old Testament that it will suffice to select a few of the more inventive, if well-known stories, and explain why they are inaccurate depictions.

The Hebrew Bible (Tanakh)		
The Law	**The Prophets**	**The Writing**
Torah (Pentateuch)	*Former Prophets*	*Poetry*
Genesis	Joshua	Psalms
Exodus	Judges	Proverbs
Leviticus	Samuel (1&2)	Job
Numbers	Kings (1&2)	
Deuteronomy		
	Latter Prophets	*Five Scrolls*
	Isaiah	Song of Songs
	Jeremiah	Ruth
	Ezekiel	Lamentations
	The Twelve	Esther
Hosea	Nahum	Ecclesiastes
Joel	Habakkuk	
Amos	Zephaniah	*History*
Obadiah	Haggai	Daniel
Jonah	Zechariah	Ezra-Nehemiah
Micah	Malachi	Chronicles (1&2)

Creation of the World

Through the clarity of modern geological and biological evidence, we know that life on Earth evolved over hundreds of millions of years. The OT's creation story is overly simplistic. In fact, nothing written in Genesis indicates any insights from an omniscient being. It appears to be a series of man-made tales desperately trying to explain what the authors didn't truly understand.

- **Genesis 1:8:** "And God called the firmament Heaven. And the evening and the morning were the second day."
- **Genesis 1:9:** "And God said, Let the waters under the heaven be gathered together unto one place, and let the dry land appear: and it was so."
- **Genesis 1:14:** "And God said, Let there be lights in the firmament of the heaven to give light upon the earth"
- **Genesis 1:16:** "And God made two great lights; the greater light to rule the day, and the lesser light to rule the night: he made the stars also."

Even with rudimentary knowledge, the Iron Age writers of Genesis should never have penned the above verses, in which God creates light before creating the sun. The authors indicated that the moon provided light, and the stars were an afterthought. And there are no lights in the firmament, as there is no firmament. Inspired by God? Not likely. This is not a hermeneutical (interpretation) issue as some religious apologists would have us believe. Some people have referred to this part of the creation story as "a comedy of errors."[165]

In general, people are cognizant that most cultures have a creationist myth, and many have borrowed parts of that myth from beliefs of cultures that have preceded them. Many unbiased reviewers believe that the Israelites' creation tale in Genesis has some strong parallels to the much older Babylonian story of creation, Enuma Elis.[166] This is not a suggestion that the Israelites copied from the Babylonian text, but they were clearly familiar with it. However, Genesis obviously sprang from the collective imaginations of some Israelite storytellers, and the influence of Enuma Elis[167] is evident, no matter how minimal the apologists suggest it is. With all the above said, the creation story in Genesis appears to be just a colorful myth to establish a rationale for Jews to honor the Sabbath each week.

Noah's Ark

Clearly, one of the hardest-to-believe tales of the Old Testament concerns a global flood! Many historians believe that it is a retelling of the great flood in Gilgamesh![168] This biblical story just doesn't match the realities of Earth's geology. There are some huge logistical issues that had to be overcome as a handful of unlearned, Stone Age people try to put all the world's animal species into a single boat – something an entire army of 21st century men and women could not do.

First, where did all the water come from? It had to be enough water to raise ocean levels hundreds or thousands of feet to cover the mountains. And later, where did it go? Such a tall tale defies the laws of physics in the natural world. It is one thing for Iron Age tribesmen (the audience of that time period) to believe this, but modern man would have to be incredibly, willfully unknowledgeable to accept it (and yes, there are people today in the 21st century who believe this extraordinary tale).

Second, in collecting animals, we are talking about the species of animals, since "species" is what categorizes animals with regard to reproduction. A sampling of all the land-based species of the Earth couldn't fit into the USS Titanic, much less a wooden ark, no matter what shape it took; and it was constructed by a few stone-age men who had zero experience with shipbuilding or navigating a crowded wooden ship in storm conditions. There are over two million species of animals living today, which have been cataloged by scientists so far; and there appear to be another estimated million species waiting to be discovered and cataloged.[169] That does not count all the species that have gone extinct since man evolved. Today, there are 6,596 known mammal species, as well as arachnids (95,966 species), insects (1.053 million species), reptiles (12,263), and birds (11,195).[170] [171] All can drown. We have not addressed the 8,776 amphibian species (although they can only swim for a brief time), and the sea animals, including corals, crustaceans, and mollusks. Let's also debunk the nonsense of apologists who say that the story is not about species but 'kinds' of animals. So, in other words, they suggest that a dire wolf would evolve into wolves, dogs, foxes, coyotes, etc. But that would take a very large pool of dire wolves and millions of years in time. Of course, the idea for the 'kinds' of animals comes from the same apologists who say that they don't believe in evolution. They cannot have it both ways.

The numbers are even worse if you follow **Genesis 7:2-3,** which requires seven pairs of all 'clean' animals:

- **[Verse 2]:** "Of every clean beast thou shalt take to thee by sevens, the male and the female; and of beasts that are not clean by two, the male and his female."
- **[Verse 3]:** "Of fowls also of the air by sevens, the male and the female; to keep seed alive upon the face of all the earth."

And finally, how did Noah and his sons find and collect these animals over multiple continents and garner all the food they would need (including other animals for the meat eaters)? Do we assume all the animals were caged to protect them? What about all the waste that these animals would create? Who cleaned out the cages? And what did the carnivores eat? And later, they had to return these animals to various places in the world such that jaguars, caimans, anacondas, and tapirs were dropped off to unknown South

America, short-faced bears, armadillos, moose, and alligators to undiscovered North America, and kangaroos, koalas (and their eucalyptus trees since the original ones would have died from the flood), and platypuses to unexplored Australia? And of course, penguins go to the unknown Antarctica. Or else, how can one explain how they arrived at those places after the global flood? Also, many of the animals would have been at the mercy of the carnivores as soon as they left the ark, because there were no other animals for the carnivores to eat; so that would force several additional animal species into extinction. And then there were the freshwater fish and similar creatures for whom the salinity of the oceans would be poisonous! And of course, with the flora all destroyed by the flood, the herbivores would have nothing to eat. And thus, many of those herbivore species would die out as well.

This incredulous fable goes way beyond our traditional way of thinking about the natural world. Why didn't the all-knowing God, who had recently created the world, its animals, and its humans, recognize that this would happen? It would have been much simpler to re-create mankind than to go through the farce of the Great Flood with a little wooden ark.

In **Genesis 8:21**, the 'omniscient' God realizes after the flood that "the imagination of man's heart is evil from his youth," and He regrets what he had done. He then allowed mankind freewill. What this tale suggests is that God tortured every man, woman, and child (except Noah's immediate family), and all the animals on Earth with drowning, all because He made a mistake. What did the innocent animals ever do but exist? For God so loved the world, He killed every human and every beast (except the relatively few on the Ark)! That is what the author(s) of the Book of Genesis would have us believe.

Tower of Babel

Genesis 11: 1-9 presents the story of the Tower of Babel. The builder's purpose was to create a city and a tower "whose top will reach into the heaven," **[Genesis 11:4]** and protect themselves from another flood, which seems like a reasonable motivation. Additionally, mankind once believed that heaven was a dome or firmament suspended above the Earth. According to the author(s) of the Book of Genesis, the Israelite God, rather than being proud of the progress of his human creation, was fearful, and he said:

- **Genesis 11:6-7:** "… the people are one; and they have one language; and this they begin to do; and now nothing will be restrained from them, which they have imagined to do. Let us go down, and there confound their language…"

And so, God confounded their language so that the people could not understand one another, and they scattered. In these verses, the Bible paints a picture of a brooding, not-so-omnipotent, not-so-omniscient God. After all, did God not know that the Tower couldn't exceed a height whereby people would have difficulty breathing (an impossibility with their limited technology), due to the low oxygen in the air? This becomes apparent to anyone who has ever climbed a path up a sizable mountain. And wouldn't God know that there was no physical heaven above the Earth!

The Tower of Babel is a type of myth known as an etiology, which is intended to explain the origin of a custom or other phenomenon — namely, the origins of the multiplicity of languages. Of course, the story is mythical; it may have been inspired by the Babylonian tower temple north of the Marduk temple, which in Babylonian was called Bab-ilu ("Gate of God").[172] The story not only paints God as weak and whiny, but it also totally repudiates the concept that the biblical text was inspired by God. And just who is God speaking to when he says, "Let **us** go down...'? Is this an indication that the human biblical author supported polytheism? Moreover, people did not speak one language at any time in Earth's history. And this passage contradicts **Genesis 10:5, 10:20,** and **10:31**. Finally, this story is set only three generations after Noah. [Noah begat Ham, who begat Cush, who begat Nimrod]. And Nimrod's kingdom was Babel **[Genesis 10:10].**[173] So, how big a city could it have been? It would have been more like a small town or hamlet. The story was meant to convey the arrogance of man, but instead, the story's author(s) reveal the cruelty, selfishness, and relative weakness of the Israelite god. Even as an allegory, this remains a bewildering tale.

Exodus

According to Martin Noth, the German biblical scholar who specialized in the early history of the Jewish people, oral traditions from various tribes were combined in the Torah (Pentateuch); and they were finally written down around the time of the Prophet Ezra (between the 5th and 4th century BCE). It is likely that the different narratives were combined into a single tale, such that a story of Passover and that of Exodus may have been separate traditions, but found themselves linked, once penned.[174]

Exodus is a tale about a significant number of Jewish slaves who have been toiling in captivity for 400 years of continuous bondage. And the estimated number of slaves leaving Egypt was over two million.[175] It's almost common knowledge now that slaves did not build the pyramids, but actually, they were built by paid labor. Furthermore, Egyptians were not known for having a public slave market, unlike their neighboring cultures in Arabia and Syria.[176] If ancient Egypt had few or no public markets for buying and selling slaves, then the story that Joseph, the Israelite patriarch, was ever sold into slavery to the Egyptians is doubtful.

Slavery was just not part of the Egyptian tradition, with the occasional exception of prisoners of war. Historians work from evidence. And there is no evidence in the archaeological and historical record to support the existence of Israelite slaves. And there is no written record of large numbers of Israelites EVER having lived in Egypt. We are talking over 2,400 years of written history by the ancient Egyptians.

The central focus of Jewish identity is the Passover, which commemorates the precursor event when Moses freed his people from slavery in Egypt. That event was the death of every firstborn male in Egypt.

- **Exodus: 12:12:** "For I will pass through the land of Egypt this night, and smite all the firstborn in the land of Egypt, both man and beast; and against all the gods of Egypt I will execute judgment: I am the Lord."

Typical for the God of the Israelites to kill every innocent, first-born animal. And given the rules of royal succession, the pharaoh would probably have been firstborn himself. Equally fascinating, according to the author(s) of Exodus, the all-knowing God of the Israelites couldn't tell the Egyptian households from the Israelite ones; so, the lamb's blood on the doors was needed. How embarrassing! There is no exact time frame for when the events of Exodus were to have occurred,[177] but many biblical scholars have suggested circa 1400 BCE. Of course, there is not a shred of evidence for the Passover, the great Exodus out of Egypt, the 10 plagues, the parting of the sea, the mass drowning of the Egyptian army, etc.[178] Additionally, outside of biblical Scripture, there is no evidence in the archaeological and historical record of Moses's existence.

In fact, the "traditional claim of Mosaic authorship" of the whole Pentateuch is untenable.[179] The only writing that existed circa 1400 BCE in that part of the world was (1) cuneiform, written on large, heavy clay tablets, (2) the Egyptian hieroglyphs, and (3) Phoenician. The original Ten Commandments are said to have been written in Hebrew, but that would be unlikely because the Hebrew alphabet hadn't been created yet. The earliest record of written Hebrew dates to the 11th century BCE[180] (approximately 300 years after Moses' time). Also, the Torah was first written in an older version of Hebrew, Paleo-Hebrew (a.k.a., Old Hebrew).[181] Later, the Torah was translated from Paleo-Hebrew to Biblical Hebrew (also known as square-script Hebrew, or classical Hebrew), probably around the middle of the 3rd century BCE.[182] Not only do the Egyptians never mention anything about the Exodus story, but they also never mention Moses. In her article for Time magazine, author and journalist Lily Rothman wrote:

> "Even scholars who [want to believe] it really happened admit that there's no proof whatsoever that the Exodus took place. No record of this monumental event appears in Egyptian chronicles of the time, and Israeli archaeologists combing the Sinai during intense searches from 1967 to 1982, years when Israel occupied the peninsula—didn't find a single piece of evidence backing the Israelites' supposed 40-year sojourn in the desert."[183]

In the early 1970s, the Israeli government funded a massive effort to locate and prove any aspect of the Exodus story in archaeological digs and historical records. Some of the best archaeologists in the world spent the next 30+ years searching for ANY evidence. They found none! Internationally renowned Egyptian archaeologist, Zahi Hawass, weighed in with his views in 2007 to a Washington Post reporter: "Really, it's a myth," Hawass said. "Sometimes, as archaeologists, we have to say that never happened because there is no historical evidence."[184]

In The Bible Unearthed, Israeli archaeologists, Israel Finkelstein and Neil Asher Silberman, dispelled any illusions that their digs had verified the story of the Exodus:

> "The process that we describe here is, in fact, the opposite of what we have in the Bible: the emergence of early Israel was an outcome of the collapse of the Canaanite culture, not its cause. And most of the Israelites did not come from outside Canaan – they emerged from within it. There was no mass Exodus from Egypt. There was no violent conquest of Canaan. Most of the people who formed early Israel were local people – the same people whom we see in the highlands throughout the Bronze and Iron Ages. The early Israelites were – irony of ironies – themselves originally Canaanites!"[185]

If over two million slaves escaped from what was then the most powerful country in that part of the world, and the entire Egyptian army was destroyed while in pursuit, this would obviously be a highly significant event. We could expect that there would be some mention of it in one ancient writing or another. But there is no such record, and no other nation or group took advantage of the situation. Additionally, there are no archaeological traces of the fleeing Israelites on any routes into and out of the Sinai. The reason is obvious: the pharaoh and his entire army were not destroyed at the Sea of Reeds (Red Sea). As was the case with the stories of Genesis, here too we appear to be dealing with legend. The Exodus tradition was hugely important, as it became a kind of "founding legend" for the nation of Israel. However, it does not appear to be actual history.[186]

The Character of Moses

Moses, the traditional author of the OT Pentateuch, the patriarch of Judaism, Christianity, and Islam, who famously penned his own death, impossibly describing the location of his tomb, appears to be a fictional individual. As stated by renowned author John Loftus, "Moses, in short, is an Osiris re-script (i.e., a monotheistic god-to-prophet rewrite of the Egyptian god, Osiris, into the fictional Judaic figure of the prophet lawgiver...)."[187]

According to archaeologist and historian, Acharya S (alias D. M. Murdock), "...The Moses fable is an ancient mythological motif found in numerous cultures. It therefore has nothing to do with any particular ethnic group, and the character of Moses is not the founder of the Jewish ideology."[188] It appears that the story of Moses, as told in Exodus and the Ten Commandments, may be motifs borrowed from other myths. Outside the Old Testament, there is no evidence that Moses ever existed, no contemporary references, no corroborating, extant sources.

It is extremely unlikely that Moses was anything more than a man-made persona[189] used to tell the imaginary legend of Exodus and the Ten Commandments.[190] The Ten Commandments were a set of biblical rules which correlated with the ethics and worship practices of the Israelites. According to William G. Dever, "the overwhelming scholarly consensus today is that Moses is a mythical figure."[191] Very importantly, the story of Moses is a cultural myth, which is a good thing, since his personality, as depicted in the Old Testament, is that of a psychopath. Consider the tale given in **Numbers 31: 16-18**, in the land of the Midianites, whereby thousands of male children and thousands of women were ruthlessly murdered; and the virgin girls kept as 'slaves' for the men.

- **Verse 17:** "Now therefore kill every male among the little ones, and kill every woman that hath known a man by lying with him."
- **Verse 18:** "But all the women children, that have not known man by lying with him, keep alive for yourselves."
- **Verse 35:** "And thirty and two thousand persons in all, of women that had not known man by lying with him."

Exodus 32:26-29 reveals that the 3,000 men, (that's not counting women or children) who choose not to follow Moses, were murdered by their own people, the Levi, the very same tribe chosen to be priests, all because Moses was incensed that some of the people wanted to go their own way.

- **Verse 27:** "And he said unto them, Thus saith the Lord God of Israel, Put every man his sword by his side, and go in and out from gate to gate throughout the camp, and slay every man his brother, and every man his companion, and every man his neighbor."
- **Verse 28:** "And the children of Levi did according to the word of Moses: and there fell of the people that day about three thousand men."

Then there is Deuteronomy, in which Moses utterly destroyed the men, women and children of every city in the region; and there were no survivors.

Deuteronomy 3: 4-6

- **Verse 4:** "And we took all his cities at that time, there was not a city which we took not from them, threescore cities, all the region of Ar'gob, the kingdom of Og in Ba'shan.
- **Verse 5:** "All these cities were fenced with high walls, gates, and bars; beside unwalled towns a great many."
- **Verse 6:** "And we utterly destroyed them, as we did unto Sihon king of Hesh'bon, utterly destroying the men, women and children of every city."

The Walls of Jericho

The story of the fall of Jericho is told in **Joshua 5:13–6:27**. It was the first battle fought by the Israelites during the conquest of Canaan. In this passage, Joshua leads the Israelites marching around the city walls once a day for six days, and then seven times on the seventh day, when the priests blow their trumpets, and the Israelites shout a battle cry. The sound of the trumpets and the shouts cause the walls to collapse, and the Israelites take the city. And of course, the Israelites revel in the destruction of another people. Except that it appears to have never happened!

Joshua 6:

- **Verse 20:** "So the people shouted when the priests blew with the trumpets: and it came to pass, when the people heard the sound of the trumpet, and the people shouted with a great shout, that the wall fell down flat, so that the people went up into the city, every man straight before him, and they took the city."
- **Verse 21:** "And they utterly destroyed all that was in the city, both man and woman, young and old, and ox, and sheep and ass, with the edge of the sword."

In 1868, General Sir Charles Warren, GCMG, (Feb 1840 – Jan 1927) of the British Royal Engineers,[192] identified Tell es-Sultan (also known as Tel Jericho) as the site of biblical Jericho.[193] General Warren had been one of the earliest European archaeologists of the biblical Holy Land, and particularly of the Temple Mount. Later, between 1907 and 1911, Ernst Sellin and Carl Watzinger, German archaeologists, excavated the site, finding the remains of two walls, which they eventually dated to the Middle Bronze Age (1950–1550 BCE).[194] Kathleen Kenyon, a British archaeologist of the Neolithic culture, re-excavated the site in the years 1952–1958, and she concluded that the destruction occurred at an earlier time, and that Jericho had been deserted throughout the mid-late 13th century BCE, the supposed time of Joshua's battle.[195] In 1995, Kenyon's work was corroborated by radiocarbon tests, which dated the destruction level to the late 17th or 16th centuries BCE.[196] A small unwalled settlement was rebuilt in the 15th century BCE, but it has been agreed among archaeologists that Tell es-Sultan was unoccupied from the late 15th century until the 10th/9th centuries BCE.[197]

The strong consensus among scholars is that the Book of Joshua holds little historical truth.[198] The story of Jericho and the Israelite conquest represents the propaganda of the Kingdom of Judah and their claims to the territory after 722 BCE.[199] Unfortunately, no archaeological evidence corroborates the biblical account of what happened in Jericho.[200] As for what did happen, "the walls of Jericho fell not because of trumpet-playing inspired by the heavens, but by events beneath the ground."[201] In other words, the calamity was caused by an earthquake that occurred long before the Israelites got there. That same fault line threatens other nearby towns today.

The Book of Daniel

The Book of Daniel purports to have been written in the 6th century BCE, and it concerns the prophetic ministry of Daniel the prophet, who was taken into Babylonian captivity at the fall of Jerusalem. The book of Daniel contains many detailed 'predictive prophecies' concerning the course of history. For reasons discussed below, it has prompted many critical scholars to date the authorship of Daniel to the 2nd century B.C., during the Maccabean revolt[202] against the Seleucid king, Antiochus IV Epiphanes[203] (215 – 164 BCE). The Maccabean Revolt was a Jewish rebellion led by Judas Maccabeus and his four brothers against the Seleucid Empire, after King Antiochus issued decrees forbidding certain Jewish religious practices. The main phase of the revolt occurred from 167 to 160 BCE, but resistance continued until 134 BCE, when the Maccabees eventually attained independence.

The Book of Daniel claims to have been written at the time of the Babylonian exile (597 – 538 BCE), but that claim is highly unlikely. It had exerted significant influence on the beginnings of Christianity by prophesying 'one like a Son of Man.' Historians believe that the detailed prophecies and other content were written after the events that they describe, making them appear predictive. This is particularly true of historical events occurring during the reign of the Seleucid king, Antiochus IV Epiphanes (2nd century BCE). There are several key indicators that support the "pious fraud" argument:

- *Historical Inconsistencies with the Babylonian timeline of the 6th century* – The historical details in the book do not align with known facts of the Babylonian period. In other words, the author of Daniel knew very little about the Babylonia period in which he supposedly lived. Not only that, but Daniel was supposed to have held a high position on the Babylonian court.
- *Daniel's overly detailed account of Antiochus IV Epiphanes* – Antiochus IV was the Greek ruler who persecuted the Jews in the 2nd century BCE, and Daniel's predictions of his reign seem to retroactively fit historical events. Thus, what was written to appear predictive was actually the author's interpretations of relatively recent past events.[204]

- *Those prophecies that exceed 164 BCE* – Whether the author of the Book of Daniel died circa 164 BCE or just stopped writing, the predictions after that date were well off the mark, with highly inaccurate predictions.[205]
- *Different authorship* – There appear to be two different authors for the Book of Daniel. Chapters 1-6 appear to be written earlier, and Chapters 7-12 later, with the 2nd author adding a series of prophecies to the earlier writings.[206] Supporting this view is that **Daniel 1** and **Daniel 8-12** are written in Hebrew, but **Daniel 2-7** are written in Aramaic. **Daniel 1-7:1** is written in the third person, but **Daniel 7:2 to 12:13** (the last verse of the Book of Daniel) is written in the first person.
- *Lack of external corroboration* – There are no external sources to validate the key stories of the book.
- *Literary style and genre* – The Book's literary style and genre are not compatible with the Jewish literature at the time of Daniel's 6th century life, but they are characteristic of later Jewish writings. The Book of Daniel is similar to apocalyptic literature, and it uses symbolic language and imagery to convey religious messages.

The Book of Daniel appears to have been written in its final form around 165 or 164 BCE. It is neither a book of history nor a book of prophecy.[207] It seems odd that the person who supposedly lived in the 6th century BCE got many of his facts about Babylon in the 6th century so wrong, but then suddenly was able to predict events in the 2nd century BCE; and for the period post-164 BCE (the year that Antiochus IV Epiphanes died), suddenly the author got nothing correct.

The following are some examples of the mis-statements from the Book of Daniel.

- **Daniel 1:1-2:** "In the third year of the reign of Jehoiakim, king of Judah, came Nebuchadnezzar , king of Babylon unto Jerusalem, and besieged it. And the Lord gave Jehoiakim, king of Judah, into his hand, with part of the vessels of the house of God: which he carried into the land of Shinar [refers to Babylon] to the house of his god; and he brought the vessels into the treasure house of his god."

The above is way off. The third year of the reign of Jehoiakim is 606 BCE. Nebuchadnezzar, who acquired the throne of Babylon in 605 BCE, besieged and sacked Jerusalem in 598 BCE, the eleventh year of Jehoiakim's reign. Actually, Jehoiakim was killed before the sack of Jerusalem, and his son, Jehoiachin (a.k.a. Jeconiah) reigned a few months before the city fell. Judah had been a vassal state of Egypt, and when Nebuchadnezzar threatened Jehoiakim, the latter had pledged allegiance to Babylon; and it became its vassal state until 601, when Jehoiakim re-allied with Egypt. So, Nebuchadnezzar attacked Jerusalem.[208] These events are confirmed by Babylonian records; no contemporary of that period would confuse these events, nor confuse the timeline.

- **Daniel 5:1-2:** "Belshazzar, the king made a great feast to a thousand of his lords, and drank wine before the thousand. Belshazzar, whiles he tasted the wine, commanded to bring the golden and silver vessels which his father, Nebuchadnezzar, had taken out of the temple which was in Jerusalem..."

However, Belshazzar was not the son of Nebuchadnezzar, nor was he the successor, and he was never the king of Babylon. Nebuchadnezzar's successors were Amel Marduk (who survived him by only two years), Neriglissar (559-555), and Nabonidus (555-538). Near the end of Nabonidus' reign, Babylon fell to Cyrus the Great (600 – 529 BCE), who founded the Achaemenid Empire (Persia). It was under Cyrus that the Jewish exiles from Judah were allowed to return and rebuild their temple.[209]

- **Daniel 5:29-31:** "Then commanded Belshazzar, and they clothed Daniel with scarlet, and put a chain of gold about his neck, and made a proclamation concerning him, that he should be the third ruler in the kingdom. That night was Belshazzar, the king of the Chaldeans, slain. And Darius the Median [Mede] took the kingdom, being about threescore and two years old."

Darius the Mede is an invention of the author of the Book of Daniel. The king at that time was Nabonidus. The Persians, not the Medes, took over the Babylonian kingdom, but they spared the life of Nabonidus. Darius the Great reigned from 522 to 486 BCE, as the third king of the Achaemenid Empire (Persia), but it was Cyrus the Great who conquered Babylon. While the author was clearly confused regarding the political chronology of this time, he managed to proclaim his own high status within the kingdom.

- **Daniel 6:**
  Verse 1: "It pleased Darius to set over the kingdom a hundred and twenty princes, which should be over the whole kingdom."
  Verse 2: "And over these three presidents; of whom Daniel was the first: that the princes might give accounts onto them, and the kings should have no damage."
  Verse 3: "Then this Daniel was preferred above the presidents and princes, because an excellent spirit was in him; and the king sought to set him over the whole realm."

This refers to the system which divided Persia into provinces or satraps; and it was Cyrus the Great, not Darius, who created approximately 20 satraps, not 120. These are mistakes that a contemporary official would not make. And, of course, there is no record of any of these "princes" being named Daniel, nor of anyone outranking them being named Daniel.

- **Daniel 9:1:** "In the first year of Darius, the son of Ahasuerus [a.k.a. Xerxes], of the seed of the Medes, which was made king over the realm of the Chaldeans;"

Now the author reverses the line of succession. Xerxes (486 – 465 BCE) was the son of Darius, and the 4th king of the Achaemenid Empire (Persia).

Daniel 9:24 tells us that 70 weeks had to elapse before everlasting righteousness would occur. That means the end of the world. And we are still waiting for that.

Daniel 11:1-4 is not very accurate, but **Daniel 11:5-39** is highly detailed, and gets progressively more so as it moves into the Seleucid era, especially regarding the ten-year reign of Antiochus.[210] However, starting with **Daniel 11 40-45,** the author of Daniel completely botches his predictions, such as predicting a war between the Ptolemies and the Seleucids, forecasting that Antiochus would conquer most of North Africa, and prophesying the death of Antiochus in Palestine. None of these events ever occurred. Indeed, Antiochus did not capture a single province in North Africa, and he was nowhere near Palestine when he died (he was in Persia). **Daniel 12** focuses on the end times for Jews, having nothing to do with Jesus Christ.

All these mistakes are highly improbable for someone who was a contemporary, much less a supposed high official. The 3rd century philosopher, Porphyry[211], was the first to famously point this out. He claimed that the *Book of Daniel* was forged by a Palestinian Jew in the time of Antiochus Epiphanes. He considered it a pseudonymous prophecy that was *'ex eventu'* (after the event), which focused on the persecution of the Jews under Antiochus IV Epiphanes.[212] None of Porphyry's works survives however, and his critique of Daniel is known to us only through St. Jerome[213] (~342-420), who interacts with Porphyry's critiques in his commentary on Daniel.

The claim by multiple biblical scholars that the Book of Daniel is a "pious fraud" underscores the belief that it was written much later than the time it purports to be set in, during the Babylonian exile; and it was intentionally crafted to bolster Jewish faith during the Maccabean Revolt by creating prophecies that seemed to predict future events, thus giving the impression of divine inspiration even though it was written after those events occurred.

Yahweh – The OT's Most Proficient Mass-Murderer

According to the stories in the Tanakh, the OT deity had an ego so fragile that he killed off thousands of species and multiple tribes/nations who did not conform to his expectations. A notoriously vengeful deity, Yahweh saw the death of humans as an appropriate punishment for even trivial offenses, or for just being part of a different tribe or nation; and he assured the death of animals whom he created for doing nothing at all. The following passages are very disturbing, and the Israelite author(s) present Yahweh as behaving as a mass murderer.

Here are just some <u>examples</u> of the divine destruction attributed to Yahweh:[214]

Biblical Reference	Fatalities	The Supposed Crime
Genesis 6:7	The "Flood" An estimated 20 million people and millions of animal species.	People being 'wicked'. The most horrible instance of crimes against humanity (and all animal species) known as, **Collective Punishment.** He drowned innocent children, pregnant women and animals.
Genesis 19: 4-5 Ezekiel 16: 46-48, and Ezekiel 16: 49-50	The towns of Sodom and Gomorrah (population of Sodom est. to be 600-1,200; Gomorrah presumably would be similar).	According to Genesis: being evil and wanting to rape two angels (who visited Sodom in the form of men). The passage suggests that a mob were interested in homosexual rape in respect to the angels. Lot — the only example of a good man in the city — offered them his virgin daughters instead, but the mob was not interested. According to Ezekiel): Their crime was being prideful (arrogant), overfed and unconcerned

		(having an abundance of idleness); neglecting the poor and needy; being haughty and committing abominations before God. This is an instance of **Collective Punishment** where God punishes the "wicked" with the innocent.
Genesis 19:26	The wife of Lot	Pausing to look back at the spectacle of God destroying entire cities, in a massive conflagration of (in direct contradiction of Yahweh's strange order not to do so).
Genesis 38:7	Er, the firstborn of Judah.	Judah was "wicked in the sight of the Lord."
Genesis 38: 9-10	Onan (Er's brother)	Disobeying God's orders to impregnate his dead brother's wife.
Exodus 9: 22-26	People and beasts in fields.	Being outside when God decided to show his strength. God hardened Pharaoh's heart, so he refused to let the Israelites go. **Collective Punishment**
Exodus 12:29	The firstborn of Egypt; all non-Israelite residents of Egypt, including cattle and other animals.	Being firstborn was when God decided to show his strength. God hardened Pharaoh's heart, so he refused to let the Israelites go (which makes it Yahweh's fault). **Collective Punishment**
Exodus 14:28	The Egyptian army and all their horses	Refusing to disobey orders to pursue the Israelites fleeing through the Red Sea, which was parted with walls of water on both sides of the path.
Leviticus 10: 1-3	Nadab and Abihu, sons of Aaron.	Offering a strange fire before the Lord.
Numbers 11:1-3	An undisclosed number of Israelites	Complaining
Numbers 11:32-34	An undisclosed number of Israelites were smitten with a great plague.	Complaining about the food and wanting to go back to Egypt for an easier life. **Collective Punishment**

Numbers 14:36-37	Ten scouts who had been sent to explore the promised land.	Spreading bad reports about this land being too difficult to conquer.
Numbers 16:27-32	Korah, Dathan, Abiram, and their respective wives and children	Claiming to be as holy as Moses and Aaron.
Numbers 16:35	250 Israelite men	Followers of Korah
Numbers 16:45-49	14,700 Israelites	Complaining about the previous assassinations concerning Korah.
Numbers 21:4-9	An undisclosed number of Israelites who sustained serpent bites.	Despairing and complaining about the lack of bread and water.
Numbers 25:9	24,000 Israelites	Sexual immorality with Moabite women and the worship of Baal. **(Collective Punishment)**
Deuteronomy 2:14-16	The entire Israelite army.	Unclear (possibly to prevent them from waging war on the children of Lot). **(Collective Punishment)**
Joshua 10: 10-11	An undisclosed number of Amorites.	Waging war against Israel, trying to protect themselves and their families from the holy slaughter that the Israelites regularly inflicted on their enemies
1 Samuel 6:19	Either 70 or 50,070 Philistines from Beth-shemesh (dependent on how the 'inerrant' Bible[215] is translated).	For looking into the Ark of the Covenant. **(Collective Punishment)**
1 Samuel 25: 37-38	Nabal	David refrained from murdering Nabal's servants or stealing from him. He expected his kindness to be repaid in the form of gifts from Nabal. But when Nabal declined, Yahweh killed Nabal before David had the chance to go "avenging thyself with thine own hand."

2 Samuel 6: 6-7	Uzzah	Touching the Ark of the Covenant while trying to prevent it from tipping over.
2 Samuel 12:14-18	David and Bathsheba's baby boy.	None. The baby was killed to punish David for his adultery with Bathsheba and subsequently arranging the death of her husband, Uriah the Hittite.
2 Samuel 24:13-15	70,000 Israelites from Dan and Beersheba.	David took a census of his lands and people. **(Collective Punishment)**
Hosea 13:16	The entire population of Samaria	"They shall fall by the sword; their infants shall be dashed in pieces; and their women with child shall be ripped up." Because they rebelled. **(Collective Punishment)**
1 Kings 13: 1-24	An unnamed prophet	The 'prophet' had been told by God not to eat bread, but another guy claimed that God had commanded him to bring the prophet home for some food. So, so Yahweh had lions devour the unnamed prophet who was lied to.
1 Kings 14: 10-18	Abijah, the son of Jeroboam.	None. Child killed by Yahweh to punish Jeroboam.
1 Kings 20: 35-36	An unnamed man devoured by lions	Refusal to strike a prophet when ordered to do so by the prophet in question.
1 Kings 22: 51-53 and **2 Kings 1: 16-17**	King Ahaziah	For Baal worship, and for seeking medical advice from a rival god.
2 Kings 1: 9-14	102 soldiers	Being impolite to Elijah and serving King Ahaziah.
2 Kings 2: 23-24	42 children	They mocked Elisha's bald head
2 Kings 17: 25-26	An unknown number of Assyrians	For not worshiping Yahweh, he sent lions to kill them.

2 Kings 19: 34-36	185,000 Assyrian soldiers	Being at war with Israel.
2 Chronicles 13:13-20	Jeroboam	Rebelling against Abijah, the king of Israel, based on dependence on David.
2 Chronicles 21:13-18	Jehoram	Doing evil in the sight of the Lord.
Jeremiah 28:15-17	Hananiah, the prophet	Being a false prophet and preaching against Yahweh's chosen.
Ezekiel 24: 15-18	Ezekiel's wife	She did nothing. Yahweh just wanted to make a point.

Cosmology Errors

We have covered how the author of Genesis was confused about the origin of light, and that heaven was a dome or firmament above the flat Earth. Apparently, the authors of Isaiah, Judges, Jeremiah, and Ezekiel were also confused. While that is to be expected of Iron Age men, let's not pretend that they were inspired by a deity.

- **Isaiah 13:10:** "For the stars of heaven and the constellations thereof shall not give their light: the sun shall be darkened in his going forth, and the moon shall not cause her light to shine."

Sure, that can happen! Constellations of stars will suddenly burn out, and the moon will not give us the light it never had.

- **Judges 5:20:** "They fought from heaven; the stars in their courses found against Sisera (the commander of the Canaanite army.)"

So, the stars fought against Sisera, indicating a targeted divine action against an enemy of Israel.

- **Jeremiah 31:35:** "Thus saith the Lord, which giveth the sun for a light by day, and the ordinances of the moon and of the stars for a light by night…"
- **Ezekiel 32:7:** "And when I shall put thee out, I will cover the heaven, and make the stars thereof dark; will cover the sun with a cloud, and the moon shall not give her light."

Everyone in 1000 BCE apparently believed that the moon emits its own light.

- **Isaiah 11:12:** "And he shall set up an ensign for the nations, and shall assemble the outcasts of Israel, and gather together the dispersed of Judah from the four corners of the earth."
- **Jeremiah 16:19:** "Oh Lord, my strength, and my fortress, and my refuge in the day of affliction, the Gentiles shall come unto thee from the ends of the earth…"

- **Acts 13:47:** "For so hath the Lord commanded us, saying I have set thee to be a light of the Gentiles, that thou shouldest be for salvation unto the ends of the earth."

Both the OT and the NT (i.e., The Acts of the Apostles) support the primitive view of a flat Earth. In the 6th Century, a Catholic monk, Cosmas, wrote *Topographia Christiana*, which he meant to describe the structure of the physical world, based on data he obtained from the Bible. Cosmas declared the world was flat and surrounded by four seas, as he tried to prove the literal accuracy of the biblical view of the universe; he did this because he wanted to refute Ptolemy's concept of a spherical universe.[216] For several centuries, there was some confusion regarding the topography of the Earth. By the time of Christopher Columbus, educated people had long accepted the views of scientists, philosophers, and mathematicians who observed that Earth was spherical.[217]

Other Disturbing OT Passages

Some passages of the Bible are disturbing for a variety of reasons, and they can be downright shocking. These passages solidify the view that the Bible, certainly the OT, is not a proper source of ethics.

Skeleton Zombies

This vision reminds modern man of a zombie horror movie. Ezekiel basically sees a valley filled with dry bones, and then they all come together and begin to form skeletons, but they remain dead.

Ezekiel 37:

- **Verse 1:** "The hand of the Lord was upon me, and carried me out in the spirit of the Lord, and set Me down in the midst of the valley which was full of bones,"
- **Verse 7:** "So I prophesied as I was commanded: and as I prophesied, there was a noise, and behold a shaking, and the bones came together, bone to his bone."
- **Verse 8:** "And when I beheld, lo, the sinews and the flesh came up upon them, and the skin covered them above: but there was no breath in them."

Cannibal Mother

This shameful narrative is about two starving women who agree to eat their own children. Though the mother who initially came up with the idea hides her own son to try and save him.

2 Kings 6:

- **Verse 28:** "And the king unto her, what aileth thee? And she answered, This woman said unto me, Give thy son, that we may eat him today, and we will eat my son tomorrow."
- **Verse 29:** "So we boiled my son, and did eat him: and I said unto her on the next day, Give thy son that we may eat him: and she hath hid her son."

Stoning

Casting stones is mentioned in several parts of the Bible. One can be stoned to death for being a rebellious son, gathering wood on the Sabbath, or being unable to prove virginity upon getting married. Stoning is a horrible, barbaric punishment whereby the victim dies of blunt trauma. The Torah and Talmud prescribe stoning as punishment for a variety of offenses, including rebelliousness against a parent, or loss of virginity, which could be caused by several factors outside the girl's control. Such extreme punishments are inconceivable today. And yet some people want to believe that the Bible provides a solid guideline of morality.

- **Deuteronomy 21:18-21:** "If a man have a stubborn and rebellious son, which will not obey the voice of his father, or the voice of his mother, and that, when they have chastened him, will not harken onto them: Then shall his father and his mother lay hold on him, and bring him out unto the elders of his city. This, our son is stubborn and rebellious; he will not hear our voice…and all the men of his city shall stone him with stones, that he die…"
- **Deuteronomy 22:20-21:** "But if this thing (that she is not a virgin) be true, and the tokens of virginity be not found for the damsel: Then they shall bring out the damsel to the door of her father's house, and the men of her city shall stone her with stones that she die…"

Treatment of Women

There are numerous passages about women that can be found disturbing: from being "unclean" from having a period or a baby (**Leviticus 12**) to **Deuteronomy 22:28–29**, which cites the Israelite custom compelling a woman to marry her rapist. Truly, being forced to marry and remain with her rapist was every woman's dream!

- **Deuteronomy 22: 28-29:** "If a man find a damsel that is a virgin, which is not betrothed, and lay hold on her, and lie with her, and they be found; Then the man that lay with her shall give unto the damsel's father fifty shekels of silver, and she shall be his wife; because he hath humbled her, and he may not put her away all his days"

The Double Standard for Sexual Crimes

A woman who had sex outside her marriage was severely punished. Indeed, the OT is clear that adulterers are to be stoned to death. But married men with mistresses and concubines are not punished, as follows:

- Abraham **[1 Chronicles 1:32]**
- Saul **[2 Samuel 3:7]**
- Gideon **[Judges 8:31]**
- Rehoboam **[2 Chronicles 11:21]**
- David **[2 Samuel 5:13]**

When a man has sex with a slave girl, it is the female who is to be punished:

- **Leviticus 19:20:** "And whosoever lieth carnally with a woman, that is a bondmaid [slave], betrothed to a husband, and not at all redeemed, nor freedom given her; she shall be scourged."

A man may forcibly take a woman from enemy captives, and make her his wife, after trying her out.

- **Deuteronomy 21:11-14:** "And seest among the captives a beautiful woman, and hast a desire unto her, that though wouldest have her to thy wife; Then thou shalt bring her home to thine house; and she shall shave her head, and pare her nails…And it shall be, if thou hast no delight in her, then thou shalt let her go whether she will; …"

A woman who doesn't scream when she is raped is to be stoned:

- **Deuteronomy 22:24:** "Then ye shall bring them both out unto the gate of that city, and ye shall Stone them with stones that they die; the damsel, because she cried out not…"

Bastard children and their descendants are to be punished:

- **Deuteronomy 23:2:** "A bastard shall not enter into the congregation of the Lord; even to his tenth generation shall he not enter into the congregation of the Lord."

Yahweh actually decrees that the punishment for a man's misdeeds is for his fiancée to have sex with another man.

- **Deuteronomy 28:30:** "Thou shalt betroth a wife, and another man shall lie with her: thou shalt build a house, and thou shalt not dwell within…"

King David had sex with Bathsheba; and so, Yahweh decreed that all his wives to be publicly raped; and his newborn child would die.

- **2 Samuel 12:11-12:** "Thus saith the Lord, Behold, I will raise up evil against thee out of thine own house, and I will take thy wives, before thine eyes, and give them unto thy neighbor, and he shall lie with thy wives in sight of this sun. For thou didst it secretly: but I will do this thing before all Israel, and before the sun."

Examples of Contradictions of the OT

Logically, if two or more statements contradict each other, then at least one of them is false. Biblical contradictions underscore the many false statements of the OT and provide some evidence that it is not inerrant. Nothing is more contradictory than Genesis with its inconsistent and physically impossible creation stories than Chapter 1 vs. Chapter 2. So, Chapter 1 says that the beasts were created first; then after the animals, man and woman were created at the same time. Then in the next chapter, the author changes the order of creation from man first, then the beasts, and then woman.

Chapter 1:

- **Genesis 1:24:** "And God made the beast of the earth after his kind, and cattle after their kind, And everything that creepeth upon the earth after his kind..."
- **Genesis 1:26-27:** "And God said, Let us make man in our image, after our likeness: and... So God created man in his own image, in the image of God created he him; male and female created he them."

Chapter 2:

- **Genesis 2:15:** "And the Lord God took the man, and put him into the garden of Eden to dress it and to keep it."
- **Genesis 2:19:** "And out of the ground the Lord God formed every beast of the field, and every fowl of the air..."
- **Genesis 2:22:** "And the rib, which the Lord God had taken from man, made he a woman, And brought her unto man."

There are many other contradictions in these first two chapters. Just to mention two more: Chapter 1 states that fruit trees were created before man, while Chapter 2 places their creation after man. Chapter 1 states that the fowl were created from the waters, while Chapter 2 states that they were formed out of the ground.

Chapter 1:

- **Genesis 1:12:** "And the earth brought forth grass, the herb yielding seed after his kind, and the tree yielding fruit, whose seed was within itself, after his kind..."
- **Genesis, 1:20:** "And God said, Let the waters bring forth abundantly the moving creature That hath life, and fowl that may fly above the earth in the open firmament of heaven."

Chapter 2:

- **Genesis 2: 7:** And the Lord God formed man of the dust of the ground, and breathed into his nostrils the breadth of life; and man became a living soul."
- **Genesis 2: 9:** "And out of the ground made the Lord God to grow every tree that is pleasant to the sight, and good for food..."
- **Genesis 2:19:** "And out of the ground the Lord God formed every beast of the field, and every fowl of the air..."

To mention some examples of contradictions that should never have happened, Genesis 8 and the story of the "worldwide flood" are unsupported in archaeology or in history. In Chapter 8, verse 4, the Ark rested on Mt. Ararat in the 7th month; but in the very next verse, it states that the mountaintops were under water until the tenth month. Then, after verse 13 describes the Earth being dry on the first day of the first month, verse 24 contradicts it and says it was the 27th day of the 2nd month.

- **Genesis 8:4:** "And the ark rested in the seventh month, on the seventeenth day of the month, upon the mountains of Ararat."
- **Genesis 8:5:** "And the waters decreased continually until the tenth month, on the first day of the month, were the tops of the mountains seen."

- **Genesis 8:13:** "And it came to pass in the six hundredth and first year, in the first month, the first day of the month, the waters were dried up from off the earth: and Noah removed the covering of the ark, and looked, and behold, the face of the ground was dry."
- **Genesis 8:14:** "And in the second month, on the seven and twentieth day of the month, was the earth dried."

Our last example focuses on the requirement of Yahweh to sacrifice animals to him. There have been many verses in the OT in which Yahweh commanded sacrifices. One example is **Exodus 29:38:42,** in which Yahweh demands two lambs per day for a year. Later, in **Jeremiah 7:22,** Yahweh denies that he ever required animal sacrifices. Wow! Someone has some explaining to do!

- **Exodus 29:38-39:** "Now this is that which thou shalt offer upon the altar; two lambs of the first Year day by day continually. The one lamb thou shalt offer in the morning; and the other lamb thou shalt offer at evening."
- **Jeremiah 7:22:** "For I spake not unto your fathers, nor commanded them in the day that I brought them out of the land of Egypt, concerning burnt offerings or sacrifices."

Cruel Punishments

Throughout the OT, Yahweh (God) was depicted as outrageously cruel, as he often inflicted punishments on the innocent. Earlier in this chapter, we already reviewed the "mass murders" attributed to Yahweh. In this section, we will just summarize the intense suffering that was caused.

Yahweh sanctioned slavery:

- **Leviticus 25:44-46:** "Both thy bondsmen, and they bondmaids, which thou shalt have, shall be of the heathen that are round about you; of them shall ye buy bondmen and bondwomen. Moreover, of the children of the strangers that do sojourn among you; of them shall ye buy, and of their families that are with you, which they begat in your land: and they shall be your possession. And ye shall take them as an inheritance for your children after you, to inherit them for a possession; they shall be your bondmen forever..."

    Yahweh caused cannibalism:

- **Jeremiah 19:9:** "And I will cause them to eat the flesh of their sons and the flesh of their daughters, and they shall eat everyone the flesh of his friend in the siege and straightness, wherewith their enemies, and they shall seek their lives, shall straighten them."

Yahweh ordered religious persecution and punishments:

- **Deuteronomy 13:13-15:** "Certain men, the children of Belial, are gone out from among you, and have withdrawn the inhabitants of their city, saying, Let us go and serve other gods, which ye have not known; Then shalt thou inquire, and make search, and ask diligently, and, behold, if it be truth, and the thing certain, that such abomination is wrought among you; Thou shalt surely smite the inhabitants of that city with the edge of the sword, destroying it utterly, and all that is therein, and the cattle thereof..."

- **1 Samuel 15:3:** "Now go and smite Amalek, and utterly destroy all that they have, and spare them not; but slay both man and woman, infant and suckling, ox and sheep, and camel and ass."
- **Isaiah 13:9,15-16:** "Behold, the day of the Lord cometh, cruel both with wrath and fierce anger...and he shall destroy the sinners thereof out of it. Everyone who is found shall be thrust through... Their children shall be dashed to pieces before their eyes; their houses shall be spoiled, and their wives ravished."

One grave issue with the savage cruelty and injustice in the OT is that it incites others to violence and cruelties. If a God can be involved in brutal, cruelties, then why should ordinary people have qualms about it? The reasoning process is well illustrated by Joseph McCabe, who reported that in the Middle Ages, Christian Europe employed more torture than in any society in history.[218] McCabe explains that the primary cause of this cruelty was the Christian doctrine of eternal punishment. Says McCabe, "if...God punishes men with eternal torment; it is surely lawful for men to use doses of it in a good cause."[219]

Divine Inspiration

The preceding text described some of the fallacies of the Old Testament. It was clearly not inspired by any deity, certainly not one that was omniprescient. That said, some Christians (and many Jews for that matter) have believed that the OT / Tanakh was the Word of God, and its texts were "inspired," although clearly not inerrant. Biblical inerrancy is primarily a Christian Protestant innovation of the last few centuries, common mostly to evangelical 'independent' denominations, as opposed to 'mainline' Protestant groups. Catholics have never viewed the Old Testament (or even the New Testament) as inerrant, if they have even read the Bible.

As you read the biblical passages, such as a deity commanding the rape and/or death of innocent people, or historical verses that are easily proven false by historical record, science, or logic, you need to ask yourself if this is the work of a perfect god? Or is it the writing of a flawed human? Is what is proposed believable?

Christian apologists have been known to cite four reasons why they believe the Bible (both Old and New Testaments) are divinely inspired. But none of them are accurate.

- ***Reason 1:*** *The Bible has a historical framework and it refers to real people (some of them) and real places (most of them).* This rationale is ridiculous. Some of those cited as real people (e.g., Moses or Darius the Mede) never existed; and the events described either did not occur (e.g., Noah's Ark or Exodus), or what occurred happened in a different era, e.g., the walls of Jericho falling down hundreds of years before the Israelites got there. Just because a place once existed doesn't mean the fable regarding that place happened! This is similar to stating Abraham Lincoln was a famous vampire hunter who lived in the 19th century CE and served briefly as President of the USA; and the proof of this claim is a monument in Washington, D.C., dating back to the early 20th century.

- ***Reason 2:*** *The Bible has many confirmations in the sciences such as biology, geology, astronomy, and archaeology.* Sadly, it doesn't. If anything, science has shown the Bible has erred time and again. Our world isn't flat; the moon doesn't make its own light; the sun doesn't revolve around the Earth; evolution is real; carbon dating has proven many Jewish and Christian relics to be forgeries, and on and on.
- ***Reason 3:*** *The Bible is written as history.* The mythical stories in the Bible are certainly not history. They are the products of fertile imaginations. The Bible has many conflicting stories, dates, and names that are erroneous, as well as multiple anachronisms. While it can be used as a supportive document with actual historical sources, academic historians do not consider either the OT or the NT to be historically accurate.
- ***Reason 4:*** *The Bible contains an unchallenged number of fulfilled prophecies.* Although it would be a legitimate claim if it weren't so easily refuted. These alleged prophecies are not prophecies at all, but they are just obscure passages taken out of context from the Old Testament and reinterpreted to fit Christian dogma as stated in the New Testament. See the next section for multiple prediction failures. And being unchallenged? Just not true.

So, if something in Scripture is false, such as a historical, scientific, or translation error, does that mean that everything in Scripture is false? Of course, not (although it might seriously challenge the concept of biblical inerrancy). However, as the list of false statements, historical and scientific errors, contradictions, forgeries, and other inaccuracies piles up, and some of them are far more important than others, you might want to rethink whether these mythical tales hold any true value.

There are many arguments that support the rejection of the concept of divine inspiration of 'Scripture'. Some religious traditions hold differing views on the nature of inspiration, such as emphasizing the divine origin of the text while acknowledging the human element involved. Generally, the rationale for rejection tends to center on historical inaccuracies, text contradictions, scientific discrepancies, copying and translation errors, and interpretation problems, all suggesting that the Bible is a product of human authorship, rather than direct divine revelation.

- *Historical inaccuracies* – Critics point to historical events described in the OT that are not supported by archaeological evidence or other historical records, suggesting the human authors did not have access to accurate information. There is also tiers of anachronisms, such as camels in Abraham's time, when camels had not yet been domesticated in the Levant region.
- *Text contradictions* – Inconsistencies among different biblical passages or versions of the same story trigger questions about the Bible's reliability as a divinely inspired text.
- *Scientific discrepancies* – Various passages in the Bible contradict established scientific knowledge, validating concerns about the accuracy of the manuscripts. See Chapter 1, Debunked by Science.
- *Copying and translation errors* – The process of copying and translating the original manuscripts across centuries introduced errors or alterations, which impacted the accuracy of the text, and produced thousands of manuscript text variants.

Additionally, we have no time stamp to show when various documents were written; there are no original documents, nor do we know the identity of the authors, since they either used a pseudonym, or the supposed author was not alive at the time of authorship.

- *Diverse and inconsistent interpretations* – The complex symbolism in the biblical manuscripts can lead to vastly different interpretations. The way in which Scripture is interpreted can significantly impact the different approaches to literal meaning, allegorical interpretations, or historical context. If the Bible truly conveyed the words and truths of God, then one would presume that God would want it to be clear, intelligible, and mistake-free to even those with the most rudimentary or no education. But that is not the case.

Any belief that the Old Testament is anything other than allegorical, not word-for-word inerrant, is a major self-deception. Only someone indoctrinated by years of reinforced propaganda and unfettered by logic or any critical analysis could believe such literal silliness. We live in the 21st century, and we have so much knowledge available to us at the click of an electronic keyboard. Only the willfully ignorant could accept such myths as true.

OT Predictions vs. NT Fulfillment

Christian apologists cite a series of fulfilled prophecies as evidence for their claims of divine inspiration. However, each supposed prophecy has proven to be unconvincing for one or more reasons, including its vagueness, prophecies after the fact, failed prophecies, unfulfilled prophecies, or non-existent prophecies.[220]

It has become almost an adage that how one interprets a prophecy is the key determinant of its fulfillment. Some prophecies are just vague predictions, and so their fulfillment could be any one of a large variety of events, which could be adjusted and adapted to match the so-called 'prediction.' Other prophecies, especially about Jesus, are seemingly fulfilled only because the authors of the gospels distort unrelated verses of the OT. Some prophecies include fabrications, like the fake genealogy numbers of "fourteen generations" found in **Matthew 1:17**. Some predictions were made after the event took place. And some prophecies clearly fail or remain unfulfilled. But it was essential for early Christianity to try to make prophetic connections with Judaism. Why? As stated by author Robert J. Miller, "Making that connection was essential in a time and culture that regarded old sacred writings with reverence and anything new in religion with suspicion."[221]

The actual nature of prophetic literature can differ dramatically. Prophecies can take the form of simple predictions or terrifying threats of future grandiose eschatology.[222] The OT's prophecies tend to markedly differ from what is stated in the NT, if a record of them exists at all. The prophecy of the OT is often a call for moral improvement, not unalterable doom. A good example is the story of Jonah, which seems like a totally fictional parable.

In the immediate decades following the crucifixion of Jesus, most believers were part of the Jewish sect that wanted to believe that Jesus was indeed the Messiah; and therefore, based on their belief, they concluded that he fulfilled the Tanakh Scriptures. These early Christians interpreted vague passages of the Old Testament as predictions of Jesus, even though that is not what was said.

What many modern Christians fail to understand is that the very authors of much of the New Testament, who portrayed Jesus as the Messiah, searched and quoted the Old Testament in order to find an obscure predictive reference to 'prove' their assertions. Many of the so-called "messianic prophecies" that Christians believe refer to Jesus were not considered messianic prophecies by the Jews.

Today, Christians who believe that Jesus fulfilled predictions of the Old Testament primarily base their views on what the gospels say about Jesus' life: He was born in Bethlehem; his mother was a virgin; he performed miracles; he was tried as a dissident by Rome, etc. But how do we know that these are facts from Jesus' life? The gospels were written many decades after Jesus had died. None of the writers of the gospels were eyewitnesses. No one knew what Jesus really said, and what he really believed. So, either these contrived 'prophecies' of the OT were not meant to be predictions of the future Messiah, or the "facts of Jesus' life" in the NT that fulfilled these prophecies were not actually true.

As explained by biblical scholar, Bart Ehrman, "...the authors of the New Testament who portrayed Jesus as the Messiah are the ones who quoted the Old Testament in order to prove it, and they were influenced by the Old Testament in what they decided to say about Jesus, and their views of Jesus affected how they read the Old Testament... The Old Testament in fact never says that the Messiah will be born of a virgin, that he will be executed by his enemies, and that he will be raised from the dead."[223]

Rationale Wiki derived some key criteria for a statement to be considered a viable Biblical prophecy, and it must fit all of the following five criteria[224]:

- Accuracy – It excludes inaccurate statements
- Plainly stated in the Bible – It cannot be a reinterpretation of the text
- Unambiguous – It cannot be meaningless musings or vague concepts
- Improbable – Lucky guesses don't count; evidence does
- Unknown to anyone – It cannot be foreknowledge

In applying the above-cited criteria to the biblical prophecies, one quickly determines that many of the predictions were historically false. Indeed, many of the predictions of the OT prophets can be readily proven to be failed prophecies. Now let's look at the prophet, Ezekiel, who had many failed predictions, some of which were just nonsensical. He predicted that Yahweh would destroy the City of Tyre. However, it never occurred. After a 13-year siege, Tyre compromised with Nebuchadnezzar. And the city of Tyre still exists today.

- **Ezekiel 26:7-9:** "For thus saith the Lord God; Behold, I will bring upon Tyrus [Tyre] Nebuchadrezzar, king of Babylon, a king of kings, from the north, with horses and with chariots, and with horsemen, and companies, and much people. He shall slay with the sword thy daughters in the field: and he shall make a fort against thee, and cast a mount against thee, and lift up the buckler against thee. And he shall set engines of war against thy walls, and with his axes he shall break down the towers."

And there was this harsh prediction where Ezekiel predicted the desolation of Egypt, where no one could even walk through it. But it never happened. From the establishment of the first Pharaonic dynasty (which predates the Israelites) to our modern day, Egypt has never been uninhabited.

- **Ezekiel 29:8-12:** "Therefore thus saith the Lord God; Behold, I will bring a sword upon thee, and cutoff man and beast out of thee. And the land of Egypt shall be desolate and waste; and they shall know that I am the Lord: because he hath said, The river is mine, and I have made it. Behold, therefore, I am against thee, and against thy rivers, and I will make the land of Egypt utterly waste and desolate, from the tower of Syene even unto the border of Ethiopia. No foot of man shall pass through it, nor foot of beast shall pass through it, neither shall it be inhabited for forty years. And I will make the land of Egypt desolate...."

Ezekiel must have really disliked Egypt. He predicted that the Nile would dry up. Again, that never happened.

- **Ezekiel 30:12:** "And I will make the rivers dry; and sell the land into the hand of the wicked; and I will make the land waste, and all that is therein, by the hand of strangers..."

There were many other failed prophecies from the "prophets": Joel, Jeremiah, Isaiah, and Zechariah. There is no point in citing all their failed predictions. Suffice it to say that the inerrancy of the OT isn't real. Yet, there is one set of prophecies that still needs to be discussed, as they are the ones that supposedly refer to Jesus. And many people just assume that they are true, without checking. That said, in 2 Samuel and reiterated in 1 Kings, it is foretold that the Davidic Line will rule Judah forever. And in **Jeremiah 33:17,** the line of kings is described as being continuous. Further, the alleged prophesy focuses on the direct descent from David in 2 Samuel.

- **2 Samuel 9:13-16:** "He shall build a house for my name, and I will stablish the throne of his Kingdom forever. If he commit iniquity, I will chasten him with the rod of men, and with the stripes of the children of men. But my mercy shall not depart away from him, as I took it from Saud, whom I put away before thee. And thine house and thy kingdom shall be established forever."
- **1 Kings 11:34-36:** "Howbeit I will not take the whole kingdom out of hand: but I will make him prince all the days of his life for David my servant's sake, whom I chose, because he kept my commandments and my statutes. But I will take the kingdom out of his son's hand, and will give it unto thee, even ten tribes. And unto his son will I give one tribe, that David my servant may have a light always before me in Jerusalem, the city which I have chosen to put my name there."
- **Jeremiah 34:17:** "For thus saith the Lord: David shall never want a man to sit upon the throne of the house of Israel."
- **2 Samuel 7:12-13:** "And when your days be fulfilled, and thou shalt sleep with your fathers, I will set up thy seed after thee, which shall proceed out of thy bowels, and I will establish his kingdom. He shall build a house for my name, and I will stablish the throne of his kingdom forever."

But the Davidic Line ended with King Zedekiah[225] in c. 586 BCE, he was the last king of Judah. And between Zedekiah and Yeshua of Nazareth, there is a 600-year gap. Further, the alleged prophecy stresses the literal descendancy from David. Additionally, according to the myth of the virgin birth, Jesus is not the son of Joseph, and again, not descended from David.

Christian apologists take extensive liberties in fabricating reasons why a given biblical prediction is true. Take **Isaiah 53:10,** for instance, where it is foretold that a key figure [which Christians believe refers to Jesus] will have children. When confronted with this clearly inaccurate, ambiguous soothsaying, Christians respond that it was meant to be metaphorical, and that Jesus had children in the spiritual sense. If declaring something metaphoric foretelling is acceptable, then any presaging can be shown to be "metaphorically fulfilled".

There is also a controversy over the prophecy that the Messiah would be born in Bethlehem. In **Micah 5:2**, there appears to be a translation error regarding Bethlehem. Some translations suggest that Micah was referring to a clan named Bethlehem Ephrathah, not a city.[226] However, Christian apologists suggest the unproven theory that the previous name of Bethlehem was Bethlehem Ephratah. The following is the King James Version:

- **Micah 5:2:** "But thou, Bethlehem Ephratah, though thou be little among the thousands of Judah, yet out of thee shall he come forth unto me that is to be rule in Israel; whose goings forth have been from of old, from everlasting.

The New International Version of the Bible gives it a totally different take:

- **Micah 5:2:** "But you, Bethlehem Ephrathah, though you are small among the clans of Judah, out of you will come for me one who will be ruler over Israel, whose origins are from of old, from ancient times."

Finally, the only "evidence" that suggests Jesus is a descendant of David is the contrived genealogies of the gospels of **Matthew [1:1-17]** and **Luke [3:23-38].** Matthew traces the genealogy of Joseph from David, and Luke traces it from Adam to David to Mary. Of course, Adam did not exist. And given that there were no records maintained by the Israelites in that Age, that most of the Israelite population were illiterate, and that it was a span of 970 years from David to Jesus, what are the odds that these contrived genealogies were remotely accurate? Some Christian apologists have declared that the records were maintained in the Temple in Jerusalem. The 1st Temple was destroyed in 586 BCE and not rebuilt until 350 BCE. Then the Romans destroyed the 2nd Temple in 70 CE. The Gospel of Matthew was written after the 2nd Temple destruction, and the Gospel of Luke was written much later. Further, the Jewish custom was to follow the patriarchal line, not the matriarchal one. And there is a big biblical problem with Matthew's genealogy. Matthew's genealogy includes Jeconiah, who had been cursed by God, and who said he would make him childless **[Jeremiah 22:30].**

Chapter Summary

The Tanakh (Old Testament) is at best a set of tribal fables handed down over many generations until they were finally written onto parchment or other suitable canvas. Archeological evidence demonstrates that the Torah could not have been completed before the 7th century BCE, as it refers to many cities and countries that did not exist before then. Moreover, it could not have been written by a single author; rather, there were multiple, unknown human authors who spliced things together.

And overall, those who conceived and wrote what became the Tanakh lived in a superstitious time, when people accepted folklore for fact. It is obvious that since Genesis is so scientifically inaccurate, apologists undergo extensive intellectual gymnastics to try to make it sound remotely credible. To believe in the inerrancy of the Book of Genesis requires the suspension of logic and reason. The OT is not a divinely inspired book; it is not the infallible word of God; it is not a history of the Israelites; and it is certainly not a reliable source of ethical truths. The OT is unreliable because it contains many errors, borrowed pagan myths, numerous forgeries, and it runs unchecked with many harmful and cruel teachings. What the OT teaches us is that Yahweh was supposed to have created the universe, but he couldn't inspire an accurate spiritual testament!

The Old Testament's central deity evolved from a polytheistic pantheon of gods who were believed to live in the firmament above the Earth, and this evolved, wrathful God promoted an atonement theory that a blood sacrifice could magically rescue the Israelite believers from the grip of evil. By continuing to treat this mistake-ridden book as the word of God, humanity must endure more error and greater misery.

In our review of the OT, it should now be obvious why it has no credibility:

- The book of Genesis is amateurish in its explanation of the creation of the world, in its narrative of a global flood, and in its portrayal of the origin of languages via the ridiculous Tower of Babel fable.
- Archaeologists have not been able to produce any evidence that the book of Exodus is even marginally accurate. There was no Israelite slavery, no Passover, no crossing of the Red Sea, and no Moses. Passover is rooted in tradition and in Jewish beliefs; but its historical authenticity is highly doubtful.
- The walls of Jericho fell from an earthquake over a century before Joshua's arrival.
- The book of Daniel is a pious fraud with multiple factual mistakes and botched predictions, and it was not written during the Babylonian captivity (6th century BCE), but during the 2nd century BCE.

And the above-cited items are a small sample of the numerous mistakes and deluded fantasies running rampant through the Tanakh / OT. And it is nearly impossible to reconcile these disparities. In the 21st century, it is very difficult to believe in the inerrancy of the Old Testament.

Old Testament prophecies provide no evidence of the "truth of Christianity" [nor did the Jewish authors mean to do so]. There is not a single prophecy in the Old Testament that specifically predicts Jesus as the Messiah. In fact, there are so many factual contortions trying to make vague OT prophecies fit NT fulfillment, with a plethora of failed prophecies, and without a single, specific prophecy that was fulfilled. It should be obvious that Christianity does not tie back to the Scriptures of Judaism, and the Jewish "prophets" were just storytellers who wrote down their tribal stories. It is clear that the Old Testament's alpha male god reflects the fears, ignorance, insecurities, and arrogance of the macho male writers who wanted full control of their property, including their wives and slaves. Further, the OT prophecies lack a connection with the contrived NT stories of their fulfillment. This will be explored further in the next chapter.

Throughout most of the latter half of the 1st century CE, Christians were essentially just one more sect of Judaism. The Romans of that time also regarded the Christians as a sect of the Jewish people. As Christianity took a path that signaled a different identity, as acknowledged by both Jews and Christians, the Roman government modified its view (late 1st century). In the early to mid-2nd century CE, the gradual process of forming a Christian identity led to a separate, independent religion from Judaism.

It must be somewhat shocking for a Christian, indoctrinated since childhood, to hear that biblical stories which were part of his/her church services, Sunday school curriculum, and other areas of religious teaching are false (as in, they didn't happen), exaggerated, contradictory, mistranslated, or misinterpreted. But that is the truth. Indeed, tiers of decent, well-meaning religious leaders have themselves been deceived.

---

[141] Throughout this book terms such as 'written' or 'penned' are used. Such descriptors are referring to an array of writing instruments, such as a single, sharpened reed straw or a quill adapted from a bird feather. Canvases include parchment, vellum, animal hides, hemp cloth, and a host of other writing surfaces.

[142] "Old Testament canon, texts, and versions," Britannica; https://www.britannica.com/topic/biblical-literature/Old-Testament-canon-texts-and-versions

[143] "Judaism," Britannica; https://www.britannica.com/topic/Judaism

[144] Elon Gilad, "When the Jews Believed in Other Gods," July 26, 2018; Haaretz; https://www.haaretz.com/archaeology/2018-07-26/ty-article-magazine/.premium/when-the-jews-believed-in-other-gods/0000017f-dc52-d856-a37f-fdd222920000

[145] Joseph Cataliotti, "Religion of Israelites | Deities, Holy Places & Evolution," Study.com; https://study.com/academy/lesson/ancient-israel-religious-beliefs-figures-places.html

[146] Joshua J. Mark, "Yahweh," World History Encyclopedia; published on 22 October 2018; Bible and Interpretation; https://www.worldhistory.org/Yahweh/

[147] Mark S. Smith, "The Origins of Biblical Monotheism: Israel's Polytheistic Background and the Ugaritic Texts," https://bibleinterp.arizona.edu/articles/MSmith_BiblicalMonotheism

[148] "Yahweh," Encyclopedia Britannica; https://www.britannica.com/topic/Yahweh

[149] Ibid.

[150] Mark S. Smith, The Early History of God: Yahweh and the Other Deities in Ancient Israel. Eerdmans; 2002; ISBN 9780802839725.

[151] Victor Harold Matthews, Judges and Ruth. p. 79; New Cambridge Bible Commentary; 2004; Cambridge University Press. ISBN 978-0-521-00066-6.

[152] Arnold Gottfried Betz, "Monotheism". p. 917. In David Noel Freedman and Allen C. Myer (eds.). Eerdmans Dictionary of the Bible; 2000; ISBN 9053565035.

[153] Rolf Jacobson, "Background of Hosea," Enter the Bible; https://enterthebible.org/courses/hosea/lessons/background-of-hosea

[154] Rainer Albertz, A History of Israelite Religion, Volume I: From the Beginnings to the End of the Monarchy. p. 61, Westminster John Knox Press; 1994; ISBN 9780664227197.

[155] D.M. Murdoch, "The Moses Fraud," taken from her book, Did Moses Exist? https://www.astrotheologyzone.com/the-moses-fraud.html

[156] Paul Krause, "How Yahweh Became God: The War God Thesis," Discourses on Minerva; Jan 24, 2022; https://minervawisdom.com/2022/01/24/how-yahweh-became-god-the-war-god-thesis/

[157] Robert Karl Gnuse, "No Other Gods: Emergent Monotheism in Israel." Journal for the Study of the Old Testament: Supplement Series. Vol. 241. p. 225. Sheffield Academic Press; 1997; ISBN 9780567374158.

[158] Joshua J. Mark, "Yahweh," World History Encyclopedia; published on 22 October 2018; https://www.worldhistory.org/Yahweh/

[159] "Tanakh," Encyclopedia Britannica; https://www.britannica.com/topic/Tanakh

[160] Felix Just, S.J., Ph.D.; "Jewish and Christian Bibles: A Comparative Chart" Catholic Resources; https://catholic-resources.org/Bible/Heb-Xn-Bibles.htm

[161] "Episode 16: Four Main Parts," Literature and History; https://literatureandhistory.com/episode-016-four-main-parts/

[162] Ibid.

[163] Ibid.

[164] "7 Missing Bible Books: Why Did Protestants Remove Them from the Bible?" Christian Pure; https://christianpure.com/learn/missing-books-protestant-removal-bible/

[165] Bill Flavell, "Five Days that Unravel the Bible," Atheist Alliance International; April 5, 2018; https://atheistalliance.org/thinking-out-loud/five-days-that-unravel-the-bible/

[166] Victor Hurowitz, "The Genesis of Genesis," Biblical Archaeology Library; https://library.biblicalarchaeology.org/article/the-genesis-of-genesis/

[167] Joshua J. Mark, "Enuma Elish - The Babylonian Epic of Creation - Full Text," 4 May 2018; World History Encyclopedia; https://www.worldhistory.org/article/225/enuma-elish---the-babylonian-epic-of-creation

[168] "The Epic of Gilgamesh: Unraveling the Mesopotamian Flood Myth," Mythology Worldwide.com; https://babylonian.mythologyworldwide.com/the-epic-of-gilgamesh-unraveling-the-mesopotamian-flood-myth/ . This refers to the flood myth in the "Epic of Gilgamesh", one of three Mesopotamian flood myths.

[169] Hannah Ritchie, "How Many Species are there?" Our World in Data; https://ourworldindata.org/how-many-species-are-there; Data source: International Union for Conservation of Nature Red List of Threatened Species (2024)

[170] Ibid.

[171] Talitha Van Niekerk, "How Many Animals Are in the World in 2024," World Animal Foundation, Aug 29, 2024; https://worldanimalfoundation.org/advocate/how-many-animals-are-in-the-world/

[172] "Tower of Babel," Britannica; https://www.britannica.com/topic/Tower-of-Babel

[173] "The Bible is Wrong About The Tower of Babel," The Church of Truth; https://thechurchoftruth.org/the-bible-is-wrong-about-the-tower-of-babel/

[174] Martin Noth, The Scheme of the Twelve Tribes of Israel; 1930; references by the Encyclopedia Britannica; https://www.britannica.com/biography/Martin-Noth]

[175] Given that the world population in 1400 BCE has been estimated to be 30 – 35 million, 2 million Israelites is a seriously large number; and yet they remained a minor tribe in the Levant. "Historical Estimates of World Population," US Census Bureau; https://www.census.gov/data/tables/time-series/demo/international-programs/historical-est-worldpop.html

[176] "Egypt Knew No Moses: Evidence On Why Exodus Never Happened"; (Jan 2023); Historum; https://historum.com/t/egypt-knew-no-moses-evidence-on-why-exodus-never-happened.194987/

[177] Ishaan Tharoor, "Was Moses Real," The Washington Post; Dec 10, 2014; https://www.washingtonpost.com/news/worldviews/wp/2014/12/10/was-moses-real/

[178] Prof. Joshua Berman, "Evidence for the Exodus," adapted from Berman's text, Ani Maamin: Biblical Criticism, Historical Truth and the Thirteen Principles of Faith (Maggid, 2020); https://aish.com/evidence-for-the-exodus/

[179] "Moses," Encyclopedia Britannica; https://www.britannica.com/biography/Moses-Hebrew-prophet/The-Covenant-at-Sinai

[180] "Hebrew Alphabet," Encyclopedia Britannica; https://www.britannica.com/topic/Hebrew-alphabet

[181] "What Language is the Torah Written In?" Universal Translation Services; Sep 30, 2022; https://www.universal-translation-services.com/what-language-is-the-torah-written-in/

182 "Hebrew Language," Encyclopedia Britannica; https://www.britannica.com/topic/Hebrew-language

183 Lily Rothman, "Exodus and the True Story of Moses, Time Magazine; Dec 12, 2014; https://time.com/3626278/exodus-and-moses/

184 "Archaeologist: No proof Red Sea parted," UPI, April 3, 2007; https://www.upi.com/Top_News/2007/04/03/Archaeologist-No-proof-Red-Sea-parted/10321175613038/

185 (Finkelstein & Silberman, The Bible Unearthed); From Ancient Origins, https://www.ancient-origins.net/history-famous-people/moses-myth-or-history-002246

186 "Is the Exodus a Myth?" December 4, 2022; Bart Ehrmann Blog; https://ehrmanblog.org/is-the-exodus-a-myth/

187 "Moses Never Existed," https://www.eoht.info/page/Moses%20never%20existed

188 Acharya S, "Moses, Theft from Egypt," Offline Illumination; https://tgpretender.co.uk/moses-theft-from-egypt/

189 John W. Loftus, "Did Moses Exist?", Jan 09,2019; Debunking Christianity; https://www.debunking-christianity.com/2016/05/did-moses-exist.html

190 Murdock, Dorothy M. (2014). Did Moses Exist? The Myth of the Israelite Lawgiver. Stellar House Publishing. Murdock's book dissects all aspects of the myth of Moses.

191 Dever, William G. (1993), "What Remains of the House That Albright Built?" The Biblical Archaeologist, University of Chicago Press: pp. 25–35, doi:10.2307/3210358, ISSN 0006-0895, JSTOR 3210358, S2CID 166003641

192 "Charles Warren," Academia Lab; https://academia-lab.com/encyclopedia/charles-warren/

193 Bart Wagemakers, Archaeology in the 'Land of Tells and Ruins': A History of Excavations in the Holy Land Inspired by the Photographs and Accounts of Leo Boer; p. 122. 2014; Oxbow Books. ISBN 978-1782972464.

194 Ibid. pp. 122-124

195 Dever, William G. (2006). Who Were the Early Israelites and Where Did They Come From? pp. 45-47. Eerdmans. ISBN 978-0802844163.

196 Hendrik J. Bruins and Johannes van der Plicht, "Tell Es-Sultan (Jericho): Radiocarbon Results of Short-lived Cereal and Multiyear Charcoal Samples from the End of the Middle Bronze Age"; p. 213. 1995.Proceedings of the 15th International Conference: doi:10.1017/S0033822200030666.

197 Jacobs, Paul F. (2000). "Jericho". In Freedman, David Noel; Myers, Allen C. (eds.). Eerdmans Dictionary of the Bible. Eerdmans. P. 691. ISBN 978-9053565032.

198 Ann E. Killebrew, Biblical Peoples and Ethnicity: An Archaeological Study of Egyptians, Canaanites, and Early Israel, 1300–1100 B.C.E. Society of Biblical Literature; p. 152. 2005; ISBN 978-1589830974.

199 Robert B. Coote, "Conquest: Biblical narrative". In David Noel Freedman and Allen C. Myers, (eds.), Eerdmans Dictionary of the Bible. p. 275; 2000; Eerdmans. ISBN 978-9053565032.

200 Maura Sala, "The Walls of Jericho," Bible Odyssey; https://www.bibleodyssey.com/articles/the-walls-of-jericho/

201 Charles Arthur, "Earthly power brought Jericho down," 10 September 1997; The Independent, https://www.the-independent.com/news/earthly-power-brought-jericho-down-1238517.html

202 "The Maccabean Revolt," World History Encyclopedia; https://www.worldhistory.org/article/827/the-maccabean-revolt/

203 "Antiochus IV Epiphanes," Encyclopedia Britannica; Antiochus IV; https://www.britannica.com/biography/Antiochus-IV-Epiphanes

204 Richard Carrier, "How do we know Daniel is a Forgery," Richard Carrier Blogs, 9 May 2021; https://www.richardcarrier.info/archives/18242

205 Richard Carrier, Ibid.

206 Philip R. Davies, "The social world of apocalyptic writing," published in The World of Ancient Israel: Sociological, Anthropological and Political Perspectives (edited by R. E. Clements).

207 Philip R. Davies, Ibid.

208 David Mandel, "Nebuchadnezzar," My Jewish Learning; https://www.myjewishlearning.com/article/nebuchadnezzar/

209 "Nebuchadnezzar," New World Encyclopedia;
https://www.newworldencyclopedia.org/entry/Nebuchadrezzar_II
210 Richard Carrier, "How We Know Daniel is a Forgery," 9 May 2021;
https://www.richardcarrier.info/archives/18242
211 Porphyry (234? – 305? C.E.) was a Neoplatonist philosopher who studied with Longinus in Athens and then with Plotinus in Rome from 263–269 C.E. and became a follower of the latter's version of Platonism. See "Porphyry," Stanford Encyclopedia of Philosophy; revised Feb 17, 2021;
https://plato.stanford.edu/entries/porphyry/
212 "The Authenticity of the Book of Daniel: A Survey of the Evidence," July 14, 2021; Jonathan McClatchie; https://jonathanmclatchie.com/the-authenticity-of-the-book-of-daniel-a-survey-of-the-evidence/
213 Translated by Gleason L. Archer, Jr., "Jerome's Commentary on Daniel," The Tertullian Project;
https://www.tertullian.org/fathers/jerome_daniel_01_intro.htm
214 "Examples of God personally killing people," Rationale Wiki;
https://rationalwiki.org/wiki/Examples_of_God_personally_killing_people
215 "Biblical literalism is the theological view held by some Christian denominations that one should regard the contents of the Bible as literally true and "inerrant".
216 Cosmas, Britannica; https://www.britannica.com/biography/Cosmas
217 Erin Blakemore, "Christopher Columbus Never Set Out to Prove the Earth was Round," Britannica; updated Aug 10, 2023; https://www.history.com/news/christopher-columbus-never-set-out-to-prove-the-earth-was-round
218 McCabe, Joseph, The History of Torture (Austin: American Atheist Press, Reprinted 1982), pp. 12, 23.
219 McCabe, ibid; pp. 20, 21.
220 "Biblical Prophecy is not Convincing Proof of its Divine Inspiration," Reddit;
https://www.reddit.com/r/DebateAChristian/comments/91vsfb/biblical_prophecy_is_not_convincing_proof_of_its/
221 Robert J. Miller, "How New Testament Writers Helped Jesus Fulfill Prophecy," part of John Loftus' anthology, The Case Against Miracles; p. 255
222 Biblical Prophecies," Rational Wiki; https://rationalwiki.org/wiki/Biblical_prophecies
223 "Jesus and the Messianic Prophecies – Did the Old Testament Point to Jesus?" Bart Ehrman Blog; November 8, 2015; https://ehrmanblog.org/jesus-and-the-messianic-prophecies/

225 Britt Mooney, "Who Is King Zedekiah in the Bible?" Christianity; April 2024;
https://www.christianity.com/wiki/people/king-zedekiah-bible.html; Zedekiah rebelled against Babylonian dominance, which prompted a siege of Jerusalem by Nebuchadnezzar, resulting in the city's fall and the temple's destruction.
226 Joseph Francis Alward, "Was Bethlehem Birth Prophesied?"; Jan 8, 1998; Skeptical Views of Christianity (archived from October 31, 2013).
https://skepticalviewsofchristianity.com/bethlehem_birth_prophecy.html

Chapter 3 – Jesus of Nazareth

The New Testament (NT) is the second division of the Christian biblical canon. It discusses the teachings of Jesus of Nazareth, as well as events relating to first-century Christianity. The words "New Testament" refer to a new covenant that Christians believe completes or fulfills what the Jews accept as their covenant that Yahweh (the God of Israel) made with the people of Israel. While Christianity traditionally claims this new covenant as being prophesied in the Jewish Book of Jeremiah, Judaism traditionally disagrees. The New Testament describes a collection of first- and second-century Christian "Scriptures" written in Greek at various times by unknown authors.

In this chapter, we will reveal an array of historical errors, contradictions, discrepancies, and logical inconsistencies that will clearly debunk the false belief that any OT prophecies regarding the messiah were fulfilled in the NT.

Who was Jesus?

We are defined in life in many ways: by our name, by our place of birth, our ethnicity, and hopefully, primarily by our deeds. Unfortunately, the information about Jesus is sketchy at best, and some of it is just wrong.

His Name Was Not Jesus

Jesus' real name, Yeshua (which translates to English as "Joshua"), is thought to be common for that time because Israeli archaeologist Amos Kloner discovered

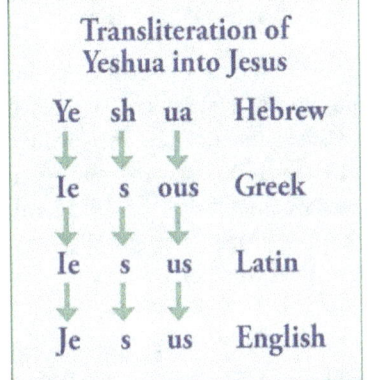

tombs of 71 'Yeshuas',[227] all from around the time of Jesus' death. Additionally, the name is in the Old Testament, referencing at least four different people.[228] The name "Jesus" is a transliteration[229] into English, not a translation. It came from the Latin form of the Greek name "Iesous". Although the New Testament was translated from Greek, there is no letter "J" in Greek, nor in Latin.[230] His name in Hebrew was indeed Yehōshūa', but he was more likely called the Aramaic word, Yēshūa'. And he would have been called Yeshua Bar Yehosef (Joshua, son of Joseph) or Yeshua Nasraya (Joshua of Nazareth).[231] The Romans were said to put 'INRI' (Iesus Nazarenus Rex Iudaeorum) on his cross, or in English, 'Joshua, King of the Jews'. So how did we get the name, "Jesus"?

Until the 16th century, there was no letter 'J' in any alphabet. Over time, both the 'I' and 'J' were used interchangeably by scribes to express the sound of both the vowel and the consonant. It wasn't until 1524 when Gian Giorgio Trissino, an Italian Renaissance grammarian, made a clear distinction between the two sounds.[232]

Even in the original King James Version (1611) of the Protestant Bible, there was no letter 'J' at all, because the letter 'J' still didn't exist in English at that time! The first English-language book to make a clear distinction between the sound of 'I' and the sound of 'J' was not written until 1634. Indeed, the letter 'J' was the last of the 26 letters to be included in the English Alphabet.[233] When English Protestants fled to Switzerland during the reign of the

Catholic Queen Mary I (mid-16th century), they drafted the Geneva Bible and used the Swiss spelling. Translators in England adopted the Geneva spelling in the 17th century.[234] The 1638 King James Bible translated the Latin word, Iesus, into the English word, Jesus.

Initially, the RCC did not follow suit. After the fall of the Roman Empire, the Catholic Church effectively appointed itself the guardian of the Latin language, and 1,500 years later, in 1978, they added the letter J to the Latin alphabet.[235] Today, even Latin versions of the New Testament refer to Jesus, rather than Iesus. Even so, for the past few hundred years, the RCC used the name Jesus whenever referring to him in English.

Ethnically, He was not Caucasian

In relating the story of Jesus, Christianity did not stop with changes to his name. His appearance has been altered to resemble a European Caucasian. Statues, pictures like the blue-eyed, fair-skinned man on the front of your grandparents' old Bible, have deceptively shaped and reshaped our perception of Yeshua of Nazareth. One could argue that it was intentional.

A photo of the image on my Bible

Some of the best-known depictions of Christ, from Leonardo da Vinci's "Last Supper" to Michelangelo's "Last Judgment" in the Sistine Chapel, were produced during the Renaissance (1350 – 1600). But the all-time most reproduced image of Jesus comes from the 20th century. The adjacent photo is from Warner Sallman's light-eyed, light-haired "Head of Christ," from 1940.[236] While no one knows exactly what Jesus looked like, the historical Jesus probably would have had the brown eyes and the brown skin like other 1st century Jews from the Galilee region of Israel. But European artists since the Renaissance have tried to distance Jesus, his parents, and their relatives from their Jewishness. Antisemitic forces, including WWII-era Nazi, tried to divorce Jesus totally from Judaism to favor an Arian stereotype.[237]

Over time European Christians have recast Jesus in their own fair-skinned image; and the myth of a white male God has enabled Christianity's footprint globally.[238] Various prominent scholars and the archbishop of Canterbury have called for a reconsideration in portraying Jesus as a white European.[239] The same pattern has occurred with Mary, otherwise known as Miriam of Nazareth. The image promoted was and remains that "white is best" – and that is not the appropriate teaching. "The whiteness of Christ took on a symbolic meaning beyond good versus evil or purity; but who could miss the symbolism that a white man was the savior of the world?" [240]

He was not Born in Bethlehem

Gospel of Matthew

The New Testament gospels do not agree about the details of Jesus' birth. Some gospels do not mention Bethlehem or Jesus' birth at all. The story in the Gospel of Matthew begins with wise men who come to the city of Jerusalem after seeing a star to the east that they interpreted as signaling the birth of a new king. It goes on to describe their meeting with the local Jewish king, Herod, of whom they inquire about the location of Jesus' birth. This gospel says that the star of Bethlehem subsequently leads them to a house where Jesus has been born to Joseph and Mary.

The Gospel of Matthew cites that after their visit, Joseph had a dream where he was warned of Herod's attempt to kill his newborn child, Jesus. When the wise men went to Herod with the news that a child had been born to be the king of the Jews, Herod decided to kill all young children to remove the threat to his throne. It then mentions how Joseph, Mary, and the infant Jesus leave for Egypt.

- **Matthew 2:23:** "…in a city called Nazareth: that it might be fulfilled which was spoken through the prophets, He should be called a Nazarene."

Gospel of Luke

Luke's version, written more than a decade or two after Matthew, is very different. Joseph and Mary journey to Bethlehem in response to a census that the Roman emperor, Caesar Augustus, required for all the Jewish people. To meet the prophecy, the Gospel of Luke declared that Joseph was a descendant of King David, and Bethlehem was the hometown where he was required to register.

The Gospel of Luke includes no flight to Egypt, no paranoid King Herod, no murder of children, and no wise men visiting baby Jesus, who is supposedly born in a manger because all the travelers overcrowded the guest rooms. After the birth, Joseph and Mary are visited not by wise men, but by shepherds.

The Actual Story

It is not necessary to reconcile Matthew's version with Luke's version, because they are both purposely constructed fables to pretend that Jesus was born in Bethlehem, as that was the "believed" prophecy for the Messiah. [See **Micah 5:2**]. First, while there is no explicit mention of a "star" in **Isaiah 60: 1-6**, some biblical scholars believe that the concept of a "light" or "brightness" in that passage, could symbolize the coming of God's glory, likely influenced the idea of the star of Bethlehem in Matthew's birth narrative. However, neither Matthew nor his audience apparently knew that no one could follow a star, as the Earth rotates. Stars rise and set relative to an observation point on the Earth (like the sun). But it is perplexing that the 'wise men' travelling west to Jerusalem and later south to Bethlehem would use a guide "in the east." Next, biblical researchers have traced the potential route of the "wise men," and they concluded that it would have taken them two to three years to arrive in Bethlehem. Third, **Matthew 2:16** claims that Herod murdered all boys younger than the age of 2. But there is no historical evidence of such an event, referred to as the 'Massacre of the Innocents'. Indeed, this has since proven to be totally fiction.[241] It appears that Matthew just wanted to associate Herod with the pharaoh of Moses' time.[242] And since Herod issued no order for the killing of innocents, there was no reason for Joseph and his family to journey to Egypt. Furthermore, biblical scholars have never been able to locate any statement from any prophet in the Old Testament to which this could refer. This is the second time that the author of the gospel of Matthew used the literary trick of a dream for Joseph (the other was supposedly about the virginity of Mary). How would Matthew, writing over 70 years after the birth of Jesus know what Joseph dreamed? Finally, the words

"Nazareth" and "Nazarene" are not found anywhere in the Tanakh/Old Testament, as there was no such prophecy.

Luke's fiction sounds a little more plausible to modern ears, but it is also not historically factual. There was never an empire-wide tax levy in the Roman Empire; and had there been, Rome would not have required anyone to travel, as they would just pay their taxes wherever they lived. Many people lived quite a distance from their original hometowns, and requiring such travel would cause economic havoc. And as with other myths, no one recorded it. That said, there was a Census of Quirinius conducted only in the Roman province of Judaea, but that occurred in 6 CE[243] – which would be 10 to 12 years after the birth of Jesus of Nazareth. And Herod died in 4 BCE. This was just Luke's way of tying Bethlehem to Joseph, which is not truly logical, because according to Christian belief, Joseph is not the true father of Jesus. And according to Jewish custom of the time, Mary's lineage, which did not trace back to David, was not germane to the prophesy.

For the record, while Jesus was not born on December 25, the pagan god Mithras was supposedly born on that date. Dec 25 is a date selected by Pope Julius I (337 – 352) in approximately 350 CE to counter a pagan festival celebrating the winter solstice.[244] And due to a Gregorian calendar mistake in 1582, Jesus was born between 6 and 4 BCE, (as opposed to the year 0 or 1), probably in Nazareth.[245]

The Crucifixion

It is a central tenant of the Jesus story that Jesus was an itinerant rabbi who preached his message throughout Judea at around 30 CE; and while doing that, he angered the Roman rulers, who feared that he was provoking unrest among the Jewish people as he often spoke of a future kingdom. However, Jewish leaders also feared him because he challenged traditional Jewish authority and teachings. While there is no consensus among scholars of that time, a situation transpired that resulted in Jesus being charged with sedition, and he was executed via crucifixion. Rabbi Yeshua of Nazareth, later to be proclaimed Christos, or Jesus Christ, was savagely nailed to a cross through his wrists. Crucifixion could take a week for a person to die, but Jesus died six hours after being nailed, probably due to his exhaustion from the scourging. According to the gospels, Jesus died at around 3 PM that afternoon.

Angry Jews on Good Friday

On Sunday, four days prior to the Last Supper meal, Jesus had a 'triumphal entry' into Jerusalem, where he was received by the Jewish people as a king. He then healed the sick and performed other miracles, as well as sharing his wisdom with the crowds. And somehow, the Romans did not notice any of this. Then, only five days later, on what we now call Good Friday, he was hated by the Jews so much that they clamored for his execution and supposedly demanded the release of the criminal, Barabbas (see next section). I thought this story sounded a bit off when I heard it as a child; it just doesn't pass any test of reasonableness. What probably happened is that the gentile Christians of that era wanted to make the Romans the benevolent ones, and relegated the Jews, who had just been defeated in the Jewish–Roman War / Revolt (66–74 CE), to the realm of villains.

This contrived story has been the catalyst for horrible recriminations against the Jews throughout the following two millennia.

Barabbas

There are several "side-stories" regarding the gospels' coverage of the crucifixion of Jesus. One in particular has been a concern to historians: the story of Barabbas, also known as Bar Abbas, a Jewish revolutionary who challenged Roman rule. The Gospel of Mark states that there was a Roman custom of releasing a prisoner in Judea during the feast of Passover in the following citations from the gospels:

- **Mark 15: 6-8:** "Now at that feast he released unto them one prisoner, whomsoever they desired. And there was one named Barabbas, who lay bound with them that had made an insurrection with him, who committed murder in the insurrection. And the multitude crying aloud began to desire him to do as he had ever done unto them."
- **Mark 15:11:** "But the chief priests moved the people, that he should rather release Barrabas onto them"
- **Matthew 27:16-17:** "And they had a notable prisoner, called Barabbas. Therefore, when they were gathered together, Pilate said unto them, Whom will ye that I release unto you? Barabbas, or Jesus which is called Christ?"
- **Matthew 27: 21-22:** "The governor answered and said unto them, Whether of the twain will ye that I release unto you? They said, Barabbas. Pilate sayeth unto them, What shall I do then with Jesus which is called Christ? They all say unto him, Let him be crucified."
- **Luke 23: 18:** "And they cried out all at once, saying, Away with this man, and release unto us Barabbas."
- **John 18:39-40:** "But ye have a custom, that I should release unto you one at the Passover; will ye therefore that I release unto you the King of the Jews? Then credit they all again, saying, Not this man, but Barabbas..."

However, there is no corroborating source(s) that attests to any such Passover practice.[246] Indeed, this story is preposterous. Pontius Pilate was a Roman governor renowned for executing his authority in accordance with Roman law, not the law of the Jews, who were a conquered people. No Roman governor would care about the Jewish Passover. Further, the name Bar Abbas is Aramaic for "son of the father." That is a name that seems like a symbolic reflection on the Jesus story; does it not?

The Cross

The cross is the main religious symbol for many Christian churches. The precise shape of the object on which Jesus was crucified cannot be proven from the Bible. New Testament writings regarding Jesus' crucifixion do not specify the shape of that cross, but subsequent early writings liken it to a capital letter 'T'. The Crux Commissa was an upright stake with a crossbeam on the top; it resembled a capital T-shaped cross, like the Greek letter, Tau.[247] The upright post was already at the place of execution, as was standard, because that post was to be used repeatedly. It had a metal nub at its top that the crossbar fitted snugly onto, and the victim was attached to the crossbar and then raised onto the upright post. This was the primary method used by the Romans. Logically, it would make no sense to try to nail a thick crossbar to an upright post (as in a little 't').

Crucifixion was humiliation, making the condemned as vulnerable as possible. Although artists have traditionally depicted the figure on a cross with a loincloth or a covering of the genitals, the person being crucified was usually stripped naked.[248]

Other myths about a Roman crucifixion Include:

- There are no other reports of breaking the legs of crucifixion victims in antiquity. Only **John 19** reports this.
- Breaking of legs was a separate non-capital punishment in the Roman Empire that Constantine abolished (in 337 CE) along with crucifixion.[249]
- No one in antiquity was reported to carry an entire cross — they only carried the cross bar, referred to as the 'patibulum' in Latin. Carrying the entire cross would have been impossible for even the strongest of men. Evidence of Roman crucifixions suggests that Jesus carried just the horizontal patibulum, which would probably have been dragged by Jesus, after having been severely scourged, as it weighed by itself around 60 pounds (27 kg).

Death and Burial

The story may seem straightforward, but our knowledge of the events is from the writers of the gospels, who wrote decades later, without revealing their names, had only hearsay as background 'evidence,' and who fabricated an incredible amount of unnecessary tangential information. The first example comes from Luke.

- **Luke 22:41-42:** "And he was withdrawn from them about a stone's cast, and kneeled down and prayed, Saying, Father, if thou be willing, remove this cup from me: nevertheless not my will, but thine be done."

This is one of several instances where a gospel writer just creates what he wants. After all, Jesus supposedly moved a 'stone's throw' away from the apostles who were with him to acquire some privacy. He wasn't yelling his prayers, so how did anyone hear him? The writer of the Gospel of Luke was not there; he wrote this passage approximately 70 years later. This portion of the Gospel of Luke is based on what?

From the writer of **Matthew 12:40,** Jesus says, "For as Jonah was three days and three nights in the belly of the great fish, so will the Son of Man be three days and three nights in the heart of the earth."

This was another 'fulfilled prophecy' that wasn't true. Some Christians pretend that the OT predicted the death and resurrection in three days, but it did not. There are no OT passages that predict the crucifixion of the Messiah. Further, can Christian apologists not count? It wasn't even two full days since Friday afternoon, much less three. Some suggest that the Jews counted differently, but they did not. They suggest that Friday was a day, Saturday was a day, and Sunday was a day. Even if one were to accept that contrived counting, the words, "and nights" blow that up. It was only two nights, and it was not in fulfillment of anything. There is nothing in the OT that predicted this. Jonah in the whale has nothing to do with Jesus' death. The Gospel of Matthew's correlation of Jesus with Jonah appears to be an extreme overreach.

- **Luke 23:42-44:** "And he said unto Jesus, Lord, remember me when thou comest into thy kingdom. And Jesus said unto him, Verily I say unto thee, today shalt thou be with me in paradise. And it was about the sixth hour, and there was darkness over all the earth until the ninth hour."

So, another private conversation that no one else could hear between Jesus and the man nailed next to him. This passage was written by the author of the Gospel of Luke, a non-witness, over seven decades later. Jesus' last words (according to the gospel) underscore that he was not God. The authors of Mark and Matthew say exactly the same thing:

- *Mark 15: 34*
- *Matthew 27:46* "My God, my God, why hast thou forsaken me?"
  If Jesus was God, then he is saying, "...why hast I forsaken myself?" Therefore, the Gospel of John, written much later than the Gospels of Mark or Matthew, fixed that; **John 29:30** says, *"It is finished,"* and that sounds much more divine.

In the synoptic narrative, while Jesus is hanging on the cross, the sky over Judaea (or the whole Earth) is "darkened for three hours, "from the sixth hour to the ninth hour (noon to mid-afternoon). And even though this darkness over the Earth occurred when it should have been sunlight, none of the Romans apparently noticed. Indeed, nothing in this story is corroborated. Some Christian apologists have tried to suggest that there was a solar eclipse. But no eclipse can last three hours![250] And "over all the Earth"? Hyperbole anyone?

- **Mark 15:33:** "And when the 6th hour was come, there was darkness over the land until the ninth hour."
- **Matthew 28:45:** "Now from the sixth hour there was darkness over all the land unto the ninth hour."
- **Luke 23: 44:** "And it was about the 6th hour, and there was a darkness over all the earth until the ninth."

The Synoptic Gospels state that the veil of the temple was torn from top to bottom. And apparently needing even more drama, the Gospel of Matthew mentions an earthquake and a rock splitting.

- **Mark 15:38:** "And the veil of the temple was rent in twain from the top to the bottom"
- **Matthew 27:51:** "And behold, the veil of the temple was rent in twain from the top to the bottom; and the earth did quake, and the rock rent."
- **Luke 23:45:** "And the sun darkened, and the veil of the temple was rent in the midst."

So, a key question remains: how does this crucifixion of the rabbi, Yeshua bar Josef, wash away sins? In the Synoptic Gospels, Jesus never says any words similar to, "I will be sacrificed so that your sins will be forgiven." Indeed, the Synoptic Gospels were not written to convince anyone that Jesus was divine. Only the forged Gospel of John, written almost a century after the days of Jesus, states Jesus was divine; but even the Gospel of John does not mention that Jesus died for our sins.

The concept of a blood sacrifice is the standard way that ignorant people (as in uneducated and superstitious) of the ancient world appeased their gods. They generally sacrificed animals. Paul was aware of Judaism's requirements for blood sacrifice rituals. And Paul contrived the Jewish sacrifice analogy as an interpretation of Jesus' death. He said as much in Romans, when he tied it back to Adam's sin in Genesis.

- **Romans 5:8-9:** "But God commandeth his love toward us, in that, while we were yet sinners, Christ died for us. Much more then, being now justified by his blood, we shall be saved from wrath through him."
- **Romans 5:19:** "For by one man's disobedience many were made sinners, so by the obedience of one shall many be made righteous."

So, the entire concept of sacrifice for the sins of mankind appears to have been fabricated by Paul of Tarsus, who used his understanding as a Pharisaic Jew regarding how blood sacrifices can save us from God's wrath. Paul never claimed that anything was revealed to him by God; he basically interpolated this on his own. Paul of Tarsus was the only person in ancient history to tell us that Jesus of Nazareth died to redeem us from our sins. Jesus never said that. He never even mentioned sinners. The phrase, "a sinner saved by grace," certainly appears to be a man-made deception. How many people have believed and been deceived by this false doctrine? It is a doctrine that seems based on faulty reasoning and the misapplication of logic.

Let's, for a moment, accept that Jesus died to remove some stain on humanity. If he did that, then the sin/stain is gone. So, what does anyone's belief in the resurrection of Jesus have to do with being 'saved'? Saved from what? We are living long after his 'sacrifice,' and the world is still awash in evil and suffering. That presents questions about the efficacy of Jesus' sacrifice and why evil and suffering haven't been abolished.[251] And why still have sacraments like Baptism and communion if Jesus' sacrifice was sufficient? These rituals imply that we need something more, and that Jesus' dying just wasn't enough.

Resurrection and Ascension

Most Christians today believe that Jesus' resurrection from the dead and ascension to heaven both happened in a material body. Christians regard the resurrection of Jesus and his ascension into Heaven as a central doctrine in Christianity. But there is no evidence of this event. Indeed, the earliest Christians believed in a "spiritual" resurrection (which, based on his writing, is what Saul of Tarsus (St. Paul) apparently believed), but over time the story evolved into a "bodily" resurrection.

Resurrection

Let's start with Paul, who wasn't a disciple of Jesus during that time. His later writing of the Resurrection was limited to this brief summary.

- **1 Corinthians 15:3-6:** "For I delivered unto you first of all that which I also received, how that Christ died for our sins, according to the Scriptures; And that he was buried, and that he rose again the third day, according to the Scriptures. And that he was seen by Cephas, then by the twelve. After that, he was seen by above five hundred brethren at once; of whom the greater part remain unto this present, but some are fallen asleep."

The above passage, written by Paul in the mid-50s CE (over 20 years after the death of Jesus), is the single entry testifying to the most fundamental belief of Christianity – that Jesus died for our sins and then rose from the dead three days later. No one else corroborated this; nowhere else is this assertion written. There were no witnesses. There is no evidence or testifying statement by anyone in support of Paul's comment. What Paul asserts is simply his theological claim, and not historical fact. Furthermore, Paul blatantly lied when he said, "according to the Scriptures." Paul cannot cite any Scripture that ever prophesied that the Messiah would rise on the third day, because there is no such citation. Nowhere in the Old Testament is it predicted that the Messiah would die and rise again. Absolutely nowhere!

Just like the 500 brethren that Paul fabricated. Paul wasn't there, and no one confirmed that tale either. Paul's claim of 500 witnesses is at best pure hearsay of rumors he heard, or at worst, he felt the need to manufacture some secondary, hearsay evidence. And isn't it quite odd that no Roman writers or officials knew anything of this incredible event? None of the five hundred wrote about it, nor informed anyone else who could write about it, including the Romans.

There was no foretelling in Jewish Scripture that its Messiah would die for their sins. And who is Cephas? Apologists say that it is another name for Peter (whom Paul had later met and knew). However, the cited verse indicates that 'Cephas' was outside the group of apostles, now 11 apostles, as Judas had supposedly departed. A century later, the author of the Gospel of John would declare Cephas as another name for Peter, but that unnamed author generally agreed to whatever Paul wrote.

It is always fascinating that Paul strived so hard to identify that the Resurrection story fulfilled some non-existent OT prophecy. He spins the tale to find something believable, no matter how obscure. However, Paul of Tarsus lacks credibility; he was wrong about so many things. On the other hand, Paul didn't write anything about the empty tomb or the alleged sightings of Jesus by the two Marys and later by the apostles. This suggests that the "tradition of the discovered empty tomb" did not yet exist. The gospels that crafted those events would be written many decades later. That takes us to the first gospel, Mark. But Mark didn't write about the Resurrection nor the Ascension. Significantly, those references to Jesus in the Gospel of Mark **(Mark 16:9-20)** were added <u>after</u> the Gospel of Mark was completed.[252] [253] [254] Nor did any prominent residents of Jerusalem, nor the Romans, write or testify about Jesus' Resurrection or Ascension.

Actually, only the authors of Matthew, Luke, and John wrote about it. Three writers testifying many decades after an event that they did not witness, nor did they apparently have any information from witnesses. None of the people referenced as having seen Jesus post-crucifixion wrote about him or mentioned him to anyone in authority. And everyone referenced by Matthew, Luke, and John was already a disciple of Jesus. This entire story depended on a miracle with no evidence.

But the author of the Matthew Gospel did introduce some comic relief in his 'zombie apocalypse,' where just about everyone got resurrected, as there was an opening of the "graves of dead saints," and these resurrected saints went into the holy city and appeared to many people. However, none of the "many" to whom Jesus or the zombies appeared said anything to anyone or submitted it to writing. And the Romans remained unaware of all the zombies moving through Jerusalem. Thus, with no records, and with the writer of the Gospel of Matthew not being an eyewitness, how did he know about any of this? Unless, of course, he invented it.

- **Matthew 27:52-53:** "And the graves were opened; and many bodies of the saints which slept arose; And came out of the graves after his resurrection, and went into the holy city, and appeared to many."

Now let's look at a basic area of contradiction that theologians and apologists have reviewed for years. This should be a simple question: how many women were at the tomb?

Mark 16:1	Matthew 28:1	Luke 24:10	John 20:1	1 Corinthians 15:4-7
"In the end of the sabbath, as it began to dawn toward the first day of the week, came Mary Magdalene and the other Mary to see the sepulcher."	It was Mary Magdalene and Joanna, and Mary the mother of James, and other women that were with them, which told these things unto the apostles."	"And when the sabbath was past, Mary Magdalene, and Mary the mother of James, and Salome, had bought sweet spices, that they might come and anoint him. "	"The first day of the week came Mary Magdalene early, when it was yet dark, to the sepulcher, and saw the stone taken away from the sepulcher. "	"He rose again the third day according to the Scriptures. And that he was seen of Cephas, then of the twelve. After that, he was seen of above five hundred brethren at once; of whom the greater part remains unto this present, but some are fallen asleep. After that, he was seen of James; then of all the apostles."
2 x women	3 (including Joana) + "other women"	3 x women (but instead of Joanna, we have Salome)	1 x woman	No women

72

And what about the supposed appearance of Jesus to the apostles? The author of the Gospel of Luke says that the first appearance of the newly resurrected Jesus happened in Jerusalem, where the apostles had gathered. However, Matthew says that it happened 60 to 80 miles away in Galilee. These contradictory stories cannot be reconciled into a consistent narrative of the Resurrection.

If the Resurrection story is the greatest event in the history of mankind, why is there such insufficient evidentiary support? And why couldn't the 'divinely revealed' Scriptures agree on basic details? Indeed, we have no evidence, much less extraordinary evidence, that Jesus of Nazareth rose from the dead. The lack of clarity undermines the credibility that the Resurrection ever occurred. Thus, disbelief in the Resurrection might certainly be a rational view. Clearly, the tale of Jesus' Resurrection was meant to validate the status of Jesus. Unfortunately, the lack of evidence suggests that the story is a myth shaped to fit the Christian movement.

Ascension

There are many potential proofs that Jesus could have provided to humanity, especially after this ridiculous comment in the Gospel of Mark.

- **Mark 16:16-17:** "And he said unto them, Go ye into all the world, and preach the gospel to every creature. He that believeth and is baptized shall be saved; but he that believeth not shall be damned."

So, the apostles are to preach to every 'creature', not every person. And with no proof and no evidence of any type, those who do not believe are to be damned. How fair and loving! And this from Jesus, not Yahweh! Also, it should be noted that the only gospel written at that time was the Gospel of Mark. So many Christian denominations today cite this passage that one cannot be saved without accepting that Jesus of Nazareth rose from the dead. Yet many people, prior to those teachings and for centuries afterward, had no access to that information due to geographic and language barriers. This presents many moral and ethical issues. Eternal suffering for disbelief, or for just being unaware. That just doesn't sound like Jesus of Nazareth! It would seem that the author of the Gospel of Mark is putting words in Jesus' mouth.

The author of Luke, who is also the author of Acts of the Apostles, couldn't even get the timing correct regarding Jesus' time span between the Resurrection and Ascendancy. First, he agrees with the Gospel of Mark (one day); but then he couldn't resist the magic number of 40 days in Acts.

- **Mark 16:**
  Verse 9: "Now when Jesus was risen early the <u>first day</u> of the week, he appeared first to Mary Magdalene, out of whom he cast seven devils."
  Verse 19: "So then after the Lord had spoken unto them, he was received up into heaven, and sat on the right hand of God."
- **Luke 24:**
  Verse 1: "Now upon the <u>first day</u> of the week, very early in the morning, they came unto the sepulcher, bringing the spices which they had prepared, and certain others with them."

Verse 51: "And it came to pass, while he blessed them, and he was parted from them, and carried up into heaven."

- **Acts 1:**

  Verse 3: "To whom also he shewed himself alive after his passion by many infallible proofs, being seen of them <u>forty days</u>, and speaking of the things pertaining to the kingdom of God."

  Verse 9: "And when he had spoken these things, while they beheld, he was taken up; and a cloud received them out of their sight."

The author of the Gospel of Luke was particularly adept at alleging that make-believe OT prophecies were being fulfilled. Of course, nowhere in the OT does it predict any of these things!

- **Luke 24:46:** "And said unto them, thus it is written, and thus it behooved Christ to suffer, and to rise from the dead on the third day."

The Christ Experience

In recasting the story of Jesus Christ, it is important to view the world through the eyes of the early Christian community in the Mediterranean world. The traditional paradigm, "to save the world from sin," just doesn't work for 21st-century mankind.

Origin of Sin and Evil

Sin is a religious concept; it is *an offense against religious law*. It is the result of an individual knowingly and willingly doing something that hurts his/her relationship with God. So, sin remains strictly religious. It is also a religious sales pitch: without it, there is no need for salvation. For a growing number of people, sin is entirely a man-made concept.

The foundation for the concept of original sin surfaced in the early 3rd century by the Christian theologian, Tertullian of Carthage (c. 155 – 220 CE),[255] who is considered the first Christian theologian to write in Latin. Tertullian actively advocated traducianism,[256] the parental generation of souls. Tertullian was one of the first to conceptualize the hereditary transmission of sin. His ideas regarding sin and traducianism were further developed and popularized into the Christian doctrine by Augustine of Hippo, who stated that even babies who die unbaptized are tainted with original sin.[257] But his proof was based on a mistranslation of **Romans 5:12** from the original Greek. This mistaken translation was the only instance in the New Testament to indicate that the guilt for the original sin of Adam (a character in Genesis that never existed) was passed on. What Paul wrote is that people die because everyone sins, not because Adam transgressed.[258] [259] Paul never mentioned the concept of original sin, nor did he allude to it.

Neither Jesus nor the apostles ever brought up original sin, and it is probably safe to say, as Jews, they did not believe in original sin. Certainly, there is no passage in Scripture that speaks definitively to the concept. Psychologist, S. Richard Bellrock, stated that "Original sin is to morality as Zeus's thunderbolt is to weather. That is, Zeus's thunderbolts do not exist; and therefore, [they] contribute nothing to our understanding of weather."[260]

The Mythology of Christianity

The view that humans are intrinsically evil is not commensurate with an ethical system based on mutual respect. And the question remains: if the world was created perfect, and people were made in the image of God, where did evil come from? After all, if God were truly all-powerful and if he were the lone deity, then the origin and continued existence of evil, as well as all the ongoing suffering in the world, would not be in alignment with the nature of a benevolent, loving deity. And that concern was supposed to have been alleviated by the idea of salvation and an afterlife.

Still, what about those verses that seem to indicate that God did, indeed, cause horrifying events to come about and evil deeds to be done? The following verses do not appear to have the inspiration of a deity; but rather they appear to be the authors' poor explanation of events:

- **Genesis 50:20** ~ "As for you, you meant evil against me, but God meant it for good in order to bring about this present result, to preserve many people alive"
- **Exodus 4:21; 7:3** ~ "I will harden Pharaoh's heart"
- **1 Samuel 16:14** ~ "An evil spirit from the Lord tormented Saul"
- **2 Samuel 12:15, 18** ~ "So Nathan went to his house. Then the Lord struck the child that Uriah's widow bore to David, so that he was very sick...Then it happened on the seventh day that the child died"
- **2 Samuel 24:1** ~ "The Lord incited David to take a census of the people" (cf. 1 Chron 21:1)
- **1 Kings 22:23** ~ "Now therefore, behold, the Lord has put a deceiving spirit in the mouth of all These your prophets; and the Lord has proclaimed disaster against you."
- **Job 1:7-8** ~ "The Lord said to Satan, "From where do you come?" Then Satan answered the Lord and said, "From roaming about on the earth and walking around on it." The Lord said to Satan, "Have you considered My servant Job? For there is no one like him on the earth, a blameless and upright man, fearing God and turning away from evil.""
- **Isaiah 45:7** ~ "I form the light and create darkness: I make peace and create evil: I, the Lord, do these things"
- **Lamentations 3:38** ~ "Who is there who speaks and it comes to pass, Unless the Lord has commanded it? Is it not from the mouth of the Most High That both good and ill go forth?"
- **Amos 3:6** ~ "If a calamity occurs in a city, has not the LORD done it?"
- **Acts 2:23** ~ "This Man, delivered over by the predetermined plan and foreknowledge of God, you nailed to a cross by the hands of godless men and put Him to death."

Considering the weight of this Scriptural testimony, should we conclude that God enacts (not simply permits) evil? But if so, for what purpose? Isn't it more likely that the ancient authors of these biblical passages simply crafted these words for their own purposes?

Redemption and Salvation

It is all about our guilt-producing mantra, 'Jesus died for our sins...' We hear it repeatedly. The concept that humans are intrinsically sinners is an insidious doctrine. Somehow, we deserve divine punishment, and Jesus becomes the victim. This story further enhances our guilt. And then we add <u>eternal</u> punishment for <u>temporal</u> sins! To be human is to be guilty and feeling guilty. And we spend a lot of time pleading with God to have mercy.[261] Paul wrote in around 55 CE:

- **Romans 5: 8-9:** "But God commendeth his love toward us, in that, while we were yet sinners, Christ died for us. Much more then, being now justified by his blood, we shall be saved from wrath through Him."
- **Romans 5: 12:** "Wherefore, as by one man sin entered into the world, and death by sin; and so death passed upon all men, for that all have sinned."

So, one sentence, which is a mistranslation of the original Greek text from one religious zealot (Paul), based on an event in the book of Genesis that didn't happen, created what became a mainstay Christian belief. And Jesus is never quoted anywhere in the Bible as saying anything about humans sinning. Generally, he taught acceptance, tolerance, and love for one's neighbor. Jesus never said anything about dying to redeem us. And if we say that he did, then we are saved? How does that translate into a requirement that we must believe in his resurrection to be saved?

The theology that developed was that mankind's only hope for salvation was based on the belief that God would come from His celestial abode to aid us. And so, we were to refer to him as Redeemer and Savior, as he saved us from the Fall of Perfection [even though it never happened]. How did he do that? By dying on a cross – a concept that may have seemed reasonable to Mediterranean Christians in the first three centuries; but that story is a bit contrived and weird in our modern era. Therefore, what the New Testament (actually, it is just Paul) is saying is that God created the problem of sin; He imposed a death sentence; and then He sacrificed Himself to resolve the problem that He, Himself, had created. Said differently, if Jesus is truly God, then God sacrificed Himself to Himself to appease Himself.[262] This is quite a circular argument. And this doctrine of substitutionary atonement (also called penal substitution), that the suffering and death of Jesus somehow paid the price for humanity's sins, undermines the basic principles of justice.[263] Moreover, such a doctrine is not at all in alignment with a loving, omnipotent and omniprescient Creator.

The view espoused by Paul is a message of guilt. We are sinners who have become victims of our own sins. And so, Jesus died to redeem our broken souls. This story of the 'sacrifice' of Jesus enhances that guilt. This is a form of ecclesiastic control of our lives. Alternatively, we should ask ourselves how a person dying 2000 years ago "pays" for our "sins"? Only we can "redeem" ourselves – by forgiving ourselves, apologizing to those we have wronged, and changing our behavior going forward. What Jesus did or didn't do two millennia ago can't absolve us from the basic truth that each of us is responsible for our own lives.

In Paul's view, God is not so much a loving deity as a punishing one. According to Episcopal Bishop John Shelby Spong (1931 – 2021), we attach guilt to everything.[264] Apparently, our natural biology is a key source of our guilt. We are sexual human beings, and we feel guilty about that. We are miserable penitents, born into sin. And we wallow in guilt. We have defined human life as sinful. So, rather than celebrating life, we are deluged with guilt.[265] Is this a healthy attitude?

Religion shouldn't be based on guilt and manipulation. As espoused by Bishop Shelby, begging for mercy is what a quivering child does in front of an abusive bully. Does mankind really need a savior? The New Testament reflects the mistrustful and at times irrational culture of its time. We need to step away from the traditional framework created by those living in the first three centuries.[266] If God is indeed all-powerful, then God can forgive without a blood sacrifice and without any preconditions. Even we lowly mortal humans forgive one another without requiring anything in return, and certainly, we have no requirements for suffering or death. The idea of a blood sacrifice is riddled with illogic containing many justice issues.

Such stories of blood sacrifice were common in many of the other religions of the time. Indeed, there are many "savior" and "resurrection" stories in the Egyptian, Greek, and Persian literature to draw from. For example, the followers of the god Mithras, a Persian deity with ties to Zoroastrianism, believed in salvation through his blood sacrifice of bulls. Mithras underwent ritual baptism, was known for his miraculous deeds, surrounded by 12 signs of the zodiac, and was called 'Light of the World' and 'The Truth.'[267] The cult of Mithras is known to have been centered in Tarsus[268] [269] (Mersin province of Turkey today), where Paul was from. Christian apologists have denied the historical tie with Mithras, stating that Mithras was not popular in the Roman world until late 1st century CE. However, the religion that Paul was exposed to in his hometown of Tarsus in Asia Minor in the province of Cilicia was not Roman Mithraism but Persian Mithraism.[270]

The Egyptian god, Osiris, died and was resurrected to symbolize rebirth and renewal.[271] Dionysius was a Greek god known for his death and resurrection. Followers of Dionysus ritually ate his flesh and drank his blood.[272] So Paul had plenty of background material to syncretically adapt pagan themes to Christianity.

The Historicity of Jesus of Nazareth

The era in which Jesus of Nazareth supposedly existed is one of the most documented periods of ancient history; and many contemporary writers documented the era in great detail.[273] There is no definitive physical or archaeological evidence of the existence of Jesus. But that is circumstantial. "The reality is that we don't have archaeological records for virtually anyone who lived in Jesus's time and place," says University of North Carolina religious studies professor Bart D. Ehrman, author of _Did Jesus Exist? The Historical Argument for Jesus of Nazareth_. "The lack of evidence … means that like 99.99% of the rest of the world at the time, he made no impact on the archaeological record."[274] Of course, the rest of the world did not perform miracles, nor were they surrounded by strange events as darkness for three hours in the middle of the day, nor zombies walking throughout the city in which one is buried.

Skepticism regarding the historicity of Jesus persists. Here are some key points against his existence:

1. **Scarcity of secular evidence from the 1st century to support Yeshua ben Yosef's existence.** Pagan authors contemporaneous to Jesus' time remain conspicuously silent about him. No birth records, trial transcripts, or death certificates. Very few references to Jesus appear in any non-Christian or non-Jewish writings of that era.

Jewish historian, Josephus,[275] and Roman historian, Tacitus,[276] and Roman gossip writer, Suetonius, make passing references to Jesus and his followers in their writings. However, these references are disputed. Indeed, the account of Josephus in a passage called, *"Testimonium Flavianum"* in his manuscript, <u>Antiquities of the Jews</u>, has been shown to be a forgery created by the Catholic Church and inserted into Josephus' document.[277] Indeed, it has been refuted conclusively for centuries; and it dates more than 60 years after the death of Jesus. Yet this passage from Josephus did not surface until centuries after his death, in the early 4th century.[278]

Roman historian Tacitus (56 – 120 CE) blamed the burning of Rome on criminals, "commonly called Christians," and they were "followers of Christos." However, the historical accuracy of this passage is such that critics question whether Tacitus wrote this account.[279] Nor were there any widespread persecutions of Christians by Nero. Indeed, at the time of the burning of Rome, there were very few 'Christians' in Rome.

Another piece of tenuous evidence comes from Suetonius, who wrote the <u>Life of Claudius</u>, dating around 110 CE, and he referred to someone named "Chresto" who caused Jews to riot in Rome. But Jesus would have been long dead by then (Claudius reigned from 41-54 CE).

The historians/writers cited above, even if their writing was not forgery, would only be referring to what they had heard – in other words, pure hearsay. There is no corroboration among them or with eyewitnesses.

2. **Unfamiliarity of Jesus' life details is apparent in the earliest New Testament writings**. Paul (Saul of Tarsus) appears unaware of the basic biographical aspects attributed to Jesus in later texts. More than that, he was oblivious to the existence of Jesus of Nazareth! He always referred to Christos (the Christ) – never once to Jesus. Paul refrains from citing Jesus' authority when it would have strengthened his reasoning. Paul never mentions Jesus' disciples or that he even had any. He never mentions any miracles. All of these things – the ministry of Jesus, his parables, his disciples, and his miracles would have to be produced later in the gospels. According to G.A. Wells, in <u>The Historical Evidence for Jesus,</u> "The… Pauline letters…are so completely silent concerning the events that were later recorded in the gospels as to suggest that these events were not known to Paul, who, however, could not have been unaware of them if they had really occurred."[280]

The first writing after Paul, the Gospel of Mark, presents only a limited view of Jesus' life; the story begins with the one-year ministry of Jesus, skipping the previous 30 years, including his family life, and ends abruptly. More details about the life of Jesus of Nazareth appear in later texts. That is why it is important to read the New Testament books in chronological order. Isn't it odd that the further away from the era of Jesus of Nazareth, as the possibility of eyewitnesses grows dimmer, many additional details of his life emerge – almost as if special-interest groups were composing and embellishing the story over time!

3. **Lack of first-hand accounts in the New Testament stories.** Pseudonymous writing was customary in the 1st and 2nd centuries, contributing to the uncertainty about the

direct experiences of the authors of the gospels.[281] And we now know that the name designations of the gospels – Mark, Matthew, Luke, and John – were not assigned until the late 2nd century, over 100 years after Jesus' death.

4. **Inconsistencies among the gospel accounts.** The earliest gospel, Mark, served as a template for the later Matthew and Luke, albeit with variations. However, these accounts contradict one another for reasons that are not limited to differing intentions and audiences. Indeed, such inconsistencies are characteristics of oral traditions that have evolved and changed with multiple retellings; they are not characteristic of written accounts, and they especially would not be typical of divinely inspired accounts.

5. **Diverse depictions of the real historical Jesus.** Scholars who claim to have unveiled the real historical Jesus present divergent portraits, including a philosopher, rabbi, revolutionary, and pacifist. This variety underscores the complexity of the discussion.

So, what is the proof that Jesus existed? There is limited evidence to be sure, but I am inclined to believe that the man, Rabbi Yeshua ben Josef of Nazareth, did exist. My rationale is the ridiculously contrived backstories by the authors of the gospels of Matthew and Luke to have him born in Bethlehem just to link him to the prophecy of the Messiah from the House of David. If he didn't exist, then why not just say that the Messiah was born in Bethlehem and that is where he grew up, and be done with it? But to contrive stories to have Jesus born in Bethlehem, grow up in Nazareth, and then die in Jerusalem suggests that there may have been a real itinerant, Jewish preacher who was executed for treason against the Roman Empire. And it was Saul of Tarsus (St. Paul) who first wrote about him; and it was he who, a growing number of historians believe, created the original tale. In one of his earliest epistles, **Galatians 1:12,** Paul states that his information came from divine revelation rather than the original apostles. In other words, he appears to have invented it.

However, for others, such as the author of *Nailed,* David Fitzgerald, the precited issues lead to one conclusion: "Jesus appears to be an effect, not a cause, of Christianity. Paul and the rest of the first generation of Christians searched the Septuagint translation of Hebrew Scriptures to create a Mystery Faith for the Jews, complete with pagan rituals like a Lord's Supper, gnostic terms in his letters, and a personal savior god..." [282]

Other Intriguing Reveals about Jesus

He Was Not Initially Believed to be Divine

It is a core Christian belief that Jesus died on the cross, was buried in a tomb, and on the third day he rose from the dead and appeared to his disciples. Some skeptics argue that Jesus did not die on the cross, but he survived or fainted. Others suggest that his body was stolen or moved by his followers, who then devised or hallucinated his resurrection. The historical evidence for the crucifixion and resurrection of Jesus is limited and ambiguous. There is no independent confirmation from non-Christian sources.

There is no empirical evidence that attests to the divinity of Jesus. As explained by Religions Wiki, "Historians would require extensive evidence to consider a historic person divine."[283] The New Testament is generally unreliable[284] and is certainly biased. German Protestant theologian, Ernst Troeltsch (February 1865 – February 1923) argued that there must be "some analogy between historical events and current events, which generally rules out supernatural causation".[285] Most mainstream historians see no <u>evidence</u> that Jesus was divine. In fact, that appeared to be a common theme in the early Christian community (1st century). Indeed, American New Testament scholar and author, Bart D. Ehrmann argues, "[...] in our earliest sources Jesus is always distinguished as a different entity from God, and as his subordinate."[286] Bart D. Ehrman contends that the historical Jesus did not claim to be divine, nor was he worshipped as such during his life; rather, his status as God the Son in the Trinity in Christian doctrine gradually progressed in the years following his crucifixion.[287]

During his lifetime, Jesus didn't refer to himself as God, and he apparently didn't consider himself to be God; nor did any of his disciples seem to believe that he was God. In the first two centuries CE, only two sources declared Jesus to be divine. One was the author of the Gospel of John – a gospel that has been determined to be a counterfeit, and it was not written by anyone who ever met Jesus. The other was Paul, who wrote the various epistles, and who apparently knew nothing about his ministry. So, the divinity of Jesus was effectively cited by one source, and all knowledge regarding Jesus by that one source was hearsay. That suggests that the divinity of Jesus of Nazareth was yet another man-made construct that evolved over time.

He Sometimes Contradicted the Old Testament

There are many contradictions in both the Old and New Testaments. What is interesting is that some Christians believe that Jesus would never contradict something from the Old Testament (which was the only approved (canonized) Scripture when he was preaching); but that is exactly what he occasionally did. The following are just three examples. Interestingly, the Scripture to be contradicted came from Deuteronomy, and it is the author of the Gospel of Matthew who penned each contradiction:

While Yahweh instructs the Jews to take oaths, Jesus says that to swear by anything is "from the evil one."

- **Deuteronomy 6:13:** "Thou shalt fear the Lord, your God and serve Him, and shalt swear by his name."
- **Matthew 5:37:** "But let your communication be Yeah, Yeah; and your Nay, Nay. For whatever is more than these cometh of evil.

The Old Testament says that God's people should show no mercy and practice an eye-for-an-eye form of justice, but Jesus directly contradicts that position.

- **Deuteronomy 19:21:** "And thine eye shall not pity; and life shall go for life, eye for eye, tooth for tooth, hand for hand, foot for foot."
- **Matthew 5:38-39:** "Ye have heard that it hath been said, eye for eye, and tooth for tooth.' But I say unto you, that ye resist not evil: but whosoever shall smite thee on the right cheek, turn to him the other also."
- **Matthew 5:44-48:** "But I say unto you, love your enemies, bless them that curse you, do good to them that hate you, and pray for them which despitefully use you, and persecute you. That ye may be the children of your Father which is in heaven..."

The author of Deuteronomy (falsely attributed to Moses) provides his thoughts regarding Yahweh's blessing, while the author of Matthew quotes Jesus providing an opposite viewpoint.

- **Deuteronomy 28:** "If ye obey the Lord your God and faithfully keep all His commandments...then He will send rain in season from his rich storehouse in the sky and bless all your work...But if ye disobey the Lord your God and do not faithfully keep all his commands and laws that I am giving you today...No rain will fall, and your ground will become as hard as iron. Instead of rain, the Lord will send down dust storms and sandstorms until ye are destroyed."
- **Matthew 5:45:** "... for he maketh his sun to rise on the evil and on the good, and sendeth rain on the just and the unjust."

Jesus Said He Would Return in His Audience's Lifetime

The prophesy of Jesus' return in the lifetimes of his apostles and others who followed him are additional examples of failed prophesies. According to the authors of the gospels, Jesus believed that the end was coming in his own generation, and he promised to return in their lifetimes. Such false predictions certainly challenge the omniscience of Jesus, and <u>if</u> he really said it, then it undermines his credibility.

- **Mark 9:1:** "Verily I say unto you, that there be some of them that stand here, which shall not taste of death, till they have seen the kingdom of God come with power."
- **Mark 13: 26, 29-30:** "And then shall they see the Son of man coming in the clouds with great power and glory... So ye in like manner, when ye shall see these things come to pass, know that it is nigh, even at the doors. Verily I say unto you, that this generation shall not pass, till all these things be done"
- **Mark 14:62:** "And ye shall see the Son of man sitting on the right hand of power, and coming in the clouds of heaven."
- **Matthew 10:23:** "But when they persecute you in this city, flee ye into another: for verily I say unto you, Ye shall not have gone over the cities of Israel, till the Son of man be come."
- **Matthew 16:28:** "Verily I say unto you, that there be some standing here, which shall not taste of death, till they see the Son of man coming in his kingdom."
- **Matthew 23:36:** "Verily I say unto you, All these things shall come upon this generation."
- **Matthew 24: 30, 33-34:** "And then shall appear the sign of the Son of man in heaven: and then shall all the tribes of the earth mourn, and they shall see the Son of man coming in the clouds of heaven with power and great glory ... So likewise ye, when ye shall see all these things, know that it is near, even at the doors...Verily, I say unto you. This generation shall not pass, till all these things be fulfilled."
- **Matthew 26:64:** "Nevertheless I say unto you, Hereafter shall ye see the Son of man sitting on the right hand of power, and coming in the clouds of heaven."
- **Luke 9:27:** "But I tell you of a truth, there be some standing here, which shall not taste of death, till they see the kingdom of God."
- **Luke 21:32:** "Verily I say unto you, this generation shall not pass away, till all be fulfilled."

Jesus' late-1st-century followers had to find a way to make sense of the predicament of having devoted their lives to a prophecy that seemed to have failed. And over the past two millennia since the prophecy was supposedly uttered by Jesus, believers have come up with a variety of explanations for why he had not come back. However, none of those contrived explanations are remotely credible.

The results of this failed prophesy remain the same; Jesus never returned. And reading all the contrived explanations provided by the Christian apologists are just too far-fetched. For the record, I do not believe that Rabbi Yeshua made any of these predictions. The author of the Gospel of Mark created these words several decades after the death of Yeshua, and much later, the authors of Matthew and Luke just dutifully copied what Mark creatively invented. And one must wonder why the authors of Matthew and Luke, writing so much later after the author of Mark, would even put this exchange in their gospels, given that most, if not all, of the audience from 30 CE were already dead.

The Power of Faith and Prayer, or Lack thereof

Jesus promises that, for anyone who has faith in God the Father, that is, "the one who sent me", prayers will be answered, and the person praying will receive whatever he asks.

- **Mark 11:24:** "Therefore I say unto you, what things soever ye desire, when ye pray, believe that ye receive them, and he shall have them."
- **Mark 16:17-18:** "And these signs will accompany those who believe: in my name they will cast out demons; they will speak in new tongues; they will pick up serpents, and if they drink any deadly thing, it will not hurt them; they will lay their hands on the sick, and they will recover."
- **Matthew 7:7-8:** "Ask, and it shall be given you; seek, and ye will find; knock, and it will be opened unto you. For every one that asketh receiveth, and he that seeketh findeth, and to him who knocketh it shall be opened."
- **Matthew 17:20:** "For truly, I say to you, if ye have faith as a grain of mustard seed, ye shall say unto this mountain, Remove hence to yonder place; and it shall remove; and nothing shall be impossible unto you."
- **Matthew 18:19:** "Again I say to you, That if two of you agree on earth as touching anything that they shall ask, it shall be done for them of my Father which is in heaven. For where two or three are gathered together in my name, there am I in the midst of them."
- **Matthew 21:21-22:** "Verily I say unto you, if ye have faith, and doubt not, ye shall not only do this removed, and be thou cast into the sea; it shall be done. And all things, whatsoever ye shall ask in prayer, believing, ye shall receive."
- **Luke 10:19:** "Behold, I give unto you power to tread on serpents and scorpions, and over all the power of the enemy: and nothing shall by any means hurt you."

To date, scientific studies have concluded that prayers are <u>not effective</u> beyond any statistical measure of coincidence. Contrary to what the author of the Gospel of Matthew says above, prayer doesn't move mountains. In many ways, this false belief is very dangerous, because people cling to their prayers, rather than do something more useful. For example, instead of getting the protection of life-saving immunizations, some Christian Fundamentalists believe that God will protect them. They cannot accept that it is just chance to not get a given disease without an inoculation, not the intervention of God. And those who do contract a disease (e.g., COVID), after praying not to get it, and die from it...; well, that was God's will! What a cop out! God's will is not mentioned in the Scripture verses above. And the next time there is an illness or unfortunate event in your family or among friends, instead of saying, "I will pray for you," just tell the truth, that you plan to do nothing because praying implies doing nothing! And it is counterproductive to personal responsibility.[288]

"The hands that help are far better than the lips that pray!"
– Robert G. Ingersoll

Jesus Didn't Understand Germs

In Mark 7, Jesus confronts the Pharisees about their tradition of handwashing before eating, essentially declaring that what defiles a person is not external things like unwashed hands, but rather their inner thoughts and actions. While that is a good spiritual teaching point, it underscores that he is an Iron Age man, as he doesn't know that the germs he ingests can hurt him. The purpose of Jews washing their hands may have been ceremonial, but it resulted in washing away some germs and in limiting the opportunities to contract a sickness. Jesus is saying that nothing you put in your body can hurt you since it was made by God, so you don't need to wash your hands. This is nonsense; germs and poisons will, in fact, kill you.

- **Mark 7: 5:** "Then the Pharisees and scribes asked him, Why walk not thy disciples According to the tradition of the elders, but eat bread with unwashed hands?"
- **Mark 7: 18-19:** "And he saith unto them, are ye so without understanding also? Do ye not perceive, that whatsoever thing from without entereth into the man, it cannot defile him; because it entereth not into his heart, but into the belly, and goeth out into the draught, purging all meats?"

Remember that there were strict Jewish rules about what food was clean vs. what was unclean. Leviticus Chapter 11 describes in detail what animals were clean and unclean. But now Jesus declares all foods clean.

- **Mark 16:18:** "They shall take up serpents; and if they drink any deadly thing, it shall not hurt them; they shall lay hands on the sick, and they shall recover."

Back in Jesus' time, during their childhoods half of all children caught and died of disease. Jesus could have told us about germ theory, but he was just as unaware as other humans of the time. [289]

Strange Comments Attributed to Him

The concept of eternal Hell for mortal mistakes began with Jesus. However, morality should not be based on fear, as it undercuts general moral behavior, and it reflects badly on the ethical views it claims to represent. The following are highly destructive teachings:

- **Mark 9:43:** "And if thy hand offend thee, cut it off; it is better for thee to enter into life maimed, than having two hands to go into hell, into the fire that never shall be quenched."

- **Mark 5:29:** "And if thy right eye offend thee, pluck it out, and cast it from thee; for it is profitable for thee that one of the members should perish, and not that they whole bode should be cast into hell."
- **Matthew 13: 41-42:** "The Son of man shall send forth his angels, and they shall gather out of The kingdom all things that offend, and them which do iniquity. And shall cast them into a furnace of fire. There shall be wailing and gnashing of teeth."

It wasn't fig season, so cursing the fig tree was irrational and petulant, especially for the Son of God:

- **Mark 11:13-14:** "And seeing a fig tree afar off having leaves, he came, if haply he might find anything thereon: and when he came to it, he found nothing but leaves; for the time of figs was not yet. And Jesus answered and said unto it, No man eat fruit of thee hereafter forever…"

If Jesus is God, then how come he lacks knowledge? Jesus doesn't know the day and hour, but the Father does.

- **Mark 13:32-33:** "But of that day and that hour knoweth no man, no, not the angels which are in heaven, neither the Son, but the Father. Take ye heed, watch and pray: for ye know not when the time is.

Sometimes, the advice attributed to Jesus was just unwise:

- **Matthew 6: 34:** "Take therefore no thought for the morrow; for the morrow shall take thought for the things of itself. Sufficient unto the day is the evil thereof."
- **Mark 10: 21-22:** "Then Jesus…said unto him, One thing thou lackest; go thy way, sell Whatsoever thou hast, and give it to the poor, and thou shalt have treasure in heaven: and come, take up the cross, and follow me. And he was sad at the saying and went away grieved; for he had great possessions." [Note: "take up the cross"? that is a bit anachronistic, as Jesus hadn't been crucified yet].
- **Matthew 12:30:** "He that is not with me is against me; and he that gathereth not with me scattereth abroad." [What about neutrality?]
- **Luke 14:26:** "If any man come to me, and hate not his father, and mother, and wife, and children, and brethren, and sisters, yea, and his own life also, he cannot be my disciple." [So, Jesus wants us to hate our families? Wow].
- **Luke 19:24-25:** "And He said unto them that stood by, Take from him the pound, and give it to him that hath ten pounds. And they said unto him, Lord, he hath ten pounds. For I say unto you, that unto every one which hath shall be given; and from him that hath not, even that he hath shall be taken away from him." [In Mark 10 above, Jesus wanted the wealthy to give up their money; but in Luke, he wants to take it from the poor.]

And sometimes, gospel passages contradict that Jesus preaches peace:

- **Matthew 10:34-36:** "Think not that I am come to send peace on earth; I came not to send peace, but a sword. For I am come to set a man at variance with his father, and a daughter against her mother, and the daughter in law against her mother-in-law. And a man's foes shall be they of his own household."

Again, these comments attributed to Jesus in Scripture may not actually have been uttered. Logically, Jesus should not have said these things; and indeed, he might not have done so. The gospels, written decades after the death of Jesus, are notoriously unreliable. Given that Jesus is said to have studied the Tanakh, he was literate. So, it begs the question, why didn't he put anything in writing and set the record straight from the beginning?

Why the Jews Reject Jesus as the Messiah

Let's define terms. "Moshiach" is the Hebrew word for "messiah." The word, moshiach, in Hebrew means "anointed." In Talmudic literature, the title, Moshiach, or Melech HaMoshiach (the King Messiah), is reserved for the Jewish leader who will redeem Israel in the 'end of days'.[290] As stated by author, Nissan Dubov, "One of the principles of Jewish faith enumerated by Maimonides is that one day there will arise a dynamic Jewish leader, a direct descendant of the Davidic dynasty, who will rebuild the Temple in Jerusalem, and gather Jews from all over the world and bring them back to the Land of Israel."[291] It is further prophesied that all nations will recognize Moshiach as the world leader, and there will be world peace.

The Jewish idea of Moshiach is a great human leader like King David, not a savior; and as predicted in **Jeremiah 23:5**, he will be a great human political leader descended from King David, not a god or demigod.[292] Further, there are prophecies and requirements of the Messiah as laid out in the Old Testament. For example, some prophecies the Jews associate with the Messiah (still to come) are:

- **Isaiah 11:12:** Many Jews will return to Israel: "And he shall set up an ensign for the nations, and shall assemble the outcasts of Israel, and gather together the disperses of Judah from the four corners of the earth." [That sort of happened in 1948].
- **Isaiah 2:4:** The Messiah will bring peace to the world: "And he shall judge among the nations, and shall rebuke many people: and they shall eat their swords into plowshares, and their spears into pruning hooks: nation shall not lift up sword against nation, neither shall they learn war anymore." [That definitely didn't happen].
- **Ezekiel 37:26-28:** The Temple will be rebuilt: "Moreover, I will make a covenant of peace with them…My tabernacle also shall be with them: yea, I will be their God, and they shall be my people. And the heathen shall know that I the Lord do sanctify Israel, when my sanctuary shall be in the midst of them for evermore." [Still waiting on this one].
- **Jeremiah 31:33:** There will be a worldwide knowledge of God: "But this shall be the covenant that I will make with the house of Israel; after those days, saith the Lord, I will put my law in their inward parts, and write it in their hearts; and will be their God, and they shall be my people." [Probably not going to happen].
- **Zechariah 14:9:** All of mankind will worship only the God of the Jews: "And the Lord shall be king over all the earth: in that day shall there be one Lord, and his name one." [Seems highly unlikely].

These events listed above did not occur during Jesus' time on Earth. Many Christians believe that these prophecies are associated with Jesus' Second Coming; however, Jews do not believe in a Second Coming of Jesus. Moreover, in addition to <u>not</u> fulfilling the Jewish prophecies, there are other reasons that the Jews do not accept Jesus as their Messiah:

- Jews believe that their Messiah will be an ordinary human, not a deity. And he will be the progeny of a human father, not the son of a god.
- He had to be descended from David on his father's side; Jews reject the false lineages crafted by the gospel writers of Matthew and Luke.
- The Jews reject that the miracles that Jesus supposedly performed provide proof that he was the Messiah, as they argue that those not from God can perform miracles as well.
- The Messiah will follow Jewish law, but Jesus said that many of its rules and commandments no longer applied.
- Jews do not believe that a "blood sacrifice" was necessary, and they deny the concept of "original sin."

One 'fact' about Jesus, that he was crucified by the Romans, is telling. And his death was probably one of the primary issues that ancient Jews had with Christian claims that Jesus was the Messiah. The Jews did not want their Messiah to be tortured and executed. That was the antithesis of the Jewish vision of their Messiah.

The beliefs that Jesus is God, the son of God, or a person of the Trinity are simply incompatible with Jewish theology, which fosters the view that Jesus did not fulfill the messianic prophecies that establish the criteria for the coming of the Messiah.[293] Judaism does not accept Jesus as a divine being or the Messiah. Belief in the Trinity, as well as several other beliefs of Christianity, are also incompatible with Judaism.

Chapter Summary

The case for the historicity of Jesus of Nazareth is very weak. There are no documents of anything that Jesus ever wrote; there are no sculptures, no paintings from that time, and very limited mentions of Jesus outside the gospels. A growing number of scholars do not believe he existed. Indeed, it is impossible to prove his existence. After all, he left no written record, and no one who knew him or witnessed his teachings wrote about it. Paul of Tarsus was the first person to write about Christ, but he acted as though he knew nothing about the historical Jesus of Nazareth, nor his family, nor his ministry. Paul only wrote about "the Christ." His writings suggest a celestial Christ rather than a real person who lived on Earth. But Paul also lied to us, inventing the pretense that Jesus died for our sins, and he rose into Heaven according to the Scriptures – of course, he had no idea what Scriptures that might be, as he invented that as well. The bottom line: for Paul to know nothing about Rabbi Yeshua of Nazareth is very telling.

The legacy of Jesus is somewhat tarnished by the false writings of the authors of the gospels. They were not truthful about his place of birth and his genealogy. They wrote that he would return in their lifetimes, that prayer had power, and nothing ingested into your mouth could hurt you – all false! They made up the passage regarding Barabbas (Bar Abbas), which would fuel hatred of the Jews in future centuries. They reported hearsay information about the crucifixion, burial, resurrection, and ascension, and they couldn't even agree on that, contradicting each other in multiple places of their gospels. Any reasonable person would conclude that the gospels are not factual history, not accurate reporting, and not even credible stories; they are, at best, allegorical tales regarding a myth, about which one person, Saul of Tarsus, declared Christos (but not Jesus) to be divine.

Dying and then being resurrected is typical of many ancient mythologies – Osiris, Mithras, and Dionysus come to mind, as the Resurrection appears to be a metaphor for spiritual rebirth and eternal life. There were no eyewitnesses to the Resurrection or any evidence that it occurred – only hearsay.

The parables and statements attributed to Jesus appear to be shaped by theological and political agendas rather than by historical truth. If Jesus were truly God, he might have delivered a flawless, universally comprehensible revelation accessible to all mankind; and it would be optimum if He had written it himself. Unfortunately, we have many thousands of competing interpretations of Jesus' messages.

---

[227] "Is this really the last resting place of Jesus, Mary Magdalene - and their son?" The Guardian; Feb 2007; https://www.theguardian.com/world/2007/feb/27/religion.israel

[228] Leah Berenson, "Jesus Wasn't Really Named Jesus So What Was His Real Name?" Mystical Raven; Dec 2023; https://mysticalraven.com/spirituality/24212/jesus-real-name

[229] Transliteration is the process of representing or intending to represent a word, phrase, or text in a different script or writing system.

[230] "Why an Ancient Roman Wouldn't Recognize Their Own Alphabet Today," Glossika; https://ai.glossika.com/blog/latin-alphabet-evolution . At the time of early Christianity, the Latin alphabet had only 22 letters, as opposed to the modern English alphabet which has 26 letters. The "missing letters" were G, J, U and W.

[231] Leah Berenson, Ibid.

[232] Stefan Ayers, "When was the Letter J invented?" Language Lovers; Aug 22, 2023; https://languagelover.org/2023/08/22/when-was-the-letter-j-invented/

[233] Claire Nowak, "Do You Know the Last Letter Added to the Alphabet? (It Wasn't Z)," Reader's Digest, Jan 2023; https://www.rd.com/article/last-letter-added-to-the-alphabet/

[234] Brian Palmer, "Was Jesus a Common Name Back When He Was Alive?" Slate; https://slate.com/news-and-politics/2008/12/was-jesus-a-common-name-back-when-he-was-alive.html

[235] Gary Arndt, "The Latin Alphabet," Everything Everywhere; Aug 2020; https://everything-everywhere.com/the-latin-alphabet/

[236] Anna Swartwood, "The Long History of How Jesus Came to Resemble a White European," University of South Carolina; July 2020; USC News & Events | University of South Carolina. This photo The Head of Christ painting by Warner Sallman, 1941.photo from The Warner Sallman collection http://www.anderson.edu/sallman/ Photo, fair use, https://en.wikipedia.org/w/index.php?curid=20132866;

[237] Anna Swartwood, Ibid.

[238] Grace Ji-Sun Kim, When God Became White, May 2024; ISBN: 9781514009390

[239] Anna Swartwood, Ibid.

[240] Ed Gaskin, "Whitewashed: How a Jewish and brown Jesus became an Aryan"; The Times of Israel, Jan 2023; https://blogs.timesofisrael.com/whitewashed-how-a-jewish-and-brown-jesus-became-an-aryan/

[241] Arthur George, The Mythology of America's Seasonal Holidays: The Dance of the Horse; (2020); Springer International Publishing; p. 218; ISBN 978-3-03046916-0.

[242] Maier, Paul L., Herod and the Infants of Bethlehem, (1998), Mercer University Press; pp. 170-171; ISBN 978-0-86554-582-3

[243] Neil Rees, "What was the Census that took Mary and Joseph to Bethlehem?" Christian Today; Dec, 2023; https://www.christiantoday.com/article/what.was.the.census.that.took.mary.and.joseph.to.bethlehem/141207.htm

[244] "Which pope declared that Jesus Christ was born on December 25?" The New Daily; Dec 14, 2017; https://www.thenewdaily.com.au/religion/2017/12/14/12-days-of-christmas-day-three

[245] The primary error in the Gregorian calendar regarding the common era of Jesus is that the calculations used to establish the "Year 1 AD" likely placed Jesus' birth a few years too late, with most historians now believing he was born closer to 4 BC; this error stems from calculations made by Dionysius Exiguus when establishing the Anno Domini system in 525 CE, which among other mistakes, skipped a "Year Zero" and jumped directly from 1 BC to 1 AD. "History of the Standard Gregorian Calendar," ANSI; Feb 10, 2016; https://blog.ansi.org/2016/02/history-of-standard-gregorian-calendar/

[246] "What is the historicity of the Paschal prisoner release custom in Mark?" Biblical Hermeneutics; https://hermeneutics.stackexchange.com/questions/96281/what-is-the-historicity-of-the-paschal-prisoner-release-custom-in-mark?

[247] Robin M. Jensen, "Five Myths about the Cross," Washington Post; April 14, 2017; https://www.washingtonpost.com/opinions/five-myths-about-the-cross/2017/04/14/dae63c1a-1fa8-11e7-be2a-3a1fb24d4671_story.html

[248] "Crucifixion," World History Encyclopedia; https://www.worldhistory.org/crucifixion/

[249] "Roman emperor Constantine I and his policy towards Christianity," Short History Website; September 21, 2016; https://www.shorthistory.org/ancient-civilizations/ancient-rome/roman-emperor-constantine-i-306-337-ad-and-his-policy-towards-christianity/

[250] Solar eclipses last from several seconds to up to approximately 7 minutes. "Solar Eclipse Duration," Western Kentucky University.edu; https://www.wku.edu/eclipse/duration.php

[251] PJ Bible, "How Historians Know Jesus Didn't Exist: The Case Against Christ," You Tube

[252] Jimmy Akin, "A Fake Resurrection in Mark's Gospel?" Catholic Answers; https://www.catholic.com/magazine/online-edition/a-fake-resurrection-in-marks-gospel

[253] Mark Woods, "Was the ending of Mark's Gospel deliberately changed?" Christian Today; https://www.christiantoday.com/article/was.the.ending.of.marks.gospel.deliberately.changed/80210.htm

[254] "Gospel According to Mark," Britannica; https://www.britannica.com/topic/Gospel-According-to-Mark

[255] "Who was Tertullian and what were his contributions to early Christianity?" Bible Chat; https://biblechat.ai/knowledgebase/theological-concepts/doctrine/who-was-tertullian-what-were-his-contributions-early-christianity/

[256] Traducianism was a doctrine about the origin of the soul that believed that the immaterial aspect is transmitted through natural generation along with the body, the material aspect of human being. In other words, "an individual's soul is derived from the soul of one or both parents." "Traducianism," New Advent (Catholic Encyclopedia; https://www.newadvent.org/cathen/15014a.htm

[257] "Original Sin," Britannica; https://www.britannica.com/topic/original-sin

[258] "Romans 5:12 Mistranslation?" Reddit; https://www.reddit.com/r/AcademicBiblical/comments/qwfc4d/romans_512_mistranslation/?rdt=45594

[259] Augustine and the Aramaic of Romans 5:12; Ad Fontes; https://adfontesjournal.com/andrew-koperski/augustine-and-the-aramaic-of-romans-512/

[260] S. Richard Bellrock, "Sin Does Not Exist: And Believing That It Does Is Ruining Us"; Sunstone; April 18, 2019; https://sunstone.org/sin-does-not-exist/ Mr. Bellrock gave the credit for the original idea for the Zeus metaphor to James Cornman who wrote it in 1968.

261 "John Shelby Spong - Re-Casting the Christ Story," *You Tube*; *Chautauqua Institution; Interfaith Lecture Series*; https://www.youtube.com/watch?v=WDNz2Ifn9k4

262 PJ Bible, "How Historians Know Jesus Didn't Exist: The Case Against Christ," You Tube

263 "10 Problems with the Penal Substitution View of the Atonement," ReKnew; Dec 10, 2015; https://reknew.org/2015/12/10-problems-with-the-penal-substitution-view-of-the-atonement/

264 Bishop John Shelby "Jack" Spong served as the Episcopal Bishop of Newark, New Jersey from 1979 to 2000. Spong was a liberal Christian theologian. From David Crumm, "Interview: Bishop John Shelby Spong on the Bible," Read the Spirit; Jan 18, 2012; https://readthespirit.com/explore/interview-bishop-john-shelby-spong-on-the-bible/

265 Bishop Spong; Ibid.

266 John Shelby Spong, The Sins of Scripture: Exposing the Bible's Texts of Hate to Reveal the God of Love; 2005; Harper One; ISBN 0-06-076205-5

267 "How Christianity Borrowed from Mithraism," More History; https://more-history.com/how-christianity-borrowed-from-mithraism/

268 Roger Pearse, "Mithras in Tarsus," June 16, 2011; https://www.roger-pearse.com/weblog/2011/06/16/mithras-in-tarsus/

269 Joshua J. Mark, "Tarsus," World History Encyclopedia; published 18 July, 2019; https://www.worldhistory.org/Tarsus/

270 "Paul And The Pagan Religion of Mithraism, Mystery Solved," Biblical Non-Orthodoxy; https://nonorthodoxy.com/paul-and-the-pagan-religion-of-mithraism-mystery-solved/

271 Richard Milner, "The Truth About Mythological Figures Similar To Jesus," Mar 3, 2022; www.grunge.com/493831/the-truth-about-mythological-figures-similar-to-jesus/

272 Milner, Ibid.

273 Dan Barker, "Debunking the Historical Jesus," March, 2006; Freedom From Religion Foundation, Inc.; https://ffrf.org/fttoday/march-2006/articles-march-2006/debunking-the-historical-jesus-2/

274 Bart D. Ehrman, "Jesus and the Messianic Prophecies – Did the Old Testament Point to Jesus?" The Bart Ehrman Blog; November 8, 2015; https://ehrmanblog.org/jesus-and-the-messianic-prophecies/

275 Jewish historian, Flavius Josephus, was a Jewish traitor who became a household member of the Roman Empire's ruling family (the Flavians) following the sacking of Jerusalem. Jeremy Rosen, "Was Josephus a hero or a traitor?" The Times of Israel, May 17, 2024

276 The Roman historian and senator, Publius Cornelius Tacitus, briefly referred to Jesus and his execution. Tim O'Neill, "Jesus Mysticism 1: The Tacitus Reference to Jesus," History for Atheists, Sep 7, 2017; Tacitus only repeated what Christians of the early 2nd century told him; that is not independent evidence.

277 Acharya S/D.M. Murdock, The Jesus Forgery: Josephus Untangled; Stellar House Publishing; https://stellarhousepublishing.com/josephus/#:~:text=Despite%20the%20best%20wishes

278 Dan Baker, "What the Bible-Belt Media Didn't Tell You about the Italian Lawsuit," Freedom From Religion, Inc.; Jan 31, 2006; https://ffrf.org/news/releases/debunkingjesus/

279 "Jesus Christ – No Historical Evidence," World Future Fund; https://www.worldfuturefund.org/History/jesushistory.html

280 G. A. Wells, The Historical Evidence for Jesus; pp. 22-23; Rowman and Littlefield Publishers, Jan 1982; ISBN 9780879754297

281 Valerie Tarico, "5 reasons to suspect Jesus never existed," AlterNet; https://www.alternet.org/5-reasons-to-suspect-jesus-never-existed/

282 Fitzgerald's quote found in Tarico's "5 Reasons to Suspect that Jesus Never Existed."

283 "Jesus existed and was deified by later Christians," Religions Wiki; https://religions.wiki/index.php/Jesus_existed_and_was_deified_by_later_Christians#cite_note-4

284 Per Religions Wiki, some historians such as Richard Carrier disregard the gospels and 'Acts' entirely as complete fiction; and they focus on the early epistles for interpretation.

285 Michael R. Licona, Jan G. Van der Watt, Historians and miracles: The principle of analogy and antecedent probability reconsidered, HTS Theologies Studies / Theological Studies; Vol 65, No 1 (2009), 6 pages.

[286] Richard Carrier, On the Historicity of Jesus, 2014; he quotes Bart Ehrmann.

[287] Bart B. Ehrmann, How Jesus Became God: The Exaltation of a Jewish Preacher from Galilee; March 2014; Harper One

[288] "The Case Against School Prayer," Freedom From Religion; https://ffrf.org/publications/brochures/schoolprayer/

[289] Brian Wilson, "Why Didn't Jesus Tell Us About Germs?" presents an argument by Richard Carrier; Debunking Christianity; https://www.debunking-christianity.com/2014/01/why-didnt-jesus-tell-us-about-germs.html

[290] Nissan Dovid Dubov ,"What Is the Jewish Belief About Moshiach (Messiah)?" Chabad.org; https://www.chabad.org/library/article_cdo/aid/108400/jewish/The-End-of-Days.htm

[291] Dubov, Ibid.

[292] "Mashiach: The Messiah," Judaism 101; https://www.jewfaq.org/mashiach

[293] Rabbi Shraga Simmons, "Why Jews Don't Believe in Jesus," Jewish World; https://web.archive.org/web/20060316040138/http://www.aish.com/jewishissues/jewishsociety/Why_Jews_Dont_Believe_In_Jesus.asp

Chapter 4 – New Testament

"It's important to acknowledge that strictly speaking, the gospels are anonymous."
- Dr. Craig L. Blomberg, <u>The Case for Christ</u>

In this chapter, we focus solely on the New Testament (NT), which is considered the cornerstone of Christianity. The 27 books of the New Testament are usually divided into five sections: (1) the Pauline epistles; (2) the gospels, which tell the story of Jesus' ministry (Matthew, Mark, Luke, and John); (3) The Acts of the Apostles; (4) the General Epistles - written by various Christian leaders to provide guidance for the earliest church communities; and (5) the Apocalypse, which includes only the Book of Revelation. All books of the New Testament were initially written in Greek.

The Pauline Epistles

Saul of Tarsus, alias Paul, is the true architect of Christianity. His canonized writing began with his Second Journey in the early 50s and ended in about 63 CE, concluding almost a decade before the first gospel (Mark) was penned. A summary of the years of Paul's journeys and his epistles is included below.[294]

Journey/ Imprisonment	Years	Epistle	Written From	Years
Paul at Damascus	37-40 CE			
First Journey	45-47 CE			
Second Journey	51-53 CE	1 Thessalonians	Corinth	52 CE
		2 Thessalonians	Unknown	52 CE
Third Journey	54-58 CE	Galatians	Ephesus	55-57 CE
		1 Corinthians	Ephesus	57 CE
		2 Corinthians	Macedonia	57 CE
		Romans	Corinth	57-58 CE
Voyage to Rome	60-61 CE			
Imprisonment in Rome	61-63 CE	Ephesians	Uknown	62 CE
		Philippians	Rome, in prison	62 CE
		Colossians	Unknown	62 CE

		Philemon	Rome, in prison	63 CE
Post-Imprisonment	63-67 CE	Hebrews	Italy, not in prison	64-65 CE
		Titus	Unknown	64-65 CE
		1 Timothy	Unknown	64-65 CE
		2 Timothy	Unknown	66-67 CE

Only a subset of these epistles can be shown to have been written definitively by the same author, Paul (the ones lightly highlighted). Scholars continue to debate the authenticity of 2 Thessalonians, Ephesians, and Colossians as written by Paul (they are shown in gray); and most biblical scholars believe that Hebrews, Titus, and 1 and 2 Timothy (highlighted in blue) were <u>not</u> written by Paul. The reasons for doubting Paul's authorship include theological inconsistencies, biographical discrepancies, and historical anachronisms (e.g., the Pastoral Letters' discussions of church polity, which some argue only became institutionalized after Paul).[295] The biggest objection to their Pauline authorship is the issue of language and style.

Paul's views seemed to stray from the teachings of Jesus in the gospels (or perhaps more accurately, the gospels strayed from Paul, since his epistles predated them) and from the early Church in Jerusalem.[296] Paul's beliefs were strongly rooted in the earliest Jewish Christianity; but they deviated from this Jewish Christianity in their emphasis on the inclusion of the gentiles into God's New Covenant.[297] Bishop John S. Spong (Episcopal Bishop of Newark) argued that "Paul's words are not the Words of God. They are the words of Paul - a vast difference."[298] George Bernard Shaw (1856 – 1950) maintained that Paul created and promoted the legend of Jesus as a risen savior. He wrote: "…The conversion of Paul was no conversion at all; it was Paul who converted the religion that has raised one-man above sin and death."[299]

Another concern is that Paul's epistles have a deficit of information regarding Mary and Joseph, the virgin birth, the place of birth, his trial before Pontius Pilate, and no mention of Jesus' Baptism by John the Baptist. There is no citation of any miracles performed by Jesus, or of Jesus' ministry and teachings in general. Paul never even references that Jesus had disciples. Paul did not comment on Jesus' crucifixion or the three hours of darkness in the middle of the day; he provides no details of the burial of Jesus; he never mentions the empty tomb, and he fails to spotlight Jesus' post-Resurrection appearances. Paul never cites the historical Jesus in any way. But he does write a lot about "Christ."[300]

There is so much about Paul's narratives that is just not credible. This is a man who never met Jesus and who was not a witness in Jerusalem during the final days of Jesus. He had no religious authority to speak for God, as he was neither an apostle (even if he declared himself one) nor a religious cleric. We have only Paul's word that he heard a voice and an apparition that caused him to stop persecuting Christians and support them. Indeed, there are three different versions of his encounter with the voice/apparition in **Acts of the Apostles** (penned by the author of the Gospel of Luke):

- **Acts 9:4-9** "Led to Damascus with three days without sight."

- **Acts 22:7-13** "Led to Damascus and immediately got his sight back."
- **Acts 26:13-18** "Made a minister and sent to the Gentiles"

Paul preached that salvation was by faith alone, except when he contradicts himself, as in:

- **Romans 2:6** "Who render to every man according to his deeds"
- **2 Corinthians 5:10** "For we must all appear before the judgment seat of Christ; that every one may receive the things done in his body, according to that he hath done, whether it be good or bad."

Jesus mentioned <u>both</u> faith and good works.

- **Matthew 16:27:** "For the Son of man shall come in the glory of his Father with his angels; and then he shall reward every man according to his works."

When it suited his purposes, Paul had no issues with fabrications. In his epistle to the Romans, he tells us that because the Jews rejected Jesus as the Messiah, salvation was offered to the gentiles. That charge is taken up by the author of Acts (who was also the author of the Gospel of Luke). Of course, the real reason why Paul preached to gentiles is that Peter and the original apostles required gentile men to be circumcised prior to joining their Jewish sect, and for Paul, this was an opportunity to expand the Christian sect under his leadership, as he did not require circumcision as a prerequisite.

- **Romans 9:30-31** "...That the Gentiles, which followed not after righteousness, have attained to righteousness. Wherefore? But Israel, which followed after the law of righteousness, hath not attained to the law of righteousness."
- **Romans 11:11** "I say then, have they stumbled that they should fall? God forbid, but rather through their fall salvation is come unto the Gentiles, for to provoke them to jealousy."
- **Acts 13:46-48** "Then Paul and Barnabas waxed bold, and said, It was necessary that the word of God should first have been spoken to you: but seeing ye put it from you, and judge yourselves unworthy of everlasting life, lo, we turn to the Gentiles. For so hath the Lord commanded us, saying, I have set thee to be a light of the Gentiles, that thou shouldest be for salvation unto the ends of the earth."

One of Paul's fantasies was that Jesus would return in his (Paul's) lifetime. And that was the clever scheme that Paul used to sell others on Christianity. Throughout his epistle to the Romans, Paul told them that 'you won't have to die,' and that was the carrot on top of the afterlife that Christianity promised in general. Indeed, the concept of an afterlife was still considered a relatively novel idea in the 1st century Mediterranean world. This immortal existence in heaven was very appealing to new converts.

The Jewish Tanakh presents no firm conception of an afterlife. Until the 3rd century BCE, to most Jews, a glorious afterlife was a distant aspiration; but by the 2nd century BCE, that began to change for some to a natural expectation. One could see the shift in attitudes in the passages of 2 Maccabees, which Catholics and Orthodox Christians accept as canonical, but which Protestants view as apocryphal. But Paul was aware of it.

Believing that Jesus was returning soon, Paul gave this poor advice to the Corinthians:

- **1 Corinthians 7:1** "It is good for a man not to touch a woman."
- **1 Corinthians 7:29-30** But this I say, brethren, the time is short: it remaineth that both they that have wives be as though they had none; And they that weep, as though they weep not; and they that rejoice as though they rejoice not; and they that buy as though they possessed not."

The Gospels of Mark, Matthew, and Luke would, in succession, take up the mantra of Christ's imminent return based on the epistles of Paul; but thankfully, they did not reiterate Paul's rants regarding sex, happiness, and sadness.

New Testament Canon Selection

Christianity existed for nearly 300 years without any official Scripture. But in the 4th century, the Christian Church initiated a process and began to declare which texts were legitimately representative of Christianity. To some extent Athanasius, Bishop of Alexandria, holds much of the responsibility for shaping the content of the New Testament, while excluding books he labeled as heresy."[301] [302] In his 39th Festal Letter (CE 367) Athanasius produced the list of books which he wanted to be regarded as Scripture;[303] and he provided them in a specific order. Then he added the following words: "In these [writings] alone the teaching of godliness is proclaimed. No one may add to them, and nothing may be taken away from them."[304] His suggested books to be included in the Christian Scripture was the earliest list which corresponds with the canon[305] of the New Testament as we now know it.[306] He named the 27 books that are currently accepted by Christians as the authoritative canon of Scripture.[307]

For whatever reason, the list created by Athanasius was accepted in Rome in 383 CE, and it was adopted by the Council of Carthage in 397 CE. The Council of Hippo in 393 was more concerned with the status of the Old Testament's Deuterocanonical books , and the canon of the New Testament does not appear to have been critically discussed at any length. Thus, the Athanasian canon was gradually accepted throughout the Christian Church. This came about through an attenuated process, which took the form of an accepted consensus, rather than a formal statement. In fact, no Ecumenical Council ever made a definitive pronouncement on the subject.[308] So effectively, one man (Athanasius) prepared a list of books to be regarded as Scripture, and the other Church leaders appear to have just accepted it.

Officially, the 27-book New Testament was first formally canonized during the Councils of Hippo (393) and Carthage (397) – both towns are located in North Africa. Pope Innocent I ratified the same canon in 405, but it seems probable that a Council in Rome in 382 under Pope Damasus agreed to the list as well. Effectively, the councils seem to have endorsed what had already become the consensus in the churches of the West.[309]

There are many books (over 50), both gospels and letters, that did not "make the cut" at the above councils, and they were exiled from inclusion in the New Testament. Some samples of these excluded books are shown below:[310]

The Mythology of Christianity

Name of Gospel	Approx Year Composed	Contents	Why It Was Left Out of the Canon (Opinion)
Gospel of Thomas	100 – 150 CE	Contains 114 sayings of Jesus, many of which are not found in the canonical gospels	Considered too unorthodox for early Christian leaders, and it had strong Gnostic overtones
Gospel of Peter	100-150 CE	Describes the birth and childhood of Jesus, as well as the role of Mary in the early Christian movement	Considered too different from the canonical gospels by early Christian leaders
Gospel of James	100-150 CE	Describes the birth and childhood of Jesus, as well as the role of Mary in the early Christian movement	Considered too focused on Mary and not enough on Jesus by early Christian leaders
Gospel of Mary	100-200 CE	Describes the teachings of Mary Magdalene, a close disciple of Jesus	Contradicted traditional views of male and female roles
Gospel of Judas	150-200 CE	Portrays Judas Iscariot as a heroic figure who betrayed Jesus only at his request	Considered heretical by early Christian leaders
The Gospel to the Egyptians	150-200 CE	A discussion between Salome and Jesus about topics such as celibacy, death, and sin	Considered heretical by early Christian leaders

The non-canonical texts were not accepted as part of the New Testament by the early Christian Church. Their exclusion might have been because the non-canonical gospels contain different data about Jesus and the early Christian movement. As such, they do not receive the same reverence as the canonical gospels, considered to be the primary sources of information about Jesus and his teachings. The non-canonical texts taught narratives which contrasted with prevailing Christian viewpoints. It was Christians of the 4th century that appointed themselves the one true universal Church of Jesus Christ, and the validators of the New Testament canon. These rejected texts were more focused on understanding Jesus of Nazareth as the developer of their souls, rather than the savior of their sins.[311]

The New Testament canon selection committee (aka, the orthodox Christian Church of the 4th century) opted to go with a quasi-historical understanding of Jesus' life, a theological understanding of his death, and a physical understanding of his resurrection.[312] The Bauer thesis is the idea that a great diversity of views existed in early Christianity. This collection of views was replaced by an orthodoxy of belief in Jesus as God, and that theology agreed with Paul of Tarsus. The consequence is that the interpretation of Jesus that prevailed in Christianity is largely arbitrary.[313] The Gospel of Mary is a great example of an early Christian text that was deemed unorthodox by the men who shaped the nascent Catholic Church; and it was subsequently erased from the history of Christianity along with other narratives that underscored women's contributions to the early Christian movement.

Approximately 40 years after the death of Rabbi Yeshua of Nazareth, his public life (spanning one year) and his teachings made their way to written substance, penned by an unknown author who wrote in the name of Mark, but who clearly had never met Rabbi Yeshua. The Gospel of Mark (circa 70-80 CE) was followed by the Gospels of Matthew (circa 80-90 CE) and Luke (circa 105-120 CE). The Gospel of John now appears to have been a forgery that was fabricated even later.

Biblical scholars have stated that none of the anonymous writers were eyewitnesses. Most assuredly, the stories and teachings of Rabbi Yeshua were shared among the Christian faithful via word of mouth. And even after the anonymous authors wrote the gospels, they were disseminated for many decades across different lands only in verbal stories. Very low literacy rates (less than 2 percent) during that time, and the sporadic persecution of early Christians within the Roman Empire probably contributed to the scarcity of Christian documents. Indeed, none of the original manuscripts have survived. We have only fragments of scribal copies of other copies of the original documents.

"They [the gospels] are not biographies," says Professor Paula Fredriksen of Boston University; "they are a kind of religious advertisement. What they do is proclaim their individual author's interpretation of the Christian message through the device of using Jesus of Nazareth as a spokesperson for their evangelists' positions."[314] For the past century, scholars have generally agreed that the gospels were not actually written by the people to whom they are attributed. To the contrary, it seems clear that the stories that form the basis of Christianity were passed down to future generations before they were collected and put into writing.

The remarks of biblical scholar, Dr. Craig L. Blomberg, concluded that the gospels are anonymous.[315] It was a fairly common practice in the ancient period to make pseudepigraphal attributions of authorship, especially with religious texts. This also occurred with several Old Testament figures (e.g., Moses). Additionally, there were gospels written in the name of almost every apostle; but most of these texts were rejected, as discussed above. D. M. Murdock asked, "Is this an admission that there were many people within Christianity engaging in forgery?"[316] As Merrill Tenney has stated, this subject of attribution is extremely important because "if it could be shown that any of the books of the New Testament was falsely attributed to the person whose name it bears, its place in the canon would be endangered."[317] Well, that ship has sailed!

The Synoptic Gospels

Nearly everything we now know, or think we know, about the life and ministry of Jesus comes from the New Testament's gospels. As was prevalent at that time, these gospels existed in the oral tradition in various Christian communities prior to being written down. Indeed, no eyewitnesses wrote anything. There were no written records about Jesus of Nazareth for anyone to study. The entire religious movement in the mid-1st century was based on oral tradition. But then some Christians wanted liturgical readings, so the authors of Mark, Matthew, and Luke wrote their respective gospels (each at least a decade or two apart), which were never intended to be a history or biography of the life of Jesus. The traditional names – Mark, Matthew,

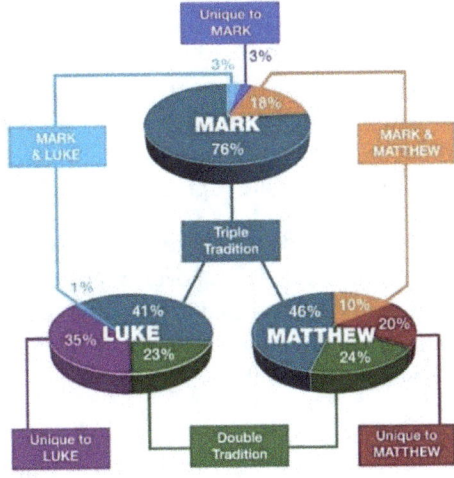

Relationships Among the Synoptic Gospels

Luke, and John – did not become associated with the gospels earlier than the 2nd century. Why? Some believe it was to forge links to some of the original apostles to provide an authoritative flavor. If so, then they should have chosen from the actual apostle names, since 'Mark' and 'Luke' were not among the names of the original twelve apostles[318] which were:

- Simon Peter,
- Andrew,
- James (son of Zebedee),
- John (son of Zebedee),
- Philip,
- Bartholomew,
- Thomas,
- Matthew (also known as Levi),
- James (son of Alphaeus),
- Thaddaeus
- Simon the Zealot,
- and Judas Iscariot

The Gospels of Mark, Matthew, and Luke are considered "synoptic" because they share similar content and narrative structures, and often (not always) the stories occur in a similar sequence and in similar or sometimes identical wording. While the synoptic writers, to some degree, did mirror each other, each had a specific audience in mind to address a defined issue. To that end, each writer selected and arranged the historical data of Jesus's life in a way best suited for their chosen aim.

Over three-quarters of Mark's content is found in both Matthew and Luke, and over 80% of Mark is found in at least one of the other two Synoptic Gospels. Additionally, Matthew (24%) and Luke (23%) have material in common.[319] Indeed, if one reads the Gospels vertically – that is, reading the entire Gospel of say, Mark, followed by the Gospel of Matthew, and then the Gospel of Luke - then the stories seem quite similar. But if you read the gospels horizontally – that is, read about the same event across all three gospels, then you will notice some alarming discrepancies. Because of these differences, we might ask which gospel, if any, provides the correct version of the events. Another concern is the timing of the Synoptic Gospels. They were written decades after the ministry of Jesus by individuals who had no visibility into the events for which they were writing. The adjacent illustration graphically depicts the relationships among the three Synoptic Gospels.

The historical evidence suggests that Mark wrote for a community deeply affected by the failure of the First Jewish Revolt against Rome. Matthew wrote for a Jewish community in conflict with the Pharisaic Judaism that dominated Jewish life in the postwar period. Luke wrote for a predominately gentile audience eager to demonstrate that Christian beliefs in no way conflicted with their ability to serve as good citizens of the empire.

The Synoptic Gospels all focus on the ministry of Jesus, but the content and order of the stories somewhat differ. Because the Synoptic Gospels look so much alike, it has been hypothesized that the content in Matthew and Luke which they did not get from Mark may have come from another source which has been lost to time. That hypothetical source has been referred to as "Q". About a decade after Mark, the Gospel of Matthew surfaced, drawing on a variety of sources, including Mark and from a collection of sayings that scholars later called "Q", for Quelle, meaning source. Q is part of the common material found in the Gospels of Matthew and Luke, but not in the Gospel of Mark. According to this hypothesis, this material was drawn from the early Church's oral gospel traditions.[320]

Q was theorized by 1900, and it has become one of the foundations of most modern gospel scholarship.[321] B. H. Streeter formulated a widely accepted view of Q: that it was written in koine Greek; that most of its contents appear in Matthew, in Luke, or in both; and that Luke more often preserves the text's original order than Matthew. In the two-source hypothesis, the three-source hypothesis, and the Q+/Papias hypothesis, Matthew and Luke both used Mark and Q as sources. Some scholars have postulated that Q's origin tied back to a plurality of sources, some written and some oral.[322] There is also an array of arguments against Q, but currently, the Q hypothesis is the dominant view among biblical scholars.

Christian apologists are fond of saying that these gospels provide separate but complementary accounts in which each views the biography from a different angle. However, this just doesn't seem plausible. First, as has been mentioned, the gospels are not biographies. These Synoptic Gospels often copied each other, and even then, they ended up contradicting each other. Since the authors of these gospels never met Jesus, and were written decades later, it is unlikely that the data they presented is truly accurate. What is interesting is that none of the Synoptic Gospels states that Jesus died for our sins. Jesus never says anything about being crucified so that our sins will be forgiven; He never mentions that he will rise again in three days after his death.

The Mythology of Christianity

Canonical Gospel	Approx Date Written	Author Background
Mark	70 – 80 CE	Gentile
Matthew	80 – 90 CE	Jew
Luke	105 – 120 CE	Greek Gentile / Hellenistic
John	140 – 165 CE	Gentile (Roman?)

Mark

The Gospel of Mark lacks the numerous speeches and religious references found in Matthew and Luke. It is a very results-oriented, action gospel whose objective is to tell Jesus' story as straightforward as possible to those who were unfamiliar with Judea or Judaism. Thus, the gospel starts with the beginning of Jesus' ministry. And he records many miracles. He refers to Jesus as the Son of Man.

We do not know Mark's heritage and ethnicity, although he is most probably a gentile. The Gospel of Mark seems to speak to the Romans, who were the leaders of the empire, and who knew about power. So, to this group comes the action-packed gospel of the powerful ministry of Jesus. Mark uses the word, *ana,* 1,375 times to tie together the endless actions of Jesus of Nazareth. They wanted a God who could powerfully meet their deepest needs.[323] The author of Mark also attempted to align a specious OT prophecy with the coming of Jesus. At the very beginning of the gospel **[Mark 1:2]**, the author has Jesus saying, "As it is written in Isaiah the prophet: 'Behold, I will send my messenger before thy face, which shall prepare thy way before thee." However, no such narrative appears in the Book of Isaiah, or anywhere else in the OT.

The Gospel of Mark appears to have been written by a non-Palestinian, non-disciple of Jesus. That is important because it categorizes this first gospel as hearsay. In his Gospel of Mark, the author demonstrates no first-hand understanding of the social and political situation of Palestine, nor does he have any familiarity with Palestine's geography. An example of the former is: "And if a woman shall put away her husband, and be married to another, she committeth adultery." **[Mark 10:12].** But in Palestine in that era, only men could obtain a divorce.[324] The Gospel of Mark made many geographic errors; one example is the following: "They came to the other side of the sea, to the country of the Gerasenes." **[Mark 5:1].** He meant Gerasa,[325] which is 31 miles from the shore of the Sea of Galilee. Then the author of the Gospel of Matthew changed the name from Gerasa to Gadara, which is 5 miles from the shore of Galilee. The errors in Judean geography and customs, and his need to explain Jewish laws and concepts, strongly suggest that the author of the Gospel of Mark was not Jewish.

Mark's Gospel differs from the other two Synoptic Gospels in that it is only 16 chapters (much shorter than the other gospels) and lacks several key details. And these missing details are not insignificant. There is no mention of the Nativity, Jesus' virgin birth, of Joseph, or any appearance of the resurrected Christ. Of course, let's not forget that Mark's writing preceded the other two gospels. Because the Gospel of Mark is so brief, early Christians worried that it was incomplete. Thus, it has been hypothesized that the verses after **16:8,** which describe Jesus' meeting with Mary Magdalene and the disciples after his resurrection, were added later to make the text more complete.[326] Indeed, the status of these verses, **Mark 16:9-20,** is still disputed.[327] The Catholic position is that the Gospel of Mark ended too abruptly, which suggested to the RCC that the original ending may have been lost. Thus, verses 16:9-20 were likely added; yet, the Catholic Church accepts the "longer ending" as canonical,[328] even though they don't know who added these verses. In contrast to Matthew and Luke, Mark focuses his attention on Jesus' death without a corresponding emphasis on retelling his teaching.

Matthew

Biblical scholars and linguists generally believe that the author of the Gospel of Matthew was a highly educated Jew who wrote in Greek, although he possessed a Jewish mindset. He borrowed heavily from the author of the Gospel of Mark and potentially from the Q document. He refers to Jesus as the Son of David.

Unlike Mark, Matthew includes a nativity account, but his account differs from that of Luke. Among the most salient differences are that Matthew tells the story from Joseph's point of view, while Luke tells it from Mary's perspective.[329] It is important for Matthew to focus on Joseph's pedigree as a descendent of the House of David, so that Jewish audiences could find clues that Jesus was the Messiah. Never mind that Joseph was not actually Jesus' father (per the same Christian gospels), and that they had to contrive a reason for Yeshua to be born in Bethlehem. (That was discussed in Chapter 2).

Similarly, to connect the Jesus as Messiah story with the Jewish prophecy fulfillment, Matthew introduced the story of the three magi. Among the biblical prophecies in the Old Testament was one from Psalms which foretells a king who would receive adoration and wealth from the rulers of distant lands:

- **Psalms 72: 10** "The kings of Tarshish and of the isles shall bring presents: the kings of Sheba and Sheba shall offer gifts."

The writer of the Matthew Gospel focuses heavily on his Jewish connections. In the Matthew version, the Romans are the protagonists. And Matthew paints the story that Jesus wants to discuss the Kingdom of Heaven, not the Kingdom of God. It is in the Gospel of Matthew that Jesus recommends giving one's possessions to the poor (**Matthew 19:16-24**). This is clearly contrary to the 'prosperity theology' of the modern mega churches and televangelists who suggest that wealth and holiness are interconnected.

Matthew has some unique narratives found nowhere else:

- This gospel has the only narrative regarding Mary and Joseph fleeing to Egypt **(Matthew 2:14)**
- It is the only gospel to state that Peter was a Rock and upon the rock he would build his Church, upon which the legitimacy of the Catholic Church succession stands **(Matthew 16:18).** (See Chapter 4).
- It is the only gospel to mention:
  - Guards posted outside Jesus' tomb
  - An earthquake after his death, so powerful it splits rocks

  - The zombie dead who rise, walk into town, and are seen by many people
  - A pact between the high priests and the guards to cover up the miracles they witnessed

Luke

The Gospel of Luke was most likely written by someone with a Hellenic (Greek) heritage, and the mindset is highly intellectual. He appears to have been a gentile physician. He refers to Jesus as the Son of Adam, and he portrays Jesus as the perfect man. This is the longest gospel, which includes some parables not found anywhere else, including the Prodigal Son, the Good Samaritan, the Pharisee, and the Tax Collector.

As mentioned, while most biblical historians are convinced that the Gospel of Luke and *Acts of the Apostles* were written by the same person; this is based on language use and style.[330] But the *Acts of the Apostles* was problematic[331] because:

- It is historically inaccurate
- It appears to be the only surviving text that describes early 2nd-century Christianity
- It strives to represent Saul of Tarsus as a heroic leader of the Christian movement; yet there are discrepancies between Paul's letters and Acts' portrayal of him, as well as potential embellishments of events
- There is a troubling lack of clarity regarding the relationships among the gentile converts and the Jerusalem Church.
- There are general inconsistencies in the narrative

Moreover, the dating of the Gospel of Luke deserves amending. A lingering view of Luke, written at the end of the 1st century, has some serious problems. Luke refers to 'many other gospels';[332] and early Church theologian, Jerome, believed those many other gospels included the gospels of the Egyptians and the Twelve Apostles, which would push the Gospel of Luke well into the 2nd century.[333] Another longstanding argument for a later date for Luke's Gospel is that the evangelist used the works of Jewish historian, Josephus, to pad out his history.[334]

In Against All Heresies (III, 11.8), written around 180 CE, Bishop Irenaeus of Lyons is the first (that we have record of) to name the four gospels, and to give reasons for their potential inclusion in the New Testament.[335] The remarks by Irenaeus represent the first mention of all four canonical gospels together. In fact, prior to this, there is no clear evidence of the existence of the canonical gospels as we have them now.

The Forgery Gospel

Christian tradition maintains that John wrote the fourth gospel as well as the three "Johannine" letters (1, 2, and 3 John), which are also a part of the New Testament and have been cited as evidence of John's leadership among early followers of Jesus. Like the Gospel of John these letters are anonymous. The author of 1 John claims to be an eyewitness who "testifies" to what he has "seen and heard" (1:2–3). The author of 2 and 3 John identifies himself only as "the elder" (**2 John 1:1; 3 John 1:1**), but it also suggests that he was a witness to the Jesus story.[336]

For several decades, scholars had assumed that the Gospel and epistles of John were written within a single, close-knit network of churches sharing a distinctive theological outlook, which they referred to as the 'Johannine community' or 'Johannine Christianity'.[337] However, no one has ever found a trace of this Johannine community — no mentions in ancient texts, and no archeological evidence. According to Hugo Menez, Assistant Professor of Religious Studies at UNC-Chapel Hill, the reason for this is that the texts in question are ancient forgeries.[338] The Gospel of John and 1 John, 2 John, and 3 John were likely written by multiple authors falsely claiming to be a single person close to Jesus. [339]

Mendez has argued that the existence of the Johannine tests cannot be addressed "apart from evidence of literary contact between all four Johannine texts and the pseudepigraphic (falsely ascribed) character of the same works. Taken together, these features cast the Gospel of John, 1 John, 2 John, and 3 John as unreliable bases for historical reconstruction, whose implied audiences and situations are probably fabrications."[340]

Traditionally, these texts have been credited to one person, who claims to be an eyewitness, a "disciple whom Jesus loved." Gullible people just assumed that it meant the Apostle John. Moreover, 1, 2, and 3 John all seem to construct the same implied author, and they show extensive signs of copying, as would be expected of ancient forgeries.[341]

The Gospel of John, as well as 1 John, 2 John, and 3 John, were likely written by multiple authors, falsely claiming a connection to Rabbi Yeshua of Nazareth. What they produced was a chain of forgeries that built upon one another to claim the religious authority of an eyewitness and a disciple. Said differently, one forger copied the strategy of another forger. The same types of false authorial claims made in the Johannine epistles are also declared in the Gospel of John.[342] There are multiple reasons to reject the Gospel of John, and in that rejection, there is a huge theological impact, as the Gospel of John is the only gospel that speaks to the divinity of Yeshua of Nazareth.

There is no anti-Christ mentioned anywhere in the New Testament, except in the letters referred to as 1 John and 2 John (in only four verses: **1 John 2:18, 22, 4:3**, and **2 John 7**). These letters appear to be clear forgeries. Yet, for many decades, zealous Christians have wasted untold time and effort in declaring every public figure they don't agree with as 'the anti-Christ' – a bogeyman drummed up in their imagination. Indeed, Roman Emperor Nero, Napoleon Bonaparte, Ronald Regan, Barack Obama, Donnie Trump, and pretty much every pope in the last few centuries have been referred to as the Antichrist.

Dating the Gospel of John

Just as we do not know who wrote the Synoptic Gospels, we do not know the identity of 'John.' He clearly was not an eyewitness. In the early 20th century, scholars believed that 'John' was written in the early 2nd century. A fragment of papyrus codex, which is only 3.5" by 2.5" (the size of a credit card), was discovered in Oxyrhynchus, which is in northern Egypt, about 160 km southwest of Cairo, near a branch of the Nile River. The front of the fragment contains parts of 7 lines from the Gospel of John, 18:31-33 in Greek, and the back contains parts of verses 37 and 38. The discovery and publication in the 1930s of a papyrus fragment known as P52[343] changed everything.

The P52 papyrus codex is the earliest physical evidence regarding the Gospel of John. The initial dating of P52 placed it around 125 CE. The theory is that for the Gospel of John to have been copied and made its way to Egypt, where P52 was found, a date no earlier than 110 CE had to be presumed for the original writing of the gospel. However, recent re-examinations of P52 suggest that this date is too early by several decades. That the Gospel of John was not written and released until [the] mid-2nd century appears viable, according to the Harvard Theological

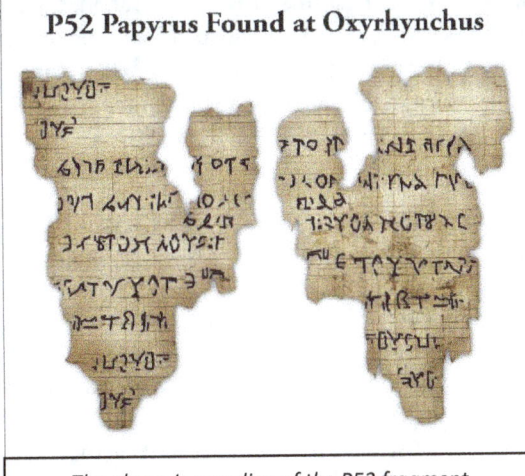

P52 Papyrus Found at Oxyrhynchus

The above is a replica of the P52 fragment

Review, because at that time "Justin Martyr, an early Christian apologist and foremost interpreter of the theory of the Logos, espoused a *logos* (the Word) Christology, without citing the Gospel of John explicitly. Such an omission by Justin would seem strange if the Gospel of John had already been written and was in circulation." [344]

Neither was the Gospel of John known to Bishop Polycarp[345] (c 101 – c 200 CE), bishop of Smyrna (in Greece) and a leading Christian figure in the 2nd century. The letter of Polycarp to the Philippians,[346] generally thought to be from around 135 CE, never quotes from John, and never even alludes to it. Yet, other New Testament writings are quoted abundantly in his letter. Polycarp doesn't once quote the Gospel of John in his writings, even though he quotes the Gospels of Mark, Matthew, and Luke. There's no explicit attestation for the Gospel of John until Bishop Irenaeus (130 - 202 CE), late in the 2nd century.[347]

A relatively early mention of John's Gospel was made by Clement Alexandrinus[348] (150 - 215 CE), as well as commentary by Tatian[349] (circa 160-185), an Assyrian Christian writer and theologian. Tatian attempted to synthesize the four gospels in his Diatessaron (meaning "Harmony of Four"), and he even attempted to remove all duplicate information among the gospels. The argument for the belief that Irenaeus himself authored John includes the fact that this Church Father was provoked passionately to defend the Gospel of John, which he did with great fervor. Even if John were composed by another, this abundance of defense suggests that the gospel had not been in existence for a long time, but it had only recently emerged in the literary and historical record.[350]

We still don't know who the actual author was, but we can easily conclude that it is impossible that the author of a document circa 150 CE was an eyewitness during the time of Yeshua of Nazareth, approximately 115 years earlier.

Why a Forgery?

Reading the New Testament closely reveals that Mendez has some textual support for his argument that the Gospel of John is an ancient forgery, as the Gospel of John presents events strongly in variance to the other gospels. For example, in Mark and Luke, only women keep vigil at the cross. And in John, the disciple runs on ahead to Jesus' tomb, yet in the Gospel of Luke, Peter goes there alone. The famous scene at the cross, when the disciple 'whom Jesus loved' stands with Mary and the women **(John 19:25-27)** never appears in any of the other gospels. Mendez calls this the "Forrest Gump effect," whereby this character has been inserted into the narrative events to give them a first-person eyewitness flavor.[351]

And we see these same theatrical comments again at the tomb visit; and the version from John does not match Matthew, which was written approximately 70 years earlier.

- **Matthew 28:1-9** In the end of the sabbath, as it began to dawn toward the first day of the week, [Sunday], came Mary Magdalene and the other Mary to see the sepulcher. And behold, there was a great earthquake, for the angel of the Lord...rolled back the stone from the door, and sat on it... And as they went to tell his disciples, behold Jesus met them..." **vs.**
- **John 20:1-2** Now on the first day of the week Mary Magdalene came to the tomb early, while it was still dark, and saw that the stone had been taken away from the sepulcher [tomb]. So she ran and went to Simon, Peter and the other disciple, the one whom Jesus loved, and said to them, "They have taken the Lord out of the tomb, and we do not know where they have laid him."

Jesus is Portrayed as a Greek.

In the Synoptic Gospels Jesus is a recognizably Jewish figure. Yet the figure of Jesus presented in John doesn't act Jewish. For example, when addressing the Jews, Jesus speaks of the Mosaic Law as "your Law" and "their Law" as though he did not follow the Jewish rules:

- **John 8:17** "In your own Law it is written that the testimony of two witnesses is true."
- **John 10:34** Jesus answered them, "Is it not written in your Law, 'I have said you are gods.'"
- **John 15:25** "But this is to fulfill what is written in their Law: 'They hated me without reason'."

Jesus' style of preaching also undergoes a radical change in the Gospel of John. In the Synoptic Gospels, he preaches in narrative parables and in short, compact sayings; but in John, the preaching includes long discourses, as if Jesus were being portrayed as a Greek. If the Gospel of John were read in isolation, then one would never guess that the parable was a common teaching method of Jesus (**John 15:1-8** being a rare example of a parable). Further, none of the parables in the Synoptic Gospels are found in John; they are all omitted.

Gospel of John and its Gnostic Terminology

The prologue of the Gospel of **John [1:1-18]** is arguably the best-known and most influential passage in the New Testament. The first eighteen verses of John are typically called the 'prologue' because they are clearly different from the rest of the gospel, with something that looks like a poem, not prose narrative. The key concepts of these verses are not found in the rest of the gospel, such as Jesus being "the Word" made flesh. In the prologue, Jesus is called the "logos" twice, and that is stated nowhere else in the Gospel of John, nor anywhere in the rest of the New Testament. Many scholars believe that the author(s) of John appended these verses as a prologue well after the initial writing.[352] It also appears that the Gospel of John was first fully accepted and used as authoritative in gnostic circles.[353]

Modern scholarship has determined that early Christianity was a diverse mosaic of beliefs, and Christian orthodoxy only settled in the 4th century, when Gnosticism lost much of its influence.[354] It is quite telling that the early Gnostics assigned profound significance to the Gospel of John, especially to the opening verses.[355] The reason why it's important to highlight this is that some of the ideas contained in the prologue to John are indeed gnostic in nature, the very thing that early Christians used to reject the Gospel of Thomas and other gospels. In his treatise, <u>Against Heresies</u>,[356] Irenaeus of Lyons quotes from a lengthy gnostic commentary on the prologue of John.[357] The Gnostics believed the prologue of John explicitly mentioned the names of several divine entities or "*aeons*".[358] An aeon is a divine entity that is considered an extension of the True God. Aeons were believed to be intermediate beings between humans and God. These *aeons* are common names in the gnostic myth, as reported by Irenaeus. In **John 1:1–18** the following *aeons* are revealed by name (as translated from the ancient Greek text of John):

- the "Beginning" or Arche,
- the Word (Logos),
- Life (Zoe), which was the "light" of
- Man (Anthropos),
- the Church (Ecclesia),
- Grace (Charis), and
- Truth (Aletheia)

The Gospel of John can be readily understood to be a refutation of everything that "orthodox" Christians of the 2nd century have tried to establish in terms of a standard history, tradition, and theology.[359] In its original form, the Gospel of John may well have been among the earliest of the gnostic gospels.[360] If early Christians reject the Gospel of Thomas by writing it off as a gnostic work, then they should have been consistent and rejected the Gospel of John for the exact same reason, as it too has significant gnostic verses. Since the Gospel of John is the bedrock for Trinitarians, and it is usually their "go-to" book of the Bible in trying to find support for the divinity of Jesus; and this represents yet another damning blow to the doctrine of the Trinity.

The Passover Meal

According to the Gospels of Mark, Matthew, and Luke, the Last Supper was the Passover meal.

- **Luke 22:8** "So Jesus sent Peter and John, saying, "Go and prepare the Passover for us, that we may eat it."
- **Mark 14:12-18** "And on the first day of Unleavened Bread, when they sacrificed the Passover lamb, his disciples said to him, 'Where will you have us go and prepare for you to eat the Passover?' And he sent two of his disciples and said to them, 'Go into

the city, and a man carrying a jar of water will meet you. Follow him, and wherever he enters, say to the master of the house, 'The Teacher says, 'Where is my guest room, where I may eat the Passover with my disciples?' And he will show you a large upper room furnished and ready; there prepare for us.' And the disciples set out and went to the city and found it just as he had told them, and they prepared the Passover. And when it was evening, he came with the twelve. And as they were reclining at table and eating, Jesus said, 'Truly, I say to you, one of you will betray me, one who is eating with me."

The above verses confirm that the meal being eaten is the Passover meal. The disciples ask where the Passover meal is to be eaten; they go there, they prepare, later Jesus arrives, and they eat a meal. However, in the Gospel of John, the final meal took place <u>before</u> the festival of Passover. John is telling us that Jesus died before the Passover meal, once again, contradicting the other gospels.

- **John 13:1-2** "It was just before the Passover Festival. Jesus knew that the hour had come for him to leave this world and go to the Father. Having loved his own who were in the world, he loved them to the end. The evening meal was in progress…"

Next, when Jesus' accusers were delivering him to Pilate, the Passover had not taken place.

- **John 18:28** Then they led Jesus from the house of Caiaphas to the governor's headquarters. It was early morning. They themselves did not enter the governor's headquarters, so that they would not be defiled, but could eat the Passover."

Finally, John explicitly states that Jesus was crucified on the day of preparation for the Passover:

- **John 19:14-15** Now it was the day of Preparation of the Passover. It was about the sixth hour. He said to the Jews, "Behold your King!" They cried out, "Away with him, away with him, crucify him!" Pilate said to them, "Shall I crucify your King?" The chief priests answered, "We have no king but Caesar."

Why did John alter the story?

- **John 1:29** The next day John saw Jesus coming toward him and said, "Look, the Lamb of God, who takes away the sin of the world!"

It's crucial to note that John is the only gospel that identifies Jesus as the "Lamb of God." In **John 1: 29**, the gospel author puts the phrase in the mouth of John the Baptist. John's Gospel portrays Jesus as the Passover lamb, slaughtered on the day of preparation for Passover, whose shed blood somehow brings salvation, just as the blood of the Passover lamb supposedly had brought salvation to the Israelite slaves in Egypt. For the author of the Gospel of John, Jesus was the Lamb of God; he died at the same time, and at the hands of the same people (the Jewish priests) as the Passover lambs.[361]

Thus, we can see that the Gospel of John was not an accurate narrative about the historical Jesus. John alters the day of the Crucifixion to make a theological point. This is one of the numerous reasons why so many New Testament scholars conclude that the Gospel of John is inaccurate and a fraud.

Anti-Jewish Views

The Gospel of John is unique among the gospels for its intense hostility towards a group simply labeled as "the Jews," an appellation that the author of John uses 73 times in his gospel,[362] and 31 of those times it is used in a very hostile sense. This usage has led to considerable disputes between Jews and Christians and accusations of anti-Semitism over the meaning of this phrase and the sentiment behind it.[363] John portrays the Jews as the enemy of Jesus and their willing acceptance of blame for Jesus' death, and Jesus calling the Jews, "children of the devil."

- **John 8:44** "Ye are of your father the devil, and the lusts of your father ye will do. He was a murderer from the beginning, and abode not in the truth, because there is no truth in him...."
- **John 19:12** "And from thenceforth Pilate sought to release Him: but the Jews cried out, saying, If thou let this man go, thou art not Caesar's friend: whoever maketh himself a king speaketh against Caesar."
- **John 19:15** "But they cried out, Away with him, away with him, crucify him. Pilate saith unto them, Shall I crucify your King? The chief priests answered, We have no king but Caesar."

The above certainly doesn't sound like a Jewish response. Historian and author, Lillian Freudmann, wrote that these passages in the Gospel of John make antisemitism respectable and encourage aggression against Jews."[364] Remember, the Jews at this time are quite angry with Rome and its ruling over them. This sounds like the words of a Roman author. Further, the Gospel of John was written in the mid-2nd century; and by that time, the Christians and Jews had separated into two distinct groups, as there was a clear break between mainstream Judaism and Christianity, with the Jews barring Christians from worshipping in the synagogues. And thus, Christians gradually came to view the religion of their spiritual founder, Jesus, with hostility and scorn.

In the other three gospels, the plot to arrest Jesus and put him to death is always presented as coming from a small group of priests and rulers, the Sadducees. In none of the other gospels do "the Jews" demand, en masse, the death of Jesus. According to noted historian and author James Everett Seaver, "Much of Christian hatred toward the Jews was based on the popular misconception that the Jews had been the active persecutors."[365]

The Gospel of John has been cited as the primary source that created the image of "the Jews" acting collectively as the enemy of Jesus, which later became fixed in Christian minds. Clearly, the Gospel of John was written to a gentile audience.

John Contradicts the Synoptic Gospels

There are over 30 direct contradictions of John against the Synoptic Gospels.[366] It should suffice to just share a handful of them:

- **Matthew 3:16 & Mark 1:10:** "It was Jesus who saw the Spirit descending."
- **John 1:32:** "It was John who saw the Spirit descending."
- **Matthew 21:12-13:** "The cleansing of the temple occurs at the end of Jesus' career."
- **John 2:13-16:** "The cleansing of the temple occurs near the beginning of his career."

- **Matthew 12:39 & Mark 8:12 & Luke 11:29:** "Jesus says that he will give no 'sign.'"
- **John 3:2 & 20:30:** "Jesus proceeds to give many such "signs."
- **Mark 6:53:** "After feeding the 5000, Jesus and the disciples went to Gennesaret."
- **John 6:17-25:** "After feeding the 5000, they went to Capernaum."
- **Mark 16:5 & Luke 24:3:** "Women entered the tomb."
- **John 20:1-2 & John 20:11:** "Women did not enter the tomb."

Embellishments of John

There are many areas where the author of John's Gospel clearly seems to have embellished what is written in the Synoptic Gospels, as he adds details to the ministry and words of Christ and the witness of others.[367] Given that the author of John wrote almost a century <u>after</u> Jesus died and well after the authors of the Synoptic Gospels, one wonders where he got the material used to embellish. The author clearly had his own agenda. Here are some examples of the many titles he embellished for Jesus:

- The Lamb of God   **[John 1:29, John 1:35]**
- Son of God,   **[John 1:34, John 1:49]**
- Rabbi   **[John 1:38, John 1:49]**
- Christ / Messiah   **[John 1:41]**
- Jesus of Nazareth   **[John 1:45]**
- King of Israel   **[John 1:49]**
- Son of Man   **[John 1:51]**

John 1 is totally inconsistent with the other gospels, which do not speak of these titles. None of the Synoptics attest to John the Baptist identifying Jesus as the "Lamb of God" or "the Son of God." In Luke, Peter identifies Jesus as the Christ only much later in the ministry when Jesus asks his disciples, "Who do you say that I am?" (Luke 9:20).

Seven "I Am" statements

In the Synoptic Gospels, Jesus is not focused on teaching about himself, but in John's Gospel, Jesus fixates on who he is and where he came from.[368] If the historical Jesus claimed to be God, how could the other gospel writers omit that? But they never mentioned it.[369] The Synoptic Gospels stand in marked contrast to the Gospel of John, whose content is comparatively distinct. In fact, over 90% of its material cannot be found in the Synoptics.[370] Jesus' principal theme throughout the Synoptic gospels is the Kingdom of God; he rarely speaks of himself. However, in John, the discourses are largely vehicles for expressing Jesus' self-consciousness and self-proclamation.

- **John 6:35** "I am the bread of life; whoever comes to me shall not hunger, and whoever believes in me shall never thirst"
- **John 8:12** "I am the light of the world. Whoever follows me will not walk in darkness, but will have the light of life."
- **John 10:7-10** "I am the door of the sheep. All who came before me are thieves and robbers, but the sheep did not listen to them. I am the door. If anyone enters by me, he will be saved and will go in and out and find pasture. The thief comes only to steal and kill and destroy. I came that they may have life and have it abundantly."

- **John 10:11** "I am the good shepherd. The good shepherd lays down his life for the sheep."
- **John 11:25-26** "I am the resurrection and the life. Whoever believes in me, though he die, yet shall he live, and everyone who lives and believes in me shall never die."
- **John 14:6** "I am the way, and the truth, and the life. No one comes to the Father except through me."
- **John 15:1-2** "I am the true vine, and my Father is the vinedresser. Every branch in me that does not bear fruit he takes away, and every branch that does bear fruit he prunes, that it may bear more fruit."

The discovery that the very chapter that asserts the author as being "the disciple whom Jesus loved" **[John 21:20]** further establishes the inauthenticity of the Gospel of John. The Gospel of John originally ended at Chapter 20, verse 31. Chapter 21 appears to have been added much later![371]

Raising of Lazarus

The raising of Lazarus in Chapters 18 and 19 of John is the climax of Jesus' ministry and is pivotal to the narrative of John. However, the Synoptic Gospels do not mention Lazarus. It appears that the story, the symbolism, and the parallels it draws are numerous embellishments:

- **John 11:4, 13-15** "Jesus knows Lazarus is ill and engages in a plot to let him die so that a greater sign can be demonstrated through the situation."
- **John:7-8** "Jesus knew he is subjecting himself to danger by going to Judea after the Jews wanted to stone him."
- **John:25-26** "Jesus uses the situation to make a declaration about himself, "I am the resurrection and the life.""
- **John 11:17, 39** "Lazarus was in the tomb for four days" – (a similar period that Jesus was dead)
- **John 11:38, 44** "Lazarus was wrapped in a burial shroud and was sealed in a tomb (similar to Jesus)."
- **John 11:45-57** "The raising of Lazarus sets in motion the plot to arrest Jesus." Note: This is opposed to the cleansing of the temple as presented in the Synoptic Gospels.
- **John 12:9-11** "The Jews also want to kill Lazarus."
- **John 12:17-18** "The crowds gathered at the triumphal entry due to the raising of Lazarus."
- **John 11:4** "Lazarus and Jesus are meant to die so that God may be glorified (both are signs)."

Proclamations that Jesus is the Messiah

In the Synoptic Gospels, Jesus' identity as the Messiah is kept secret during his ministry; Jesus only discloses his fate to be killed and be resurrected to his closest disciples, and only at the end of his ministry. In John, Jesus is announced as the Messiah at the very onset of his ministry **(John 1:41)** and publicly makes prophetic proclamations about his resurrection **(John 2:19-21)**. This is such a striking inconsistency between John and the Synoptic Gospels.

John's Materials Differ Radically from the Synoptic Gospels

The Synoptic Gospels include many of the same stories, generally in the same sequence, and share the same points of view. And they significantly predate the Gospel of John, 90% of whose content doesn't match the other gospels.

The Spear Piercing the Side of Jesus.

- **John 19:34** "Instead, one of the soldiers pierced Jesus' side with a spear, bringing a sudden flow of blood and water."

This is an obvious embellishment introduced by John for his own reasons. Take away the spear thrust, and there is little in the gospels that would have resulted in the death of Jesus in only three hours. Perhaps, that is why he added it. Crucifixion doesn't kill a person by itself; it is the exhaustion resulting from prolonged hanging on the cross, sometimes taking several days to die, not a few hours.

The Guards Prostrating to Jesus.

The Synoptics depict the picture of Jesus as being reluctant to be crucified, like most rational humans. They each mention Jesus begging his Father to be saved from death when he is in the Garden of Gethsemane. Luke even has Jesus sweating drops of blood just before his arrest. All of this is in stark contrast to John, who portrays Jesus as willingly handing himself over to the authorities:

- **John 18:3-6** "So Judas came to the garden, guiding a detachment of soldiers and some officials from the chief priests and the Pharisees. They were carrying torches, lanterns and weapons. Jesus, knowing all that was going to happen to him, went out and asked them, 'Who is it you want?' 'Jesus of Nazareth,' they replied. 'I am he,' Jesus said. (And Judas the traitor was standing there with them.) When Jesus said, 'I am he,' they drew back and fell to the ground."

The Gospel of John does not mention the concerns of Jesus as written in the Synoptics. John's version projects the power of Jesus: from the outset, Jesus is in charge, just his voice is enough to cause the soldiers to retreat, and fall prostrate on the ground.

It is strange to think that the authors of the Synoptics would not have been aware of incidents such as the spear piercing the side of Jesus and the soldiers prostrating to him in the Garden of Gethsemane, had they really taken place. It is even more inconceivable that they would have intentionally omitted such remarkable accounts from their gospels. One must therefore conclude that such stories are later embellishments by whomever authored John.[372]

Material Differences

The Synoptics are basically descriptive in their approach, like reporters of a story, but making no claims on eyewitness accounts. John is reflective in separating himself from the events he describes; but he pretended to be an eyewitness, which he clearly was not, given the dating of the P52 fragment.

The Gospel of John omits much of the synoptic content: the temptation of Jesus, Jesus' transfiguration, no examples of casting out demons, the Sermon on the Mount and the Lord's Prayer, and no narrative parables. But John has included a significant amount of material <u>not</u> discussed in the Synoptic Gospels, including seven additional miracles, as well as material contradictions to the Synoptic Gospels, including the length of Jesus' public ministry. John, who wrote many decades after the Synoptics, prescribes a public ministry that extends over <u>3 to 4 years</u>, with multiple trips from Galilee to Jerusalem, while the Synoptics describe <u>one year</u> of public ministry and <u>one trip</u> to Jerusalem.

John wrote from a post-resurrection perspective, emphasizing that the apostles could not fully understand the true nature of what was happening with Jesus of Nazareth. John makes more use of symbolism and double meanings, such as **John 2:25** (temple/body); **John 7:37:38** (water/spirit); and **John 12:32** (lifted up / exalted).

Book of Revelation (The Lie)

If you've read the Book of Revelation, it might not surprise you that it had a very contentious trajectory to canonicity. Amazingly, the controversy was not about the fact that the book is a cryptic enigma in which a beast with seven heads and ten horns emerges from the sea. Indeed, the book of Revelation was initially met with an enthusiastic reception in the late 2nd century, largely thanks to the false belief that its author was John the Apostle. This idea was accepted for quite a while until a 3rd-century author claimed it to be a forgery, and others disagreed with its message of a literal thousand-year reign by Christ on Earth.[373]

There was a significant variety of opinion among Christian patriarchates (regional Churches) about what writings should be considered authoritative and thus canonized. Revelation was eventually affirmed as a book of the New Testament. But centuries later, many early Protestant leaders like Martin Luther and John Calvin rejected its apostolic and prophetic authenticity; and even today, it is the only New Testament book not read in the Divine Liturgy of the Eastern Orthodox Church.[374] The name of Revelation's author is not exactly known, but he appears to have been a devout Jew and mystic who was exiled to the isle of Patmos, off the coast of Greece. Thus, he is often referred to as John of Patmos.[375]

There are three key points in myth-busting the Book of Revelation:

1. It is <u>not</u> a prophecy about the end of the world, but it is a view regarding how the author's own world ended with the sack of Jerusalem by the Romans. Revelation is an anti-Roman narrative, and a piece of mystic propaganda wrapped in one. "The message: God would return and destroy the Romans who had destroyed Jerusalem."[376]
2. The number 666 is <u>not</u> about the devil, but rather it is about Emperor Nero. John of Patmos used the Jewish numerology system to spell out Nero's imperial name.[377]
3. Its author hated Rome, but he was <u>not</u> at all fond of the early Christians. There was not one agreed-upon version of Christianity in the first two centuries. John of Patmos was a devout Jew who obsessed over Jesus as the Jewish Messiah, but he railed against the message that Paul and the gentile 'Christians' were preaching.

There were many books similar to Revelation which did <u>not</u> make the cut into the Christian Bible. How did Revelation make it when it clearly was not a text that supported the Christian views of the 4th century (when the canonization of the Bible occurred)? Elaine Pagels, a religion historian, traces that decision largely to Bishop Athanasius,[378] (yes, him again), the prominent but pugnacious church leader who championed Revelation about 360 years after the death of Jesus.[379] Pagels says, "Athanasius (296 – 373 CE) was so fiery that during his 46 years as bishop he was deposed and exiled five times."[380]

During the 4th century, many Christian leaders opposed including Revelation in the New Testament. Indeed, Athanasius's predecessor, Bishop Dionysius of Alexandria, said the book was "unintelligible, irrational, and false."[381] However, for Athanasius, the Book of Revelation was a useful political tool which he used against other Christians who dared to question him. There is evidence that Athanasius was guilty of violence, strong-arm tactics against his opponents, and various 'barbaric behaviors.'[382] According to author Elaine Pagels, Rome was no longer the enemy; those who questioned church authority were aligned with the anti-Christ in Athanasius's reading of Revelation.[383]

Adam Gopnik wrote in The New Yorker, "Revelation very nearly did not make the cut. In the early 2nd century, many bishops in Asia Minor voted to condemn the text as blasphemous. It was only in the three-sixties (360s CE) that the Church council, under the control of the fiery Athanasius, inserted Revelation as the climax of the entire New Testament."[384]

In her article, "The Untold Truth of the Book of Revelation", Kathy Benjamin wrote, "But Revelation (not Revelations) is probably the most difficult book in the Bible to interpret accurately. It's lousy with symbolism and numerology and all these coded messages (that few can decipher). It was both a rousing propaganda message and revenge fantasy all in one."[385]

Revelation 13: 15-18 mentions the "mark of the beast." Other references to it can be found in **Revelation 14:9, 11, 15:2, 16:2, 19:20, and 20:4**. Obviously, there has been a lot of speculation about the mark of the beast; this puzzling mark has become quite exaggerated. In recent times, zealous, conservative Christians have focused on the concern that no one "may buy or sell" without it. What rubbish! In the 1960s, some Christians in my hometown decried UPC codes in grocery stores as "the mark," and that concern regarding bar codes continued into the 21st century.[386] The 'mark' became RFID tags on animals,[387] integrated circuit chips on 'smart cards'; and most recently, digital currency was declared to be 'the mark.'[388] [389] Apparently, when some religious conservatives do not understand a given technology, they follow their tendency to declare it to be the mark of the beast.

Further, many of these Christians have strived diligently to connect the anti-Christ to their unwarranted fears of the "beast." But the reality is, there is no mention of the anti-Christ in the Book of Revelation – none! For some, the idea of an anti-Christ is central to the apocalyptic viewpoint (even though there is no rational reason for this). The only mention of such a being came from the forgeries of the letters of 1 John and 2 John. What is so embarrassing for Christianity is that no one knows what the mark is, or what it will do. And as Steve Shives proclaimed in his podcast, it has been and so far remains an "almost inexhaustible inspiration for fiction and religious paranoia."[390]

The Book of Revelation should never have been included in the Christian New Testament. It has plagued Christianity ever since it was first put to writing. That the Book of Revelation was included in the New Testament canons is yet another indictment regarding how the early Christian Church in the 4th century loosely vetted, selected, and declared what books would be included in the New Testament.

Miracles of the New Testament

A miracle (from the Latin *mirari*, to wonder) …is an event that is not explicable by natural causes alone.[391] For some, it is about the <u>probability</u> of an event occurring. The more miraculous the event, the more improbable it is. Professor Lawrence Shapiro, University of Wisconsin, Dept of Philosophy, wrote, "The best evidence for the presence of supernatural activity is that activity's vast improbability."[392] Shapiro further explained that there could be alternative explanations, including natural causes, for these incredible events. Similarly, assumptions about God are ultimately unevidenced speculation.

Prior to the Age of Enlightenment, Christian Europe did not question the reality of miracles, nor did Catholics or Protestants. Many people prior to that period, and some people well beyond that Age, were generally religious and quite superstitious.

In his manuscript, "On Human Nature and Understanding" (1739), Philosopher David Hume established himself as the leading source for modern views against the occurrence of miracles. Hume defined a miracle as a violation of the laws of nature, and he posited that evidence for miracles comes from the <u>independent</u> testimony of others, while evidence against miracles is experienced personally every day through the unchanging laws of nature.[393] Hume says that people must weigh the evidence based on experience and logic. According to Hume, the probability of people inaccurately claiming that they'd seen Jesus' resurrection far outweighed the probability that the event had occurred in the first place.[394]

Let's look at three philosophical razors which can be useful tools in making the complex seem less so: Occam's razor, Hitchens' razor, and Sagan's razor. In philosophy, a razor is a principle or rule of thumb that enables one to eliminate (shave off) unlikely explanations for a phenomenon or avoid unnecessary actions. The first tool for discerning the credibility of miracles is Occam's Razor,[395] a problem-solving principle that recommends searching for unambiguous explanations constructed with the smallest possible set of elements.[396] Thus, Occam's razor (named after William of Ockham, c. 1287–1347) directs us to use our experience and intellect to reason it out:

> *"Explanations which require fewer unjustified assumptions are more likely to be correct; avoid unnecessary or improbable assumptions."*

Occam's razor tells us that the simplest answer is usually the correct one. Evolutionary biologist Richard Dawkins once stated that he thought that every discussion among atheists and theists should start with a review of Occam's razor. He believed that "this simple tool could be critical in cutting away something like half the possible arguments as irrelevant, thus focusing the discussion."[397] A simple tool, but a powerful one! However, opposing views may not coalesce into the same conclusion. Let's continue to what has come to be known as the Hitchens Razor, named after Christopher Eric Hitchens (April 1949 – December 2011), a British and American author and journalist:

"What can be asserted without evidence can also be dismissed without evidence."[398]

And American astronomer, planetary scientist, and science communicator, Carl Sagan (November 1934 – December 1996) once famously pronounced:

"Ordinary claims require only a small amount of fair evidence;
Extraordinary claims require extraordinary levels of evidence."[399]

These philosophical razors are focused on evidence. It becomes a hard truth that without collaborating evidence, the miracle claims are empty assertions which offer no rationale for belief. So, we move on to another excellent tool, Bayes' Theory, which is a mathematical process to determine conditional probability, or the likelihood of an outcome occurring based on a previous outcome in similar circumstances.[400] In the 18th century, Presbyterian Reverend Thomas Bayes developed his formula initially as an attempt to defend Christianity. Bayes' theorem can help us understand how our assumptions affect our beliefs. The problem is that Bayes' theorem requires the existence of some credible evidence—or data—before it can be correctly used in evaluating miracle claims.[401] Thus, for Bayes' Theorem to be a credible and useful tool to apply to testimonial evidence regarding stated miracle claims, there has to be some actual existing evidence, and for the more spectacular claims, there needs to be overwhelming evidence. And in terms of the biblical miracles, it is a non-sequitur, because there is no evidence!

In his narrative regarding the use of Bayes' theorem, author John Loftus correctly asks why the virgin birth of Jesus was so readily accepted without any credible evidence. Not only was there no objective evidence, but there was no second-hand testimony either.[402] Joseph's so-called dream, described by an anonymous author 80 years later, is hardly evidence. Without evidence to compare, Bayes' theorem cannot help with miracle claims. Since Joseph put nothing in writing, and as far as we know, he mentioned his dream to no one, this is an instance of hearsay based on a rumor.

Jesus' resurrection is another miracle event without evidence. The claim that Jesus died for our sins is <u>not</u> supported in any other Scripture. Paul was a Pharisaic Jew who was indoctrinated with the Jewish legalistic practices of blood sacrifice rituals. Sacrifice was a standard way to appease ancient gods. To Jews of the 1st century, a blood sacrifice was an act of obedience to their God, Yahweh. And so, it appears that Paul applied this analogy of a sacrifice to Jesus' crucifixion as an act of obedience to atone for the sins of mankind.[403] Paul was familiar with the book of Genesis, which he thought provided an explanation for the origin of sin and death, and he extrapolated that story to contrive the salvation myth. He followed up his pronouncement about dying for our sins with comments in his epistle to the Romans:

- **Romans 5:8** "But God commendeth his love toward us, in that, while we were yet sinners, Christ died for us."

We must ask ourselves, did the miracle event of the Resurrection occur as reported? Or is it more likely that there is some other explanation? In some cases, what might have been viewed as a miracle at a given time in history might receive a naturalistic explanation at some date in the future when science and technology advance.

If we can pinpoint the actual identity(ies) of the witness(es) to an event, then we need to look at the credibility of the witness(es) and their motivation(s). When it comes to Jesus' resurrection, the reports were highly biased; they came from unlearned, superstitious people, again, if the authors told the truth of what they heard. Human perception has many cognitive biases. Even with all the information available to us in the 21st century, we are routinely deceived, we misperceive that which we witness ourselves, and at times, we self-deceive. Distortions of reality are part of our human makeup.

Stories of Jesus' miracles did not surface in the Christian tradition until the Gospel of Mark in the eighth decade of the 1st century – approximately 40 years after the death of Jesus of Nazareth. And stories of Jesus' supernatural birth (virgin Mother) did not surface until the Gospel of Matthew in the 9th decade of the 1st century. The concept of a virgin birth of a god was a common theme in that era, and eventually, some Christian writers wanted a god as cool as some other pagan deities, who were born of virgins. There just is no objective evidence for any miracles described in the NT (or the OT for that matter). No miracle has ever been proven. The following are some thoughts on miracles:

"All of the tales of miracles, with which the Old and New Testament are filled, are fit only for imposters to preach and fools to believe."
– Thomas Paine (1737 – 1809), <u>The Writings of Thomas Paine</u>

"In those parts of the world where learning and science have prevailed, miracles have ceased; but in those parts of it that are barbarous and ignorant, miracles are in vogue."
– Ethan Allen, 1794, <u>Reason, the Only Oracle of Man</u>

"It is impossible to use electric lights and the wireless and to avail ourselves of modern medical and surgical discoveries, and at the same time to believe in the New Testament world of spirits and miracles.
– Theologian Rudolph Bultmann (1884-1976) [404]

"A miracle is an event described by those to whom it was told by people who did not see it."
– Elbert Hubbard, American writer and philosopher, <u>The Philistine</u>
(1909)

The Bible was written in a pre-scientific age when many natural phenomena (e.g., thunder, lightning, pestilence, earthquakes) were attributed to direct divine action. The cited 'miracles' were meant to authenticate a connection of Jesus to the divine (God the Father). We now know that there are perfectly natural explanations for these and many other phenomena. The following is a list of the so-called miracles of Jesus Christ, according to the four gospels. Not one of the miracles was witnessed by the gospel authors. And those miracles cited only by 'John' are part of his forgery.

Miracles Cited in the New Testament

#	Miracle	Mark	Matthew	Luke	John
1	Jesus Turns Water into Wine at Wedding				2:1-11
2	Jesus Heals an Official's Son in Galilee				4:43-54
3	Jesus Drives Out an Evil Spirit	1:21-27		4:31-36	
4	Jesus Heals Peter's Sick Mother-in-Law	1:29-31	8:14-15	4:38-39	
5	Jesus Heals Many Sick in Gennesaret	1:32-34	8:16-17	4:40-41	
6	First Miraculous Catch of Fish			5:1-11	
7	Jesus Cleanses a Man with Leprosy	1:40-45	8:1-4	5:12-14	
8	Jesus Heals a Centurion's Paralyzed Servant		8:5-13	7:1-10	
9	Jesus Heals a Paralytic Man	2:1-12	9:1-8	5:17-26	
10	Jesus Heals a Man's Withered Hand	3:1-6	12:9-14	6:6-11	
11	Jesus Raises a Widow's Son from the Dead in Nain			7:11-17	
12	Jesus Calms a Storm on the Sea	4:35-41	8:23-27	8:22-25	
13	Jesus Casts Demons into a Herd of Pigs	5:1-20	8:28-33	8:26-39	
14	Jesus Heals a Hemorrhaging Woman	5:25-34	9:20-22	8:42-48	
15	Jesus Raises Jairus' Daughter Back to Life	5:21-24, 35-43	9:18, 23-26	8:40-42, 49-56	
16	Jesus Heals Two Blind Men		9:27-31		
17	Jesus Heals a Man Unable to Speak		9:32-34	11:14-15	

#		Mark	Matthew	Luke	John
18	Jesus Heals an Invalid at Bethesda				5:1-15
19	Jesus Feeds 5,000 +	6:30-44	14:13-21	9:10-17	6:1-15
20	Jesus Walks on Water	6:45-52	14:22-33		6:16-21
21	Jesus Heals Many Sick	6:53-56	14:34-36	6:17-19	6:02
22	Jesus Heals a Woman's Daughter	7:24-30	15:21-28		
23	Jesus Heals a Deaf and Dumb Man	7:31-37			
24	Jesus Feeds 4,000+	8:1-13	15:32-39		
25	Jesus Heals a Blind Man at Bethsaida	8:22-26			
26	Jesus Heals a Man Born Blind Healed				9:1-12
27	Jesus Heals an Epileptic Boy	9:14-29	17:14-20	9:37-43	
28	Miraculous Temple Tax in a Fish's Mouth		17:24-27		
29	Jesus Heals a Blind, Mute Man		12:22-23		
30	Jesus Heals a Disabled Woman			13:10-17	
31	Jesus Heals a Man with Dropsy			14:1-6	
32	Jesus Cleanses Ten Lepers			17:11-19	
33	Jesus Raises Lazarus from the Dead				11:1-45
34	Jesus Restores Sight to Bartimaeus	10:46-52	20:29-34	18:35-43	
35	Jesus Heals the Blind and Lame		21:14		
36	Jesus Withers the Fig Tree	11:12-14	21:18:22		
37	Jesus heals a servant's severed ear.			22:50-51	
38	Second Miraculous Catch of Fish at the Sea of Tiberias (Galilee)				21:1-4
39	Resurrection	16	28	24	20-21

Unreliability of the New Testament

Is the New Testament the literal, inspired word of God? Or is it the corrupted result of numerous scribes who have altered the original texts? Even the original texts included the prejudices of the men who wrote them.

Many Christians incorrectly believe in the inerrancy of the New Testament, meaning that everything is true and it is free of any errors. When those who believe that the New Testament is inerrant are confronted with an irreconcilable contradiction (of which there are many), they usually shift their argument to one of "the New Testament contains no contradictions of consequence." Thus, while they then acknowledge the existence of contradictions [only because they cannot prove otherwise], they don't consider them to significantly impact the overall truth of what the New Testament is teaching. But many times, these contradictions are quite material.[405]

The New Testament was written originally in Greek, not Aramaic, and not Latin. There are multiple manuscripts that comprise the New Testament. Christian theologians have been faced with a massive arrangement of textual variants. The New Testament has been hand-copied and translated more than any other ancient book; and with each copy, there are many spelling, grammar, and translating errors, as everything was copied or translated by hand. There are more than 30,000 changes made to the Bible. Several thousand of these changes represent differences among the Greek texts used, as well as the translation of vernacular texts used in various languages. Additionally, there are several revised versions. Other changes were simply made for consistency. Moreover, a huge issue with translations is that sometimes the translators are inconsistent with the language they are translating. After all, translating and copying such large texts inevitably led to human errors. But sometimes the changes are deliberate.[406] Thus, every time the New Testament was copied or updated, or translated, changes occurred, and some were quite meaningful alterations. As early as the 3rd century, the scholar and theologian, Origen of Alexander[407] (c. 185 – c. 253) called out the corruption in the copied texts of the New Testament:

> "...the differences among the manuscripts [of the gospels] have become great, either through negligence of some copyists or through the audacity of others; they either neglect to check what they have transcribed, or in the process of checking, they lengthen or shorten, as they please."[408]

Sometimes we need to remind ourselves that the New Testament was not compiled and canonized until the late 4th century. And there were many political and as well as religious arguments about it. Pope St. Damasus I, in 382, issued the Decree of Damasus in which he listed the canonical books of the New Testament (and those of the Old Testament), unchanged from what Bishop Anastasius had compiled. What Christians refer to as the Holy Bible is just the compiled books of Damasus, which were originally composed by Bishop Anastasius.

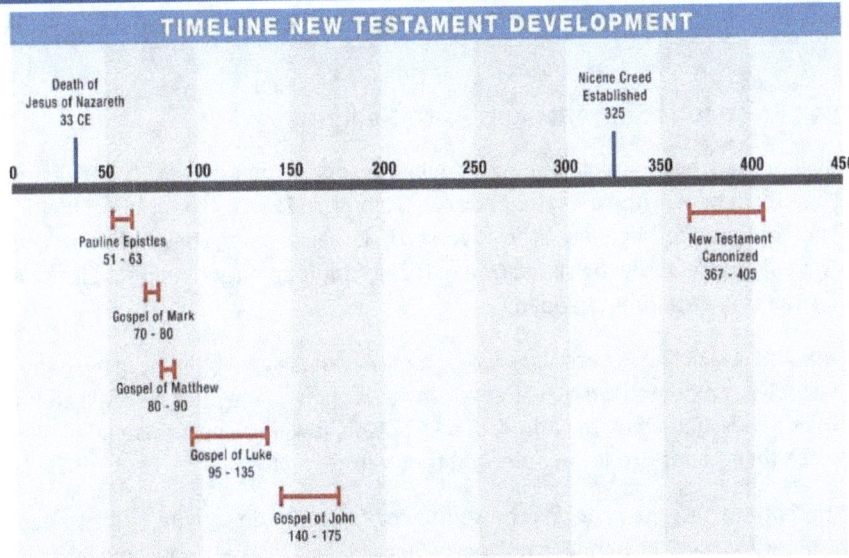

TIMELINE NEW TESTAMENT DEVELOPMENT

The above timeline depicts the enormous time lags from the death of Jesus to the writings about him which made their way into the New Testament. All writings were based on hearsay. There were no witness testimonies! Except for Paul of Tarsus, all authorship was obscured, as it was written by self-serving men with unknown agendas.

The claim that mistakes are negligible and have limited theological consequences is simply not true. The following are just three examples of corruptions in the New Testament: (1) the role of women, (2) faith healing, and (3) Jesus the Omniscient.

The Role of Women

- **1 Corinthians 14:34-25** "Women should remain silent in churches. They are not allowed to speak, but must be in submission, as the law says. If they want to inquire about something, they should ask their husbands at home; for it is disgraceful for a woman to speak in the church."

Based on this verse, women have not been allowed to lead or preach in many Christian churches, especially the RCC. However, Paul does not appear to have originated this verse; most likely, it was added by later clerics who sought to exclude women from church leadership. Indeed, Paul had previously written in the same epistle about women openly prophesying and praying. Additionally, the placement of this text can differ by manuscript. Professor Alan Johnson explained: "A growing number of modern scholars believe that verses 34-35 are a later interpolation added at an early stage in the manuscript transmission."[409]

Adding his voice, Richard Hays, a New Testament scholar, wrote: "All things considered, this passage is best explained as a gloss [an additional insertion] introduced into the text by the second- or third-generation Pauline interpreters who compiled the pastoral epistles."[410]

The evidence favors the scenario that verses 34 and 35 were added, and they were <u>not</u> part of the original epistle. Yes, based on this, women have been barred from assuming self-actualizing roles in church leadership; and they have been marginalized as active members of the laity.

Handling Poisonous Serpents and Faith Healing

The Gospel of Mark has multiple endings, depending on the manuscript. The oldest copies of the New Testament, known as the Codex Vaticanus (c. 350 CE) and Codex Sinaiticus (c. 260 CE) manuscripts, respectively, stop at verse 16:8. Later versions have additional verses, and they are not necessarily the same. One of these additional [fraudulent] copies says that Christians can survive serpent handling:

- **Mark 16:17-28** "And these signs will accompany those who believe: In my name they will drive out demons; they will speak in new tongues; they will pick up snakes with their hands; and when they drink deadly poison, it will not hurt them at all; they will place their hands on sick people, and they will get well."

This inappropriate passage provides the source for "speaking in tongues," "faith healing," and for American churches handling poisonous snakes (and several people dying) as part of their Christian service, notwithstanding that these verses were added to the original document much later.

Satan

Most Christians assume that Satan, the evil adversary of God, is just as much present in the Old Testament as he is in the New Testament. After all, there was that clever snake that tempted Eve in Genesis. But such beliefs underscore how perceptions change over time. Well, the term *satan* is indeed of Hebrew origin. Whenever satan is used in the Old Testament, it is preceded by the ancient Hebrew article ha –, as in ha-satan, which in ancient Hebrew was used as a verb, meaning "to obstruct" or "to oppose"; and when used as a noun, it means "adversary" or "accuser." The phrase is used nine times in the Tanakh, and in five of those uses, ha-satan is used to describe <u>not</u> an immortal demon, but rather "a human being who is a military, political, or legal enemy of Israel."[411] And the snake in Genesis was just a clever snake.

References to the Christian Satan occur in the New Testament 34 times; half in the gospels and half in the epistles and Book of Revelation.[412] Satan is nothing more than a religious version of the Bogeyman, designed to frighten adults. The problem is that the concept of the Christian Satan appears illogical to many people. Christians believe that Satan is the enemy of their omniscient and omnipotent God; but being omniscient, their God would already know what Satan would try to do; and being omnipotent, he would have the power to destroy him. But he did not, and he has not. If Satan is the root of all ills that beset humans, then the Christian God is responsible for the consequences. For his inaction, God would be grossly negligent. It is no different than your local police force being aware that a serial criminal resides at 123 Elm Street in your town, yet refusing to arrest him, no matter how many times the criminal strikes.

The Hell Invention

The very concept of Hell is in direct contrast to the idea that the divine creator is a God of love. We humans are in a mortal existence of relatively short time spans; any mistakes made in our brief existence do not deserve an eternity of punishment. Indeed, early Christianity generally believed that when a person died, if deserving, then their soul entered the Kingdom of God; and if they were not deserving, they just ceased to exist. Until the late 6th century, there was no concept of an everlasting, fiery Hell as we know it today.

Ambiguities and mistranslations from Greek in New Testament passages have led to significant disagreement among Christians. However, most acknowledge that Pope St. Gregory I (C. 590 – 604), was one of the earliest RCC leaders to discuss Hell as a place of everlasting anguish in his Dialogues, Chapters 42 – 44.[413] The RCC soon learned that fear was a great tool for the control of desperate people. Indeed, the fire and brimstone teachings prevalent in Evangelical Churches today stem from and have their origin in Gregory I's branding of Hell. Later, Dante Alighieri's (1265-1321) *Divine Comedy* (Inferno was the first of the three-part epic poem) was completed in 1320, and the RCC discovered that the threat of Hell was a great control mechanism. Later, many of the Protestant sects used Hell in a similar way.

But there is no basis for Hell. The RCC created a fear-based view where believers were held strictly accountable in their short mortal lifespan and could be eternally enslaved in death. And no proof of Hell was necessary; just fear of it kept people in line. After all, fear is the ultimate weapon of control. But it is all a scam! The fear of Hell has no control once people think for themselves and realize that they have no reason to fear its existence.

There are alternative views, however. Pope John Paul II stated in 1999, "Hell is not a place of fire and eternal suffering."[414] [415] He described Hell as a separation from God, and only symbolically described as a fiery place of torment... He referred to the descriptions of torment as "improper use of Biblical images." And Pope Francis I stated in 2016, "Hell is not 'a torture chamber.' Rather, it is the horror of being separated forever from the "God who loves us so much."[416]

One can argue that the concept of Hell is completely incompatible with Yeshua's message. Paul of Tarsus, a key inventor of the Christian religion, never mentioned Hell. And Hell as a place of torment is not in the Bible – anywhere! In the Old Testament, the Hebrew word *Sheol* (which occurs in 65 instances) simply means place of the dead, just like the Greek *Hades*. It has been mistranslated as Hell. Indeed, that is true of the King James Version of the Bible, which translates *Sheol* as "Hell." Most modern translations do not make that mistake.

Another term that has been mistranslated is the Greek word Gehenna, which is used 11 times in the New Testament, but it refers to a garbage dump outside of Jerusalem. It comes from the Hebrew *Ge Hinnom* (Valley of Hinnom), which the Jews of the 1st century believed was a place of child sacrifice in times long past their era. By Jesus' time, it was seen as a cursed place. But it was still only a garbage dump, and it was <u>not</u> a place of eternal suffering. In the New Testament, the New International Version, New Living Translation Version, and New American Standard Bible (among others) mistranslate *Gehenna* as "Hell". However, as previously stated, if translated accurately from the Greek, no reference to Hell is found in the New Testament anywhere. "Hell is a terrible mythology that must be eradicated from human consciousness."[417]

And while we are on the topic, why would a loving deity want any of mankind to suffer at all? To prove our commitment and our faith? If our deity is kind and wants only the best for us, then suffering through all of life's trials seems rather perverse. So, we convince ourselves that we suffer in our current, ephemeral life so that we will have it so much better in the spiritual life that awaits us? Maybe, if it is true, but doubtful, as it is very unlikely.

Chapter Summary

Christianity is based on certain assertions, even though none of them are objectively provable. Many Christians see the New Testament as a fulfillment of the prophecies of the Old Testament. Indeed, Christianity made itself dependent on Judaism to validate its beliefs and help to establish its credibility. To borrow a term from today's media, this is a "retroactive reconstruction," also called retroactive continuity,[418] whereby the gospel writers cherry-picked Old Testament prophecies against which they attempted to recontextualize in the life of Jesus. They effectively attempted to adapt the life of Jesus to manipulate and fulfill these cherry-picked OT prophecies. However, many of the OT prophecies cited as examples are not actually referring to the Messiah, and those that are do not refer to Jesus of Nazareth. None of Jesus' miracles were verified; nothing about his divinity has been proven. The validity of the religious claims doesn't match the historical reality.

There were many additional prophecies in the New Testament, and they were not fulfilled either. The prediction that the generation to whom Jesus spoke would not pass away prior to the Second Coming [**Matthew 23:36 and Luke 9:27**] never occurred. The prediction that Jesus would spend three days and three nights in a tomb [**Matthew 12:40**] did not happen (it was actually two days and two nights; and Matthew's "prediction" was made many decades after the event had already occurred). And Jesus has failed to respond to many Christians who asked for things in his name. [**John 14:13-14**]. The many false prophecies cast doubt on all claims in the entire Bible

While many Christians perceive the OT as an allegory, they desperately want to believe that the NT is the absolute truth! But the lax methods and cult of personality (i.e., regarding Bishop Athanasius) used by the early Christian Church to collect, vet, approve, and canonize its NT Scriptures in the late 4th century resulted in books containing forgeries and lies being included in what some refer to as the "holy text." Just look at the way the story of Jesus has been contrived and distorted – his name, place of birth, his years of ministry, the type of cross he was nailed to, his death, and burial. There is absolutely no evidence of his resurrection and ascension. The statements attesting to his divinity are nothing more than hearsay.

The earliest Christian narratives are the letters (epistles) of Paul (alias Saul of Tarsus) – a man who never met Jesus, who did not mention a single action or sermon of Jesus, and who wrote of him as if he were a spiritual figure, not a man of flesh and blood who was a doer of deeds. Paul was followed, decades later, by the gospels, which are not history; but instead, they are exaggerated, religious propaganda, as they were written to inspire, without the constraint of accuracy.

Most biblical scholars agree that the Synoptic Gospels were written in the late 1st century or early 2nd century by non-witnesses. Thus, the entire premise that the New Testament is a collection of the teachings of Jesus of Nazareth is invalid. Texts written decades after a series of events took place, written by writers who did not witness the events, nor who have any original scripts from the events, would be of little value to independent thinkers in our modern world. This mistake-ridden book of hearsay does not appear to have been inspired by any deity. The gospels are not records of historical events, and they were written with exaggeration and propaganda during an era when fables were commonly exchanged and elaborated, written for illiterate, superstitious audiences who were susceptible to belief in such myths.

It can be distressing to discover that what we have always accepted in Scripture to be true is not remotely accurate. While it is difficult to accept for many Christians who have been indoctrinated into their belief system, the reality remains: no one who ever met Jesus of Nazareth wrote about him; and no one who ever wrote about him had met him! Nor did Jesus himself write any texts regarding his own thoughts. If Jesus of Nazareth were truly the Son of God, he might have provided us with his own flawless, unambiguous writings and guidance. Obviously, that did not happen!

---

[294] Provided by Matthew McGee, "Chronology of Apostle Paul's Journey and Epistles," Chronology of Apostle Paul's Journeys and Epistles (matthewmcgee.org); www.matthewmcgee.org/paultime.html

[295] "Which Letters did Paul Write?" SATA; https://sats.ac.za/blog/2021/03/01/which-letters-did-paul-write/#:~:text=The%20implication%20is%20that%20the,deutero%2DPauline%20letters%20(lit. An article reciting work from Mark A. Powell, Introducing the New Testament. A Historical, Literary, and Theological Survey. 2nd ed. 2018;

[296] "Differences Between Gospels and Epistles, " Religions Wiki;
https://religions.wiki/index.php/Differences_between_the_Gospels_and_the_epistles

[297] "The Gentile mission and St. Paul," Britannica;
https://www.britannica.com/topic/Christianity/The-contemporary-social-religious-and-intellectual-world

[298] Bishop John S. Spong, Rescuing the Bible from Fundamentalism, p. 104, Harper San Francisco, 1991

[299] "George Bernard Shaw Quotes," AZ Quotes; https://www.azquotes.com/quote/1032521

[300] Bob Seidensticker, "What Did Paul Know About Jesus? Not Much" Patheos; Dec 17, 2012; updated Jan 7, 2015. https://www.patheos.com/blogs/crossexamined/2012/12/what-did-paul-know-about-jesus-not-much/

[301] Elaine Pagels, Ibid

[302] Kathy Benjamin, "The Untold Truth of the Book of Revelation," Grunge; Aug 14, 2021; https://www.grunge.com/150322/the-untold-truth-of-the-book-of-revelation/?utm_campaign=clip

[303] "367 Athanasius Defines the New Testament," Christian History Institute; https://christianhistoryinstitute.org/magazine/article/athanasius-defines-new-testament

[304] Carsen Peter Thiede, "367 Athanasius Defines New Testament," Christian History Institute; https://christianhistoryinstitute.org/magazine/article/athanasius-defines-new-testament Note: Dr. Carsten Peter Thiede lives in West Germany and is a member of the advisory board of Christian History.

[305] The term "canon", which is Greed for a "rule" or "standard," when applied to the Bible, it denotes the collection of books that are accepted as authoritative.

[306] Alan M. Linfield, "Notes and Queries," Guardian.co.uk;
https://www.theguardian.com/notesandqueries/query/0,5753,-

1885,00.html#:~:text=Their%20eventual%20exclusion%20was%20not,too%20shallow%20in%20spiritual%20content.

[307] "Who decided which books to include in the Bible?", July 9, 2022; Biblword; https://www.biblword.net/who-decided-which-books-to-include-in-the-bible/

[308] Ibid.

[309] "Athanasius Lists the New Testament Writings," Grace Communion International; https://www.gci.org/articles/athanasius-lists-the-new-testament-writings/

[310] Keith Long, "The Canonical vs. Non-Canonical Gospels: Why Some Books Didn't Make the Cut," Bart Ehrman Blog; Dec 1, 2022; https://www.bartehrman.com/canonical-vs-non-canonical-gospels/

[311] Keith Long, "The Canonical vs. Non-Canonical Gospels: Why Some Books Didn't Make the," BartEhrman.com; https://www.bartehrman.com/canonical-vs-non-canonical-gospels/

[312] Ibid

[313] "Bauer thesis," Religions Wiki; https://religions.wiki/index.php/Bauer_thesis

[314] "Gospels: Their Meaning, Purpose, and Similarities and Differences," Facts and Details; https://europe.factsanddetails.com/article/entry-638.html

[315] Strobel, Lee. The Case for Christ; p. 26; Zondervan, 1998.

[316] D.M. Murdock/Acharya S, "When Were the Gospels Written," Stellar House Archives; https://stellarhousepublishing.com/gospel-dates/

[317] Tenney, Merrill C. New Testament Survey, p. 102, Michigan: Wm. B. Eerdmans Publishing Company, 1985.

[318] Allyson Holland, "A Biblical Guide to the 12 Disciples of Jesus," Crosswalk; Updated Oct 10, 2024; https://www.crosswalk.com/faith/bible-study/who-were-the-12-disciples-and-what-should-we-know-about-them.html

[319] "Synoptic Gospels," New World Encyclopedia; https://www.newworldencyclopedia.org/entry/Synoptic_Gospels

[320] Mournet, Terence C. Oral Tradition and Literary Dependency: Variability and Stability in the Synoptic Tradition and Q. (2005). pp. 54–99; ISBN 9783161484544.

[321] Robert W. Funk, and Roy W. Hoover; The Five Gospels; Harper; San Francisco. 1993. "Introduction," pp. 1–30.

[322] Terence C. Mournet, Oral Tradition and Literary Dependency: Variability and Stability in the Synoptic Tradition and Q; 2005; pp. 192–286. ISBN 9783161484544.

[323] "Why Are There Four Gospels?" Christianity.com; Feb 4, 2024; https://www.christianity.com/jesus/is-jesus-god/the-gospels/why-are-there-four-gospels.html

[324] Frank Zindler, "Did Jesus Exist?" American Atheists; https://www.atheists.org/activism/resources/did-jesus-exist/ ; reprinted from the Summer 1998 edition of American Atheist magazine.

[325] Frank Zindler, Ibid.

[326] Jimmy Akin, "A Fake Resurrection in Mark's Gospel?" Catholic Answers; https://www.catholic.com/magazine/online-edition/a-fake-resurrection-in-marks-gospel

[327] Michele Gama Sosa, "The Biggest Differences Among the Gospels," Oct 24, 2022; Grunge; https://www.grunge.com/1068628/the-biggest-differences-between-the-gospels/

[328] Sosa, Ibid.

[329] Ibid

[330] Gary Cottrell, "Who wrote Luke and Acts?" World Press; Feb 14, 2012; https://garycottrell.wordpress.com/2012/02/14/who-wrote-luke-and-acts/

[331] Greg Boyd, "Is the Book of Acts Reliable?" Re/Knew; Dec 20, 2018; https://reknew.org/2018/12/is-the-book-of-acts-reliable/

[332] Charles Waite, History of the Christian Religion to the Year Two Hundred; Oregon: Dr. Carroll Bierbower, 1992. 385-6. Waite notes that the German critic Schleiermacher determined Luke's Gospel to have been compiled from 33 different manuscripts, and he shows the very divisions upon which these are delineated (Waite, 379-380).

[333] D.M. Murdock/Acharya S, "When Were the Gospels Written," Stellar House Publishing; https://stellarhousepublishing.com/the-gospel-dates-when-were-the-gospels-written/

[334] Carrier, Richard, "Luke and Josephus," The Secular Web; 2000; www.infidels.org/library/modern/richard_carrier/lukeandjosephus.html

[335] "Irenaeus of Lyon Insists on Only Four Gospels," HistoryofInformation.com; https://www.historyofinformation.com/detail.php?entryid=190

[336] Candida Moss, "Everyone's Favorite Gospel is a Forgery," Published on Mar 14, 2020; The Daily Beast; https://www.thedailybeast.com/everyones-favorite-gospel-the-gospel-of-john-is-a-forgery-according-to-new-research/

[337] Hugo Mendez," Did the Johannine Community Exist?" Journal for the Study of the New Testament, Volume 42, Issue 3, Mar 2, 2020. [Abstract in Sage Journals]. https://journals.sagepub.com/doi/full/10.1177/0142064X19890490

[338] Ibid.

[339] "Was the Bible's Gospel of John author fake?" University of North Carolina at Chapel Hill; March 9, 2020; https://college.unc.edu/2020/03/gospel-of-john/

[340] Hugo Mendez, "Did the Johannine Community Exist?", Ibid.

[341] Ibid

[342] Candida Moss, "Everyone's Favorite Gospel is a Forgery," Updated Mar 14, 2020; Daily Beast; https://www.thedailybeast.com/everyones-favorite-gospel-the-gospel-of-john-is-a-forgery-according-to-new-research/

[343] "The St. John Fragment," HistoryofInformation.com; https://historyofinformation.com/detail.php?id=1410#:~:text=Dating

[344] "The Use and Abuse of P52: Papyrological Pitfalls in the Dating of the Fourth Gospel," Brent Nongbri, Harvard Theological Review, Cambridge University Press: **02 August 2005;** https://www.cambridge.org/core/journals/harvard-theological-review/article/abs/use-and-abuse-of-p52-papyrological-pitfalls-in-the-dating-of-the-fourth-gospel/676A4EA909EB03046F89DB8CE1F050BE

[345] "St. Polycarp,' Encyclopedia Britannica; https://www.britannica.com/biography/Saint-Polycarp

[346] "Epistle of Polycarp to the Philippians; New Advent, https://www.newadvent.org/fathers/0136.htm

[347] "The Gospels are Finally Named! Irenaeus of Lyons," The Bart Ehrman Blog; Nov 18, 2024; https://ehrmanblog.org/the-gospels-are-finally-named-irenaeus-of-lyons/

[348] "St. Clement of Alexandria," Encyclopedia Britannica, Titus Flavius Clemens, or Clement of Alexandria, was a Christian apologist and missionary theologian in the late 2nd and early 3rd centuries.

[349] "Tatian," New World Encyclopedia; https://www.newworldencyclopedia.org/entry/Tatian

[350] D.M. Murdock/Acharya S, "When Were the Gospels Written," Stellar House Publishing; https://stellarhousepublishing.com/the-gospel-dates-when-were-the-gospels-written/

[351] Candida Moss, "Everyone's Favorite Gospel is a Forgery," Daily Beast; updated Mar 14, 2020; https://www.thedailybeast.com/everyones-favorite-gospel-the-gospel-of-john-is-a-forgery-according-to-new-research/

[352] Ibid

[353] "John and 'the Gnostics'," Oxford Academic; March 2004; https://academic.oup.com/book/32575/chapter-abstract/270378938?redirectedFrom=fulltext

[354] Rebecca Denova, "Gnosticism," World History Encyclopedia; 09 April 2021; https://www.worldhistory.org/Gnosticism/

[355] James M. West, "Gnostic Enigmas in the Gospel of John," Gnostic Sophistries; August, 2012; https://ogdoas.wordpress.com/2012/08/13/gnostic-enigmas-in-the-gospel-of-john/

[356] Irenaeus of Lyons, Ex Fontibus Company, Alexander Roberts (editor); Against Heresies, – March 28, 2012; https://www.earlychristianwritings.com/text/irenaeus-book1.html

[357] Irenaeus of Lyons, vol. 1, Ibid; p. 328

[358] "The Pleroma and the Aeons," Gnosticism Explained; https://gnosticismexplained.org/the-pleroma-and-the-aeons/]

[359] James M. West, "Gnostic Enigmas in the Gospel of John," Gnostic Sophistries; WordPress.com; revised Dec 20, 2023; https://ogdoas.wordpress.com/2012/08/13/gnostic-enigmas-in-the-gospel-of-john/

360 Ibid.

361 Ibid

362 Rebecca Denova, "Origins of Christian Antisemitism in the Gospels," World History Encyclopedia; Nov 28, 2023; https://www.worldhistory.org/article/2335/origins-of-christian-antisemitism-in-the-gospels/

363 Michele Gama Sosa, "The Biggest Differences Between the Gospels," updated Feb 28, 2023; Grunge; https://www.grunge.com/1068628/the-biggest-differences-between-the-gospels/

364 Lillian C. Freudmann, Anti-Semitism in the New Testament; University Press of America, Inc.; Lanham, MD; 1994

365 "Antisemitism in the New Testament." Religion Wiki; https://religion.fandom.com/wiki/Antisemitism_in_the_New_Testament;

366 Theophilus Josiah, "Contradiction of John," Issues with John.com; https://issueswithjohn.com/contradictions-of-john/

367 Theophilus Josiah "Embellishments of John," Issues with John.com; https://issueswithjohn.com/embellishments-of-john/

368 Excerpt from Bart D. Ehrman, Jesus, interrupted: Revealing the Hidden Contradictions in the Bible (and Why We Don't Know About Them); HarperOne; 2009

369 Bart D. Ehrman, Ibid.

370 "Is the New Testament the Preserved Word of God?" Many Prophets Message, https://manyprophetsonemessage.com/2013/12/09/is-the-new-testament-the-preserved-word-of-god/

371 Brent Nongbri, "The Twenty-first Chapter of the Gospel According to John", Variant Readings; October 6, 2018; https://brentnongbri.com/2018/10/06/the-twenty-first-chapter-of-the-gospel-according-to-john/#:~:text=I%20think%20it%27s%20fair%20to,existed%20at%20an%20earlier%20period

372 Many Prophets One Message, "Ten Reasons Why We Must Reject the Gospel of John," May 12, 2015; https://www.manyprophetsonemessage.com/2015/05/12/ten-reasons-why-we-must-reject-the-gospel-of-john/

373 Benito Cereno, "The Most Controversial Books That Were Included in the Bible," Jan 7, 2020; Grunge.com; https://www.grunge.com/182424/the-most-controversial-books-that-were-included-in-the-bible/

374 Ibid.

375 Elaine Pagels, Revelations: Visions, Prophecy & Politics in the Book of Revelation.

376 John Blake, CNN, "4 big myths of Book of Revelation," https://signposts02.wordpress.com/2013/01/08/4-big-myths-of-book-of-revelation/

377 Elaine Pagels, Ibid.

378 "St Athanasius," Encyclopedia Britannica; https://www.britannica.com/biography/Saint-Athanasius

379 Elaine Pagels, Ibid.

380 Elaine Pagels, Ibid.

381 Kathy Benjamin, "The Untold Truth of the Book of Revelation," Grunge; https://www.grunge.com/150322/the-untold-truth-of-the-book-of-revelation/

382 Andries Van Niekerk, "Athanasius was Justly Deposed for Violence," From Daniel to Revelation, Mar 2020; https://revelationbyjesuschrist.com/athanasius-excommunicated/

383 Elaine Pages, Ibid

384 Adam Gopnik, "The Big Reveal," The New Yorker, Feb 27, 2012; https://www.newyorker.com/magazine/2012/03/05/big-reveal

385 Kathy Benjamin, "The Untold Truth of the Book of Revelation," Grunge; August 14, 2021; https://www.grunge.com/150322/the-untold-truth-of-the-book-of-revelation/

386 Amy Sullivan, "Are Texas Schools Forcing Students to Bear the Mark of the Antichrist?" New Republic, November 27, 2012; https://newrepublic.com/article/110542/barcode-mark-beast-resurfaces-texas

387 Mike Winger, "Stop your 'Mark of the Beast' Nonsense," YouTube, June 2022.

388 Gethsemane Church, "Cryptocurrency & the Mark of the Beast," Medium, Sep 17, 2024; https://medium.com/@thegethsemanechurch/cryptocurrency-the-mark-of-the-beast-84fee9f8f9ca

389 "Bitcoin and the Mark of the Beast," Christian Evidence; Dec 29, 2017; https://www.christianevidence.net/2017/12/is-bitcoin-mark-of-beast.html

390 Steve Shives, "Five Stupid Things About the Mark of the Beast," YouTube, January 2014

391 "Miracles," Standford Encyclopedia of Philosophy; revised May 2024; https://plato.stanford.edu/entries/miracles/

392 Lawrence Shapiro, The Miracle Myth: Why Belief in the Resurrection and the Supernatural Is Unjustified; 2016; New York, Columbia University Press

393 Edited by Daniel von Wachter, "Hume's Arguments against Miracles," https://philpapers.org/browse/humes-argument-against-miracles

394 "Miracles," Internet Encyclopedia of Philosophy; https://iep.utm.edu/miracles/

395 Credited to William of Ockham (circa 1287–1347), an English Franciscan friar

396 "Occam's Razor," Britannica; https://www.britannica.com/topic/Occams-razor

397 Richard Dawkins, "Why is Occam's Razor not the starting point of any discussion about religion?" Richard Dawkins Foundation for Reason and Science; Sep 2012; https://richarddawkins.net/2012/09/why-is-occams-razor-not-the-starting-point-of-any-discussion-about-religion/

398 Christopher Hitchens, God is Not Great: How Religion Poisons Everything (New York, NY: Atlantic Books, 2008), p. 150.

399 "The Sagan Standard: Extraordinary Claims Require Extraordinary Evidence," Effectiviology; https://effectiviology.com/sagan-standard-extraordinary-claims-require-extraordinary-evidence/

400 Adam Hayes, "Bayes' Theorem: What It Is, the Formula, and Examples"; Investopedia; March 2024; https://www.investopedia.com/terms/b/bayes-theorem.asp.

401 John W. Loftus, "What's Wrong with Using Bayes' Theorem on Miracles?" Jan 2022; The Secular Web; https://infidels.org/kiosk/article/whats-wrong-with-bayes-theorem/

402 Loftus, Ibid.

403 "Jesus did not die for your sins," The Church of Truth; https://thechurchoftruth.org/jesus-did-not-die-for-your-sins/

404 Rudolph Bultmann, "New Testament and Mythology", in Kerygma and Myth: A Theological Debate; p. 5; H.W. Bartsch (ed), R.H. Fuller (trans). New York: Harper & Row, 1961; https://www.religion-online.org/book/kerygma-and-myth/

405 Many Prophets One Message, "Does the New Testament Contain Contradictions?", Jan 16,2014, https://manyprophetsonemessage.com/2014/01/16/does-the-new-testament-contain-contradictions/

406 Many Prophets One Message, "Is the New Testament the Preserved Word of God?", Dec 9, 2013 https://www.manyprophetsonemessage.com/2013/12/09/is-the-new-testament-the-preserved-word-of-god/

407 "Origen," Britannica; https://www.britannica.com/biography/Origen

408 Bruce Metzger, The Text of the New Testament: Its Transmission, Corruption, and Restoration, 4th edition (2005), p. 200

409 Alan F. Johnson, The IVP New Testament Commentary Series; 1 Corinthians (InterVarsity Press, Downers Grove, IL, 2004), p. 271.

410 Richard Hays, Interpretation: A Bible Commentary for Teaching and Preaching; "1 Corinthians" (John Knox Press, Louisville, KY, 1997), p. 247

411 Stephanie Hertzenberg, "Is Satan in the Old Testament?" Belief Net; https://www.beliefnet.com/faiths/christianity/is-satan-in-the-old-testament.aspx

412 Joel Beeke, "Satan in the New Testament," Reformation Heritage Books; https://joelbeeke.org/satan-in-the-new-testament/

413 Gregory the Great, Dialogues (1911) Book 4. pp. 177-258; https://www.tertullian.org/fathers/gregory_04_dialogues_book4.htm#C44

414 John Paul II, General Audience at the Vatican, 28 July, 1999. https://www.vatican.va/content/john-paul-ii/en/audiences/1999/documents/hf_jp-ii_aud_28071999.html

[415] "Pope John Paul II Rejects Reality of a Literal Hell,"
https://www.ovrlnd.com/Cults/poprejectshell.html

[416] Tom Nash, "Did the Pope Really Say Hell Doesn't Exist?" Catholic Answers;
https://www.catholic.com/qa/did-the-pope-really-say-hell-doesnt-exist

[417] R C Hogan, "Yeshua and Hell," Yeshua Before 30 CE; 2006; https://30ce.com/jesusonhell.htm

[418] Retroactive continuity refers to a literary device in which the form or content of a previously established narrative is changed. "A Short History of 'Retcon'," Merriam-Webster;
https://www.merriam-webster.com/wordplay/retcon-history-and-meaning

Chapter 5 – History of Catholicism and its Popes

During the past 2,000 years in which the papal system underwent extensive evolution, the Roman Catholic Church (RCC) has significantly impacted Western history, and it has directed its huge influence well beyond its religious sphere. At times, it preserved important knowledge through its monastic scriptura;[419] other times, it stifled freedom of thought and intellectual achievement. It played a substantial role in crafting the Renaissance, as the Church maintained libraries, provided education, and sponsored paintings and sculptures. On the other hand, it has severely hindered scientific advancements, and it has promoted violence, torture, and war against those who were not in full alignment with its specific orthodoxy. Note: the term, Roman Catholic, did not come into popular use until the 17th century, and the RCC didn't use that term for itself until the 20th century.

This chapter's focus on the popes is due to the doctrine of the Catholic Church that the pope is the "Vicar of Christ" on Earth, and he can exercise his supreme power over the entire Christian Church. The term, Vicar, refers to a representative, deputy, or substitute; anyone acting "in the person of" or agent for a superior. The concept of "papal supremacy" dates to the 6th century, after the fall of the Western Roman Empire and the rise of the bishops of Rome as the rulers of Christendom. Thus, a study of the popes reveals how these men have shaped the Catholic Church and ruled as God's representatives on Earth. For convenience, we can present the approximately 300 Popes (264 popes and 40 antipopes) in six major eras or "ages," which align to key events in European and world history.

The origin of the term, bishop, is obscure, but it generally refers to the pastoral leader of a given Christian group. Over time, as the bishop of Rome assumed supremacy in the Church, the position became known as the pope.[420] The office of the pope is referred to as the papacy, and his ecclesiastical[421] the jurisdiction is called the Apostolic See.[422]

Christianity began as a Jewish sect, and its center of gravity, or home base, was Jerusalem, not Rome, the latter of which was one of the first gentile cities to develop a significant following. However, when Jerusalem was destroyed in 70 CE by the Roman Imperator (Commander), Titus (thereafter to become the Roman Emperor in 81 CE), the prime locale of the Christian Church gradually shifted to Rome, which was the center of the empire; and due to the efforts of St. Paul (Saul of Tarsus) and his followers, it shifted to the gentiles. Over the first three centuries (and well beyond), the Church devoted much of its attention to combating the numerous perceived heresies it encountered. This refers to any belief or theory that is strongly at variance with established beliefs or customs, particularly the accepted orthodoxy of Christianity.

Movement Toward Papal Supremacy

Over time the Roman Church developed a reputation with other churches for doctrinal correctness. To be more accurate, the Church of Rome simply ended up on the majority side of most issues, as the Church leaders often decided their beliefs via voting at councils. There were also other key regional churches, such as in Antioch, Alexandria, and Constantinople. The leaders at these locations were referred to as patriarchs; it was a title that Rome avoided in favor of the title, bishop. Even in the early Church, there were several attempts at manifestations of Roman ecclesiastic authority over other churches. As early as 195 CE, Bishop Victor of Rome tried unsuccessfully to exercise his self-appointed authority over other churches by excommunicating[423] the Quartodecimans, a group of bishops led by Polycrates of Ephesus, for their mistake in observing Easter on the same date as the Jewish Passover. However, the rest of the Church felt that Bishop Victor's punishment was too harsh, and Bishop Victor was compelled to relent.

But there continued to be pushback against the bishops of Rome. In the mid-3rd century, Stephen tried to assert his doctrinal authority as bishop of Rome, but other bishops weren't having it. Bishop Cyprian in North Africa argued, "You are Peter…" [NT reference, **Matthew 16: 18-19**] was not a charter of supreme leadership, but it applied to all bishops. At the Third Council of Carthage (256 CE), Bishop Cyprian asserted that the Bishop of Rome should not consider himself a "bishop of bishops". While Bishop Cyprian was prophetic in his assertions regarding the bishop of Rome, the Council of Nicea[424] (325 CE) would further solidify Rome's ascendancy to Christian leadership.

One of the key underpinnings of Catholicism is the role of the pope. Catholics believe that the pope is head of the Catholic Church on Earth. Among other things, it means that he can set forth Church rules, even if those rules are not supported in Scripture (e.g., the Marian dogmas and priest celibacy). And as of 1870, the Pope can speak *ex cathedra* (with infallibility) on matters of faith and dogma (as can the magisterium, consisting of bishops and popes together as the official teaching authority of the RCC). There are several claimants to using the name, pope, for the first time. We will discuss those in a moment. First, let's discuss who was <u>not</u> the first pope, not even the first bishop of Rome.

The RCC twisted the connection with the apostle Peter, as the first bishop of Rome, to validate their giving so much authority, and ultimately power, to the papacy.[425] Catholics want to believe that St. Peter was the first pope, and they are taught it is so by Church tradition. However, anytime the Catholic Church declares something is "Church tradition", it usually means that the Church lacks hard evidence. After all, according to tradition, St. Patrick drove the snakes out of Ireland, and no one truly believes that story either.

Scripture says nothing about Peter being the head of the Church on Earth. However, there is a reference to Jesus being head of the Church [in **Ephesians 1:22-23, 5:23;** and **Colossians 1:18**]. Moreover, Paul teaches that Christ, not Peter, is the foundation of the Church [**1 Corinthians 3:11**]. It all comes down to a purposeful misunderstanding of the words from **Matthew 16:18-19**, stating that Peter was the rock upon which Jesus would build his church.[426] But it is doubtful that Peter, as the Christian leader, is the meaning of this verse; and there is no other evidence supporting Peter. According to **Matthew 18:18**, the teachings of all the apostles were equally accepted and binding, and that they had no leader other than Jesus of Nazareth. Thus, Peter had no authority over the other apostles. And frankly, this story gets even more contrived.

Peter and the other disciples were not Christians. They were Jews who followed the teaching of the Rabbi Yeshua (Jesus) of Nazareth. Moreover, there is no historical evidence that Peter ever went to Rome, much less was martyred in Rome; and he certainly was never a Christian bishop. The Book of Acts is silent about Peter. Paul makes no mention in his epistles of Peter being in Rome, and for good reason – because he wasn't there!

Nevertheless, the Catholic Church declared that "by tradition" Peter was the first bishop of Rome, based on the writing found only in **Matthew 16: 18-19** as interpreted by the Roman Catholic Church; and thus, Peter and his successors were to be the representatives of Jesus on Earth. That said, the Christian patriarchs in other cities challenged that assertion.

A letter attributed to the bishop of Rome, St. Linus, referred to the martyrdom of Peter and Paul; however, this letter turned out to be a 6th-century forgery.[427] This begs the question as to why the RCC thought it was necessary to create a false report about those respective 'martyrdoms.'

Initially, the Christian community was relatively informal; but all organized religions tend to gravitate to a growing power structure and vertical hierarchy. There were many external persecutions, heresies, and other challenges to adjudicate; and so over time, the bishop of Rome became a key unifying figure for the Christians. When the bishop of Rome, Stephen (254 – 257), put forth the idea that he had primacy over the other bishops, the bishops of Caesarea (Bishop Firmilian) and Carthage (Bishop Cyprian) soundly rejected Bishop Stephen's claim. At the Council of Carthage (256), Cyprian had strongly asserted that bishops of Rome should not strive to exercise "tyrannical" powers.[428] [429] But when Emperor Constantine had declared in the Edict of Milan that Christians had the official freedom to worship and the Council of Nicea in 325 established the key tenets of religious belief, the bishop of Rome's influence grew, even though he did not convene or lead the council. Later, another bishop of Rome, Leo I (440 – 462)[430], tried to use **Matthew 16:19** to affirm his primacy over the other bishops.

These claims of superiority of the bishops of Rome were continually challenged by the patriarchs of Constantinople. But such claims were one of many irritants between the East and West. In 1054, Eastern Orthodoxy would separate from Roman jurisdiction in the Great Schism.

Over time, the Church's doctrine of "papal supremacy" established the pope as the pastor of the entire Roman Catholic Church, and this doctrine effectively decreed that the pope has full, supreme, and universal power over the entire Church. The term papal supremacy dates back to the 6th century, and it co-existed with the rise of the bishops of Rome to not just their ecclesiastic authority over Catholicism; but it gained consideration to be the ultimate power within the Christian community, which at the time, was referred to as Christendom.[431]

The term "Pontifex Maximus" was a term used by the pagan priests of Rome, and it came to be associated with the emperors of Rome. According to the Byzantine historian Zosimus, in 381, Emperor Gratian (367 to 383), chose to reject the title[432] and its cloak of office as impious, because he was a Christian emperor; and he didn't feel that the title was appropriate for him.[433] Bishop of Rome Damasus (366-384) had no such qualms, and he took the title; but it was his successor, Siricius (384-399 A. D.), who used the appellation of Pontifex Maximus and its derivative term, pontiff, as "a distinctive title".[434]

Roman bishops quickly adopted the worldly pretensions of the Roman emperors for pomp and rituals. Pope Gregory I (590 – 604) asserted in the 590s that "the care of the whole church" had been placed in the hands of Peter and his successors in Rome (i.e., to himself). Throughout the first seven centuries, some non-Roman bishops applied the term, papa, or pope, to themselves. However, in 1075, Pope Gregory VII declared in his *Dictatus papae* (Papal Dictates) that the term, pope, was exclusively reserved for bishops of Rome;[435] and he asserted his power to depose emperors and kings. *Dictatus papae* stated that the pope "indubitably becomes holy through the merits of the blessed Peter."[436]

During the reign of Pope Innocent III (1198–1216), a power-hungry pontiff who viewed his authority through a far-reaching lens, the title "vicar of Peter" was transitioned to "vicar of Christ."[437] Between the 11th and 14th centuries, the Roman papacy became head of the Church in a very imperial fashion, a development that pushed titles of papal power to a new level of institutional structure, far removed from their scriptural foundations. Thus, the pope not only served as the head of Roman Catholic Christianity, but he was viewed as the leader of Christendom throughout medieval Europe.[438]

So why did the Catholic Church insist on tying things back to Peter? Because the Church believed it gave them a cornerstone of legitimacy in connecting with Yeshua of Nazareth, and it provided a justification for the supremacy of each succeeding bishop of Rome. And thus, the Catholic Church formulated its connection with the apostle Peter to give itself power. The Church of Rome maneuvered to gain power over other churches. But it was the prestige of the city of Rome in the Christian world that positioned the bishop of Rome (otherwise referred to as the Pope) as the leader of the Catholic Church. The latter *flipped the script* to try to gain legitimacy in order to promote the concept of the supremacy of papal authority. That said, today the pope has a level of authority that has no basis in any manuscripts mentioned in or as part of the New Testament.

	Evolution of Papal Primacy	
Year(s) CE	**Occurrence**	
195	Bishop Victor of Rome tried unsuccessfully to exercise his self-appointed authority over other churches by excommunicating the Quartodecimans.	
254-257	Bishop Stephen of Rome tried to advance the claim of doctrinal authority over the entire Church, but the patriarchs of Carthage and Caesarea rejected Stephen's claim.	
384	Pope Siricius used the appellation of Pontifex Maximus as "a distinctive title", and its derivative term, pontiff.	
590s	Pope Gregory I asserted that "the care of the whole church" had been placed in the hands of Peter and his successors in Rome.	
1075	Pope Gregory VII declared in his Dictatus papae (Papal Dictates) that the term, pope, was exclusively reserved for bishops of Rome; and he asserted his power to depose emperors and kings.	
1200	Pope Innocent III (1198–1216) transitioned his title from "vicar of Peter" to "vicar of Christ."	
1870	At the instigation of Pope Pius IX, the First Vatican Council decreed that the Roman pontiff speaks with infallibility on matters of faith and morals.	

Papal Infallibility

Alongside the evolution of Roman and papal primary is the concept of papal infallibility. In the 21st century, infallibility is defined as being "exempt from error in judgment, knowledge, or opinion."[439] The origin of this concept was not dogmatic, nor even ecclesiastic; instead, it was firmly rooted in the insecurities of a cleric of the Franciscans, a Roman Catholic religious order founded in the early 13th century. Pope Nicholas III's father was Matteo Rosso,[440] of the Orsini family, who was a close friend of St. Francis Assisi, the founder of the Franciscans. Pope Nicholas issued many of his bulls and letters on the topic of the Franciscans,[441] including the idea of apostolic poverty, whereby the papacy would own all the Franciscans' wealth. The theory of a specific papal infallibility was first raised by the Franciscan philosopher, Pietro Olivi (c. 1248-1298). He argued that Saint Francis' teaching on poverty exemplified the lifestyle that Christ taught the apostles. Pope Nicholas III (1277-1280) was persuaded to issue the bull, *Exiit qui seminat* (1279), which stated that it was an official teaching of the Roman Church that the Franciscan way was the way of Christ. Olivi maintained that no subsequent pope could change the teaching of Nicholas III on the superiority of Franciscan poverty. Thus, the concept of papal infallibility was meant to <u>restrict</u> the power of future popes to change doctrine.[442] It simply meant that a pope could not refute the words of his predecessors.

According to historian and researcher, Brian Tierney, "there is no convincing evidence that papal infallibility formed any part of the theological or canonical tradition of the Church before the thirteenth century". Eventually, but only after much reluctance, it was accepted by the papacy because it suited the popes to accept it.[443] However, Avignon Pope John XXII (1313-1334) did not want his power limited. John XXII later condemned the whole Franciscan theory of evangelical poverty in two letters: *Ad conditorem canonum* (1322) and *Cum inter nonnullos* (1323), asserting scriptural evidence to show that Christ and the Apostles had owned property.[444] The English philosopher and Franciscan, William of Ockham (1287 – 1347) opposed Pope John XXII. He argued that the current pope was bound to the declarations of Nicholas III.[445] Guido Terrena (sometimes spelled Terreni), a Carmelite philosopher, supported John XXII regarding the concept of papal infallibility, but he did so as a way to increase the sovereign power of the pope.[446]

The concept of infallibility arose again over the issue of papal canonization of saints, which asserted itself in the medieval Church. The centralization of the canonization process in Rome was inevitable. In 1170, Pope Alexander III had decreed that no one could be declared a saint without the permission of the Supreme Pontiff.[447] Later, as popular support to some saints grew in the Middle Ages, the papacy had the role of deciding which saints were to be canonized. In the 13th century, the Franciscans and the Dominicans began to push for the canonization of saints who had belonged to their respective orders, and each religious order claimed that popes could not err in their decisions about canonization.[448] While the RCC has never officially defined canonization of a saint as an act of infallibility, the consensus of theologians has been that it is.[449]

- In the late 14th century, the RCC faced its Western Schism (1378-1417); and from that spun the Conciliar movement. This was an attempt to modify and limit papal control over the RCC by means of general councils (not by a sovereign pope); and it was a response to growing centralization of Church administration, as well as perceived abuses of power.[450] The Conciliarists believed that the pope could err; however, they held that a Church council could not. William of Ockham had argued for papal infallibility as a means of limiting the pope's power. But increasingly, it was the anti-Conciliarists who took up the idea of papal infallibility, but only when the pope was speaking on matters of faith and morals.[451]

It was in the 19th century that the papal infallibility again surfaced, when Pope Pius IX (1846 -1878) decreed the doctrine of the Immaculate Conception in 1854 in his bull, '*Ineffabilis Deus*,' which he declared to be infallible.[452] Yet, he had no authority to do so, and Darwin would show that the concept of original sin was bogus, since there was no first man nor first woman. Later, at the First Vatican Council (1869 – 1870), Pius IX bullied the attending cardinals to proclaim that the pope was infallible when speaking on matters of faith and morals. Cardinal St. John Henry Newman (1801-1890) worried about the growing cult of the pope and criticized those Catholics who emphasized papal infallibility. Newman had always believed in papal infallibility, but he opposed the church's public declaration of it. He warned that the Church was not ready for the Pope's infallibility.[453]

In 1964, Pope Paul VI (1963 – 1978) commented on infallibility in his encyclical, '*Luman gentium*'. In that document, Paul VI asserted that infallibility on matters of faith and morals can also reside in the body of bishops when that body exercises the supreme magisterium with the pope. The following is the relevant part of the encyclical:

> "Although the individual bishops do not enjoy the prerogative of infallibility, they nevertheless proclaim Christ's doctrine infallibly whenever, even though dispersed through the world, but still maintaining the bond of communion among themselves and with the successor of Peter."[454]

Similarly, in the Catechism of the Catholic Church[455] (CCC), #891, it states:

> "The infallibility promised to the Church is also present in the body of bishops, when together with Peter's successor, they exercise the supreme Magisterium."

What the above assertion is saying is that the infallibility promised to the Catholic Church also resides in the body of bishops, but only when that body exercises the supreme magisterium in conjunction with the pope.[456] So, rather than clarify, that pronouncement by Pope Paul VI obfuscated the overall intent even further, because the bishops must agree with the pope. And thus, one must ask, what is the point of the bishops having infallibility for matters of faith and morals if they must agree with the pope, who already has infallibility for matters of faith and morals?

While this encyclical from Pope Paul VI helps assuage any fears of Gallicanism,[457] whereby a local bishop might seek independent governing authority from the ecclesiastical authority of Rome, it did not resolve the issue regarding how the Church can avoid an "ultra-papalism" where the pope is regarded as an absolute monarch whose every utterance is treated as an infallible decree.[458] Years later, on May 7, 2005, Pope Benedict XVI specifically warned against this possibility:

"The power of teaching in the Church involves a commitment to the service of obedience to the faith. The pope is not an absolute monarch whose thoughts and desires are law. On the contrary: The pope's ministry is a guarantee of obedience to Christ and his word."[459]

Catholic Tradition

Catholicism teaches that all its practices originated during the time of the apostles, whether or not those doctrines are supported in the Scriptures. **1 Timothy 3:15** is often cited in support of this thesis: [the Church is to be] "...the pillar and support of the truth." The Catholic Church appears to interpret this passage to mean that "it has the right and authority to develop and determine doctrine."[460] The word, tradition, as used ecclesiastically, refers to doctrine transmitted from one generation to another, that is not directly tied to Scriptures, but it is associated with the verbal teachings of Jesus of Nazareth or his apostles.[461] Never mind that there is no corroborating evidence regarding those verbal teachings (the RCC refers to it as "undocumented"), outside of the New Testament, which is itself hearsay, as Jesus and his apostles never wrote anything down. And the Catholic Church doesn't just transmit doctrine from one generation to another, but it develops doctrine over time, and then its leaders vote on it. So, in the RCC, "truth" has been and continues to be determined by the majority rule of selected voters.

The RCC is somewhat unique in Christian Churches in that it doesn't rely on "sola scriptura" to determine its doctrine. The RCC believes that its tradition is equivalent to Scripture, since it originally canonized the Bible (that is, the RCC determined which books they accepted, and which they did not).

The Catechism of the Catholic Church states, "The apostles entrusted the 'sacred deposit' of the faith (*depositum fidei*), contained in the Sacred Scripture and Tradition, to the whole of the Church. By adhering to [this heritage] the entire holy people, united to its pastors, remains always faithful to the teaching of the apostles, to the brotherhood, to the breaking of bread and the prayers. So, in maintaining, practicing, and professing the faith that has been handed on, there should be a remarkable harmony between the bishops and the faithful." (CCC # 84).

John Henry Cardinal Newman (1801 – 1890), an Anglican priest who later converted to Catholicism and became a cardinal, tried to explain in his book, An Essay on the Development of Christian Doctrine, that there have been over the last 19 centuries, "apparent inconsistencies and alterations in its doctrines;"[462] but they were not material enough to interfere with the general course of the religion. He rationalized that just because the "... Church was not aware of later dogmas, does not mean that it was not unconsciously cognizant of them."[463] Such equivocation basically meant that the knowledge of the apostles, including things they didn't know they knew, was somehow passed on to future leaders of the RCC, as continued revelations occurred. In his writing, Cardinal Newman provided some examples of doctrines of the RCC that developed over time: purgatory, original sin[464] (see next chapter), and Baptism.[465] Even when there is no evidence to support a given supposition, such as St. Peter acting as the first bishop of Rome, the RCC claims it to be true. Unfortunately, the issue of Catholic tradition has been significantly impacted by forged documents that run rampant in Catholic canons and teachings. For example, some writings used to justify the RCC hierarchy as apostolic institutions are themselves fraudulent. [466]

Papal History

The Early Years (33 – 476 CE)

This period of history can be conveniently divided into two parts: (1) the Persecution phase, and (2) the Religious Freedom phase.

Up until Constantine's Edict of Milan in 313 CE, Christians were viewed negatively throughout the Roman Empire and were subject to persecution from time to time. Romans punished Christians (and Jews) for treason, various rumored crimes, illegal assembly, and for introducing an alien cult that led to Roman apostasy. This new and unknown religion was often regarded as a politically subversive cult. Romans thought the Christian cult comprised subversives, not because of the god they worshiped, but because Christians would <u>not</u> worship Roman gods and goddesses.[467] However, it is a myth to believe that Christians were constantly persecuted; and that persecution was directed by imperial policy. Indeed, there were persecutions centrally directed by five Roman Emperors (i.e., Nero, Domitian, Decius, Valerian, and Diocletian, with the latter being the most vicious); however, most persecutions were localized,[468] and not directed by a central authority.[469] The myth of constant Christian persecution largely stems from two works written in the early 4th century CE after religious tolerance was decreed in the Roman Empire. Tasked with charting the history of Christian suffering in prior centuries, Lactantius, a Christian Latin teacher, and Eusebius, the bishop of Caesarea, both associated any local, regional or empire-wide persecutions to the emperors of that time.[470]

The early bishops of Rome / popes had no temporal powers; and they were often focused on addressing the many and varied *heresies* they encountered. In general, the early Christian *heresies* centered around the twin issues of the nature of the Trinity and, more specifically, the nature of Jesus Christ.[471] Most early bishops of Rome generally appeared to be decent leaders of their Christian laity, although little is known about most of them, especially for the first two centuries. The Catholic Church would later declare all of them to be martyrs *by Church tradition*, even in instances when they clearly weren't; and later, the Catholic Church declared these 'martyrs' to be saints by acclamation.

Once Emperor Constantine I declared religious freedom, Christianity began to convene numerous meetings of religious councils to combat *heresies*. Emperor Constantine's Edict of Milan (312 CE) had declared toleration of <u>all</u> religions in the empire. Christians met in Nicaea (today it is Iznik,[472] Turkey) for their first ecumenical[473] council, which was called by and presided over by the pagan, Emperor Constantine I. The primary purpose of the Council was to resolve a conflict among the Christians over Arianism,[474] first proposed by Arius of Alexandria, that affirmed that Jesus of Nazareth was not divine, but a created individual. As stated by Arthur McGiffert, "Constantine himself, of course, neither knew nor cared anything about the matter in dispute, but he was eager to bring the controversy to a close…"[475] Arius lost the vote; and the Council incorporated the non-scriptural word, *homoousios*, which means "of one substance" into the Apostle's Creed to show the divinity of Jesus of Nazareth and his equality with the Father. Emperor Constantine exiled Arius, which established a precedent for secular authorities meddling in Christian ecclesiastic affairs. Additionally, all Arian writings were turned over to the Roman Empire to be burned, and Constantine ordered a penalty of death for those who refused to surrender Arian writings.[476], Constantine also involved himself in Christian elections, presiding over the process, and on at least one occasion, he imposed his candidate for Bishop of Rome – all because he wanted a united empire.

The controversy over Arianism had surfaced in the late 3rd century, and it continued in the early 4th century; and for some, it held sway through at least the last of the 6th century. Roman emperors, Constantius II and Valens, became Arians, as did prominent leaders and warlords among the Goths, Vandals, and Lombards. While Arius did not win the vote at the Council of Nicea, a substantial number of early Christians believed that Jesus of Nazareth was not divine; and by extension, Arians do not believe in the traditional doctrine of the Trinity. Arius wanted to emphasize the transcendence and sole divinity of God. God alone is, for Arius, without beginning, unbegotten, and eternal. The Arian controversy, as it has become known, was to dominate imperial, ecclesiastical, and civic policies for more than 200 years.

TIMELINE OF THE CATHOLIC PAPACY

		KEY HISTORICAL EVENTS	RELIGIOUS IMPLICATIONS
1. CLASSICAL AGE 600 BCE - CE 476	**PERSECUTION OF THE CHRISTIAN CULT CE 33 - 313**	St Paul writes his epistles (52 -64) In 64, Emperor Nero blames Christians for the Great Fire of Rome The Synoptic Gospels are written (70 - 96) Emperor Decius leads empire-wide persecution of Christians (250) The Persecution of Diocletian occurs (303-304) Constantine's Edict of Milan (313) establishes religious freedom	The myth of constant persecution largely stems from two works written in the early 4th century by Lactantius, a Christian teacher, and Eusebius, bishop of Caesarea. These authors lived in the reign of Emperor Constantine; and they decided to chart the history of Christian suffering to that point. They both associated persecutions with the emperors under whom they occurred. But the reality is that the persecutions of Christians in the first three centuries was, with some notable exceptions, haphazard, highly localized, and not generally directed by imperial policy.
	RELIGIOUS FREEDOM IN ROMAN EMPIRE CE 313-476	The Edict of Thessalonica (380) renders Christianity the state religion of Rome Romans and Goths defeat Attila the Hun at Chalons (451) Fall of the Western Roman Empire (476)	The early popes were largely spiritual leaders, with no real temporal power. They concerned themselves with in-fighting against multiple heresies, which seemed to sprout up everywhere and often.

Principally, the dispute between Trinitarianism and Arianism was about two things:[477]

1. Has the Son always existed eternally with the Father, or was the Son begotten at a certain time in the past?
2. Is the Son equal to the Father or subordinate to the Father?

For Constantine, these were just minor theological points that stood in the way of his uniting his empire, but for the Christian theologians who demand rigorous religious orthodoxy, it was of paramount importance.[478] And the representatives of the bishop of Rome voted for divinity, which further solidified the bishop of Rome as a 'thought leader' for Christian orthodoxy. Interestingly, the First Council of Nicea attempted, but failed to establish, a uniform date to celebrate Easter.[479]

The Council of Nicea did not end the controversy, which became violent. The Arians fought back and managed to regain imperial favor, albeit briefly. Of the aftermath of the Council of Nicaea, noted historian Will Durant writes, "Probably more Christians were slaughtered by Christians in ... 342-343 [CE] than by all the persecutions of Christians by pagans in the history of Rome."[480] Although claiming to be Christian, many of these believers fought and slaughtered one another over their differing views of Christianity.

Still later, when Emperor Theodosius declared Nicene Christianity as the state religion (in 380 CE) via the Edict of Thessalonica, as opposed to Arian Christianity, which was still widely practiced at the time, the character of many of the bishops shifted from humble pastors to men of ambition who wanted to exercise their power and control. Also, this imperial edict first used the term, *catholic*, [universal] Christians, which had been coined by Church father, Saint Ignatius, bishop of Antioch (c. 50–140) in his Letter to the Smyrnaeans (circa 110 AD).[481] In 330 CE, Emperor Constantine moved his capital to New Rome (later called Constantinople); and the bishop of Rome became the center of power in Rome. By the end of the 4th century, there were five key Christian districts: Rome, Constantinople, Jerusalem, Antioch, and Alexandria.

While all these districts were nominally the most powerful districts of Christianity, Rome and Constantinople emerged as the most dominant, and more importantly, as strong rivals. In 607 CE, Emperor Phocas (602 - 620) decided to declare Rome as "Head of all the Churches,"[482] although the emperor would appoint the bishop of Rome, a right that he would eventually delegate; Emperor Phocas had also favored Rome by giving the pope permission to convert the Roman Pantheon into a Christian Church.[483] It is important to note that Phocas was a usurper emperor known for his vicious, tyrannical behavior. He supported Rome more to embarrass the patriarch of Constantinople than to support the Roman pope, Gregory I, who had previously supported him.[484] Emperor Phocas was soon deposed and executed; but the bishop of Rome clung to his new title.

Some decades later, Pope Leo (440 – 461) declared that he was appointed by God (back to the erroneous reference to Peter as the Rock), and that he (the pope) was God's representation on earth. Papal selection evolved to an election process (and it took over a thousand years to work that out), although temporal authorities sometimes appointed the pope, or at least approved the elections prior to the pope's consecration; and they held a tacit veto power on the election, right up to the beginning of the 20th century.

Ostrogothic Papacies (493 – 537)

In the wake of the fall of the Western Roman Empire, the pope began to assume regional civil authority, as well as an ecclesiastical one. However, the Ostrogoths gained hegemony over Rome. Like the Roman emperors, they interfered with the papal selection process, either appointing the pope or strongly influencing his selection. Theodoric the Great (493 – 526)[485] (who was a Christian Arian) and his successors, Athalaric (526 - 534) and Theodahad (534 - 536), were particularly active in influencing and guiding the papal inductees. This interference ended only when the Byzantines reconquered Rome and the Italian territories during the Gothic War.

The Ostrogothic kings continued to meddle in the selection of the new popes and excessively dominated their elections. Simony (the selling of ecclesiastic privileges) and bribery were too often a common event; and the quality and skill set of the papal candidates seemed less important regarding their chances of being elected, compared with their ability to corrupt the officials of the foreign kings as well as in their powers of clever deception."[486]

Byzantine Papacies (537 – 752)

With the decree of Emperor Justinian (527 - 565), the Byzantines replaced the domination of the Ostrogoth Kingdom. Justinian asserted that any newly elected bishop of Rome or papa could only be consecrated in that position after the emperor had validated his election. The Christian papacy remained at Rome; but for 215 years the popes required the approval of the Byzantine Emperor for their episcopal consecrations.[487] Justinian did recognize the Roman see[488] as the highest ecclesiastical authority,[489] in reward for their agreement to this arrangement.

Many popes were chosen by the Byzantine emperor, or his liaisons. Justinian I personally selected three popes – a practice continued by his successor until distance and convenience delegated the confirmation process to the Exarchate of Ravenna (former capital of the Western Roman Empire). Except for Pope Martin I[490] (who was punished with exile), no pope in this age challenged the authority of the Byzantine emperor. However, as heresies continued to surface, there were multiple theological conflicts between the popes of Rome and the patriarchs of Constantinople, which would often gravitate to become a source of friction between the pope and the emperor. In 741, Pope Zachary (741 – 752) became the last pope to seek the approval of a Byzantine emperor.[491]

The Lombards in northern Italy conquered the Exarchate of Ravenna in 751.[492] The Byzantine Empire was not able to assist, and so in 752 Pope Stephen II (752 – 757) appealed to the Franks.

Frankish Papacy (756 – 857)

After defeating the Lombards, the Franks acquired a tract of land in central Italy, which their leader, Pepin the Short, gifted to the pope. This land, initially referred to as the Donation of Pepin, became known over time as the Papal States, and the Pope became a temporal ruler of those Papal States.[493] Moreover, Francia replaced the Byzantines as the protector of Rome, and as such, it had enormous influence on the selection and administration of the popes for approximately 100 years. Sadly, one of the worst things that could have happened to the Catholic Church was the Pope's secular power over the Papal States. Over succeeding centuries, that enormous temporal power would become highly corrosive.

After the death of Pope Stephen II in 757 CE, lay Roman nobles began inserting themselves into the election of the pontiff, an unfortunate development that would continue for 200 years. Additionally, each new pope had to swear loyalty to the Frankish monarch, the latest secular authority to insert itself into the affairs of the Church, appropriating the privileges asserted by the Byzantines.[494] That said, even though the pope was considered subordinate to the emperor, Pope Leo III crowned Charlemagne, the first of the Carolingian rulers. That event set a precedent that all emperors were supposed to be crowned by the Pope.

Indeed, over time, this relationship between the secular rulers of Europe and the Catholic Church became symbiotic, favoring the rulers (monarchs and popes), to the detriment of the common men and women. The secular rulers needed the RCC to anoint them and declare their legitimacy, while the RCC needed the rulers to either protect them or simply leave them alone and refrain from interference. From feudal times to the 19th century, this became the subscribed method for control of the people, who were told it was a sin to go against their rulers, who had been figuratively anointed by God, and it was blasphemy to go against the Church. This kept everyone in their place: the slaves remained enslaved, the poor remained poor, and the aristocrats remained wealthy.

The famous verse from **Matthew 22:21**, "Render unto Caesar the things which are Caesar's, and unto God the things which are God's," was used repeatedly to justify taxes to the secular leaders and tithing to the Church. At its extreme, some rulers moved toward absolute monarchies, which declared they needed neither the pope nor their nobles to approve their monarchies, as they were self-legitimized through a concept of 'the divine right of kings'[495] to rule by the grace of God.

TIMELINE OF THE CATHOLIC PAPACY cont

		KEY HISTORICAL EVENTS	RELIGIOUS IMPLICATIONS
2. EARLY MIDDLE AGES CE 476 TO 1,000	OSTROGOTHIC PAPACY 493 - 537	The Anno Domini calendar is invented (525) Franks invade northern Italy (537)	The Ostrogothic Leaders (Theodoric, Athalaric or Theodahad) either appointed the popes, or strongly influenced their selections.
	BYZANTINE PAPACY 537 -752	Justinian I's reconquest of Italy (554) Seige of Constantinople by the Umayyad Caliphate (717-718) Charles Martel triumphs over the Saracens at Battle of Tours (732)	A period of Byzantine domination when popes required the emperor's approval for their consecration. The emperor eventually delegated the papal apointments to the Exarchate of Ravenna. Theological conflicts between pope and emperor/patriarch of Constantinople were common.
	FRANKISH PAPACY 756 - 857	Donation of Pepin [Papal States] made to the pope (756) Vikings raid Lindisfarne in England (793) Charlemagne is crowned "Emperor of the Romans" by Pope Leo III (800)	This was an era of political, spiritual, and martial conflict among the Franks, the Lombards, and the Roman nobles. This shift away from the Byzantines occurred after the Lombards conquered the Exarchate of Ravenna, the last Byzantine holding in Italy.
	SAECULUM OBSCURUM (THE PORNOCRACY) 904 - 963	Normandy is founded (911) Otto I was crowned Emperor of the Holy Roman Empire (962)	Popes were under the corrupt influence of the Theophylacti family. It is a period of papal immorality and depravity, spanning six decades and involving 12 popes.
	CRESENTII ERA 974 - 1012	The Althing of Iceland embraces Christianity (1000)	Roman nobles associated with the Cresenti family ruled Rome and selected the popes. There were a rival to the Theophylactii.

In many ways, the Frankish interference in the papal selection process was mild compared to the turmoil created by the Roman aristocrats. As Carolingian power (Franks) waned in the late 9th and early 10th centuries, the papacy once again found itself at the disposal of powerful local nobles.[496] There were two Roman aristocratic families that dominated Rome and the papacy: the Counts of Tusculum, also known as Theophylacti, and the Crescentii. Their corrupt actions and criminality seemed more like rival gang warfare.

Saeculum Obscurum (904 – 964)

This period was referred to as *Saeculum Obscurum*,[497] the Dark Age, which began with Pope Sergius III in 904, and it persisted through the papacy of Pope John XII (955 – 964). Also called the Papal Pornocracy, this era followed the chaos that occurred after the death of Pope Formosus in 896 and the Cadaver Synod.[498] During this time, the popes were under the control of the powerfully corrupt family, the Theophylacti, and their cronies. The counts of Tusculum were Roman nobles who arbitrated Roman politics (including religion) on and off for more than a century. In addition to the papal influence, they held secular power through consulships and senatorial memberships.[499]

Theophylact I (c. 864 – 924) was a medieval count of Tusculum who was the effective ruler of Rome from 905 to his death in 924. His wife, Theodora (870 – 916),[500] prevailed upon him to support her lover as pope; and he was installed as John X in 914. Also, Theophylact was the father of the notorious, Marozia (890 – 932/937), a Roman noblewoman, who was the alleged mistress of Pope Sergius III, and who was given the unprecedented titles, *senatrix* and *patricia* of Rome by Pope John X.[501] Her first son, John, became Pope John XI. Marozia later married Alberic I, Duke of Spoleto, and in 909 they had a son, Alberic II, who is said to have had his mother killed and who imprisoned his half-brother, Pope John XI, until the latter's death.[502]

Later, Alberic II forced the other Roman nobles to elect his only son, Octavian, to the papacy upon the death of the current pope. In December 955, Pope Agapetus II died, and Octavian became Pope John XII, a man of corrupt morals. Pope John XII was only 18 when he became pope; he reached out to Otto I, the Great; and he crowned Otto and his wife, Adelaide, as Holy Roman emperor and empress on Feb. 2, 962.[503] But when Emperor Otto ordered John to take an oath of obedience to him, Pope John XII refused. Otto then deposed John for instigating an armed uprising against the emperor and for Pope John's "dishonorable conduct" in refusing to take the oath. After much maneuvering by Pope John XII, he died in 964, allegedly in the arms of his mistress, ending a private life of gross immorality.[504] The death of this pope whose drinking, gambling, incest, and murders marked one of the lowest points of the papacy, ended the Saeculum Obscurum.[505]

The Theophylacti had placed family members or non-family puppets in eleven papacies following Pope Sergius III. The heirs of Theophylact, the Tusculani, were the rivals of the Crescentii in controlling Rome, and they ensured the placement of several popes. Their eventual heirs were the Colonna family, which was a branch of the Theophylacti.[506] From the early 10th century through the early 19th century, the Roman Catholic Church made some grievous missteps – from the Pornocracy, the Crusades, the Inquisitions, to witch-hunting, etc. – and elected some of its most wicked popes.

Crescentii Era (974 – 1012)

It was the Crescentii who ruled Rome and selected the popes for the next 37 years. Crescentius I de Theodora (d. 984?) led a revolt in 974 against Pope Benedict VI, who was imprisoned and then purportedly strangled by order of Crescentius.[507] Crescentius was then appointed as the successor, the antipope, Boniface VII, who was soon expelled by the new pope, Benedict VII, who had been appointed by Otto II, and who was the grandson of Marozia.[508]

In 985, Crescentius' son, John, assumed the title of Patricius of Rome, and he appears to have controlled the election of the new pope, John XV. Ten years later, upon the death of Pope John XV, Emperor Otto III (994 – 1002)[509] nominated his German cousin, who became Pope Gregory V. In 996, Crescentius Numentanus, probably John's brother, led an uprising against Pope Gregory, but Otto III had him reinstated in 998. Otto besieged Crescentius, and then captured and executed him on April 29, 998.[510]

After the brief papacy of Pope Sylvester II, the first French pope, John Crescentius, son of Numentanus, ensured the election of Pope John XVII (May – Nov, 1003), who was his puppet; but Pope John XVII only lasted five months.[511] Next, John Crescentius helped elect Pope John XVIII (1004 - 1009),[512] who abdicated after five years and died soon thereafter. Pope John XVIII was followed by Pope Sergius IV (1009 – 1012), also hand-picked and appointed through the influence of John Crescentius.[513] Pope Sergius died one week after John Crescentius. And the papacy's Crescentii Era came to an end.

Tusculani Papacy (1012 – 1048)

The influence of the Theophylacti family re-emerged in Rome and supplanted the Crescenti; and they remained in power for approximately 35 more years, starting with Pope Benedict VIII (1012 – 1024),[514] previous known as Theophylactus II, count of Tusculum. The papacy of Pope Benedict VIII marked the return of the Tusculani family and the fall of their rival, the Crescentii. Gregory VI (an antipope) opposed Benedict VIII, and he compelled the latter to flee Rome. However, the Holy Roman Empire's (HRE's) Henry II restored Pope Benedict to his position, and Pope Benedict remained on good terms with Henry II throughout his almost 12-year papacy.[515]

Upon the death of Pope Benedict VIII, his brother, Romanus, became Pope John XIX (1024 – 1032), although he had never been ordained as a Catholic priest, but had been a consul and senator. Like his brother, he bought the office. In only two days, he passed through the necessary clerical stations, from priest to bishop to pope. He was considered greedy, immoral, and incompetent.[516] His papacy spanned over 8 years.

The Counts of Tuscany then passed the papacy over to their young (age 20), immoral progeny, Theophylactus III, nephew of John XIX and son of Alberic. Benedict IX claimed the papacy three times: from 1032 to 1044 (pope # 145) after which he fled Rome when he provoked a Roman insurrection; from April to May 1045 (pope # 147) when he sold the papacy to his godfather, who became Gregory VI; and from 1047 to 1048 (pope # 150), after which he was deposed, excommunicated and expelled. Benedict was known for his violent temper and his debauchery. Other than an antipope in 1058, Benedict IX was the last of the popes from the powerful Tusculani family.[517]

TIMELINE OF THE CATHOLIC PAPACY cont		
	KEY HISTORICAL EVENTS	**RELIGIOUS IMPLICATIONS**
3. HIGH MIDDLE AGES CE 1000 TO 1250 — **TUSCULAN PAPACY 1012 - 1048**	Cnut the Great is crowned King of England (1016) / Count of Castile, Fernando the Great, becomes King of Leon (1037) / "The city of Oslo is founded by King Harald Hardrada of Norway (1048)"	The feudal system flourished. The nobility furnished the upper ranks of the Church almost exclusively. The Counts of Tusculum (or Theophylacti family) continued to produce popes and antipopes. The reforms (initiated by Pope Gregory VII) was a reaction to these crime families.
THE HOLY ROMAN EMPIRE (HRE) AND THE CRUSADES 1048 - 1257	The Great Schism separates the Western and East Orthodox Churches (1054) / Norman conquest of England (1066) / "Pope Urban calls for the First Crusade (1095)"	"Emperor Henry III appointed three German successors to Pope Leo X (who died in 1054) without elections. There were many disputes between the pope and the HRE, with the Investiture Controversy being the most prominent. The rules for papal elections continued to evolve.

The unprecedented actions of Pope Benedict IX (the only pope to serve multiple papal 'terms'), resulted in tremendous turmoil in Rome. So, when Henry III arrived in Rome in 1046 seeking coronation as the Holy Roman Emperor, he encountered three different popes.[518] Henry called for the Council of Sutri,[519] where all three papal claimants were deposed; and he appointed Pope Clement II (1046–47).[520] Benedict would again renew his claim to the papacy by seizing Rome in November 1047, when Clement II died; but he was quickly deposed. The Tusculani family still held local power in Rome. In April 1058, they violently emplaced Giovanni Mincio as Pope Benedict X;[521] but he was expelled in January 1059, and the RCC now considers him an anti-pope.

Holy Roman Empire (HRE) (1048 – 1257) and the Crusades (1095 – 1291)

After the brief reigns of Pope Clement II (289 days) and Pope Damasus II (23 days), the HRE's Henry III appointed Pope Leo IX (1049-1054) and his two successors – all Germans, without the formality of an election. However, two events occurred which enabled Pope Nicholas II (1059–61) to reset the process for the papal elections in 1059:[522] (1) the death of Emperor Henry III, and (2) his successor being a child emperor. Thus, Pope Nicholas labored to ensure that all future elections would occur at conclaves, under the purview of the College of Cardinals,[523] while limiting the role of any secular ruler. Pope Nicholas set out procedures where the cardinal bishops elected the pope, with the cardinal priests and deacons providing their concurrence. It was a better system, but the turmoil of the 12th century with its schisms and antipopes caused additional upheaval. Adjustments to the electoral process were made at the Third Council of the Lateran[524] (1179); but some abuses continued.

Meanwhile, a protracted strife with the Holy Roman Empire surfaced, known as the Investiture Controversy.[525] Traditionally, the secular rulers had maintained some control over the appointments of Church offices. Various monarchs exercised their tacit authority to appoint (invest) local church officials such as bishops and monastery abbots. Pope Gregory VII (1073 – 1085) pushed back against this practice, and Pope Calixtus II (1119 – 1124) signed the Concordat of Worms in 1222 with Emperor Henry V, which differentiated between royal and spiritual powers and enabled the emperor to retain a limited role in selecting bishops. However, this Concordat largely transformed the relationship between Church and state;[526] and it heavily favored the Church.

This period also overlapped with what would later be described as the Great East-West Schism, as well as the crusades (1095 – 1291), which was a series of religious wars spanning approximately 200 years in a failed attempt generally to wrest control of the "Holy Land" from Muslim domination. Additionally, there were Christian crusades directed at 'pagans' in the Baltic countries. The crusades were launched with papal leadership fortified by the operational harshness and vigor of European nobility. While the Catholic popes would continue to struggle with temporal rulers throughout the Middle Ages, the crusades, albeit ultimately quite unsuccessful and highly regrettable, temporarily enhanced papal prestige in Christian Europe. Yet 1.7 million people would die in the warfare or from accompanying diseases, starvation, and banditry.

Wandering Popes (1257 – 1309)

Political instability in Italy during the latter half of the 13th century compelled the papal court to relocate to several different towns, including Viterbo, Orvieto, and Perugia. The popes brought with them the Roman Curia, which comprised the administrative institutions of the Holy See and the central body through which the affairs of the RCC were conducted. The College of Cardinals met in the city where the last pope had died to hold their papal elections. Host cities enjoyed a boost to their prestige and certain economic advantages, but the municipal authorities risked being consumed into the administration of the Papal States if they enabled the pope and his entourage to overstay their welcome.

More than two years after the death of Pope Clement IV (1265 – 1268), the cardinals had still not elected a successor. The local magistrate locked the electors in the episcopal palace and provided only life-sustaining rations until the cardinals elected Gregory X (1271 – 1276). At the Council of Lyon (1274), Gregory proposed that the cardinals meet in a conclave[527] with strict regulations regarding the electoral process. Pope Boniface (1294 – 1303) ordered that Gregory's rules be enshrined into canon law. However, with the schisms and antipopes of the next century, papal elections proved annoyingly difficult for the RCC to achieve conformity.

According to Cambridge Emeritus Professor of History of Christianity, Eamon Duffy: "Aristocratic factions within the city of Rome once again made it an insecure base for a stable papal government."[528] Pope Innocent IV was exiled from Rome for six years, and all but two of the papal elections in the 13th century took place outside the city of Rome. The skyline of Rome itself was then dominated by the fortified war-towers of the aristocracy (a hundred towers were built in Innocent IV's pontificate alone); and the popes increasingly spent their time in the papal palaces at Viterbo and Orvieto."[529]

Avignon Papacy and the Western Schism (1309 – 1417)

Pope Clement V was highly stressed from continual riots in Rome due to the factionalism of rival clans, as well as his fear of the unruly cardinals. So, he moved the papal see to Avignon, which at the time belonged to a vassal of the pope, the Duke of Anjou. While not officially on French soil, the pope sought the protection of the French king. That protection came with the obligation for the pope to support King Philip IV's political persecution of the Knights Templar. In total, seven French popes resided in Avignon, France, spanning 73 years:

1. Pope Clement V (1305–1314),
2. Pope John XXII (1316–1334),
3. Pope Benedict XII (1334–1342),
4. Pope Clement VI (1342–1352),
5. Pope Innocent VI (1352–1362),
6. Pope Urban VI (1362–1370),
7. Pope Gregory XI (1370–1378).

The Avignon papacy was severely negative to the reputation of the papacy. Indeed, the court of the Avignon popes significantly increased its financial abuses and practices to augment its coffers. To the people, the popes were perceived as living in extravagance, and because they were not in Rome, they were viewed as disinterested in the suffering of Christians who underwent the terrible trauma of the Black Death (1346 – 1353), where 30 to 50 million people perished, perhaps 50% of Europe's population.[530]

In 1377, in response to the steadily increasing influence of the French monarchy, Pope Gregory XI moved the papal residence back to Rome, where he died soon thereafter. However, the French cardinals did not agree with the choice of his elected successor, Urban VI, an Italian, and they withdrew to a conclave of their own, where they elected one of their number, Robert of Geneva, who became Clement VII. This was the beginning of the period of difficulty from 1378 to 1417, which is often referred to as the "Western Schism" or "the great controversy of the antipopes," when the Roman Catholic Church was divided in allegiances among the various claimants to the office of pope. Benedict XIII (in Avignon) and Gregory XII (in Rome) followed Clement VII, and collectively they were known as the Pisan popes (due to the Council of Pisa in 1409); but they were later declared to be antipopes by the RCC.

TIMELINE OF THE CATHOLIC PAPACY cont

		KEY HISTORICAL EVENTS	RELIGIOUS IMPLICATIONS
4. LATE MIDDLE AGES CE 1250 TO 1450	THE WANDERING POPES 1257 - 1304	The Seventh Crusade is defeated in Egypt, Louis IX of France captured (1250) / Marco Polo and his family begin their trip to the East (1260) / The Knights Templar were suppressed, tortured, and killed (1307-1312)	Political instability from factions of the Roman nobility compelled the papal court to move to various locations, e.g., Viterbo, Orvieto, & Perugia. The College of Cardinals would meet in the city where the last pope died to hold the papal elections.
	AVIGNON PAPACY 1309 - 1377	The Great Famine of Europe (1315-1317) / The Hundred Years' War between England and France begins (1337) / Black Death Kills 200 million (1347-1351)	During this period, the papacy was located in France and under control of the French king. This involved seven French popes; the last, Pope Gregory XI, moved the papal residence back to Rome.
	WESTERN SCHISM 1378 - 1417	John Hus is burned at the stake (1415); it led to the Hussite Wars in Bohemia. / The Council of Constance (1414 - 1418) ended the Western Schism.	The Pisan cardinals served as antipopes to the popes in Rome. The schism ended with the election of Pope Martin V at the Council of Constance.

At one point, three men each claimed simultaneously to be the one, true pope. They were not in any theological disagreements, as much as they were embroiled in political ones. But throughout Europe, the Catholic Church was severely weakened and suffered diminished prestige, as the Western Schism produced confusion and bordered on utter chaos.[531] In 1417, the Council of Constance (1414-1418) finally resolved the controversy.[532]

Renaissance Papacy (1417 – 1517)

It has been cited many times that the Renaissance arrived in different countries at different times. On the Italian peninsula, it arrived early. Rome was seemingly coming out of a long decline. The Avignon papacy had returned to Rome, and the Western Schism was finally resolved at the Council of Constance, which also oversaw the election of Pope Martin V, who returned the papacy to Rome in 1420.

Popes were generally of the nobility (which is a trend that would continue until the 20th century), but they often lacked assets of their own, and so, to promote their family interests, they often turned to nepotism. The word nepotism originally referred specifically to the practice of creating cardinal-nephews, when it appeared in the English language about 1669.[533] According to Professor Eamon Duffy, "the inevitable outcome of all of this was a creation of a wealthy, privileged cardinal class, with strong dynastic connections."[534] The college of cardinals was dominated by (1) cardinal-nephews who were relatives of the popes that elevated them, (2) crown-cardinals—representatives of the Catholic monarchies of Europe, and (3) members of the powerful Italian noble families.

During this era, popes were more frequently called upon to arbitrate disputes between competing colonial powers than to resolve theological disputes. Columbus's discovery in 1492 upset the unstable relations between the kingdoms of Portugal and Castile (Spain), whose jockeying for possession of colonial territories along the African coast had for many years been regulated by the papal bulls, which were public decrees issued by a Catholic pope. The name is derived from a leaden seal (*bulla*) that was appended to the end of the document to authenticate it. Pope Alexander VI, himself a Spaniard, responded with three bulls, which were highly favorable to Castile[535].

The Papal States took on the look of a nation state, and the papacy took an increasingly active role in European wars and diplomacy. Pope Julius II, the so-called " Warrior Pope", did not fail to use violence, bloodshed, and an array of bullying tactics to increase the territory and property of the papacy.[536] The popes of this period used the papal military not only to enrich themselves and their families but also to enforce and expand upon the longstanding territorial and property claims of the papacy as an institution. During this era of the "Renaissance papacy," the popes were increasingly financially dependent on the revenues from the Papal States themselves, but even that did not generate enough wealth. In Rome, the Renaissance was guided by the papacy, which commissioned magnificent buildings, paintings, and sculptures. Moreover, the popes were often involved in petty, martial conflicts. With ambitious expenditures on war and construction projects, popes turned to new sources of revenue from the sale of indulgences and bureaucratic and ecclesiastical offices.

As stated by Professor Duffy, "the Renaissance papacy invokes images of a Hollywood spectacular, all decadence and drag."[537] That said, none of the Renaissance popes were considered saintly men; some were inept, but their conduct was far worse. Sixtus IV (1471 – 1484), Innocent VIII (1484 – 1492), Alexander VI (1492 – 1503), Julius II (1503 – 1513) and Leo X (1513 – 1521), who ruled successively for 50 years,[538] were among the worst popes in history. It should be noted that Pius III actually was pope for 26 days in 1503; and while not one of the wicked popes, he accomplished very little. The avarice, sexual depravities, murderous misconduct, and the criminal appetites of these Renaissance popes not only directly led to the Reformation, but collectively, they brought the papacy to its lowest level of prestige in its history.

Reformation and Counter-Reformation (1519 – 1648)

The Reformation movement established several national churches within Europe outside of papal control. They challenged the Catholic Church theologically and practically. It was the corrupt papacy and the abuses of the Catholic clergy that led to and provided the basis for Martin Luther's 95 Theses, which ignited the Protestant Reformation. The out-of-control gimmick of indulgences to reduce one's time in purgatory was a flagrant abuse, but it was a big fundraiser for the Catholic clergy. Indulgences were a distinctive feature of the penitential system of both the medieval Roman Catholic Church, which granted full or partial remission of the punishment of sin. A penitent could provide money to the Church in exchange for the remission of sin for himself or a loved one, even if the latter was deceased.

TIMELINE OF THE CATHOLIC PAPACY cont

		KEY HISTORICAL EVENTS	RELIGIOUS IMPLICATIONS
5. EARLY MODERN AGE CE 1450 - 1750	RENAISSANCE PAPACY 1418 - 1517	Joan of Arc burned at stake (1431) / Guttenberg Press (1440) / Fall of Byzantine Empire (1453) / A misogynistic book, Malleus Maleficarum, ignites witch-hunting hysteria (1486)	During this era, many popes continued to promote their family interests through nepotism. The Papal States transformed into a nation state; but many of the Renaissance popes were decadent and unfit for office. The prestige of the papacy was severely undermined by its corruption and frequent scandals.
	REFORMATION / COUNTER-REFORMATION 1517 -1580	Martin Luther posted his '95 Theses' (1517) / Yeshua' or 'Iesu' changed to 'Jesus' (mid-1600s)	The Reformation was a backlash to the corrupt activities of the Rennaissance popes. The Counter-Reformation did little to mediate the issues; they just shifted back to the Catholic hierarchy's reinforced conservative values.
	AGE OF ENLIGHTENMENT C. 1640 - 1750	The Thirty Years' War ends in 1648 / Newton presents his Theory of Gravity (1687) / "Union of England and Scotland to form Great Britain (1707)" / Voltaire publishes his novella, Candide (1759)	The Enlightenment was an intellectual movement which emphasized reason over superstition, and science over faith. The popes of this period held a predominately hostile view of most Enlightenment ideas, such as the separation of church and state and religious tolerance.

The concept of purgatory is the achievement of medieval Christian imagination regarding a place where souls go to suffer and purify prior to going to heaven. As part of the Counter-Reformation, the Catholic Council of Trent defined purgatory as "a temporary state or place of purification after death for those who die in God's grace, but who still need to be purified from the effects of their sins before entering into the fullness of heaven." In 1999, Pope John Paul II said of purgatory, "The term does not indicate a place, but a condition of existence." Either way, the concept of purgatory is shared among the RCC, Eastern Orthodox, and Anglicanism.[539]

During the Counter-Reformation (1560 – 1648), the RCC did institute some minor internal reforms and gave up some secular power. Pope Paul III (1534 – 1549) called the Council of Trent (1545 -1563), which, over three separate sessions, was effectively the formal Catholic reply to the doctrinal challenges of the Protestant Reformation. The Council redefined Catholic doctrine and made decrees for self-reform. For example, it decreed that the appointment of relatives to Church offices was forbidden. It affirmed that both faith and works were necessary for salvation, clarified the importance of sacraments (which it formalized), and improved clergy discipline and education. The Council of Trent declared that the doctrine of transubstantiation was to be a dogma of faith. It reaffirmed the authority of the Catholic Church, codified Scripture, reformed some abuses, and of course, it took the step of condemning Protestant theology.

The Protestant Reformation might never have happened if the Church had simply addressed Martin Luther's objection to the sale of indulgences, instead of trying to silence him. However, Luther proceeded from that criticism to a rejection of the Church entirely. Central to his claim was that salvation could be found by faith alone, and for communion with God, one needed only the Bible.

The Council of Trent reaffirmed what books of the Bible constituted "Holy Scripture". The Lutherans had rejected certain books, and by this time, Luther had published his own translation of the Bible. To counter this, the Council of Trent asserted its own 'authoritative' version of Scripture. So, in April 1546, the Vulgate (Latin) translation of Saint Jerome was affirmed as the *only authoritative text*.[540] The Council determined that the Church's interpretation of the Bible was the final word. The Council banned heretical and faulty translations (that is, non-Catholic translations); and it required that any vernacular translations must have ecclesiastical approval (which it had no intention of giving).

During this period, the Church continued to adjust its electoral rules. Gregory XV (1621 – 1623) issued ecclesiastical legislation (again) specifying the detailed procedures of the conclave. However, secular authorities still had a hand in the selection of Christ's Vicar on Earth via the right of veto. During the papal selection process, a cardinal from a given jurisdiction would inform the conclave of the inadmissibility of a papal candidate. Secular interference with papal elections finally ended in the early 20th century. [541]

In all, the Council of Trent was too little, too late. The RCC now had competing Christian Churches in Western Europe. Over time, that would result in a bloody Thirty Years' War (1618 – 1648) in which 4.5 to 8 million people died;[542] at the end of which, entire countries had left the sphere of Catholicism. One of the consequences of those changes is that the RCC no longer had total control over the lives of the people. And it was about to be confronted by scientific and political changes, which revealed some serious misbeliefs.

Index of Prohibited Books

To prevent the spread of Protestant thought, the *Index Librorum Prohibitorum* (Index of Prohibited Books) was established by Pope Paul IV in 1557 and was approved by a Church decree in 1563, which began by specifically naming the works of Reformers such as Luther, Zwingli, John Calvin, and others. The Index was detailed in its prohibitions, but it essentially stated that any book condemned by the Holy Office or by one's priest or bishop was to be rejected by a Catholic in good standing with the Church. Unrepentant reading of books on the Index was understood as a grave sin and an act of rebellion that imperiled one's soul. The Index continued in effect until 1966 when it was permanently suspended by Pope Paul VI,[543] because it was considered contrary to the teaching of Vatican II concerning freedom of inquiry. (New Catholic Encyclopedia v. 7, 2nd ed, 2003).[544]

The Index's avowed purpose was to protect Church laity from reading works that were considered dangerous or contrary to faith or morals. The list condemned both religious and secular texts; and it graded works based on how dangerous or repugnant they were deemed to be. The Index also banned all books by a particular author or publisher in many cases. The following is a small sample of some of the many books banned by the Catholic Church, which made the Index of Prohibited Books listing:[545]

• Alighieri Dante	Divine Comedy
• Henri Bergson	Creative Evolution
• Edward Gibbons	The Decline and Fall of the Roman Empire
• Victor Hugo	Les Misérables
• Victor Hugo	The Hunchback of Notre Dame
• Immanuel Kant	Critique of Pure Reason
• John Locke	An Essay Concerning Human Understanding, Vol 1, 2 and 3
• Niccolo Machiavelli	The Prince
• John Milton	Paradise Lost
• Francois-Auguste Alexis	History of the French Revolution
• Voltaire	Philosophical Dictionary

The banning of books is a Catholic tradition that goes back to Pope Gelasius I, who around 496, decreed what has been called the First Roman Book Index.[546] As shown in the above sampling of book authors and titles, the Index was not limited to theology books; it also banned books of love stories to political theory. And all writings of some authors – including David Hume, Thomas Hobbes, Émile Zola, and Jean-Paul Sartre – were prohibited.[547] So clearly, the expressed Church goal of protecting its laity from "contamination of the faith" seems to really be about control, and in the cases of some authors, petty retaliation.

Age of Enlightenment 1640 - 1740

By the mid-17th century, the "age of reason" or "enlightenment" produced a crop of thinkers, writers, and politicians radically opposed to the RCC and its influence in the world. François-Marie Arouet (1694 – 1778), known by his pen name Voltaire, was one such individual. Although educated by Catholic Jesuits, Voltaire embraced anti-Catholic beliefs, and he worked tirelessly to destroy the "infamous thing," his moniker for the Church.[548]

The Age of Enlightenment challenged the strongly held view of the Catholic Church that revelation and faith were the primary sources of truth. There were two key forces in the Enlightenment that challenged Christian (both Catholic and Protestant) thought: scientific and political, and these challenges were transformational.

Science

The revolution of scientific thought challenged the standard interpretations of the Bible. It came about by the application of reason. While v (1473 – 1543) had developed his heliocentric theory[549] In the early 16th century, it wasn't published until after his death in 1543. Nicolaus Copernicus proposed that the planets orbit around the Sun; that Earth is a planet which, besides orbiting the Sun annually, also turns once daily on its own axis; and that very slow changes in the direction of this axis account for the precession of the equinoxes. This view represented a paradigm shift from the Ptolemaic model of the heavens, which posited that the cosmos had the Earth at its center, stationary. The Church considered it speculative at best. However, Giordano Bruno (1548 – 1600) went beyond the heliocentric theory (which still maintained a finite universe with a sphere of fixed stars) to describe his theories of an infinite universe and the multiplicity of worlds.[550] He was burned at the stake in Rome at the behest of Pope Clement VIII. Later, when Galileo (1564 – 1642) declared he could demonstrate the validity of the heliocentric theory through observations with his telescope, he was tried by the Catholic Inquisition in 1633 for his subversive views, threatened with death, and underwent house arrest for the rest of his life.[551]

Francis Bacon (1561 – 1626) was the first great advocate of empiricism and the separation of science and theology.[552] Empiricism is the theory that all knowledge is derived from sense experience. Stimulated by the rise of experimental science, it developed in the 17th and 18th centuries, expounded in particular by John Locke, George Berkeley, and David Hume. Isaac Newton (1643 – 1727) applied logic and mathematical calculation to explain how the universe worked. Observation, reason, and hypothesis became the new standard for intellectual thought; it was called the scientific method. Pioneered by Francis Bacon's inductive reasoning and Galileo Galilei's experimental methods, the scientific method emerged as a systematic way of investigating phenomena and testing hypotheses, and it became central to Enlightenment thought. This new approach to knowledge surfaced, gained many advocates, and effectively changed how people viewed the world. There was no longer any need for religion to explain the natural world. Indeed, the teachings of the Church were often at odds with new scientific discoveries, and the religious teachings were often revealed as false.

It was during this era that the contentious relationship between the Church and science came into sharp focus. The Galileo affair stands as a vivid example of conflict between scientific inquiry and theological interpretation. But the full picture is more nuanced. While there were some clergy actively seeking to reconcile faith and reason, most took a defensive posture, furious that anyone would challenge the supremacy of the RCC. It was also a time of exploration and discovery, and the Church turned its attention to opportunities to advance its influence globally through evangelization.

Politics

Scientific enlightenment gave rise to political enlightenment, whereby the concept of human rights and 'natural law' became part of a new vision. Hugo Grotius (1583 – 1645) was one of the first to express the idea of a society of states governed by natural laws and mutual agreement. [553] Grotius influenced such notable men as John Locke (1634 – 1704), who penned essays regarding self-government by a mutually-agreed structure of law. He espoused individual freedoms and the separation of church and state, advocacy of religious toleration, and general empirical and scientific temperament.[554] His writings had a profound influence on the framers of the U S Constitution.

The intransigent Catholic Church had very different views. Most Catholic theologians met Enlightenment reasoning with suspicion. The Enlightenment views clearly undermined Catholic tradition, and it placed reason over the Church's espoused truths of faith. We must recall that many of the senior clergy of the Church, including its popes, came from noble families. Those senior clergy supported monarchical governments and corresponding forms of social order. Many of them still had a medieval mindset. The Biblical exegesis of the Catholic Church was not only what they understood, but challenges to that mindset terrified the RCC, and it most certainly threatened their supremacy. The Catholic Church still believed that political freedom was not a right, and we should recall that the pope was the secular emperor of the Papal States. Indeed, even after its disastrous handling of the Reformation, the Catholic Church still wanted all governments to be subordinate to it.

An emphasis on reason and empiricism was often viewed as an attack on the Catholic faith. The RCC's response was to become highly defensive and attempt to reassert its authority, similar to its response to the Protestant Reformation. And we know how well that worked out.

Revolutionary Papacy (1775 -1848)

In many ways, the events of the revolutionary period were the greatest fears of Catholicism come to pass. This was a period of expansion and shifting dynamics.

Napoleon Bonaparte invaded Italy in 1797 and immediately defeated the papal troops. Pope Pius VI agreed to peace terms which included a large indemnity, several works of art from the Vatican collection, and the turnover to France of Bologna, Ferrara, and Romagna.[555] Later, the French Army took over Rome, and Pope Pius VI was taken prisoner;[556] and he was then brought to the citadel of Valence in France, where he died.[557]

The next pope, Pius VII, initially appeared conciliatory towards Napoleon, signing the French Concordat of 1801 and officiating at Napoleon's imperial coronation. But the Concordat was very slanted toward France, and by 1808, relations between Napoleonic France and the papacy had deteriorated. Napoleon annexed the remaining parts of the Papal States, and the Pope excommunicated everyone involved in the annexation.[558] The Pope was then arrested and would remain a prisoner of the French until February 1814.[559]

Suffice it to say that the papal experiences with Napoleon and his Republican troops were not received well. It is no surprise that Pope Leo XII (1823 – 1829) and Pope Gregory XVI (1831 – 1846) held strong anti-liberal, reactionary sentiments, along with the ruling European aristocracies. Further, the movement toward Italian unification grew steadily. To no one's surprise, the 19th-century popes opposed the unification of Italy.

Pope Gregory XVI was especially conservative and hoped to restore his ecclesiastical authority over the laity and their governments (apparently through wishful thinking). His papal bull, *Mirari vos*, in 1832 condemned liberalism. Pope Gregory refused to modernize the Papal States; he rejected the very idea of democracy; and, of course, as with his immediate predecessors, he hated the concept of separation of church and state.

The Vatican Adjustment (1848 – 1929)

When Pope Pius IX was elected in 1848, he seemed to promise a more progressive papacy. However, revolutions were erupting throughout Europe. In 1849, a Roman Republic was declared, and Pope Pius IX fled the city. Napoleon III saw an opportunity and, in cooperation with Austria, he sent troops to restore Papal rule in Rome. Pope Pius IX was reinstated three years after his departure, but he would shed himself of any liberal tendencies, as he pursued harsh policies even more repressive than those of his predecessors. He became opposed to everything "modern." He was involved in an 1858 kidnapping scandal of a Jewish boy, Edgardo Mortara. [560] [561] He repulsed a Jewish delegation with insults, and he then rescinded the civil rights of Jews and confined them to a Jewish ghetto.[562] Pope Pius IX proclaimed in 1854 the Immaculate Conception of Mary, that she was "free of all stain of original sin."

He said he spoke "with infallibility," but he did not (yet). Later, he published the encyclical, *Quanta cura*, which included the *Syllabus of Errors,* a list of what Pius IX considered to be *terrible evils*. These "evils" included the separation of church and state, freedom of conscience, civil rights, religious liberty, and democracy. This document put many loyal Catholics in opposition to their own modern governments.

In 1869, Pius IX convened the Vatican I Council; and he demanded that the cardinals give formal approval to his theory of papal infallibility, or speaking *ex cathedra,* as an official dogma to which Catholics could only reject upon pain of a mortal sin. This effort conveniently ignored the past when many popes had spoken in error, and their misstatements were reversed by later popes. Although technically, Pius IX's declaration of infallibility for the Immaculate Conception predated the Vatican I Council, it was "grandfathered" in. Unfortunately, the notion of papal infallibility would drive a spiritual wedge between Catholicism and the rest of the world. Interestingly, not long after his 'infallible' edict of Mary's Immaculate Conception and freedom from original sin, Darwinism would prove the entire human race was free of original sin.

The very concept of papal infallibility would probably have shocked the early Christians. The apostles displayed no such prominence among Christians. As Cardinal St. John Henry

Newman wrote, "In the course of time, first the power of the bishop displayed itself, and then the power of the pope."[563]

The legations of the Papal States in 1850: (1) Romagna, (2) Marche, (3) Umbria, (4) Marittima and Campagna; and Rome.

When the Franco-Prussian War broke out, Napoleon III recalled the French garrison from Rome. Then the French suffered a crushing defeat to the Prussians at the Battle of Sedan. This deprived the Papal States of its secular protector. The Italians held a plebiscite in October 1870, which agreed to annex the Papal States and Rome to the Kingdom of Italy; and they did so, against the protests of Pope Pius IX. Thus, at the barrel of a gun, the Pope's temporal powers were suddenly obliterated. The new Italian king, Victor Emmanuel, offered to give the pope a face-saving authoritative position; Pius IX responded by excommunicating the king. The petulant pope vowed to be a "prisoner of the Vatican," which the king never intended. Pope Pius IX retreated to Vatican City, where he resided and refused to come out.

Subsequent popes until 1929 also refused to negotiate with the Italians. Finally, on 11 February 1929, the Lateran Treaty was signed by Italian dictator, Benito Mussolini and Pope Pius XI, and it was ratified by the Italian parliament to recognize Vatican City as an independent state.

In the late 20th century, the Catholic Church wanted to canonize Pope John XXIII. However, to squelch dissent among some conservative cardinals, Church leaders thought it appealing to canonize a conservative pope along with the progressive John XXIII. They strongly considered Pius XII, who acquiesced with Mussolini and Hitler in not vigorously opposing the Jewish holocaust. The Church felt that Pius XII was too controversial, and so it substituted Pius IX. The canonization of now Saint Pope John XXIII was fast-tracked, but the beatification of Pius IX has been repeatedly postponed[564] as this intolerant throwback to the Middle Ages was found "wanting in patience, justice, and charity toward subordinates."[565]

World Wars

Pope Benedict XVI during WWI and Pope Pius XII in WWII made themselves available to both sides of the respective conflicts to serve as mediators to broker a peace, or at least to try and limit the war. Neither was used in that capacity. During WWI, there was no religious element; it was Christian country against Christian country. The opposing sides simply did not feel that they needed mediation by the pope.

For Pius XII, there were two distinct phases to the Second World War. His initial concern was to end the war or to prevent it from spreading. Like Benedict XV in the First World War, he made himself available to both sides to help broker peace or otherwise limit the war. In WWII, the Allies were angry that Pius XII was not more forceful in his condemnation of the Jewish death camps, while the Axis Powers considered Pius XII to be a sympathizer of the

Allies. Pope Pius had apparently thought that his strictly neutral position would put him in an appropriate position to fashion a compromise, and so he strived hard to give that impression. Unfortunately, his failure to denounce the German invasion of Poland and the atrocities committed there set the stage for his continued silence.[566]

For the latter part of the war, the pope focused on thwarting the extension of communism in Europe. Pius XII feared the destabilization of European society, which could result from war. The papacy took a strong anti-Communist stance during the Cold War, and Catholics who supported communism were excommunicated by Pope Pius XII in July 1949,[567] although many priests in communist-run countries (at the time), such as Poland and Hungary, ignored Pius' decree and welcomed communists into their churches. The decree was finally revoked in 1983.[568]

When war in Vietnam erupted, the Church initially called the cause just, but it grew increasingly pacifist as the 1960s wore on. At the same time, significant changes were taking place within the Church as the 1962-1965 Second Vatican Council modernized and freed up discourse within its rank and file. During this era the liberation theology surfaced. This was a movement within Latin American Catholic theology and spirituality since the 1950s and 1960s that reads the Christian gospel from the standpoint of the poor.[569] The RCC, which historically has often been on the wrong side of history, criticized liberation theology, "as naive purveyors of Marxism and advocates of leftist social activism."[570] The movement sought to apply religious faith by aiding the poor and oppressed through involvement in political and civic affairs.[571]

Cold War and Beyond

Beginning with Pope John XXIII's 1963 *Pacem in terris* (Peace on Earth) encyclical calling for nuclear disarmament, the Church began to take a stronger and more vocal stance against the nuclear arms race. Throughout the 1980s, in addition to its anti-Communist stance, the Vatican took a stronger position in promoting human rights and economic development.

U.S. President Ronald Reagan and Pope John Paul II forged an important partnership in the 1980s in their efforts to discredit the Soviet Union. The United States and the Vatican announced the establishment of diplomatic relations in 1984.[572] But since the end of the Cold War, experts say the Vatican and U.S. administrations have struggled to find common cause. There have been long-standing tensions on a number of issues, including Washington's handling of counterterrorism policies. The Vatican strongly opposed the U.S.-led intervention in Iraq. Yet some say this rift over the war has been overstated. Other issues of common cause include reviving the Middle East peace process and curbing the spread of nuclear arms. But the Catholic Church and the White House continued to clash on several important social issues, including the use of the death penalty, as well as global programs that permit abortion.[573]

USA - Vatican relations remained uneven following Joseph Ratzinger's accession as Pope Benedict XVI, particularly as the Obama administration pursued a more liberal social agenda.[574] The Vatican had increased its pressure on major global political players, including the United States, to take a firm stance on climate change policy. In Pope Benedict XVI's revisions to the "seven deadly sins," he included polluting the environment as a sin – a sign many experts interpreted as politically significant. In an August 2007 address, Benedict urged the Catholic Church worldwide to become more environmentally conscious, saying abuse of the environment is against God's will. Experts say Benedict's speech was only the latest in a series of increasingly forceful statements about tending to environmental concerns, and that by defining the issue in moral terms, he substantially upped the ante for policymakers in countries where the Catholic Church is influential.

The beginning of the Obama administration signaled that there would be sharp disagreements on issues that collide with the Vatican's views on the sanctity of life. Shortly after the 2008 presidential election, Pope Benedict spoke with Obama to make clear that the Vatican would oppose attempts to loosen policy on embryonic-stem-cell research; and unsurprisingly, Vatican officials were quick to criticize Obama's move to end restrictions on stem-cell funding in March 2009. Even before the stem-cell decision, Obama had upset the Vatican by rescinding the Mexico City Policy, a Reagan-era rule preventing humanitarian groups receiving U.S. funding from promoting or performing abortions.

Meanwhile, the pope was strongly criticized on a March 2009 trip to Africa for saying the distribution of condoms would not solve the AIDS epidemic. The RCC continued to prohibit the use of contraception of any kind. Pope Benedict never weighed in on whether he supports the use of condoms for married couples when one member is infected with a sexually transmitted disease. The Church has encouraged a strong "conscience clause" within the U.S. President's Emergency Plan for AIDS Relief (PEPFAR), a major funding initiative targeting some of the worst-affected countries with HIV. The clause allows groups like Catholic Relief Services to refuse to execute the condom education and distribution portion of the programs.[575] As proclaimed by the New York Times, the saving of over 25 million lives in Africa wasn't pro-life enough for the Catholic Church.[576]

Pope Francis was elected pope in March 2013 shortly after Pope Benedict XVI resigned. While the latter had been a staunchly conservative pontiff, Pope Francis has shown himself to be far more progressive. Francis has called for spiritual renewal within the Church and greater attention to the plight of the poor; and he sternly condemned the forces that diverted the Church from its ministry.[577] Pope Francis's ministry of engagement has caused a great deal of discomfort, especially with many staunchly conservative U S Catholic bishops, who debated for months whether the Eucharist should be withheld from pro-choice Catholics. Indeed, some bishops threatened House Speaker Nancy Pelosi (D-Calif.) as well as President Joseph Biden, both staunch Catholics, who dared to support a woman's right to her own body.

In 2022, Pope Francis acknowledged the unprecedented hostility he has encountered from US conservative bishops, who have openly opposed the pope's pastoral priorities, especially regarding welcoming LGBTQ people into the Church and combating climate change. Some have characterized the conservative bishops as wanting to return to the pre-Vatican II era. Pope Francis, in turn, described them as "backwardists," with his warning, "A Church that does not develop its thinking in an ecclesial way is a Church that goes backward."[578] In August 2023, Pope Francis stated that American conservative bishops have "replaced [their] faith with ideology."[579]

Pope Francis pleaded with world leaders and Christians everywhere to "put an end to the senseless war against creation."[580] Pope Francis denounced the exploitation of natural resources; he called upon the world to transform their collective hearts, lifestyles, and public policies to avoid what he declared to be "a calamitous destruction of natural resources".[581] Since its release in October 2015, the Pope's apostolic exhortation, *Laudato Si,*" made it clear that climate change was at the forefront of Pope Francis' concerns.[582] Eight years later, *Laudate Deum* extended and renewed the plea that everyone should be better stewards of our environment.

TIMELINE OF THE CATHOLIC PAPACY cont

			KEY HISTORICAL EVENTS	RELIGIOUS IMPLICATIONS
6. LATE MODERN AGE CE 1750 – PRESENT	REVOLUTIONARY ERA 1775 – 1848		American Revolution (1775 - 1783) / French Revolution (1789 - 1799) / S. Americans revolt against Spanish rule (1810)	"The Catholic Church displayed its official bias against revolutionary movements, e.g., Pius VI condemned the French Revolution and was highly critical of the principles of freedom that inspired the American Revolution."
	VATICAN ADJUSTMENT 1848 – 1929		American Civil War (1861 - 1865) / Gov't of Italy reclaims its Papal States (1870) / World War I (1914 - 1918) / The League of Nations (1920) was formed / Concordat of Worms (1122) resolves the Investiture	As of 1870 the popes were no longer sovereigns of the Papal States. Popes of this era were generally uncompromising throwbacks with very anti-modern views. They had difficulty reconciling their papal authority with constitutional government.
	CONTEMPORARY ERA CE 1929 –PRESENT		World War II (1939 - 1945) / Communist Victory in China (1949) / Astronaut Neil Armstrong walks on the moon (1969) / Fall of Berlin Wall ends Cold War (Nov 1989) / Soviet Union collapses (1991) / Terrorist attack on NYC (2001) / Russia invades Ukraine (Feb 2022)	Beginning with Pope John XXIII the Church took a more progressive stance. The Second Ecumenical Vatican Council brought many welcome changes; and it reached out to other religions. It also marked its abandonment of its earlier opposition to liberal democracy. Pope Paul VI continued the ecumenical efforts of John XXIII. Then the papacies of John Paul II and Francis I provided some stability and identity to the Church.

The illustration, *Timeline of Evil*, presented on the following page, graphically depicts a timeline regarding various horrors of Christianity and the Catholic Church.

Chapter Summary

This chapter presented a brief history of the Roman Catholic Church (RCC), focusing on the popes. As early as the late 2nd century, the bishop of Rome attempted to force his hegemony over the other Christian bishops. Far too often, the early Roman Church seemed more focused on acquiring levels of papal supremacy than they were on the spiritual well-being of the Church. They established Church tradition to further their claims for legitimacy for the leadership of the Church. That was followed by the concept of papal infallibility; and yet the Catholic Church has proved very fallible in its decisions "of faith and morals."

The timelines shown throughout this chapter illustrate the Catholic chronology of activities and outcomes and the chain of events that occurred in each papal era, as well as reflect on the timing of other contemporaneous occurrences. While many of the bishops of Rome and popes were decent men, striving to do what they thought was right, at around 900 CE, things went horribly wrong for the RCC. The papacy became currency for the ruling Roman aristocrats, and their criminal families fought each other for the privilege of controlling that position. Criminal offenses in the papal palace became the norm, and some of the most immoral and wicked men claimed the position and title of pope.

In the 11th century, just as the papacy was trying to separate itself from its horrendous past 150 years, the RCC initiated the Great Schism (with the Eastern Orthodox Church); and then the RCC quickly followed that mistake with two centuries of unnecessary upheaval, cruelty, and bloodshed, much of it inflicted on the innocent – the crusades. After years of corruption and the reign of truly sinful popes (Innocent III, Gregory IX, Boniface VIII, and Urban VI), the RCC entered its arguably worst period with its five corrupt Renaissance popes who reigned in succession (Sixtus IV, Innocent XIII, Alexander VI, Julius II, and Leo X). There seemed to be no crime that was beyond these five pontiffs. The despicable escapades of these "vicars of Christ" were the catalyst for the Protestant Reformation.

Rather than focusing primarily inward to reform itself, the RCC redoubled its efforts with its inquisitions, witch hunts, book banning, and all types of reactionary methods that it used to lash out at anyone seen as not supporting its orthodox agendas, as the RCC decried that it was no longer the primary Christian Church in the Western World. And the ultra-conservative, passive-aggressive attitudes of the pontiffs did not change until the latter half of the 20th century. There were multiple efforts to sanitize some of the historical actions of the RCC. But the RCC has recognized many of its past misdeeds and issued extensive apologies to those wronged, or to their progeny. That is discussed in detail in the next chapter. Sadly, given the contemptuous treatment of Pope Francis I and his progressive ideas, there appears to be nothing to prohibit the RCC from returning to its old ways – except the collective will of the Catholic laity!

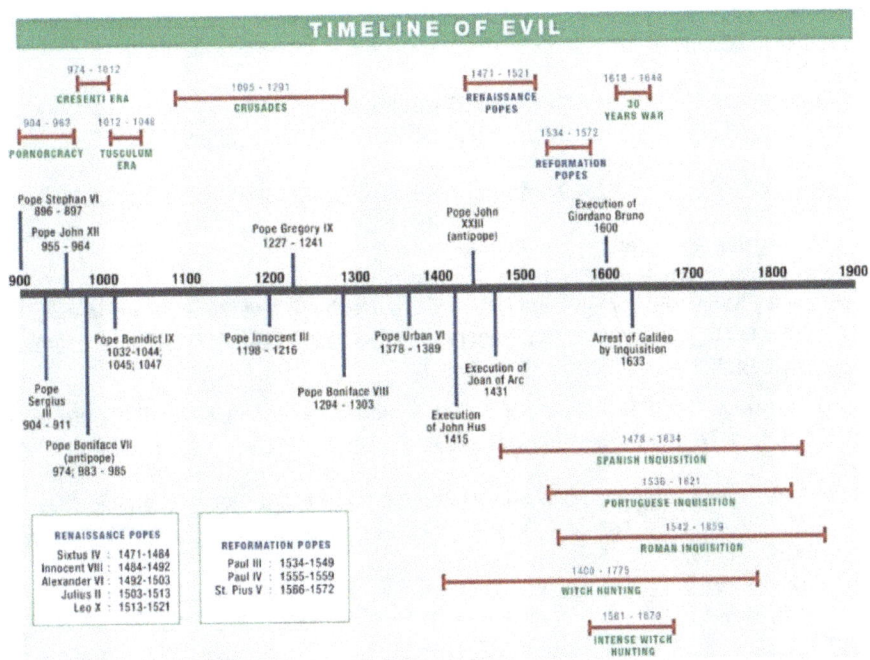

(A comprehensive listing of all the Catholic bishops of Rome / popes is provided in **Appendix 1.**)

[419] V. M. Traverso, "How we have books: A brief history of the monastic scriptorium," Aleteia; Aug 2023; https://aleteia.org/2023/08/25/how-we-have-books-a-brief-history-of-the-monastic-scriptorium

[420] The origin of pope is the Latin word, papa (not pater, which means father).

[421] Ecclesiastical refers to belonging to or connected with the Christian religion; it is not secular.

[422] The word *see* comes from the Latin, *sedes*, meaning "seat," and which refers to the episcopal chair occupied by a bishop who has responsibility over a specified area.

[423] Excommunication is a form of ecclesiastical censure by which a person is excluded from the communion of believers, the rites of a church, and the rights of church membership, but not necessarily from membership in the church as such.

[424] "Council of Nicea," Encyclopedia Britannica, The article on the Council of Niceas was researched and updated by Melissa Petruzzello.

[425] Jonathan Wynne-Jones, "St Peter was not the first Pope and never went to Rome, claims Channel 4," Channel 4 Telegraph; https://www.telegraph.co.uk/news/worldnews/1582585/St-Peter-was-not-the-first-Pope-and-never-went-to-Rome-claims-Channel-4.html?

[426] Don Wright, "Peter Was Not the First Pope," Brown Street; Jan 8, 2022; https://www.brownstreetcoc.org/peter-was-not-the-first-pope/

[427] Johann Peter Kirsch, "Pope St. Linus," Catholic Encyclopedia, Vol 9. Pp. 272-273 (New York NY; Robert Appleton Co; 1913); https://en.wikisource.org/wiki/Catholic_Encyclopedia_(1913)/Pope_St._Linus

[428] "Council of Carthage (AD 257), Fathers of the Church", New Advent; Source: Translated by Henry Percival. From Nicene and Post-Nicene Fathers, Second Series, Vol. 14. Edited by Philip Schaff and Henry Wace. (Buffalo, NY: Christian Literature Publishing Co., 1900.) Revised and edited for New Advent by Kevin Knight. <http://www.newadvent.org/fathers/3818.htm>.

[429] "St. Stephen I," Encyclopedia Britannica; https://www.britannica.com/biography/St-Stephen-I-pope

[430] Denis Kaiser, "Leo the Great on the Supremacy of the Bishop of Rome," Andrews University Seminary Student Journal, Volume 1, Number 2, Fall 2015 Andrews University, denis@andrews.edu, August 2015.

[431] "The Development of Papal Supremacy," Lumen Learning; https://courses.lumenlearning.com/atd-herkimer-westerncivilization/chapter/the-development-of-papal-supremacy/#:~:text=Papal%20supremacy%20is%20the%20doctrine,the%20Pope%20enjoys%2C%20by%20divine

[432] Livius.org, Articles of ancient history, "Pontifex Maximus," https://www.livius.org/articles/concept/pontifex-maximus/

[433] Roger Pearse, "When did Roman emperors cease to use the title of 'Pontifex Maximus'?, posted April 19, 2121; https://www.roger-pearse.com/weblog/2021/04/19/when-did-roman-emperors-cease-to-use-the-title-of-pontifex-maximus/

[434] Ministry Magazine, "The Roman Pontifex Maximus," Robert Leo Odom, *Editor, The Watchman Magazine, Nashville,* TN https://www.ministrymagazine.org/archive/1943/06/the-roman-pontifex-maximus

[435] George Ryan, "The Dictatus Papae: 27 Powers Reserved Only for the Pope," uCatholic; May 13, 2020; https://ucatholic.com/blog/the-dictatus-papae-27-powers-reserved-only-for-the-pope/ By George Ryan -May 13, 20206286 1

[436] "Petrine Theory," Britannica; https://www.britannica.com/topic/Petrine-theory

[437] "Innocent III. Mover, Shaker and Entrencher of the Papacy," Uncommon Faith; May 16, 2023; https://uncommonfaith.org/2023/05/16/innocent-iii-mover-shaker-and-entrencher-of-the-papacy/

[438] "Petrine Theory," Ibid.

[439] Vincent Ryan Ruggiero, "The Befuddling Concept of Infallibility," Catholic Journal; Aug 15, 2022; https://www.catholicjournal.us/2022/08/15/the-befuddling-concept-of-infallibility/

[440] Pope Nicholas III, New Advent; https://www.newadvent.org/cathen/11056a.htm

441 "Nicholas III," Catholic Online; https://www.catholic.org/saints/saint.php?saint_id=1022

442 Paul Collins, "Papalism triumphant: John Paul II," from Papal Power; Chapter 4, published by Harper Collins 1997, pp 97-123; https://www.churchauthority.org/papalism-triumphant-john-paul-ii-paul-collins/

443 Brian Tierney, Origins of Papal Infallibility 1150-1350: A Study on the Concepts of Infallibility, Sovereignty and Tradition in the Middle Ages, p. 281; Leiden: E. J. Brill, 1972.

444 "Pope John XXII," Britannica; https://www.britannica.com/biography/John-XXII

445 "William of Ockham: Defending the Church, Condemning the Pope," Philosophy Now; https://philosophynow.org/issues/56/William_of_Ockham_Defending_the_Church_Condemning_the_Pope

446 Thomas Turley, "Guido Terrena, Infallibilists in the curia of Pope John XXII," Journal of Medieval History Volume 1, Issue 1, April 1975, Pages 71-101; https://www.sciencedirect.com/science/article/abs/pii/0304418175900329

447 "The History of Canonization," EWTN; https://www.ewtn.com/catholicism/library/history-of-canonization-13746

448 Rebecca Rist, Ibid

449 "Are Canonizations Infallible?" Catholic Answers; https://www.catholic.com/qa/are-canonizations-infallible

450 Antony Black, "The conciliar movement," Cambridge University Press; 28 March 2008; https://www.cambridge.org/core/books/abs/cambridge-history-of-medieval-political-thought-c350c1450/conciliar-movement/56E860FCC4FEB77B2DD653DB3973045A

451 Rebecca Rist, Ibid

452 "Immaculate Conception," Religions; https://www.bbc.co.uk/religion/religions/christianity/beliefs/immaculateconception.shtml

453 "Papal Infallibility," John Henry Newman: A Biography; July 2009; Oxford Academic; https://academic.oup.com/book/37016/chapter-abstract/322499686?redirectedFrom=fulltext

454 "Dogmatic Constitution on the Church, Lumen Gentium," Chapter 3, Paragraph 25; https://www.vatican.va/archive/hist_councils/ii_vatican_council/documents/vat-ii_const_19641121_lumen-gentium_en.html

455 Catechism of the Catholic Church, 2nd Edition; Doubleday; New York; April 1995; promulgated by Pope John Paul II.

456 Vincent Ryan Ruggiero, "The Befuddling Concept of Infallibility," Catholic Journal; Aug 15, 2022; https://www.catholicjournal.us/2022/08/15/the-befuddling-concept-of-infallibility/

457 "Gallicanism," Encyclopedia.com; https://www.encyclopedia.com/philosophy-and-religion/christianity/roman-catholic-and-orthodox-churches-branches-schisms-and-heresies/gallicanism. Gallicanism was essentially a French ecclesiastical doctrine advocating restriction of papal power.

458 "In the Era of Synodality, 'Lumen Gentium' Delivers a Key Message About Episcopal Authority," National Catholic Register; https://www.ncregister.com/commentaries/lumen-gentium-and-episcopal-authority

459 "In the Era of Synodality…" Ibid.

397 Bob Williams, "Examining Catholic Doctrines", Bible Lessons.com; https://www.biblelessons.com/catholic.html

461 Ibid.

462 John Henry Cardinal Newman, An Essay on the Development of Christian Doctrine, p. 9; University of Notre Dame Press, Notre Dame, Indiana; https://www.gutenberg.org/files/35110/35110-h/35110-h.htm

463 Ibid, p. xxiii

464 Newman, Ibid, p. 126

465 Newman, Ibid, p. 127

466 Bob Williams, "The Problem of Forgeries", Bible Lessons.com; https://www.biblelessons.com/catholic.html

[467] Kevin P. Considine, "Why did the Romans Persecute Christians,", U.S. Catholic, July 12, 2022. https://uscatholic.org/articles/202207/why-did-the-romans-persecute-christians/

[468] Shushma Malik, *"Myth busting Ancient Rome – Throwing Christians to the Lions,"* The University of Queensland and Caillan Davenport, *The University of Queensland;* 22 Nov 2016: https://hpi.uq.edu.au/article/2016/11/mythbusting-ancient-rome-%E2%80%93-throwing-christians-lions

[469] Posted by Dr. Stephen Flick, July 14, 2024, "Persecutions in Church History," Christian Heritage Fellowship, Persecution of the Early Christian Church - Christian Heritage Fellowship, Inc. https://christianheritagefellowship.com/persecution-of-the-early-christian-church/

[470] Shushma Malik and Caillan Davenport, "Myth busting Ancient Rome – Throwing Christians to the Lions," The Conversation; https://theconversation.com/mythbusting-ancient-rome-throwing-christians-to-the-lions-67365

[471] Dr. C. George Boeree, "Early Christian Heresies," Shippensburg University; https://webspace.ship.edu/cgboer/heresies.html

[472] "Iznik," Encyclopedia Britannica; https://www.britannica.com/place/Iznik

[473] Ecumenical refers to an array of different Christian churches; also called interdenominational; its goal is Christian unity.

[474] "Arianism", Encyclopedia Britannica,

[475] Arthur Cushman McGiffert, A History of Christian Thought, Vol 1, p. 258, 1954

[476] *"Emperor Constantine's Edict against the Arians". fourthcentury.com. 23 January 2010. Archived from the original on 19 August 2011. Retrieved 20 August 2011.*

[477] Denis E. Groh, "The Arian Controversy—How It Divided Early Christianity," The Biblical Archaeological Society; https://library.biblicalarchaeology.org/article/the-arian-controversy-how-it-divided-early-christianity/

[478] "Athanasius: 5-time exile," Blue Letter Bible; Feb 14, 2013; https://blogs.blueletterbible.org/blb/2013/02/14/athanasius-5-time-exile/

[479] "First Council of Nicaea," Encyclopedia Britannica; https://www.britannica.com/event/First-Council-of-Nicaea-325

[480] Will Durant, The Story of Civilization, Vol 4: The Age of Faith; p. 8, Dec, 1980.

[481] "St. Ignatius of Antioch," Britannica; https://www.britannica.com/biography/Saint-Ignatius-of-Antioch

[482] Andrew Ekonomou, Byzantine Rome and the Greek Popes: Eastern Influences on Rome and the Papacy from Gregory the Great to Zacharias, A.D. 590-752; Lexington Books, Feb, 2007.

[483] C. Keith Hansley, "Emperor Phocas (r. 602-610) Gave the Ancient Roman Pantheon To Pope Boniface IV," The Historian's Hut, Sep 10, 2027; https://thehistorianshut.com/2017/09/10/emperor-phocas-r-602-610-gave-the-ancient-roman-pantheon-to-pope-boniface-iv; and also, https://www.britannica.com/biography/Saint-Boniface-IV

[484] Andrew Ekonomou, Ibid.

[485] Joshua J. Mark, "Theodoric the Great," World History Encyclopedia, Oct 2014; https://www.worldhistory.org/Theodoric_the_Great/

[486] Sir Henry Hoyle Howorth. Saint Augustine of Canterbury. p. 406; London: J. Murray; 1913.

[487] Nick Kampouris, "The Story of the Last Greek Pope in Rome," Greek Reporter; https://greekreporter.com/2025/04/22/last-greek-pope-rome/

[488] "Holy See," Britannica; https://www.britannica.com/topic/Holy-See The word see comes from the Latin sedes, meaning "seat," which refers to the episcopal chair occupied by a bishop and the area over which he has responsibility.

[489] "Justinian I – Religious Relations with Rome" New World Encyclopedia; https://www.newworldencyclopedia.org/entry/Justinian_I

[490] Pope St. Martin I, PopeHistory.com, https://popehistory.com/popes/pope-st-martin-i/

[491] "Pope St. Zachary," PopeHistory.com; 2024l https://popehistory.com/popes/pope-st-zachary/

[492] "Lombards and Byzantines," Encyclopedia Britannica, https://www.britannica.com/place/Italy/The-Lombard-kingdom-584-774

493 "Papal States," Britannica; https://www.britannica.com/place/Papal-States

494 "The Medieval Papacy," Britannica, https://www.britannica.com/topic/papacy/The-medieval-papacy

495 "Divine Right of Kings," Britannica; https://www.britannica.com/topic/divine-right-of-kings

496 "The Medieval Papacy," Britannica, Ibid.

497 Christopher R. Altieri, "A breezy (and cautionary) history of the papal 'dark age'", The Catholic World Report, Nov 22, 2021; https://catholiccitizens.org/issues/papacy-history-of/97422/a-breezy-and-cautionary-history-of-the-papal-dark-age/

498 Elizabeth Harper, "The Cadaver Synod: When a Pope's Corpse Was Put on Trial," Atlas Obscura, March 3, 2014; https://www.atlasobscura.com/articles/morbid-monday-cadaver-synod

499 Sandra Miesel "When Harlots Ruled the Church," The Catholic World Report; August 27, 2023; https://www.catholicworldreport.com/2023/08/27/when-harlots-ruled-the-church/

500 "The Woman who Ruled the Papacy," Medievalists Net; https://www.medievalists.net/2023/09/woman-who-ruled-papacy/

501 "Marozia, the De Facto Ruler of the Papacy," The Royal Women; https://theroyalwomen.com/2021/12/26/marozia/

502 "Alberic II of Spoleto," Pantheon World; https://pantheon.world/profile/person/Alberic_II_of_Spoleto

503 "Pope John XII," Encyclopedia Britannica; https://www.britannica.com/biography/John-XII

504 Pope John XII, Ibid.

505 Josh West, Pope John XII: The Youngest and Worst Pope in History, Medium; https://joshwest63.medium.com/pope-john-xii-the-youngest-and-worst-pope-in-history-b701a9949eaf

506 "Colonna Family", Palazzo Colonna; https://www.galleriacolonna.it/en/the-colonna-family/

507 "Benedict VII," Encyclopedia Britannica; https://www.britannica.com/biography/Benedict-VI

508 "Benedict VII," Encyclopedia Britannica; https://www.britannica.com/biography/Benedict-VII

509 "Otto III," Encyclopedia Britannica; https://www.britannica.com/biography/Otto-III

510 "Crescentii Family," Encyclopedia Britannica, https://www.britannica.com/topic/Crescentii-family

511 "Pope John XVII – the 140th Pope," PopeHistory.com; https://popehistory.com/popes/pope-john-xvii/

512 "Pope John XVIII," Pope History; https://popehistory.com/popes/pope-john-xviii/

513 "Pope Sergius IV," Flocknote; https://sttmformation.flocknote.com/note/14370064

514 Mann, Horace (1907). "Pope Benedict VIII". In Herbermann, Charles (ed.). Catholic Encyclopedia. Vol. 2. New York: Robert Appleton Company.

515 Debra Booton McCoy, "Pope Benedict VIII: The First Tusculum Pope," Catholic 365; September 2, 2021; https://www.catholic365.com/article/12854/pope-benedict-viii-the-first-tusculum-pope.html

516 "Pope John XIX," Pope History; https://popehistory.com/popes/pope-john-xix/

517 "Pope Benedict IX," Encyclopedia Britannica, https://www.britannica.com/biography/Benedict-IX

518 "Pope Benedict IX – The 145th, 147th & 150th Pope," PopeHistory.com; https://popehistory.com/popes/pope-benedict-ix/

519 "Council of Sutri in 1046," from "Episode 28 – Three Popes with One Stone," History of the Germans Podcast; https://historyofthegermans.com/2021/08/19/episode-28-thre-popes-with-one-stone/

520 Baumgartner, Frederic J. (2003), Behind Locked Doors: A History of the Papal Elections; p. 18; ISBN 0-312-29463-8.

521 "Pope Benedict X," Encyclopedia Britannica, https://www.britannica.com/biography/Benedict-X

522 Ibid.

523 The College of Cardinals has three orders: (1) the Episcopal Order (Cardinal Bishops), (2) the Presbyteral Order (Cardinal Priests), and the Diaconal Order (Cardinal Deacons).

524 "Third Lateran Council," Encyclopedia Britannica; https://www.britannica.com/event/Third-Lateran-Council This council required a two-thirds majority of the College of Cardinals for papal elections.

525 "Investiture Controversy," Encyclopedia Britannica; https://www.britannica.com/event/Investiture-Controversy

[526] Michael Griffith, "Investiture Controversy," World History Encyclopedia; April 2021; https://www.worldhistory.org/Investiture

[527] Papal conclave is *the assembly of cardinals in the Roman Catholic Church to elect a new pope and the system* of strict seclusion to which they submit. "Papal Conclave," Encyclopedia Britannica; https://www.britannica.com/topic/papal-conclave

[528] Eamon *Duffy, Saints & Sinners (3 ed.). New Haven Ct: Yale Nota Bene/Yale University Press, 2006: p. 156. ISBN 978-0-300-11597-0.*

[529] Duffy; Ibid.

[530] "Black Death," Britannica; https://www.britannica.com/event/Black-Death

[531] "Western Schism," Encyclopedia.com; https://www.encyclopedia.com/religion/encyclopedias-almanacs-transcripts-and-maps/western-schism

[532] "Council of Constance," New Advent; https://www.newadvent.org/cathen/04288a.htm

[533] "Nepotism," Oxford English Dictionary. September 2003; https://www.oed.com/dictionary/nepotism_n?tl=true

[534] Eamon Duffy, *Saints & Sinners* (3 ed.). New Haven Ct: Yale Nota Bene/Yale University Press; 2006; *p. 193*

[535] In 1516, Aragon and Castille were united as Spain under Charles, grandson of Ferdinand and Isabella.

[536] Jackson J. Spielvogel, Western Civilization: Volume B: 1300 to 1815; 7th (seventh) edition; p. 368; published in 2008 by Wadsworth Publishing

[537] Eamon Duffy, *Saints & Sinners* (3 ed.), p. 193

[539] Camilla Klein, "What Christian Religions Believe in Purgatory?" Christian Educators Academy; https://christianeducatorsacademy.com/what-christian-religions-believe-in-purgatory/

[540] "Vulgate," Britannica; https://www.britannica.com/topic/Vulgate

[541] The royalty veto of popes was last exercised in 1903 when Austria blocked the candidacy of Cardinal Rampolla. At that conclave, Cardinal Sarto was elected; as Pope Pius X (1903 – 1914) he abolished the right of royal exclusion.

[542] Joshua J. Mark, "Thirty Years' War," World History Encyclopedia; https://www.worldhistory.org/Thirty_Years'_War/ Note: the majority of deaths were attributed to famine and disease caused by the warring parties.

[543] "Index of Prohibited Books," World History Encyclopedia; https://www.worldhistory.org/article/2018/index-of-prohibited-books/

[544] The New Catholic Encyclopedia can be accessed at: https://www.newadvent.org/cathen/

[545] "Banned Literature," Loras College Library; https://library.loras.edu/bannedliterature/index

[546] "Index Librorum Prohibitorum," Encyclopedia Britannica; https://www.britannica.com/topic/Index-Librorum-Prohibitorum

[547] Britannica, Ibid.

[548] "Voltaire and Religious Intolerance," The Online Library of Liberty; Carmel, IN, Liberty Fund, Inc., https://oll.libertyfund.org/pages/voltaire-religious-intolerance

[549] "Nicolaus Copernicus," Standford Encyclopedia of Philosophy, https://plato.stanford.edu/entries/copernicus/

[550] Giovanni Aquilecchia, "Giordano Bruno" Encyclopedia Britannica, https://www.britannica.com/biography/Giordano-Bruno

[551] Mark Cartwright, "Galileo Galilei" World History Encyclopedia, Sep 5, 2023; https://www.worldhistory.org/Galileo_Galilei/

[552] Stanford Encyclopedia of Philosophy, "Francis Bacon," *First published Mon Dec 29, 2003; substantive revision Fri Dec 7, 2012*

[553] Yasuaki Onuma, "Hugo Grotius," Encyclopedia Britannica; https://www.britannica.com/biography/Hugo-Grotius

[554] Graham A J Rogers, "John Locke," Encyclopedia Britannica; https://www.britannica.com/biography/John-Locke

[555] Hales, E.E.Y., Revolution and Papacy, Doubleday & Co., 1960, p. 101

556 Ibid. p. 115

557 Ibid. p. 128

558 Ibid. p. 189

559 Ibid. pp. 222-223

560 "The Kidnapping of Edgardo Levi Mortara," American Jewish Archives; https://www.americanjewisharchives.org/snapshots/the-kidnapping-of-edgardo-levi-mortara/

561 "A beatification too far," Jewish Telegraphic Agency; https://www.jta.org/2000/08/27/lifestyle/a-beatification-too-far

562 JTA Staff "A beautification too far," Jewish Telegraphic Agency; August, 2000; https://www.jta.org/2000/08/27/lifestyle/a-beatification-too-far

563 "An Essay on the Development of Christian Doctrine," pp. 18-149, University of Notre Dame, Notre Dame, IN, 1989.

564 Richard Boudreaux, "Jews Disturbed by Beatification of Pope Pius IX," Los Angeles Times, Sep 3, 2000; https://www.latimes.com/archives/la-xpm-2000-sep-03-mn-14969-story.html

565 "Pius IX The Problem Pope," SJA Defend; https://www.sdadefend.com/History/pius_ix.htm

566 Peter C. Kent, Lonely Cold War of Pope Pius XII, Published by McGill-Queen's University Press 2002, ISBN: 9780773569942 https://doi.org/10.1515/9780773569942-009

567 In his "Decree Against Communism," Pius XII authorized his 'Holy Office' to expel from the church any Catholic who joined or even collaborated with "godless" Communists. "Pope Pius XII Excommunicates all Catholic Communists," History.com; https://www.history.com/this-day-in-history/pope-pius-xii-excommunicates-communist-catholics-decree

568 Ibid.

569 "Liberation Theology," JesuitResource.org; https://www.xavier.edu/jesuitresource/jesuit-a-z/terms-l/liberation-theology#

570 "Liberation Theology," Encyclopedia Britannica; https://www.britannica.com/topic/liberation-theology

571 Ibid.

572 "U.S. Relations with the Holy See," U S Department of State; Bureau of European and Eurasian Affairs; August 27, 2020

573 Lee Hudson Teslik and Toni Johnson, "US-Vatican Relations," Council on Foreign Relations, https://www.cfr.org/backgrounder/us-vatican-relations

574 Lee Hudson Teslik and Toni Johnson "U.S.-Vatican Relations," Council on Foreign Relations, https://www.cfr.org/backgrounder/us-vatican-relations

575 Jodi Enda, "Negotiating with People's Lives," Catholics For Choice; https://www.catholicsforchoice.org/wp-content/uploads/2014/01/EndaArticle1.pdf

576 "It's Not Pro-Life to Oppose a Program That Has Saved 25 Million Lives," New York Times, Sep 5, 2023; https://www.nytimes.com/2023/09/05/opinion/abortion-pepfar.html

577 "Francis," Britannica; https://www.britannica.com/biography/Francis-I-pope

578 "Pope Francis blasts reactionary American Catholics who oppose church reform," National Catholic Reporter; Aug 28, 2013; https://www.ncronline.org/vatican/vatican-news/pope-francis-blasts-reactionary-american-catholics-who-oppose-church-reform

579 "Pope says conservative U.S. Catholics have replaced faith with ideology," Los Angeles Times; Associated Press
Aug. 28, 2023; https://www.latimes.com/world-nation/story/2023-08-28/pope-backward-us-conservatives-replaced-faith-ideology

580 "Pope demands end to 'senseless war against Creation,' Catholic World News; May 25, 2023; https://www.catholicculture.org/news/headlines/index.cfm?storyid=58783

581 Catholic World News, Ibid.

582 "Pope Francis makes it clear: Climate change must be a priority for all Catholics (especially Americans)," America Magazine; October 04, 2023; https://www.americamagazine.org/politics-society/2023/10/04/laudate-deum-pope-francis-climate-change-246201

Chapter 6 – Selected Concerns of Catholicism

The Roman Catholic Church (RCC) is the original and largest branch of Christianity with approximately 1.3 billion Catholics worldwide.[583] Its history spans two millennia. It is led by the pope, as the bishop of Rome; the Holy See (RCC's sovereign central government located at the Vatican City) is assisted by the Roman Curia, a group of departments, congregations, and councils with specific functions and responsibilities relating to Church matters such as liturgy and worship, religious education, missionary activities, doctrine of the faith, or bishops and clergy.[584]

The RCC has had a lasting impact on art, architecture, philosophy, ethics, education, and humanitarian efforts with a rich tradition of liturgy and central acts of worship. In the 21st century, it faces a daunting list of challenges, including:

- Priest shortages, caused by celibacy requirements and refusal to accept females in the priesthood
- Declining membership and mass attendance (especially in Europe)
- Ending sexual abuse (both child molestation and female adult sexual assault)
- Financial strains
- Social and cultural changes
- Secularization of society

There has been an array of criticisms inflicted upon the RCC: the infallibility of the pope, the Church's seeming obsession with Mary and the saints, the role and treatment of women, etc. The following are brief discussions on a host of topics that are specific to the Roman Catholic Church.

Reading the Bible

The Catholic Church has a very long history of suppressing the reading of the Bible, especially the New Testament. Prior to the mid-20th century, not only were there historic prohibitions against translating any portions of the Bible into one's native language but even reading it was viewed as the work of the devil. Historical individuals such as John Wycliffe (c. 1330-1384) firmly believed that the Bible should be available to all Christians in their own language and that they did not need the mediation of priests to interpret the Bible.[585] [586] Censorship of the Bible included restrictions and the prohibition of possessing or reading, or using the Bible, or any particular editions or translations of it. In most cases, the bans on pious lay people possessing or publicly reading certain Bibles were related to vernacular scripture editions not derived from the Vulgate (the Latin version). Violators of Bible prohibitions have at times been punished by confiscating the Bibles used or distributed, imprisonment, banishment, burning, and execution.[587]

Why did the RCC take such an immutable stance over the centuries? The RCC believed that it, and only it, could interpret the Scriptures. Per the <u>Catechism of the Catholic Church</u>, "The task of interpreting the Word of God authentically has been entrusted solely to the magisterium of the Church, that is, to the Pope and to the bishops in communion with him." [588]

Pope Damasus (366 – 384) commissioned Jerome of Stridon (344? – 420) to undertake what became the Vulgate Bible translation (from its original Greek to Latin).[589] Although Jerome's translation was not immediately accepted, from the mid-6th century, all the separate books were commonly bound in a single cover, usually containing much of Jerome's Old Testament translation from the Hebrew, as well as Jerome's translation of the gospels from their original Greek text. The remainder of the New Testament was taken from older Latin versions, which may have been slightly revised by Jerome.[590] Various editors produced revised texts of the Vulgate over the years. For example, the University of Paris produced a key edition in the 13th century. Its primary purpose was to provide a standard for theological teaching. The earliest printed Vulgate Bibles were all based on this Paris edition.[591] A key benefit of having a common Latin text was that it enabled clerics to reference a text that was uniform.

The following are some examples of the Catholic Church's unwillingness to enable its own laity to read the Bible and its prohibition from translating it into a vernacular language.

- **The Council of Toulouse (1229)** – The Council was called by the local bishop, Folquet de Marselha,[592] to address the perceived threat from the rapid growth of Catharism, also known as Albigensian, for Albi, a city in southern France where it flourished. Catharism was a belief that the universe was a battleground between good, which was the spirit, and evil, which was matter. Human beings were believed to be spirits trapped in physical bodies.

The Council resolved that a search in each parish was to be made for heretics; and that If found, their houses should be destroyed, and the residents imprisoned, and that non-Latin translations of the Bible or any unauthorized copies be destroyed.[593] The Council pronounced:

> **"We prohibit also that the laity should be permitted to have the books of the Old and the New Testament; … expressly forbidding their having the other parts of the Bible translated into the vulgar tongue" (Allix, <u>Ecclesiastical History</u>, II, p. 213)."** [594]

- **Council of Tarragona (1234)** – Declared "No one may possess the books of the Old and New Testaments in any Romance language [i.e., French, Spanish, Italian, Portuguese and Romanian]; and if anyone possesses them, he must turn them over to the local bishop within eight days after promulgation of this decree, so that they may be burned…"[595]

- **John Wycliffe (1330-1384)** – Wycliffe was an Oxford-educated theologian who challenged the Roman Catholic Church hierarchy and claimed the Christian Scriptures were the supreme authority, not the pope. As Steven Lawson explained, "superstition and error were hallmarks of the 14th century, and even the clergy had little knowledge of the Bible."[596] John Wycliffe began his own translation from Latin to English in the early 1380s, with the first version appearing in 1382. Although most people could not read English, they could understand it when read to them. The Bible in the vernacular was a direct challenge to Church authority, which could not control how the Scriptures were to be presented and understood if others held a copy in their own language.[597]

- **Pope Gregory XI (1376)** – Pope Gregory ordered that all literature on the Bible should be placed under ecclesiastical direction. As a result, only the Vulgate edition and a few poor-quality translations in some national languages were tolerated.[598] [599]

- *Council of Constance (1415)* – In session 8 on the 4th of May, the Council of Constance pronounced John Wycliffe a heretic, condemned his memory, and ordered his bones to be exhumed. The archbishop of Canterbury, Arundel, posthumously condemned him again. By the Council's decree, Wycliffe's bones were exhumed, publicly burned, and the ashes thrown into the Swift River.[600]

- *William Tyndale (1536)* – For translating the Bible into English, William Tyndale was burned at the stake. Before his death, Tyndale wrote, "The Church forbade owning or reading the Bible to control and restrict the teachings and to enhance their own power and importance." [601]

- *Pope Pius IV (1555 – 1559)* – His Tridentine Index placed severe restrictions on the ownership of vernacular Bibles. In 1564, the Church published the ten "Tridentine Rules" to clarify its prohibitions on books, which were not necessarily enumerated in the <u>Index of Prohibited Books</u>, including against all heretical and superstitious writings; and the Church also established the punishment of excommunication for those in possession of such works. Over 300 years later, those restrictions were relaxed by Pope Leo XIII (1878 - 1903) in 1896.[602]

- *The Council of Trent (1545 – 1564)* – Because printing presses were creating multiple copies of the New Testament in various vernacular languages, the RCC placed the Protestant Bible on its list of prohibited books; and it forbade any person to read or possess a copy without a license from a bishop or Inquisitor. Rule 4 stated: "…Those, however, who presume to read or possess them [The Bible written in a language other than Latin] without such permission may not receive absolution from their sins till they have handed them over to the ordinary."[603] This rule was approved by Pius IV in 1563.[604] Most people couldn't read, nor understand the Latin Vulgate Bible. And of course, what Catholic layperson is going to visit the local 'Inquisitor' and confess that he had a copy of the New Testament in his own language! Even the Catholic clergy had to obtain a license from their bishops before they were allowed to read the Bible. Booksellers were forbidden to have Bibles in stock for sale under pain of severe punishment.[605]

- *Pope Clement XI (1700 – 1721)* – Issued a papal bull, *Unigenitus*, in 1713, against Jansenism and condemned item-by-item the works of Jansenist theologian, Pasquier Quesne, who wrote *Réflexions morales*. In that document, Pope Clement condemned the direct reading of the Bible by Catholic laity. This Papal bull condemned 101 propositions of Pasquier Quesnel, including propositions 80 and 82:[606]

"80. The reading of Sacred Scripture is for all."
"82. The Lord's Day ought to be sanctified by Christians with readings of pious works and, above all, of the Holy Scriptures. It is harmful for a Christian to wish to withdraw from this reading."
This papal bull, *Unigenitus*, has never been revoked; but if the Catholic Church discussed it today, it would probably be subjected to many qualifications.[607]

- *Pope Pius VII (1800 -1823)* – In 1816, Pope Pius VII referred to the distribution of Christian Bibles as "a most crafty device by which the very foundations of religion are undermined."[608] in his letter of June 29, 1816, Pius VII called Bible societies "a pestilence against which we must take all measures within reach of papal authority."[609] Again, in 1816, he penned the following: "...The Roman Church, accepting only the Vulgate edition according to the well-known prescription of the Council of Trent, disapproves the versions in other tongues and permits only those which are edited with the explanations carefully chosen from writings of the Fathers and Catholic Doctors, so that so great a treasure may not be exposed to the corruptions of novelties, and so that the Church, spread throughout the world, may be 'of one tongue and of the same speech.' " [610] Pope Pius VII also wrote, "The day the Church abandons her universal tongue (Latin) is the day before she returns to the catacombs."[611]

- *Pope Leo XII (1823 – 1829)* – In 1824, he called the Protestant Bible the "Gospel of the Devil" in an encyclical letter in 1824, and he condemned the distribution of the Bible.[612] Pope Leo may have been unaware that the Protestant and Catholic New Testaments were basically identical. Further, no one has ever produced credible evidence that Protestants were purposely mistranslating the New Testament to subvert Catholics. Leo XII's *Ubi primum* (3 May 1824) referenced the misleading commentary material, stating:

- "You have noticed a society, commonly called the Bible Society, boldly spreading throughout the whole world. Rejecting the traditions of the holy Fathers and infringing the well-known decree of the Council of Trent, it works by every means to have the holy Bible translated, or rather mistranslated, into the ordinary languages of every nation. There are good reasons for fear that (as has already happened in some of their commentaries and in other respects by a distorted interpretation of Christ's gospel) they will produce a gospel of men, or what is worse, a gospel of the devil!" [613]

- *Pope Pius VIII (1829 – 1830)* – He was very critical of new translations of the Christian Bible and of Bible societies. Regarding Bible translations and the work of non-Catholic Bible societies, he wrote in his encyclical, *Traditi humiliate,* in 1829, again repeating the unproven assertions that there were notes and inserts in the Protestant Bibles.

   "We must also be wary of those who publish the Bible with new interpretations contrary to the Church's laws. They skillfully distort the meaning by their own interpretation. They print the Bibles in the vernacular and, absorbing an incredible expense, offer them free even to the uneducated. Furthermore, the Bibles are rarely without perverse little inserts to ensure that the reader imbibes their lethal poison instead of the saving water of salvation."[614]

- **Pope Gregory XVI (1831 – 1846)** — This reactionary pope railed against the publication, distribution, reading, and possession of Bibles (even Catholic ones) translated into the vulgar (vernacular) language.[615]

- **Pope Pius IX (1846 – 1878)** – In Item 14 of his encyclical, *Qui pluribus, On Faith and Religion*; he writes: "This is the goal too of the crafty Bible societies which renew the old skill of the heretics and ceaselessly force on people of all kinds, even the

167

uneducated, gifts of the Bible. They issue these in large numbers and at great cost, in vernacular translations, which infringe the holy rules of the Church. The commentaries which are included often contain perverse explanations; so, having rejected divine tradition, the doctrine of the Fathers and the authority of the Catholic Church, they all interpret the words of the Lord by their own private judgment, thereby perverting their meaning... Gregory XVI of happy memory, our superior predecessor, followed the lead of his own predecessors in rejecting these societies in his apostolic letters. It is our will to condemn them likewise."[616]

- **Leo XIII (1878 - 1903) –** In his Apostolic Constitution *Officiorum* (1897) Pope Leo XIII issued the following restrictions on the use of common-language Bibles: "All native-language versions, even those published by Catholics, are absolutely prohibited unless they have been approved by the Apostolic See or edited under the supervision of bishops, with explanatory notes taken from the Church Fathers and learned Catholic writers...All versions of the Holy Books made by any non-Catholic writer whatsoever and in any common language are prohibited, especially those published by Bible Societies, which have been condemned by the Pontiff of Rome on several occasions."[617]

Some Catholic apologists have stated that Catholics were prohibited from joining Bible Societies because these groups might not be using Scriptures approved by RCC sources, or the Bibles had additional comments, and thus were anti-Catholic. Yet, generally, the Bibles were published "without note or comment."[618] Since the Catholic hierarchy wouldn't produce the New Testament in a vernacular language of the common people, the Protestants did so. The Bible societies distributed Bibles for free or for a token price. But instead of rejoicing at this, the popes were angry and condemned the Bible societies.

A common concern was that without the direction of the clergy, the laity would misinterpret the Scriptures. For example, **Ephesians 2:8-9** states, "For by grace you have been saved through faith. And this is not of your own doing; it is the gift of God, not a result of works..." This passage draws a big distinction between many Protestant sects that believe that faith alone will get one to salvation, versus the Catholic belief that it takes faith and good works.

The following is an excerpt from the original Catholic Encyclopedia:[619]

> "Indeed, the reckless distribution of the Scriptures in too many cases becomes an occasion for the profanation of the written Word, rather than for the growth of religion. Instances of abuse of the Bible could be collected freely from the letters of missionaries, Catholic and non-Catholic alike.

> "But for deeper reasons than this, the attitude of the Church toward the Bible societies is one of unmistakable opposition. Believing herself to be the divinely appointed custodian and interpreter of Holy Writ, she cannot without turning traitor to herself, approve the distribution of Scripture 'without note or comment.' The fundamental fallacy of private interpretation of the Scriptures is presupposed by the Bible societies."

Several Catholic apologists have said that the Vulgate version was written in Latin because until the last two-to-three centuries, that was the language of the people. They further lament that languages such as English went through so many changes that it didn't even have a common syntax and uniform spelling for many centuries, and the Church wanted to spare Christians the false view. But it is a spurious argument. Within three centuries after the fall of Rome (476 CE), Latin had become a dead language (except for the educated clergy of the Catholic Church and some nobles); and it had been replaced by the Romance and Germanic languages;[620] although there was a brief resurgence of interest in Latin during the Renaissance period. Yes, all languages go through an evolutionary process (even Latin); but by the late Middle Ages, most European languages could be readily written and read by those who were literate in those languages. It should also be noted that, until the 13th century, most parish priests and many bishops were illiterate.[621] They simply memorized their responses [in Latin] for mass, and if they forgot, they could just make up some strange Latin-like sounds, as their parishioners had no idea what they were saying anyway. The problem was partially tackled by the Fourth Lateran Council in 1215. It took a few decades for the education process to take place, but when bishops started demanding literacy, many priests became motivated to learn. However, complaints of the illiteracy of some parish priests continued through the end of the 14th century.[622]

Let's briefly revisit the differences between the Catholic and Protestant Bibles. The Protestant Bible has 66 books, and the Catholic Bible has 73. Catholic Bibles contain additional Old Testament books referred to as the Deuterocanonical books (Catholic term for second canon) or the Apocrypha (Protestant term which refers to books of doubtful authenticity in authorship). The other Scripture material is basically the same. Interestingly, the King James version (KJV), published in 1611, included the Apocrypha. But the KJV excluded the Apocrypha by 1885.[623]

The Protestant Bible, of course, was compiled during the Reformation; and one of its key leaders, Martin Luther opted to exclude seven books of the Old Testament: (1) Baruch, (2) Judith, (3-4) 1 and 2 Maccabees, (5) Sirach, (6) Tobit and (7) Wisdom (although he translated them). The Catholic Council of Trent reaffirmed its Deuterocanonical books. Note: all seven books were included in the Septuagint, a 3rd-century Greek translation of the Old Testament. However, Martin Luther deleted them, because he is said to have believed that they lacked the authority of the gospels; and for Luther, they had less theological value than the rest of Scripture. Luther argued that these books were not included in the Jewish Canon; thus, they were not divinely inspired. The Protestants were trying to align themselves with the Jewish tradition, and they excluded books from the Hebrew canon. Of course, the irony of Luther's rationale is that he is renowned for being highly anti-Semitic.

In many ways, the Protestants were emulating the early Christians, whose leaders met in councils in the 4th century to approve and ratify books for the New Testament as the authoritative Scriptures of the Church. Either way, the Protestant Bible was a subset of the Catholic Bible.

One might assume that John Wycliffe was correct; the RCC wanted to restrict the availability of the Bible to enhance its own teaching and to control the people. We all are familiar with the dictum, knowledge is power,' and the RCC didn't want to share its 'knowledge,' nor subject itself to explanations of its interpretations. But there may be another explanation which accompanied the RCC's desire for control. While everyone understands that the Old Testament is a repackaging (a translation and adaptation) of the Jewish Tanakh,[624] it is also true that the New Testament is, to a large extent, a Jewish document as well. Many of the contributors to the New Testament were Jewish. For example, the Gospel of Matthew was clearly written by a Jew to address a Jewish audience.

The most prolific New Testament writer, St. Paul, alias Saul of Tarsus, wrote a significant portion of the 27 New Testament books. His Jewish background is indisputable. Paul's Jewishness is evident in the focus of his writing as well. This is true of many New Testament writers. Paul considered himself part of a new Jewish sect, and he apparently hoped to convince others of his vision of redemption.[625] The pages of the New Testament clearly follow a general framework found in Judaism. Its authorship, content, and focus reflect a Jewish tradition. Indeed, the Synoptic Gospels reveal a pattern of historical narratives that are interwoven with instructions found in the Torah.[626] According to Samuel Sandmel of the Hebrew Union College:

> "The controversies between Jesus and the Scribes/Pharisees have no reference outside the community of Israel; Jesus' preaching of the coming kingdom could have had meaning only for Jews; the synagogues in which Jesus reads from the prophets, heals the sick, and forgives sins are Jewish houses of worship for believing Jews and not unconverted gentiles...."[627]

The New Testament is a book that strives to document what its framers viewed as a fulfilled prophecy. "It is written" occurs multiple times as the New Testament writers reinforce their arguments with quotations from the Hebrew Scriptures. Indeed, one purpose of the New Testament was to record the fulfillment of the prophecies and the teachings contained in the Old Testament.[628] But as Robert J. Miller so aptly puts it, "...the 'miracle' of fulfilled prophecy is an artifact of the ingenuity of Christian writers."[629] In other words, there were no fulfilled prophecies.

During the 4th century, soon after Christians were enabled to practice their religion in the Roman Empire without constraint, there was a push to fully separate Christianity from Judaism.[630] Some scholars believe the separation began with the Jewish revolt against Rome (66–74 CE); and it was completed by the end of the Bar Kokhba revolt (132–135 CE). Professor Bernard Starr points out that the Church may have wanted to conceal from its Christian membership that Christianity was originally a Jewish sect, and that Rabbi Yeshua's (Jesus') disciples had continued to maintain their Jewish identities. Would Christians with access to the New Testament have noticed that the word "Jew" appears 202 times, including 82 of those citations in the gospels? Or that the word "Christian" never appears in the gospels at all, since Christianity was still considered a Jewish sect when the Synoptic Gospels were written?[631]

The process of erasing the Jewish identity of Rabbi Yeshua and his disciples continued through the Middle Ages and even modern times, with paintings of Jesus and his followers shown as fair-skinned Europeans with Christian artifacts and practices. These images did not remotely resemble their Jewish heritage and lives in rural villages in Galilee.[632]

The posture of the Catholic Church changed after 1943 when Pope Pius XII issued the encyclical, *Divino afflante spiritu*. This not only enabled Catholics to study Scripture, but it also encouraged biblical reading.[633] Although biblical study by the Catholic laity still remains the exception rather than the rule, at least the Catholics who wish to indulge in reading their Scriptures can do so without concern for Church admonitions or its excessive punishments.

Original Sin

The term, original sin, ties back to Adam's and Eve's fall from grace. Its origin appears to have been based on a mistranslation of Paul's epistle, **Romans 5:12:** "Therefore, as sin came into the world through one man and death through sin, and so death spread to all men because all men sinned." (See Chapter 3). In other words, humanity was linked to sin. However, Jerome of Stridon (c. 347 – c. 419) mistranslated the original Greek passage to the Latin Vulgate version as, "Adam… in whom all men sinned…" That slight difference was viewed by Augustine to mean that all men were guilty of Adam's sin.

The concept of original sin was not truly part of early Christianity. The phrase is not found in Scripture, and Jesus never mentioned it. However, the Christian theologian, Augustine of Hippo (354 – 430 CE), fully formed the concept of original sin in his writings, which were based on Paul's **Romans 5:12-19**, and consequently links sin and death to Adam's transgression.[634] In his book, *Confessions* 8:12, Augustine advanced the idea that God created everything perfect; Adam fell from that state of perfection when he sinned; and the sin affected everyone as it was passed on to every human being since.[635] However, in many ways, Augustine was just trying to refute Pelagius (c. 354 – 418), a monk and Christian theologian, who taught that all humans were basically "good" by nature, and that people could choose to obey God and act morally. But Augustine was determined to prove the monk wrong, and he penned a document, *On the Grace of Christ and on Original Sin*.[636] Unfortunately, Augustine had a lot of influence on Christian theology. Almost a millennium later, the concept was taken up by the Council of Trent, in its Fifth Session, in the mid-16th century (1546).[637] [638]

In many ways, original sin was another invented tenet used by the RCC to control its followers by convincing them they were inherently sinful and needed the Church to help them reach salvation. Jonathan Merritt of the *Religion News Service* refers to original sin as a "theological construct" which was derived over time.[639] This means that while it wasn't explicitly mentioned in Scripture, it was derived from stitching together various passages. It was a concept aggressively advanced by Augustine, who was an extremely troubled man. One can forgive Augustine for believing that God created only perfection, and Adam and Eve fell from that state of perfection. After all, that is what he had been taught in his reading of Genesis. But as for his belief that the results of their sin were passed on to every generation of their progeny, Augustine was influenced by the mistranslation of **Romans 5:12-19**, to which he applied his own 5th century views. Further, the "fall from perfection" was not original to the Christian experience. Augustine of Hippo may not have understood that Genesis was partially modeled after the Babylonian creation myth that the Israelites encountered during their captivity in the 6th century BCE.

The logic of original sin became twisted since the story of Adam and Eve states that they never knew Good nor Evil – until they ate the fruit. Thus, they were innocent of the crime because eating the fruit was not evil, and it certainly was not a sin. They were only being curious. Conceptually, newly created Adam and Eve would have had the moral intelligence of young children. Further, **Genesis 22-23**, reveals Yahweh's true issue: that "man is become one of *us*, to know good and evil: and now, lest he put forth his own hand, and take also of the tree of life, and eat, and live forever." So, the omniscient and omnipotent God feared that mankind would know the difference between good and evil and would live forever! Wow! And exactly who is "us"?

Second, it is highly irrational for the descendants of Adam to be held guilty for this sin, based on what Adam supposedly did. Third, if God is omniscient, then he must have known before he even created Adam and Eve that they would do this. If he knew that beforehand, then why would he create the tree in their vicinity in the first place? [640]

Fourth, neither Jesus of Nazareth, nor his disciples, nor the early Christian Church's (first three centuries) leaders (including Paul) ever mentioned original sin, as the concept hadn't been "invented" yet. Moreover, neither Judaism, which authored Genesis, nor Islam, which adopted much of the Old Testament, supports the concept of original sin. Fifth, if there was no fall, then there was no need for humanity to be rescued or saved. We cannot be restored to a status humanity never possessed.

Last, and this is a crucial point: we know evolution is a fact, and that Adam and never existed. Thus, there was never a first man nor a first woman. So, no Adam; no Garden of Eden; and no state of perfection from which to fall.

Most Christians are not aware of the history and origin of original sin, and even among those who profess to believe in it, many do not appear to fully understand what is being taught. They do not realize that the concept is not mentioned in the Bible, and that it didn't become a dogma of the RCC until the 5th century.

Like so many tenets of faith that were derived over a prolonged timeline, the nascency of original sin comes from the fertile imagination of St. Augustine. And with that myth busting, Mary's immaculate conception can also be denied as a hoax. In the Foreword of Cardinal Newman's manuscript, <u>An Essay on the Development of Christian Doctrine</u>, Ian Ker wrote that "for St. Paul to know anything [about the doctrine of the Immaculate Conception], "...must less believe it, would be fanciful, not to say ludicrous."[641]

The Trinity

The early Church had a problem: it taught that Yeshua was the son of God, and yet it said that Christians worshipped only one God. Further, if Yeshua was God, was he always God? Or had he been God since his death and resurrection, or from the beginning of creation? And if the latter, how does he become the son of God, if he was already God, because that would make him the Son of Himself!

The New Testament refers to Yeshua as the Son of God approximately fifty times; no gospels nor epistles ever referred to him as God the Son. The phrase, Son of God (as in the original Greek), is in the genitive case; this indicates that Rabbi Yeshua originated from and belongs to God the Father. God the Son is not a biblical term; indeed, it does not appear in the Greek, Hebrew, or Aramaic texts. On the other hand, God the Son is a Babylonian term. The Babylonians made Nimrod a god, and when he died, they deified his son, Tammuz, as God the Son. The Babylonians set the precedent for making God a man, and man a God. This polytheistic trinitarianism was intertwined with Greek religion and philosophy, and it appears to have slowly worked its way into Christian thought and creeds some 300 years after Jesus.

The current mainstream teaching in Christianity is that God is a co-equal, co-eternal, one-substance Trinity, and that Jesus (Yeshua) is God. Yet, the historical record is overwhelming that the Christian Church of the first three centuries did not worship God in a three-in-one Godhead. The early Church worshipped one God, the Father, and believed in a subordinate Son. It is an undeniable historical fact that, following the death of Jesus Christ, the early Christians did not include the Trinity in their theological beliefs. It took over 300 years to formulate the main elements of this doctrine. It should be obvious that the Trinity was created by the early Church as a way of reconciling worship of Jesus, while also claiming monotheism.

Why did they need to worship Yeshua of Nazareth anyway? The only gospel in the New Testament that spoke to the divinity of Yeshua of Nazareth was the Gospel of John, which we now know was written in the mid-to-late 2nd century, and with modern technology reviews, it appears to be a forgery. (See Chapter 3). The only other documents that proclaim the divinity of Jesus of Nazareth came from the epistles of Paul, who referred only to "the Christ."

The Council of Nicaea (in 325 CE) had been convened primarily to resolve the debate over Arianism. The Council of Nicaea concluded that the Son was one substance (*homoousios*) with the Father. He is not *like* God but is *fully* and eternally God. What Nicaea left out, of course, was that the Holy Ghost was part of the Godhead. The controversy leading up to that Council was primarily focused on the nature of Yeshua of Nazareth and his relationship to God the Father.

Disagreements soon centered around the nature of the Holy Ghost. The Council of Nicaea did not produce a Trinity; at best, it produced only a duality. Additionally, Paul and other writers of the Bible had not recognized the doctrine of the Trinity.[642] However, the Council of Nicea did produce a statement, "We believe in the Holy Ghost." According to author Karen Armstrong, "This seems to have been added to Athanasius's creed almost as an afterthought. People were confused about the Holy Ghost. Was it simply a synonym for God, or was it something more?"[643]

The word 'Trinity' appears nowhere in the Bible. The newly introduced Holy Ghost was not yet considered an equal member of the Godhead until the First Council of Constantinople in 381 CE, after five decades of political debate.[644] The use of the word, Trinity, was a construct used to articulate Christianity's belief in the oneness of God. And so, at the Council of Constantinople, the belief in the Holy Trinity was officially agreed upon by Church leaders throughout the Roman Empire. There were many precedents for this tritheism, as it is a recurring religious convention found among older world religions: in Egypt, Samaria, Mesopotamia, and even Hinduism.[645]

Once a decision was reached regarding the Trinity, Roman Emperor Theodosius would tolerate no dissenting views. He issued his own edict that read: "We now order that all churches are to be handed over to the bishops who profess Father, Son and Holy Ghost of a single majesty, of the same glory, of one splendor, who establish no difference by sacrilegious separation, but (who affirm) the order of the Trinity by recognizing the persons and uniting the Godhead."[646]

Developing the narrative of the concept of the Trinity fell to a number of Church leaders, including Athanasius of Alexander. The essential foundation of this doctrine was threefold:

1. Christ was with God in the beginning and was God (**John 1:1**)
2. Christ and God the Father are unified (**John 10:30**)
3. New Christians are to be baptized in the name of Father, Son, and Holy Ghost (**Mt 28:19**)

With the deity of Christ officially recognized, the Council of Constantinople in 380 CE extended the concept to the identification of the Holy Ghost within the Godhead. This was accomplished by expanding the Nicene Creed, making the creed fully Trinitarian; and it re-condemned Arianism. This solidified the orthodox doctrine of the full humanity of Jesus Christ. The Council of Chalcedon (AD 451) focused on the relationship of Jesus' humanity to his divinity (known as the *hypostatic union*), and it issued a declaration which became the orthodox statement on the person of Jesus. *Hypostatic union* means that Jesus is one person with two natures and is simultaneously fully God and fully human.

The concept of the Trinity of divine beings was not an idea put forth by Jesus. Instead, it was conceived by the Christian Church to resolve its problem of monotheism. The Trinity denies that Jesus Christ is His Father's only Son. Instead, it teaches that Jesus Christ is the eternally begotten Son of God, which is man-invented, and is illogical. The incoherence of one God in three distinct persons violates the principle of non-contradiction.[647] In other words, God cannot be one being and three persons, simultaneously. Even the most steadfast Christian apologists cannot logically explain the concept of the Trinity.

The Trinitarian fathers could not accept the clear truth of the Bible that Jesus is God the Father's only (birthed) Son; and therefore, it was necessary that the Son had a beginning before God the Father created all things through His Son. To accept this central truth of the Bible would have destroyed their monotheistic doctrine, and so instead, they invented a non-biblical, confusing concept that Jesus is 'the <u>eternally</u> begotten' Son of the Father. It seems ridiculous to imply that God the Father is continually in a state of begetting His Son. This is clearly an ambiguous attempt to rationalize the divinity of Jesus within the constraints of monotheism.

The concept of the Trinity brings confusion and contradiction into the death and resurrection of the Son of God. Scripture is clear that God the Father cannot die because He alone is truly eternal, having no beginning and no end (**Deuteronomy 32:40, Psalm 90:2, 1 Timothy 1:17, 6:16**). However, it was certainly possible for the Son to die.

The Trinity teaches that the Son is co-equal to His Father; however, Scripture clearly states that the Son of God is not co-equal, but is subordinate to the Father. The following are just two of many Scriptures which unambiguously state that Jesus Christ has always remained subordinate to His Father, right from His birth when he was begotten by His Father, before the foundation of the world.

- For by Him all things were created that are in heaven and that are on Earth, visible and invisible, whether thrones or dominions or principalities or powers. All things were created through Him and for Him. *[Colossian 1:16].*
- But I want you to know that the head of every man is Christ, the head of woman is man, and the head of Christ is God. *[1 Corinthians 11:3]*

Another issue with the Trinity doctrine is that it remains nonsensical to most people. That is why the RCC enshrined the doctrine of the Trinity as a "mystery," a divine truth beyond human understanding. Indeed, the doctrine of the Trinity was so irrational, the language needed to explain it was not up to the task of describing it. The Catholic Church was forced to coin new words, such as *'homoousios,'* a Greek term meaning "one substance." Since such words did not mean very much to the average reader/listener; thus, one could understand what the three Persons (hypostasis [Gr]) of the Godhead having "one substance" meant, only if one already had some idea that they were somehow linked.

This doctrine has been problematic for Christianity since its inception. It evolved over many decades, indeed centuries, to try to resolve fundamentally contradictory claims about Yeshua of Nazareth. Its illogic has led to multiple "schisms." To some extent, the Trinity doctrine was constructed originally <u>not</u> to understand the nature of God, but as a weaponized vendetta against alternative views of that era (e.g., Arianism, Macedonianism, etc.). This construct was designed specifically to refute other theologies and to exclude those who adhered to them.

Trinitarian theology has spent hundreds of years wrestling with this inherent inconsistency, and it has ended up with the general guidance, "just accept this difficult concept even if it makes no sense to you". Maybe it is time to admit that the Trinity doesn't make logical sense, rather than suggesting that it is people's lack of understanding that is at fault?

Theology professor, Louis Berkhof, wrote: "The Church confesses the Trinity to be a mystery beyond the comprehension of man. The Trinity is a mystery, not merely in the biblical sense of what is a truth, which was formerly hidden but is now revealed, but in the sense that man cannot comprehend it and make it intelligible."[648] Indeed, the Encyclopedia Americana stated that it was "beyond the grasp of human reason."[649] Professor Millard Erickson, Southwestern Baptist Theological Seminary, wrote that the Trinity "is not clearly or explicitly taught anywhere in Scripture, yet it is widely regarded as a central doctrine, indispensable to the Christian faith..."[650] The bottom line: the Trinity appears to be a theological construction, unsupported in Scripture, nor anchored in logic.

The Holy Ghost

The Bible, from Genesis to Revelation, speaks about one Father God and His only begotten and obedient Son. Many times, the Bible says that the Son sits at His Father's right hand; but nowhere does it say that the Holy Ghost sits next to the Father, or the Son.

In the earliest surviving New Testament, there is no mention of the Holy Ghost. Further, in the early 1960s, the 2nd Vatican Council changed the name, Holy Ghost, to the Holy Spirit. The term "Holy Spirit" had never been used by the RCC prior to that. The terms 'the Spirit of God' and 'the Holy Spirit' [which are anachronisms that were added retroactively] occur approximately 120 times in the Bible. These terms, depending on their context, appear to refer to the presence and power of God the Father or to directly to God the Father. For example: *"And the angel answered and said to her, 'The holy spirit will come upon you, and the power of the Highest* (Father God) *will overshadow you; therefore, also, that Holy One who is to be born will be called the Son of God."* **[Luke 1:35].**

There are a few Scriptures where the term 'the Holy Spirit' refers to the person of God the Father. For example: "Now the birth of Jesus Christ was as follows: After His mother Mary was betrothed to Joseph, before they came together, she was found with child of the Holy Spirit" **[Matthew 1:18].** Here, *'the Holy Spirit'* refers to the Person of God the Father, who is holy and a spirit. There are several examples where Scriptures have been changed to try to justify the Trinity. Here are just two:

> "For there are three that bear witness in heaven: the Father, the Word, and the Holy Spirit; and these three are one." [1 John 5:7]

This particular verse does not appear in any of the early Greek Manuscripts of the Bible dated before the 10th century. **1 John 5:7** was inserted into translations of the Bible, first into the Roman Catholic Latin Vulgate, and then subsequently into the KJV and other popular versions of the Bible to support the doctrine of the Trinity.

> "Go therefore and make disciples of all the nations, baptizing them in the name of the Father and of the Son and of the Holy Spirit." [Matthew 28:19].

This verse, although found in Greek manuscripts of the Bible, was corrupted under the influence of the RCC. It contradicts the original teaching in the Bible that baptizing should always be done in the name of the Son only. The Apostles never baptized converts "in the name of the Father, the Son and the Holy Spirit," but always solely baptized them "in the name of our Lord Jesus Christ," as in **Acts 2:38, 8:16, 10:48,** and **19:5**. There is not one single example in the whole of the Bible where people were baptized with any other words. Matthew wrote his gospel circa 80 CE, and the concept of the Holy Ghost would not surface for another two centuries; yet the Gospel of Matthew was changed retroactively, including the King James version.

The Roman Catholic Church itself admitted that it had changed the exact Baptismal words. Consider the following quotes:

- "The baptismal formula was changed from the name of Jesus Christ to the words Father, Son, and Holy Spirit by the Catholic Church in the second century."[651]
- "Everywhere in the oldest sources it states that Baptism took place in the name of Jesus Christ." "The baptismal formula was changed from the name of Jesus Christ to the words Father, Son, & Holy Ghost by the Catholic Church in the second century."[652]
- *"The early church always baptized in the name of the Lord Jesus until the development of the Trinity doctrine in the 2nd century."*[653]

Even this admission by the RCC appears incredibly disingenuous, as there was no agreed-upon 'Trinity' until the 4th century. The only thing relevant to this discussion, which occurred in the late 2nd century, was that Theophilus of Antioch mentioned the triad of God, the Word, and Wisdom. Other Church Fathers refer to the "divine triad." One of these was Tertullian, who, because he wrote in Latin, provided the origin of the English word "Trinity" (i.e., *trinitas*).[654] But other than these terms being coined, nothing changed until the 4th century. The terms used in the 2nd century don't reflect trinitarian belief. They do not profess a triune or tri-personal God, as they did not consider in using such terms to be referring to persons equally divine. A common strategy for defending monotheism in this period was to emphasize the unique divinity of the Father.[655]

None of the manuscripts of the Bible are totally error-free, and where a verse in a manuscript contradicts other clear verses found elsewhere in Scripture, as in the case of **Matthew 28:19,** then it is right to investigate and question the authenticity of that verse. Yeshua of Nazareth said: "All authority has been given to Me in heaven and on earth. Go therefore and make disciples of all the nations, baptizing them in my name." *[Matthew 28:18-19].*

There is no hiding the fact that the concept of the Trinity was developed three full centuries after Jesus died. The Trinity doctrine would evolve over time as an orthodox Christian response to Arianism. To condemn Arianism, the Council of Nicea in the early 4th century had to produce a statement of belief that Jesus of Nazareth and God the Father were equal. And, as previously mentioned, there was no concept of the Holy Ghost being an equal part of the Trinity until the late 4th century. And so for over three centuries, Baptism was performed in the name of Jesus.

In the 4th century, Cappadocian theologians including, Basil of Caesarea, Gregory of Nyssa, and Gregory of Nazianzus, together formulated orthodox Trinitarian doctrine and made it possible for the Council of Constantinople (381) to affirm the divinity of the Holy Spirit. The Cappadocians made a clear distinction between *hupostasis* and *ousia* (which can be translated to *particular* and *universal*), thereby establishing orthodox trinitarian vocabulary.[656]

The Saints

A saint, originally known as a 'hallow', is a person who is recognized as having an exceptional degree of holiness or closeness to God.[657] The first persons honored as saints were the martyrs. Pious legends of their deaths were considered affirmations of the truth of their faith in Christ. By the 4th century, however, "confessors"—people who had confessed their faith not by dying, but by word and life deeds—began to be venerated publicly.[658] In the early Church, saints were often proclaimed by acclamation, which is an overwhelming vocal approval or assent without ballot. And sometimes, they were proclaimed locally (and nowhere else). Originally, the Church did not have a highly developed process for proclaiming saints. But that would change. From the 5th through the 12th centuries, canonizations were performed by the local bishop. However, "because of the abuses evidenced in the granting of veneration to individuals," papal intervention was introduced.[659] In 1170, Pope Alexander III (c. 1100/1105-1181) decreed that no one could be declared a saint without the permission of the Supreme Pontiff.[660]

When the Church formalized canonization in the 13th century, the traditional saints were grandfathered in. Being a hierarchical, structured religion, the Catholic Church (after hundreds of years without a process) created a much stricter process for the canonization of its saints. Canonization is the act by which the Catholic Church declares that a person who has died was a saint, upon which declaration, the person is included in the "canon", or list of recognized saints. Pope John XV (985 – 996) began the canonization process, starting with St. Ulrich of Augsburg. In the 12th century, the RCC centralized the process. Later, in 1234, Pope Gregory IX (1227 – 1241) asserted that only a pope had the authority to declare a saint.[661] Finally, in 1588, Pope Sixtus V (1585 – 1590) formalized the canonization process[662] which did not dramatically change in the next 450 years. Further, Pope Urban VIII (1622 – 1644) issued a decree in 1642 that gave Rome centralized control[663] of the canonization process.

One of the more humorous requirements for canonization for sainthood is that the prospective candidate must be Catholic. Really? Mary, Joseph, Mary Magdalene, and the twelve disciples (including Matthias, who replaced Judas Iscariot) – all deemed to be saints – were never Catholic; they were Jews!

Today, the formal canonization process includes a five-year, post-death waiting period before the process of canonization can begin. The process has four steps.[664] First, the local bishop conducts an investigation into the candidate's life, and he officially agrees to accept a candidate for consideration; if so, the candidate is called a "Servant of God". Second, the Congregation for the Causes of Saints scrutinizes the evidence, and once a candidate is formally recognized by the pope, he or she can be called "Venerable". Third, once a verified miracle occurs in the candidate's name, then he or she becomes beatified (is known as "Blessed"); an exception is made for martyrs who do not require the first verified miracle. Fourth, upon the verification of a second miracle (or the first one for martyrs), then the pope announces the candidate as a "saint." In total, two miracles are generally required for canonization, and nearly all miracles in our modern age turn out to be unexplained medical cures.[665] So, if the consulted doctors cannot explain the cure or how quickly the cure took, then it was a miracle!

The canonization process begins with veneration, then beatification, and then sainthood. The advantages of this canonization process for the "saints" are unknown, as they are dead and are already believed to be in the Christian heaven. Catholics pray to saints that they intercede with God on their behalf. They could do that regardless of whether the deceased individual was canonized as a saint or not. The Catholic Church believes that the saints are important because they are role models worthy of imitation, provide a guide for today's Catholics to live their lives, and they are heavenly helpers for those who pray for their intercession.[666] The RCC doesn't explain why such intercessions might be needed, as its all-perfect God already knows everything. Additionally, the RCC teaches that canonization becomes an infallible statement that a given individual is in Heaven.

Theoretically, saints are more than just people who live a good life; they must demonstrate virtues of justice, temperance, fortitude, and prudence as well as the theological virtues of faith, hope, and charity.[667] In spite of its lofty goals for sainthood, and while it has admittedly been an evolved process, the Catholic Church (both East and West) has demonstrated with some of its past selections that it has set a relatively low bar for sainthood, one that is more skewed toward a political rationale. Let's review a sample of some of its more questionable saint selections:

- o **St Constantine** (306 - 337), Emperor of the Roman Empire, Emperor Constantine never bothered to learn and understand the Christian religion. His only concern was that his subjects should be united under one religion. It was all about power and control. This brutal emperor had his brother-in-law, his teenage nephew, his eldest son, and his wife all murdered. He interfered continually with the ecclesiastical side of the Church. Although declared a saint of Orthodox Christianity, Constantine may not have actually been a converted Christian. Norbert Brox, a professor of church history, asserts that "Constantine did not experience any conversion; there were no signs of a change of faith in him. He never said of himself that he had turned to another god [because he worshiped the deity, Sol Invictus (the victorious sun god)]." [668]

- • **St. Olga** (890 - 969) of Kiev is known for her subjugation of the Drevlians, a tribe that had killed her husband, Prince Igor. Olga invited the rival leaders to meet with her, and then she had them buried alive. Next, she massacred thousands of people who came to her husband's funeral. After she agreed to peace with a neighboring town (Iskorosten), she had the town burned to the ground, and its fleeing citizens enslaved. Later, she strongly promoted Christianity. A saint of Orthodox Christianity. [669]

- • **St. Vladimir** (956 – 1015) (Grand Prince of Kiev), was notorious for his barbarism and immorality (rapine). He tried to unite his kingdom under Slavic paganism as a usurper. Renowned for his licentious behavior, at one time he had a concubine of several hundred women. Fleeing from his brother, he went to the kingdom of Polotsk; when the daughter of the king refused to marry him, he raped her, and then he killed her father. [670] He had his brother Yaropolk killed, and he raped his widowed sister-in-law. He agreed to be baptized a Christian for political reasons. Afterwards, he began forced conversions throughout his kingdom. A saint of Orthodox Christianity. [671]

- • **St. Olaf II Haraldsson** (995 – 1030), King of Norway. He converted his nation to Christianity using force. This bloodthirsty Viking viciously tortured, maimed, and killed those who refused to convert or who continued to follow their old religion. He lost his kingdom and died in battle (having nothing to do with his religion); he was soon declared a martyr and then a saint by the Roman Catholic Church (canonized one year later by a local Bishop Gremkjell). [672]

- • **Pope St. Pius V** (1566 - 1572), having served as the Inquisitor General, used the Inquisition during his papacy to search out and eliminate all known Protestants from the Italian peninsula. A publicly avowed enemy of nepotism (for others), he appointed his nephew a cardinal. He is famous for excommunicating Queen Elizabeth I, who wasn't even Catholic; and in a papal bull, he commanded English Catholics to resist the queen's rule; and it stated that those who remained loyal to Elizabeth would also be excommunicated. [673]

- • **St. Junipero Serra** (1713 - 1784), a Franciscan monk, led a movement in California to bring thousands of native Americans to Catholic missions, where the natives became a source of slave labor. Families were separated, and disease was rampant. Junipero Serra's Franciscans punished any transgression of their moral code by the neophytes with brutal beatings.[674] Serra was canonized a saint in 2015, but many feel that he was integral to a system that decimated the population of Native Americans in the colonial era. [675]

The theme of the above saint selections points to politics. If you do something which helps the Catholic Church, even if the means are despicable, then the RCC rewards you with sainthood.

Finally, there are those whose saintly actions were make-believe, as there is no evidence that they even existed; and to the credit of the modern RCC, they have been removed as saints. In 1969, Pope Paul VI removed 93 saints from the liturgical calendar,[676] due to a lack of evidence for their existence. It is unfortunate that the RCC doesn't require more evidence for some of its other beliefs. Among the more well-known saints removed by Paul VI are the following:

- St. Christopher (*Saint of Travelers*)
- St. Ursula (*Myth of 4th century Britain*)
- St. Nicholas (*Goodbye, Santa*)
- St. George (*Sorry, England, the dragon slayer is no more*)
- St. Barbara (*Myth of 4th century Greece*)

The Papal Saints

Given that the men selected as popes are the "Vicars of Christ" on Earth and given that they are "elected" by a quorum of their righteous peers, pious leaders of the RCC, you would think that the majority of them would have led decent lives and thus become saints, in an almost de facto effort. But that is not the case at all.

According to the Catholic Church, there have been 267 popes/bishops of Rome (up to Pope Leo XIII). In reality, there have been 264, if we count Pope Benedict IX once (not three times), and if we are truthful, that Peter was never the bishop of Rome. Of the 264 popes, 82 have been recognized as saints. That is 31% overall.

The original 34 bishops/popes were all declared saints, as 30 of them were considered martyrs (according to Catholic tradition). Never mind that most of those martyrdoms were not substantiated; indeed, in many cases, there was clear evidence that they were not martyred. There is substantiated evidence for only two bishops of Rome (Fabian and Sixtus II) being martyred for the entire span of the Catholic Church's existence. For the sake of statistical wonderment, if we remove the 28 popes for whom no evidence of martyrdom exists, that would bring us to 54 out of 264 popes, or 20.45%.

Since the 11th century, when its canonization process for sainthood was inaugurated, the Catholic Church has only canonized eight popes as saints (approximately 5 % over that 1,000-year time period), including the not-so-saintly Pope Pius V. Of course, there are eight more beatified popes for that time period that are "in the queue." But as time progresses, it becomes less likely that they will be canonized. Of the eight canonized saints from the last ten centuries, four of them lived in the 20th century. Thus, with <u>so many</u> of the early "bishops of Rome" declared saints due to their unsubstantiated martyrdoms, and <u>so many</u> popes in the 4th to 9th centuries declared saints via acclamation by the local population (a sort of peer pressure, mob rule), and <u>so few</u> popes declared saints once a process was put into place to verify their lives, what does that say about the men chosen to be the popes of the RCC? Generally, the above statistics do not speak well of the overall quality and saintliness of the men chosen historically to be God's representative on Earth.

Heresies and Schisms

Since the early days of Christianity, many disputes have arisen among members of the Church. In the first three centuries of Christianity, heresy and schism were not clearly distinguished. Heresy is understood today to mean the denial of revealed truth as taught by the Church.[677] And heresy is defined in relation to orthodoxy, which has been in the process for centuries of clarifying beliefs in opposition to people or doctrines that are perceived as incorrect. Heresy is distinguished from both apostasy and schism.[678] Apostasy is considered the total abandonment of the Christian faith after it has been accepted,[679] while schism is a formal and deliberate breach of Christian unity, without being based essentially on doctrine.[680]

The Catholic Church makes a distinction between material and formal heresy. Material heresy means, in effect, "holding erroneous doctrines through no fault of one's own" due to ignorance, and is neither a crime nor a sin since the individual has made the error in good faith. Formal heresy is "the willful and persistent adherence to an error in matters of faith" on the part of a baptized person.[681] A Catholic who embraces a formal heresy is considered to have automatically separated his or her soul from the Catholic Church. Here, "matters of faith" means dogmas which have been proposed by the infallible magisterium[682] of the Church and, in addition to this intellectual error, "pertinacity in the will" in maintaining it in opposition to the teaching of the Church must be present.[683]

All that said, there was extensive diversity among the early Christian Church, each group presenting its own version of Christianity. There was no actual orthodox belief early on, as each Christian group developed its own distinct views. Heresy assumes a dominant Nicene Christianity, but that orthodoxy vs. heresy dichotomy just didn't exist until the mid-4th century. Thus, heresy was a sort of insider term, and it was weaponized to differentiate between "us vs. them," as various Christian sects competed for domination as the centrist view.

Heresies have been a major source of conflict within Christianity throughout its two-millennia history. Christian Churches have responded to heresies in a variety of ways, including theological debate, excommunication, and even violence. Heresies tend to result in schisms in the Church. Of these, there were four schisms which significantly fragmented Christianity: (1) Arianism, (2) the Separation of the Oriental Orthodox, (3) the Great Schism, and (4) the Protestant Reformation.

Arianism (4th – 7th century CE)

Arianism was the first of the great Christological heresies to threaten the unity of the Church seriously. Arianism proposed that Jesus, as the Son of God, was created by God. It was proposed early in the 4th century by the Alexandrian priest, Arius. Arianism is often considered a form of Unitarian theology because it stresses a belief in God the Father at the expense of the Trinity, the doctrine of three distinct persons in one Godhead.[684]

These disagreements divided the Church into various factions for over 55 years, from the time of the First Council of Nicaea in 325 CE until the First Council of Constantinople in 381 CE and for several centuries beyond that.[685] Arius's Christology was a form of Adoptionism theology. His basic view was that the Son came into being through the will of the Father, and thus, the Son had a beginning. Although the Son was before all eternity, he was not eternal, and Father and Son were not of the same essence.[686]

An opposing view was advanced by Bishop Athanasius regarding the divinity of the Son before he took on flesh. Thus, at the heart of Athanasius's Christology was a religious focus. That led him to conclude that the divine nature in Jesus was identical to that of the Father, and that Father and Son have the same substance. He insisted on the need for the Nicene homoousios to express the Son's unity with the Father.[687] Athanasius defended the divinity of the Son (and by extension the Holy Ghost) against those whose theological beliefs saw this as nonsensical.[688]

Separation of the Oriental Orthodox (mid-5th century).

The six autocephalous (self-governing) Oriental Orthodox Churches (Coptic, Syriac, Armenian, Ethiopian, Eritrean, and Malankara) split from the rest of Christianity in 451 CE, following the Council of Chalcedon. The schism between Oriental Orthodox and the rest of the Church resulted in part from the refusal of Dioscorus, the Patriarch of Alexandria, to accept the Christological dogmas promulgated by the Council of Chalcedon on Jesus's two natures (divine and human). Most Christians accepted the council's statement that Christ has two natures (human and divine) within one person. Church leaders who rejected this teaching broke away to form the Oriental Orthodox Churches. Oriental Orthodoxy emphasizes the one nature of Christ, although it rejects Eutychian monophysitism.[689]

The Oriental Orthodox Churches accepted that Christ had two natures, but they insisted that those two natures are inseparable and united. Dioscorus would accept only "of" or "from" two natures, but not "in" two natures. To the leadership of the remainder of the Christian Church, the Dioscorus proclamation was tantamount to Nestorianism, which they rejected.

There were many attempts at reconciliation, including an extreme attempt in 518 whereby the new Byzantine Emperor, Justin I, who had accepted the results of the Chalcedon Council, demanded that the entire Church in the Roman Empire accept the Council's ruling, or he would replace all of the non-Chalcedonian bishops, including the patriarchs of Antioch and Alexandria.[690] This was not the only time that interference in ecclesiastical affairs by Byzantine emperors exacerbated a bad situation.

Great Schism (1054 onward)

Caused by numerous factors, the three most important issues were: (1) the doctrinal differences between the Eastern (Orthodox) and Western (Roman) Churches, (2) the Eastern Church's rejection of universal papal authority proclaimed by Rome, and (3) the growing sociopolitical differences between the Eastern and Western Churches. However, what triggered the Great Schism was a change introduced into the Nicene Creed unilaterally by the RCC. This was a pivotal moment in Christianity, and it affected "Christendom" for centuries.

The final countdown for the Great Schism began with the Norman invasion of southern Italy in 1016, and for subsequent decades, there was a suppression of Greek practices in the region's churches, which had a strong Byzantine influence. Archbishop Leo of Ochrid wrote a comprehensive critique of the Latin beliefs and practices divergent from those of the Eastern Church, especially the filioque, mandatory clerical celibacy, and the use of unleavened bread in the Eucharist.[691]

The original Nicene Creed said only "from the Father" and this is what early Christians, and particular the Eastern Church, believed. However, the RCC did not think that it properly emphasized the divinity of Jesus and his equality with the Father, so it added "and the Son" at a Western council called by Charlemagne in 809. This is referred to as the *filioque* (Latin for 'from the Son'). After resisting Germanic pressure for over 200 years to formally adopt the filioque, in 1014 the RCC used the term in public worship at the coronation of Henry II, Holy Roman Emperor. Forty years later, the RCC would accuse the Greek Christians of being heretical for <u>not</u> using the filioque. And so, in 1054 the Constantinople Patriarch, Michael Cerularious (1043 – 1058) was excommunicated in the name of Pope Leo IX (1049 – 1054); and Patriarch Cerularious excommunicated Pope Leo.

The filioque was just a final outrage committed between two sparring Churches. These two halves of the Christian universe had been in various rifts for the past 800 years. From Constantinople's perspective, the biggest issue was the reassertion of papal claims to have jurisdictional authority over <u>all</u> Christian Churches.[692] To potentially resolve the filioque, mandatory clerical celibacy, and the use of unleavened bread in the Eucharist, Pope Leo sent an RCC delegation to Constantinople. For unknown reasons, the delegation was led by Cardinal Humbert of Silve Candida; he was known as a hot-head and anti-Byzantine cleric.

Humbert refused to greet Patriarch Michael Cerularius with the proper protocol, and then Cerularius refused future audiences with Cardinal Humbert. The latter served Patriarch Michael with a bull of excommunication and returned to Rome, where he learned that Pope Leo IX had died soon after he had departed for Constantinople. The next Pope, Victor II (1055 – 1057), could have revoked Humbert's excommunication, but he chose not to.[693] Although in 1965, Pope Paul VI and Patriarch Athenagoras I lifted their Church's mutual anathemas, the RCC and Orthodox Churches are still not in communion with each other.

Protestant Reformation (1519 onward)

The Protestant Reformation began in Wittenberg, Germany, on October 31, 1517, when Martin Luther (1483 – 1546), a Catholic monk and a teacher, published a document (that is, nailed his written thoughts) which he called *Disputation on the Power of Indulgences*, or *95 Theses*.[694]

The reformation was caused by a combination of several factors: more than a century of dissatisfaction with the Catholic Church, whose popes and bishops were demonstrating an increasing abuse of spiritual power for political and material gain; and the desire of Henry VIII for a divorce, accompanied by the Pope's refusal to grant him one.[695] Among the various abuses of the clergy, money-generating practices such as the sale of indulgences was the catalyst that prompted Martin Luther to call for change.

Many ordinary people were particularly worried about what would happen to them when they died. The RCC was teaching that most of them were not good enough to go straight to heaven, so they would be sent instead to a place called "Purgatory." This concept was invented in the 12th century. In Purgatory, they would be given a second chance to work off their sins and would eventually become good enough to go to heaven. However, this post-death purification effort was not biblical teaching; but it was a theological interpretation by zealous Catholics. Over time, the Church offered to speed up the process by selling what they called "indulgences which served as a sort of voucher that gave them time off from purgatory.[696] Indulgences became a cash-cow for the RCC, and its abuse is what motivated Martin Luther to publish his document.

The Protestant Reformation that occurred in Europe during the 16th century was caused by the overall corruption in the RCC and the inappropriate use of papal power. The Reformation prompted the rest of the Western world to question their Church's authority. There was a strong undercurrent of secular rulers, such as King Henry VIII, who simply needed an excuse to break free of papal limitations.

The Renaissance popes had been highly corrupt and had abused their power. Clerical discipline was lax. Priests were supposed to be celibate; but many kept concubines and had illegitimate children who then had to be supported out of church funds. Worship services were conducted in Latin, which ordinary people did not understand. People began to question the legitimacy of the pope's claim to be Christ's representative (or "vicar") on Earth.[697]

Protestantism emerged as one of the four major branches of Christianity, alongside the RCC, Oriental Orthodox, and Eastern Orthodox Churches. And there were several long-lasting effects, including:[698]

- The establishment of many Protestant Churches, groups, and movements, such as Lutheranism, Calvinism, Anglicanism, and the Society of Friends (i.e., Quakers), among many others.
- Translation of the Bible into German, French, English, and other languages.
- The Counter-Reformation - a movement within the Roman Catholic Church to reform and revive itself.
- Improved training and education for some Roman Catholic priests.
- The end of the sale of indulgences.
- Creation of an alternative branch of Christianity competing with the RCC in Western Europe and the Americas.

Inquisition and Witches

Inquisitions

The Tribunal of the Holy Office of the Inquisition was originally intended to maintain Catholic orthodoxy. The Catholic Inquisition was a judicial procedure and a group of institutions whose aim was to combat heresy, apostasy, blasphemy, witchcraft, and deviant customs; in short, it was to suppress dissent within the Catholic Church. Violence, torture, or the simple threat of their application, were used by the Inquisition to extract confessions and denunciations from heretics.[699] An analysis of Inquisition records indicated that while most sentences consisted of penances (like wearing a cross sewn on one's clothes or going on a pilgrimage), convictions of unrepentant heresy were handed over to the secular courts, which generally resulted in execution or life imprisonment.[700]

The first Inquisition was established in 1184 in Languedoc, France, with the aim of combating religious deviation, such as apostasy or heresy, particularly among the Cathars. The Inquisition was permanently established in 1229 (Council of Toulouse), and it was largely run by the Dominicans.[701]

The English term, "inquisition," can apply to any one of several institutions that worked against heretics or other offenders of the canon law of the RCC (Canon Law Penal Sanctions).[702] The canon law of the Catholic Church is how the Church organizes and governs itself; it is the system of laws and ecclesiastical legal principles made and enforced by the hierarchical authorities of the Catholic Church. It generally refers to a judicial process, not an organization. For over 600 years, the Inquisition in various European countries and in the New World (Central and South America and Catholic-colonized Caribbean islands) enforced rigid RCC orthodoxy. In many ways, the Inquisition embodied the power of religion over the State. The words of **John 15:6** were often the rationale for the death of unrepentant heretics: "If a man abide not in me, he is cast forth as a branch and is withered; and men gather them, and cast them into the fire, and they are burned."

The Spanish Inquisition was just one of many such institutions within the RCC, but it is the most infamous. Under the supreme council of the Spanish Inquisition were 14 local tribunals in Spain and several in the colonies. Hundreds of thousands of Spanish Jews, Muslims, and later Protestants were forcibly converted, expelled from Spain, or executed.[703] Because the Spanish Inquisition had no budget, it relied on the confiscation of property from those denounced to acquire funds.[704] Thus, it had a financial motivation to find its victims guilty. The Inquisition expanded geographically in the 16th century, along with Spanish conquests; and it took root in Mexico in 1570. In 1574, some Protestants were burned at the stake there, and the Inquisition then came to Peru, where Protestants were likewise tortured and burned alive.[705] The tribunals in Mexico and Peru were particularly harsh;[706] and they would continue through 1820.

Additionally, the inquisition was activated whenever the RCC felt the need to repress new scientific thought. Galileo is a well-known case, but the Church also condemned other scientific endeavors, such as the study of human anatomy. Translating the RCC's own Scriptures into a vernacular language that the people could understand also drew the attention of the Inquisition.

The Emperor Napoleon almost succeeded in terminating the Inquisition in countries such as Spain and Italy; and he released its chained prisoners in 1808. In 1810, after Napoleon's second capture of Rome, he decided to transfer all of the Vatican's archives to France. Napoleon also demanded that Inquisition records from the Vatican archives be sent to Paris, so he could prove that the Inquisition was evil; but more than 30 crates of Inquisition documents were lost in transit. The first convoy contained 3,239 cases; and there were two further convoys containing Inquisition files, including those of Galileo,[707] which did survive the trip. Napoleon also liberated the Jews in the papal states; and he removed their travel restrictions.

Napoleon's closure of inquisition tribunals in Spain may have been brief, but it had major implications in revealing the previously secret inquisitorial archives. Although some major destruction of archival materials did occur, many Spanish inquisition records were preserved, seized, and immediately reviewed to develop a more accurate "source-based" historical perspective.[708] Later, when Napoleon was deposed, the European "old order" returned to power with King Ferdinand VII in 1814, and the Inquisition was reinstated. Six years later, it was temporarily halted, but it would soon begin again for a final decade.

Modern historians estimate that in more than 350 years of active effort, some 150,000 people were prosecuted for various offenses under the Spanish Inquisition, and between 3,000 and 5,000 were executed.[709] The last execution of the Inquisition took place in Spain in 1826, which occurred via the garroting of the Catalan school teacher, Gaietà Ripoll, for purportedly teaching Deism in his school.[710] The practices of the Inquisition were finally outlawed in 1834.

Later, the Inquisition altered its name to Congregation for the Doctrine of the Faith. In 2005, the head of the Congregation for the Doctrine of the Faith, Joseph Aloisius Ratzinger, was elected Pope Benedict XVI.

Witches

Throughout the medieval era, mainstream Christian teaching had disputed the existence of witches and denied any power to witchcraft, condemning it as pagan superstition.[711] Concern and prosecution of witchcraft became more pronounced during the Renaissance period. And while that occurred almost a century prior to Martin Luther's rebellion against Catholic abuses, the most intense witch-hunting coincided with the Protestant Reformation and Counter-Reformation,[712] and it occurred on both sides (Catholic and Protestant). Indeed, the largest witch hunts occurred in Protestant Germany. The creation of the concept of devil-worship, followed by its persecution, enabled the Christian Churches to more easily subordinate people to authoritarian control and to denigrate women openly. What was passed off as witchcraft was simply a fictional creation of these Christian Churches.

In 906, the Canon *Episcopi*,[713] an RCC ruling, declared that belief in the existence and operation of witchcraft was heresy. This early ecclesiastical statement describes witchcraft as the practice of pagan religion, and it ascribes the acts of witches to dreams and fantasies. This document would initially limit the scope of Inquisitions to heretics and apostates. When the Inquisition came into being, it initially had no interest in witchcraft because it appeared related to the practice of another religion.

On June 13, 1233, Pope Gregory IX (1227 – 1241) had authorized the killing of witches via his papal bull, *Vox in Rama*.[714] Fortunately, that particular perversion just didn't catch on. This was the same pope who recommended the wanton extermination of all domestic cats across Europe. Approximately 250 years later, at the request of Inquisitor Heinrich Kramer, in 1484, Pope Innocent VIII (1484 – 1492) issued a papal bull, *Summis desiderantes affectibus*, declaring that witches did indeed exist; and the bull authorized their "correcting, imprisoning, punishing, and chastising;"[715] and thus, it became a heresy to believe otherwise. As the Inquisitions proceeded through the 1400s, their focus shifted from Jews and heretics towards so-called witches. Indeed, in that era, witchcraft was seen as the most extreme form of heresy.[716]

Church authorities tortured and killed thousands of women (that is, approximately 80% were women),[717] [718] and a significant number of men, in an effort to get them to confess that they flew through the sky, had sexual relations with demons, turned into animals, or engaged in various sorts of black magic. These images depicted what Christians imagined went on at a gathering of witches. People typically fear what they don't understand. Thus, witches were doubly feared because they were allegedly agents of Satan seeking to undermine Christian society, and because no one really knew what witches did or how. In the place of real knowledge or information, Christian leaders contrived evil acts and created stories that led to hate and fear of witches. Almost everything that was "known" at the time about witches was pure fiction; they were inventions by Church authorities who told the laity that witches were a threat. It was in this environment of widespread suspicion, fear, and intolerance that witch hunting thrived, often creating a mass hysteria among the population.[719]

One of the most famous developments of the Inquisition's witch-craze was the publication of the *Malleus Maleficarum (Hammer of Witches)*[720] by Heinrich Kramer in 1487. This Dominican monk wrote a lurid, fictitious account of what they said witches were really like. The *Malleus Maleficarum* is a guidebook for identifying and prosecuting witches. It became the leading manual during the witch hunts in Europe. The book promoted the persecution of women, as it linked witchcraft to heresy. In reality, many of the so-called witches were just marginalized members of society with no power, such as widows, the elderly, alcoholics, the mentally ill, or the outspoken.[721] Although widely used, the *Malleus's* violent and misogynistic content led to its eventual ban in many countries. Indeed, soon after it was published, it was condemned by the Inquisition theologians in Cologne for recommending illegal procedures.[722] Even the Spanish Inquisition cautioned its members not to believe everything the *Malleus* said.[723] But the Inquisition had the papal approval to proceed.[724]

As stated by writer, Austin Cline, Regional Director for the Council for Secular Humanism, "The persecution of witches reached its zenith at a time when Christianity's attitudes against sex had long since turned into full-blown misogyny."[725] It is amazing and sad how celibate men became so obsessed with the sexuality of women. As it is stated in Malleus Maleficarum: "All witchcraft comes from carnal lust, which is in women insatiable." Another section describes how witches were known to "...collect male organs in great numbers, as many as twenty or thirty members together, and put them in a bird's nest..."[726]

Confessions of witchcraft, extracted under torture or threat of torture, commonly came attached to denouncements of other possible witches, which kept the Inquisitors in business. The complete toll of victims is impossible to learn. Various accounts say 5,000 witches were killed in the province of Alsace, 900 in the city of Bamberg, about 2,000 in Bavaria, 311 in Vaud, 167 at Grenoble, 157 at Wurzburg, and 133 in a single day in Saxony. Some smaller villages were exterminated.[727] The period of the European witch trials with the most active phase and the largest number of fatalities seems to have occurred between 1560 and 1630. [728]

It should not be surprising that just about every torture victim eventually confessed.[729] When people are tortured, and especially when the torture involves sexual abuse, it doesn't take long for the victim's world to become reduced to nothing but the pain, and a desire for the pain to end. When the only important thing is the cessation of pain, the victim will tell the torturers whatever they want to hear. It may not be the truth, but if the pain lessens, then at that moment, that's all that matters.

The "heretics" who were the earlier targets of the Inquisition were rarely executed at first. They typically had a chance to repent and submit to the Church; only after relapsing into heresy did they generally become subject to execution. Even then, they might still be given another chance to repent. Those declared to be witches received few reprieves, and only rarely were accused witches allowed to go free after repenting. It was believed that their evil was too much of an existential threat to Christian society, and they had to be completely excised, not unlike cancer, which has to be cut out lest it kill the entire body. There was simply no tolerance or patience for the witches.[730]

The Protestant and Catholic Churches' creation of witchcraft and devil worship has exacted a heavy and bloody toll on humanity. The centuries of obsession with witchcraft underscore the terrible power of supernatural beliefs. Biblical passages such as **Exodus 22:18** contributed significantly: "Thou shalt not suffer a witch to live." Lest anyone imagine that the persecution of witches has been relegated to the distant past, it must be noted that with these Christian precedents already established, witch hunts – and killings – continue well into our own "enlightened" times. Modern witchcraft persecutions were driven largely by religious fundamentalism and are further exacerbated by factors such as civil conflict, poverty, and resource scarcity.[731]

Scotland had more than its share of witch hunts. The persecutions began in the early 16th century, and they spanned two centuries, during which approximately 4,000 people were accused of witchcraft, a vast majority of them women. They were brutally tortured and coerced into false confessions. Two-thirds of those accused were executed. In 2022, Nicola Sturgeon, former First Minister of Scotland, issued a formal apology for the "egregious historical injustice" of the witch hunts, commenting that "the deep misogyny that motivated it has <u>not</u> [been consigned to history]. We live with that still."[732]

"Those who can make you believe absurdities can make you commit atrocities" – Voltaire

Marian Doctrine

Since the Middle Ages, devotion to Mary has been very strong among the laity, and it reached a high pitch in 1854 when Pius IX tried to declare an infallible dogma in the papal bull, *Ineffabilis Deus*, regarding the Immaculate Conception. The Marian Doctrine[733] consists of four dogmas that are taught by the Roman Catholic Church:

1) Mary is the "Mother of God";
2) She was free of original sin from the moment of her conception;
3) She was a perpetual virgin; and

4) She was assumed body and soul into Heaven

In many ways, the four Marian dogmas are harmless, even though they cannot be proven, and indeed, there is not one shred of Christian Scripture that provides support for these dogmas. However, they do demonstrate how hard the RCC had to work to get these four dogmas accepted. Embellishments to the legend of Mary seem to have taken form in the 5th century, and they have continued through the 20th century. The story of the virgin birth is covered in the Gospels of Matthew and Luke, but the Marian dogmas are based on Catholic tradition. Indeed, Scripture has very little to say about Mary. She appeared with others on the day of Pentecost. And Paul said she was "a descendent of David" **(Romans 1:3)**, which is effectively hearsay.[734] Later, the writer of the Gospel of Luke invented a genealogy for her in order to try and back up Paul's misinformation.

The first point that Mary is the mother of God is generally accepted by all the Christian sects, even though the Trinity caused some concern, as she was the mother of Jesus only, not God the Father, nor the Holy Spirit. In 431, the Council of Ephesus solemnly declared Mary to be the mother of God.[735] [736]

That she was born without original sin is amusing, since we all were. It was noted that Pius IX "tried" to declare her Immaculate Conception as an infallible dogma, but the Church had not yet passed its declaration of infallibility for popes, which would occur in 1870 at the 1st Vatican Council. Later, Darwinian evolution proved him very fallible. It took a very long time for this "Marian dogma" to develop, and even such Church stalwarts as St. Bernard of Clairvaux[737] and St. Thomas Aquinas[738] saw no theological justification for the immaculate conception. There has been continual and unnecessary internecine fighting among Church leaders regarding if Mary ever sinned, since the Church believed she still needed a Savior: "My spirit has rejoiced in God my Savior" (Luke 1:47). However, the post-Reformation Council of Trent affirmed Mary's freedom from all personal sins.[739]

That Mary was a virgin, as speciously predicted in **Isaiah 7:14,** written circa 730 BCE, is a difficult concept to grasp. This clear "add-on" to the story of Jesus was totally unnecessary, but it may have helped seal the religion in the eyes of some believers in the 1st-century Mediterranean region. First, there were many such stories from pagan deities, including Mithra, Heracles, Dionysus, Tammuz, Adonis, and others.[740] Virgin birth and an obsession with virginity were common themes in that time period. Second, there is the translation issue, which occurred when the text was translated into Greek from the Hebrew 'ha-almah', which means 'young girl' (not virgin). Third, contrary to what Isaiah wrote, the baby's name was <u>not</u> Immanuel, probably because Isaiah had a different historical context in mind. Fourth, there is the total lack of evidence; there is not even second-hand testimony. The only supporting document is the Gospel of **Matthew [1:19-24],** mentioning Joseph's dream, written 80 years later by someone Joseph never knew, as Matthew clearly invented the dream. These hearsay stories and lack of evidence speak quite negatively to the credibility of the gospels.

But the RCC won't let it stop there. In its <u>Catechism of the Catholic Church</u> (CCC #499) it states, "And so the liturgy of the Church celebrates Mary as *Aeiparthenos,* the 'Ever-virgin.'" Ever-virgin means that *before, during,* and *after* the birth of Jesus, Mary remained a virgin. Indeed, the RCC Catechism spells it out: Mary "remained a virgin in conceiving her Son, a virgin in giving birth to him, a virgin in carrying him, a virgin in nursing him at her breast, always a virgin." (RCC #510). Yet the New Testament never claimed that Mary remained a virgin after the birth of Jesus. It was accepted early in Church tradition that Mary held off having sex with Yoseph prior to her impregnation by God. Yet the New Testament explicitly affirms her virginity only until the birth of Jesus and mentions Jesus' siblings.

> "Is this not the carpenter's son? Is not this mother called Mary? And his brethren, James, and Joses, and Simon, and Juda? [Matthew 13:55]

> "Is not this the carpenter, the son of Mary, the brother of James, and Joses, and of Juda and Simon? And are not his sisters here with us? [Mark 6:3].

The concept of perpetual virgin not only goes against the New Testament, but it is contradictory to Jewish views held in that time period, as well as contrary to later Catholic views. It appears to have had its genesis in Augustine of Hippo's unhealthy view of human sexuality in the early 5th century.[741] However, marriage is not incompatible with pious living. Nevertheless, it is unfathomable that the RCC wants us to believe Mary was always a virgin, and she failed in her duties as Yosef's wife. Indeed, if Yosef and Miriam (Mary) were married in appearance only, then they were unfaithful to the concept of marriage. How the Roman Catholic Church condones such a notion, much less promotes it, seems preposterous!

After much debate, the Second Council of Constantinople in 553 CE gave Mary the title, "Ever Virgin."[742] So, according to the RCC, the perfect woman is a virgin who does not have sexual relations with her husband!

Nowhere was it documented how and when Mary died. By the 7th century, speculation began regarding the bodily ascension of Mary into heaven by both Western and Eastern Christian Churches. And those discussions continued and strengthened. In November 1950, Pope Pius XII declared the Assumption of the Blessed Virgin Mary as an infallible declaration in *Munificentissimus Deus* (the only use of papal infallibility since the concept was declared in 1870), whereby Mary was assumed into Heaven, body and soul. Eastern Orthodox Christians believe that Mary died a natural death; then her body was resurrected and later reunited with her soul. Either way, does it really matter? The Marian doctrine and all the mental contortions to which the Catholic Church had to submit simply underscore the very type of theological legalism that Rabbi Yeshua of Nazareth preached against.

The Focus on Sacraments and Rituals

The Council of Trent (1545 – 1563), held in what is now Trento, Italy, codified and officially confirmed the seven sacraments. Yes, it took the RCC 1,500 years to finalize their sacraments. The Council of Trent was called in response to the Protestant Reformation; for over 18 years (with multiple adjournments due to military events), it attempted to adjudicate a number of Church issues that had lapsed under continual ambiguity for several centuries.[743] Although it did address some self-reform issues, which were so badly needed, the Council of Trent focused more on the clarification of the RCC's ecclesiastic doctrine vis-à-vis the Protestant assaults. Chief among them were the sacraments.

Over the many centuries of its development, the RCC had widely fluctuated as to what constituted a genuine sacrament. The number of sacraments varied from five to twelve.[744]

The Council of Florence defined seven sacraments, and it provided a summary of each. In Session 8 (22 Nov 1439), it stated:

> "Three of the sacraments, namely baptism, confirmation and orders, imprint indelibly on the soul a character, that is a kind of stamp which distinguishes it from the rest. Hence, they are not repeated in the same person. The other four, however, do not imprint a character and can be repeated."[745]

However, it was not until a session of the Council of Trent in 1549 that the concept of seven sacraments became fixed as an article of faith[746].

Baptism

The origin of Baptism is found in the Jewish cultural milieu, which encompassed John the Baptist and Jesus of Nazareth. Jews were practicing a purification ritual by immersion in a special bath called a mikveh.[747] Similar to Baptism, mikveh is a spiritual cleansing and a ritual washing, meant to symbolize purification.[748] This biblical ritual has been practiced regularly by Jews for over a thousand years prior to the arrival of Jesus.

It was Cyprian of Carthage who originally associated infant Baptism with the idea of original sin. In his writings, Augustine of Hippo strengthened this connection, arguing that the Catholic Church would not have baptized children if they did not need it. Augustine's new emphasis on original sin appears to have had the unintended effect of emphasizing the urgency of Baptism. Children were thus to be baptized as soon as possible.

Baptism was the sacrament of initiation. It has its roots in the Jewish tradition. The New Testament does not give us a liturgy of Baptism, and neither do the earliest non-biblical sources. In the early Church, the three Sacraments of initiation: Baptism, Confirmation, and Eucharist, were celebrated in the same ceremony by adult catechumens at the Easter Vigil.[749] From the 8th to 12th centuries, the rite of initiation consisted of Baptism, Confirmation, and first Holy Communion, being three parts of one whole, not always experienced at the same time.[750]

Holy Eucharist

The Swiss Reformation Leader, Huldrych Zwingli (1484 – 1531),[751] who founded the Swiss Reformed Church, had promoted the doctrine of consubstantiation similar to Martin Luther's views. Thus, at a session in 1551 – 1552, the Catholic delegates at the Council of Trent announced their decree "Concerning the Most Holy Sacrament of the Eucharist," citing the real presence of and the doctrine of transubstantiation.[752] The latter term denotes the idea that bread and wine are changed in substance into the flesh and blood of Christ, as *"trans"* is Latin for "across". On the other hand, consubstantiation is a Protestant term which denotes that bread and wine are not changed in substance, but that Christ is present with the elements. *"con"* is a form of Latin *"cum"* for "with". The Council proclaimed that Jesus Christ is entirely present in both the consecrated bread and the consecrated wine in the Eucharist. This was a re-validation of canon 1 of the Fourth Council of the Lateran, which had decreed the concept of transubstantiation in 1215.[753]

Penance

The Council of Trent extensively codified the sacrament of Penance in its second meetings (1551-1552). The word "penance" was derived from the Latin *"poena"* (penalty). It refers to disciplinary procedures imposed by the RCC. It involves the confession of one's sins to a priest, who then pronounces "absolution". The priest then provides requirements for satisfaction (the confessor's penance), exacted in order to effect a reconciliation between the offender and the Church. This ritual is a human construct. According to John Henry Cardinal Newman, the sacrament of Penance "was a later development as the complement of Baptism."[754]

Confirmation

The term "confirm" appears to have come into usage in the 5th century CE at Gallic councils of Riez, Orange, and Arles III. Confirmation was a ritual performed by a bishop after another minister baptized on a separate occasion. In practice, the bishop had been the primary minister of an elaborate rite of initiation.[755] Confirmation developed throughout the early Middle Ages, after a letter from Pope Innocent I (401–417) to Decentius of Gubbio, whereby Innocent permitted presbyters (i.e., priests) to anoint those whom they baptized to bestow the Holy Ghost, but not on the forehead; the latter was reserved for bishops. This letter influenced the decision in the West to restrict confirmations to bishops, whereas the Eastern Churches permitted presbyteral confirmation [756]

Confirmation is a ritual that is seen as a sealing of the covenant created in Baptism. The ceremony typically involves laying on the hands. The earliest preserved independent rites of Confirmation come just before the 11th century. It was bequeathed sacrament status in the 12th century. Later, in 1274, the Second Council of Lyon listed Confirmation among the sacraments of the Church.

Originally, Confirmation had been part of a threefold rite with Baptism and one's first Communion. However, the establishment of Confirmation as a separate rite sent the Catholic theologians looking for reasons to justify it. Pope Innocent's reference to the apostles' laying on hands was considered problematic, as that would imply that the Holy Ghost was not given in Baptism; and this was unanimously rejected. Instead, the RCC maintained that while the Holy Ghost was given in Baptism, it was in Confirmation given with a fullness that equipped Christians for spiritual battle.[757] The sacrament is called Chrismation in Eastern Christianity. In the East, it takes place immediately after Baptism; in the West, it occurs when a child reaches the age of reason or early adolescence, or in the case of an adult, Confirmation occurs immediately after Baptism in the same ceremony.[758]

During the Reformation, Confirmation invited the critique of the Protestant reformers. For those Protestant Churches that baptized children, Confirmation was understood as a completion of a process of initiation that started with Baptism, even though the two rites were separated in time by several years. This has remained an important element in the understanding of Christian initiation in some Protestant Churches.

Today, Confirmation marks membership in the Church, and it is a reaffirmation of baptismal vows to remain in the Church and follow its teaching. It is regarded by Catholics, Orthodox

Christians, and some other Christians as a sacrament. In the Catholic Church, after an individual reaffirms the vows, a bishop lays hands on him or her.[759] Confirmation is an expression of salvation.

Matrimony

The RCC contends that marriage is a Church institution. And the RCC claims marital jurisdiction over all who have been baptized in that communion. The doctrine was not defined as a dogma of faith until 1563, when the Council of Trent declared that marriage was properly one of the seven sacraments, and it spelled out the implications of the dogma.[760] Criticism of the doctrine by Luther and others had made it seem an indispensable pillar of Catholic teaching.

Marriage between Catholics is considered a sacrament (Council of Trent). Marriage between two non-Catholics is but a mere contract. The Catholic Church permits no valid cause for divorce. However, it has been shown on many occasions that one can get an annulment for a plethora of circumstances. An annulment is a declaration that one's original marriage was never valid (and it goes well beyond consummation). Then, following the annulment, Catholics may remarry. Modern Catholic clergymen appear as adept with legalistic manipulation as were the ancient Pharisees.[761]

Holy Orders

Prior to the sacrament of Holy Orders, the RCC grappled with clerical celibacy. In 404 CE, the bishop of Rome, Innocent I, started the concept that priests should be celibate. Arguments over celibacy contributed to the schism between the RCC and the Eastern Orthodox Church. These discussions continued in spite of New Testament Scriptures stating in **Timothy 4:1-3** that forbidding marriage was a doctrine of the devil. In 1022, Pope Benedict VIII (1012 – 1024) banned priests from getting married because of monetary reasons. He didn't want the priests' sons inheriting Church property. At that time, women didn't inherit property.[762]

According to historical records, in 1074 Pope Gregory VII (1073 – 1085) began enforcing the rule that anyone to be ordained must first pledge celibacy.[763] In 1095, to emphasize that priests could not have wives, Pope Urban II (1080 – 1099), the pope who started the crusades, had some priests' wives sold into slavery; children were abandoned.[764] In 1123, at the First Lateran Council, Pope Calistus II (1119 – 124) decreed that clerical marriages were invalid. Pope Innocent II (1130 – 1143) confirmed the previous councils' decrees prohibiting marriage at the 2nd Lateran Council in 1139. Indeed, the RCC had existed for a thousand years before it definitively took its formal stand in favor of celibacy in the 12th century at the Second Lateran Council held in 1139, when a rule was approved forbidding priests to marry. In 1563, the Council of Trent reaffirmed the tradition of celibacy.[765] [766]

The entire debate on priest celibacy had its origin in the Church retaining property when the priests died. By ensuring that clerics remained unmarried and without heirs, the RCC protected its properties from being passed down through family dynasties.[767] In the 21st century, to address the priest shortage, Pope Francis suggested that he would review the

Catholic Church's position on celibacy for priests. However, Pope Francis died in early 2025 without any action on this topic.

The requirement for ordination celibacy is specific to the RCC. Other Churches in union with Rome (Ukrainian, Melkite, and others) have different disciplines whose origins reach far back into their traditions. They allow married clergy, but with certain restrictions, especially for ordination to the episcopate.[768]

Originally, priests were set up to be assistants to the bishops to administer the Eucharist, acting in "persona Christus" ("in the person of Christ").[769] An official who becomes a priest must be ordained by a bishop. Ordination of priests took some time to finalize, from the 8th through the 15th centuries. It was clearly an evolved process.

'Apostolic succession'[770] is considered an essential premise for ordination, because the ritual of successors and assistants being appointed by those who preceded them in the ministry is the key element of the legitimacy of the holy orders of each Church. As a member of a holy order, one must be ordained by someone who was himself ordained. There are three "degrees" of ordination (or holy orders): deacon (minister who assists priests), presbyter (a priest), and bishop. Bishops and presbyters are priests and have the authority to celebrate the Eucharist.[771] And all priests must be male, just because the original twelve apostles were male, according to the RCC.

The Council of Trent confirmed Holy Orders as a sacrament and confirmed the need for celibacy of the clergy. During the third period of the Council of Trent (1562 – 1563), it decreed that every diocese must provide for the proper education of its future clergy in seminaries under RCC guidance.

Extreme Unction

In previous ages, the sacrament was known by a variety of names, e.g., the holy oil or unction of the sick. By the Middle Ages, perhaps due to the high mortality rate and the fear of death, this sacrament of the sick gradually lost its healing communal dimension and became associated with the "last rites" of the Church before death. Thus, it was called Extreme Unction or "final anointing."[772] *Extreme Unction* did not become a term used in the West until the 12th century, and has never been used in the East.[773] It involves the application of consecrated oil by a properly ordained priest to the eyes, ears, nostrils, lips, hands, and feet of the failing victim.

The Council of Trent defined and explained the sacrament of Extreme Unction, which is the ritual anointing of the seriously ill. In 1551, the Council of Trent affirmed that "only priests (bishops and presbyters) are ministers of the Anointing of the Sick."[774] In 1965, the Second Vatican Council reclaimed the original meaning of the sacrament, when it decreed that "'Extreme Unction,' which may also and more fittingly be called 'Anointing of the Sick,' is not a sacrament intended only for those who are at the point of death, for as soon as any of the faithful is in danger of death from sickness or old age, this is already a suitable time for them to receive this sacrament."[775]

Purgatory

For the first millennium of Christianity's existence, Christians were far from clear about where their souls would go after death.[776] Purgatory was not a historical doctrine of the Church. It was still in doubt in the 5th century CE, even though St. Augustine of Hippo[777] and Pope St. Gregory I wrote about it. Indeed, in his "*Dialogues*," Pope Gregory spoke about fire being purgatorial, and about the need for purification after death for certain souls, helping to establish the idea within the Church.[778] He also referred to the cleansing fire as a matter of unquestioned belief. As a result, Pope St. Gregory I has been referred to as "the inventor of purgatory."[779] The most prominent modern historian of the idea of Purgatory, Jacques Le Goff, dates the term, purgatorium, to around 1170; *Le Goff* argues that the doctrine of *Purgatory* did not appear in the Latin theology of the West prior to the late 12th century.[780] According to Le Goff, the view of Purgatory in the Middle Ages was a physical place where souls went. At the Second Council of Lyon in 1274, the Catholic Church defined, for the first time, its teaching on Purgatory,[781] in two points:

- Some souls are purified after death;
- Such souls benefit from the prayers and pious duties that the living do for them.

Purgatory became central to late medieval religion and was associated with indulgences and other penitential practices, such as fasting. Indulgences removed part of the temporal punishment of the living or the dead. The Eastern Orthodox Church rejected the concept of Purgatory. The doctrine of Purgatory and the effectiveness of prayer for those in Purgatory were affirmed in the papal bull of July, 1439, *Laetentur caeli* (Let the Heavens Rejoice!). The Roman Catholic Church believed (then and now) that the living faithful can help souls complete their purification from sins by praying for them, and by gaining indulgences[782] for them as an act of intercession.

The Late Middle Ages saw the growth of considerable abuses, such as the unrestricted sale of indulgences by professional "pardoners" sent to collect contributions for papal projects such as the rebuilding of Saint Peter's Basilica in Rome. In the Catholic Church, Purgatory is today considered a place (or a form of existence), where less than pure souls go through a purifying fire to make them worthy of the beatific vision in heaven.

Some Protestant sects believe that the concept of Purgatory and those beliefs and acts that are often attached to it (prayer for the dead, indulgences, meritorious works on behalf of the dead, etc.) fail to recognize that Jesus' death was sufficient to pay for all sins. Thus, to their way of thinking, Purgatory is not necessary.

Limbo

The traditional teaching concerning Limbo was considered part of the category of "common doctrine" in the past because it had been alluded to by the Catholic Magisterium over the centuries, as well as taught by theologians. The name, Limbo, originates from the Latin word limbus, meaning "border" or "edge", which was considered by medieval theologians to be a state or place reserved for the unbaptized dead, including good people who lived before the coming of Christ.

Similar to Purgatory, the concept of Limbo had its origin in the writings of St. Augustine of Hippo, who seemed to stumble into it vis-à-vis his opposition to the Pelagians, who did not believe in original sin. When confronted about innocents such as children who died prior to Baptism or good people who lived prior to Jesus Christ, Augustine suggested they did not deserve harsh punishment, though they cannot immediately achieve salvation.[783] On the other hand, St. Augustine denied any notion of such an intermediary place or Limbo.

In the 13th century, St. Thomas Aquinas laid the foundation for the "Limbo" explanation. He emphasized that original sin was inherited rather than a sin freely committed. Since Hell was the place of eternal punishment for unrepentant mortal sinners who had rejected God, and since the unbaptized could not enter Heaven, those unbaptized infants should be in another place, perhaps in a state of limbo. St. Thomas Aquinas added that these souls do not have the knowledge of what they have missed. Essentially, they would be left in a state of ignorant bliss. Aquinas's theological speculation was regarded as a reasonable explanation.[784]

The concept of Limbo has been a long, drawn-out affair in the Catholic Church. The following are a few quotes from the Catholic leaders over the centuries:[785]

- "The idea that infants can be granted the rewards of eternal life without even the grace of Baptism is utterly foolish." – (Pope Saint Innocent I, Letter to the Bishops of the Church, A.D. 417)

- "The souls of those who die in mortal sin or with original sin only, immediately descend into Hell, yet to be punished with different punishments." – (Pope Gregory X, Second Council of Lyons, 1274)
- "The souls of those who depart this life in actual mortal sin, or in original sin alone, go down straightaway to Hell to be punished, but with unequal pains." – (Pope Eugene IV, Council of Florence, *Laetentur Caeli*, July 6, 1439)
- "Where do infants go who die without Baptism? Infants who die without Baptism go to Limbo, where they do not enjoy the sight of God, but also do not suffer. This is because having original sin, and it alone, they do not merit heaven, but neither do they merit Purgatory or Hell." – (Catechism of Pope Saint Pius X, first published in 1910)

The teachings about Limbo, which is fast becoming a theological anachronism, was taught for centuries, right up through the 1960s. And in 2007 Pope Benedict effectively "closed" Limbo.[786] In its backpedaling, the RCC has declared Limbo was never formally part of the Church doctrine, in spite of the reality that it has been an unchallenged element of the RCC belief system.

In a long-awaited document, the RCC's *International Theological Commission* said Limbo reflected an "unduly restrictive view of salvation". The 41-page document was published by the U.S.-based <u>Catholic News Service</u>, which is part of the U.S. Conference of Catholic Bishops. Pope Benedict, authorized the publication of the document, called "The Hope of Salvation for Infants Who Die Without Being Baptized."[787] This document reflects significant evolution on the topic of Limbo. This papal-approved document did not formally abolish the concept of Limbo, but it represented a move away from its necessity in Catholic theology.[788] This is similar to the RCC's stance on original sin. Indeed, while Catholicism accepts Darwinism, it still illogically clings to the original sin of Adam and Eve.

Shift from Latin

Before the Vatican II Council, the liturgy of the Mass was conducted exclusively in Latin (referred to as the Tridentine Mass, which had been promulgated by Pope Pius V in 1570). However, it remained a language that the Catholic laity were generally unfamiliar with, and which hampered their full engagement during the Catholic mass service. Thus, to foster that full participation by the laity, Vatican II voted on December 1962 to allow vernacular languages.[789] Following Vatican II, the use of vernacular languages gained momentum globally, and the use of Latin diminished over time; but some parishes continued to conduct their masses in Latin. Interestingly, the progressive Pope John XXIII who called the Vatican II Council, initially opposed the movement away from Latin. Nine months prior to Vatican II, Pope John XXIII had issued a forceful decree, *Veterum sapientia*, which strongly promoted Liturgical Latin.[790]

Thus, it was a monumental shift for the RCC to move away from Latin Tridentine Mass. That shift is underscored by the declaration of Pope St. Pius V in 1570, who promulgated the Tridentine Mass via his decree (papal bull), *Quo primum*. In should be noted that the RCC had used Latin for its Church masses since the early 3rd century; the Tridentine mass merely standardized it.[791] In making his decree, Pope St. Pius V wrote: "By this our decree, to be valid IN PERPETUITY, we determine and order that NEVER shall anything be added to, omitted from, or changed in this Missal."[792] Pope St. Pius V concluded his decree with the following statement: "No one whosoever is permitted to alter this notice of Our permission, statute, ordinance, command, precept, grant, indult, declaration, will, decree, and prohibition. Should anyone dare to contravene it, let him know that he will incur the wrath of Almighty God and of the Blessed Apostles Peter and Paul."[793]

And there were these quotes:

> "If anyone says that the Mass ought to be celebrated in the VERNACULAR only, ... let him be anathema (cursed) – the Ecumenical Council of Trent (1570)

> "The use of the Latin language is a clear and beautiful sign of unity, and an efficacious remedy against any corruptions of true doctrine " – Pope Pius XII

> "Latin is the immutable language of the Western Church." – Pope John XXIII

In 1969, Pope Paul VI promulgated the Novus Ordo Mass, also called the Ordinary Form of the Mass. Once released, Pope Paul VI's new Roman Missal effectively replaced the traditional Tridentine Latin Mass as the new normal form of the RCC mass.[794] In his *Missale Romanum*, Paul VI states that the new liturgical norms are to be "firm and effective, now and in the future, notwithstanding, to the extent necessary, the apostolic constitutions and ordinances issued by our predecessors, and other prescriptions, even those deserving particular mention and derogation."[795]

In July 2007, Pope Benedict XVI issued his decree, *"Summorum pontificum"*, which liberalized the use of the 1962 version of the Roman Missal, stating that it was never abrogated, and was thus to be considered as the "extraordinary form of the Roman Rite." However, in July 2021, Pope Francis reversed the decree of Pope Benedict XVI via his *motu proprio*,[796] *Traditionis custodes*,[797] stating that "the liturgical books promulgated by Saint Paul VI and Saint John Paul II, in conformity with the decrees of Vatican Council II, are the unique expression of the *lex orandi* of the Roman Rite," and that all provisions contrasting to that were abrogated.[798] Pope Francis' document emphasized the importance of the vernacular language in fostering participation and understanding of those who attend Mass. Of course, the RCC "traditionalists", especially many of the conservative American bishops, were incensed with anger and have pushed back against Pope Francis. There has been a lot of infighting among the RCC clergy because attendance at Mass is well down from previous decades.

Apologies of the Catholic Church

While increasingly common in the past 60 years or so, the RCC's ecclesial apologies are a relatively modern phenomenon. Like the papacy, top Protestant leaders also have gradually issued institutional *'mea culpas'* for their Churches' historical wrongs. Many of the apologies on behalf of Christian denominations are for grave offenses: genocide, sex abuse, slavery, war, and other despicable crimes.

The pivot to significant apologies came in the aftermath of World War II, following a declaration by Germany's Protestant Churches that they failed to oppose the Nazis adequately. It was among the first in a series of recognitions that Christian institutions themselves committed wrongs. Jeremy Bergen, Professor of religious and theological studies at Ontario's Conrad Grebel University College, told the *Washington Post*, "For 1,900 years, Churches didn't apologize for the bad things they did."[799] That certainly changed with Pope John Paul II and Pope Francis I. Jeremy Bergen explained that in the 1990s, Church apologies increased as more attention was paid to human rights following the Cold War.[800]

To his credit, Pope John Paul II issued many public apologies.[801] During his long reign as Pope, he apologized to many who had suffered at the hands of the Catholic Church over the centuries. Indeed, he officially made public apologies for over 100 abuses. A partial list include:

- Christians involved in the African slave trade[802]
- The Inquisitions[803] [804]
- The religious wars that followed the Protestant Reformation[805]
- Burnings at the stake, such as Jan Hus (1415)[806]
- Treatment of and relations with the Jews[807] [808]
- Muslims killed by the Crusaders[809]
- The Crusaders' Sack of Constantinople (1204)[810]
- Massacre of French Protestants[811]
- The discrimination against women[812]
- Treatment of and condemnation of Galileo[813]
- The inactivity and silence of many Catholics during the Holocaust[814]
- Catholic Church sex abuses (against children and women)
- Behavior of Catholic missionaries against the aboriginal children of Australia[815]
- The general mistreatment of indigenous peoples of colonized lands[816]

- For sexism, racism, hatred of Jews, and violence in defense of Catholicism[817]

Many of the injustices and crimes attributed to the RCC are focused on a given country. The following is a sample of some modern apologies focused on specific countries or groups of people.

Canada

A Canadian government-funded commission issued findings that detailed a history of physical and sexual abuse of indigenous children in the country's Catholic-run residential schools. And thousands of these children died at these schools.[818] The pope specifically asked forgiveness for "projects of cultural destruction and forced assimilation promoted by the governments of the time."[819]

In April 2022, Pope Francis apologized to Canada's indigenous community on Canadian soil for the role the Catholic Church played in overseeing decades of abuse.[820] From 1870 – 1997, more than 150,000 children and young adults went through the Indian residential school system in Canada, seventy percent of which were operated by the Catholic Church or Catholic religious orders. These schools were known around the indigenous communities for their intentional suppression of indigenous culture, widespread physical abuse, and neglect.

Chile

Pope Francis defrocked a once-prominent priest, Rev. Fernando Karadima, whose case had been at the center of public outrage about clerical sexual abuse and its concealment in Chile. His case has proved particularly toxic for Pope Francis, who long defended the bishop accused of covering it up, Juan Barros. However, Pope Francis decided to send Archbishop Charles Scicluna of Malta to Chile to listen to the victims who accused Bishop Juan Barros of a cover-up.[821] The sex crimes investigators sent to Chile was the beginning of an about-face that was to result in all 34 of the Roman Catholic bishops in Chile offering their resignations.[822] In a separate case, Santiago Cardinal Ricardo Ezzati stepped down in 2019 after being accused of covering up at least five cases of sexual abuse by members of the clergy.[823]

In January 2018, Francis apologized to Chileans during his first visit to the country as pope. Fast forward from January to April, and the release of the 2,300-page report, and Pope Francis was once again apologizing — and inviting victims to the Vatican to deliver the apology in person, says *The Washington Post*.[824]

France

The numbers are staggering: it has been reported that independent inquiries have found more than 216,000 people who have been victims of sexual assault perpetrated by the French Catholic clergy in the 70 years leading up to 2020.[825] The inquiry found the total number of children abused in France could rise to 330,000 (80% were boys), when considering abuses committed by lay members of the RCC, such as teachers at Catholic schools.[826]

An independent commission was set up at the request of the RCC in France. The long-awaited 2,500-page report by the *Independent Commission on Sexual Abuse in the Church* detailed how the Church hierarchy had repeatedly silenced the victims and failed to report or discipline the clergy members involved.[827] The above-cited figures include abuses committed by some 3,000 priests and other people involved in the RCC — wrongdoing that Catholic authorities covered up over decades in a "systemic manner," according to the president of the commission that issued the scathing report, Jean-Marc Sauvé.[828]

Germany

There were 497 children and teenagers identified as the victims of sexual assault in the Archdiocese of Munich alone, in the 74-year period leading up to 2019.[829] Pope Benedict XVI (2005 – 2013) had been accused of overlooking sexual abuse while he was the archbishop of Munich. Cardinal Ratzinger had long claimed to have been unaware of the abuses linked to a particular priest. After it came out that he had been present at a meeting to discuss that exact thing, it put his whole 'plausible deniability' thing in doubt. "In a total of four cases, we came to the conclusion that the then-archbishop, Cardinal Ratzinger, can be accused of misconduct," said one of the report's authors, Martin Pusch.[830] The following month, Pope Benedict XVI responded to the charges in a letter in which he expressed "my profound shame, my deep sorrow, and my heartfelt request for forgiveness".[831]

In 2019, to help stop sexual abuse and its cover-ups within the RCC, Pope Francis ordered a four-day summit of almost 200 Church leaders, plus Vatican officials and experts, to discuss ways of dealing with abuse. The following year, he restated his "commitment of the Church to eradicate this evil." [832]

Ireland

It was in 2015 that we learned that more than 800 babies were buried in a mass, unmarked grave on the site of a Catholic-run, mother-and-baby home in Tuam, County Galway. The former workhouse was converted into a facility for housing unwed pregnant women and their children in 1925, and it was active until 1961.[833] 796 children were known to have died there.[834] There were dozens of laundry/workhouses that lasted for 231 years, and they are estimated to have cumulatively housed somewhere around 300,000 women.[835] The Magdalene Laundries in Ireland, also known as Magdalene asylums, were institutions usually run by Roman Catholic orders,[836] but the Church of Ireland and Presbyterian Churches also ran some of the laundries.

Many female residents were forced to work from sunrise to sunset to pay off their debt to the Church for their sins of flirting, mental illness, and getting pregnant out of wedlock (including cases of sexual assault). Most survived on meager food rations, and some were locked in solitary confinement when not working. The last laundry closed in 1996.[837]

John Paul II's successor, Pope Benedict XVI, also apologized for clerical abuse, most significantly in a 2010 pastoral letter to Irish faithful. He said he was "truly sorry" for the hurt and blamed Irish bishops, though he was silent on the Vatican's responsibility.[838] When Pope Francis visited Ireland in 2018, he apologized for abuses that included the mother-and-baby homes. Pope Francis issued a sweeping apology for the "crimes" of the Catholic

Church in Ireland, saying Church officials didn't respond with compassion, truth, or justice to the many children and to the women who were abused over generations.[839]

Israel / Judaism

While this is not specific to Israel, an apology to worldwide Jews was long in coming, and clearly needed. The RCC needed to confront the crimes that it committed against the Jews over the past 19 centuries. In 1965, the Catholic Church officially disavowed the false belief that the Jews were responsible for the death of Jesus, but it has persisted as a source of tension in relations between the RCC and the Jewish community. Pope John Paul II made several apologies to the Jewish people for the suffering they endured at the hands of Christians. On March 16, 1998, the Pope and the Vatican issued a document called "We Remember: A Reflection on the Shoah."[840]

In March 2000, John Paul II visited Yad Vashem (the Israeli national Holocaust memorial) in Israel, and he touched a very holy site in Judaism, the Western Wall in Jerusalem, placing a letter inside it.[841] Pope Paul II prayed and touched the wide beige stones of the ancient wall, where he deposited his letter, which was a signed plea for God's forgiveness for centuries of Catholic torment of the Jewish people.[842] In 2011, conservative Pope Benedict XVI declared that there was no basis in Scripture for the belief that the Jewish people were responsible for the death of Jesus.[843]

And then, there was the matter of Pope Pius XII. The Vatican was reluctant to refer to him. At the same time, Jewish leaders pointed out the damage that his silence had caused.

USA

In 2018, headlines of an abuse case that spanned parishes across Pennsylvania horrified readers everywhere: more than 1,000 victims (children) had been sexually assaulted by priests for years, and a 1,365-page report from a grand jury put the spotlight on all the horrors. In response, Pope Francis issued a formal apology saying: "With shame and repentance, we acknowledge as an ecclesial community that we were not where we should have been... We showed no care for the little ones; we abandoned them." Pope Francis also said that Catholic leaders were to blame following a grand jury report that found more than 1,000 children were sexually abused by approximately 300 "predator priests" in Pennsylvania for decades.[844]

The following year, *The Guardian* reported that Pope Francis had done something about it and gotten rid of the so-called "pontifical secrecy" that had protected so many, along with putting in other practices that made it an offense to try to silence victims.[845] Additionally, the RCC has moved to defrock hundreds of priests in recent years after credible allegations of abuse have come to light.[846]

While it seems horrible to state and worse that it occurred, child abuse and its cover-ups ran rampant in the USA in the 20th century. And it certainly was not limited to the USA, nor was it limited to the 20th century. But it is relatively recent that knowledge of it being so widespread is coming into the light. It has been a rapidly escalating sexual abuse crisis that has spread across several continents, from Australia to Latin America.[847]

A so-called zero tolerance policy adopted by the United States Conference of Catholic Bishops in 2002 has done little to halt the controversy, although it may have helped to limit the pervasive cover-ups. Outside the United States, too, investigations have disturbed religious society in numerous other countries, from Australia to Chile, Argentina, Mexico, Germany, and the Netherlands. In February 2019, Pope Francis spoke out against what he described as the "sexual slavery" that nuns all too frequently suffered at the hands of Catholic priests.[848]

Sadly, patterns of sexual abuse against adults and minors of both sexes have occurred for centuries. The pervasiveness of the problem suggests that it may be deeply rooted in the RCC's history. In fact, several explanations proffered in heated debates are wrapped in historical judgments and past events. Some RCC critics have identified a rigid Church structure and antiquated norms of sex and gender, including clerical celibacy and a male priesthood.[849]

The term "pedophile" means different things to different people. And the term doesn't just apply to men, but overwhelmingly, the statistics suggest that it is relatively uncommon in women. There is some consensus on the clinical definition, and most psychologists agree that a pedophile is someone who has a sexual interest in pre-pubescent children, typically those under the age of 12. It is estimated that within a statistically-significant population of men that between 1-2% have pedophilic tendencies, according to Prof Philip Jenkins from the Institute of Studies of Religion at Baylor University in Texas.[850]

This most heinous of crimes is not an issue that the RCC grapples with alone. Unfortunately, there are multiple organizations, from Baptist Churches to the Boy Scouts, which continue to wrestle with this issue. Further, there is as of yet no way to identify a pedophile in advance. There are no tests to take or a clinical pre-evaluation. After all, the majority of pedophiles and child sex offenders identify as heterosexual.[851] However, once abuse is reported, Churches and other organizations should listen to the abused, and once evidence is determined, they should hold that abuser accountable, report him to the proper law enforcement authorities, and not transfer him from parish to parish. The RCC still does not appear to have fully reviewed its own role in child molestations and sexual predation of women.

Chapter Summary

This chapter has been a discussion on various practices and issues of the 2,000-year old Roman Catholic Church, from its prohibitions against reading of the Bible, especially in a non-Latin vernacular language even for its own New Testament; its insistence on the existence and consequences of original sin (even after it has formally acknowledged the reality of the theory of evolution); its fabrication of the Trinity, Satan, and Hell; the manner in which it has selected some questionable saints, and its pitiful few papal candidates for sainthood; its many heresies and schisms; the horror of its inquisitions and savage witch hunts; its focus on sacraments and rituals; its creation of Purgatory and Limbo; and of course, its apologies for its past grave offenses. Many other religious organizations committed similar offenses and also tried to cover them up, but unlike the RCC, most of them have yet to apologize, nor provide compensation to many victims (See Chapter 7).

Indeed, it is important to recognize that the Roman Catholic Church has been undergoing changes. Since WWII, the RCC has recognized the Big Bang theory, the theory of evolution, promoted the unsupervised reading of the Bible, conducted its rituals and Masses in the local vernacular languages, has terminated the Index of Prohibited Books, has renamed and altered the mission of the Inquisition, has dismissed the notion of Limbo, has redefined Hell as a separation from God and not a physical place, has reached out to other Christian denominations, and has removed its declaration that the RCC is the only path to salvation.

These are marvelous steps, which have been long in coming. Now, if the RCC can open itself to female clergy, fully confirm its welcome to LGBTQ+ people, accept the reality that there never was original sin, and shy away from its stern views regarding papal supremacy and infallibility, then it will be in better alignment with modern thinking and better prepared for its future.

A summary analysis of the primary heresies of the Catholic Church is provided in **Appendix 2.**

---

583 "Catholic Churches," World Data.com; https://www.worlddata.info/religions/catholics.php

584 "Roman Catholicism," Britannica; https://www.britannica.com/topic/Roman-Catholicism

585 Mark Sweetnam, "How We Got Our Bible (6): John Wycliffe and the English Bible," Truth and Tidings; https://truthandtidings.com/2010/01/how-we-got-our-bible-6-john-wycliffe-and-the-english-bible/

586 B L Clifton, "The Story of John Wycliffe"; Feb 2, 2016; Bible, Church History; https://blclifton.com/the-story-of-john-wycliffe/

587Bernard Starr, "Why Christians Were Denied Access to Their Bible for 1,000 Years," HuffPost; May 20, 2013; https://www.huffpost.com/entry/why-christians-were-denied-access-to-their-bible-for-1000-years_b_3303545

588 Catechism of the Catholic Church (CCC), paragraph 100, p. 35; Second Edition; Doubleday, New York. 1994.

589 "Pope St. Damasus I," New Advent; www.newadvent.org/cathen/04613a.htm

590 "Vulgate," Encyclopedia Britannica; https://www.britannica.com/topic/Vulgate

591 "Vulgate," Ibid.

592 "Folquet de Marselha," Alchetron; Oct 07, 2024; https://alchetron.com/Folquet-de-Marselha. Folquet had highly negative relations with his diocese, primarily due to his support of the Albigensian Crusade, which was popularly perceived as a war of aggression against Catharism. The Albigensian Crusade was a military and ideological campaign initiated by Pope Innocent III to eliminate Catharism in Languedoc, what is now southern France.

593 Peters, Edward (1980). Heresy and Authority in Medieval Europe. London: Scolar Press. pp. 194–195. ISBN 0-85967-621-8.

594 Taken from David Cloud, "Did Rome Forbid Vernacular Versions?" Way of Life Literature; Feb 15, 2004; https://www.wayoflife.org/database/did_rome_forbic_vernacular_versions.html

595 "Did Rome Forbid Vernacular Versions?" Way of Life Literature, Publisher of Bible Study Materials, https://www.wayoflife.org/database/did_rome_forbic_vernacular_versions.html. The Catholic Church did not produce a Bible in English until 1582, two full centuries after John Wycliffe provided the English people with their first Bible, and it was a half century after Tyndale wrote his English masterpiece.

596 Steven Lawson, "The Bible Convictions of John Wycliffe"; publisher: Ligonier Ministries, Aug 2021; ISBN: 978164893298

597 "John Wycliffe," New History Encyclopedia; https://www.worldhistory.org/John_Wycliffe/

598 "Censorship of the Bible," DetailedPedia; https://www.detailedpedia.com/wiki-Censorship%20of%20the%20Bible

[599] Timothy L. Hall, "Censorship of the Bible," EBSCO; https://www.ebsco.com/research-starters/religion-and-philosophy/censorship-bible

[600] "Council of Constance 1414-18," Papal Encyclicals Online; https://www.papalencyclicals.net/councils/ecum16.htm

[601] "William Tyndale," World History Encyclopedia; https://www.worldhistory.org/William_Tyndale/

[602] "Index Librorum Prohibitorum", Encyclopedia Britannica; https://www.britannica.com/topic/Index-Librorum-Prohibitorum

[603] "Canons and Decrees of the Council of Trent/Second Part/Concerning Prohibited Books," WikiSource; https://en.wikisource.org/wiki/Canons_and_Decrees_of_the_Council_of_Trent/Second_Part/Concerning_Prohibited_Books

[604] By H. J. Schroeder, Canons and Decrees of the Council of Trent, p. 274.

[605] "Did Rome Forbid Vernacular Versions?" Way of Life Literature, Publisher of Bible Study Materials; https://www.wayoflife.org/database/did_rome_forbic_vernacular_versions.html

[606] "Pope Clement XI's Papal Encyclical "Unigenitus", Puritan Board, 1713"; 2019; https://puritanboard.com/threads/pope-clement-xis-papal-encyclical-unigenitus-1713.97954/

[607] Ibid.

[608] Rev C. A. Salmond, D.D., The Popes of the Nineteenth Century; Protestant Truth Society; p 9 & p.39; Log College Press, London; https://static1.squarespace.com/static/590be125ff7c502a07752a5b/t/604e51b9652486643e82fad4/1615745467286/Salmond%2C+Charles+Adamson%2C+The+Popes+of+the+Nineteenth+Century.pdf

[609] Lourens de Vries, "The Book of True Civilization: The Origins of the Bible Society Movement in the Age of Enlightenment;" United Bible Societies; https://translation.bible/wp-content/uploads/2024/07/de-vries-2017-the-book-of-true-civilization-the-origins-of-the-bible-society-movement-in-the-age-of-enlightenment.pdf

[610] "Why Did the Catholic Church Prevent Vernacular Bible Translations?" Virgo Sacrata; https://www.virgosacrata.com/vernacular-bible-translations.html

[611] Ibid.

[612] Pastor Steve Wohlberg, "Papal Rome against the Bible," White Horse Media; https://www.whitehorsemedia.com/papal-rome-against-the-bible/

[613] "Ubi Primum," Papal Encyclicals Online; para. 17; https://www.papalencyclicals.net/Leo12/l12ubipr.htm

[614] "Traditi humilitati", Papal Encyclicals Online; para 5; https://www.papalencyclicals.net/pius08/p8tradit.htm

[615] Steve Wohlberg, "Papal Rome Against the Bible," White Horse Media; https://www.whitehorsemedia.com/papal-rome-against-the-bible/

[616] Qui Pluribus, Papal Encyclicals Online; https://www.papalencyclicals.net/pius09/p9quiplu.htm

[617] **"A Record of Opposition to Bible Education," Watchtower Online Library;** https://wol.jw.org/en/wol/d/r1/lp-e/101982163

[618] David Cloud, A History of the Churches from a Baptist Perspective, Nov 2023; Popes Condemned the Bible Societies (wayoflife.org)

[619] James M. Gillis, "Bible Societies," Catholic Answers; https://www.catholic.com/encyclopedia/bible-societies

[620] "When Did Latin Die? And Why?" Global Language Services; Jan 2024; https://www.globallanguageservices.co.uk/did-latin-die/#:~:text=Historians%20have%20since%20stated%20that,spoken%20language%20was%20rapidly%20evolving.

[621] "Medieval Priests," WordPress.com; March 8, 2020; https://aprilmunday.wordpress.com/2020/03/08/medieval-priests/

[622] "Medieval Priests," Ibid.

[623] History of the English Bible, <u>BYU Library</u>; https://guides.lib.byu.edu/englishbibles#:~:text=1611%3A%20The%20King%20James%20Bible,to%20be%20Printed%20in%20America.

[624] The Tanakh, or Hebrew Bible, contains the same books as a Christian Protestant version of 'the Old Testament' with some small variations in verse numbering, except the books are not in the same order.

[625] Alan F. Segal, <u>Paul the Convert</u> (New Haven: Yale University, 1990), p. xiv.

[626] Catherine Damato, "Is the New Testament Jewish?", <u>Jews for Jesus</u>, https://jewsforjesus.org/answers/is-the-new-testament-jewish

[627] Samuel Sandmel, <u>A Jewish Understanding of the New Testament</u> (New York: Ktav, 1974), p. 90.

[628] <u>The Universal Jewish Encyclopedia,</u> vol. 8, p. 174. https://archive.org/details/the-jewish-encyclopedia-vol.-8

[629] Robert J. Miller, "How New Testament Writers Helped Jesus Fulfill Prophecy," part of John Loftus' anthology, <u>The Case Against Miracles</u>; p. 258.

[630] Rebecca Denova, "The Separation of Christianity from Judaism," <u>World History Encyclopedia</u>; https://www.worldhistory.org/article/1785/the-separation-of-christianity-from-judaism/

[631] Bernard Starr, Contributor, "Why Christians Were Denied Access to Their Bible for 1,000 years," <u>HuffPost, The Blog</u>; https://www.huffpost.com/entry/why-christians-were-denied-access-to-their-bible-for-1000-years_b_3303545

[632] Bernard Starr; <u>Ibid</u>.

[633] Msgr. Daniel Kutys, "Changes in Catholic Attitude Toward Bible Reading," The United States Conference of Catholic Bishops' (USCCB's); https://www.usccb.org/offices/new-american-bible/changes-catholic-attitudes-toward-bible-readings

[634] "Concept of Original Sin," <u>Swindon Church</u>; https://swindonchurch.org/2024/07/25/concept-of-original-sin-from-early-christian-thought-to-contemporary-theology-part-1/#:

[635] Peter Nathan, "The Original View of Original Sin"; <u>Foundations</u>; Summer 2003; https://foundations.vision.org/original-view-original-sin-1140

[636] "Early Christian History: Theology — Original Sin," <u>Early Christian History</u>; https://earlychristianhistory.net/orig-sin.html

[637] "Concerning Original Sin," First Decree; The Council of Trent; http://www.thecounciloftrent.com/ch5.htm

[638] Matthew Bellisario, "Dogmatic Theology: The Council of Trent: Original Sin," <u>Dominican Trad</u>; Feb 25, 2020; https://dominicantrad.blogspot.com/2020/02/dogmatic-theology-council-of-trent.html

[639] Jonathan Merritt, "Jesus didn't believe in 'original sin' and neither should we," <u>Religion News Service</u>; Jan 13, 2017; https://religionnews.com/2017/01/13/author-jesus-didnt-believe-in-original-sin-and-neither-should-we/

[640] <u>Ibid</u>.

[641] Newman, <u>Ibid</u>, p. xxii

[642] "How Paul Surprisingly Denied the Trinity Doctrine," <u>Becoming Christians</u>; https://becomingchristians.com/2015/12/03/how-paul-surprisingly-denied-the-Trinity-doctrine/

[643] Karen Armstrong, <u>A History of God: The 4,000-Year Quest of Judaism, Christianity and Islam</u>; p. 115; Aug 9, 1994; Ballantine Books; ISBN-13: 978-0345384560

[644] "History of Trinitarian Doctrine," <u>Stanford Encyclopedia of Philosophy Archive</u>; https://plato.stanford.edu/archives/sum2024/entries/Trinity/Trinity-history.html

[645] "20 Biblical Traditions Heavily Influenced by Other Ancient Cultures," History Collection; Mar 20, 2019; https://historycollection.com/20-biblical-traditions-heavily-influenced-by-other-ancient-cultures/

[646] Richard Rubenstein, <u>When Jesus Became God</u>; p. 223, 1999.

[647] "Law of non-contradiction," <u>Philosophical Terms</u>; https://philosophyterms.com/law-of-non-contradiction/ This is a logic principle that states that contradictory propositions cannot both be true in the same sense at the same time,

[648] Louis Berkhof, <u>Systematic Theology</u>; 1996; p. 89.

[649] "The Trinity," <u>Encyclopedia Americana</u>; 1980, Vol. 27.

[650] Millard J. Erickson, <u>God in Three Persons: A Contemporary Interpretation of the Trinity</u>; Baker Pub Group; Jan, 1995, p. 12

[651] <u>The Catholic Encyclopedia,</u> p. 263; Published by Robert Appleton Company, New York; 1914. This encyclopedia was created and designed with the Catholic Church. The new online version can be found at: https://www.newadvent.org/cathen/ ; the 1986 version of the *Catholic Encyclopedia* doesn't mention the history of the baptism words.

[652] <u>Britannica Encyclopedia</u>, 11th Edition, Vol 3 (p. 82 and pp 365-366)

[653] Maurice Arthur Canney, <u>Encyclopedia of Religions,</u> p. 53

[654] "Who Was Tertullian", <u>GotQuestion.org</u>; https://www.gotquestions.org/Tertullian.html

[655] "History of Trinitarian Doctrines," <u>Stanford Encyclopedia of Philosophy</u>; https://plato.stanford.edu/entries/Trinity/Trinity-history.html

[656] "Trinity," <u>Encyclopedia.com</u>; updated Jun 08 2018; https://www.encyclopedia.com/philosophy-and-religion/christianity/christianity-general/Trinity

[657] *Wilson, Douglas; Fischer, Ty (2005). <u>Omnibus II: Church Fathers Through the Reformation</u>. Veritas Press. p. 101. ISBN 978-1-932168-44-0. Archived from the original on 10 March 2024. Retrieved 31 March 2021. The word 'hallow' means 'saint,' in that 'hallow' is just an alternative form of the word 'holy' (as in 'hallowed be Thy name').*

[658] Stephanie Mann, "Two kinds of Saints," reported in <u>Simply Catholic</u>; https://www.simplycatholic.com/two-kinds-of-saints/

[659] Robert J Sarno, "Canonization of Saints: History and Procedure," <u>Omnilogos</u>; https://omnilogos.com/canonization-of-saints-history-and-procedure/

[660] "The History of Canonization," <u>EWTN Global Catholic Network</u>; https://www.ewtn.com/catholicism/library/history-of-canonization-13746

[661] Michael Lipka and Tim Townsend, "Papal Saints: Once a given, now are extremely rare," <u>Pew Research Center</u>; April 24, 2014; https://www.pewresearch.org/short-reads/2014/04/24/papal-saints-once-a-given-now-extremely-rare/

[662] Fr. William P. Saunders, "The Canonization Process", <u>The Arlington Catholic Herald,</u> Oct 10, 2018; https://www.catholicherald.com/article/columns/the-canonization-process/

[663] "Canonization of Saints (History and Procedure), <u>Encyclopedia.com</u>; https://www.encyclopedia.com/religion/encyclopedias-almanacs-transcripts-and-maps/canonization-saints-history-and-procedure

[664] Pat McCloskey, <u>Franciscan Media;</u> "Stages in the Canonization Process," May 9, 2020; https://www.franciscanmedia.org/ask-a-franciscan/stages-in-the-canonization-process/

[665] <u>Ibid</u>.

[666] Eric Stoltz, "What is the purpose of Saints in Catholic theology?" <u>Quora</u>; https://www.quora.com/What-is-the-purpose-of-Saints-in-Catholic-theology

[667] "7 Characteristics of Saints," <u>WordPress.com</u>, Aug 21, 2012; https://catechesisinthethirdmillennium.wordpress.com/2012/08/21/7-characteristics-of-the-saints/

[668] Norbert Brox, <u>A Concise History of the Early Church</u>, 1966, p. 48.

[669] "St. Olga". *Encyclopedia Britannica*, 17 Jul. 2024; https://www.britannica.com/biography/Saint-Olga

[670] Meagen Fairholm, "Religion and Ruthlessness: The Politics of Vladimar of Kiev"; pp. 192-193; file:///C:/Users/chuck/Downloads/Vol.+31+-+Article+9+-+Fairholm+p+189-208.pdf

[671] Jane Caecila, "Vladimir the Great: pagan, philanderer, saint," <u>Dance's Historical Miscellany;</u> 8 April 2014; https://www.danceshistoricalmiscellany.com/vladimir-great-pagan-philanderer-saint/

[672] DB Kelly, "The Worst Things Saints Have Ever Done", May 13, 2023, <u>Grunge,</u> <u>History,</u> Static Media publishing; https://www.grunge.com/804649/the-worst-things-saints-have-ever-done/

[673] "Pope Pius V's Bull Against Elizabeth I", <u>Elizabethan World Reference Library</u>. *Encyclopedia.com*. 15 Aug 2024; https://www.encyclopedia.com

[674] "The case against Junipero Serra, <u>48 Hills</u>; August 17, 2015; https://48hills.org/2015/08/the-case-against-junipero-serra/

[675] History Extra, The official website for BBC History Magazine, "7 Controversial Saints in History"; https://www.historyextra.com/period/medieval/controversial-bad-saints-thomas-becket-history-cardinal-john-newman-sinners/

[676] "Once a Saint, Always a Saint? Kind Of -- Unless You're Demoted," ABC News; https://abcnews.go.com/International/saint-saint-kind-demoted/story?id=23477573

[677] Cross and Livingstone, (eds.), "Heresy", The Oxford Dictionary of the Christian Church (2nd edition), 1974, Oxford University Press; https://www.oxfordreference.com/display/10.1093/acref/9780199659623.001.0001/acref-9780199659623-e-2683

[678] Ibid.

[679] Dominic M. Prümmer, Handbook of Moral Theology Mercer Press 1963, sect. 201ff

[680] Cross & Livingstone (eds) Oxford Dictionary of the Christian Church, 1974 apostasy, schism

[681] Ibid.

[682] Magisterium refers to the Catholic Church's authority or office to give authentic interpretation; and it rests with the pope and his bishops / cardinals.

[683] Dominic M. Prummer, Handbook of Moral Theology, Section 201, 1963, Mercier Press.

[684] Joseph Tamayo, "The Arian Heresy and Its Relation to Our Present Age", Inside the Vatican; https://insidethevatican.com/magazine/the-arian-heresy-and-its-relation-to-our-present-age-part-1/?gad_source=1&gclid=EAIaIQobChMI4fqBsevKiAMVl0B_AB27eS78EAAYASAAEgL3pfD_BwE

[685] "Arianism," Britannica; https://www.britannica.com/topic/Arianism

[686] Ibid

[687] Ayres, Lewis, Nicaea and its Legacy, An Approach to Fourth-Century Trinitarian Theology, 2004.

[688] Ryan Reeves, "Who was Athanasius and Why Was He Important?" The Gospel Coalition; May, 2016; https://www.thegospelcoalition.org/article/who-was-athanasius-and-why-was-he-important/

[689] "What is the Oriental Orthodox Church?" Got Question? https://www.gotquestions.org/Oriental-Orthodox-Church.html

[690] "Oriental Orthodoxy," New World Encyclopedia; https://www.newworldencyclopedia.org/entry/Oriental_Orthodoxy

[691] "The Great Schism," Orthodox Church in America – Volume III, Church History, Eleventh Century; https://www.oca.org/orthodoxy/the-orthodox-faith/church-history/eleventh-century/the-great-schism

[692] Ibid

[693] Ibid

[694] Robb S. Harvey, Free Speech Center, Middle Tennessee State University; July 27, 2024; https://firstamendment.mtsu.edu/article/protestant-reformation/#:~:text=The%20Reformation%20did%20not%20arise,in%20the%20late%20fourteenth%20century

[695] "The Reformation and its Impact," Durham World Heritage; https://www.durhamworldheritagesite.com/learn/history/reformation#:~:text=The%20reformation%20was%20a%20combination,to%20grant%20him%20one%3B%20and

[696] Ibid.

[697] Gerald Bray, "5 Questions about the Reformation," Crossway, Oct 2020; https://www.crossway.org/articles/5-questions-about-the-reformation/

[698] "Reformation Causes and Effects," Encyclopedia Britannica; https://www.britannica.com/summary/Reformation-Causes-and-Effects

[699] Jordan Bishop, "Aquinas on Torture". New Blackfriars. pp, 229–237; 24 April 2006

[700] Peters, Edward (1989). Inquisition. p. 67, U of California Press. ISBN 9780520066304.

[701] "The Council that almost banned the Bible," European Catholics in English; 31 March 2025; https://catholicus.eu/en/the-council-that-almost-banned-the-bible-the-controversial-decision-that-could-have-changed-history/

[702] "Code of Canon Law, Book VI; Penal Sanctions"; Vatican Archives; https://www.vatican.va/archive/cod-iuris-canonici/eng/documents/cic_lib6-cann1364-1399_en.html;

[703] "Spanish Inquisition Key Facts," Britannica; https://www.britannica.com/summary/Spanish-Inquisition-Key-Facts

[704] Stephanie Jelks, "The Spanish Inquisition: Origins, History, & End of the Institution," The Collector; Dec 16, 2022; https://www.thecollector.com/what-was-the-spanish-inquisition/

[705] "Inquisition," Feb 8, 2024; History.com; https://www.history.com/topics/religion/inquisition

[706] "Spanish Inquisition," Britannica; https://www.britannica.com/topic/Spanish-Inquisition

[707] Michal J A Paszkiewicz, "Napoleon and the Galileo files," All Posts; Nov, 2023; https://www.cricetuscricetus.co.uk/post/napoleon-and-the-galileo-files

[708] "Introduction to inquisition polemics and histories," Inquisitio; The University of Notre Dame; https://inquisition.library.nd.edu/genre-polemics-and-histories-introduction

[709] Stephanie Jelks, "The Spanish Inquisition: Origins, History, & End of the Institution," Dec 16, 2022; The Collector; https://www.thecollector.com/what-was-the-spanish-inquisition/

[710] Stephen Law, Humanism: A Very Short Introduction. p. 23; 2011; Oxford: Oxford University Press. ISBN 978-0-19-955364-8.

[711] Behringer, Witches and Witch-hunts: A Global History, p. 31 (2004). Wiley-Blackwell.

[712] Brian P. Levack, The Witch-Hunt in Early Modern Europe; pp. 110-111; (London/New York, 2013 ed.)

[713] "Canon Episcopi (or Capitulum Episcopi)," Encyclopedia.com; https://www.encyclopedia.com/science/encyclopedias-almanacs-transcripts-and-maps/canon-episcopi-or-capitulum-episcopi

[714] Natasha Sheldon, "Thou Shalt not suffer a Cat to Live": Why Pope Gregory IX's Vox in Rama Implicated Cats in Devil Worship," History Collection; May 5, 2018; https://historycollection.com/thou-shalt-not-suffer-a-cat-to-live-why-pope-gregory-ixs-vox-in-rama-implicated-cats-in-devil-worship/

[715] "Summis desiderantes affectibus of Innocent VIII (1484)," Unam Sanctam Catholicam; https://unamsanctamcatholicam.com/2024/09/18/summis-desiderantes-affectibus-of-innocent-viii/

[716] William Bradford Smith, "Chapter 3 The Persecution of Witches and the Discourse on Toleration in Early Modern Germany," Brill; https://brill.com/edcollchap-oa/book/9789004371309/BP000012.xml?language=en

[717] "Witch Hunt," Britannica; https://www.britannica.com/topic/witch-hunt

[718] Anne Llewellyn Barstow, "On Studying Witchcraft as Women's History: A Historiography of the European Witch Persecutions," Journal of Feminist Studies in Religion; Vol. 4, No. 2 (Fall, 1988), pp. 7-19; https://www.jstor.org/stable/25002078 Published By: Indiana University Press

[719] "Witch Trials & Witchcraft," Library of Congress – Research Guides; https://guides.loc.gov/feminism-french-women-history/witch-trials-witchcraft

[720] Peiye Yang, "Hammer of Witches," International Journal of New Developments in Engineering and Society
ISSN 2522-3488 Vol. 5, Issue 1: 35-38, DOI: 10.25236/IJNDES.2021.050107, published by Francis Academic Press, UK; https://francis-press.com/uploads/papers/Albv71GrYhXbZo5ylJ8Edi5l38UDicti82gSilLJ.pdf

[721] "What Was 'The Malleus Maleficarum', or 'The Hammer of Witches'?" The Collector; https://www.thecollector.com/malleus-maleficarum-or-hammer-of-witches/

[722] "Malleus Maleficarum," Britannica; https://www.britannica.com/topic/Malleus-maleficarum

[723] Karen Jolly, Edward Peters, and Catharina Raudvere, Witchcraft and Magic in Europe, Volume 3: The Middle Ages (History of Witchcraft and Magic in Europe). P. 241. Bloomsbury Academic; 2001; ISBN 0-4858-9103-4.

[724] "Malleus Maleficarum," Britannica; https://www.britannica.com/topic/Malleus-maleficarum

[725] Austin Cline, "Persecuting Witches and Witchcraft," Learn Religions; April 5, 2023; https://www.learnreligions.com/persecuting-witches-and-witchcraft-4123033

[726] "The Malleus Maleficarum Quotes," Goodreads; https://www.goodreads.com/work/quotes/757149-malleus-maleficarum

[727] "Holy Horrors: Witch-Hunts," Church and State; https://churchandstate.org.uk/2012/10/holy-horrors-witch-hunts/

728 Robert W. Thurston, <u>Witch, Wicce, Mother Goose: The Rise and Fall of the Witch Hunts in Europe and North America</u>. p. 79; Edinburgh: Longman; 2001; ISBN 978-0582438064.

729 Austin Cline, "Persecuting Witches and Witchcraft," <u>Ibid.</u>

730 Arran Birks, "The 'Hammer of Witches': An Earthquake in the Early Witch Craze," <u>The Historian</u>; Published in London at QMUL; https://projects.history.qmul.ac.uk/thehistorian/2020/01/24/the-malleus-maleficarum-an-earthquake-in-the-early-witch-craze/

731 Dr. Brendan Walsh, "'Witches' are still killed all over the world. Pardoning past victims could end the practice," <u>The University of Queensland</u>, Australia; May 10, 2024; https://www.uq.edu.au/research/article/2024/05/%E2%80%98witches%E2%80%99-are-still-killed-all-over-world-pardoning-past-victims-could-end-practice

732 Maria Cramer, "Scotland Apologizes for History of Witchcraft Persecution," <u>New York Times</u>; https://www.nytimes.com/2022/03/09/world/europe/scotland-nicola-sturgeon-apologizes-witches.html

733 "The Four Marian Dogmas," <u>The Catholic News Agency</u>, Sep 13, 2024; https://www.catholicnewsagency.com/resource/55423/the-four-marian-dogmas

734 John MacArthur, "Exposing the Heresies of the Catholic Church: Mary Worship", Feb, 2013; https://www.gty.org/library/blog/B130227

735 Pope John Paul II, "Church Proclaims Mary Mother of God," <u>EWTN</u>, (Irondale, AL); https://www.ewtn.com/catholicism/library/church-proclaims-mary-mother-of-god-8055

736 "Council of Ephesus - 431," <u>Papal Encyclicals Online</u>; https://www.papalencyclicals.net/councils/ecum03.htm

737 Fr. Edward Lee Looney, "Ten Marian Facts About St. Bernard of Clairvaux," <u>Catholic Culture</u>; https://www.catholicculture.org/culture/library/view.cfm?id=10978

738 Dave Armstrong, "St. Thomas Aquinas and Mary's Immaculate Conception," June 13, 2024; <u>National Catholic Register</u>; https://www.ncregister.com/blog/dave-armstrong-aquinas-and-immaculate-conception

739 Pope John Paul II, "Mary Was Free From All Personal Sin," <u>EWTN</u>, (Irondale, AL); https://www.ewtn.com/catholicism/library/mary-was-free-from-all-personal-sin-8041

740 Garrett S. Griffin, "Other Gods Born to Virgins on December 25 Before Jesus Christ," Dec 8, 2016; <u>Griffin</u>; https://gsgriffin.com/2016/12/08/other-gods-born-to-virgins-on-december-25-before-jesus-christ/

741 Frank A James, "Augustine's Sex-Life Change: From Profligate to Celibate," <u>Christianity Today.com</u>; https://www.christianitytoday.com/1987/07/augustines-sex-life-change-from-profligate-to-celibate/

742 Paul Senz, "Why Mary's Perpetual Virginity Matters," <u>Catholic Answers</u>, 2/2/2021; https://www.catholic.com/magazine/online-edition/why-marys-perpetual-virginity-matters

743 "Council of Trent," <u>Encyclopedia Britannica</u>; https://www.britannica.com/event/Council-of-Trent

744 "Where Did the Seven Sacraments Come From?" <u>Christian Courier</u>; https://christiancourier.com/articles/where-did-the-seven-sacraments-come-from

745 "Council of Basel-Ferrara-Florence, 1431-49 A.D.," <u>Papal Encyclicals Online</u>; https://www.papalencyclicals.net/councils/ecum17.htm

746 Wayne Jackson, "Where Did the Seven Sacraments Come From?" <u>Christian Courier</u>; https://christiancourier.com/articles/where-did-the-seven-sacraments-come-from

747 Shoshanna Lockshin, "What is a Mikveh?" <u>My Jewish Learning</u>; https://www.myjewishlearning.com/article/the-mikveh/

748 "Mikvah (Baptism): The Connection Between Immersion, Conversion and Being Born Again," <u>The Messianic Prophecy Bible Project</u>; https://free.messianicbible.com/feature/mikvah-baptism-the-connection-between-immersion-conversion-and-being-born-again/

749 "The History and Development of the Sacrament of Confirmation," <u>Loyola Press</u>; https://www.loyolapress.com/catholic-resources/sacraments/confirmation/history-and-development-of-sacrament-of-confirmation/

750 Sharon Ely Pearson, "How We Got Here from There: A Historical Perspective on Confirmation," <u>Building Faith</u>; https://buildfaith.org/how-we-got-here-from-there-a-historical-perspective-on-confirmation/

751 "Huldrych Zwingli," Encyclopedia Britannica; https://www.britannica.com/biography/Huldrych-Zwingli

752 "The Council of Trent – Session XIII - The third under the Supreme Pontiff, Julius III, celebrated on the eleventh day of October, 1551," EWTN Global Catholic Television Network; https://www.ewtn.com/catholicism/library/thirteenth-session-of-the-council-of-trent-1479

753 "Main outcomes of Lateran Councils?" Bible Hub; https://biblehub.com/q/main_outcomes_of_lateran_councils.htm

754 John Henry Cardinal Newman, An Essay on the Development of Christian Doctrine, p. 63; University of Notre Dame Press, Notre Dame, Indiana

755 "Confirmation," Encyclopedia.com; May 21 2018; https://www.encyclopedia.com/philosophy-and-religion/christianity/christianity-general/confirmation

756 Ibid.

757 Knut Alfsvag, "The Role of Confirmation in Christian Initiation," Brill; 14 Sep 2022; https://brill.com/view/journals/jyt/22/2/article-p251_006.xml?language=en

758 "Catholic Confirmation Explained," About Catholics; https://www.aboutcatholics.com/beliefs/catholic-confirmation-explained/#:~:text=Confirmation%20is%20aSacrament

759 "Christian Confirmation," Facts and Details; https://europe.factsanddetails.com/article/entry-775.html

760 'Marriage as a Sacrament," Cambridge University Press; https://assets.cambridge.org/97811071/46150/excerpt/9781107146150_excerpt.pdf

761 Wayne Jackson, "Where Did the Seven Sacraments Come From?" Christian Courier; https://christiancourier.com/articles/where-did-the-seven-sacraments-come-from

762 Helen L Owen, "When Did the Catholic Church Decide Priests Should Be Celibate?" History News Network; Oct 2001; https://www.historynewsnetwork.org/article/when-did-the-catholic-church-decide-priests-should

763 "A Brief History of Celibacy in the Roman Church," Future Church; https://futurechurch.org/future-of-priestly-ministry/optional-celibacy/history-of-celibacy/

764 Future Church; Ibid; https://futurechurch.org/future-of-priestly-ministry/optional-celibacy/history-of-celibacy/

765 A brief history of Celibacy…. Ibid.

766 Helen L. Owen, "When Did the Catholic Church Decide Priests Should Be Celibate?" History News Network; Oct 2001; https://www.historynewsnetwork.org/article/when-did-the-catholic-church-decide-priests-should

767 "The Case for Marriage Among Catholic Priests," WheelerMethodist.org; https://wheelermethodist.org/blog/should-catholic-priests-marry/

768 John W. O'Malley, "The History Behind Celibacy and the Priesthood," America Magazine; Oct 28, 2002; https://www.americamagazine.org/faith/2002/10/28/history-behind-celibacy-and-priesthood?

769 "Catholic Priests," Facts and Details; https://europe.factsanddetails.com/article/entry-780.html

770 "Apostolic Succession," Encyclopedia Britannica; https://www.britannica.com/topic/apostolic-succession

771 "Ordination," Independent Catholic Church; https://independentoldcatholicchurch.org/ordination/

772 "History of the Sacrament of Anointing," Holy Martyrs Catholic Church; https://holymartyrs.net/about-us/sacraments/anointing-of-the-sick/history-of-the-sacrament-of-anointing/

773 "Extreme Unction," New Advent; https://www.newadvent.org/cathen/05716a.htm

774 CCC, paragraph 1516, p. 421

775 "Anointing the Sick," Ave Maria Press; https://www.avemariapress.com/engagingfaith/history-of-the-sacrament-of-the-anointing-of-the-sick

776 "A Brief History of Purgatory," Time; https://time.com/6273511/a-brief-history-of-purgatory/

777 "Craig Truglia, Saint Augustine and the existence of Purgatory," Orthodox Christian Theology; Nov 20, 2014; https://orthodoxchristiantheology.com/2014/11/20/saint-augustine-and-the-existence-of-purgatory/

778 Dr. Eitan Bar, "The Doctrine of 'Hell' in Late Christianity," Eitan Bar; https://eitan.bar/articles/the-doctrine-of-hell-in-late-christianity/

779 John Roskoski, "The Afterlife (part 2); Purgatory," Catholic 365; Feb 24, 2022; https://www.catholic365.com/article/14771/the-afterlife-part-2-purgatory.html

780 Jacques Le Goff, The Birth of Purgatory, translated by Arthur Goldhammer; University of Chicago Press, 1984. The book is online; the Library of the Central European University Budapest, Scolar Press; https://monoskop.org/images/a/a5/Le_Goff_Jacques_The_Birth_of_Purgatory_1984.pdf

781 "What Is Purgatory?" The Spiritual Life; https://slife.org/purgatory/

782. Catechism of the Catholic Church (CCC), p. 413, Sections 1478-1479; Doubleday, New York; Apr, 1995.

783 "Limbo," Britannica; https://www.britannica.com/topic/limbo-Roman-Catholic-theology

784 "Whatever Happened to Limbo," Catholic Straight Answers; https://catholicstraightanswers.com/whatever-happened-to-limbo/

785 Taylor Marshall, "The Doctrine of Limbo in Catholic Tradition," New Saint Thomas Institute; https://nsti.com/wp-content/uploads/2014/10/Limbo-Paper-March-31-2015.pdf

786 "Pope Benedict 'closed' Limbo and no one complained," National Catholic Reporter; https://www.ncronline.org/opinion/guest-voices/pope-benedict-closed-limbo-and-no-one-complained

787 Philip Pullella, "Catholic Church buries limbo after centuries," Reuters; August 9, 2007; https://www.reuters.com/article/world/catholic-church-buries-limbo-after-centuries-idUSL20287216/

788 "Limbo: Waiting Around for the Coming of Christ," Historic Mysteries; February 28, 2024; https://www.historicmysteries.com/myths-legends/limbo/39250/

789 "Use of Vernacular In Worship Approved," Blog at WordPress.com; https://vaticaniiat50.wordpress.com/2012/12/10/use-of-vernacular-in-worship-approved/

790 Jeff Ostrowski, "Mass in the Vernacular?" February 6, 2024; Corpus Christi Watershed; https://www.ccwatershed.org/2024/02/06/mass-in-the-vernacular-seven-7-considerations/

791 Scott P. Richert ," What Is the Tridentine Mass?" Learn Religions; https://www.learnreligions.com/what-is-the-tridentine-mass-542958

792 "The Unchanged Sacrifice of the Mass and Decree of Quo Primum," Latin Mass CTM-org; http://www.latinmass-ctm.org/priest/priest_unchanged.htm

793 "Quo primum," Papal Encyclicals Online; https://www.papalencyclicals.net/Pius05/p5quopri.htm

794 "Novus Ordo (Ordinary Form of the Mass)," Roman Catholic Diocese of Peterborough; https://www.peterboroughdiocese.org/en/life-and-faith/novus-ordo--ordinary-form-of-the-mass-.aspx

795 "Missale Romanum," The Vatican; https://www.vatican.va/content/paul-vi/en/apost_constitutions/documents/hf_p-vi_apc_19690403_missale-romanum.html

796 "Motu proprio," Catholic Answers Encyclopedia; https://www.catholic.com/encyclopedia/motu-proprio . Motu proprio translates to, 'on his own impulse.' A motu proprio rescript begins by giving the reasons for issuing it, and it then indicates the law or regulation made or the favor granted. It is less formal than a constitution and carries no papal seal.

797 "Traditionis custodes," Vatican; https://www.vatican.va/content/francesco/en/motu_proprio/documents/20210716-motu-proprio-traditionis-custodes.html

798 "The Hidden Story Behind Traditionis Custodes", Inside the Vatican; https://insidethevatican.com/magazine/the-hidden-story-behind-traditionis-custodes/?gad_

799 D B Kelly, "Times Popes Have Apologized for Actions of the Catholic Church," Grunge; July 31, 2022; https://www.grunge.com/947338/times-popes-have-apologized-for-the-actions-of-the-catholic-church/

800 D B Kelly, Ibid

[801] Richard Boudreaux, "Pope Apologizes for Catholic Sins Past and Present," Los Angeles Times; Mar 13, 2000; https://www.latimes.com/archives/la-xpm-2000-mar-13-mn-8338-story.html

[802] E. J. Dionne Jr., "Pope Apologizes to Africans for Slavery," The New York Times, Aug. 14, 1985; https://www.nytimes.com/1985/08/14/world/pope-apologizes-to-africans-for-slavery.html

[803] "The Pope's Apology for the Inquisition," BBC (March 12, 2006); https://www.jewishwikipedia.info/understand.html

[804] Ivan J. Kauffman," Facing the Inquisition: A pope seeks pardon," Dec 10, 2007; America Magazine; https://www.americamagazine.org/issue/637/other-things/facing-inquisition

[805] "Pope apologizes for Reformation wrongs," LaCroix International; https://international.la-croix.com/news/religion/pope-apologizes-for-reformation-wrongs/2519

[806] "Pope Francis takes significant step forward with Jan Hus comments," 06/15/2015; Radio Prague International; https://english.radio.cz/pope-francis-takes-significant-step-forward-jan-hus-comments-8257068

[807] Sarah Delaney, "Pope Asks Pardon For Sins Of Church," The Washington Post; March 12, 2000; https://www.washingtonpost.com/archive/politics/2000/03/13/pope-asks-pardon-for-sins-of-church/9efdf34b-7912-489f-a6d0-b01eb57c64d6/

[808] Rory Carroll, "Pope says sorry for sins of church," The Guardian; Mar 13, 2000; https://www.theguardian.com/world/2000/mar/13/catholicism.religion

[809] Rory Carroll, Ibid

[810] Harry Karapalides, "This Date in History: An 800 Year Apology," Cosmos Philly; May 4, 2001, posted May 4, 2020; https://cosmosphilly.com/this-date-in-history-an-800-year-apology/

[811] Rory Carroll, Ibid

[812] "Pope John Paul II apologizes for church's oppression of women," National Library of Medicine; Spring 1995; https://pubmed.ncbi.nlm.nih.gov/12290462/

[813] Rory Carroll, Ibid

[814] William Drozdiak, "Vatican Apologizes to Jews – Church Cites Failings in Fighting Holocaust," Washington Post; Mar 16, 1998; https://www.washingtonpost.com/archive/politics/1998/03/17/vatican-apologizes-to-jews/ce5ea6e9-bd97-4022-b639-288342b63455/

[815] "Apology to Indigenous People from Religious Orders of Australia," Catholic Religious Australia (CRA); https://www.catholicreligious.org.au/apology-to-indigenous-people-from-religious-orders-of-australia

[816] "Pope Francis Apologizes for Church's Colonial Sins," Foreign Policy; https://foreignpolicy.com/2015/07/10/pope-francis-apologizes-for-churchs-colonial-sins/

[817] "Church apologies: Top leaders say sorry for historical sins," AP News; https://apnews.com/article/pope-francis-canada-religion-sexual-abuse-by-clergy-11563ae36c003eaf46ed68a928b41317

[818] Scott Neumann, "The pope's apology in Canada was historic, but for some Indigenous people, not enough," NPR, July 25, 2022; https://www.npr.org/2022/07/25/1113498723/pope-francis-apology-canada-residential-schools-indigenous-children

[819] Newmann, Ibid

[820] Hada Messia and Alex Hardie, "Pope apologizes to indigenous people of Canada," April 1, 2022; CNN; https://www.cnn.com/2022/04/01/world/pope-apology-indigenous-canada/index.html

[821] Gerard O'Connell, "Pope Francis sends special prosecutor to Chile to investigate charges against Bishop Barros," America Magazine; Jan 30, 2018; https://www.americamagazine.org/faith/2018/01/30/pope-francis-sends-special-prosecutor-chile-investigate-charges-against-bishop

[822] Pascale Bonnefoy, "Pope Defrocks Fernando Karadima, Priest at Center of Abuse Outrage in Chile," The New York Times; Sep 29, 2018; https://www.nytimes.com/2018/09/29/world/americas/chile-pope-francis-fernando-karadima.html

[823] "Fernando Karadima, Chilean priest at center of abuse scandal, dies," National Catholic Reporter; July 27, 2021; https://www.ncronline.org/news/vatican/fernando-karadima-chilean-priest-center-abuse-scandal-dies

824 Scott Neumann and Sylvia Poggioli, "Pope Apologizes For 'Serious Mistakes' In Handling Of Chile's Sex Abuse Scandal": April 12, 2018; NPR; https://www.npr.org/sections/thetwo-way/2018/04/12/601742861/pope-apologizes-for-serious-mistakes-in-handling-of-chile-s-sex-abuse-scandal

825 "French Church abuse: 216,000 children were victims of clergy" – BBC; 5 October 2021; https://www.bbc.com/news/world-europe-58801183

826 French Church, Ibid

827 "Aurelien Breeden, "Over 200,000 Minors Abused by Clergy in France Since 1950, Report Estimates," The New York Times; Oct 5, 2021; https://www.nytimes.com/2021/10/05/world/europe/france-catholic-church-abuse.html

828 Associated Press, "About 333,000 children were abused within France's Catholic Church, a report finds," NPR, October 5, 2021; https://www.npr.org/2021/10/05/1043302348/france-catholic-church-sexual-abuse-report-children

829 "Report on abuse in Munich diocese: 497 victims in 74 years," Vatican News; https://www.vaticannews.va/en/church/news/2022-01/sex-abuse-report-munich-ratzinger-marx-holy-see-statement.html

830 "Pope Benedict XVI implicated in report on sexual abuse in German diocese," PBS News; Jan 20, 2022; https://www.pbs.org/newshour/world/pope-benedict-xvi-implicated-in-report-on-sexual-abuse-in-german-diocese

831 "Letter of Pope Emeritus Benedict XVI regarding the report on abuse in the Archdiocese of Munich-Freising," Holy See Press Office; Vatican City; 6 Feb 2022; https://press.vatican.va/content/salastampa/en/bollettino/pubblico/2022/02/08/220208b.html

832 Harriet Sherwood, "Former pope Benedict accused of inaction over child sexual abuse cases," The Guardian; https://www.theguardian.com/world/2022/jan/20/former-pope-benedict-accused-inaction-child-sexual-abuse-cases

833 Associated Press, "Pope Apologizes for Catholic Church 'Crimes' in Ireland," Voice of America News; https://www.voanews.com/a/pope-apologizes-for-catholic-church-crimes-in-ireland/4545031.html

834 Nicole Winfield and Pietro De Cristofaro, "Pope apologizes for 'crimes' against Irish women, babies," Associated Press News; August 26, 2018; https://apnews.com/article/36b31ae6dfc3439ea2a45f07769136cb

835 Associated Press, "Pope Francis apologizes for 'crimes' of the Catholic Church in Ireland," CBC; Aug 26, 2018; https://www.cbc.ca/news/world/dead-babies-remembered-ireland-pope-visit-1.4799531

836 Erin Blakemore, "How Ireland Turned 'Fallen Women' Into Slaves". History. (21 July 2019); https://www.history.com/news/magdalene-laundry-ireland-asylum-abuse

837 Erin Blakemore, "How Ireland Turned 'Fallen Women' Into Slaves," History.com; https://www.history.com/articles/magdalene-laundry-ireland-asylum-abuse

838 David Batty, "Pope Benedict Apologies for Irish priests' child sex abuse," The Guardian; 20 Mar 2010; https://www.theguardian.com/world/2010/mar/20/pope-benedict-apologises-irish-priests

839 De Cristofaro, Ibid.

840 "We Remember: A Reflection on the Shoah," PBS; 16 March 1998; https://www.pbs.org/wgbh/pages/frontline/shows/pope/encyclicals/jews.html

841 "Pope John Paul II: Relations with Jews and Israel," Jewish Virtual Library; https://www.jewishvirtuallibrary.org/pope-john-paul-ii-relations-with-jews-and-israel

842 Richard Boudreaux and Tracy Wilkinson, "Pope Leaves an Apology At Jews' Revered Wall," Los Angeles Times; March 27, 2000; SF Gate; https://www.sfgate.com/news/article/pope-leaves-an-apology-at-jews-revered-wall-2792689.php

843 "Pope: 'Jews Are Not Responsible For Killing Jesus'" NPR - Faith Matters; March 4, 2011; https://www.npr.org/2011/03/04/134264425/Pope-Jews-Are-Not-Responsible-For-Killing-Jesus

844 Erik Ortiz, Pope apologizes for priest sex abuse scandal with 'sorrow and shame', NBC News; Aug 20, 2018; https://www.nbcnews.com/news/pope-francis/pope-francis-apologizes-catholic-priest-sex-abuse-scandal-sorrow-shame-n902121

[845] Harriet Sherwood, "Pope issues law to force priests and nuns to report sexual abuse," The Guardian; 9 May 2019; https://amp.theguardian.com/world/2019/may/09/pope-issues-law-to-force-priests-and-nuns-to-report-sexual-abuse

[846] Erik Ortiz, Ibid.

[847] Sheena McKenzie, Barbie Nadeau and Livia Borghese, CNN, "Pope on Pennsylvania sex abuse report: We abandoned the little ones," August 20, 2018; https://www.cnn.com/2018/08/20/europe/pope-francis-letter-sexual-abuse-intl/index.html

[848] Wietse de Boer, "The Catholic Church and Sexual Abuse, Then and Now," Origins; https://origins.osu.edu/article/catholic-church-sexual-abuse-pope-confession-priests-nuns

[849] Boer, Ibid

[850] Wesley Stephenson, "How many men are pedophiles?" BBC News; 30 July 2014'; https://www.bbc.com/news/magazine-28526106

[851] "Are Most Child Sex Offenders Heterosexual?" Stop Abuse Campaign; https://stopabusecampaign.org/2017/03/10/are-most-sex-abusers-heterosexual/

Chapter 7 – Protestantism

The Protestant Reformation in the 16th century was initially a movement to curb the selling of indulgences and relics as well as to remedy some other relatively minor abuses. But as the Reformation grew, its doctrinal and core issues broadened well beyond these relatively moderate abuses. Indeed, disputes arose over a variety of religious practices (e.g., veneration of the saints and the taking of sacraments), ecclesiastical structures, the expensive construction of St. Peter's Basilica in Rome, and especially the supremacy of the pope.[852] But after Martin Luther and Jean (John) Calvin split with the Roman Catholics, the Protestants continued to debate theological issues among themselves, and they began to split off from each other; and that fragmentation process has continued through today.

The 16th century saw the advent of Lutherans, Calvinists, Anglicans, Anabaptists, Huguenots, Presbyterians, and Puritans. In the 17th century, the Baptists surfaced, and the Baptists have repeatedly split into multiple sub-groups, now well over 30 separate groups; the Amish, Quakers, and Congregationists originated in the 17th century as well. The 18th century ushered in the Methodists, Dutch Reformed Church, Unitarians, Episcopalians, and the Shakers.[853] The 19th century gave rise to Jehovah Witnesses, the Church of the Latter-Day Saints, the Church of Christ, and Adventists.[854] The latecomers included the Assemblies of God in the 20th century, as part of the Pentecostal movement, and later in the century the Charismatic movement. There have been many other new denominations; but this is not an attempt to write a comprehensive listing of all the denominations of the Christian sects. That said, one thing became obvious: Christians divide into multiple denominations because they generally disagree about almost everything.

In today's world, Christians cannot even agree on which denominations are truly Christian. The Church of Latter-Day Saints (Mormons) consider themselves Christian, as do the Jehovah's Witnesses, Church of God, and Christian Scientists; however, some Southern Baptists, the largest evangelical Protestant group in the USA,[855] have been known to classify each of them as cults.[856] In any case, Southern Baptists are moving away from the cult appellation directed at other denominations.

A common consensus held by most religious experts is that if a Christian denomination is to be considered Protestant, in general, it should acknowledge the following three fundamental principles of Protestantism.[857] Of course, there are exceptions, such as Liberal Protestants do not necessarily support *sola scriptura*.

- **Scripture Alone** (*Sola scriptura*) – Emphasized by Luther, this is the belief that the Bible is the highest source of authority for believers. U.S. Protestants are split on this issue in that 46% of those surveyed by *Pew Research* in 2017 said that the Bible is the sole source of religious authority for Christians – a traditionally Protestant belief. In other words, these Christians treat the Bible as the words of their God. Meanwhile, 52% say Christians should look both to the Bible and to the Church's official teachings and tradition for guidance; this is the position held by the RCC during the time of the Reformation as well as today. On the US Catholic side, 75% say that in addition to the Bible, Christians need guidance from Church teachings and tradition.[858]

What is interesting about this is that it was early Catholicism that canonized the Scriptures, and it wasn't particularly diligent in vetting them. Additionally, there is some effort involved in reading the Bible and understanding what it says: there's historical contexts, the literary structure of the author's content, the context of the writing, the sociological and political background, etc. All that may require external inputs, even if those external sources just explain why the verses are saying what they are saying.

- **Justification by faith alone** (*Sola fide*) – This is the view that believers are justified, or pardoned for sin, solely on the condition of faith in Jesus Christ, rather than a combination of faith and good works. For Protestants, good works are a necessary consequence rather than a cause of justification.[859] Yet, in the *Pew Research* survey of 2017, almost half of U.S. Protestants (46%) say faith alone is needed to attain salvation (the belief held by Protestant reformers in the 16th century); but slightly over half (52%) say both good deeds and faith are needed to get into heaven – which is a historically Catholic belief. Indeed, 81% of U.S. Catholics say both good deeds and faith are needed to get into heaven.[860]

Some Protestant denominations do use their faith as their impetus for good works. As an example, Methodist Churches have always emphasized that ordinarily both faith and good works play a role in salvation; in particular, the works of piety and the works of mercy, in Wesleyan-Arminian theology, are "indispensable for our sanctification." [861] Methodists believe that good works are the external result of true faith.

- **Universal priesthood of believers** – The universal priesthood of believers implies the right and duty of the Christian laity to read the Bible in the vernacular; but it also has the expectation that each person take part in all the public affairs of their Church. It is generally opposed to a hierarchical system which puts the essence and authority of the Church in an exclusive priesthood, and that makes ordained priests the necessary mediators between God and the people.

While most Protestant sects reject the full hierarchy of the Catholic Church, a number of Protestant Churches, including Lutheran Churches, the Moravian Church, and the Anglican Communion, affirm that they ordain their clergy in line with the apostolic succession,[862] and in 1922, the Eastern Orthodox Ecumenical Patriarch of Constantinople recognized Anglican orders as valid.[863] However, the Roman Catholic Church has rejected the validity of Anglican apostolic succession as well as that of other Protestant Churches.

Overall, in the United States, 500 years after the Reformation, the high-level views of Catholics and Protestants are more alike than they are different. Of course, that is a massive generalization; there are many Protestant sects, each with their own special views, and some of them are not truly in alignment with mainstream Protestantism.

Protestant Intolerance During the Reformation

Martin Luther kicked off the Protestant Reformation, and he was soon joined by John Calvin. While each believed in their own version of freedom of conscience, both men were quick to persecute others. Indeed, German priest and theologian, Martin Luther (1483 - 1546); Swiss theologian, Ulrich Zwingli (1484 – 1531); French theologian, John Calvin (1509 – 1564); French Calvinist, Theodore Beza (1519 – 1605); Scottish theologian, John Knox[864]

(1514 – 1572), Archbishop of Canterbury, Thomas Cranmer[865] (1489 – 1556) and Bishop of London, Nicholas Ridley[866] (1500 – 1555) — all advocated the right of the civil authorities to punish the 'crime' of heresy.[867] Luther, Beza, and Calvin were particularly intolerant of dissent. The primary doctrine of Protestantism was the right of private judgment in matters of religious belief. That said, it is illogical to assert that an individual may interpret the Bible to suit oneself, and in the next moment to torture and/or execute that same individual for having done so. Yet, that is what sometimes occurred during the early decades of the Reformation.

In England the advocates of religious toleration long continued to be in a minority; but it finally became governmental policy through the Toleration Act of 1688, in which the English Parliament granted freedom of worship to Protestant non-conformists (i.e., non-Anglicans) such as Baptists and Congregationists; although it <u>excluded</u> Roman Catholics, Jews, non-trinitarians such as Unitarians, and atheists from its religious toleration.[868]

Intolerance in America

In the early to mid-17th century, many of the non-conformist Protestants fled from Ireland and England to America, where they established their religious settlements. The amazing thing is that so many of those fugitives did not learn the lesson of toleration, as they did not grant it to others. Often, when they found themselves in a position to do so, they persecuted other Christians, such as the Society of Friends, or Quakers.[869] In Massachusetts, for successive convictions, a Quaker would suffer the loss of one ear and then the other, the boring of the tongue with a hot iron, and sometimes death. In Boston, three Quaker men and one woman were hanged.[870]

English writer, William Penn (1644 – 1718), who was persecuted by Protestants in England, founded the tolerant colony of Pennsylvania, based on Quakerism. That Christian sect has an honorable record of tolerance, and it is one of the most individualistic of Protestant sects. Pennsylvania Quakers were leaders of the abolitionist movement in the United States, and they were the first religious group to condemn slavery.[871]

In the 17th century, the most notable instances of practical toleration were found in the colony of Maryland, founded by Lord Baltimore (1605 – 1675) in 1632 for persecuted Catholics, and the colony offered asylum to Protestant sects. As it turned out, relatively few English Catholics made the long trek across the Atlantic. The colony was founded to be a refuge for Catholics, but it held greater appeal for Protestant dissenters, such as Quakers and Puritans, who disagreed with the Church of England.[872] Lord Baltimore (Cecil Calvert) allowed several hundred Puritans, unwelcome in Episcopalian Virginia, to enter Maryland in 1648. On April 21, 1649, the colony's assembly passed the Maryland Toleration Act,[873] which made it illegal for Marylanders to use derogatory religious terms for each other, including "heretic, schismatic, idolater, popish priest, Jesuit papist, or any other name or term in a reproachful manner relating to matters of religion."[874] This act protected all trinitarian Christians in Maryland, but it denied protection for non-trinitarians.[875]

Then the dictator, Oliver Cromwell (1599 – 1558), who was a Puritan, came to power in England in 1649. Under the authority of the English Parliament, Puritans seized control of the colony of Maryland. These Puritans were staunch Reformed Protestants and were unfriendly toward Catholicism, even after they themselves had been treated fairly. They repealed the Maryland Toleration Act in 1654, and they banned Catholics from openly worshiping. When Cecil Calvert regained control of the colony of Maryland, the Act was reinstated, before being repealed permanently in 1692.[876] After the Maryland rebellion of 1689, a new Protestant governor was in place, and the Maryland assembly openly passed a wave of repressive, anti-Catholic religious and civil measures. Catholic worship was banned, and Catholics were barred from voting.[877] During the 40+ years the Catholics had governed Maryland, they had not been guilty of any religious oppression.[878] Unfortunately, religious freedom would not return to Maryland until after the American Revolution, with its secular constitution.

Christian Diversity

According to writer and lecturer, Chris Hitchens (1949 – 2011), "Religion is the outcome of unresolved contradictions in the material world."[879] However, religion is also full of contradictions and fallacies vis-à-vis the natural world. Let's consider why there are so many religions! As people "seek the truth", and as they find fault with a particular religion, they alter it or even discard it for a new one. After all, many religions are simply re-adaptations of the religions that went before them, whereby people chose portions of a religion they liked and rejected other portions, as they cherry-pick key aspects from multiple religions, very similar to the ancient Greeks and Romans. That helps to explain why Christmas was set for Dec 25, a Roman pagan holiday[880], and why All Saints Day Eve (October 31) aligns with the Celtic holiday honoring the dead – Halloween, or All Hallow's Eve or Hallow E'en in Ireland. It also helps to explain why there are thousands of Protestant denominations, and new ones crop up each year. Without the overly strict controls that the Catholic Church once forced on its laity for over a millennium, there is nothing to retard still greater diversity among Christian beliefs.

How do Christians classify themselves? For all its issues, starting around 300 CE, Catholicism defined Christianity for the next 1200 years. And there remain three basic groups of Catholic Churches: (1) the Oriental Orthodox Churches[881], (2) the Eastern Orthodox, which is officially the Orthodox Catholic Church[882], and (3) the Roman Catholic Church (RCC). But in antiquity, there was no mainstream, orthodox Christianity. In those first 2 ½ centuries after Paul jump-started Christianity, there was no central church authority, but there was tremendous diversity of thought and practice. The belief that Christianity was united from the start is just not accurate. Additionally, Christianity did not develop uniformly throughout the Mediterranean area. Each independent group developed its own distinct doctrines, although these diverse thoughts often overlapped and blurred.

Christian Churches next gravitated to five ancient patriarchates located in Rome, Constantinople, Alexandria, Antioch, and Jerusalem. The Oriental Orthodox Churches were part of the first three ecumenical councils – Nicea, Constantinople, Ephesus; but they did not accept the results of the 4th Council – Chalcedon (in today's Turkey) in 451; so they split off, due to their perceived differences regarding the divine and human natures of Jesus Christ.[883] Much later, the Eastern Orthodox split off in the schism of 1054[884] as the Roman Church became entangled in its own excesses. Until that time, the Eastern and Roman Churches were considered two branches of the same body, albeit with disagreements between the two branches having long existed. In the 1950s, both the Roman Catholic and Eastern Orthodox Churches independently began dialogue with the Oriental Orthodox Churches to resolve their ancient Christological disputes.[885]

In the 16th century, the Protestant Reformation unleashed a torrent of new Christian denominations, as those that split with the centralized RCC couldn't agree with their fellow Protestants regarding their interpretations of Scripture, diverse Church practices, doctrinal disagreements, the role of the clergy, and the authority of the Bible. Various Protestant sects emerged, and as disagreements occurred, they tended to fracture, split off, and form new Churches, rather than promote compromise and reach a reconciliation.

There are more than 200 Christian denominations in the USA alone, and there are over 45,000 globally.[886] [887] The process of continual fracturing among Protestant Christians has led to the formation of numerous denominations, each holding different beliefs. The largest US denomination is the Baptists, who constitute almost 30% of all American Protestants. As stated by Dan Barker, "there are thousands of Christian denominations and sects – all using inspired Scripture to validate their conflicting doctrines."[888]

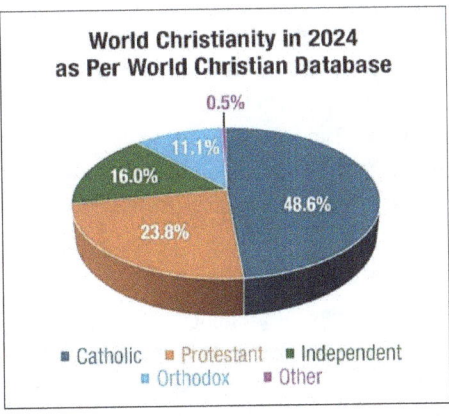

Globally, there are approximately two billion Christians. The adjacent illustration on global Christianity shows a decomposition by major Christian groups. As the United States has become more diverse demographically, its religious landscape has shifted in the past few decades. However, the United States does have a relatively high percentage of Christians.

Christian Denominations - United States[889]

- Roman Catholics - 61,900,000 (source: *2020 US Religion Census*)
- Eastern Orthodox - 3,000,000 - 6,000,000 (source: *Wikipedia*)
- Protestants - 140,000,000 (source: *Public Region Research Institute*)

Although Protestantism has more total members than Catholicism in the U.S., no single Protestant denomination has as many members as Roman Catholicism.

Major American Protestant Denominations

Mainline Protestants

Some consider mainline Protestant Christian denominations as those Protestant denominations that were brought to the United States by its historic immigrant groups. The largest of these include the Episcopal (English), Presbyterian (Scottish), Methodist (English and Welsh), and Lutheran (German and Scandinavian) Churches. In 1989, William Hutchison coined the term "Seven Sisters of American Protestantism,"[890] to refer to seven major denominations that comprise mainline Protestantism: (1) American Baptist Churches USA,

(2) the Christian Church (Disciples of Christ), (3) the Episcopal Church, (4) the Evangelical Lutheran Church in America, (5) the Presbyterian Church (USA), (6) the United Church of Christ, and (7) the United Methodist Church. Like many Protestant sects, mainline denominations are theologically pluralistic.

Most mainline denominations teach that the Bible is God's word in function, but they tend to be open to new ideas and societal changes. While the majority mainline Protestants believe that Jesus is the way to salvation, some would accept that perhaps there are other ways to salvation as well. They believe that people involved in other religious traditions, even outside of Christianity, may have access to God's grace and to salvation through their own means. Additionally, mainline Protestants have been increasingly open to the ordination of women. Mainline Protestant Churches tend to belong to inclusive organizations such as the National Council of Churches and the World Council of Churches. From the perspective of evangelicalism, mainline denominations are often considered "liberal." But a more accurate categorization would be that they have embraced theological pluralism.[891] When a distinction is made between evangelical and mainline Churches, it's not a hard and fast distinction. There are even evangelical, mainline Protestants.

Zwinglianism

The theology of Zwingli, or Zwinglianism, was concentrated in Switzerland. Like Martin Luther, Ulrich Zwingli was a Catholic priest. Along with John Calvin and Martin Luther, he was a key leader in the Protestant Reformation, but his influence has been overshadowed by Luther (who outlived him) and by the next-generation Swiss reformers, such as Calvin and Heinrich Bullinger (1504 – 1575), who succeeded Zwingli in December 1531.[892]

By 1525, the Protestant Reformation took firm root in Switzerland. In April 1525, Zurich leaders officially abolished the ritual of mass, and the Bible was read and preached in the language of the people. Zwingli saw to it that the communion service was open to the congregation and clergy alike. Venerating Mary, selling indulgences, and praying for the dead were no longer practiced.[893] Zwingli met Martin Luther in 1529; they agreed on most issues, but they could not agree on the Eucharist. Luther supported consubstantiation, and Zwingli believed that communion was symbolic. Zwingli is considered the founder of the Swiss Reformed Church, which has evolved into the Protestant Church of Switzerland (PCS).[894]

Lutheranism

Luther's actions were the catalyst of the Protestant Reformation. Martin Luther developed a new Christian discourse of faith, which clearly deviated from the teaching and interpretations of the Roman Catholic Church. He railed against the RCC's sale of indulgences; and Luther ardently believed in an individual's personal interpretation of the Bible, and in providing a Bible in the German language. Luther had published his German translation of the New Testament in 1522; and he and his collaborators completed the full translation of the Old Testament in 1534, when the entire Bible was published.[895]

While he promoted some radically new ideas, Luther also advocated intolerance, persecution, and violence. Luther wrote a ferocious pamphlet in 1525 against the peasants who were fighting to improve their standard of living under the oppressive German princes. Luther advised the princes: "Let everyone who can, smite, slay, and stab, secretly or openly, remembering that nothing can be more poisonous, hurtful, or devilish than a rebel. It is just as when one must kill a mad dog."[896] Luther called on the secular authorities to suppress his theological opponents, and he advocated the sword to protect his version of religion and morality.

Luther wrote negatively about Jews throughout his career.[897] Although Luther rarely encountered Jews during his life, his attitudes reflected a theological and cultural tradition that saw Jews as a rejected people guilty of the murder of Christ, while he lived in a locality that had expelled Jews roughly 90 years earlier.[898] Martin Luther's hateful and anti-Jewish sentiments have often been identified as highly influential on modern anti-Semitism. Sadly, despite his early attempt at reaching out to people of Jewish faith, the famous reformer altered his stance; and he embraced a most aggressive strategy against Jews at large.[899]

Philipp Melanchthon (1497 – 1560) was a German theologian in the Lutheran Church. He was a friend of Martin Luther and succeeded him. In 1530, Philipp Melanchthon called Anabaptists "irreligious fanatics and murderous revolutionaries, enemies of temporal government, however peaceful they may seem."[900] Melanchthon accepted the chairmanship of the secular Inquisition that suppressed the Anabaptists in Germany with imprisonment or death, as he was convinced that God had destined all Anabaptists to Hell.[901]

In a memorandum of 1531, composed by Melanchthon and signed by Luther, the Anabaptist rejection of the ministerial office was described as "an insufferable blasphemy." In a memorandum of 1536, again composed by Melanchthon and signed by Luther, the distinction between the peaceful and the revolutionary Anabaptists was removed. Melanchthon, this time, argued that even the passive action of the Anabaptists in rejecting government, oaths, private property, and marriages outside the faith was itself disruptive of the civil order; and it was therefore seditious.[902]

Saxony was the center of the Lutheran Reformation. A regular inquisition was set up in Saxony, with Melanchthon as the judge, and under it, many persons were punished, some with death, some with life imprisonment, and some with exile.[903] Melanchthon, with Luther's approval and sanction, professed the view that heretics who denied infant Baptism, original sin, and the 'Real Presence' (consubstantiation) in the Eucharist should be put to death.[904] Later, Melanchthon changed his mind regarding the 'Real Presence.'[905]

The Church of England

The Church of England was established in 1534, after King Henry VIII renounced papal authority because the pope wouldn't grant his marriage annulment to Catherine of Aragon. Thus, English law (Act of Supremacy) established the Church of England as England's national church.[906] The Church of England was increasingly intolerant of Catholics and, at times, of Puritans through 1690, even promoting the execution of Catholic priests during the reign of Elizabeth I.[907] In 1559, the *Act of Uniformity* was passed under Queen Elizabeth's rule, which mandated the use of a specific Book of Common Prayer and other liturgical practices, often enforcing adherence through penalties for non-conformity. The law required all English subjects to attend services in the Church of England. Those who refused to do so, known as *recusants*, were fined one shilling for every Sunday or holy day they missed. By 1581, with growing paranoia over Catholicism as a political threat, Elizabeth's government introduced the *Act to Retain the Queen's Subjects in Their Due Obedience*. This Act escalated the penalties for recusancy with fines of 20 pounds per month. Anyone found attempting to convert others to Catholicism could be charged with treason, and the punishment was death.[908]

Members of the Church of England, known as Anglicans, believe the Protestant Bible to be the highest and supreme authority in matters of faith. Their theological positions can be found in the historic Anglican Formularies (rites and prayers): (1) the Book of Common Prayer, (2) the 39 Articles of Religion, (3) the Ordinal (which contains ordination services for bishops, priests, and deacons), and (4) the Book of Homilies (an officially-approved collection of sermons) offering commentary on those formularies.[909]

The King James Bible, commissioned in 1604 and printed in 1611, was intended to "allow access to the knowledge" and included several new pieces of information contributed by 54 "King-approved" advisers.[910] However, after its publication, it was condemned by many scholars, including the eccentric Puritan, Hugh Broughton (1549 – 1612) and the English philosopher, Thomas Hobbes (1588 – 1642), for being wildly inaccurate and an "abominable translation."[911]

Episcopal Church

After the American Revolution, the Anglican Church in the United States had to separate from the Church of England because its clergy were required to swear allegiance to the British monarch as Supreme Governor of the Church of England. The Episcopal Church describes itself as "Protestant, yet Catholic,"[912] and it asserts apostolic succession, tracing its bishops back to the apostles via holy orders. It has continued to use the Book of Common Prayer, which was updated in 1979, and it remains in communion with the Anglican Church.

Since the 1960s and 1970s, the Episcopal Church has pursued a more liberal course, although there remains a wide spectrum of liberals and conservatives within the Episcopal Church. In 2015, the Church's General Convention passed resolutions allowing the blessing of same-sex marriages and approved two official liturgies to bless such unions.[913] It has opposed the death penalty and supported the civil rights movement. The Episcopal Church has called for the full legal equality of LGBT people.[914] In view of this trend, the conventions of four dioceses of the Episcopal Church voted in 2007 and 2008 to leave the Episcopal Church.[915] Later, in 2012, many members and parishes of the historic Diocese of South Carolina left the Episcopal Church, eventually becoming a diocese of the Anglican Church in North America.

The Episcopal Church had experienced notable growth in the first half of the 20th century; but like many mainline churches, it continues to experience a decline in membership in more recent decades.[916]

Methodism

Also referred to as the Methodist movement, Methodism is a Protestant Christian sect whose origins, doctrine, and practice derive from the life and teachings of John Wesley (1703–1791), a former Anglican priest.[917] Methodism originated as a revival movement within Anglicanism with roots in the Church of England in the late 18th century, and it became a separate denomination soon after Wesley's death.

Methodists view Scripture as their primary religious authority, but Methodists look to Christian tradition, including the historic creeds. Most Methodists teach that salvation is achievable for all. This is the Arminian doctrine[918] (named after Dutch theologian, Jacobus Arminius) which promotes the role of free will in obtaining salvation, and it rejects the doctrines of predestination and unconditional election. This is opposed to the Calvinist position that God has pre-ordained the salvation of a select group of people. However, some early leaders of the Methodist movement were considered Calvinistic Methodists, as they held to the Calvinist position of predestination.

Initially, the Methodists did not wish to separate from the Anglican Church but were seeking reform. However, as converts grew, the rift with the Church of England widened. In 1784, John Wesley responded to the shortage of priests in America due to the Revolutionary War by ordaining priests with the power to administer the sacraments. This occurred immediately after the refusal of the Anglican Bishop of London to ordain and send a Methodist. This action was used as the primary reason for the split of Methodism from the Church of England after John Wesley's death.[919]

The Wesleyan Methodist Church grew rapidly, numbering 450,000 members by the end of the 19th century.[920] However, just before, during, and after the 19th century, the Methodist Church was beset by a number of schisms. The Methodist New Connexion broke off in 1797, the Primitive Methodists in 1811, the Bible Christians in 1815, and the United Methodist Free Churches in 1857. In 1907, the Methodist New Connexion, the Bible Christians, and the United Methodist Free Churches joined to form the United Methodist Church; and in 1932, the Wesleyan Methodist Church, the Primitive Methodist Church, and the United Methodist Church came together to form the Methodist Church. Today, the World Methodist Council (WMC) is an association of Churches in the Methodist tradition, and it comprises more than 40.5 million Methodists in 138 countries.[921]

In the 20th century, several attempts were made to reunite the Methodist Church with the Church of England. Those attempts were rejected by the Church of England's General Synod in 1972. However, dialogue and informal relations continued. In 2003, a covenant between the two churches was signed, and it commits each Church to work more closely with the other towards full unity.[922]

The United Methodist Church, once the second-largest Protestant denomination in the United States, has long been divided into factions over LGBTQ inclusion and even weighed splitting into two separate Churches over the issue. In 1984, the Church banned "self-avowed practicing homosexuals" from becoming members of the clergy and later prohibited performing or celebrating same-sex unions.[923] Then, in May 2024, the United Methodist Church General Conference repealed bans on LGBTQ clergy and same-sex marriage. The United Methodist Church has lost a quarter of its churches (7,600 of them) in the USA in the past five years (2019 – 2024) over LGBTQ+ rights.[924] And the fallout continues.

Calvinism

In 1541, John Calvin (1509 – 1564) was invited back to Geneva. In the first five years of John Calvin's "leadership", 58 people were executed and 76 were exiled for their religious beliefs. Calvin allowed no art other than music, and even that could not involve instruments. Under his rule, Geneva became the center of Protestantism and sent out pastors to the rest of Europe, which led to Presbyterianism in Scotland, the Puritan Movement in England, and the Reformed Church in the Netherlands. In 1555, he achieved absolute supremacy as the leader in Geneva.[925] Calvin was able to infuse the Church of Geneva with his harsh disciplinarian views.

The official acts of the City of Geneva from 1541 to 1559 exhibit run rampant with censures, fines, imprisonments, and executions. When the City was struck with a pestilence in 1545, more than twenty men and women were burnt alive for witchcraft, believing they had conspired to spread the horrible disease. From 1542 to 1546, fifty-eight judgments of death and seventy-six decrees of banishment were passed.[926] Most historians typically view Calvin as the most intolerant of the Reformers. With often harsh language, he relegated himself to the ranks of megalomaniacs and religious tyrants.[927]

Calvin determined that the moral guidance of the Old Testament still applied. And killing people who went against his pure doctrine seemed a moral necessity. He dismissed the admonition from Jesus to "love your enemies". Calvin did not patiently discuss his differences with people who promoted competing ideas. Calvin requested beheadings, made death threats, and praised God for enabling the torture of heretics.[928] Calvin is known to have justified capital punishment of heretics through the following verses:

- **Leviticus 24:16.** "And he that blasphemeth the name of the Lord, he shall surely be put to death; and all the congregation shall stone him; as well the stranger, as he who is born in the land, when he blasphemeth the name of the Lord, shall be put to death."

And Paul's instructions for dealing with people who theologically disagree with you were equally ignored:

- **2 Timothy 2:24-25** "A servant of the Lord must not quarrel but must be kind to everyone, be able to teach, and be patient with difficult people. Gently instruct those who oppose the truth. Perhaps God will change the people's hearts, and they will learn the truth."

Michael Servetus expressed his theological leanings in a 1531 publication, which encountered strong opposition. In his book, he rejected the Trinity as a philosophical construct. He also advocated Arian and Anabaptist views.[929] After escaping the RCC Inquisition, he came to Geneva, where he was recognized, arrested on the order of John Calvin, given a trial for heresy, and then condemned to be burned at the stake. John Calvin was an "expert witness" at the trial against Servetus.[930]

Theodore Beza (1519 – 1604) succeeded John Calvin as the spiritual leader in the Republic of Geneva. In the various controversies into which he was drawn, Beza often showed an excess of irritation and intolerance. Beza was not tolerant of the Anabaptists and other left-wing reformers, and he took a strict attitude towards them. In September 1554, Beza wrote a manuscript to refute the principle of tolerance; regarding the latter, he defended the City of Geneva's roasting of Servetus. Beza contended that the toleration of error is indifference to truth, and he felt that it destroyed all order and discipline in the Church. He wrote that even the enforced unity of the papacy is much better than anarchy; and heresy is much worse than murder, because it destroys the soul.[931]

Presbyterianism

The followers of John Knox (1514 – 1572) were members of his Presbyterian Church, which insisted on the traditional Scottish Church laws emphasizing the supremacy of God and the Scriptures as the guiding principle in worship. Knox developed a system of Calvinist theology, which was adopted as the ruling ideology of the Scottish Reformation. This system taught salvation through faith in the sacraments and Scripture, as opposed to merit or deeds.

Presbyterians believe in the doctrines of original sin, justification by faith alone, a priesthood of all believers, the sole authority of the Scriptures, predestination, and eternal security. The beliefs of the Presbyterian Church are all contained within the document, *The Book of Confessions*, which was first published in 1983 and was revised in 2023.[932] The *Book of Confessions* is Part 1 or the Constitution of the Presbyterian Church (USA). At the end of this constitution is an article of faith that outlines the major beliefs of this denomination, which is part of the Reformed tradition.[933]

John Knox, a prominent leader in the Scottish Reformation, was known for his intolerance, especially regarding the celebration of mass. He's thought of as a misogynist (he declared that women were inferior to men), and as an insolent, arrogant person given to harshness and even cruelty.[934] Knox vehemently attacked Catholic practices, advocated for the removal of Catholic clergy from power, and publicly criticized Catholic monarchs like Mary, Queen of Scots. Knox's opposition to Catholicism led to a climate of hostility against Scottish Catholics during the 16th century.

Puritanism

This was a religious reform movement in the late 16th and 17th centuries that sought to "purify" the Church of England of remnants of the Roman Catholic "popery" that the Puritans claimed had been retained after the religious settlement from the reign of Queen Elizabeth I.[935] Puritans were dissatisfied with what they considered a limited extent of the English Reformation, and with the Church of England's toleration of certain practices associated with the Roman Catholic Church.

Puritanism was never a formally defined religious division within Protestantism; and the term, Puritan, was rarely used after the turn of the 18th century. It appears that the Puritans wanted to reform the human condition through religion, to wipe out poverty, and to make a heaven on earth in which everyone was free to discover God's will for themselves. But Puritans did not believe that other religions could achieve that goal. They believed that only their reformed version of Anglican Christianity could do so.[936] The Puritans were not escaping their society nearly as much as they wanted to build a new, reformed society. And they were very authoritarian in pursuit of their goals.

The time span for Puritan New England was 1630 to about 1720. The Pilgrims who arrived in 1620 were not Puritans; it was the group who arrived in 1630 who began Puritan colonization. The settlements founded by these Puritans were based on the same religious practices of Congregationalism.[937] The Congregationalist Churches, widely considered to be a part of the Reformed (Calvinist) tradition of Christianity, are theologically descended directly from the Puritans.[938] In the 1690s, several of the Puritan leaders died, and with the influx of many non-Puritan colonists in the following two decades, Puritanism died off, but Congregationalism continued. In the 21st century, the Congregational tradition is represented by the United Church of Christ, the National Association of Congregational Christian Churches, the Conservative Congregational Christian Conference, the Evangelical Association, and many unaffiliated local churches.[939]

Baptists

Baptists are a denomination of Protestant Christianity distinguished by baptizing only professing Christian believers and doing so by complete immersion. Modern Baptist Churches trace their history to the English Separatist movement in the 17th century, which occurred over a century after the foundation of the Church of England during the Protestant Reformation.[940] This view of Baptist origins has the most historical support, and it is the most widely accepted.[941] Baptist Churches have their origins in a movement started by John Smyth and Thomas Helwys in Amsterdam.[942]

Both Roger Williams and John Clarke are variously credited as founding the earliest Baptist Church in North America. Williams established his church in Providence, RI in 1639; John Clarke started his church in Newport, RI. According to historian William Brackney, "There is much debate over the centuries as to whether the Providence or Newport church deserved the place of 'first' Baptist congregation in America. Exact records for both congregations are lacking."[943]

The First Great Awakening energized the Baptist movement, and the Baptist community experienced spectacular growth. Baptists became the largest Christian community in many southern states. In May 1845, the Baptist congregations in the United States split over slavery and missions. The Home Mission Society prevented slaveholders from being appointed as missionaries.[944] The split created the Southern Baptist Convention (SBC), while the northern congregations formed their own umbrella organization, now called the American Baptist Churches USA (ABC-USA). The SBC is a cooperation of fully autonomous, independent churches with commonly held essential beliefs that pool some resources for missions.[945] The ABC-USA was established in 1907 as the Northern Baptist Convention, and it was later named the American Baptist Convention from 1950 to 1972.

After the American Civil War, another split occurred when some freedmen set up independent black congregations, regional associations, and state and national conventions. The National Baptist Convention, USA (NBC USA or NBC), is a Baptist Christian denomination headquartered in Nashville, Tennessee, and it is affiliated with the Baptist World Alliance. It is one of the largest predominantly and traditionally African American Churches in the United States, and it became the second-largest Baptist denomination in the world.[946]

Church of Jesus Christ of Latter-day Saints

The Church of Jesus Christ of Latter-day Saints, informally known as the LDS Church or Mormon Church, was founded during the Second Great Awakening in 1830 by Joseph Smith in western New York. Joseph Smith published the Book of Mormon in 1830 when he was 25 years old, although he stated that he had "discovered" it on gold plates in 1823.[947] [948] While some Mormon followers view Joseph Smith as a prophet, a sizable number of historians and other critics have labelled him a con artist and fraud. He faced multiple criminal charges in New York, Ohio, Illinois and Missouri.[949]

Originally called the Church of Christ, today it is headquartered in Salt Lake City, Utah. Church theology is restorationist and nontrinitarian. The LDS Church identifies as Christian and includes a belief in the doctrine of salvation through Jesus Christ and his substitutionary atonement on behalf of mankind.

For Mormons, the ideal of salvation is to live forever as a family in the highest heaven of the celestial kingdom. Mormons believe that human beings obtain salvation both through the grace of God and their own actions. Part of the work of salvation has been done by the atonement of Jesus Christ, in that all human beings are guaranteed resurrection; but to attain the full quality of eternal life, believers also have work to do.[950]

The Church has been criticized throughout its history, including disputes over the Church's historical claims, treatment of minorities, and its finances. The LDS Church's practice of polygamy was controversial until it was curtailed in 1890, and then officially rescinded in 1904.[951]

Adventism

Adventism is a branch of Protestant Christianity that believes in the imminent Second Coming (or the "Second Advent") of Jesus Christ.[952] The largest Church within the movement is the Seventh-day Adventist Church, which was founded in 1863. It is best known for its teaching that Saturday is the Sabbath; and thus, Saturday is the appropriate day for worship. However, the second coming of Jesus Christ, along with Judgment Day based on the three angels' message in **Revelation 14:6–13**, remain core beliefs of Seventh-day Adventists. The denomination grew out of the Millerite movement in the United States during the mid-19th century.

Much of the theology of the Seventh-day Adventist Church corresponds to common evangelical Christian teachings, such as the Trinity and the infallibility of Scripture. However, it has some distinctive teachings such as the unconscious state of the dead and its doctrine of an investigative judgment (which asserts that the divine judgment of professed Christians has been in progress since 1844).[953] The Church emphasizes diet and health, advocating vegetarianism, and its holistic view of human nature. The Church believes that God rested on the seventh day, after he created the world and everything in it. The second coming of Christ and the resurrection of the dead are among official beliefs.[954]

The Seventh-day Adventist doctrine of creationism is based on their belief that the opening chapters of Genesis should be interpreted as literal history. Adventists' beliefs include: all earthly life originated during a six-day period some 6,000 years ago, and a global flood destroyed all land-based animals and humans, except for those saved on Noah's Ark. Adventists oppose theories which propose interpreting the days of creation allegorically.[955]

Assemblies of God

While relatively latecomers to the Protestant denominations, the Assemblies of God USA was founded in 1914, and boasts close to 13,000 churches within the U.S. with nearly three million members. There are approximately 86 million Assemblies of God adherents worldwide, making the Assemblies of God (AG) the world's largest Pentecostal denomination.[956] The World Assemblies of God Fellowship (WAGF) is a global cooperative body of over 170 Pentecostal denominations that was established on August 15, 1989. In time, self-governing general councils separated from the original fellowship or formed independently in various nations throughout the world, originating either from indigenous Pentecostal movements or as a direct result of the indigenous mission strategy of the General Council.[957]

The doctrinal position of the Assemblies of God is framed in a trinitarian Pentecostal and evangelical context. The Assemblies of God believe that the Bible is divinely inspired and the infallible, authoritative rule of faith and conduct. The Assemblies of God Church ordains women as pastors, which many Christians consider liberal and progressive. Pentecostal and Charismatic denominations have traditionally allowed women to serve in pastoral ministry.[958] Currently, about one-quarter of Assemblies of God Church pastors are women.

The Assemblies of God is the world's largest Pentecostal group, and it considers itself a fellowship rather than a denomination. The Four Core Beliefs of the Assemblies of God are Salvation, Baptism in the Holy Spirit, Divine Healing, and the Second Coming of Christ.[959]

The Great Awakenings

The Great Awakenings refer to key waves of dramatic religious revival and religious enthusiasm among Protestants in the United States. Some characterized these revivals as occurring in three waves, and some prefer to group them as four waves of 'Awakenings.' Each

Movement	Dates	Purpose
1st Great Awakening	c. 1730 – 1755	Spiritual revival of church members
2nd Great Awakening	c. 1790 – 1840	Spiritual revival to extend membership
3rd Great Awakening	c. 1855 – 1930	Activism
4th Great Awakening	c. 1960 – 1980	Political Realignment

of these "Great Awakenings" was characterized by widespread Protestant revivals, a sharp increase of interest in religion, a profoundly emotional sense of spirituality and redemption on the part of those affected, a resulting increase in church memberships, and the formation of new religious movements and denominations.[960]

The First Great Awakening movement occurred in Germany, Great Britain, and the American colonies in reaction to the secular rationalism that was being emphasized during the era when passion for religion was waning. Secular rationalism was a philosophy that combined rationalism and secularism to promote reason and critical thinking over religious authority. The ideas of the Enlightenment had just made their way to the American colonies, and the Enlightenment thinkers emphasized a scientific and logical view of the world while downplaying religion. Also, the American colonies were religiously divided. In New England, the Congregational Churches were dominant, whereas in the religiously tolerant Middle Colonies, the Quakers, Dutch Reformed, Anglican, Presbyterian, Lutheran, Congregational, and Baptist Churches all competed with each other for parishioners. In the Southern Colonies, the Anglican Church was officially established, though there were significant numbers of Baptists, Quakers, and Presbyterians.[961]

During this time, many Christian preachers traveled from town to town, preaching the gospel, emphasizing salvation from sins, and promoting enthusiasm for Christianity.[962] This Great Awakening focused on people who were already church members, though not exclusively. They changed their rituals and actualized their self-awareness; and the people involved began reading their Bibles at home. The new style of preaching ignited passion and emotional reactions rather than listening in a detached manner. This new preacher style was referred to as "New Lights," while the established preachers were referred to as the "Old Lights." The New Light ministers rejected the rationalism of the Enlightenment and appealed to the passions of the audience members rather than their reason, which resulted in emotional reactions and often their conversions.[963]

Many critics of that time thought the emotional appeal of the "New Light" evangelical ministers would lead to social chaos. Thus, the main source of opposition was conservative pastors of the established churches, particularly Anglicans and Congregationalists. These "Old Light" ministers preferred rational sermons and religious practices/rituals, and they rejected the passionate New Light theology and style of the evangelical preachers. To some extent, the Old Light ministers successfully banned the New Light ministers from preaching in several churches and towns.[964]

By the late 1740s, the Great Awakening revivals were lessening; but the movement's effects were long-lasting as the fervor continued to spread throughout the colonies, albeit at a much slower pace. The revivals had weakened the hold of the established churches in colonial America, and large numbers of Christians joined new evangelical Churches like those of the Baptists or Methodists.

The Second Great Awakening began after the American Revolution, but unlike the first Great Awakening, the 2nd focused more on the unchurched. It was during this time that the Holiness Movement started, as well as the Latter-Day Saints, Adventism, and the Restoration Movement. The Second Great Awakening made 'soul-winning' the primary function of Protestant ministries; and it stimulated several moral reforms, including temperance and the emancipation of women.[965]

During this period, the Methodist circuit riders and local Baptist preachers made enormous gains in increasing church membership. Additionally, Baptists and Methodists in the South preached to slaveholders and slaves alike. Conversions and congregations started with the First Great Awakening resulted in Baptist and Methodist preachers being authorized among slaves and free Africans well before 1800.[966] Also, the unique frontier institution known as the 'camp meeting' began. This second wave of evangelical revivalism led to the founding of numerous colleges and seminaries and to the organization of mission societies across the country.

The Third Great Awakening was a period of religious activism. Similar to the first two 'Great Awakenings,' it was a period that saw a resurgence in religious interest and vigor. It was characterized by the rise of the Pentecostal movement, and it helped reinvigorate religious education through the founding of various Bible colleges and seminaries.[967] It was during this Awakening that there was a shift from emphasis on personal to social sin. It was more of a belief that poverty is not a personal failure ("the wages of sin"); but it was a societal failure that can be addressed by the state.[968] During this period the Jehovah's Witnesses was founded, and Pentecostalism began, which in turn would lead to the Charismatic movement.

The Fourth Great Awakening oversaw attacks on materialist corruption and the rise of pro-life, pro-family movements. The Fourth Great Awakening is said to have begun in the mid-20th century, although it is controversial. Mainline Protestant denominations weakened sharply during this period in both membership and influence; however, some of the most conservative religious denominations (such as the Southern Baptists) grew rapidly in numbers, had grave internal theological battles and schisms, and became politically powerful.[969]

Single-issue movements began to emerge about halfway through this religious phase, e.g., the right-to-life movement emerged during the mid-1970s. That was followed by the Jesus Movement, the Moral Majority, and later by the Christian Coalition, and its focus on a US political realignment in the 1990s.[970] However, the rapid rise of religious "nones" in the 2000s may be the proverbial "nail in the coffin" for future religious revivals.[971]

Topics Specific to Protestantism

Plunder and Suppression of Catholicism

Throughout the latter half of the 16th century, some Protestant princes and other nobility found it hard to resist the temptation to loot Catholic monasteries, convents, and churches. This occurred in Scandinavia, the British Isles, the Northern Netherlands, a large area of Germany, and in many of the Swiss cantons. In Sweden, Gustavus Eriksson Vasa (12 May 1496 – 29 September 1560), also known as King Gustav I, removed from the custody of the Catholic Church all its landed properties. The proportion of land held by the Swedish Crown increased during his reign from 5.5% to 28%; that of the Catholic Church decreased from 21% to nothing.[972] And for many, once enriched with the pillage of the RCC, it remained in their interests to strongly resist the return of Catholicism to their lands.[973]

The Catholic Mass was abolished in Zurich in 1525.[974] Under Zwingli, attendance at sermons for the entire population was compulsory under pain of punishment. Indeed, all church worship that deviated from the prescribed regulations was punishable. Catholics and their priests were not allowed to hold their Catholic masses or the laity to attend them, even outside the district of Zurich. Moreover, it was actually forbidden, 'under pain of severe punishment, to keep pictures and images even in private houses.' [975]

Predestination

Predestination, in theology, is the idea that God, being omniscient and omnipotent, has predetermined the fate or destiny of individuals, including their salvation or damnation, before the foundation of the world.[976] In modern usage, predestination is distinct from both determinism and fatalism, and is subject to the free decision of the human moral will; but the doctrine also teaches that salvation is entirely due to the eternal decree of God.[977]

Calvinists have taken the term, predestination, to mean that God selected certain individuals in eternity past, and God predetermined that he would save them; and everyone else is condemned without recourse. Amazingly, according to the Calvinists, the preselected ones can't avoid it; and anyone not selected has no choice in the matter either. It's all predestined, or so they would have us think. The dour Calvinist view of predestination removes any reason for motivation to improve as an individual.

In trying to answer the question, "If God is choosing who is [to be] saved, doesn't that undermine our free will to choose and believe in Christ?" Calvinist apologists intellectually tie themselves in a knot, and then they exclaim that mankind cannot know the mysteries of God. And in trying to respond to pushback that the concept of predestination, where God chooses some and not others, is unfair, the Calvinist apologists retort that no one deserves to be saved. The Calvinist rejoinder is that we have all sinned **[Romans 3:23]** and are all worthy of eternal punishment **[Romans 6:23].** As a result, God would be perfectly just in allowing all of us to spend eternity in Hell.[978]

That response appears convoluted and harsh. No one deserves to spend eternity in Hell because of actions in an ephemeral mortal life. And didn't God supposedly create all of humanity in His image? It is just illogical to believe that a deity would predestinate humans in or out of their salvation.[979]

Biblical Inerrancy

The concept of inerrancy formed during the 19th and 20th centuries in the United States. Its fullest articulation may have occurred when the "Chicago Statement on Biblical Inerrancy" (CSBI) was produced at an international Summit Conference of evangelical leaders, held in Chicago in the fall of 1978. Sponsored by the International Council on Biblical Inerrancy, the Chicago Statement was signed by nearly 300 noted *evangelical scholars*.[980] According to the statement, the "Holy Scriptures in the Bible speak with "infallible divine authority in all matters upon which it touches."[981] There is no distinction made between the Old and New Testaments. Biblical inerrancy has been particularly influential among U.S. Christian Fundamentalists, who sometimes use the doctrine of inerrancy to argue against gender equality, homosexuality, social justice, and other topics thought (by them) to violate the God's infallible word.[982] Australian theologian and New Testament scholar, Michael F. Bird, has recommended that conservative Christians find a comfortable level of nuance in their views of inerrancy,[983] because if they define inerrancy too narrowly, they will make indefensible claims and raise additional questions which will put the declarants in a quandary that they cannot explain.

The issues that most people have with the concept of inerrancy of the Bible is very straightforward: there are no original manuscripts; and those we do have are copies of copies; and those hand-copied manuscripts contradict each other, have undergone multiple translations, and some were purposely altered. There are mistakes of history, of cosmology, of biology; and archeological findings have disproven the "Scriptures" time and again. How could any deity inspire these writings?

No matter how hard the Christian apologists work through their intellectual acrobatics, the biblical Scripture was written by superstitious, Iron Age men; and other men, often for political reasons, decided what was Scripture and what was not. In Misquoting Jesus, renowned New Testament scholar Bart Ehrman noted that "there are more variants among the ancient documents than there are words in the New Testament."[984] His statement highlights the diversity of sources and the complexities of early Christian writings. Why are believers so addicted to the concept that the Scriptures are inspired? There is absolutely no evidence for it. Neither the OT nor the NT has the ring of authenticity!

The Pentateuch (Torah) was completed during the Babylonian exile. The Nevi'im (Prophets) were finalized during the Persian era, approximately 323 BCE. The conclusion of the last section of the Bible, Ketuvim (Writings), is believed to have had its final canonization in the 2nd century CE, although this is still debated.[985] So, the Old Testament was finalized by Jewish leaders in the 2nd century, and the Catholic bishops decided what composed the New Testament Scripture and what did not in the 4th century CE. And thus, the decisions of the Jews and Catholics of those eras regarding the OT and NT, respectively, is what some Protestant groups consider inerrant! Many Jews and most Catholics do not believe in the inerrancy of the Old or New Testament, respectively.

Protestant Church Scandals in the United States

Sexual abuse within religious settings has been the focus of prior research for at least the last fifty years. However, most research has focused on the Roman Catholic Church, not Protestant Christian Churches. It is relatively recent that an overall pattern of sexual offenders and offending behaviors has been uncovered across multiple Protestant Churches. Researchers reviewed the three largest faith-based insurance companies that insure nearly 160,000 churches. These faith-based insurance companies reported 7,095 insurance claims of sexual abuse by clerical members, church employees, and congregation members from 1987 to 2007; that is an average of 260 claims of sexual abuse per year[986] over those two decades!

Most recently, the Houston Chronicle published a series titled "Abuse of Faith," uncovering sexual abuse and cover-up within the largest Protestant Christian organization in the U.S. (i.e., the Southern Baptist Convention (SBC)).[987] They identified 380 sexual abusers and 700 alleged victims over 20 years. According to the *Houston Chronicle*, victims of sexual abuse had pleaded for the SBC to act, saying it was allowing sexual predators to move from church-to-church. But the SBC in 2008 rejected all proposals to produce a registry, saying the organization could not tell its 47,000 member churches whom to hire or ordain.

Eventually, about 220 "church leaders" were convicted.[988] Moreover, the investigators found that 35 Southern Baptist ministers were hired at their churches, despite being accused of sexual misconduct or abuse, demonstrating a disturbing pattern of poor institutional oversight in responding to alleged sexual abuse.

This study cataloged sex offenders of both children and young adults into three types: on-site offenders, off-site offenders, and serial offenders. It has been demonstrated that there are distinct sex abusers who operate within U.S. Protestant Christian Churches. Each type of abuser is unique in how they offend, how often, and who they target. With most abusers being identified as serial offenders, churches must develop better policies and procedures to prevent and identify instances of sexual abuse.

Though there has not been a strong research focus on Protestant Christian sexual abuse in the past, studies are now focusing on clergy sexual abuse and related issues.[989] It is not my intent to describe multiple, sordid situations within Protestant Churches where abuse has occurred. Let's just recognize that these repulsive, immoral acts are not found solely in the RCC. But wherever they occur, church officials must listen to the victims and root out these outrages against children and women.

Protestant Movements

Reformed Christianity

Reformed Christianity, originally referring to Calvinism, is a major branch of Protestantism that began early in the Protestant Reformation during the 16th century.[990] Today, it is largely represented by the Continental Reformed, Presbyterian, and Congregational traditions, as well as some Baptist traditions.[991] The five points of Reformed Christianity are often presented via the acronym, TULIP. These five points are part of a much larger theology, but they serve as a helpful introduction to the beliefs of Reformed Theology.[992]

- **T**otal Depravity – The fall corrupted every aspect of human nature; this refers to the old concept of original sin.
- **U**nconditional Election – God's election of sinners to salvation is not conditioned on anything outside of God's nature. In other words, our actions or decisions don't influence our salvation.
- **L**imited Atonement – Rather than making redemption possible for everyone, Christ actually accomplished the redemption only of those for whom he selected.
- **I**rresistible Grace – The Holy Spirit will regenerate all those for whom Christ died. While unbelievers may resist the external call of the gospel, the elect among them will hear and respond to the internal call.
- **P**erseverance of the Saints – Those who have been chosen by God, those for whom Christ died and who have been called out of death and into life, God will preserve by His grace until the end. Once saved, always saved.

Reformed theology emphasizes the authority of the Bible and the sovereignty of God, and it provides a framework for understanding the Bible based on God's covenants with people. Reformed Churches emphasize simplicity in worship. As articulated by John Calvin, the Reformed Churches believe in a spiritual presence of Christ in the Lord's Supper.[993]

Reformed Christians also believe that God predestined some people to be saved and others to eternal damnation. God's choice is held to be unconditional, and it is not based on any characteristic or action on the part of the person chosen.

Evangelicalism

Evangelicals are a diverse group of Protestant Christians who share certain beliefs and practices; it is a worldwide inter-denominational movement. The term "evangelical" comes from the Greek word, *euangelion*, which means "the good news" or the "gospel." Generally, evangelicals believe in the Bible as the literal word of God; and they believe in the importance of conversion and a personal relationship with Jesus Christ. Evangelicals emphasize the importance of sharing the New Testament gospels with others. They also believe in the necessity of being born again, which is a defining characteristic of the evangelical movement. Evangelicals can belong to many different denominations, including Baptist, Pentecostal, Lutheran, Methodist, and more. Evangelicals can support a broad range of views.

According to the National Association of Evangelicals (NAE), historian David Bebbington provided a summary of evangelical distinctives, identifying four primary characteristics of evangelicalism:[994]

- The belief that lives need to be transformed through a "born-again" experience and a life-long process of following Jesus
- A high regard for, and obedience to, the Bible as the ultimate authority
- The expression and demonstration of the gospel in missionary (e.g., active evangelism) and social reform efforts
- A stress on the sacrifice of Jesus Christ on the cross as making possible the redemption of humanity

Comprising almost a quarter of the U.S. population,[995] evangelicals are a diverse group drawn from a variety of denominational backgrounds, including some non-denominational churches, Pentecostal, Baptist, Lutheran, Reformed, Methodist, Mennonite, Plymouth Brethren, and Quaker.[996] Interestingly, Martin Luther preferred the designation of *evangelical*, if only to separate the Lutherans of the day from the Calvinists, who considered themselves *reformed*.

By the beginning of the 20th century, Protestant Churches became divided over new intellectual and theological ideas, such as Darwinian evolution and historical criticism of the Bible. Those who embraced these new ideas eventually became known as Modernists, and those who rejected them became known as Fundamentalists, who defended the doctrine of biblical inerrancy and adopted a dispensationalist theological system for interpreting the Bible.[997] As a result of the Fundamentalist–Modernist controversy of the 1920s and 1930s, Fundamentalists lost control of the mainline Protestant Churches, and they separated themselves from non-Fundamentalist churches.[998] Meanwhile, Evangelicalism became the driving force behind the rise of Protestantism in the U S South.

Evangelicalism is not a single entity that is easy to stereotype, although many have tried. They have diverse views, such as limited inerrancy of the Bible, implied understanding of scientific issues, and willingness to cooperate with non-Evangelicals. Although they are considered conservative overall in relation to the rest of Christian denominations, Evangelicals run the range from traditional, to moderate, to progressive within their own movement in terms of their views on social and science topics.

Fundamentalism

All forms of fundamentalism reflect the absolute authority of a revelatory text such as the Jewish Tanakh, the Christian New Testament, or the Muslim Quran. What seems to spark fear in Fundamentalists is that something might be left to chance. Thus, a key characterization of fundamentalism is its absolute surety. It occurs when a set of beliefs becomes a reflexive creed, an unshakable certainty that one's faith beliefs are accurate and true, without benefit of any supporting evidence whatsoever.

As previously mentioned, Christian Evangelicals are a very broad, diverse group, and Christian Fundamentalists have been a subset of that. The latter are very conservative, open to literal interpretations, have tendencies toward intolerance, and can be judgmental even toward other conservative Christians. Christian Fundamentalism is a movement in American Protestantism that arose in the late 19th century / early 20th century in reaction to theological modernism, whose original goal was to accommodate new developments in the theory of biological evolution.[999] Christian Fundamentalism had its origin in 19th-century millennialism in the U.S.[1000] It emphasized the literal interpretation of the Bible, the imminent physical Second Coming of Jesus, and His resurrection. Fundamentalists tend to be insular, separating themselves from others who do not share their specific beliefs. Fundamentalist theology tends to strongly stress Biblical inerrancy and Biblical literalism.[1001]

Christian Fundamentalism is a movement that has manifested itself in various Protestant denominations at various times, including Presbyterians, Southern Baptists, and Missouri Synod Lutherans. It also can include denominations in the Reformed tradition, such as Reformed Anglican, Reformed Baptist, and Continental Reformed.[1002] In the 21st century, Christian Fundamentalism has effectively separated from the Evangelicals as its own separate branch, and by comparison, Evangelicals seem much more moderate.

Restoration Movement

The Restoration Movement is a Christian movement that began on the United States frontier during the Second Great Awakening (1790–1840) of the early 19th century. The pioneers of this movement were seeking to reform its Church from within, and they sought the unification of all Christians in a single body,[1003] patterned after what they believed to be the early 2nd-century Christian Church of the New Testament.[1004] The Restoration Movement affirms biblical authority and binds it to a strong commitment to church unity.

Those in the Restoration movement believe that names, creeds, and ecclesiastical traditions divide believers from one another, and they renounce denominational exclusivity. They believe that creeds and doctrinal statements are unnecessary and divisive, and individual congregations task themselves with studying and interpreting the Bible for themselves. External authority over the local church has been staunchly resisted. [1005]

The Restoration Movement has not produced the unity it originally sought, being itself subject to fracturing. The Restoration Movement has since divided into multiple separate groups, of which the three main groups are: (1) the Church of Christ, (2) the Christian Church (Disciples of Christ), and (3) the independent Christian Church/Church of Christ congregations.[1006]

Holiness Movement

The Holiness movement is an influence within Christianity that teaches that a person can achieve perfect holiness, or sinless perfection, while on earth. This doctrine teaches "entire sanctification," which usually comes via a spiritual experience that those in the Holiness movement refer to as the "second work of grace" or the "second blessing."[1007] The Holiness movement is opposed by Reformed *thinkers,* who assert that original sin still exists in even the most faithful person. These Reformed *thinkers* probably didn't get the memo that there was no original sin.

Beginning in the 19th century, the Holiness Movement grew out of a Methodist background in America during the Third Great Awakening. As the name suggests, there was a lot of emphasis placed on one's personal holiness. Because of growing tensions with traditional Methodists, those in the Holiness Movement broke away from the Methodist Church and developed their own denominations.[1008]

Some denominations are strongly associated with the Holiness movement, such as the Church of God (Holiness), from which we get the religious rite of serpent handling. However, it is not a single church entity, but rather Holiness is a theological perspective found across several denominations. One of the largest denominations within the Holiness Church is the Church of the Nazarene. Another is the Salvation Army. The founding of the Salvation Army in 1878 helped to rekindle Holiness sentiment in the cradle of Methodism.[1009] Today, the Salvation Army is both a Protestant Christian Church and an international charitable organization, headquartered in London, England. It remains aligned with the Wesleyan-Holiness movement.

Modernism (Liberal Protestantism)

Modernism was the conscious adaptation of the Christian religion to modern conditions of life. Modernists wanted to apply their religious beliefs to the most pressing social issues. Thus, the height of U. S. Protestant modernism came in the period between the 1890s and the 1920s, when the USA transformed itself from an agricultural nation into an industrial powerhouse, and when the country was transitioning to global political leadership. Additionally, Darwinism had won over the scientific community; and it threatened to undermine one of the central bases of the Christian faith. But Protestant modernizers remained convinced that the theory of evolution could be accommodated to religious belief, as they interpreted the biblical accounts of Genesis as providing rough metaphors for the process of evolution. And they saw no reason why God could not act as the driving force behind the processes Darwin described.[1010] But other Protestants would vehemently reject the new scientific theories.

This countervailing view resulted in the trial of John Scopes, a high school teacher in Dayton, TN, for teaching evolution in 1925 when he was filling in as a temp. Backed by the ACLU, fiery Clarence Darrow joined the defense team, as William Jennings Bryan, a three-time losing presidential candidate, joined the prosecution. While the case made headlines in the press, it resolved nothing. The jury found Mr. Scopes guilty, which Darrow had requested, and fined him $100, which the ACLU paid. The Tennessee Supreme Court later reversed the decision (on a technicality).[1011] Over four decades later, in 1968, the U. S. Supreme Court in "Epperson v. Arkansas", 393 U.S. 97, invalidated an Arkansas statute prohibiting the teaching of human evolution in the public schools, in a unanimous landmark decision.[1012]

Today, Christian modernism is a movement that interprets Christian teaching by prioritizing modern knowledge, science, and ethics. It emphasizes the importance of reason and experience over doctrinal authority, such as the Bible or 'sacred tradition.' It has a perceived need to adapt Christianity to a modern intellectual context. With today's knowledge of evolution, big bang theory, the universe cosmology, etc., the Old Testament is neither historically, archaeologically, nor scientifically defensible; and to Christian modernists it is clearly only an allegory. Most Christian modernists have concluded that "none of the New Testament writings can be said to be apostolic in the sense in which it has been traditionally held to be so."[1013] These Christians placed less emphasis on miraculous events associated with the life of Jesus than on his teachings.[1014] The United Church of Christ (UCC) is an example of a modernist Christian Church,[1015] renowned for its progressive stance on social issues.

Pentecostalism

Pentecostalism is a Protestant Christian movement which emphasizes direct personal experience of the Holy Spirit through Baptism.[1016] The term Pentecostal is derived from Pentecost, an event that commemorates the descent of the Holy Spirit upon the apostles while they were together in Jerusalem. Pentecostalism is a renewalist religious movement which places special emphasis on a direct personal experience with God through Baptism. Pentecostals follow the traditions of Protestant evangelical faith, including salvation through grace, the authority of the Bible, and universal priesthood.[1017]

In many ways, Pentecostalism is an umbrella term that includes a wide range of different theological and organizational perspectives. Many Pentecostals embrace the term, evangelical, while others prefer restorationist. Moreover, Pentecostalism is theologically close to the Charismatic Movement; indeed, some Pentecostals use the two terms interchangeably. Pentecostalism is well known for its acceptance of speaking in tongues (also known as *glossolalia),* divine healing, and prophecies as evidence of the Holy Spirit. When Pentecostal Christians speak in tongues, they believe that their born-again spirits are speaking, not their minds. They believe that the Holy Ghost could not give them this supernatural communication with the Father until they received new spirits.[1018] Most meetings are for praying and spirited singing, dancing, shouting "in the spirit," and raising hands and arms in prayer. Also, anointing the sick with oil can be part of the worship service.

The Pentecostal movement encompasses various Christian denominations and churches which share a common emphasis on the direct experience with the Holy Spirit. It is divided between Holiness Pentecostals, who affirm three definite works of grace, and Finished

Work Pentecostals, who are partitioned into trinitarian and non-trinitarian branches, the latter giving rise to Oneness Pentecostalism.[1019] There are multiple Oneness Pentecostal denominations; two examples include the United Pentecostal Church International and the Pentecostal Assemblies of Jesus Christ.[1020]

Charismatic Movement

The Charismatic movement is interdenominational. The movement is deemed to have begun in 1960 in the U S Episcopal Church, and it had spread to other mainstream Protestant denominations, including Evangelical Lutherans and Presbyterians by 1962. Some Methodists became involved in the Charismatic movement in the 1970s. [1021]

Charismatic Christians believe in an experience of Baptism with the Holy Spirit joined with the spiritual gifts of the Holy Spirit. Charismatic Christianity is distinguished from Pentecostalism by making the act of speaking in tongues no longer necessary as evidence of Baptism, and giving prominence to a diversity of spiritual gifts. In fact, many in the Charismatic movement have deliberately distanced themselves from Pentecostalism for cultural and theological reasons.

Charismatics generally believe that the Holy Spirit has already been present in a person from the time of regeneration (i.e., when they were born again); and they prefer to call subsequent encounters with the Holy Spirit by other names, such as "being filled".[1022] In contrast to Pentecostals, Charismatics tend to accept a range of supernatural experiences (such as prophecies, miracles, healing, or "physical manifestations of an altered state of consciousness") as evidence of having been baptized or filled with the Holy Spirit.[1023]

Pentecostals are also distinguished from the Charismatic movement in that Pentecostals have traditionally placed a high value on evangelization and missionary work. On the other hand, Charismatics have tended to see their movement as a force for revitalization and renewal within their own church traditions.[1024]

Green the Church Movement

The Green the Church movement is a sustainability initiative aimed at expanding the role of churches as centers for environmental and economic resilience, and in enlisting religious leaders to engage church groups in the climate fight. The national Green the Church program is a partnership between the grassroots organization's parent, Green for All, in addition to churches and the U.S. Green Building Council, which is sharing strategies on how to make places of worship, church centers, and related facilities more sustainable.[1025] This program has been very successful in a variety of churches, especially traditionally Black Churches which started the movement, and which are embracing sustainability through Green The Church to use sustainable food and energy practices to fight the global climate change crisis.[1026] Dr. Ambrose Carroll, Senior Pastor of the Church by the Side of the Road in Berkeley, CA, and CEO and Founder of Green The Church, referred to this movement as the next "big tent movement of our day."[1027] The Green Church movement invokes religious teachings to advocate for responsible stewardship on our planet, and it advocates for responsible and sustainable technology use.

New Religious Movements and Christian Cults

The moniker, New Religious Movement (NRM), has been applied to many new religions since the early 18th century. These NRMs see themselves as alternatives to mainstream religions such as Christianity and/or they have an apocalyptic (i.e., an eschatological belief in 'the end of times') or millenarian dimension; the latter refers to Christ establishing a 1,000-year reign of the saints on the earth.

Seventh-day Adventists and Jehovah's Witnesses are two products of millennialism, the belief in a future (and typically imminent) thousand-year age of blessedness, beginning with or culminating in the Second Coming of Christ. The origins of both groups were Adventism. Millennialism is also a key theme in the teaching of groups such as the Plymouth Brethren and the Latter-day Saints (Mormons). Seventh-day Adventists arose out of the Millerite movement, the followers of William Miller who expected the end of the world around 1843 or 1844. Several of the Millerites claimed the gift of prophecy.

The Watch Tower Bible and Tract Society publications (the legal and administrative group of the Jehovah's Witnesses) had made a series of predictions about Christ's Second Coming and the advent of God's kingdom, each of which has proven unfulfilled. However, the predictions for 1878, 1881, 1914, 1918, and 1925 were later reinterpreted as a confirmation of the eschatological framework of the Bible Student movement and Jehovah's Witnesses, with many of the predicted events viewed as having taken place invisibly.[1028] Thus, disinformation can be reappraised as prophecy confirmation.

A cult is a movement or group held together by a shared commitment to a leader and/or a distinctive ideology. Today, it is a pejorative term, and it is often used when a group operates outside the norms of a society and/or places controls on its members. Indeed, "control" is the operative word to describe cults. Religions tend to acquire the cult designator when they become overly controlling, punish doubts or questions, and when everyone pays homage to and provides unquestioning loyalty to a single, authoritarian individual. This has been the case for a handful of Christian religions. Other cult characteristics include dogmatic beliefs and a high level of commitment to those beliefs. Generally, members of a religion come and go freely, whereas cults tend to somewhat restrict the movements of their members. Thus, the hallmarks of a cult include: authoritarian leadership, indoctrination, exclusivism, and opposition to independent thinking.

As the Christian Churches are increasingly more fragmented, some men and women believe that they can do a better job; and they establish new sects or movements which mirror their own peculiar thoughts and inclinations. To lend some legitimacy to their efforts, they often select and misuse scriptural readings. While often heretical to the teaching of traditional Christianity, they draw from the same Scripture, employ the same language, and often use similar rituals. Thus, some of these cults are associated with mainstream Christianity.

Most religions start out as cults; Christianity certainly did. The Romans first considered it a Jewish cult, and then later it gained its own independent notoriety. Throughout history, a cult becomes a religion when its membership becomes so numerous (or just so highly visible) that it requires recognition by a government authority – much like Christianity in the 4th century Rome, or Mormonism in the USA in the late 19th century.

There have been some notorious organizations in the 20th century, which most Christians accept as cultist, including the following:

- **People's Temple** led by Jim Jones who, due to legal pressure, moved his followers to Guyana, wherein approximately 912 of its members committed suicide in a place they called Jonestown in November 1978, after attempting to create a utopian society.[1029]
- **The Family International** (aka Children of God; aka Family of Love) led by David Berg in California in the 1960s and 1970s. Sometimes called Moses David by his followers, David Berg preached anti-establishment beliefs, and he also prophesied the end of the world. According to writer, Mina Elwell, "The Children of God abused all its members, and children were no exception."[1030]
- **Heaven's Gate:** A new religious movement and doomsday cult which committed mass suicide in 1997, because they believed such action would provide them with access to an alien spacecraft. The theology of Heaven's Gate has been described as a mixture of Christian millenarianism and ufology.[1031]
- The **Branch Davidians** were an offshoot group of the Davidian Seventh-day Adventist Church, led by David Koresh, alias Vernon Howell; 80 members died in Waco, Texas, in February 1993 from a confrontation with the FBI and a resulting fire.[1032]
- The **Unification Church** (now known as the Family Federations for World Peace) is a new religious movement (NRM) derived from Christianity and founded by Sun Myung Moon in the 1950s. Its members are called Unificationists or sometimes informally referred to as 'Moonies'. Although Jesus was able to create the conditions necessary for humanity's spiritual salvation, he did not marry (as far as we know), and thus, according to Moon, Jesus did not complete God's plan. Followers believe that they can help establish God's kingdom on Earth by accepting the blessing of their marriage in one of the mass wedding ceremonies for which the church has become well known.[1033]

Decline in Church Membership

According to Gallup's survey[1034] in 2021, 47% of Americans were members of a church. This was the lowest percentage Gallup has ever measured in its 80-year history. In 1937, when Gallup first measured that statistic, 73% of U.S. citizens were church members, and church membership peaked in 1947 at 76%, while remaining fairly steady for the following four decades. Then in 1988, the percentage dipped below 70% for the first time. Church membership has been on a decline ever since. Additionally, there has been an even sharper decline in church attendance. Only 21% of Americans say that they attend religious services weekly; another 20% attend at least monthly; and the majority of Americans attend church seldom (26%) or never (31%).[1035]

Religious demography is generally a zero-sum game. The growth of one group usually translates to the shrinkage of other groups. This decline in church membership appears to be primarily the result of more Americans expressing no religious preference. For the past 20 years, the percentage of Americans who do not identify with any religion has grown from **8%** in 1998–2000 to **13%** in 2008–2010, to **21%** in 2020, to **29%** by 2024. This trend toward the "Nones" appears to account for more than half of the 20-point decline in Christian church membership. So that rise in the Nones is bad news for U.S. Christian churches, pretty much across

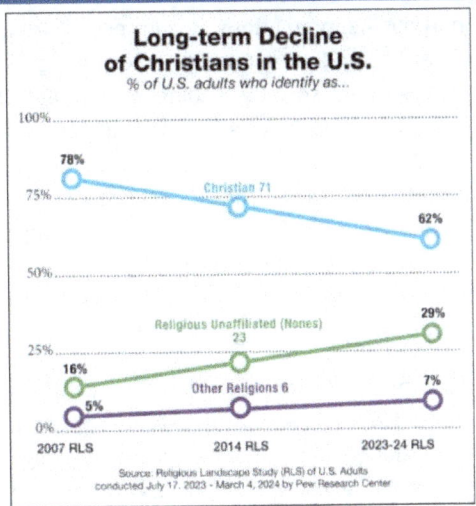

Long-term Decline of Christians in the U.S.
% of U.S. adults who identify as...

Source: Religious Landscape Study (RLS) of U.S. Adults conducted July 17, 2023 - March 4, 2024 by Pew Research Center

denominations, with mainline Protestants continuing to show the most significant decline. However, nearly all Christian denominations are showing declining numbers in church attendance, as well as other faiths.[1036] As one example, as of 2024, the Southern Baptist Convention has sustained membership decline for the *17th straight year*, dropping below 13 million for the first time since the mid-1970s.[1037]

Religiously unaffiliated refers to those who disdain organized religion – the atheists, agnostics, and even some deists. Grouped together, they can be referred to as Humanists. Their growth in numbers reflects a seismic shift in the religious sensibilities of the US population. Religion is about binding together, and a deity is not needed to make life meaningful to them. Humanists are non-religious people who strive to lead fulfilling, meaningful and ethical lives, using reason and empathy to guide their decisions and actions. They strive to base their understanding of the world on reason and science, rejecting supernatural or divine beliefs.[1038] They tend to take action to solve real-world problems, not to depend on prayer. And they hold themselves and other humans fully accountable.

The decline of Christianity is even sharper and has been going on for much longer across Europe, as compared to the United States. Increased secularization, high-profile church scandals, and younger generations not being raised [fully indoctrinated] in a church, all contribute to a steady loss of numbers throughout the West.[1039] But the drivers of this religious change go much deeper. Just look at the large group of US white Evangelical Christians who have become a Republican voting bloc, with a carefully constructed worldview, and a minority persecution complex. The term, "evangelical," has become a political label in our riven society, and the evangelical movement has become inundated with culture wars. Sarah McCammon, an NPR journalist, explained in her book, The Evangelicals: Loving, Living, and Leaving the White Evangelical Church, how a rising generation of the children of evangelicalism are now fleeing their Church, who are thinking for themselves, and who are deconstructing what feels like the "alternative facts" of their childhood. This has become a generational tipping point.

Of course, there are many underlying reasons for the dissatisfaction of younger church members, including the irrelevancy of the Church; its lack of acceptance for people of color in some denominations; treatment of immigrants and LGBTQ individuals; sexual abuse cover-ups and predatory behavior; its political alignments; its toxic culture; and, not least of all, growing societal secularism. The latter refers to the disillusionment and cynicism that members feel. As American theologian and ethicist, Russell D. Moore, explained it, "the trends in secularization mean that people do not need the Church in order to see themselves as Americans or as good people or even as 'spiritual'. And they certainly do not need the Church in order to carry out their political affiliations—even when those political affiliations are those preferred by the Church.[1040] There is compelling data from sociologists and demographers that the politicization of the American religion is a critical driver pushing people <u>away</u> from religious affiliation.[1041]

Additionally, it is no coincidence that the acceleration of the decline of Christianity, at least in the United States, has been accompanied by a strong correlation to the rise of and dependency on the Internet. While not suggesting that the Internet is the key cause, there is a definite correlation between Internet use and religious decline. Information has become more freely available; and that puts pressure on religious myths, while providing access to the truth! People can now compare how the myths and beliefs of other denominations can differ significantly with those of their own sect. If nothing else, it sometimes prompts some critical thinking as not all versions can be correct. That said, the Internet also offers information bubbles that enable people to confirm their pre-existing opinions, while avoiding discussions which conflict with those beliefs. Thus, those information bubbles serve as echo chambers for their unconfirmed, unproven beliefs.

As the above illustration clearly shows, as a percentage of the U S adult population, the number of Christians has been declining, while the number of religiously unaffiliated has been significantly rising.[1042] In *Pew Research Center* telephone surveys conducted in 2018 and 2019, 65% of American adults described themselves as Christians; this is down 12 percentage points over just the previous decade. Meanwhile, the religiously unaffiliated share of the population, stood at 26%, up from 17% in 2009.[1043] And in 2022, the *Pew Research Center* cited that with current trends, Christian population within the USA will drop below 50% within the next fifty years.[1044] And since the majority of current immigrants to the USA are Christian, blocking and removing immigrants in the United States will probably accelerate the decline of Christianity in the USA. And in the next chapter, we will discuss the reasons for the decline.

Chapter Summary

In the 16th century, Protestantism became a counterbalance to the RCC in the West. As we covered earlier in this chapter, while it began as a movement to address RCC abuses, many Protestant denominations quickly became as intolerant as Catholicism. There were numerous theological and ritual opinions among the many and growing Protestant sects, which is why there have been so many religious movements and revivals.

Much like early Christianity of the first three centuries, early Protestantism was not a single, unified, coherent movement. Instead, it was a movement of many sub-groups, characterized by conflict and internal disagreements. The only thing the early Protestants shared was the "dangerous idea" (as cited by author Alister McGrath) that the Bible is the main source of authority for the Christian religion, and that all Christians have the right to interpret it for themselves. And thus, Protestants eventually discovered that they were unable to reach consensus on important matters of doctrine,[1045] because the Bible is open to so many diverse interpretations.

What is truly amazing is the acceptance among some Christians for biblical inerrancy that ignores the obvious mistakes of logic, history, and science found in Genesis, Exodus, and other biblical writings, as though the stories were dictated by God to an unerring recorder. And Protestant denominations, which fully disagree with the Catholic Church on so many topics, accept the canonization of New Testament Scriptures by ancient Catholic bishops who clearly made at least some of their decisions based on the politics of the time. Meanwhile, Catholicism, which compiled the New Testament, doesn't believe in the inerrancy of either the Old or the New Testament.

Various Protestant denominations that rose up in the 16th and 17th centuries against the abuses they associated with Roman Catholicism; but very soon, these same Protestant sects focused on the torture and killing of heretics; established inquisitions and witch-hunting efforts; stole Church properties from the RCC; and demonstrated significant intolerance not only to Catholic Christians, but to fellow Protestant Christians, who may have harbored moderately different theological beliefs.

The United States has seen four multi-decade periods of "great awakenings" or religious revivals among the Protestant denominations. On the other hand, the sheer number of Christian denominations, as many as 45,000 worldwide today, suggests that the Christian religion is seriously fracturing into many various subgroups. Moreover, while there remain many Protestant sects and a substantial Church membership today, the size of the Protestant Christian body has started to recede significantly, in alignment with the rise of the Nones. In general, Christianity (Catholicism and Protestantism) is in decline, as the world is becoming more diverse and more secular.

Many Christian sects tend to emphasize certain parts of the Bible while downplaying others. This selective approach, which is seen in almost every Christian denomination, can lead to a distorted understanding of Christian doctrine. Further, Christianity's adaptations to and by local cultures and practices have led to multiple syncretisms and the dilution of its core teachings. On the other hand, the claim by some that Christianity is the only path to salvation is exceptionally difficult to reconcile in a pluralistic world.

Some Christian denominations continue to limit the role of women in leadership positions, sparking debates about gender equality within the faith. Further, Christianity's stance on LGBTQ+ rights and relationships varies widely, causing significant controversy both within the Church body and in broader society.

Clearly, Christianity is not a monolithic belief system. As demonstrated by the innumerable Protestant denominations, each with its unique interpretations of Scripture and theology, Christian diversity usually leads to disagreements and division among believers. This has fueled theological differences, often called heresies by one or the other, as well as schisms throughout Christian history.

A listing of the primary Protestant denominations, including a synopsis of their beliefs and the name of their founders, is provided in **Appendix 3, Protestant Christian Religions**.

[852] "U.S. Protestants Are Not Defined by Reformation-Era Controversies 500 Years Later," Pew Research Center; August 31, 2017; https://www.pewresearch.org/religion/2017/08/31/u-s-protestants-are-not-defined-by-reformation-era-controversies-500-years-later/

[853] "Christian Denominations," Preceden; https://www.preceden.com/timelines/50595-christian-denominations

[854] "Timeline of the Protestant Reformation," Coming in the Clouds; a PDF; https://comingintheclouds.org/wpclouds7/wp-content/uploads/2017/07/Protestant-Reformation-Timeline.pdf

[855] Southern Baptists descended from Baptists who settled in the American colonies in the 17th century; in 1845 Southern Baptists split with their northern counterparts over slavery. June 7, 2019. Dalia Fahmy, "7 Facts about Southern Baptists," Pew Research Center; June 2019; https://www.pewresearch.org/short-reads/2019/06/07/7-facts-about-southern-baptists/

[856] Neil J. Young, "Southern Baptists vs. the Mormons," Slate, Dec, 2007; https://slate.com/human-interest/2007/12/how-the-southern-baptist-convention-has-tried-to-keep-its-members-from-becoming-mormons.html

[857] J. Gordon Melton, ed., Encyclopedia of World Religions. (2005). New York: Facts On File. ISBN 0-8160-5456-8. Archived from the original on 23 March 2021.

[858] "U.S. Protestants Are Not Defined by Reformation-Era Controversies 500 Years Later," Pew Research Center; Aug 2017; Ibid

[859] Johann Jakob Herzog and Albert Philip Schaff; The New Schaff-Herzog Encyclopedia of Religious Knowledge. p. 419. (1911); archived from the original on 6 September 2015. Retrieved 27 June 2015.

[860] "U.S. Protestants Are Not Defined by Reformation-Era Controversies 500 Years Later," Pew Research Center; Aug 2017; Ibid

[861] Henry H. Knight III, "Wesley on Faith and Good Works". (9 July 2013). Catalyst Resources. Retrieved 16 September 2017.

[862] Christopher R. Guidry and Peter F. Crossing (1 January 2001). World Christian Trends, AD 30-AD 2200: Interpreting the Annual Christian Mega Census. P. 307; William Carey Library. . ISBN 9780878086085.

[863] John Robert Wright, Marsha L. Dutton, and Patrick Terrell Gray, (2006). One Lord, One Faith, One Baptism: Studies in Christian Ecclesiality and Ecumenism; p 273; 2006; Wm. B. Eerdmans Publishing. ISBN 9780802829405.

[864] "What Did John Knox Do in the Protestant Reformation?" Christianity.com; https://www.christianity.com/wiki/people/what-john-knox-do-protestant-reformation.html; John Knox stated that "women were inferior to men. He is reported to have said women were incompetent to rule in church and government."

[865] Was convicted of heresy by Queen Mary 1, an ardent Roman Catholic.

[866] Bishop Ridley was executed by Queen Mary I because he supported Lady Jane Grey to be queen.

[867] Dave Armstrong, "Protestant Inquisitions: Reformation Intolerance & Persecution," Patheos; Nov 22, 2021; https://www.patheos.com/blogs/davearmstrong/2017/09/protestant-inquisitions-reformation-intolerance-persecution.html

[868] "Toleration Act 1 William & Mary, Ch.18 (1689)," Encyclopedia.com; https://www.encyclopedia.com/politics/encyclopedias-almanacs-transcripts-and-maps/toleration-act-1-william-mary-ch-18-1689

[869] John L. Stoddard, Rebuilding a Lost Faith, p. 207; New York: P. J. Kenedy & Sons, 1922.

[870] Stoddard, Ibid., p. 208

[871] "Anti-Slavery," Quakers in the World; https://www.quakersintheworld.org/quakers-in-action/11/-Anti-Slavery

[872] Thomas Kidd, Baylor University, "The Founding of Maryland"; Bill of Rights Institute; https://billofrightsinstitute.org/essays/the-founding-of-maryland

[873] "Maryland Act Concerning Religion," Teaching American History; https://teachingamericanhistory.org/document/maryland-act-concerning-religion/

[874] Kidd, Ibid.

875 "The Neglected Tale of America's First Religious Freedom Law," Liberty Magazine;
https://www.libertymagazine.org/article/the-neglected-tale-of-americas-first-religious-freedom-law
876 "Maryland Toleration Act; September 21, 1649," American Battlefield Trust;
https://www.battlefields.org/learn/primary-sources/maryland-toleration-act-september-21-1649
877 Kidd, Ibid.
878 John Tracy Ellis, American Catholicism, pp. 38-39; Doubleday; Garden City, New York;
879 "People - Christopher Hitchens – Quotations," Atheist Frontier;
https://www.atheistfrontier.com/people/christopher-hitchens/quotations.pl
880 Sol Invictus is the pagan Roman holiday celebrating the birth of the sun god, Invictus, the patron god of Roman soldiers.
881 The six Oriental Orthodox Churches include Coptic, Armenian, Syrian, Ethiopian, Indian and Eritrean (the latter two being relatively recent). These six churches adhere to miaphysite Christology and theology, and are viewed as being in communion with each other.
882 The Orthodox Catholic Church is a fellowship of "autocephalous" churches, which are canonically and administratively independent, with the ecumenical patriarch of Constantinople originally holding titular or honorary primacy. Autocephaly refers to having their church leader, or head bishop, not reporting to any higher-ranking bishop.
883 "Eastern Orthodoxy," Encyclopedia Britannica; https://www.britannica.com/topic/Eastern-Orthodoxy
884 The Eastern Orthodox and Roman Catholic churches had many disagreements; but in 1054 a dispute between Pope Leo IX and the Patriarch of Constantinople, Michael Cerularius, in which both leaders excommunicated the other, precipitated a final separation, although the excommunications were each lifted in 1965.
885 "Eastern Orthodoxy," Ibid.
886 Donavyn Coffey, "Why does Christianity have so many denominations?" Live Science; July 29, 2022; https://www.livescience.com/christianity-denominations.html#:~:text=Pentecostal%2C%20Presbyterian%2C%20Lutheran%2C%20Baptist,Christianity%
887 "How Do You Define A Denomination," Center for the Study of Global Christianity;
https://www.gordonconwell.edu/center-for-global-christianity/research/quick-facts/
888 Dan Barker, Godless; p. 222-242; 2008; Ulysses Press; Berkley, CA; eISBN: 978-1-569-75148-0
889 "The State of Church Membership: Trends and Statistics [2024]," Churchtrac;
https://www.churchtrac.com/articles/the-state-of-church-membership
890 Joe Carter, "9 Things You Should Know About Mainline Protestantism," July 17, 2021; The Gospel Coalition; https://www.thegospelcoalition.org/article/know-mainline-protestantism/
891 Joe Carter, Ibid.
892 Joe Carter, "9 Things You Should Know About Ulrich Zwingli." The Gospel Coalition; Aug 28, 2019;
https://www.thegospelcoalition.org/article/9-things-know-ulrich-zwingli/
893 "Who was Ulrich Zwingli?" Got Questions? https://www.gotquestions.org/Ulrich-Zwingli.html
894 "Ulrich Zwingli and the Reformation in Switzerland," ReformationSA.org;
https://www.reformationsa.org/history-articles/ulrich-zwingli-and-the-reformation-in-switzerland
895 "The Martin Luther Bible Translation," Christian History for Everyman; https://www.christian-history.org/martin-luther-bible.html
896 Randal Rauser, "The Intolerable Martin Luther," RandalRauser.com; Aug 20, 2011;
https://randalrauser.com/2011/08/the-intolerable-martin-luther/
897 Robert Michael, Holy Hatred: Christianity, Antisemitism, and the Holocaust. p. 109; New York: Palgrave Macmillan, 2006.
898 Mark Edwards, Luther's Last Battles. p. 121; Ithaca: Cornell University Press, 1983.
899 Albrecht Classen, "Toleration, Tolerance, or Intolerance in the Works of the Young Martin Luther," Research Gate;
https://www.researchgate.net/publication/324937268_Toleration_Tolerance_or_Intolerance_in_the_Works_of_the_Young_Martin_Luther

900 Rich Preheim, "Bad history perpetuates animosity," Anabaptist World; Jan 3, 2015;
https://anabaptistworld.org/bad-history-perpetuates-animosity/

901 Will Durant, The Reformation, (Volume 6 of 10-volume, The Story of Civilization, 1967), p. 423;
New York: Simon & Schuster, 1957.

902 Dave Armstrong, "Luther Favored the Death Penalty for Anabaptists," February 3, 2016;
https://www.patheos.com/blogs/davearmstrong/2016/02/luther-favored-death-penalty-for-anabaptists.html

903 Preserved Smith, The Social Background of the Reformation, p. 177; New York: Collier Books,
1962

904 Dave Armstrong, "Home Catholic History and Religion Philip Melanchthon: Death for Denying the
Real Presence," Patheous.com; https://www.patheos.com/blogs/davearmstrong/2017/01/philip-melanchthon-death-denial-real-presence-later-denial-real-presence.html

905 "The Protestant Inquisition 'Reformation'," Catholic Apologetics Information;
http://www.catholicapologetics.info/apologetics/protestantism/protin.htm

906 "1534 The Act of Supremacy," Christian History Institute;
https://christianhistoryinstitute.org/magazine/article/act-of-supremacy

907 "Elizabeth's Act of Uniformity (1559)," Hanover Historical Texts Project;
https://history.hanover.edu/texts/engref/er80.html

908 "The Catholic Threat," Revision World; https://revisionworld.com/gcse-revision/history-gcse-revision/elizabethan-era/religious-settlement/catholic-threat

909 Barton Gingerich, "The Anglican Church: 10 Things Christians Should Know," Christianity.com;
March 7, 2023; https://www.christianity.com/church/denominations/the-anglican-church.html

910 "How Did the King James Version Come Down to Us?" Christian Publishing House;
https://christianpublishinghouse.co/2022/12/15/how-did-the-king-james-version-come-down-to-us/

911 Leah Berenson, "10 Ways the Bible Has Changed Throughout History," Premier Daily; April 10,
2024; https://thepremierdaily.com/changes-to-the-bible/

912 "What makes us Anglican?" The Episcopal Church; May 1, 2004;
https://web.archive.org/web/20170606011423/http://www.episcopalchurch.org/library/article/what-makes-us-anglican

913 Duke Helfand, "Conservative worshipers prepare for their exodus," Los Angeles Times. October
10, 2009. Retrieved December 26, 2018. https://www.latimes.com/archives/la-xpm-2009-oct-10-me-stlukes10-story.html

914 "General Convention wrap-up: Historic actions, structural changes," Episcopal News Service; July
7, 2015; http://episcopaldigitalnetwork.com/ens/2015/07/07/general-convention-wrap-up-historic-actions-structural-changes/

915 David W. Virtue, "Diocese Votes Overwhelmingly to Leave the Episcopal Church," Catholic Online;
https://www.catholic.org/news/national/story.php?id=30578

916 "Mainline Protestant churches no longer dominate," Episcopal New Service; March 30, 2005;
https://web.archive.org/web/20071231190210/http://www.episcopalchurch.org/3577_60792_ENG_HTM.htm

917 "Methodist Church," BBC's Religions;
https://www.bbc.co.uk/religion/religions/christianity/subdivisions/methodist_1.shtml

918 Stephen Ashby, "Reformed Arminianism"; Four Views on Eternal Security; p. 137; Grand Rapids:
Zondervan, 2002

919 "History of Methodism," First United Methodist Church; https://firstumchurch.com/methodism-101

920 "Methodism," Britannica; https://www.britannica.com/topic/Methodism

921 "Methodism," Britannica; Ibid.

922 "Methodist Church," BBC– Religions;
https://www.bbc.co.uk/religion/religions/christianity/subdivisions/methodist_1.shtml

923 Justin Gamble, "United Methodist Church lifts 40-year ban on LGBTQ clergy," CNN; https://www.msn.com/en-us/news/us/united-methodist-church-lifts-40-year-ban-on-lgbtq-clergy/ar-AA1nZu5G?ocid=feedsansarticle

924 Liam Adams, "Here's what a massive exodus is costing the United Methodist Church: Splinter Explainer," USA Today Network; April 16m 2024; https://www.usatoday.com/story/news/nation/2024/04/16/united-methodist-church-splintering-costing-millions/73334300007/

925 "John Calvin," Biography.com; updated Sep 14, 2022; https://www.biography.com/religious-figures/john-calvin

926 Philip Schaff, History of the Christian Church, Vol. 8: Section 107. This is taken from Phil D, "Discipline in Calvin's Geneva," The Puritan Board; Nov 13, 2019; https://www.puritanboard.com/threads/discipline-in-calvins-geneva.100030/

927 "Religious Toleration," Christian Library; https://www.christianstudylibrary.org/article/religious-toleration

928 "John Calvin Killed Rival Theologians: Bad Bible Interpretation Justified It," Re-enacting the Way; March 15, 205; https://www.reenactingtheway.com/blog/john-calvin-had-people-killed-and-bad-bible-interpretation-justified-it

929 "Religious Toleration," Ibid.

930 Mark Talbot, "The Servetus Affair, The Story of Calvin and His Critics," Desiring God; Sep 26, 2009; https://www.desiringgod.org/articles/the-servetus-affair

931 "Theodore Beza: Why it's Right to Punish Heretics," Zwinglius Redivivus; https://zwingliusredivivus.wordpress.com/2011/09/19/theodore-beza-why-its-right-to-punish-heretics/

932 The Book of Confessions; Mar 17, 2023; https://pcusa.org/resource/book-confessions

933 Mary Fairchild, "Presbyterian Church Beliefs and Practices," Learn Religions; June 25, 2019; https://www.learnreligions.com/presbyterian-church-beliefs-and-practices-700522#:~:text=The%20official%20creeds,%20confessions,%20and%20beliefs

934 David F. Wright, "John Knox and the Scottish Reformation: Christian History Interview — Prophet Without Honor?" Christian History Institute; https://christianhistoryinstitute.org/magazine/article/john-knox-prophet-without-honor

935 "Puritanism", Britannica; https://www.britannica.com/topic/Puritanism

936 "The Puritans and Freedom of Religion, Oct 27, 2008; The Historic Present; https://thehistoricpresent.com/2008/10/27/the-puritans-and-freedom-of-religion/

937 "When did "Puritan New England" die out?" The Historic Present; Jan 3, 2012; https://thehistoricpresent.com/2012/01/03/when-did-puritan-new-england-die-out/

938 Perry Miller and Thomas H Johnson, eds., The Puritans: A Sourcebook of Their Writings. p. 296; Courier Corporation. (2014).

939 "Congregationalism," Britannica; https://www.britannica.com/topic/Congregationalism/Wales-Ireland-and-Scotland

940 William H. Brackney, Baptists in North America: an historical perspective. p. 22; Blackwell Publishing; 2006; SBN 978-1-4051-1865-1.

941 Jeff Robinson, "Anabaptist kinship or English dissent? Papers at ETS examine Baptist origins," Baptist Press; Dec 14, 2009; https://web.archive.org/web/20130619030031/http://www.bpnews.net/printerfriendly.asp?ID=31878

942 J. Gordon Melton and Martin Baumann, Religions of the World: A Comprehensive Encyclopedia of Beliefs and Practices; p. 298; ABC-CLIO, US, 2010,

943 William H. Brackney; Baptists in North America: an historical perspective. p. 22. Ibid.

944 Joe Early, ed. Readings in Baptist History: Four Centuries of Selected Documents; pp. 100-101; B&H Publishing; 2008; ISBN 9780805446746.

945 "Southern Baptist Convention," International Mission Board; https://www.imb.org/southern-baptist-convention/

946 "National Baptist Convention (NBC)", The Martin Luther King, Jr. Research and Education Institute; https://kinginstitute.stanford.edu/national-baptist-convention-nbc

947 "Joseph Smith, 1805-1844," PBS: https://www.pbs.org/americanprophet/joseph-smith.html

948 "How Mormonism Went Mainstream," Time, https://time.com/6315969/mormonism-history-america-essay/

949 "Legal Trials of Joseph Smith", Encyclopedia of Mormonism. MacMillan. 1992. p. 1346. via BYU.edu.

950 "Salvation and Atonement," Religions; updated 2009-10-05; https://www.bbc.co.uk/religion/religions/mormon/beliefs/salvation_1.shtml

951 "The Church of Jesus Christ of Latter-day Saints," Britannica; https://www.britannica.com/topic/Church-of-Jesus-Christ-of-Latter-day-Saints

952 Frank S. Mead, Samuel S. Hill, and Craig D. Atwood, "Adventist and Sabbatarian (Hebraic) Churches". Handbook of Denominations in the United States (12th ed.). pp. 256-276. 2006; Nashville, Tn: Abingdon Press.

953 Anthony MacPherson, "Investigative Judgment," Encyclopedia of Seventh-Day Adventists; Sep 26, 2022; https://encyclopedia.adventist.org/article?id=7FOL#:~:text=%EE%80%80Seventh-

954 "Official Beliefs of the Seventh-day Adventist Church," Seventh-day Adventist Church; https://www.adventist.org/beliefs/

955 "What Do Adventists Believe?" Seventh day Adventist Church; https://www.adventist.org/beliefs/

956 "Welcome to the Assemblies of God," Assemblies of God (AG); https://ag.org/en

957 William W. Menzies and Robert P. Menzies, Spirit and Power: Foundations of Pentecostal Experience; p. 28; Zondervan Academic, USA, 2011.

958 Daniel Isaiah Joseph, "Assemblies of God vs. Pentecostalism: What's the Difference"; Christianity FAQ; https://christianityfaq.com/assemblies-of-god-pentecostalism/

959 Joe Carter, "9 Things You Should Know About the Assemblies of God," The Gospel Coalition; August 14, 2021; https://www.thegospelcoalition.org/article/9-things-assemblies-god/

960 "The Four 'Great Awakenings' in American Christian History," Brewminate: A Bold Blend of News and Ideas; Oct 8, 2021; https://brewminate.com/the-four-great-awakenings-in-american-christian-history/

961 John Howard Smith, The First Great Awakening: Redefining Religion in British America, 1725–1775. Fairleigh Dickinson University Press. P.1; 2015; ISBN 978-1-61147-714-6.

962 "Great Awakening," History.com; August 6, 2024 | Original: March 7, 2018; https://www.history.com/topics/european-history/great-awakening

963 William Kidd, "The Great Awakening," Bill of Rights Institute; https://billofrightsinstitute.org/essays/the-great-awakening

964 William Kidd, "The Great Awakening," Ibid.

965 "Second Great Awakening," Britannica; https://www.britannica.com/topic/Second-Great-Awakening

966 "The Slave Experience: Religion," 13.org on PBS; https://www.thirteen.org/wnet/slavery/experience/religion/history2.html

967 "The Third Great Awakening - Timeline Movement," The Association of Religious Data Archives; https://www.thearda.com/us-religion/history/timelines/entry?etype=3&eid=51

968 Robert William Fogel, "The Phases of the Four Great Awakenings," University of Chicago Press; https://press.uchicago.edu/Misc/Chicago/256626.html%20TARGET=fogel

969 Martin E. Marty, Modern American Religion. Vol. 3: Under God, Indivisible, 1941–1960; Chicago: University of Chicago Press; 1966, pp. 434–455.

970 Robert Fogel, "The Fourth Great Awakening and the Political Realignment of the 1990s," September 11, 1995; American Enterprise Institute; https://www.aei.org/research-products/speech/the-fourth-great-awakening-and-the-political-realignment-of-the-1990s/

971 "The Fourth Great Awakening - Timeline Movement," The Association of Religious Data Archives; https://www.thearda.com/us-religion/history/timelines/entry?etype=3&eid=6

972 A. G. Dickens, Reformation and Society in 16th-Century Europe, p. 191; London: Harcourt, Brace & World, 1966.

973 Hilaire Belloc (C), Characters of the Reformation, pp. 9-10; Garden City, New York: Doubleday Image, 1958.

[974] A. G. Dickens (P), <u>Reformation and Society in 16th-Century Europe</u>, p. 117; London: Harcourt, Brace & World, 1966.

[975] Johannes Janssen (C), <u>History of the German People From the Close of the Middle Ages</u>; pp. 134-135; translated by A. M. Christie, St. Louis: B. Herder, 1910 (originally 1891).

[976] Ed Jarrett, "What Is Predestination?" <u>Christianity.com</u>; Feb 23, 2024; https://www.christianity.com/wiki/christian-terms/what-is-predestination.html

[977] "Predestination," <u>Britannica</u>; https://www.britannica.com/topic/predestination

[978] "What is Predestination," <u>Got Questions?</u> https://www.gotquestions.org/predestination.html

[979] "Ennis P, "Biblical Predestination Not Focused On Individuals Or Minutia," <u>Now Think About It</u>; January 24, 2022; https://www.nowthinkaboutit.com/2022/01/biblical-predestination-not-focused-on-individuals-or-minutia/

[980] "The Chicago Statements," <u>Defending Errancy</u>; https://defendinginerrancy.com/chicago-statements/

[981] "The Chicago Statements," <u>Ibid</u>.

[982] Geoffrey Smith, "What is biblical inerrancy?" <u>Religious New Services (RNS)</u>; July 20, 2021; https://religionnews.com/2021/07/20/what-is-biblical-inerrancy-a-new-testament-scholar-explains/

[983] Michael F. Bird, "What Is the Inerrancy Debate and How Should We Think about It?' Oct 12, 2021; <u>Zondervan Academic</u>; https://zondervanacademic.com/blog/what-is-the-inerrancy-debate-and-how-should-we-think-about-it

[984] "The New Testament Gospels in a Nutshell," <u>Bart Ehrman Blog</u>; https://ehrmanblog.org/the-new-testament-gospels-in-a-nutshell/

[985] "Jewish Holy Scriptures: Canonization," <u>Jewish Virtual Library</u>; https://www.jewishvirtuallibrary.org/canonization

[986] Andrew S Denney, "Child Sex Abusers in Protestant Christian Churches: An Offender Typology," <u>Qualitative Criminology</u>; Loyola University New Orleans; Published on Jan 02, 2023; https://www.qualitativecriminology.com/pub/osa148h6/release/? data taken from Associated Press, 2007.

[987] Robert Downen, Lise Olsen, John Tedesco, "Abuse of Faith: Investigation reveals 700 victims of Southern Baptist sexual abuse over 20 years," <u>Chron</u>; Updated Feb 9, 2019; https://www.chron.com/news/investigations/article/Investigation-reveals-700-victims-of-Southern-13591612.php

[988] Downen et al, <u>Ibid</u>

[989] Andrew S. Denney, <u>Ibid</u>.

[990] Scott M. Manetsch, "Switzerland's Original Reformer Was Creative, Combative, and Frequently Controversial," <u>Christianity Today</u>. (23 May 2022). Retrieved 22 November 2022; https://www.christianitytoday.com/2022/05/zwingli-gods-armed-prophet-swiss-reformation-bruce-gordon/

[991] "What is Reformed?" <u>Christian Reformed Church</u>; https://www.crcna.org/welcome/beliefs/reformed-accent/what-reformed

[992] Clayton Kraby, "The Five Points of Calvinism – Defining the Doctrines of Grace," <u>Reasonable Theology</u>; https://reasonabletheology.org/five-points-calvinism-defining-doctrines-of-grace/

[993] Phett Dodson, "The Lord's Supper - A Reformed and Confessional View," Gospel Reformation Network; Sep 21, 2020; https://gospelreformation.net/the-lords-supper/

[994] "What is an Evangelical?" National Association of Evangelicals.Org; https://www.nae.org/what-is-an-evangelical/#:~:text=Evangelicals%20take%20the%20Bible%20seriously,to%20sinners%20by%20Jesus%20Christ.

[995] David Masci and Gregory A. Smith; "5 facts about U.S. evangelical Protestants," <u>Per Research Center</u>; March 1, 2018; https://www.pewresearch.org/short-reads/2018/03/01/5-facts-about-u-s-evangelical-protestants/

[996] Frances FitzGerald, <u>The Evangelicals: The Struggle to Shape America.</u> (2017). p. 2; Simon and Schuster. ISBN 978-1-4391-3133-6.

[997] Frances FitzGerald, <u>The Evangelicals: The Struggle to Shape America. Simon and Schuster</u>, Ibid. p. 5.

998 George M. Marsden, <u>Reforming Fundamentalism: Fuller Seminary and the New Evangelicalism</u>, pp. 3-4; (1987), Grand Rapids: William B. Eerdmans.

999 "Christian fundamentalism," <u>Encyclopedia Britannica</u>; https://www.britannica.com/topic/Christian-fundamentalism

1000 "Christian fundamentalism summary," <u>Britannica</u>; https://www.britannica.com/summary/Christian-fundamentalism

1001 Nancy T. Ammerman, "North American Protestant Fundamentalism," pp. 1–65. In Martin E. Marty and R. Scott Appleby (eds.), <u>Fundamentalisms Observed. The Fundamentalism Project</u>, (1991). Chicago, Il; London: University of Chicago Press; ISBN 0-226-50878-1.

1002 "Fundamentalism," <u>A Study of Denominations</u>; https://www.astudyofdenominations.com/movements/fundamentalism/

1003 Robert Oldham Fife, "The Restoration Movement and the Ecumenical Movement", Leaven, vol. 7, no. 4. (Fall 1999), p. 212.

1004 A. J. L. Waskey, "Restoration Movement," <u>New Georgia Encyclopedia</u>; https://www.georgiaencyclopedia.org/articles/arts-culture/restoration-movement/

1005 Jim Estep, "What Is the Restoration Movement?" <u>Christian Standard</u>; May 22, 2019; https://christianstandard.com/2019/05/what-is-the-restoration-movement/

1006 "The Restoration Movement: A History of Separation," <u>Christian Standard</u>; https://christianstandard.com/2024/03/the-restoration-movement-a-history-of-separation/

1007 "Holiness Movement - Timeline Movement," <u>The Association of Religious Data Archives (ARDA)</u>; https://www.thearda.com/us-religion/history/timelines/entry?etype=3&eid=13

1008 Sophia Bricker, "What Is the Holiness Movement and Is it Biblical?" <u>Christianity.com</u>; Updated July 23, 2021; https://www.christianity.com/wiki/christian-terms/what-is-the-holiness-movement-and-is-it-biblical.html

1009 "The Holiness Movement," <u>Britannica</u>; https://www.britannica.com/event/Holiness-movement

1010 "Protestant Modernists," <u>Encyclopedia.com</u>; https://www.encyclopedia.com/history/dictionaries-thesauruses-pictures-and-press-releases/modernists-protestant

1011 Professor Douglas O. Linder, "State v. John Scopes ("The Monkey Trial"): An Account," <u>UMKC School of Law</u>; https://www.famous-trials.com/scopesmonkey/2127-home

1012 "Epperson v. Arkansas," <u>Oyez</u>; https://www.oyez.org/cases/1968/7

1013 Shubert M. Ogden, "Sources of Religious Authority in Liberal Protestantism," <u>Journal of the American Academy of Religion</u>; pp. 405-406; Oxford University Press, Sep 1976.

1014 Linda Woodhead and Paul Fletcher (eds), "Christianity", <u>Religions in the Modern World: Traditions and Transformations</u>, pp. 186 and 193; ISBN 978-0-415-21783-5

1015 Amanda Williams, "The Most Liberal Christian Denominations," <u>Christian Website</u>; https://www.christianwebsite.com/most-liberal-christian-denominations/

1016 "Pentecostalism," BBC; https://www.bbc.co.uk/religion/religions/christianity/subdivisions/pentecostal_1.shtml

1017 <u>Ibid</u>.

1018 Ray E Horton, "Understanding Speaking in Tongues," <u>Pentecostal Theology</u>; March 3, 2021; https://www.pentecostaltheology.com/understanding-speaking-in-tongues/

1019 "Oneness Pentecostalism," <u>Apostolic Archives International, Inc.</u>, https://www.apostolicarchives.com/articles/article/8801925/180091.htm

1020 "Oneness Pentecostalism," <u>Evidence Unseen</u>; https://evidenceunseen.com/world-religions/oneness-pentecostalism

1021 Janine Ungvarsky, "Charismatic movement (Christianity)," EBSCO; 2025; https://www.ebsco.com/research-starters/religion-and-philosophy/charismatic-movement-christianity

1022 Willliam W Menzies, and Robert P Menzies, <u>Spirit and Power: Foundations of Pentecostal Experience</u>; p. 39; (2000); Zondervan. ISBN 978-0-310-86415-8.

1023 Margaret M. Poloma, and John C. Green, <u>The Assemblies of God: Godly Love and the Revitalization of American Pentecostalism</u>, p. 64; (2010), New York: New York University Press, ISBN 978-0-8147-6783-2.

[1024] William W Menzies, Ibid. p. 40

[1025] Betsy Lopez-Wagner, " Green the Church: On a Mission of Faith for Sustainability," Earth Justice; https://earthjustice.org/article/green-the-church-on-a-mission-of-faith-for-sustainability

[1026] Nicolette Higgs, "How green theology is energizing the black community to fight the climate crisis," CNN US; November 22, 2019; https://www.cnn.com/2019/11/22/us/green-the-church-black-community-fights-climate-change/index.html

[1027] "An Interview with Dr. Ambrose Carrol on the Green the Church Movement," The Green Church; https://www.greenthechurch.org/an-interview-with-dr-ambrose-carrol-on-the-green-the-church-movement

[1028] "Unfulfilled Watch Tower Society predictions," Detailed Pedia; https://www.detailedpedia.com/wiki-Unfulfilled%20Watch%20Tower%20Society%20predictions

[1029] "Peoples Temple." Britannica; https://www.britannica.com/topic/Peoples-Temple

[1030] Mina Elwell, "The Children Of God: 16 Disturbing Facts About The Cult," Grunge; updated Feb, 2023; https://www.grunge.com/476981/the-untold-truth-of-the-children-of-god-cult/

[1031] "Heaven's Gate cult members found dead," History.com; https://www.history.com/this-day-in-history/march-26/heavens-gate-cult-members-found-dead

[1032] "Branch Davidian," Britannica; https://www.britannica.com/topic/Branch-Davidian

[1033] "Unification Church," Britannica; https://www.britannica.com/topic/Unification-Church

[1034] Jeffrey M. Jones, "U.S. Church Membership Falls Below Majority for First Time," Gallop; March 29, 2021; https://news.gallup.com/poll/341963/church-membership-falls-below-majority-first-time.aspx

[1035] "How Religious are Americans?" Gallup; March 24, 2024; https://news.gallup.com/poll/358364/religious-americans.aspx

[1036] Jeffry M. Jones, "Church Attendance Has Declined in Most U.S. Religious Groups," Gallup; March 25, 2024: https://news.gallup.com/poll/642548/church-attendance-declined-religious-groups.aspx

[1037] Aaron Earls, "Southern Baptist Churches' Membership Declines to Below 13 Million," The Roy's Report; May 7, 2024; https://julieroys.com/southern-baptist-churches-membership-declines-to-below-13-million/

[1038] "What is humanism?" Humanists International; https://humanists.international/what-is-humanism/

[1039] "The State of Church Membership: Trends and Statistics [2024]," Churchtrac; https://www.churchtrac.com/articles/the-state-of-church-membership

[1040] Russell Moore, "Losing Our Religion," Moore to the Point email newsletter. April 15, 2021; https://www.russellmoore.com/2021/04/15/losing-our-religion/

[1041] David Campbell, "The Perils of Politicized Religion," American Academy of Arts and Sciences; Summer, 2020; https://www.amacad.org/publication/daedalus/perils-politicized-religion

[1042] "Religious Identity," Pew Research Center; Feb 26, 2025; https://www.pewresearch.org/religion/2025/02/26/religious-landscape-study-religious-identity/

[1043] "In U.S., Decline of Christianity Continues at Rapid Pace," Pew Research Center; October 17, 2019; https://www.pewresearch.org/religion/2019/10/17/in-u-s-decline-of-christianity-continues-at-rapid-pace/

[1044] Bob Smietana, "Fewer than half of Americans may be Christian by 2070, according to new projections," Religious News; Sep 13, 2022; https://religionnews.com/2022/09/13/fewer-than-half-of-americans-may-be-christian-by-2070-according-to-new-projections/

[1045] Alister E. McGrath, Christianity's Dangerous Idea; 2007; HarperCollins; Smithsonian Book;

Chapter 8 – The Dangers of Organized Religion

Contrary to claims by Christian apologists, the Christian persecutions of the Roman Empire were relatively mild, except for the centrally directed persecution by Emperor Diocletian. However, when the roles were reversed, and when Christians were in leadership positions throughout the Roman Empire, they released an unprecedented reign of terror, whereby pagan temples were destroyed, storehouses of ancient knowledge burned, and pagans, Jews, and even non-orthodox Christian sects were tortured and murdered.

In February 380 CE, Roman Emperor Flavius Theodosius declared Nicene Christianity the exclusive religion of the Roman Empire, requiring that "all the various nations, which are subject to our clemency and moderation should continue in the profession of that religion, which was delivered to the Romans by the divine Apostle, Peter." Non-Christians were referred to as "loathsome, heretics, stupid and blind".[1046] Christianity found itself at the forefront of the Roman Empire in politics and war.

In 395 CE, the Roman state unleashed a totalitarian reign of terror. At the behest of Christian leaders, new edicts induced new persecutions against pagans. Encouraged by Christian monks and with the consent of Eastern Roman Emperor Flavius Arcadius (383-408 CE), hordes of the Christian Goths sacked and burned many Hellene (Greek) cities (e.g., Dion, Delphi, Corinth, Argos, Sparta, Messene, Olympia, etc.), slaughtered or enslaved innumerable gentile Hellenes, and burnt down all the temples, including burning their priests alive.[1047] The mob rule of Christian zealots against those it considered pagans continued for several more decades. In 415 CE, Hypatia of Alexandria, the world's leading mathematician and astronomer, was torn to pieces with glass fragments by a hysterical Christian mob; she was a Neo-Platonist, which zealot Christians considered pagan – her only crime. Soon thereafter, the famous Library of Alexandria was destroyed. Of course, condoning violence using religious justification contradicted Jesus's teachings of non-violence.

Seven hundred years later, the Christian West would institute its holy war against the Saracens, and soon thereafter, they would craft together papal inquisitions to suppress heresy. This Christian authoritarian position actually continued with the Protestant Reformation. For example, it was Martin Luther who persecuted Anabaptists and other Christian Protestant sects. Even religious refugees fleeing to the New World, such as the Puritans, carried their rigid authoritarianism and intolerance with them.

At times, the newly formed Protestants tried to combine religious and political authority, advocating Christian governments, similar to Islamic theocracies. In 1814, Thomas Jefferson argued: "In every country and in every age, the priest has been hostile to liberty. He is always in alliance with the despot, abetting his abuses in return for protection to his own."[1048] Thus, he and many other US founding fathers sought a total separation of church and state.

Theocracies

When a country governs itself through its state's religion, it creates a theocracy, which can quickly link with civil oppression. Today, Christians often associate theocracies with Islamic countries renowned for their zeal in invoking harsh Sharia Law.[1049] Islam can seem particularly vexing as it prescribes in minute detail how individuals must conduct themselves throughout their lives, not just how often and where to pray. And while non-Muslims may be somewhat tolerated in such a country, they are certainly not treated well, and they are often subjected to the same harsh laws. Europe has also seen several Christian theocracies over the centuries, such as the Papal States and the Church of England. Anytime religious authorities get in bed with intolerant secular rulers, abuse can occur. The Spanish Inquisition was officially a weapon of the Roman Catholic Church; but it was originally sponsored by Queen Isabella (1474 – 1504 CE), an ardent and over-zealous Catholic monarch who wanted to rid Spain of those who followed the Jewish and Islamic faiths.[1050]

Some people falsely believe that in modern times, Western countries do not promote religious politics. If so, how did the Nazis and Fascists round up and kill millions of Jews in the 1930s and 1940s in the midst of those good Christians living there? The Concordat of 1933 was signed by Hitler (who was a Roman Catholic) and the Vatican, increasing Hitler's power to round up and kill Jews, while doing little to protect the Catholic community in Germany from constant interference.[1051] Apartheid in South Africa was the creation and directive of the Dutch Reformed Church, using Christian Scripture to justify its repugnant decrees.[1052] The dictatorship in Greece, 1967-1974, proclaimed a "Greece for Christian Greeks," supported by the Greek Orthodox Church, which had a well established reputation for being reactionary, repressive, and a staunch ally of the established order.[1053] The Greek Junta (4 x colonels) was a totalitarian regime, renowned for its abolition of political freedoms, its imprisonment of its citizens, and its liberal use of torture and exile.[1054]

In our modern world, there are emerging theocrats who are garnering enormous power, such as nuclear weapons in the hands of Iran and Israel, and jihadists in Afghanistan, Yemen, and Syria. Today, the Russian Orthodox Church strongly supports the dictatorship of Vladimir Putin in Russia. In Israel, zealots steadily steal more and more land from the disenfranchised Palestinians. And in the USA, we have a series of isolated Boards of Education that insert foolish ideas about 'creationism'; and some Fundamentalist Christians have demanded a Christian theocracy in the USA. Fortunately, the USA has a national constitution that requires the separation of church and state (the only one in the world). Nowhere in the U S Constitution is the name of "God" mentioned, and certainly not Christianity, or any other specific religion. After all, many of our founding fathers, while born into Christian families, were deists (e.g., Thomas Jefferson, Benjamin Franklin, Thomas Paine, James Madison, James Monroe, George Washington, and Ethan Allen);[1055] [1056] and deists believe that while there is a supreme deity, he doesn't directly intervene in the affairs of people. Regardless of one's beliefs, the only guarantee of religious freedom, including freedom from religion, is a secular state.

Having lived in a secular country for their entire lives, many Americans do not fully comprehend the impact on their freedoms that a theocracy would have. Theocracies benefit the ruling oligarchs; they do not have the best interests of the people in mind. We have established that there are over 200 Christian denominations in the United States and over 45,000 globally. So, which Christian sect would sponsor the establishment of Christian Nationalism in the US? If the various denominations could agree on religious matters, they wouldn't be different denominations. Just look at the ill-advised movements in states to put the Ten Commandments in the public schools. Never mind that the Ten Commandments have nothing to do with US law, and they are religious edicts, not moral guidelines. And which version of the Commandments should be posted? There are more Roman Catholics in the US than any other individual denomination; so should it be the Catholic version? But there are more Protestants in total; does that mean the Protestant version should be posted? And what about our neighbors who follow Hindu, Islamic, or other religions?

Any rudimentary review of current or past theocracies will uncover how oppressive religiously-governed countries can be, especially to their own people. How many groups of politically marginalized people would go under the heel of religious oppression? How many more women and LGBTQ members are to be disparaged, bullied, and oppressed? Autocracies spawn the intentional suppression of knowledge, book burnings, inquisitions, bigotry, witch hunts, bombings, and all forms of intimidation.

Theocracies are religious bullies that want to dominate citizens' thoughts as well as activities. And sadly, if people believe that they have God on their side, then history has shown that they justify their harsh regimes as the will of God. Indeed, as underscored in religious wars, what evil will they not do? Just look at the righteous Christian crusades, during which the Christian crusaders sacked a major Christian city (Constantinople) in 1204,[1057] and where the crusaders committed multiple atrocities against women and children, as well as against Jews and Muslims, in the name of Jesus Christ! Equally horrible, look at the wars in Europe in the 17th century between the Catholics and Protestants.

Separation of Church and State

The phrase "separation of church and state" originated in the early days of the United States and is often associated with Thomas Jefferson. Roger Williams, the Protestant theologian and founder of Rhode Island, was the first to use the metaphor of a "wall of separation" between church and state in his 1644 book, The Bloody Tenet of Persecution.[1058] Then President Jefferson famously used the phrase in his 1802 letter to the Danbury Baptist Association.[1059] This wall of separation protects religions from oversight by government, and it protects the government from the encroachment of religion. As Dr. Teresa Smallwood, the Postdoctoral Fellow & Associate Director, Public Theology and Racial Justice Collaborative, tersely asserts, "A wall of separation is a shield from contact, either literal or perceived."[1060]

On one hand, the Founding Fathers were Christians or deists, and they built a constitutional framework that would enable states (whose powers were "numerous and indefinite") to determine to what degree religion and government might intermingle. On the other hand, they were highly influenced by Enlightenment thinkers and explicitly prohibited the federal government from comingling with any religion.[1061] In *Everson v. Board of Education* (1947), which first applied the First Amendment's establishment clause to the states, the Supreme Court relied on Jefferson's metaphor in announcing a strict standard of separation between church and state. Justice Hugo L. Black concluded his opinion for the Court's majority with the pronouncement that "the First Amendment has erected a wall between church and state. That wall must be kept high and impregnable. We could not approve the slightest breach..."[1062]

The separation of religion from the state is a concept that defines the political relationships between the federal government and religious organizations. In the United States, the First Amendment of the Constitution is considered the cornerstone of religious freedom. The First Amendment's Establishment Clause and Free Exercise Clause prevent the government from establishing a religion, favoring one religion over another, or interfering with the practice of religion, as well as providing freedom from religion. The Bill of Rights, adopted in 1791 as ten amendments to the Constitution of the United States, was one of the earliest political expressions against the political establishment of religion. Another was the Virginia Statute for Religious Freedom, also authored by Jefferson and adopted by Virginia in 1786.[1063]

The text of the 1786 Virginia Statute for Religious Freedom, upon which the 1st Amendment is based, gives great insight into our nation's right of religious freedom. It reads: "... no man shall be compelled to frequent or support any religious worship, place, or ministry whatsoever, nor shall be enforced ... in his body or goods, nor shall otherwise suffer on account of his religious opinions or belief; but that all men shall be free to profess, and by argument to maintain, their opinion in matters of religion, and that the same shall in no wise diminish, enlarge, or affect their civil capacities."[1064]

There are those who insist that the First Amendment doesn't direct the separation of church and state because that exact phrase is not in the amendment nor in the Constitution. Well, 'Trinity' is not in the New Testament, yet many Protestants and all practicing Catholics believe in it. However, the separation of church and state metaphor is deeply rooted in early American fears of government involvement in religion. Religious liberty is intrinsic to the US Constitution and in numerous federal statutes. The freedoms it guarantees are enshrined in the First Amendment's opening 16 words which stipulate that "Congress shall make no law respecting an establishment of religion or prohibiting the free exercise thereof."[1065] These words contain two key clauses that work together for the protection of all Americans: (1) the Establishment Clause and (2) the Free Exercise Clause. The former ensures that the US Federal Government remains neutral toward religion, and it cannot favor any particular religious point of view. The latter clause means that Americans are free to practice their religion however they wish, subject to non-infringement on others.

No other nation, much less a new one, had ever dared divorce religion from government so completely; and Congress fittingly used the concepts of "religion," "establishment," and "free exercise" broadly, not narrowly.[1066] This separation principle enables all Americans to practice their deeply held beliefs in private and in public.[1067] It is an essential principle of religious liberty that we prevent the government from interfering with religion, or having the government force religious views on its people. Specifically, separating of church and state is what enables and guarantees religious liberty to exist.

An important point is that this Amendment to the Constitution also guarantees freedom from the rules and dogmas of other people's religious beliefs so that you can follow the demands of your own conscience, whether that takes a religious form or not. As stated in *Learn Religions*, "Forcing people to accept some particular idea or adhere to behavioral standards from someone else's religion means that their religious freedom is being infringed upon."[1068] The US Government can neither favor nor disfavor any religious group nor the religious beliefs espoused by a particular religious group.

Some Americans will point to "In God We Trust" on our coins. It started with our two-cent coin[1069] in 1864 after Treasury Secretary Salmon P. Chase convinced President Lincoln that such a move would shore-up support for the North. In 1866, the motto was placed on silver dollars, half-dollar coins, and the quarter-dollar coins (and relatively briefly till 1889 on our nickel 3-cent coins). The motto faded away in the late 1800s. However, the motto was restored on May 18, 1908 for all coins that had previously included it (assuming that the coin was still in circulation).[1070] In 1909, the motto was added to the U. S. dime and U. S. penny, and it was added to the U. S. nickel in 1938.

People might also mention "Under God" in the Pledge of Allegiance. But most of those same Americans fail to realize that "Under God" was not added to the national pledge of allegiance (originally penned by Francis Bellamy in 1892) until 1954, and it was added as purely anti-Soviet propaganda.[1071] "Under God" was a Cold War relic, and much the same for "In God We Trust," which President Eisenhower agreed to add to paper currency in 1955;[1072] and then he signed into law our national motto in July 1956.[1073] U.S. politicians in the 1950s wanted to assert a sense of moral superiority over the "godless" communists in the USSR – never mind that the majority of Russians were actually members of the Russian Orthodox Christian Church (only the Soviet government was truly nontheistic). Since that decade, religious and secular groups continue to argue about the constitutionality of a motto that refers to a deity, given that the US founding fathers were dedicated to maintaining the separation between religion and government.

The Constitution Framers' experiences with religious establishments primarily stemmed from the Church of England, which enforced religious uniformity through its arbitrary laws that punished dissenters. This history made it clear that to avoid similar conflicts, the new American government needed to ensure freedom of religion.[1074] In 1797, President John Adams signed an international treaty stating that "the United States of America is not in any sense founded on the Christian Religion."[1075] And the treaty met with unanimous approval of the US Senate.

The extent to which the government and religion are separated in the United States is still debated. A 2021 *Pew Research Center* survey found that the majority of Americans support church/state separation almost 3 to 1, while over 4 to 1 never want to declare any religion as the 'official religion' of the USA.[1076] However, there are pockets of support, especially among ultra-conservative Christians, for increased integration of church and government.[1077]

American politics is strongly impacted by religious beliefs; however, as the USA continues to trend secularly, the religious influence should diminish over time. The growth in the religiously unaffiliated is a 30 million-person increase since 2009. This lack of religious affiliation is more prevalent among younger generations; 34% of Generation Z identify this way. As the Baby Boomer population continues to decline in size, the prevalence of religious tradition declines as well. [1078]

"Lighthouses are more useful than churches"
– Ben Franklin

"This would be the best of all possible worlds if there were no religion in it"
– John Adams

"Christianity is the most perverted system that ever shone on man"
– Thomas Jefferson

When Separation of Church and State is Not Achieved

Without the separation of religion from government, true religious freedom would not be possible. Unfortunately, many of the attacks on this principle come from the religious side. There have been several attempts to create insular religious communities in the United States – communities which promote one version of religion and try to enforce their own moral codes. Governments, including state, county, and local, cannot pass laws that have a primary purpose of advancing their religion or their religion's views, such as segregation in public places based on one's sex, or establishing a dress code based on one's religious beliefs.[1079]

Christian nationalism is a movement that has gained momentum in conservative circles in recent years. The basic premise is a blend of government and religion, specifically Christianity, that is far more religiously intense today than has been the case throughout American history. It advocates a theocratic vision for the United States. There is a widening schism between religious adults and non-religious adults. The real danger of this schism is creating the conditions for a serious upheaval in American society. Conservative Christians have a deep sense of victimhood, and they fear a secular America; some have indicated their willingness to end democracy to promote their version of Christianity. If religious conservatives convince themselves that they cannot win democratically, many people fear that they will opt to abandon democracy altogether.[1080]

U S Republicans are increasingly claiming the mantle of "Christian Nationalists." A 2022 poll suggested that although 57 percent of Republicans recognize that declaring the U.S. a "Christian nation" is unconstitutional, almost 60 percent of those same Republicans would still support it. To achieve its agenda, the GOP is already instituting increasingly undemocratic processes and efforts to overturn legitimate elections, and it is installing religious zealots in positions of power. Christian nationalism is effectively a mash-up of Fundamentalist religion and politics.

Given the diversity of Christianity in the USA (and in the world), it is not readily apparent which version of Christianity would establish itself to dominate the US government. For example, there is a clear, and many believe a misguided, movement among some MAGA-dominant state governments to post the Ten Commandments in every school of their state(s). Louisiana's law was set to go into effect in January 2025 (it is under judicial review). Several other states – ND, SD, OK, TN, and TX – are promoting bills for their legislatures to demand similar outcomes.[1081] Not only are these bills clearly unconstitutional from a federal perspective, but the legislatures must decide which Christian version of the Commandments they will support.

The threat of a theocracy in the USA is real. Some Christian groups in the U.S. are on a path to becoming a violent and repressive force (as in Iran). The agendas of any theocracy cannot help but corrupt and suppress its country and its people. A modest study of modern and past theocratic societies would quickly illuminate the reality regarding how religiously-governed countries oppress their own people. Think how gut-wrenching it would be to witness our society crumbling beneath the stranglehold of religious oppression?

It would appear that the Republican Party is losing control of the reactionary forces it has unleashed. Indeed, it is amazing how religion can facilitate erroneous rationalizations, such as removing basic rights from others. It prevents people from living in peace, both as a community and in their own lives. It forces entire groups of people to work tirelessly to preserve rights that should be available to them already. It cites holy texts as excuses to discriminate against women, LGBT people, and foreigners.[1082]

Sometimes, strongly held beliefs morph into a cult. An example of such is the New Apostolic Reformation (NAR), a term coined by Peter Wagner, founder of several independent Charismatic churches. NAR is a theological belief system that combines elements of Pentecostalism, Evangelicalism, and the Seven Mountain Mandate to advocate Christian dominion over all aspects of society. Dominion theology, also known as dominionism, is a group of Christian political ideologies that seek to institute a nation governed by Christians and based on their understandings of biblical laws. Its end goal is to terminate the separation of church and state in the USA and establish a Christian theocracy. As Paul Rosenburg wrote, "Unlike earlier incarnations of the Christian right, the explicit goal of the widely-discussed, but little-understood NAR is to install theocracy with a democratic facade, based on the Iranian model."[1083]

The Seven Mountain Mandate is an extremist dominionist movement among Pentecostal and Charismatic Christians[1084] that there are seven aspects of society that believers seek to influence or dominate: family, religion, education, media, arts and entertainment, business, and government.[1085] Unsurprisingly, the NAR movement is highly supportive of President Trump and his MAGA agenda. Of course, one can wonder how those who advocate Christian values can support organizations and movements whose actions are clearly contradictory to those teachings. Yet, there appears to be significant overlap of the MAGA followers and supporters of the NAR movement. They seem to share a vision that intertwines religious beliefs with the governance of the United States. The dangers associated with this movement are metastasizing.

The Issues with Organized Religion

Organized religion has Bronze Age (Judaism) and an Iron Age (Christianity) origin. Both Ages ran rampant with ignorance, superstition, inequality, misogyny, and violence. The gods of the time sanctioned slavery. Women and children were literally possessions of men. Sacred texts of the New Testament, Torah, and Koran all preserve and protect fragments of Iron Age culture, putting a god's endorsement on some of the very worst human impulses.

Organized religion is simply a structured system of worship. It uses rituals in the context of a faith system. Its structure standardizes the practice of worship and defines religious doctrine. It involves designated behaviors, beliefs, worldviews, and revelations. It generally encompasses supernatural and spiritual elements. Religion comes from the Latin word *religare*, which means "to bind". At its heart, organized religion is a form of bondage, as it is a divider. It promotes a form of tribalism that includes insiders and outsiders. The latter can be depicted as enemies of God and not worthy of trust or friendship. That goes against a pluralistic, secular society striving to work together. Organized religion promotes an agenda of uncertainty and fear behind a storefront of good deeds. And it is all about control, and manipulating others based on their own interpretations, and their ulterior goals (such as acquiring financial wealth). Additionally, much of the religious doctrine that we've been taught is a myth, and as shown throughout this book, it can't withstand the critique of logical examination.

The devotions of many religious followers hinge on the idea that there is some reward waiting for them in an afterlife. For Hindus, it includes escaping the grueling tasks of reincarnation; for the Christian, it is a perfect place of infinite peace and happiness; and for the Buddhist, it is reaching Nirvana. So, if you acquire enough credits (for the things you do, or don't do) in this lifetime, you can qualify for the award (reincarnation, salvation, nirvana, eternal life, heaven, etc.). Without the promises of compensation in the afterlife (for which there is no evidence they even exist), would most religious devotees be as zealous in their belief systems?

Recruiting in a cult offers acceptance and purpose, and in many ways, that is how organized religion operates. Questions are deflected, as you are indoctrinated; your independent thinking is reduced. In times of stress, you say silly things such as, "God will protect me from Covid," and "AIDS was sent by God as a punishment for our sins." Rather than being logical, independent, and practical thinkers who can address the myriad issues that vex mankind, with organized religion we remain fixated on meaningless rituals, superficialities, and questionable Scriptures written long ago. Organized religion increases our gullibility, which only serves to promote the agendas of corrupt, power-hungry people. The greed and machinations of man can pervert what should be a positive spiritual experience into something that's ugly and divisive. Unfortunately, organized religions can promote superstition, fanaticism, and intolerance.

It is difficult to maintain a democracy of the people when the people's votes are effectively hijacked by two to three special interest issues, which someone they trust has deemed "spiritual issues". Examples in the USA include millions of people voting against their own self-interest to try and disallow abortion, same-sex marriage, or to put the Bible reading and the Ten Commandments in their secular public schools. Meanwhile, these same people who want to impose their morality on others act as though they couldn't care less about the homeless, the economy, the sick, injustice, pestilence, the environment, or the potential for war with other nations.

Religion often keeps people shackled to outdated belief systems that hinder human progress, rather than helping procure society's evolution and growth. It prevents some from progressing beyond their own antiquated thinking. Religion can perpetuate societal ignorance, and it can block humanity's progression. And that severely impacts the quality of our lives, health, and environment.[1086]

Religion has a multi-level, nuanced influence on people's lives. For some, religion can be a source of comfort and guidance. For others, it is an opportunity to socialize with others of similar interests. It can bring some people together, but it can also be a source of division, stress, and anxiety. Some religious proponents argue that religion provides inspiration and hope; but it is a false hope that is based on superstitious beliefs from the Iron Age. And as famed author, Randy Gage so succinctly wrote: "Happy, well-adjusted people don't need religion. But like governments, religions need you to need them."[1087] Americans have been losing confidence in organized religion, as membership and church attendance have been dropping annually. Another factor that has dramatically affected organized religion is religion's relationship with ultra-conservative politics for the past four decades.

Religion is not based on sound logic and common sense; instead, religious dogma tends to be self-contradictory. The primary reason that many Jews and Christians believe what they believe is because they were taught it as children, and they chose to continue with their beliefs, bereft of logic. That, in turn, demonstrates why mankind is plagued with so many seemingly intractable problems. Our true nature is based on logical and independent thinking; but instead of showing practicality in addressing life's issues that worry us, we remain fixated on meaningless religious dogma and rituals. In short, as a society, we're being willfully ignorant, and that ignorance helps to promote the needs of greedy, evil, and power-hungry people.

> *"Religion is to the common people true, to the wise false, and to the rulers useful"*
> – Seneca (C. 1 BCE – 65 CE)

Christian Persecution Complex

The Christian persecution complex is "the belief, attitude, or worldview that Christian values and Christians are being oppressed by social groups and governments in the Western world."[1088] This belief is actively promoted by some American churches. As stated by Professor of Theology, Grace Ji-Sun Kim, "...evangelicals' claims of persecution in the U.S. are unfounded and rooted in intersecting legacies of racism, sexism, heterosexism, and colonialism."[1089] Indeed, the concept that Christianity is under attack is prevalent in contemporary arguments for religious exemptions. In the U.S., conservative politicians frequently characterize "issues such as same-sex marriage and the ACA's contraceptives mandate as attacks on Christians or Christianity..." [1090]

Many conservative Christians believe they are subject to religious discrimination in the United States. In a report from the Public Religion Research Institute, three-quarters of Republicans and Trump supporters and nearly eight out of 10 white evangelical Protestants agreed with the statement: "discrimination against Christians is as big of a problem as discrimination against other groups, including blacks and minorities." [1091]

Of course, the idea that Christians whose religious practices are constitutionally protected in the U.S., and who make up the majority (albeit a shrinking majority) of the population of the U.S., are being persecuted in America is just patently absurd. What is true is that the white conservative Christians face an increasingly hostile cultural climate as a backlash to their attacks on gays, abortion, and immigration. Many of the conservative Christians cannot seem to register the differences between their cultural views from their religious ones. Another reason for their feelings that they are under attack is that some politicians and their religious leaders have been telling them that it is so. The politicians want to mobilize their votes, and the religious leaders want to explain away why so many fellow Christians are leaving their churches.

Conservative Christians' understanding of discrimination tends to be fanciful and totally misaligned with reality. They need to better understand the transforming cultural landscape in which they are shedding their dominance. As they lash out and weaponize their feelings of insecurity, others stoke their victim complex to lead them down a path of conspiracies (e.g., voter fraud, deep state, etc.), and lies upon lies.

Lack of Critical Thinking

A person's exercise in thinking clearly, deeply, and productively is a valuable life skill. However, research shows that such skills are declining, and there has been a deterioration in people's ability to think critically and reflectively.[1092] Critical thinking is the process of analyzing available facts, evidence, observations, and arguments to make sound conclusions or informed choices.[1093] Lack of critical thinking skills can be the result of several factors: lack of basic skills due to indoctrination to a given system of belief, cognitive biases, social pressure, and misinformation, failure to consider alternative choices, and fear.

Indoctrination

Today, indoctrination has become a pejorative term; originally, the word had no negative connotation. It just meant to instruct the truths or doctrines. Now, the term is used when people are taught an orthodox set of beliefs, while never being exposed to alternative points of view. It can be succinctly defined as a means of imposing a desired ideology without open discussion. Such an instance would include the indoctrination of children into a given religious belief system. In the words of Cambridge neuropsychologist Nicholas Humphrey, "this kind of religious (and cultural) indoctrination is nothing less than brainwashing, [...as] children have a right not to have their minds addled by nonsense."[1094]

With the lagging exception of the United States, most developed societies have grown predominantly secular over the past century, while orthodox religion is growing throughout the developing world. It has become clear that religion will have geopolitical consequences well into the 21st century. And over the past two decades, a number of psychological studies have been conducted to better understand how our brains process belief systems.

Reasonable, critical-thinking adults tend to believe that when an idea doesn't work, or worse, when it leads to very negative consequences, those who promote the idea will eventually admit their mistake and correct their course of action. But what tends to happen in religion is the opposite. A good example is the 19th-century Millerites (followers of William Miller) who predicted the end of the world on March 21, 1843. When it didn't occur, they concluded that their calculations were just off a bit, and they revised their prediction to March 21, 1844, and when that didn't occur, to Oct 22, 1844.[1095] Dubbed "The Great Disappointment," it was yet another speculative prophecy that never materialized.

Unfortunately, religion is self-perpetuating as it is enforced by family and in some cases by the local community, as with religious summer camps and Sunday schools. Being taught to suppress critical thinking begins early for most religious Fundamentalists. Indeed, indoctrination can be a major roadblock to critical thinking. When an individual is constantly fed a one-sided view on things such as theological beliefs, it stifles critical thinking. The combination of aggressive indoctrination along with the brain's vulnerability to believing unsupported facts can create extreme gullibility, a trait that previously might not have existed. Due to the brain's neuroplasticity, or ability to be sculpted by lived experiences, religious Fundamentalists (and this includes Fundamentalists of all religions) become hardwired to accept and to believe far-fetched statements.[1096]

Education involves a review of facts and learning about what is true and what is not true. Whereas indoctrination is aimed at influencing people to believe in a given tale without the benefit of any evidence, based on the opinions of the group or teacher. Belief in anything that has no credible evidence is harmful. In general, religions promote beliefs in something or someone that offer no evidentiary support for their claims. It is only through reason and evidence that we can determine which claims are likely true and which are likely false. But if you believe a claim based on something other than evidence and solid logic, then it can create a false premise or delusion. Believing things on the basis of anything other than evidence and critical thinking causes people to misconstrue what's true and what is in their best interests. Religion establishes the habit of believing implausible ideas based on superstitious myths, which helps facilitate the rejection of scientific truths, such as evolution and global climate change. Organized religion is the perpetrator of false comforts, and it works diligently to relieve us of responsibility for our own actions.

This rewiring of one's brain begins when children are first taught to accept Biblical stories as objective truths, rather than as metaphors for living life practically. Mystical explanations train young minds to readily accept biblical stories and not demand evidence for supernatural beliefs. Thus, the neural pathways that promote healthy skepticism and rational thought are not properly developed.[1097] And the brain structures that support critical thinking and logical reasoning don't fully mature. This inevitably leads to a greater susceptibility to lies and gaslighting[1098] by manipulative people in their lives, including religious leaders and government politicians. Religion can encourage and enforce a style of thinking that compels its adherents to accept irrational claims. And that is the biggest issue with religion: belief in outrageous claims sometimes prevents us from thinking critically and using our brains. Indeed, a research study reported by *Medical News Today* found that "religion activates the same reward-processing brain circuits as sex, drugs, and other addictive activities."[1099]

When adults realize that there is no evidence to support the religious beliefs acquired as a child, they often continue with their general beliefs because they don't want to discard the immortality of the eternal life they were promised. Giving up one's rational thought to accept a concept of everlasting life without any evidence whatsoever that eternal life exists is what makes this proposition such a "sophisticated form of mind control." [1100]

The Mythology of Christianity

Most people have beliefs that reflect their indoctrination as children, as religions permeate our culture. In addition to some religious education at home, they may have been sent to churches/temples/mosques for specific religious indoctrination, or to parochial schools that teach religion as part of their curriculum. Indeed, many of us were nurtured into a particular religion, without realizing that we were not given a choice. Most individuals will never question their parents' choices, because they have been irreversibly imprinted. And most of us generally agree that parents have a right to determine the education of their children. Therefore, early religious indoctrination is seldom discussed. But this is not about vilifying religious indoctrination, and certainly not meant as an attack on religious schools or religious families. The issue is what is being taught – the unsubstantiated religious content, which is positioned as the factual truth.

Public schools should be a venue for education, not indoctrination. Religion has no place in our public schools, from the "under God" in our Pledge of Allegiance to the Ten Commandments to other forced religious observances. Teaching children to seek evidence and base their beliefs on facts rather than faith helps develop a rational mindset. Additionally, this approach will prepare young minds for real-world problem-solving, where evidence-based decisions are expected. It also helps in distinguishing between reliable and unreliable sources of information.

> *"Religion is an illusion that humans created as a form of wish fulfillment"*
> *– Sigmund Freud*

Cognitive Biases

There are several cognitive biases that affect our ability for rational thought. For example, the Dunning-Kruger effect is a bias in which people wrongly overestimate their knowledge or ability in a specific area.[1101] This troublesome cognitive bias facilitates manipulative people to deliver unchallenged falsehoods to poorly educated, non-skeptical people. In many cases, not only are these individuals uninformed, but they are unlikely to seek new information on their own. This bias occurs when people lack information to know they don't have enough knowledge. Said differently, the problem isn't just that they are misinformed; it's that they are completely unaware that they might be deceived. This simple but befuddling concept has been demonstrated dozens of times in well-controlled psychology studies and in a variety of contexts.[1102]

Generally, humans can rationally process information when they can give equal weight to multiple viewpoints. On the other hand, many people are often unable to process information in a rational, unbiased manner once they have developed an opinion about an issue.[1103] Therefore, people have a built-in tendency to accept information that is consistent with their existing beliefs, confirming what they already believe, even if it is illogical. This is what psychologists refer to as a confirmation bias. So, individuals who have this bias, and many of us do, tend to focus on evidence or other information which supports their views, while giving little weight to evidence or information that is contrary to their beliefs. Or in the absence of evidence, such as with religion, the individual tends to fall back on his or her own pre-existing beliefs. Thus, a person with a confirmation bias favors information that confirms or at least doesn't challenge his/her previously existing views; and so he/she only seeks information that confirms those views or discredits information that doesn't support them.[1104] Confirmation bias may lead people to cling strongly to false beliefs.

Researchers at Ohio State University, Johns Hopkins University, and Stanford recently uncovered a phenomenon they termed "illusion of information adequacy," whereby people make what they consider an informed decision without considering that there might be additional information crucial to that decision. Similar to the Dunning-Krueger effect, this phenomenon occurs with people who have limited and inadequate information that aligns; and they overestimate their ability to render a decision without looking for additional input.[1105]

Cognitive dissonance is another bias that affects everyone at some point. It occurs when a person holds two related, but contradictory, cognitions or thoughts. The term was coined by psychologist Leon Festinger, who developed the concept in 1957.[1106] An example would be someone who wishes to protect others and believes a given pandemic is real (e.g., Covid-19), and thus wants to wear a face mask in public; but that same person might be asked not to wear the face mask at church services because his/her pastor has declared that God will protect his parishioners, and has banned masks during services. Holding such conflicting values and beliefs generally leads to mental discomfort and unpleasant feelings of unease.

Religious fundamentalism correlates to what some neuroscientists refer to as "magical thinking," which occurs when someone makes connections among actions and events when no such connection actually exists. Religious fundamentalism promotes a much greater reliance on intuitive thinking than upon analytical thought.[1107] The former leads to incorrect assumptions; for example, religious fundamentalism is linked to science denial. Since science provides a method to determine truth through empirical measurement and hypothesis testing, science denial is commensurate with the denial of objective truth and its tangible evidence. Thus, religious fundamentalism promotes faulty thinking while it discourages its adherents from exposure to different ideas.[1108] In that way, the Fundamentalist ideology controls the reasoning processes of its followers.

This kind of mindset encouraged by religion is a dangerous thing – basically, it is belief over evidence, even when that evidence offers unquestionable authority. It can create a group identity which often denigrates people outside the group. It motivates people to action, but sometimes these actions can have terrible consequences. Additionally, the truth matters, and far-fetched religious tales without evidence are basically deception.

Cognitive biases such as the Dunning-Kruger effect, confirmation bias, the illusion of information adequacy, and cognitive dissonance all contribute to the way we distort reality to fit our existing beliefs. We are wired with many different cognitive biases that make it difficult to separate perception from reality.[1109] Psychologists have proven that people can convince themselves of almost anything, but most of us understand that believing something doesn't make it true. Reality exists independent of one's thoughts or beliefs. When people cling to their subjective opinions over objective facts, they often make decisions that harm themselves or others.

There is an unfortunate disconnect in our world between provable facts and superstitious beliefs. Since faith is a belief without benefit of evidence, reliance on faith can erode our critical faculties. We humans need to think critically about every claim, and practice skepticism daily. We live in a society built on technology, yet many of our fellow citizens do not understand it.

So, when the facts do not align with personal beliefs, people sometimes distort reality to fit their existing beliefs. Belief in the creation story of Genesis does not negate the reality of evolution. And even though some people think it is a hoax, climate change is a scientifically-proven phenomenon supported by overwhelming data. In the latter case, no matter how strong one's disbelief, it does not negate the fact that the planet is warming, nor does it stop the potential consequences from unfolding.

Examining One's Own Belief System

It should come as no surprise that the best predictor of one's religion is one's childhood geography and one's parentage. People tend to follow the religion of their parents, and unsurprisingly, that particular religion is the very one that people believe is the true, correct one! Please forgive the generalization, but when you think of religion in India, you tend to think of the Hindus[1110] (996 million Hindus), even though the same country has over 200 million Muslims. When you think of religion in Indonesia (242 million Muslims) or Pakistan (240 million Muslims),[1111] then you think of the Muslim communities; and the prevailing religion in the USA is Christianity (216 million) or 62% of the 2024 population. So, where you live and the religion of your parents significantly influence what religion you adopt.

As mentioned in Chapter 1, anthropologists estimate that over the last ten millennia, humans have worshipped approximately 18,000 different gods, goddesses, animal spirits, and things (e.g., the sun)?[1112] What is the probability that your religion is right and everyone else's religion is wrong? And yet, most of the world's major religions assume that their views are the absolute truth, even when faced with irrefutable evidence disproving at least some of the rationalities of their beliefs.

As author Dan Barker stated in his book, Godless, "Most people suspend rationality when they examine their own belief system, but they are quick to analyze holes in other belief systems."[1113] For example, did Christians or Muslims do a thorough examination of the Vedas before they rejected Hinduism? Generally, they did not. Are Hindus and Christians well-versed in the Koran? Again, generally, they are not. Is it just easier to think that the other religions are somehow false? When Christians do take the effort to read and examine the Koran, they quickly discern some issues, but they have difficulty turning the same lens of scrutiny onto their own religion.

When you meet a non-theist, do you assume that he or she lacks morals? Or that he or she has some sinister worldview? Actually, atheists simply do not believe in a god; it is the absence of theism. It is not a belief system, and there is no atheist worldview. Non- theists are as moral or as immoral as anyone else. On the other hand, theism is a belief system. Indeed, most people are atheists with regard to a given religion that they do not accept. I believe that it is fair to say that Muslims do not believe in Hinduism; and thus, they are atheistic to that religion; and Hindus do not accept the god of Christianity, and vice versa.

Religious Fundamentalism has characteristics that have been around for at least as long as religion itself. Desiderius Erasmus (1466 -1536), a Dutch Catholic theologian and philosopher, was a leading voice in the Humanist movement, whose written works contributed to the theological and cultural transformations of Europe. His critical approach to biblical scholarship and his promotion of tolerance and reform within the Christian tradition embodied anti-Fundamentalist teaching.[1114] He was highly skeptical of the human mind's ability to discern the truth because he was well aware of human tendencies to leap to conclusions, rule out competing evidence, and confirm prior beliefs.[1115]

We are what we are because we have been indoctrinated into a given religion, not because we chose our religion after a comprehensive analysis of all religions. But perhaps as a critically thinking adult, it is time to perform an analysis to determine if you are on the right path, or are you mindlessly repeating what has been drilled into you? For example, it is difficult for the stories in Genesis to lead to a beneficial interpretation if they are assumed to be the truth and not a teaching allegory. And by insisting that an obviously fabricated story is the inerrant truth, then mankind's search for truth becomes a mirage.

Terror-Management Theory

The fear of death is a major influence on many human behaviors and beliefs. Our existential dread drives us to latch onto beliefs that connect us to something greater than our mortal selves. For physicists, grappling with the implications of quantum mechanics and the potential for an observer-dependent reality can be unsettling at times, but also comforting. Consciously influencing how our universe is viewed by others can provide a sense of purpose and continuity beyond physical death. Similarly, those in the healthcare community can reflect on how they improve and save lives. However, the occupations of most people lack a sense of greater societal purpose; and they live without a clear legacy that will live on after them.

Terror Management Theory (TMT) is a psychological theory that explores how humans cope with their fear of mortality. It suggests that our awareness of death shapes our cultural beliefs, values, and behaviors. TMT posits that people strive to maintain their self-esteem and subscribe to cultural perspectives to minimize existential terror related to their own mortality.[1116] The theory suggests that existential terror is one reason why we adopt cultural ideologies, such as religion. Indeed, some of us tend to rally around those who share our religious beliefs. To mitigate fear, some people cling to philosophies that give their lives meaning and direction in a chaotic world.[1117] Terror management theory is particularly relevant to current political events because it provides a scientific explanation for tribalism, especially in the USA (e.g., MAGA faithful vs. progressives).

Terror Management Theory proposes that humans manage the fear of their own deaths by adhering to their beliefs in religion, which give meaning, purpose, and value to their lives; and it offers a small measure of immortality. According to terror management theory, individuals may manage their fear by seeking symbolic immortality through cultural beliefs, conforming to societal values, and constructing meaning in their lives. Terror management fuels the belief in an immortal soul, and it motivates religious faith. Similarly, the awareness of death fuels faith in supernatural immortality (e.g., afterlife), supporting beliefs about a supernatural god and spirits, and promoting social behaviors designed to bolster and protect the perceived legitimacy of such religious beliefs.[1118]

It was this fear that enabled the conversion of Christians in the first two centuries. Christianity offered something that no other religion in the Mediterranean basin had offered: an afterlife. At that time, the Jewish faith did not promote a heavenly eternity for everyone. In spite of their many religions, the Romans had no concept of life forever continuing after death. Even the Egyptians only suggested that some chosen few could attain the afterlife, as it was not universally attainable for all.[1119] Of course, the Christian leadership was selling a product that they didn't have, and certainly one for which couldn't provide real evidence. A part of the afterlife motif of religion is the faulty notion that you are meant to suffer in this life, to demonstrate your worthiness for the next life.[1120] Selling a potentially much better deal in the next life is how organized religions get you to need them.

Europe's nationalist surge, the United Kingdom's Brexit, and the USA's Trumpism are just the most recent manifestations of TMT, which was first proposed by social psychologists in the 1980s and derived from cultural anthropologist Ernest Becker's *The Denial of Death* (1973).[1121] Becker believed that many human actions are motivated by a fear of death. The awareness of humans regarding the inevitability of their own death produces a high level of cognitive dissonance which results in terror. Not only do death reminders increase one's focus on nationalism and religion, but they may also influence voting habits in favor of more conservative presidential candidates.[1122] By emphasizing existential threats, a candidate may create a psychological condition that makes the brain respond positively to him, rather than negatively to his divisive rhetoric.[1123]

The Fear of End Times

An extension of the fear of death for many Christians is the unnatural fear of the 'end times'. This is another control mechanism used by some religious leaders to manage and sway their congregations. All these prophecies of war, pestilence, and famine are just regurgitations of the human experience, through which our species has already undergone and persevered. It is hard to imagine an era worse than the Black Death (bubonic plague) that struck medieval Europe from 1347 to 1352, killing an estimated 30 - 50 million people.[1124] With medical science, we should be better prepared for such pandemics. Hopefully, we humans have grown in our understanding, and we will not resort to blaming others as when Christians blamed the Jews for the spread of the Black Death, whereby a wave of violent riots ensued, and "entire Jewish communities were killed by mobs or burned at the stake en masse." [1125]

For some religious believers, we are currently living in what could be called a set of end-time fables. When they were indoctrinated, they probably didn't realize that many previous generations had been similarly indoctrinated. And all the other end-of-time predictions never happened. Yet the story perpetuates itself because it is in the interest of some religious leaders for that to happen. If our world does explode in fire and agony, it will probably be due to humans destroying themselves via misplaced hatred.

Mental health professionals are cognizant of "rapture anxiety," a type of religious trauma which can lead to high anxiety, depression, and paranoia, because any minute you could be left here on earth. The concept of rapture is an eschatological position held by some Christians regarding an end-time event when all dead Christian believers will be resurrected, joined with Christians who are still alive, and together will rise "in the clouds."[1126] It is known theologically as dispensational[1127] pre-millennialism, and is not prevalent in mainline Protestant or Catholic denominations, but it is found in some evangelical and most Fundamentalist Christian Churches. The term, *rapture*, is found nowhere in the Bible; its theology dates from the 1800s. Much of the focus on the end of times comes from the Book of Revelation, which was discussed in Chapter 4, and was about the Roman Empire and has nothing to do with the modern world.

The Theory of Stupidity

Dietrich Bonhoeffer, a German Lutheran neo-orthodox theologian and anti-Nazi dissident, wrote the following words just prior to his arrest in Nazi Germany in 1943:

> "Against stupidity, we have no defense. Neither protests nor force can touch it. Reasoning is of no use. Facts that contradict personal prejudices can simply be disbelieved — indeed, the fool can counter by criticizing them, and if they are undeniable, they can just be pushed aside as trivial exceptions. So the fool, as distinct from the scoundrel, is completely self-satisfied. In fact, they can easily become dangerous, as it does not take much to make them aggressive. For that reason, greater caution is called for than with a malicious one." [1128]

Bonhoeffer was executed by the Nazis in April 1945. His views have been recorded as the 'theory of stupidity.' He wrote: "To prevent willful malice, you can always erect barriers to stop its spread. Against stupidity, you are defenseless."[1129] He identified that herd behavior is among the pre-eminent causes of stupidity. Numerous scientific studies have shown how individual humans can be swayed by the crowd to adopt positions which go against all logic, and often, they are contrary to their own self-interests. For Bonhoeffer, stupidity was not the problem of the individual. Instead, it was a matter of many individuals in a mob mentality. As stated by author Peter Burns, "madness finds its force in crowds.[1130]

The point to the theory of stupidity is that often people do not use their critical-thinking skills. They react negatively to things they do not understand, or to evidence that is contrary to what they believe. They may act without considering the consequences of their actions; or they may lack the prerequisite foresight to make prudent decisions. A stupid person lives in absolute certainty that he is correct in his religious worldview, and such people often make impulse decisions because they lack the skills to consider alternatives.

Objective Morality

> *"One of the greatest tragedies in mankind's entire history may be that morality was hijacked by religion."*
> – Arthus C. Clarke

First, let's define terms. Objective morality is the idea that right and wrong exist factually, without placing any importance on context or opinion. The most common argument favoring objective morality relies on a view through the lens of a deity. This argument relies on the teachings of religious texts including the New Testament, Tanakh, and Quran, all of which have many passages about right and wrong. For instance, people who practice Christianity may believe the Bible labels certain actions as "sins."[1131] They believe that the

Bible sets up a morality for everyone to follow, and without it, we would be spiritually rudderless. If God is dead, is everything permitted? They wonder how we can possibly have morality without a deity?

However, religion should <u>not</u> dictate our ethics or morality, as it is not the ultimate measure of truth. Look back at the 100,000 years before Christianity. There were many known civilizations, and not one of them condoned murder, rape, stealing, and lying. Part of our secular cooperation in past societies was to forbid evil activities. We do not refrain from immoral conduct as a society because we fear some invisible deity. We do it because in our society, we know it is the right thing to do. Contrary to the views of some, people are basically good, moral beings. Human solidarity demands that we look upon each other as brothers and sisters. We must cooperate and secularly forbid evil activities such as murder. We are dependent on one another; and we have expectations of each other.

The key components of human morality, which include fairness, empathy, and kindness, are dependent not on rational thought, nor unique to human nature. Instead, those attributes have evolved as impulses in multiple mammalian groups, including humans, to further cooperation and survival.[1132] Primatologist Frans de Waal has presented decades of research to show how bonobos look after disadvantaged members of their groups, care for their elderly, and peacefully settle disputes.[1133] These are traits found in multiple mammal species. Animals do not consult a rule book of ethics any more than humans. Morality is not some thin covering over an unpleasant and troublesome human nature; rather, it is our natural inclination to do right to others.

And if we want to compare secular morality to a religious one, then look at the Judeo-Christian Bible. It is a foolish notion to think that such a book prescribes morality. There are many biblical directives to do evil, including murder, rape, enslavement, and torture. The Bible doesn't have a strong grasp of ethics. It is a hollow argument that the reason we don't kill, steal, and rape is because we fear a god's punishment! A deity does not necessarily imply accountability. The threat of damnation is a phony morality. We don't require a celestial master to establish our morality. What a profound insult to all humans! Religion does not dictate our ethics or our morality. The Bible, especially the Old Testament, is hardly an appropriate source for today's morality. If one actually reads the Judeo-Christian Bible, then that person would have to re-examine his/her beliefs, as many of the texts would embarrass and repulse most good men and women, such as the following passage:

Psalm 137:9 is an example: "Happy shall be he that dashes little ones against stones" [really?]

Morality implies avoiding or minimizing harm; yet the Bible runs rampant with horrors, such as **Psalm 137:9.** This is not a suggestion here of unfortunate collateral damage during wartime; but it is saying that believers should rejoice in directly killing innocent babies (even if they are offspring of an enemy group). The Old Testament's Yahweh was positioned by Iron-Age writers to appear to be a mass murderer. The greatest evils of the world have been committed in the name of a god. Hinduism, Judaism, Christianity, and Islam all have multiple instances where atrocities were committed in the name of their respective deities. Of course, evil has occurred outside of religious influence in the secular world, but not to the same extent.

So, to answer the question, does morality flow from religion? Clearly, it does not. We do not need to depend on any deity in order to cooperate with and help one another. How did Cro-Magnons survive as a species and outlast other primates 40,000 years ago? Neanderthals were stronger and had larger brains, but Cro-Magnons worked together in organized teams and effectively outcompeted them through their organizational efforts.[1134]

Atheism's lack of a divinely mandated moral code is one basis for theistic criticisms. But the Judeo-Christian Bible does not provide absolute moral guidance. As stated by Dan Barker, "human values are not absolute; they are relative to the human need."[1135] And in The God Delusion, author Richard Dawkins underscores clearly how the behavior and values that are presented as exemplary in the Bible would, in many cases, be reprehensible by current moral standards. The Bible does not give us any definitive moral values; for if it did, why cannot the various Christian denominations agree on what those values are? Non-theists often base their morals on reason, empathy, and what's good for people and society. They find meaning and fulfillment in living a life based on their own moral and ethical values, not requiring the promise of afterlife rewards to guide them. Most non-theists believe in being kind and helping others. You don't need to believe in a god to be a good person.

Is there any truth to the theist stereotype that suggests that atheists are untrustworthy and lack a moral compass? Do atheists care less, or at least think differently about morality than religious people do? In a new study from the University of Illinois-Chicago, social psychologists looked into these questions based on what values people view as relevant for morality, as well as what moral principles they rely on when making a moral judgment. It also explored potential differences in moral values among religious believers and disbelievers. Tomas Ståhl, UIC assistant professor of psychology, examined the matter in two large-scale, cross-national surveys comparing Americans and Swedes, in addition to two smaller U.S. surveys.[1136]

Stahl found religious disbelievers' views about morality were comparable in the U.S., a highly religious country by Western standards, and Sweden, one of the most secular countries in the world. Religious believers' views about morality were also similar across the two countries. "In both the U.S. and Sweden, people who do not believe in God have similarly strong moral concerns as religious believers about not harming vulnerable individuals, and about fairness," Ståhl said.[1137]

Slavery is another moral topic that underscores that the gospels were written by humans who were locked into the 1st and 2nd century culture; they couldn't conceive that there was anything wrong with slavery. Nor did Jesus speak out against slavery. Christians today point with pride that many Northern abolitionists of the 19th century were Christians. And that is to their credit! The militant abolitionists wanted their churches to condemn slavery as an extraordinary sin that infected every aspect of life and created an insurmountable barrier to personal and national salvation. Although that creed gradually gained numerous adherents, it remained a minority doctrine even within the Northern churches. Meanwhile, during that same time period in the same country, Southern pulpits were laden with preachers who used the Bible passages to strongly support slavery.

Slavery was just part of the natural order, according to some biblical writers. The very thought that the Bible prescribes a steady morality doesn't hold up to logic or 21st-century ethics. There are many specific biblical injunctions to do evil. Even though the New Testament is far more benign than the Old Testament, you still have to selectively choose the good passages and downplay the bad. In **Romans 14:11,** the master/slave relationship is ingrained in the Judeo-Christian world. And in **Ephesians 6:5,** Paul tells us that the Christ condones slavery: "Slaves, be obedient to those who are your master… with fear and trembling, in singleness of your heart as onto Christ."

Some of the greatest evils that have occurred took place in the name of religion. As Adolf Hitler, a Roman Catholic, stated in his manifesto, Mein Kampf, "Hence today I believe that I am acting in accordance with the will of the Almighty Creator: by defending myself against the Jew, I am fighting for the work of the Lord."[1138]

Judaism, Islam, Hinduism and Christianity all have negative episodes in their respective history. It is not hard to think of examples, both recent and ancient, where atrocities were committed. But you can name a single atrocity committed in the name of atheism? Conversely, can you name anything of goodness or value that came from Christianity, Judaism, or Islam, which a member of another religion or an atheist cannot duplicate? Of course, some atrocities have occurred by non-religious, secular forces, but that was driven by evil men, and not by atheism. As a species, we must emancipate ourselves from the spiritual shackles of organized religion. Nowhere in the Bible is there any mention of inalienable rights. When theists want to understand those rights, they point to Jefferson, Locke, or Paine, but never the Bible.[1139]

> *"Wherever morality is based on theology, wherever right is made dependent on divine authority, the most immoral, unjust, infamous things can be justified and established."*
> — **Ludwig Feuerbach (1804 – 1872), German Anthropologist and Philosopher, The Essence of Christianity**

> *"Atheism is a non-prophet organization."*
> – **George Carlin**

Christian Nationalism

Christian nationalists believe the United States was founded as a Christian nation and that the government should maintain this religious identity.[1140] Their core belief is that the destiny of the United States is coupled to their version of Christianity, and they believe that their quest for political power is divinely inspired. This belief system is deeply imbricated with increased distrust in government programs and susceptibility to conspiracy theories. Christian nationalists are demanding unwarranted influence in the U.S. government, our culture, and our society. Indeed, Christian nationalists seek a reformation of the United States[1141] into what they perceive as a country based on Christian principles, and which should be governed accordingly by Christian leaders (and preferably white Christian leaders). It is a deliberate intertwining of religious identity with political identity to the detriment of all.

Religious belief and practice have grown increasingly partisan in recent decades, indicating that an individual's religious beliefs exert a strong influence on their political choices. Christian nationalism is an interrelated set of convictions that intertwine "ideas about

American history, triumph, the providential acquisition of land, moral order, divinely ordained boundaries, loss, and persecution."[1142] It emphasizes "Christian values and principles." But what are the values and principles of the Christian sect(s)? The divisive nature of Christian nationalism fundamentally opposes inclusivity and acceptance as preached by Jesus of Nazareth. In short, Christian nationalism distorts both American and Christian values

Christian nationalists seem to be adrift from their Christian faith's historic teachings and practices. Some conservative Christians are ignorant of history and of the historical past of their religion, in particular. They are out of step with the teachings of Christianity. They tend to focus on a pending apocalypse (the 'end of times'), and they encourage political domination. Indeed, Christian nationalists seem to be completely disassociated from accountability for their actions as they careen toward their misinterpreted version of Christian eschatology.[1143]

Organizations that analyze elections and voter choice generally assume that voters maximize the probability of a desired outcome by making a series of rational judgments that compare what the voter wants to what each candidate promises. That has been seen as the logical process for free elections. This encompasses civic duty, social responsibility, and personal empowerment as part of a rational voting process. But in the polarized political system of the 2020s, some Americans voted for a candidate that favored one or two issues important to them, while ignoring everything else. If a person's religious leader voices their support for a particular candidate, who perhaps is anti-abortion, then their followers may feel pressured to support that candidate, even though that same candidate, if elected, may work against the interests of those individual voters in other areas.

In 2024, many U S Christians voted for candidates who favored anti-abortion, anti-gay, and anti-immigrant policies. These voters did not vote regarding what was best for the national economy, education, national defense, public works, or maintaining programs that were important to them personally (e.g., Medicaid, Medicare, USAID, etc.). They couldn't see past their religious agenda. Now, as they lose key benefits, even their jobs, dealing with high prices caused by unnecessary tariffs, or see programs in which they had been positively invested, reduced or discarded, they wonder what went wrong.

In 2021, Texas passed a law requiring public schools to display donated "In God We Trust" posters. In 2023, Texas lawmakers approved unlicensed religious chaplains to counsel students. In 2025, the Republican-controlled state has been trying to mandate the Ten Commandments be displayed in every classroom, which is a proposal modeled after a Louisiana law that was blocked in federal court. A decade ago, Southern Methodist University religious studies professor, Mark Chancey documented that Bible classes in Texas public schools were being taught from a Fundamentalist viewpoint with materials "designed to evangelize rather than provide an objective study of the Bible's influence."[1144] It is a constitutional violation for a state government to employ public schools to indoctrinate students into one particular faith, or one version of a given belief system. This also is in variance to the concept of parental rights, and this indoctrination is a form of child abuse. Finally, it must be repeated that American law is based on the secular Constitution, not the Bible.

Christian nationalism now poses an actual threat to American democracy itself, as it strives to contort religion into a tool of power and weaponize the Bible. In spite of approximately 2,000 biblical passages that refer to protecting the vulnerable and calling for an accounting upon those of wealth and power who cause suffering, some self-righteous Christians are trying to twist these passages for their own self-serving interests.

Whenever I hear about U S Christian nationalism, I wonder what Rabbi Yeshua would think about a country of over 350 million fortunate Americans who have such great resources and so many freedoms; but who tend to ignore the plight of the poor, the disenfranchised, and marginalized, the suffering of animals, and the needs of newly arrived foreigners whose dream is just to come to the United States and live peacefully. The Christian nationalist extremists want nothing less than a reformation of the United States, whereby the US Government declares the United States a Christian nation with laws based on "Christian values," which probably will not include tolerance, compassion, and kindness to strangers.

Anti-Abortion

Through the overthrow of Roe v. Wade in 2021, the conservative-leaning U S Supreme Court positioned abortion as one of America's most polarizing issues; and it shifted the responsibility for abortion rights to individual states. As a result, Republican-controlled state legislatures have accelerated their efforts to criminalize abortions. However, the right to an abortion appears to be protected by the 13th Amendment's abolition of involuntary servitude.[1145] [1146] This Amendment has been used in legal arguments against child labor, human trafficking, and compulsory military service. Forcing women to have a baby they do not want is very similar. Some states banned abortion procedures after six weeks,[1147] even though many women don't even know that they are pregnant in that brief time span. The fear of criminal prosecution has led doctors to hesitate to end life-endangering pregnancies, in spite of the medical dangers to the women.

Many women who need abortions are young, poor, isolated, and terrified, and some are the victims of rape. Rather than criminalize women who want an abortion, state governments might consider passing laws that financially support families, such as with the child tax credits that some in Congress couldn't wait to end. Unfortunately, many conservative Christians are so focused on this single issue that they find it quite difficult to consider the rights of the women they are condemning. Yet the Bible doesn't condemn abortion. Not once. One has to wonder from where the conservative Christians are drawing their arguments.

In the U.S., opposition to reproductive freedoms comes mainly from ultra-conservative Christians, with most Americans supporting abortion access and other reproductive needs. In fact, only 36% of Americans support a total ban on abortion.[1148] But the religious beliefs of the ultra-conservative Christians, more than any other group, are shaping societal attitudes toward reproductive rights. It is within this group of Christians that the pro-life agenda resonates so strongly; this belief not only denies an individual woman her personal rights but also has a severe impact on her reproductive health.

In 2024, Alabama's Supreme Court declared that embryos created through in vitro fertilization (IVF) were children, and therefore IVF procedures were subject to the state's

273

abortion ban and denied. The basic premise underlying the Alabama decision seemed contradictory; after all, shouldn't anti-abortion activists support people who want to have babies?[1149] Indeed, the anti-abortion movement claims to be all about support for motherhood.

Much of the current furor over fertility treatments has its origin in a Vatican teaching of the Catholic Church, which prohibited Catholics from using the then-nascent technique of IVF. The 1987 Vatican document, *Donum Vitae,* established a moral framework with regard to IVF. It said that "the gift of human life must be actualized in marriage through the specific and exclusive acts of husband and wife, in accordance with the laws inscribed in their persons and in their union."[1150] In other words, IVF separates the marital act from procreation, and the RCC felt that it was morally wrong. At that time, most Protestant sects had initially disagreed with the Catholic Church. However, in recent years, that has abruptly changed. For example, in June 2024, the Southern Baptist Convention voted to formally oppose IVF.[1151]

One motivation for this hostility to IVF appears to be homophobia. Even though IVF has helped many childless, heterosexual couples, it is the perception of some conservative Christians that assisted reproduction is a threat to traditional family structures, largely because the techniques can help LGBTQ people form families. Indeed, it is a growing perception among these judgmental busybodies that IVF is a tool that can be readily used by lesbians.[1152] Well, God forbid!

Anti-Homosexuality

Despite many efforts to compel Christian Churches to take a more inclusive approach towards gender and sexuality, they are often rebuffed by conservatives. The Old Testament has a few rebukes against same-sex relationships, but as stated several times, it was written in an age of cruelty and ignorance. The New Testament has been less vocal in its comments on same-sex relationships. Indeed, Jesus never mentioned homosexuals or transgender people, nor did anyone else in the New Testament, except Paul. It was Paul who focused on sexual morality, as he did in the following two epistles:

- **1 Corinthian 6:9-10** "Know ye not that the unrighteous shall not inherit the kingdom of God? Be not deceived; neither fornicators, nor idolaters, nor adulterers, nor effeminate, nor abusers of themselves with mankind, nor thieves, nor covetous, nor drunkards, nor revilers, nor extortioners, shall inherit the kingdom of God."
- **Romans 1:26-27** "For this cause God gave them up unto vile affections: for even their women did change the natural use into that which is against nature: and likewise also the men, leaving the natural use of the woman, burned in their lust one toward another; men with men working that which is unseemly, and receiving in themselves that recompense of their error…"

First, let's be honest about the ambiguity of these passages, especially in 1 Corinthians. Paul is not exactly specific about what he is railing against. Second, Paul condemns same-sex lust, not love. Like other ancient writers, Paul described same-sex behavior as excessive sexual desire on the part of people who could be content with opposite-sex relationships. I don't know any gay men or women who would be content with an exclusively heterosexual relationship (any more than heterosexuals would be content with gay relationships). Paul probably didn't have long-term, loving, same-sex relationships in mind, nor would he have understood such relationships. While he did describe same-sex behavior as "unnatural," Paul is the same person who said men having long hair goes against nature. Most Christians have read that as a reference to cultural conventions.[1153] And finally, homosexuality is not a chosen, changeable identity; it is how some people were made. That is a 20th-century fact wholly unknown to anyone in Paul's day, nor in earlier times in which the Old Testament was written. Christians of the 21st century have no excuse for treating the LGBTQ community as anything other than fellow human beings. If conservative Christians need to blame someone for creating humans with a homosexual identity, then they need to blame their God.

It is conservative Christians who are cherry-picking not only what to read in their Scripture, but also which items to follow. After all, Paul also admonished the fornicators, adulterers, thieves, drunkards, and extortioners as well; but the Christian conservatives tend to overlook those other categories (perhaps it is hitting a little close to home), and instead they concentrate on the LGBTQ community. The way that many Christians cherry-pick and use some of these biblical verses is actually an abuse of Christian Scripture.

The Bible is not a weapon to be twisted into various forms to satisfy pre-existing social and political ways of thinking. The obsession over homosexuality among conservative Christians is quite strange, especially in that there are probably a mere five or six mentions of what can loosely be described as homosexuality in the entire Bible.[1154] That said, there is a growing array of evangelical pastors In the United States speaking out in favor of full acceptance of LGBTQ+ people and their relationships, although it is within the confines of traditional, monogamous, and lifelong marriage.[1155]

Anti-Immigration

Christian nationalism is inversely related to pro-immigrant views.[1156] And according to multiple surveys, most Americans disapprove of Trump's immigration policy. Biblical passages in the New Testament encourage Christian believers to welcome strangers. The Bible (both Old and New Testaments) is unambiguous regarding the treatment of immigrants. **Matthew 25: 34 – 46** provides specific guidance on how to treat the suffering and marginalized people who come to our borders, many of them desperate. There is a strong Christian precedent for demonstrating a compassionate approach to immigration and to help the tired, the poor, and the sick. Conservative Christians are supposed to honor the Bible and its Scripture. You would think that Christians would be at the forefront of the acceptance of new immigrants, based on their biblical guidance. However, more than any other religious demographic, that is not the case.

One has to ask, why do so many conservative Christians embrace the MAGA rhetoric on immigration? Many Christians want to believe that America is a Christian nation, but actually we are a secular nation with a pluralistic society. Further, most Christians are aware that the percentage of Christian Americans continues to drop each decade. And ironically, most immigrants coming across the border are Christians. However, the conservative Christians who bemoan the loss of their majority, as we move resolutely and immutably toward a more secular society, have consistently supported Trump's draconian policies on immigration and refugees. Indeed, 68 percent of white evangelicals say America has no responsibility to house refugees.[1157] The hypocrisy is striking! As stated by writer John Fea, "Evangelical American Christian nationalists will talk about spreading the gospel around the world, but God forbid if their converts who accept Jesus as savior try to come here." [1158]

Not all Christian groups adhere to the MAGA religious hypocrisy with their delusion of an imagined past. As of March 2025, 27 religious groups have sued the Trump administration for infringement on their religious liberty "to honor and worship God through love and support of their immigrant neighbors."[1159] Their legal counsel, Kelsi Corkran, is with the Georgetown University Law Center's Institute for Constitutional Advocacy and Protection. He stated that his clients feel that they have a religious obligation "to embrace and serve the refugees, asylum seekers, and immigrants in their midst..." [1160]

As stated by Duke Divinity School faculty member, Jay Augustine, "Because Christian nationalism is largely premised on the hierarchical nature of race, as a social construct, it is directly aligned with white supremacy. Christian nationalism is about the preservation of power that has historically belonged to white Protestants."[1161] Therefore, Christian nationalists have a very negative view of immigrants. Indeed, 81% of white Christian nationalists believe in the far-right conspiracy tale of the Great Replacement Theory[1162] (The inventive international plot to diminish the influence of and replace white people).[1163] As the United States becomes more diverse, the tolerance for that diversity has declined among those who believe that white, conservative Christians should be in charge.

Imagine escaping conflict, oppression, and various horrors in one's country to arrive at another country where many fellow Christians serve up similar attacks, such as placing people in indefinite detention and even forcibly separating children from their parents.

"The measure of the greatness of a society is found in the way it treats those most in need, those who have nothing apart from their poverty."
– Pope Francis

Challenging Religion in Society

Church pastors have joked for decades that a certain segment of people showed up to church primarily to be "hatched, matched, or dispatched." Today, there is a clear trend for the postponement of marriage, and young couples do not appear to be in any hurry to have children. So, 'matching' and 'hatching' demographics are not producing more Christians, and 'dispatching' (via death) is just removing the elderly Christians from the membership. Meanwhile, the sheer number of Christians who remain and fill the pews has been dropping significantly. Christianity is still the largest religion in the United States, but its numerical high of approximately 90% of the US population in the 1970s has declined to 73.7% by 2016, and 62% in 2024. The purpose of this section is to understand why that has occurred.

According to researchers, churches are closing at an alarming rate in the United States. Of course, there have been church closings every year, as well as new churches starting up. Back in 2014, *Lifeway Research* estimated 4,000 Protestant churches were "planted", while 3,700 closed – a modest net gain. But in 2019, 3,500 openings were more than offset by 5,000 closures.[1164] These statistics cover all churches. But the largest Protestant denomination, the Southern Baptist Convention (SBC), now has fewer churches to attract potential new members. In Lifeway Research's analysis of the 2022 Annual Church Profile of the Southern Baptist Convention, 1,253 congregations that were part of the Convention in 2021 were no longer connected in 2022. The loss of churches has been accompanied by a significant decline in church attendance as well as membership.[1165] About 40 million Americans have left churches and other religious institutions in the last 25 years.[1166]

The phenomenon of megachurches (those with 2,000 or more members) has undergone significant change as well. The megachurches originally grew at the expense of local neighborhood churches. Now that so many neighborhood churches are closing, and many of the megachurches have closed as well, the remaining 1,800 or so U.S. megachurches are moderately growing in membership.[1167] The decline in the number of megachurches began in the 2010s as the number of Boomers began aging out;[1168] And to some extent, it continues; but megachurches are all about innovation, and the decline should stabilize in the coming years.

Church congregations of most Christian denominations in the U.S. are dwindling, and churches are closing throughout the United States. While Covid-19 may have accelerated the decline, there is a much broader, long-running trend of people moving away from religion. A study by *Pew Research* found that the number of Americans who identified as Christian was 62% in 2024, with 29% of the US population being classed as "religiously unaffiliated". Approximately 7% of Americans identified with Judaism, Islam, Hinduism, and Buddhism. "Since the decade of the 1990s, a growing number

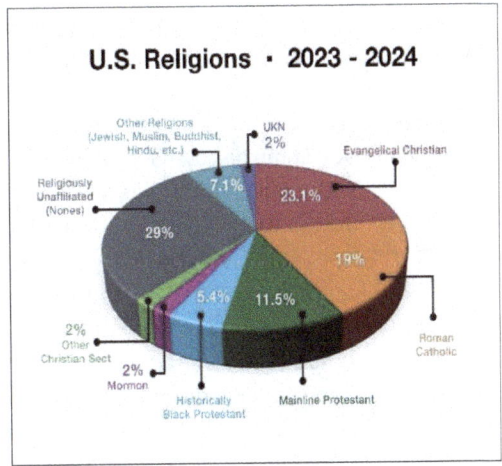

of Americans have left Christianity to join those who describe their religious identity as atheist, agnostic or 'nothing in particular'," [1169] – the Nones. The above illustration depicts a high-level decomposition of religion in the USA in 2024.

Moreover, people tend to be moving away from organized religion. Some people who still identify with a religious tradition are opting not to be members of a specific congregation. Indeed, only 60 percent of Americans who consider themselves religious are part of a congregation; that is down from 70 percent only a decade ago, according to researcher and pollster, *Gallup*.[1170]

Additionally, the age gap has widened significantly over the past several decades. Today, there are only insignificant differences between middle-aged Americans (age 50 – 64) and seniors; but there is a substantial gap between Americans over the age of 50 (15%) and those under the age of 50 (33%).[1171] There is an important dynamic underway in the U.S.: "nearly one in five (19%) Americans switched from their childhood religious identity to become unaffiliated as adults; and relatively few (3%) Americans who were raised unaffiliated are joining a religious tradition."[1172]

In all the scenarios identified by *Pew Research*, Christianity's share of the U.S. population is expected to decline. According to the report, "depending on whether religious switching continues at recent rates, speeds up, or stops entirely," *Pew Research* projections show Christians shrinking from 64% of Americans of all ages in 2020 to between 54% and 35% by 2070.[1173]

There is a plethora of reasons why Christianity is declining in the United States. One thing is clear: the US religious landscape is being reshaped, and that effort is accelerating. And it is rarely just one thing that causes someone to disaffiliate with their religion. Like most major decisions in life, there are usually multiple reasons that combine to guide a person to become a non-believer. Here are 15 key drivers for the faith decline and disaffiliation (in no particular order):

1. *Growing secularization.* Once people's basic needs, including knowledge, are met, and strong secular institutions are in place, there is less need for religion. And scientific advancements have accelerated the pace of secularization. As secularism strengthens, it encourages a societal shift towards values that emphasize individual liberties and equality, leading individuals to question the role of traditional religious institutions. The constant exposure to alternative viewpoints and the questioning promoted by social media can lead to doubts and reevaluation of one's faith. Moreover, some discover that a focus on such things as environmental causes, social justice, or personal growth is a far more fulfilling means to contribute to this world than participation in religious rituals. Some find their spirituality in nature or perhaps in acts of service to others. Their actions give them purpose.

2. *Politics of the Religious Right.* Religion has been weaponized throughout history, and today it is being used to support legislation that targets marginalized groups. MAGA and Trumpism have produced a backlash. As Christian militancy and Trumpism merge, younger moderate Christians are joining the ranks of the Nones. "An increasing number of Americans have an allergic reaction to the mixture of religion and conservative politics, including the MAGA movement," said David Campbell, a political scientist at Notre Dame University.[1174] Indeed, in surveys that ask why a former believer left their church, Trumpism was named as one of the top five reasons. Thus, Christianity is slowly declining as a tool to control the population.

3. *LGBTQ Intolerance and Bigotry* – It is about the acceptance of LGBTQ people and the behavior of other Christians toward them. Many people do not want to ignore the mistreatment of marginalized persons. That is not what their religion is about. Surprisingly, in a survey conducted by ex-Baptist Pastor Brandon Flanery, with 1,200 responses, 21.7% of respondents cited bigotry toward LGBTQ people as their primary reason for their disaffiliation.[1175] It is particularly offensive when conservative Christians in the 21st century display their ignorance by referring to same-sex relationships as 'a choice'.

4. *Doubts about Religious Scripture.* An in-depth analysis of religious history, well beyond the superficial teachings, exposed the historical inaccuracies and contradictions within religious Scripture. This is especially true of the Fundamentalist Christians who take the Bible literally. Once they actually read about the horrors and errors in the Old Testament and learn about the logical contradictions of the New Testament, and they realize that the prophecies were

false, it is difficult for them to return to their status quo. Such a critical review generally leads to more questions than answers, and it often creates intellectual dissonance in the minds of the reader.

5. *Intellectual Integrity.* Some former believers found the scientific explanations with their documented evidence to be far more compelling than the literal interpretations of religious texts penned by ancient men. It is impossible to reconcile those alternative "truths." The Internet provides 24/7 access to well-reasoned explanations of ethics and scientific discoveries, broadening perspectives, and challenging one's previously held beliefs. Many value critical thinking over blind faith. The vast amount of information and contradictory messages can cloud one's understanding of any religion. This overload leads to confusion and doubt, especially when the religious teachings aren't as clear.

6. *Disillusionment with Organized Religion.* This takes many forms. Some noticed the total lack of compassion for the homeless, including immigrants, exposing a gaping disconnect between their Church's rhetoric and its actions; others witnessed the hypocrisy within their Churches, including scandals and disagreements, or a focus on Church procedures over compassion. Yet for others, it was the materialism of their pastors and the opulent lifestyle of the Church leadership that eroded the trust they had in their Church. Further, some Churches commercialize spirituality, pressuring their congregation to contribute more and more financially. Indeed, Church members who were struggling to pay for their own housing were expected to tithe without any transparency or accountability from their Church regarding how its money was spent.

7. *Doctrinal Disagreements.* This can occur over a range of issues, such as allowing Catholic priests to marry, women to take a more participatory role in leading congregations, inclusion of LGBTQ members in their clergy, or pushing back on their Churches' stance on birth control. The latter was especially true of Catholicism, which continues to oppose the dispersal of prophylactics to stop the spread of AIDS. When individuals perceive their Church policies as unjust or out of touch with contemporary societal norms, it can lead to disillusionment. The discord between personal ethics and institutional stances, especially on social and political issues, is prompting some to reconsider their affiliation with Christianity.

8. *Childhood Indoctrination and Disillusionment.* As children, we are often taught to believe certain things without question, especially religious beliefs. As we mature, we start to question the views and myths taught to us as children. Later, we may discover that the faith in which we were indoctrinated does not align with our personal values, experiences, or perspectives. Such doubts and realizations can lead to severe anger and disillusionment, and ultimately, disbelief.

9. *Unanswered Prayers.* Some people undergo very difficult times, and during those times when their prayers are not remotely answered, it can shake their faith. They cannot help but wonder why their God is good and all-powerful, yet he does not intervene. So, when people put such emphasis on prayers and then realize that they are ineffective, they begin to question the existence and relevance of their deity.

10. *Abuse and the Handling of Abuse.* Multiple cases of sexual abuse against children and women have been well-documented across the world, including the United States. Relatively recently, investigations of abuse have now focused on Protestant

denominations. Similarly to the abuses uncovered in Roman Catholicism, the first impulse of the Protestant Churches has been to cover it up. Moreover, taking the complaints of the victims to heart and taking decisive action against the perpetrators of the abuse has not been the standard response.

11. *Immense Suffering and Evil in the World.* It is difficult to reconcile wars, natural disasters, horrific diseases, and existing evils to a benevolent, all-powerful God, who doesn't seem to care. It is a crisis of faith to accept that God allows such horrible suffering and pain. And why did God even enable evil to enter the world? It seems logically inconsistent that anything that is imperfect could come from a perfect God.

12. *The Prosperity Gospel's Emphasis on Material Wealth.* It is a clear distortion of the beliefs of Christianity. Faith is about believers honoring their God, not private jets and financial success. It has little to do with spiritual values, and it has turned off a significant number of people. It is a highly flawed and unbiblical view of the relationship between mankind and a deity.

13. *Our Universe is just too Ancient and Massive.* With a universe of billions of stars and trillions of planets, it is just too overwhelmingly vast to believe that it was all made just for humans on planet Earth, and that we are the pinnacle of all creation. With a universe of approximately two trillion observable galaxies, it defies credulity to accept that a deity created it for mankind, who remain stranded on one small, disaster-ridden planet.

14. *The Fallacies of the New Testament.* The only written Scripture for Christians comes from the New Testament, which is a compendium of writings by fallible humans, none of whom were eyewitnesses to any events of the birth, ministry, and death of Jesus of Nazareth. It is a document of hearsay and conjecture, written decades after the death of Jesus by unnamed authors, and filled with inconsistencies, contradictions, translation errors, and some purposely false statements.

15. *Questioning the Existence of God.* The most profound questions often revolve around the existence of one's invisible, non-communicative deity. For some, the lack of tangible evidence for God's existence becomes a void too large to overcome. For others, they engage in deep philosophical inquiries, weighing the arguments for and against theism. Ultimately, the scales of rational thought tip towards skepticism, leading them to step away from Christianity.

Religious ideologies can arouse powerful moral emotions in believers. As an example, no other force in our society so vigorously organizes women against women as does religion regarding reproductive rights or gender equality. We need to fight back against the corrosive power of religion in modern life.

> *"When a man is freed of religion, he has a better chance to have a normal and wholesome life,"*
> – Sigmund Freud

Chapter Summary

The term, organized religion, refers to a faith system with a relatively comprehensive structure that defines doctrine, standardizes worship practices, and administers the religious organization. Organized religion derails itself when it deviates from religious expectations and panders to external, human influences. Organized religion can become an existential threat, especially to democracies, including the USA, as it becomes weaponized within the political agendas and culture wars. Even though the separation of church and state is constitutionally protected in the United States, there are those on the Christian extreme right who are working tirelessly to rescind that protection and who are endangering religious freedom. Rigid adherence to fanciful (non-evidenced) religious beliefs has altered politics and religion in ways that are rigidly opposed to the open-mindedness and willingness to compromise that stimulate and energize democracy. However, the First Amendment to the U S Constitution encourages diversity and guarantees freedom.

Extreme cultish organizations such as the New Apostolic Reformation want to establish a Christian autocracy in the United States, under the banner of Christian nationalism. Christian nationalists appear to have convinced themselves that they have a special claim on America, and their particular brand of religious faith should have dominion over the American government. However, the USA was never a Christian nation. Even as Christian nationalists strive to hold power as the dominant segment in US politics, they are becoming an ever-shrinking minority in American society. Their forged alliance with the MAGA movement remains a transactional relationship, even as Trump is increasingly suggesting that he has been chosen, almost as a messianic figure.[1176] It seems appropriate to refer to this group of Christians as political Christianity, as they tend to prioritize political issues over the core teachings of Jesus Christ.

Morality doesn't flow from a deity, nor should it. True morality should arise from an innate human sense of right and wrong, and not from the promise of celestial rewards or the fear of eternal punishment. Research has shown that doing the right thing for others is our natural inclination. Morality exists independent of deities; and indeed, I would suggest that morality exists among humanity in spite of the directives of the numerous, diverse religions, not because of them.

There are many reasons why organized religion induces a lack of critical thinking, from childhood indoctrinations to cognitive biases. Religious zealots tend to live and move within their own religious enclaves, starting with home schooling, or going to religious parochial schools, and attending church services, meetings, and/or Sunday schools. They can even attend colleges that cater to their brand of ultra-conservative Christian subculture. One driving force is fear. They fear that they might no longer be the key political demographic; they fear they are under attack; they fear that their numbers are dropping; and they fear the 'end times.' The Christian right does not believe in facts, evidence, agreed-upon reality, and verifiable truths. They tend to live in their own reality. Moreover, those with ingrained beliefs are generally slow to change their minds, no matter what evidence they are shown. The current focus on anti-abortion, anti-same sex relationships, and anti-immigration is just a dog whistle to distract reactionary Christians while U.S. constitutional freedoms are being attacked and eroded.

Institutional Christianity is slowly dying. In the 21st century, it faces steep declines. In the United States, Christianity is projected to drop well below 50% of all adults in the next 30 to 40 years. By the 22nd century, Christianity will begin its death spiral. That is what is already occurring in many countries and some states, which have been slowly but surely moving from red to purple to blue. With their reactionary worldview dying, the conservative Christians are desperate to impose their particular version of Christianity on everyone else.

Organized religions often have established beliefs and teachings that assert a doctrinal approach, which tends to shield their members from new ideas or alternative perspectives. In our rapidly changing world, such an immutable stance often conflicts with modern societal values, particularly in areas such as gender equality, scientific understanding, and the rights of marginalized members of society. Resistance to change will continue to retard our societal progress, rendering it quite difficult for religious communities to engage constructively and to thrive within the evolving world.

[1046] Mike Magee, "Christian Atrocities: Three Centuries Of Pagan Persecution," Church and State; 21 August 2010; https://churchandstate.org.uk/2016/06/christian-atrocities-three-centuries-of-pagan-persecution/

[1047] Mike Magee, Ibid.

[1048] "Extract from Thomas Jefferson to Horatio G. Spafford," Jefferson Qotes and Family Letters; https://tjrs.monticello.org/letter/302

[1049] Sharia is a religious law forming part of the Islamic tradition. It is derived from the Quran and Hadith; it demands very harsh punishments for certain crimes.

[1050] Lori Nykanen, "QUEEN ISABELLA AND THE SPANISH INQUISITION," University of Central Florida; (2014). HIM 1990-2015. 1680; https://stars.library.ucf.edu/honorstheses1990-2015/1680

[1051] Robert A Krieg, "The Vatican Concordat With Hitler's Reich," American Magazine; Sep 1, 2003; https://www.americamagazine.org/faith/2003/09/01/vatican-concordat-hitlers-reich-concordat-1933-was-amb

[1052] "The Dutch Reformed Church and its contribution to Apartheid," European Academy of Religion and Society; Dec 7, 2021; https://europeanacademyofreligionandsociety.com/news/the-dutch-reformed-church-and-its-contribution-to-apartheid/

[1053] Alexandros Sakellariou, "Authoritarianism and the Greek Orthodox Church," Rosa Luxemburg Stiftung; https://www.rosalux.de/en/news/id/40997/authoritarianism-and-the-greek-orthodox-church

[1054] Alexander Stroem, "Playing God: The "Other Coup" of the Greek Military Junta (1967-1974)," Retrospect Journal; Feb 2, 2025; https://retrospectjournal.com/2025/02/02/playing-god-the-other-coup-of-the-greek-military-junta-1967-1974/

[1055] Steve Wiener, "Deism & the Founding Fathers | Definition, Religion & Beliefs," Study.com; https://study.com/academy/lesson/deism-the-founding-fathers-definition-beliefs-quiz.html

[1056] "Our Founding Fathers were Deists," Sarasota Herald-Tribune; July 18, 2002; https://www.heraldtribune.com/story/news/2002/07/18/our-founding-fathers-were-deists/28718041007/

[1057] This was a redirection of what has been dubbed "the Fourth Crusade" led by the French and Venetians.

[1058] Wendy McElroy, "Roger Williams: The Separation of Conscience and State," The Future of Freedom Foundation; Dec 1, 2013; https://www.fff.org/explore-freedom/article/roger-williams-the-separation-of-conscience-and-state/

[1059] Hana M. Ryman and J. Mark Alcorn, "Establishment Clause: Separation of Church and State," Free Speech Center at Middle Tennessee State University; Oct 17, 2023; https://firstamendment.mtsu.edu/article/establishment-clause-separation-of-church-and-state/

[1060] Teresa Smallwood, "The Conundrum of the Separation of Church and State," August 26, 2021; Divided We Fall; https://dividedwefall.org/separation-of-church-and-state/?gad_source=1&gclid=EAIaIQobChMIvaG7wl-oigMVzizUAR1C0QKYEAAYASAAEgLyffD_BwE

1061 Jon Miltimore, James Madison: Architect of the Separation of Church and State," Foundation for Economic Education; July29, 2019; https://fee.org/articles/james-madison-architect-of-the-separation-of-church-and-state/?gad_source

1062 John S. Baker, Jr., "Wall of Separation," Free Speech Center at MTSU; https://firstamendment.mtsu.edu/article/wall-of-separation/

1063 "Virginia Statute for Establishing Religious Freedom (1786)," Encyclopedia Virginia; https://encyclopediavirginia.org/entries/virginia-statute-for-establishing-religious-freedom-1786/

1064 James Lankford and Russell Moore, "The Real Meaning of the Separation of Church and State," Time.com; Jan 16, 2018; https://time.com/5103677/church-state-separation-religious-freedom/

1065 "Bill of Rights: The 1st Ten Amendments," Bill of Rights Institute; https://billofrightsinstitute.org/primary-sources/bill-of-rights?gad_source=1&gclid

1066 Jon Butler, "Does the First Amendment Separate Church and State?" Origins; The Ohio State University; https://origins.osu.edu/history-news/does-first-amendment-separate-church-and-state

1067 David Calloway, "What Is Separation of Church and State?" Freedom Forum; https://www.freedomforum.org/separation-of-church-and-state/#:~:text=

1068 "The Difference Between Freedom From Religion and Freedom of Religion," Learn Religions; https://www.learnreligions.com/freedom-from-religion-249685

1069 Joshua McMorrow-Hernandez, "The Story Of IN GOD WE TRUST On United States Coins," CoinValues.com; https://coinvalues.com/blog/the-story-of-in-god-we-trust-on-united-states-coins

1070 "Why Do Coins Say "In God We Trust"? GovMint, Dec 07, 2021; https://www.govmint.com/coin-authority/post/why-do-coins-say-in-god-we-trust

1071 Becky Little, "Why Eisenhower Added 'Under God' to the Pledge of Allegiance During the Cold War," History.com; June 22, 2022; https://www.history.com/news/pledge-allegiance-under-god-schools

1072 Sarah Begley, "How 'In God We Trust' Got on the Currency in the First Place," Time; Jan 13, 2016: https://time.com/4179685/in-god-we-trust-currency-history/

1073 Thomas Kidd, "The Origin of 'In God We Trust'", History News Network; https://www.historynewsnetwork.org/article/the-origin-of-in-god-we-trust

1074 Eleanor Stratton, "First Amendment & Religious Freedom," U S Constitution.net; Sep 3, 2024; https://www.usconstitution.net/first-amendment-religious-freedom/

1075 "Constituents' Letters Published About Legislative Prayer, 1st Amendment," Secular AZ; Oct 15, 2021; https://secularaz.org/prayer-lte/

1076 "In U.S., Far More Support Than Oppose Separation of Church and State," Pew Research Center; https://www.pewresearch.org/religion/2021/10/28/in-u-s-far-more-support-than-oppose-separation-of-church-and-state/

1077 Pew Research, Ibid.

1078 Grace Scott, "The (Lack of) Separation of Church and State," The Review; Jan 29, 2023; https://virginiapolitics.org/online/the-lack-of-separation-of-church-and-state

1079 Eleanor J. Bader, "Separating Church and State Still an Issue in the US," TruthOut; Nov 8, 2014; https://truthout.org/articles/separating-church-and-state-still-an-issue-in-the-us/

1080 Brynn Tannehill, "American Christianity Is on a Path Toward Being a Tool of Theocratic Authoritarianism," The New Republic; October 6, 2022; https://newrepublic.com/article/167972/american-christianity-path-toward-tool-theocratic-authoritarianism

1081 Scott Bomboy, "The newest debate over the Ten Commandments in public schools," National Constitution Center; Dec 4, 2024; https://constitutioncenter.org/blog/the-newest-debate-over-the-ten-commandments-in-public-schools

1082 Shanna Babilonia ,"The Problem With Faith: 11 Ways Religion Is Destroying Humanity," The Mind Journal; Aug 4, 2015; https://themindsjournal.com/the-problem-with-faith-11-ways-religion-is-destroying-humanity/

1083 Paul Rosenberg, "Fighting demons: The New Apostolic Reformation is waging a holy war against democracy," Salon; https://www.msn.com/en-us/news/opinion/fighting-demons-the-new-apostolic-reformation-is-waging-a-holy-war-against-democracy/ar-AA1sAqDI?ocid=msedgdhp&pc=EDGEXST&cvid=47b4e6bbb3574b93834e105a5bc13634&ei=63

[1084] Jack Wellman, "What is the Seven Mountain Mandate and is it Biblical?" What Christians Want to Know; https://www.whatchristianswanttoknow.com/what-is-the-seven-mountain-mandate-and-is-it-biblical/

[1085] Will Carless, "As Trump support merges with Christian nationalism, experts warn of extremist risks". USA TODAY, March 7, 2024.

[1086] Shanna Babilonia ,"The Problem With Faith: 11 Ways Religion Is Destroying Humanity," The Mind Journal; Aug 4, 2015;
https://themindsjournal.com/the-problem-with-faith-11-ways-religion-is-destroying-humanity/

[1087] Randy Gage, "The Danger of Organized Religion," Randy Gage; Dec 25, 2019;
https://randygage.com/the-danger-of-organized-religion/

[1088] Linda Hoover, "Effects of Negative Media on Evangelical Christians' Attitudes Toward Evangelism," p.23; Antioch University - Santa Barbara;
https://aura.antioch.edu/cgi/viewcontent.cgi?article=1205&context=etds

[1089] Grace Ji-Sun Kim and Susan M. Shaw, Contributor, "Christians In The U.S. Are Not Persecuted," HuffPost; May 18, 2017; https://www.huffpost.com/entry/christians-in-the-us-are-not-persecuted-an-intersectional_b_59161b18e4b02d6199b2ef05

[1090] Noah Ben-Asher, "Faith-Based Emergency Powers". Harvard Journal of Law and Gender; p. 22; Sep 21, 2017; 41: 269–300 , SSRN 3040902.

[1091] Emma Green, "Most American Christians Believe They're Victims of Discrimination," The Atlantic; https://www.theatlantic.com/politics/archive/2016/06/the-christians-who-believe-theyre-being-persecuted-in-america/488468/

[1092] Tara Well, "The Decline of Critical Thinking Skills," Psychology Today;
https://www.psychologytoday.com/us/blog/the-clarity/202306/the-decline-of-critical-thinking-skills?msockid=100c0b969ca362882ebc1e209d86634e

[1093] Eoghan Ryan, "What Is Critical Thinking? | Definition & Examples," Scribbr; May 20, 2022;
https://www.scribbr.com/working-with-sources/critical-thinking/

[1094] Nicholas Humphrey, "Why Evolution is True; a lecture to Amnesty Internation; Oct 14, 2020;
https://whyevolutionistrue.com/2020/10/14/a-superb-article-against-the-religious-indoctrination-of-children/

[1095] "Church history: The Great Disappointment," Grace Communion International;
https://archive.gci.org/articles/the-great-disappointment/

[1096] Dr. Bobby Azarian, "Why Evangelicals May Be Hardwired to Believe Trump's Falsehoods," Psychology Today; https://www.psychologytoday.com/us/blog/mind-in-the-machine/201912/why-evangelicals-may-be-hardwired-believe-trumps-falsehoods

[1097] Dr. Azarian, Ibid.

[1098] Gaslighting is a term that refers to a strategic attempt to get others to question their direct experience of reality.

[1099] Ana Sandoiu, "Religion is like 'sex, drugs, and rock 'n' roll'," Medical News Today; July 20, 2018; fact checked by Sandra Collier; https://www.medicalnewstoday.com/articles/322539

[1100] Winston Wu, "Debunking Christian Circular Arguments and Assumption," Debunking Skeptics; Revised in 2011; https://www.debunkingskeptics.com/DebunkingChristians/Contents.htm

[1101] "Dunning-Kruger Effect," Psychology Today;
https://www.psychologytoday.com/us/basics/dunning-kruger-effect

[1102] David Dunning, "The Psychological Quirk That Explains Why You Love Donald Trump," Politico Magazine; May 25, 2016; https://www.politico.com/magazine/story/2016/05/donald-trump-supporters-dunning-kruger-effect-213904/

[1103] "Confirmation bias," Britannica; https://www.britannica.com/science/confirmation-bias

[1104] Kendra Cherry, "What Is Confirmation Bias?" Very Well Mind; May 19, 2024;
https://www.verywellmind.com/what-is-a-confirmation-bias-2795024

[1105] Allan Rose Hill, "Why people who are wrong think they're right," MSN;
https://www.msn.com/en-us/news/opinion/why-people-who-are-wrong-think-they-re-right/ar-AA1s3auq

[1106] Reviewed by Danielle Wade, "What is cognitive dissonance?" Medical News Today;
https://www.medicalnewstoday.com/articles/326738

[1107] Bobby Azarian, PhD., "How Religious Fundamentalism Hijacks the Brain," Psychology Today; October 10, 2018; https://www.psychologytoday.com/us/blog/mind-in-the-machine/201810/how-religious-fundamentalism-hijacks-the-brain?msockid=3cc18bfa362b663d14f39eb6378a67d9

[1108] Azarian, Ibid.

[1109] Michael Krivich, "Reality Doesn't Care What You Think: Why Facts Trump Perception," MSN; https://www.msn.com/en-us/news/opinion/reality-doesn-t-care-what-you-think-why-facts-trump-perception/ar-AA1qFBiy

[1110] "Religious Composition of India," Pew Research Center; September 21, 2021; https://www.pewresearch.org/religion/2021/09/21/religious-composition-of-india/

[1111] "Muslim Population by Country 2024," World Population Review; https://worldpopulationreview.com/country-rankings/muslim-population-by-country Note: these are 2021 population numbers.

[1112] "How many gods have humans invented and what purpose do they serve?" Internet Infidels Discussion Board; https://iidb.org/threads/how-many-gods-have-humans-invented-and-what-purpose-do-they-serve.28353/

[1113] Dan Barker, Godless; 2008; Ulysses Press; Berkley, CA; eISBN: 978-1-569-75148-0

[1114] "Dutch humanist Desiderius Erasmus of Rotterdam," World History Edu; September 30, 2024; https://worldhistoryedu.com/dutch-humanist-desiderius-erasmus-of-rotterdam/

[1115] "Desiderius Erasmus," Stanford Encyclopedia of Philosophy; Sep 27 2017; https://plato.stanford.edu/entries/erasmus/

[1116] "Terror Management Theory," Psychology Today; https://www.psychologytoday.com/us/basics/terror-management-theory?msockid=3cc18bfa362b663d14f39eb6378a67d9

[1117] Bobby Azarian, "A neuroscientist explains what could be wrong with Trump supporters' brains," Raw Story; https://www.rawstory.com/amp/neuroscientist-explains-wrong-trump-supporters-brains-2649240855

[1118] Kenneth E. Vail III, Melissa Soenke, and Brett Waggoner, "Chapter 11 - Terror Management Theory and Religious Belief," Handbook of Terror Management Theory; 2019, Pages 259-285; https://www.sciencedirect.com/science/article/abs/pii/B9780128118443000111#

[1119] Philip Chrysopoulos, "What Did Ancient Egyptians Believe About Death and Afterlife?" Greek Reporter; January 20, 2025: https://greekreporter.com/2025/01/20/ancient-egyptian-afterlife/

[1120] Randy Gage, "The Danger of Organized Religion," Randy Gage; Dec 25, 2019; https://randygage.com/the-danger-of-organized-religion/

[1121] Edited by Pam Weintraub, "How the fear of death makes people more Right-wing," Aeon; https://aeon.co/ideas/how-the-fear-of-death-makes-people-more-right-wing

[1122] "A Complete Psychological Analysis of Trump's Popular Support," New American Journal; January 9, 2019; https://www.newamericanjournal.net/2019/01/a-complete-psychological-analysis-of-trumps-popular-support/

[1123] "A Complete Psychological Analysis of Trump's Popular Support," Ibid.

[1124] "Black Death," Britannica; https://www.britannica.com/event/Black-Death

[1125] Britannica; Ibid.

[1126] Paul N Benware, Understanding End Times Prophecy: A Comprehensive Approach. 2006; Chicago: Moody. p. 208; ISBN 978-0-8024-9079-7.

[1127] Lisa Loraine Baker, "What Is Dispensationalism and Who Believes It?" Christianity.com; Jun3 3, 2022; https://www.christianity.com/wiki/christian-terms/what-is-dispensationalism-and-who-believes-it.html

[1128] "Bonhoeffer on Stupidity (entire quote)," Plato's Cave; https://www.platoscave.org/2021/10/bonhoeffer-on-stupidity-entire-quote.html

[1129] "Bonhoeffer on Stupidity (entire quote)," Ibid.

[1130] Peter Burns, Bonhoeffer's Theory of Stupidity Explains The World Perfectly," Medium; https://medium.com/lessons-from-history/bonhoeffers-theory-of-stupidity-explains-the-world-perfectly-957cbb3fbac1

[1131] Ariane Resnick, "What Is Objective Morality?" Very Well Mind; https://www.verywellmind.com/what-is-objective-morality-5525515#:~:text=Trending%20VideosObjective

[1132] Jack Maden, "Where Do Morals Come From?" Philosophy Break; June, 2019; https://philosophybreak.com/articles/where-do-morals-come-from/

[1133] Jack Maden, Ibid.

[1134] Sara Novak, "Cro-Magnon vs. Neanderthal: What Is the Difference?" Discover Magazine; Dec 28, 2023; https://www.discovermagazine.com/the-sciences/cro-magnon-vs-neanderthal-what-is-the-difference

[1135] Dan Barker, Godless, p. 210; 2008; Ulysses Press; Berkley, CA; eISBN: 978-1-569-75148-0

[1136] "Do atheists have a moral compass?" UIC Today; Feb 24, 2021; https://today.uic.edu/do-atheists-have-a-moral-compass/

[1137] Ibid.

[1138] "Extracts From Mein Kampf by Adolf Hitler," Yad Vashem: the World Holocaust Remembrance Center; https://www.yadvashem.org/docs/extracts-from-mein-kampf.html; taken from Mein Kampf, p. 60.

[1139] Dan Barker, Godless; p. 216; 2008; Ulysses Press; Berkley, CA; eISBN : 978-1-569-75148-0

[1140] "What is Christian Nationalism and why it raises concerns about threats to democracy," PBS News Hour; Feb 1, 2024; https://www.pbs.org/newshour/show/what-is-christian-nationalism-and-why-it-raises-concerns-about-threats-to-democracy

[1141] "Christian nationalism," Britannica; https://www.britannica.com/topic/Christian-nationalism

[1142] Brubaker Rogers. 2012. "Religion and Nationalism: Four Approaches." Academia.edu; https://www.academia.edu/5099840/Religion_and_Nationalism_Four_Approaches

[1143] Jon Ward, "A Christian author says 'Christian nationalism' is out of step with the historic faith," Yahoo.com; Sep 27, 2022; https://www.yahoo.com/news/a-christian-author-says-christian-nationalism-is-out-of-step-with-the-historic-faith-200856187.html

[1144] Svante Myrick, "Opinion: In Texas, religious freedom and parental rights are only for Christians," The Hill; Dec 16, 2024; https://thehill.com/opinion/education/5039377-religious-indocrination-in-texas-schools/

[1145] Andrew Koppelman, "Forced Labor: Why the Thirteenth Amendment Protects Abortion Rights," Washington Monthly; Jan 12, 2023; https://washingtonmonthly.com/2023/01/12/forced-labor-why-the-thirteenth-amendment-protects-abortion-rights/

[1146] "Federal judge says constitutional right to abortion may still exist, despite Dobbs," Politico; https://www.politico.com/news/2023/02/06/federal-judge-constitutional-right-abortion-dobbs-00081391

[1147] Jaclyn Diaz and Nina Totenberg, "Texas Law That Bans Abortion Before Many Women Know They're Pregnant Takes Effect," NPR; Sep 1, 2021; https://www.npr.org/2021/09/01/1033171800/texas-abortion-ban-supreme-court-

[1148] Susan M. Shaw, "Why Christians should support reproductive justice, including abortion access," Baptist News Global; https://baptistnews.com/article/why-christians-should-support-reproductive-justice-including-abortion-access/

[1149] Kiera Butler, "How the Christian Right Became So Hostile to IVF," Mother Jones; Feb 28, 2024; https://www.motherjones.com/politics/2024/02/ivf-anti-abortion-catholic-church/

[1150] Peter Pinedo, "What is the Catholic Church's position on IVF?" Catholic News Agency; Washington, D.C. Newsroom, Feb 28, 2024; https://www.catholicnewsagency.com/news/256946/what-is-the-catholic-church-s-position-on-ivf

[1151] John Stonestreet and Jared Hayden, "Is IVF Challenging Pro-Life Views Among Christians?" Christianity.com; June 19, 2024; https://www.christianity.com/newsletters/breakpoint/is-ivf-challenging-pro-life-views-among-christians.html

[1152] Amanda Marcotte, "Alabama's targeting of IVF is the Christian right's attempt to control motherhood," Salon; Feb 23, 2024; https://www.salon.com/2024/02/23/alabamas-targeting-of-ivf-is-the-christian-rights-attempt-to-control-motherhood-and-theocracy/

[1153] Matthew Vines, "10 Reasons God Loves Gay Christians," Time; June 11, 2014; https://time.com/2842044/gay-christians/

[1154] Michael Coren, Contributing Columnist, "Why are conservative Christians so obsessed with homosexuality? ," Toronto Star; Updated July 4, 2024; https://www.thestar.com/news/canada/conservative-christians-are-obsessed-with-homosexuality-strangely-jesus-never-explicitly-mentioned-it/article_7777a9db-28c4-575e-b8e8-97cb05575745.html

[1155] John G. Stackhouse, Jr., "Evangelicals, LGBTQ+, and the Bible: What's (Been) Going On?" University of Chicago, Divinity School; Apr 15, 2016; https://divinity.uchicago.edu/sightings/articles/evangelicals-lgbtq-and-bible-whats-been-going

[1156] Samuel Stroope, Heather M. Rackin, and Paul Froese, "Christian Nationalism and Views of Immigrants in the United States: Is the Relationship Stronger for the Religiously Inactive?" Sage Journals; Feb 16, 2021; https://journals.sagepub.com/doi/full/10.1177/2378023120985116

[1157] Tara Isabella Burton, "The Bible says to welcome immigrants. So why don't white evangelicals?" Vox; Oct 30, 2018; https://www.vox.com/2018/10/30/18035336/white-evangelicals-immigration-nationalism-christianity-refugee-honduras-migrant

[1158] John Fea, "Why are evangelicals so afraid of immigrants?" The Christian Post – Voices; April 30, 20; https://www.christianpost.com/voices/why-are-evangelicals-so-afraid-of-immigrants.html

[1159] Liz Theoharis ,"Faith Leaders Resist Trump's Christian Nationalism in a Battle of Theologies," Truthout; March 3, 2025; https://truthout.org/articles/faith-leaders-resist-trumps-christian-nationalism-in-a-battle-of-theologies/

[1160] Ibid.

[1161] Christen Thomason, "The theology behind the Christian nationalist view on immigration," Baptist News Global; July 22, 2024; https://baptistnews.com/article/the-theology-behind-the-christian-nationalist-view-on-immigration/

[1162] "Replacement Theory," Britannica; https://www.britannica.com/topic/replacement-theory

[1163] Christen Thomason, Ibid.

[1164] Aaron Earls, "Protestant Church Closures Outpace Openings in U.S.," Lifeway Research; May 25, 2021; https://research.lifeway.com/2021/05/25/protestant-church-closures-outpace-openings-in-u-s/

[1165] Aaron Earls, "Southern Baptists Lost More Than 1,200 Congregations in 2022," Lifeway Research; April 2, 2024; https://research.lifeway.com/2024/04/02/southern-baptists-lost-more-than-1200-congregations-in-2022/

[1166] Jonathan Chang and Meghna Chakrabarti, "'The great dechurching': Why so many Americans are leaving their churches," Wbur; Jan 24, 2024; https://www.wbur.org/onpoint/2024/01/24/the-great-dechurching-why-so-many-americans-are-leaving-their-church

[1167] Scott Neuman, "Megachurches are getting even bigger as churches close across the country," NPR; July 14, 2023; https://www.npr.org/2023/07/14/1187460517/megachurches-growing-liquid-church?utm_source=Pew+Research+Center&utm_campaign=6e020ff510-EMAIL_CAMPAIGN_2023_07_19_03_28&utm_medium=email&utm_term=0_-6e020ff510-%5BLIST_EMAIL_ID%5D

[1168] Matthieu Lasserre, "The US megachurch movement is on the decline," LaCroix International; https://international.la-croix.com/news/religion/the-us-megachurch-movement-is-on-the-decline/19163

[1169] "Religious Landscape Study," Pew Research Center; https://www.pewresearch.org/religious-landscape-study/

[1170] Ryan P. Burge and Percy Bacon Jr., "It's Not Just Young White Liberals Who Are Leaving Religion," FiveThirtyEight; Apr. 16, 2021; https://fivethirtyeight.com/features/its-not-just-young-white-liberals-who-are-leaving-religion/

[1171] Betsy Cooper, Daniel Cox, Rachel Lienesch, Robert P. Jones, Ph.D., Exodus: Why Americans are Leaving Religion—and Why They're Unlikely to Come Back; PPRI; Sep 22, 2016; https://www.prri.org/research/prri-rns-poll-nones-atheist-leaving-religion/

[1172] Ibid.

[1173] David O'Reilly, "What Is the Future of Religion in America?" Pew Trust Magazine; Feb 7, 2023; https://www.pewtrusts.org/en/trust/archive/winter-2023/what-is-the-future-of-religion-in-america

[1174] Francis Wilkinson, "Trumpism Is Emptying Churches," <u>Bloomberg</u>; April 7, 2024; https://www.bloomberg.com/opinion/articles/2024-04-07/trump-s-brand-of-christian-conservatism-is-driving-people-from-church

[1175] Brandon Flanery, "I asked people why they're leaving Christianity, and here's what I heard," <u>Baptist News</u>; December 13, 2022; https://baptistnews.com/article/i-asked-people-why-theyre-leaving-christianity-and-heres-what-i-heard/

[1176] Chauncey DeVega, "Religion scholar on the 'civil war' within Christianity — and the urgency of stopping Trump," <u>Salon</u>; https://www.salon.com/2024/01/09/religious-scholar-on-the-civil-war-within-christianity--and-the-urgency-of-stopping/

Book Summary

Religion has exhibited a strong, at times complicated influence on human societies. Christianity has been a cornerstone of Western civilization for two thousand years, helping to shape its culture and values; and at times, it has provided hope and solace to people throughout the world. For many religious-minded people, their religion is not just a belief; it is a cultural identity that often manifests itself in ritual behaviors and superstitious beliefs. Unfortunately, organized religions have not always been a force for good; in fact, often they have been mechanisms used universally by both religious and secular rulers to control people. And they most certainly have been a source of division and strife among humanity. For humans to move forward as a species, to free our minds from this archaic worldview, and to achieve whatever our imaginations conceive, we must unshackle ourselves from the tyranny of organized religion.

It is true that faith comforts many; however, science offers a more convincing explanation of the universe than does creation through an invisible deity. While there is no definitive evidence supporting our creation via a divine deity, there is clear, indisputable evidence that our world formed from natural causes, and humans and other animals evolved via natural selection. Since there was never a first man or woman, then there was no Adam nor Eve; and there was no state of perfection from which to fall. So, the concept of original sin was clearly a fanciful invention.

There is insufficient evidentlary support for the veracity of the Bible. Both the New and Old Testaments have severe shortcomings that clearly deny that they are inspired by any deity. Indeed, some of these tribal fables are so amateurishly nonsensical, and they are so scientifically and historically mistaken, that they are not remotely credible. And that is before we even take into account the errors of text contradictions, historical discrepancies, and translation errors. Obviously, the Bible is the invention of fallible, imperfect humans. Additionally, is there any other narrative source that has injected and spread more confusion than the Bible?

Many of the stories in the Old Testament (e.g., Exodus, Jericho, Daniel, Ester, etc.) are overly embellished or never happened. According to Christianity, the New Testament was supposed to record the fulfillment of the prophecies of the Old Testament. However, the events cited in the New Testament fail to meet a single prediction of the Old Testament. Some of the so-called prophecies of the Old Testament, as declared by Saul of Tarsus (St. Paul) and others, did not even exist, and those that did exist were either not fulfilled or were false prophecies.

The doctrines and dogmas of Christianity, as well as the focus on rituals, the sacraments, the saints, Marian doctrine, the Trinity, and Hell, clearly evolved over the years within the societies that were influenced by the Church leaders. There were no divine revelations. They are all man-made constructs. Neither the Old nor the New Testament is remotely inerrant! No original text of any book in the Old or New Testament exists. The origin of the Bible is hand-written copies of tribal tales, and there are many forgeries.

The Mythology of Christianity

The historical Jesus may or may not have existed, but there is no evidentiary case for his divinity. Additionally, there is no empirical evidence for any of the claimed miracles attributed to him. The stories of his ministry (i.e., the gospels) are all hearsay without a single eyewitness report. No one who wrote about Jesus ever met him, and all but St. Paul wrote anonymously. There is no actual evidence whatsoever that Jesus of Nazareth was resurrected. The religious claims simply do not match historical reality. The lax methodology of the Catholic Church in vetting and canonizing its New Testament Scriptures 300 years after the death of Jesus resulted in the inclusion of lies and forgeries; and the Christian Church often selected testaments more for political reasons than religious ones. The Gospel of John appears to be fraudulent; the Book of Revelation was written by a Roman-hating, Christian-loathing, mystic Jew, whose narrative described the end of the Roman Empire.

Assertions of biblical events must stand on their own merits. We should not accept any statement for which there is insufficient or non-existing evidence. Truth is not about hereditary beliefs; it is based on testing and eye-witness accounts. If something is true, we don't require faith, because we can use reason to test and prove it. Superstition cannot be allowed to triumph over evidence. The truth matters!

For much of its history, Christianity was directed by the Catholic Church, and the largest portion of that was the Roman Catholic Church, which often advocated more for the supremacy of its popes and dominance of its particular religious brand than for the teachings of Jesus of Nazareth. The RCC invented the concept of the Trinity, Satan, Hell, Purgatory, Limbo, and the infallibility of the pope. The cruelty, abuse, and control wielded by the RCC spawned many other Christian Churches via the Reformation in the 16th century, and most of those Protestant denominations were equally intolerant of other beliefs. Together, both groups of Christian Churches (Catholic and Protestant) unleashed inquisitions and witch hunts, burned 'heretics,' repressed women and homosexuals, and promoted their specific versions of Christianity – to the detriment of all others.

Even as mankind entered what was termed the Age of Enlightenment and modern thought, Fundamentalist religious zealots were clearly indoctrinated and ensnared into a false belief system from which they could not free themselves. That has changed little in our Modern Era. What has emerged is organized religious superstition with its false ideologies and self-serving belief system that has become a major threat to critical thinking and reason. Today, organized religion strives desperately to render superstition as scientifically validated, without any evidence.

Today, the nonsense of Christian nationalism is threatening the USA. Once serving as the beacon for democracy, the principles upon which the USA was known are being hijacked by the religious ultra-conservatives, as they attempt to create a Christian theocracy. Christian nationalism is directly interwoven with white supremacy and all its hate. Simply put, white Christians are not entitled to any special privileges over people of other faiths or no faith.

Today, the over 45,000 different Christian denominations worldwide present clear evidence that the Christian religion has seriously fractured, while the overall size of the Protestant Christian body has started to recede significantly, in alignment with the rise of the Nones. In general, Christianity (Catholicism and Protestantism) has been in a significant decline in Europe and the United States. The world has become far more diverse and secular.

Organized religion claims with absolute certainty that it knows all; it makes claims about God, an afterlife, how the world was created, and what each of us must do to achieve eternal life. Yet, it can produce no evidentiary support for any of it. It cites vague verses in its books (Tanakh, Koran, the Vedas, and the Christian Bible) which can be interpreted to support almost anything. At its heart, organized religion is a form of bondage to a cult. It is a tool to propagate ignorance in order to gain power and control for political and religious leaders. And it is about manipulating the masses.

I don't care if you believe in Jesus Christ, Allah, the Easter Bunny, or the Flying Spaghetti Monster, as long as that faith is not imposed on others. After all, we humans need to work together and take care of each other. We are stewards of the planet and must care for it, and all the people and animals that dwell here. But organized religion poisons those goals with its greed and quest for power.

Organized religion is based on misinformation, false data, and blatant lies. It encourages faulty thinking that inserts mysticism and superstition into an investigation of cause and effect. It removes accountability, misplaces responsibility, and proclaims a false supremacy. There is no evidence for any of it. Organized religions are based on myths that enslave minds.

Prior to his death, the renowned scientist, Carl Sagan, warned humanity that ignorance and technological power were a combustible mixture that boded ill for our future. He pointed out that organized religion can obscure our capacity to distinguish truth from deception, knowledge from opinion, and evidence from faith – leading to a societal preference for simple lies over complex truths. He warned that magical religious thinking could undermine scientific literacy which is sorely needed for society's survival. Thus, the choice of scientific enlightenment over religious obscuration is paramount.

Appendices

1. Catholic Popes over the Centuries
2. Catholic Heresies
3. Protestant Christian Religions

Appendix 1 - Catholic Popes Over the Centuries

There are a few reliable records from the first three centuries. The dates in which various bishops held their positions are estimated, and the chronology of the early Roman bishops is heavily disputed. Much of the data is declared to be "According to Catholic Tradition," especially the martyrdoms during relatively peaceful periods in the Roman Empire. Similarly, the term *papa, pontiff,* or *pope* wasn't used until the second half of the 4th century. Until that point, I refer to these Church leaders as bishops of Rome. Finally, since Peter was never in Rome and never a bishop, the list of bishops/popes starts with Linus, and he is referred to as the 2nd bishop only to align the numbering used by the Catholic Church.

The term *anti-pope* refers to bishops of Rome who were elected or appointed by secular authority while the previously elected bishop was still alive. Sometimes it was difficult to know which was the legitimate pope and which was the imposter. The Church's rules for election took well over 1,500 years to solidify.

Dates	Name	Notes
67-76	**#2** **St. Linus**	There is little information on Bishop St. Linus; he has assumed legendary status. He is said to have been born in Volterra, Italy. There is no mention of Christian persecutions between Nero (June 68) and Domitian (Sep 81 CE); if no persecutions, then it is unlikely that there were any martyrs.
80-90	**#3** **St. Anacletus I**	*Martyr According to Catholic* Tradition, but not substantiated.
90-99	**#4** **St. Clement I**	*Martyr According to Catholic* Tradition, but not substantiated.
99-107	**#5** **St. Evaristus**	*Martyr According to Catholic* Tradition, but not substantiated.
107-115	**#6** **St. Alexander I**	*Martyr According to Catholic Tradition,* but his martyrdom was never substantiated.
115-125	**#7** **St. Sixtus I**	*Believed to have been born in Rome. Martyr According to Catholic Tradition;* but it is more likely he died of natural causes. *[PopeHistory.com].*
125-136	**#8** **St. Telesphorus**	*Martyr According to Catholic Tradition.* Born in Calabria, he spent a lot of energy fighting "heretics".

He reluctantly agreed to the creation of Easter and the worship on Sundays. His martyrdom is unproven. *[PopeHistory.com]*.

136-140	**#9** **St. Hyginus**	*Martyr According to Catholic Tradition*; but there were no Roman persecutions in 140 CE, so probably not a martyr. He was born in Greece. *[PopeHistory.com]*.
140-154	**#10** **St. Pius I**	*Martyr According to Catholic Tradition*; but his martyrdom is completely unsubstantiated. He was born in Aquileia, Italy; and he became bishop of Rome while Hyginus was still alive. He fought against Gnosticism and the Marcionites. *[Encyclopedia Britannica]*. He decreed that Christians should celebrate Easter on Sunday after the first full moon in March . *[PopeHistory.com]*.
155-166	**#11** **St. Anicetus**	*Martyr According to Catholic Tradition*; but his martyrdom is unconfirmed. He appears to have been from Syria. Also, a validation of his dates is impossible. He combatted *the heresies of Valentinus and Marcion. [Encyclopedia Britannica]*.
167-175	**#12** **St. Soter**	*Martyr According to Catholic Tradition*; but there is no account of his death. He was from Fundi, Italy, and he fought against the heresy of Montanism, which emphasized prophecy and rigid moral norms. *[Encyclopedia Britannica]*.
175-189	**#13** **St. Eleutherius**	*Martyr According to Catholic Tradition.* He appears to have been from Epirus, and his dates are unconfirmed. There is no evidence that he was martyred. He continued Bishop Soter's battles with Montanism. *[PopeHistory.com]*.
189-199	**#14** **St. Victor I**	*Martyr According to Catholic Tradition.* It isn't likely he died a martyr, given the attitude of the Roman Emperor at that time *[PapalArtifacts.com]*. African born, Bishop Victor is known for obtaining the release of many Christians who had been deported to the mines of Sardinia. *[CatholicNewsAgency.com]*.
199-217	**#15** **St. Zephyrinus**	*Martyr According to Catholic Tradition.* Not a traditional martyr; his opponents just made his life miserable. He hailed from Rome. *[PopeHistory.com]*. Said to have appointed his own successor, Calixtus. He failed to condemn Montanism or favor the Logos

293

doctrine (emphasizing the distinction of the three persons of the Trinity) - two concerns championed by Hippolytus. This led toward a schism in the Christian community. *[Encyclopedia Britannica]*.

218-222	**#16** **St. Calixtus**	*Martyr According to Catholic Tradition.* Born in Rome, he was the principal advisor of Zephyrinus; there is no evidence that he was martyred. In reaction to the election of Calixtus, Hippolytus was elected as an alternative, after wrongly accusing Calixtus of *heresy*. Some refer to Hippolytus as the first antipope, but the term, *pope*, did not yet exist.
222-230	**#17** **St. Urban I**	*Martyr According to Catholic Tradition.* But he died of natural causes. Born in Rome, he was bishop during the reign of Roman Emperor, Severus Alexander, a time of peace for the Church. *[Encyclopedia Britannica]*.
21 Jul 230 - 28 Sept 235 **(5 yrs)**	**#18** **St. Pontian**	*Martyr According to Catholic Tradition.* Born in Rome, Pontian summoned the Roman synod that condemned Origen, a theologian of the early Greek Church. Pontian abdicated his position after 5 years, and he was banished during a Roman persecution along with Hippolytus. They spent their last days in the mines of Sardinia, where they are said to have reconciled. They are said to have died of "ill treatment" in the mines. *[Encyclopedia Britannica]*.
21 Nov 235 - 3 Jan 236 **(43 days)**	**#19** **St. Anterus**	*Martyr According to Catholic Tradition*; but there has been a fierce debate regarding whether Anterus was martyred or died of natural causes. Born in Petilla, Italy, he was Bishop of Rome for only 40 days (about 1 and a half months). *[PopeHistory.com]*.
10 Jan 236 - 20 Jan 250 **14 yrs**	**#20** **St. Fabian**	Martyred during Emperor Decius' persecution of Christians. He was born in Rome to a noble family, and he was known as an able administrator *[Encyclopedia Britannica]*.
Mar 251 - Jun 253 **(2+ yrs)**	**#21** **St. Cornelius**	*Martyr, according to Catholic Tradition,* but there is no confirming evidence of his martyrdom. Born in Rome, he was elected nearly a year after his predecessor's death, in a very contentious election, opposed by Novatian. Cornelius' attitude toward 'lapsed' Christians set the standard for later Catholic theology. *[New World Encyclopedia]*.

251	**Novatian** (anti-bishop of Rome)	Born in Rome and elected bishop of Rome by his followers in reaction to Cornelius's election, and who was viewed as too liberal toward 'lapsed' Christians; he was excommunicated that same year by a council of 60 bishops. Founder of the *"heresy,"* Novatianism.
25 Jun 253 - 5 Mar 254 **(< 1 yr)**	**#22** **St. Lucius I**	Born in Rome, and briefly exiled from Rome in 253 during a Christian persecution. He continued Cornelius' policy toward apostates who had denounced Christianity. He was not martyred.
12 May 254 - 2 Aug 257 **(3 yrs)**	**#23** **St. Stephen I**	*Martyr According to Catholic Tradition;* his martyrdom cannot be confirmed. Born in Rome, his most important action was his defense of the validity of Baptism performed by Novatianist priests. Bishop Stephen insisted that re-baptism was unwise and unnecessary. His view ultimately prevailed, and Bishop Stephen claimed doctrinal authority over the Church, based on his position as Bishop of Rome. [*New World Encyclopedia*].
30 Aug 257 - 6 Aug 258 **(< 1 yr)**	**#24** **St. Sixtus II**	Martyred; beheaded during Valerian's persecution. Born in Athens, Greece, Bishop Sixtus II oversaw issues related to heretics and the Christian lapsi. [*PopeHistory.com*].
22 Jul 259 - 26 Dec 268 **(9+ yrs)**	**#25** **St. Dionysius**	*Martyr According to Catholic Tradition.* Upon the death of Emperor Valerian in 260, the new emperor, Galienus, issued an edict of toleration, restoring Christian properties. This peace lasted approximately 40 years and was referred to as "Little Peace of the Church." Born in Terra Nova, Italy, Bishop Dionysius worked to bring order to the Church, but he wasn't martyred.
5 Jan 269 - 30 Dec 274 **(6 yrs)**	**#26** **St. Felix I**	*Martyr According to Catholic Tradition.* Born in Rome, Felix is known to have died a peaceful death; there was some confusion regarding another Felix who may have been killed. [*PopeHistory.com*].
4 Jan 275 - 7 Dec 283 **(9 yrs)**	**#27** **St. Eutychian**	*Martyr According to Catholic Tradition.* From Luna, Italy, Eutychian's cause of death was most likely via natural causes. Little is known of Eutychian, but he did emphasize the sacred rites of burial.
17 Dec 283 - 22 Apr 296 **(12+ yrs)**	**#28** **St. Caius,**	*Martyr According to Catholic Tradition. From Salona, Dalmatia,* Caius appears to have died a natural death. Although initially tolerated, Caius feuded with

	also called Gaius	Emperor Diocletian. Bishop Caius worked and lived in the catacombs for years.
30 Jun 296 - 25 Oct 304 (< 8 yrs)	**#29** **St. Marcellinus**	*Martyr According to Catholic Tradition.* Emperor Diocletian became increasingly hostile toward Christianity. Born in Rome, Marcellinus stepped down as Bishop of Rome, but when other bishops pleaded for him to reclaim his position, he acquiesced. Diocletian was furious and renewed the bloody persecution of Christians. However, there is no proof that Marcellinus was put to death. Because of Marcellinus' alleged apostasy in trying to satisfy Diocletian, the general peace was disturbed and not restored until Miltiades in July 311. *[Encyclopedia Britannica].*
27 May 308 - 16 Jan 309 (< 1 yr)	**#30** **St. Marcellus I**	There was a 3.5-year interval between Marcellinus and Marcellus. The severe penances that Marcellus, a Roman by birth, imposed on certain apostates returning to the Faith (post Diocletian persecutions) led to rioting. In 309, Emperor Maxentius banished Marcellus from Rome for disturbing the peace. He died in exile. *[Encyclopedia Britannica].*
18 Apr 309 - 17 Aug 310 (1+ yrs)	**#31** **St. Eusebius**	*Martyr According to Catholic Tradition.* He was the bishop of Rome for four months, but the exact dates are suspect. He was from Achaea, Greece. There was a lot of internal dissension within the Roman Church regarding the re-admittance of the apostates (*lapsi*) during the persecution of Diocletian; issues that started with Marcellus continued with Eusebius. When the dissension boiled over in public, Emperor Maxentius exiled both leaders of opposing Christian groups, Eusebius and Heraclius. The Catholic Church viewed the banishment as extreme suffering and venerated him as a martyr. *[Catholic Encyclopedia].*
309-310	**Heraclius** **(anti-bishop)**	A Roman, he served in opposition to Bishop Eusebius.
2 Jul 311 - 11 Jan 314 (2+ yrs)	**#32** **St. Melchiades** **or Miltiades**	It was during Miltiades' time as bishop that Roman Emperor Constantine issued the Edict of Milan (313), granting Christianity legal status in the Roman Empire. Originally listed as a martyr according to Catholic tradition; however, the Roman calendar amended that mistake. Miltiades was from Africa.

31 Jan 314 - 31 Dec 335 (< 22 yrs)	**#33** **St. Sylvester I**	From Avellino, Italy, he was Bishop of Rome during the First Council of Nicaea (325), which condemned the Alexandrian Christian bishop, Arius, founder of Arianism, a heretical doctrine teaching that God the Son (Jesus) was neither equal with God the Father, nor eternal. Although invited to the Council of Nicea, Sylvester sent two legates to represent him.
18 Jan 336 - 7 Oct 336 (9 mos)	**#34** **St. Mark**	The records are sparse on Bishop Mark (Marcus) of Rome. The Arian controversy was raging in the Eastern Church during the time of Bishop Mark; yet no historical record indicates that Mark was involved in attempting to resolve it.
6 Feb 337 - 12 Apr 352 (15 yrs)	**#35** **St. Julius I**	Born in Rome, Bishop Julius supported Bishop Athanasius of Alexander, a great opponent of Arianism, who had been exiled. He tried to convene a synod to confront Arianism, but the Arian bishops did not attend. Julius declared that Christmas was to be celebrated on December 25.
17 May 352 - 24 Sept 366 (14 yrs)	**#36** **Liberius**	Born in Rome, Bishop Liberius condemned Arianism, and he was briefly exiled in 357 by the Arian Roman emperor, Constantius II, for not condemning Athanasius. However, Liberius was restored to his post as bishop later that year. Liberius was the first bishop of Rome <u>not</u> to be named a saint.
357	**Felix II** (anti-bishop)	Nominated by Emperor Constantius II to replace the exiled Liberius, Felix, an Arian, was rejected by the Roman clergy.

Catholic Popes

Prior to Damasus I, none of the bishops of Rome were designated pope, papa, or pontiff. The following bishops of Rome are all considered to be popes or antipopes. Those that are shown in a red background are considered by this author to be the "bad popes" - corrupt men who many believe were unfit for the position. Those shown in green were the Avignon popes, and those shown in yellow are the antipopes.

Pontificate	Name	Notes
1 Oct 366- 11 Dec 384 (> 18 yrs)	**#37** **St. Damasus I**	Born in Eqitania, Lusitania (now Portugal), Pope Damasus was very active in suppressing *heresies*. He commissioned the Vulgate translation of the Bible (from Greek to Latin). When Western Roman Emperor Gratian abdicated the title of "Pontifex Maximus," Bishop Damasus became the first official

pontiff. He was the first pope to refer to Rome as the Apostolic See. He introduced Latin as the preferred language of the Catholic Mass. In 380, the Western and Eastern Roman emperors declared Christianity to be the state religion of the joint empires.

Pontificate	Name	Notes
[366-367]	**Ursinus** (antipope)	Born in Rome, he was elected by a minority dissatisfied with Pope Damasus, but he was banished from Rome by Emperor Valentinian.
11 Dec 384 - 26 Nov 399 **(15 yrs)**	**#38** **St. Siricius**	First Bishop of Rome to employ the title "Papa" ("Pope"). A Roman, Pope Siricius, tried to assert papal authority by accompanying his decretals (decrees or proclamations) with threats of sanctions against anyone who contravened them. His papal "decretal" in 386 commanded the celibacy of priests; it was the first decree on the topic, but it wasn't universally followed.
27 Nov 399 - 19 Dec 401 **(2 yrs)**	**#39** **St. Anastasius I**	Born in Rome, Anastasius I condemned the writings of the theologian, Origen. He also fought against the *heresy* of Donatism.

		Fifth Century
Pontificate	**Name**	**Notes**
22 Dec 401 - 12 Mar 417 **(15 yrs)**	**#40** **St. Innocent I**	From Campania, Italy, Pope Innocent I was viewed as an arbitrator of ecclesiastical disputes in the East and West of the Roman Empire. He defended John Crysosdom, patriarch of Constantinople. He was a strong defender of the primacy of Rome within the Church. He compelled the Roman Emperor, Honorius, to suppress Montanism in Africa. During his papacy, the Visigoth Sack of Rome (in CE 410) under Alaric occurred.
18 Mar 417 - 26 Dec 418 **(< 2 yrs)**	**#41** **St. Zosimus**	In his brief rule as pope, Zosimus, who was from Messurga, Italy, was embroiled in a wide range of conflicts centering on the *heresy*, Pelagianism, which held that God's divine grace played only a small part in an individual's salvation.
418 - 419	**Eulalius** (antipope)	After the death of Pope Zosimus, Eulalius, who was from Rome, was elected by Roman deacons who barred entry to higher clergy into the Lateran Palace; but his claim was soon rejected after he lost the emperor's support.

29 Dec 418 - 4 Sep 422 (3+ yrs)	**#42** **St. Boniface I**	Pope Boniface was elected by the higher clergy and recognized by the emperor as the true pope. Pope St. Boniface faced an antipope throughout the early years of his papacy. Not much is known about Pope Boniface, including his birth location and family name. His papacy was noted for his peaceful diplomacy and for his zealous support of Bishop Augustine of Hippo, particularly in the fight against Pelagianism, a *heresy* that denied original sin.
10 Sep 422 - 27 Jul 432 (10 yrs)	**#43** **St. Celestine I**	Born in Campania, Italy, Celestine I was pope during the Council of Ephesus. He spent his tenure combating an array of *heretical* ideologies. He vigorously attacked Nestorianism and Pelagianism.
31 Jul 432 - Aug 440 (8 yrs)	**#44** **St. Sixtus III**	As a conciliator in 433, he helped settle a Christological dispute after the Council of Ephesus (431) between Patriarchs Cyril of Alexandria and John of Antioch. Born in Rome, he maintained calm relations with the Eastern Romans. While he had previously been suspected of being conciliatory toward Pelagianism, Pope Sixtus repelled attempts for its followers to reconcile with Rome.
29 Sep 440 - 10 Nov 461 (21 yrs)	**#45** **St. Leo I** **(Leo the Great)**	Allegedly Leo I who was born in Rome convinced Attila the Hun to turn back his invasion of Italy. Later, he was credited with convincing the Vandals to spare the lives of Roman citizens when Rome was again sacked. Pope Leo was a strong proponent of papal supremacy. He strived to safeguard Christian orthodoxy. He held that papal power was granted by Jesus to the successors of St. Peter. And he considered himself Pontifex Maximus.
19 Nov 461- 29 Feb 468 (6 yrs)	**#46** **St. Hilarius**	From Sardinia, Pope Hilarius continued most of Pope Leo's policies. He fought against Emperor Anthemius' edict of 467 that enabled toleration for several sects of the Church. He was responsible for a major change in the liturgy (ritual) of the Catholic Mass.
3 Mar 468 - 10 Mar 483 (15 yrs)	**#47** **St. Simplicius**	Born in Tivoli, Italy, Pope Simplicius combatted the Monophysitism *heresy*, a doctrine teaching that Jesus had only one nature, not two (human and divine). During his tenure as pope, the Western Emperor Romulus Augustulus, was deposed by

Odoacer, which effectively ended the Western Roman Empire.

13 Mar 483 - 1 Mar 492 (< 9 yrs)	**#48** **St. Felix III** **(Felix II)**	Felix was a Roman who was sometimes called Felix II. Felix excommunicated Acacius, Patriarch of Constantinople, in 484 for publishing with the emperor Zeno a document called the <u>Henotikon</u>, which appeared to favor Monophysitism, a doctrine previously denounced at the Council of Chalcedon (451). The Acacian Schism between the East and West, which lasted for 35 years, began after he rejected the <u>Henotikon</u>.
1 Mar 492 - 21 Nov 496 (4+ yrs)	**#49** **St. Gelasius I**	From Mons Ferratus, Africa, Pope Gelasius was a prolific author of spiritual opinions. He strongly affirmed the primacy of Rome and put forth the doctrine of the Two Powers, which insisted that the emperor bow to the will of the pope in all spiritual matters. The doctrine of Two Powers became the prevailing Church attitude for centuries after his death.
24 Nov 496 - 19 Nov 498 (2 yrs)	**#50** **Anastasius II**	Born in Rome, his attempt to end the Acacian schism inadvertently set up the groundwork for the Laurentian schism, which occurred when the Eastern Roman Emperor, Anastasius I, favored Laurentius for pope, and the Gothic King, Theodoric, supported Symmachus.
22 Nov 498 - 19 Jul 514 (15+ yrs)	**#51** **St. Symmachus**	Born in Sardinia, Laurentius submitted and became bishop of Nocera, Italy, but his supporters continued their dissent regarding a number of Symmachus' papal decisions. A synod convoked by the Gothic king, Theodoric, did not resolve the issue. Thus, Theodoric allowed Laurentius to return to Rome, which triggered four years of public violence. The division among the Roman Church was not restored until Pope Hormisdas.
498-506	**Laurentius** (antipope)	In 501, supporters of Laurentius of Rome evicted the pope from the Lateran Palace. The Gothic king, Theodoric, investigated their accusations against Symmachus in 502. Theodoric allowed the antipope, Laurentius, to return to the Lateran, where he remained until he was again banished by the king several years later.

Sixth Century

Pontificate	Name	Notes
20 Jul 514 - 19 Jul 523 (9 yrs)	#52 St. Hormisdas	Born in Frosinone, Italy, Pope Hormisdas was the father of Pope Silverius (536 - 537). In 519, he resolved the Acacian Schism with Byzantine Emperor Justin I and with Patriarch John of Cappadocia. This schism lasted 35 years [484 - 519]. This effort helped reunite Rome and Constantinople (for a time).
13 Aug 523 - 18 May 526 (2+ yrs)	#53 St. John I	At the direction of the Gothic King, Theodoric, Pope John went to Constantinople to meet with the Byzantine Emperor, Justin, to try and compel him to relax his decree against Arians. But Pope John was only partially successful. Upon his return to Rome, Pope John was imprisoned by King Theodoric (who was an Arian Christian), and the pope died in prison. Born in Tuscany, Italy, he was declared a martyr by Catholic tradition.
13 Jul 526 - 22 Sep 530 (4 yrs)	#54 St. Felix IV (Felix III)	Sometimes called Felix III. Upon the death of Pope John, Felix, who was from Samnium, Italy, was voted bishop of Rome at the behest of the Gothic King, Theodoric. Felix cultivated favorable relations with the Goths such that a Gothic imperial edict required cases against members of the Christian clergy to be tried in an ecclesiastical court. He fought against the *heresies* of Semi-Pelagianism and Arianism. He recommended Boniface II as his successor.
Sep - Oct, 530	Dioscorus (antipope)	Effectively, both Dioscorus and Boniface II were consecrated at the same time. But 60 out of 67 Roman priests rejected Boniface II's selection by Pope Felix IV. Instead, they elected Dioscorus from Alexandria, Egypt; but he died three weeks later. Boniface II could just as easily have been declared the antipope.
22 Sep 530 - 17 Oct 532 (2 yrs)	#55 Boniface II	Pope Felix IV had requested Boniface of Rome as his successor. This was a period of significant ecclesiastical intrigue, and the election of Boniface II was highly contentious. After receiving a pledge of obedience from his electors in December 530, Pope Boniface II passed a decree granting himself the right to appoint his successor, but universal disfavor compelled him to rescind it (531).

2 Jan 533 - 8 May 535 (2+ yrs)	**#56** **John II**	Born in Rome, John II was first pope not to use his personal name, Mercurius, was due to Mercury being a Roman god. Prior to the election, the Senate outlawed simony in papal elections. Disputed elections, by decree of the Gothic king, could be submitted to the judgment of officials at Ravenna.
13 May 535 - 22 Apr 536 (< 1 yr)	**#57** **St. Agapetus I**	His father was a priest in Rome. When the Byzantines were preparing to invade Italy, the Goths sent Pope Agapetus to visit Emperor Justinian in Constantinople to try to deter the emperor from reconquering Italy. His effort failed, and he died in Constantinople.
8 Jun 536 - 11 Mar 537 (< 1 yr)	**#58** **St. Silverius**	Elected due to the influence of the Ostrogoth king, Pope Silverius of Frosinone, Italy received the consent of the Roman clergy. He was a victim of the intrigues of the Byzantine empress, Theodora. In 537, the Byzantines occupied Rome, and when surrounded by an Ostrogoth army, the Byzantines accused Pope Silverius of treason and exiled him because he had secreted messages to the Ostrogoths. He was deposed on 11 Mar 537; he soon died in exile on the island of Palmaria. And the RCC declared him a saint!
29 Mar 537 - 7 Jun 555 (18 yrs)	**#59** **Vigilius**	Nominated by the Byzantine empress, Theodora, Roman born, Vigilius was elected pope; and he was recognized by the Roman clergy after the death of the exiled Pope Silverius. He was the Pope during the Second Council of Constantinople.
16 Apr 556 - 4 Mar 561 (5 yrs)	**#60** **Pelagius I**	Pelagius had openly condemned Pope Vigilius for allowing himself to be pressured to accept Emperor Justinian I's religious policies, which were perceived in Rome as encouraging Monophysitism. Vigilius retaliated by excommunicating him. Later, just as Vigilius had done, Pelagius accepted Justinian's policy of Monophysitism under duress by endorsing the Second Council of Constantinople. He was from Rome, but he was elected pope as the candidate of Emperor Justinian I. During a Gothic siege, Pope Pelagius I used his private wealth to help the hungry in Rome.
17 Jul 561 - 13 Jul 574 (13 yrs)	**#61** **John III**	His papacy was marked by war with the Lombards, who reintroduced Arian beliefs to Italy. Most historical records about Pope John III were destroyed

during a Lombard attack. He appears to have been born in Rome.

Pontificate	Name	Notes
2 Jun 575 - 30 Jul 579 (4 yrs)	#62 Benedict I	He had an 11-month delay awaiting imperial confirmation. Born in Rome, he promoted the use of Latin, reintroduced traditional papal vestments, and was called "pope of the aesthetics." His papacy was marked by Lombard invasions, famine, and plague.
26 Nov 579 - 7 Feb 590 (10 yrs)	#63 Pelagius II	Another Roman, Pope Pelagius II enjoyed a friendly relationship with the Eastern Roman Emperor in Constantinople. He battled multiple heresies, and he defended Rome against the Lombards.
3 Sep 590 - 12 Mar 604 (13+ yrs)	#64 St. Gregory I (Gregory the Great)	There was a 6-month delay for imperial confirmation from the Ostrogoth king. First pope to formally employ the titles *"Servus servorum Dei"* and "Pontifex Maximus". Both the Lombards and the Byzantines in Ravenna posed serious threats. Roman born Pope Gregory eventually reached an accord with the Lombards. He always supported the primacy of the papacy and clerical chastity. He was an enthusiastic supporter of the Byzantine usurper emperor, Phocas. He was also the pope who created the false narrative that Mary of Magdala (known as Mary Magdalene) was a prostitute. In 1969, the RCC admitted the mistake.

	Seventh Century	
Pontificate	Name	Notes
13 Sep 604 - 22 Feb 606 (1+ yrs)	#65 Sabinian	There was a multi-month delay for imperial confirmation. Beginning with Pope Sabinian, who was from Blera, Italy, the Byzantine Empire would control the Roman popes for the next 200 years. Pope Sabinian appointed 27 new bishops. His tenure as pope was filled with pestilence, periods of starvation, and continual threats of invasion from the Lombards, to whom he reluctantly paid a large sum not to invade Rome.
19 Feb 607 - 12 Nov 607 (266 days)	#66 Boniface III	Born in Rome, Boniface III decreed that no one may discuss the appointment of a successor while a pope lives; and elections may begin no sooner than the third day after his death. He was able to get the Byzantine Emperor Phocas to proclaim that Rome was "head of all Churches."

25 Aug 608 - 8 May 615 (6+ yrs)	**#67** **St. Boniface IV**	Born in Abruzzo de' Marsi, Italy, Boniface IV was the first pope to bear the same name as his predecessor. His papal tenure was beset by the *heretical* bishops who supported Monophysism as well as by famine and plagues. He backed a controversial decision that condemned Nestorianism.
19 Oct 615 - 8 Nov 618 (3 yrs)	**#68** **Adeodatus I** **(St. Deusdedit)**	Sometimes called Deusdedit, Pope Adeodatus II, from Rome, was the first pope to use lead seals on papal documents, which became known as papal bulls. While Pope, there was an unsuccessful resumption of the Byzantine War against the Lombards in Italy. After Rome suffered an earthquake in 618, the pope labored to help those in need, focusing on the city's lepers.
23 Dec 619 - 25 Oct 625 (< 6 yrs)	**#69** **Boniface V**	From Naples, Italy it took almost a year for Boniface V to be elected. He immediately faced an issue with the Exarch of Ravenna, who attempted to take control of Rome, but who died in a mutiny of his own soldiers. Pope Boniface decreed that anyone could turn to a church for help, and the concept of church sanctuary began.
27 Oct 625 - 12 Oct 638 (13 yrs)	**#70** **Honorius I**	Born in the province of Campania, Italy, Pope Honorius's lack of a strong condemnation of Monophysitism was itself condemned at the Third Council of Constantinople in 680. That said, Honorius chose not to challenge Monophysitism out of concern for creating a greater controversy. As Pope, he sponsored a restoration program for important Christian edifices. He helped end the theological controversy between East and West over the Nestorian Church.
28 May 640 - 2 Aug 640 (2 mos)	**#71** **Severinus**	Elected in 638, Pope Severinus of Rome did not receive imperial confirmation until after protracted refusal to sign the Eastern emperor's *heretical* profession of faith (i.e., Monothelitism). He eventually acquiesced to the empire's modified terms.
Aug 640 - 12 Oct 642 (< 2 yrs)	**#72** **John IV**	Born in Zadar, Dalmatia (now in Croatia), Pope John IV's election was confirmed by the Exarch of Ravenna. He perpetuated Pope Severinus' condemnation of Monothelitism. He encouraged Irish and Scottish clergy to be vigilant regarding the

Pelagian *heresy*. He sent an emissary to help the Balkan Christians during the Slavic invasions.

24 Nov 642 - 14 May 649 (6+ yrs)	**#73 Theodore I**	Hailing from Palestine, Pope Theodore's election was confirmed by the Exarch of Ravenna. Monothelitism continued to overshadow the papacy, causing strained relations with the Byzantines. Pope Theodore was admired for helping the poor of Rome.
Jul 649 - Jun 653 (4 yrs)	**#74 St. Martin I**	Born in Tuscany in the Byzantine Empire, Pope Martin did not await imperial confirmation. Pope Martin called a Lateran Council, which condemned Monothelitism. The pope was deposed and exiled in 653, and he was brought to Constantinople. He died at Cherson in 655. He is the last pope that the Catholic Church considers a martyr, even though the <u>Christian</u> Byzantines were the ones to imprison him for political reasons.
10 Aug 654 - 2 Jun 657 (< 3 yrs)	**#75 St. Eugene I**	Born in Rome, Eugene I was elected pope while Pope Martin I was still jailed, and Pope Martin had assented to his election after the fact. Emperor Constans II demanded tolerance for the Monothelites, but Pope Eugene refused. Emperor Constantius threatened the pope, but he was otherwise engaged with martial reverses against the Muslims. Pope Eugene died before the emperor could exact revenge.
30 Jul 657 - 27 Jan 672 (14+ yrs)	**#76 St. Vitalian**	As with his predecessor, his papacy was noted for the dispute with the Byzantine Emperor, Constans II, over Monothelitism, which Roman popes condemned. When the Eastern emperor was killed in 668, Pope Vitalian supported the emperor's son, Constantine IV, over his rival, Mezezius. Once emperor, Constantine IV returned to the orthodoxy of the Roman Church. Pope Vitalian was from Segni, Italy.
11 Apr 672 - 17 Jun 676 (4 yrs)	**#77 Adeodatus II**	Sometimes called Pope Adeodatus (without a number) when Pope Adeodatus I is called Pope Deusdedit. Born in Rome, he was a monk prior to the papacy. He played no role in the political events of the day or in the resolution of Monothelitism, although he did condemn it. His attention was devoted to the restoration of churches in disrepair.

2 Nov 676 - 11 Apr 678 (1+ yrs)	**#78 Donus**	Known for his restoration and beautification of local churches, Roman-born Pope Donus helped end many of the issues with Constantinople. Additionally, he ended a schism begun by Archbishop Maurus of Ravenna.
27 Jun 678 - 10 Jan 681 (2+ yrs)	**#79 St. Agatho**	He was pope during the Third Council of Constantinople (also called the Sixth Ecumenical Council (680 - 681). Originally from Palermo, Sicily, Pope Agatho participated through his legates. The council was called to heal the decades-long schism between the Monothelites and those who considered it *heresy*. The emperor promised to abolish the taxes paid by popes upon their consecration.
17 Aug 682 - 3 Jul 683 (< 1 yr)	**#80 St. Leo II**	Elected in 681, but there was a long delay (1 year, 7 months) in imperial confirmation. Born in Sicily, Leo II fought against various *heresies*. He kept mostly a positive relationship with the Eastern Roman emperor. In ratifying the condemnation of Pope Honorius for not aggressively opposing Monothelitism, he clarified that Honorius did not support the *heresy*.
26 Jun 684 - 8 May 685 (316 days)	**#81 St. Benedict II**	Again, there was an 11-month delay in consecration, awaiting imperial confirmation. In order to reduce future time gaps between election and imperial confirmation, Roman born Benedict II received a decree from the emperor abolishing the requirement of imperial confirmation, replacing it with confirmation by the Exarch (of Ravenna) in Italy. But ratification by the emperor did continue.
12 Jul 685 - 2 Aug 686 (1 yr)	**#82 John V**	Born in Antioch, Syria, Pope John V was elected by the general population of Rome. He was immediately consecrated without imperial confirmation, because Emperor Constantine IV had removed the requirement. He was in ill health throughout his brief papacy.
21 Oct 686 - 21 Sep 687 (< 1 yr)	**#83 Conon**	Hailing from Thrace, Pope Conon was a compromise candidate for the papacy. He sent notice of the election to the Exarch of Ravenna. Due to feuding between the clergy and the military, it took over two months for the two sides to agree on Conon to be pope.

Pontificate	Name	Notes
21 Sep, 687 - 15 Dec, 687	**Theodore** (antipope)	Following the death of Conon, he was a rival of Paschal for the papacy.
Sep 687	**Paschal** (antipope)	In September 687, the Roman population tried to enthrone Archdeacon Pascal of Rome to the papacy.
15 Dec 687 - 8 Sep 701 (13+ yrs)	**#84 St. Sergius I**	Pascal and Theodore were elected by factional intrigues, but the Roman clergy and people chose Sergius, from Palermo, Sicily and who alone was consecrated, but only after he gave the imperial Exarch his bribery payment. Theodore submitted to Pope Sergius; Paschal refused to yield, and he died in prison several years later. Sergius and the Lombard King Cunipert resolved the Aquilian schism, unifying the Church in Italy.

	Eighth Century	
Pontificate	**Name**	**Notes**
30 Oct 701 - 11 Jan705 (3 yrs)	**#85 John VI**	When Lombard Duke Gisulf of Benevento invaded Roman territory, Pope John VI, of Ephesus, Greece, persuaded him to withdraw his forces. At the sight of Romans suffering, the Pope sent priests to the Lombard camp, offering ransom. He also intervened when a Byzantine commander crossed into Roman territory. Pope John VI is also known for many building projects.
1 Mar 705 - 18 Oct 707 (2+ yrs)	**#86 John VII**	Born in Calabria, Italy, he was the second pope to bear the same name as his predecessor. He was known for his devotion to Mary and for his energetic restorations of Roman churches. He enjoyed a good relationship with the Lombards, but there was tension with Byzantium.
15 Jan 708 - 4 Feb 708 (20 days)	**#87 Sisinnius**	Syrian born Pope Sisinnius reigned for less than 3 weeks. He ordered that the damaged parts of the walls of Rome (these were defensive walls that the Roman people built around their cities) to be rebuilt, and he consecrated a bishop for the island of Corsica. Then he grew very ill and died of the gout.
25 Mar 708 - 9 Apr 715 (7 yrs)	**#88 Constantine**	Another Syrian, Pope Constantine strongly objected to Byzantium's canons, established by the Eastern Roman Council (Quinisext), which was assembled by Emperor Justinian II. Pope Constantine was summoned to Constantinople in 710, but no

compromise was reached. Justinian II was assassinated in 711, and his successor, Anastasius II, restored orthodoxy in 713.

19 May 715 - 11 Feb 731 (< 16 yrs)	**#89** **St. Gregory II**	Gregorius Sabellus became Pope Gregory II, who is best known for opposing the Byzantine Emperor Leo III in the Iconoclasm controversy - the deliberate destruction of religious icons. Roman born Gregory's active role in secular politics helped establish the temporal power of the pope, and by extension, his right to interfere in political matters. And the rift between Rome and Constantinople grew wider.
18 Mar 731 - 28 Nov741 (< 11 yrs)	**#90** **Gregory III**	The last pope from Syria. He was elected by a unanimous decision of papal electors who did not cast formal votes. As an unassuming priest, Gregory III was only the third pope in history to be elected via acclamation. He was immediately confronted with the Iconoclastic (destruction of religious images) controversy. He encouraged the Christianization of the German tribes. When in 739 the Lombards sacked the Exarchate of Ravenna and threatened Rome, Gregory appealed to the Franks for aid.
3 Dec 741 - 22 Mar 752 (10+ yrs)	**#91** **St. Zacharias**	Born in Santa Severino, Italy, he reached peace with the Lombards. He maintained friendly relations with the Eastern Roman Emperor and with the Franks, supporting Pepin III the Short, with whom he established the Carolingian-papal alliance.
23 Mar 752 - 25 Mar 752 (Never took office as Pope.)	Pope-elect **Stephen**	Sometimes known as Stephen II, he died three days after his election and was never consecrated into the office of Pope as such. Some papal lists still include his name. In the 16th century, the Vatican sanctioned his addition to the list of popes; however, he was removed in 1961. <u>He is no longer considered a pope by the Catholic Church</u>.
26 Mar 752 - 26 Apr 757 (5 yrs)	**#92** **Stephen II** **(Stephen III)**	Sometimes called Stephen III. Roman born Stephen II received Donation of Pepin (756), which became known as the Papal States, becoming a temporal sovereign over central Italy. Establishing the pope as a temporal ruler would have long-lasting, negative consequences on Catholicism.
29 May 757 - 28 Jun 767 (10 yrs)	**#93** **St. Paul I**	Pope Paul, from Rome, was the brother of Stephen II and a member of the Orsini family. After Stephen II's death, Pope Paul prevailed over a faction that

wanted Theophylact to become pope. Paul was chosen to continue Pope Stephen II's policies of good relations with the Franks and to deal with the threats of the Lombards. He vigorously protested Emperor Constantine V Copronymus' revival of Iconoclasm (destruction of images/icons).

Jun - Aug 767	**Constantine II** (antipope)	A Roman layman, he was forcibly imposed by the Tuscans (by his brother, Toto of Nagi) as pope while Pope Paul I still lived. In one day, the Church officials made him a deacon, a priest, a bishop, and then the pope. He was deposed by the Romans with the aid of the Lombards, who killed Toto. Constantine II was imprisoned, tortured, and excommunicated.
July 768	**Philip** (antipope)	Philip was a Roman monk who was secretly elected by the Lombard envoys of King Desiderius, but he was deposed by the Romans. He held office for one day. Philip retired to his monastery.
7 Aug 768 - 24 Jan 772 **(3+ yrs)**	**#94 Stephen III (Stephen IV)**	Sometimes called Pope Stephen IV, he was born in Syracuse, Sicily, and was canonically elected after usurpers were deposed. The Lateran Council (769) forbade laymen from participating in papal elections, and it allowed only cardinals to become popes. Note: this rule would be violated multiple times.
1 Feb 772 - 26 Dec 795 **(< 24 yrs)**	**#95 Adrian I**	Related to popes, Stephen IV and Sergius II, Roman born Pope Adrian had to contend with the sporadic efforts by the Lombards to encroach on papal lands. He was the pope during the Second Council of Nicaea. He opposed the *heresy*, Adoptionism, which was the doctrine of dual sonship of Jesus. He maintained an amicable rivalry with Emperor Charlemagne. He strived to maintain his independence in the growing estrangement between Rome and Constantinople.
26 Dec 795 - 12 Jun 816 **(20+ yrs)**	**#96 St. Leo III**	Born in Rome, and elected the day after Pope Adrian's death, Pope Leo III was consecrated the next day. He notified Charlemagne after the fact. He crowned Charlemagne Imperator Augustus on Christmas Day, 800, thereby initiating what would become the office of Holy Roman Emperor, requiring the imprimatur of the pope for its legitimacy (and vice versa). However, this alignment with the Western Empire further alienated Rome from Constantinople.

Ninth Century

Pontificate	Name	Notes
12 Jun 816 - 24 Jan 817 (6 mos)	**#97 Stephen IV (Stephen V)**	Born in Rome, he sent a notice of election to the emperor after consecration. He is sometimes referred to as Pope Stephen V. He required the citizens of Rome to offer their allegiance to the Frankish King, Louis, whom Pope Stephen IV crowned as emperor.
25 Jan 817 - 11 Feb 824 (7 yrs)	**#98 St. Paschal I**	A lifetime Roman, Pope Paschal supported new missionary expeditions from the Frankish Empire. Pope Paschal secured from the Frank monarch, Louis I the Pious, the Church's hegemony over the Papal States, the independence of Rome, and the right of Romans to hold elections. Pope Paschal contended with a revival of Iconoclasm in the East. Additionally, he oversaw extensive building activity in Rome.
May 824 - Aug 827 (3+ yrs)	**#99 Eugene II**	Born in Rome, Pope Eugene II was the candidate preferred by Roman nobles who illicitly participated in the election process. A concordat with the emperor (824) reinforced Pope Stephen III's decree (in 769) that lay persons were to be excluded from papal elections. No papal elections could be made contrary to the canons, and no pope could be consecrated without the Emperor's envoys present.
Aug 827 - Sep 827 (40 days)	**#100 Valentine**	A Roman, his election as pope underscored the growing influence of the Roman nobility in the affairs of the Church. Allowing the lay nobility to participate in papal elections would eventually lead to control of the papacy by the Roman aristocracy in the 10th century.
Oct 827 - 25 Jan 844 (16+ yrs)	**#101 Gregory IV**	Born in Rome, Pope Gregory IV was elected in 827 due to the influence of Roman nobility, but he was belatedly approved for consecration by Louis the Pious. Pope Gregory IV intervened in several feuds among Louis the Pious and his extended family. He is known for his mediation between Lothar, the co-emperor, and Lothar's half-brother, Charles the Bald. Sergius II became pope on the same day that Pope Gregory IV died.

Jan 844 - 27 Jan 847 (3 yrs)	#102 Sergius II	Elected by a majority and consecrated, despite an attempt by a mob to impose another candidate. Roman Pope Servius II did not seek imperial confirmation, so the emperor's son, Louis, verified the election's validity after the fact. Due to his severe gout, his papacy was dominated by his brother, Bishop Benedict of Albano, to whom Pope Sergius II delegated most of his papal business. During his time as pope, the Saracens launched a raid (846) on Rome in which they pillaged the basilicas of St. Peter and St. Paul.
Jan - May, 844	John VIII (antipope)	In opposition to Pope Sergius II.
10 Apr 847 – 17 Jul 855 (8+ yrs)	#103 St. Leo IV	Born in Rome, Pope Leo IX was consecrated without imperial confirmation, due to the siege of Rome. He is remembered for repairing damages at multiple Roman churches that had occurred during the Saracen raid in 846; and he took precautions against future raids. Pope Leo also formed a league of maritime republics, which jointly defeated the Saracens in the naval Battle of Ostia.
6 Oct 855 - 17 Apr 858 (2+ yrs)	#104 Benedict III	The legates who were sent to confirm Benedict's election to the emperor instead betrayed the Pope and nominated the excommunicated Cardinal Anastasius instead. Pope Benedict was imprisoned, but then he was restored to the papacy within a few months due to the protests of the Roman clergy and people. He is remembered for his doctrinal decisions and his role in stabilizing the papacy in tumultuous times. Pope Benedict was born in Rome.
Jan - Mar, 855	Anastasius III Bibliotheca (antipope)	In opposition to Benedict III. Anastasius III was set up as pope by Louis II.
24 Apr 858 - 13 Nov 867 (9+ yrs)	#105 St. Nicholas I	The papal election was influenced by Emperor Louis. Pope Nicholas, who was from Rome, held a synod in 862, restoring the rights of Roman nobles to vote in papal elections. He struggled with King Lothar of Lorraine over the latter's request for a marriage annulment; and he deposed two bishops who supported King Lothar. Pope Nicholas consistently supported the supremacy of Rome, which Constantinople rejected. Pope Nicholas triggered the Photian schism by excommunicating Photius (863)

after the Byzantine emperor appointed him Patriarch of Constantinople. Pope Nicholas resisted Carolingian domination in ecclesiastical matters, and he claimed the right to legislate for all Christendom.

14 Dec 867 - 14 Dec 872 (5 yrs)	#106 Adrian II	A relative of Pope Stephen V and Pope Sergius II, Adrian II of Rome was pope during the Fourth Council of Constantinople (869), to which he sent delegates. To help reunite East and West, Pope Adrian II accepted the Council's canon, which established the patriarch of Constantinople as second to the Roman see.
14 Dec 872 - 16 Dec 882 (10 yrs)	#107 John VIII	Born in Rome, and considered an able pope, John VIII focused much of his papacy on attempting to reverse the Saracen gains in southern Italy. Pope John VIII crowned Charles II the Bald as Western Emperor. He fortified Rome against the Saracens and founded a papal navy. He was threatened by many plots, and in Dec 882, he was apparently assassinated.
16 Dec 882 - 15 May 884 (1+ yrs)	#108 Marinus I (Martin II)	Marinus I was born in Gallese, in the Papal States. Consecrated without confirmation of the emperor, Pope Marinus I was the first bishop of another diocese (Caere) to be elected Bishop of Rome. It was considered quite scandalous at the time. Pope Marinus condemned Photius I, patriarch of Constantinople.
17 May 884 - 17 Sep 885 (1+ yrs)	# 109 St. Adrian III	Born in Rome, Adrian III wasn't elected until five months after the death of Pope Marinus I. Pope Adrian III was loved in Rome because he helped the Roman people through a severe famine. He fought against the corruption of the aristocracy. He was assassinated on his way to the Diet of Worms (in present-day Germany) to name the heir of Charles III, Holy Roman Emperor. At that time, the pope reigned under the patronage of the Holy Roman Emperor; yet the emperor needed the pope's recognition.
Sep 885 - 14 Sep 891 (6 yrs)	#110 Stephen V (Stephen VI)	Sometimes called Stephen VI, he was born in Rome. He was consecrated without imperial confirmation, but the election was accepted by the emperor. During his papacy, the Carolingian empire disintegrated. Stephen V refused to recognize Photius as patriarch of Constantinople (this was Photius' second term as patriarch). Rome and the Papal States were threatened by Saracens in the

south of Italy and Hungarian marauders in the north, and with infighting among the Italian nobles. With his papal treasury exhausted, Stephen V fell back on his family wealth to help the poor, ransom captives, and repair churches.

Born in Ostia in the Papal States, Pope Nicholas had declined to make Formosus Archbishop of Bulgaria in 867 since it was still considered uncanonical for a bishop to transfer to another diocese. This rule did not prevent his own eligibility as a papal candidate in 872. For political reasons, Pope John VIII had banished Formosus from Rome and laicized (withdrew clerical status) him under threat of excommunication. This sentence was revoked under Pope Marinus, who restored him as Bishop of Porto. In 891, he was elected pope without incident, but the validity of his papacy was challenged posthumously by several of his successors. Indeed, he was posthumously ritually executed following the Cadaver Synod.

A twice-defrocked cleric elected by a mob, Roman born Pope Boniface VI died fifteen days later. His election was apparently declared null by Pope John IX in 898 on the grounds that he was not a priest in good standing at the time of election. Nonetheless, he has been retained in the Catholic Church's list of popes.

Roman Pope Stephen VI exhumed the corpse of Formosus and condemned the dead pope for illicitly moving from the See of Porto to that of Rome, an ironic charge considering Stephen himself had been Bishop of Anagni before becoming pope. It became known as the Cadaver Synod [Synodus Horrenda]. Formosus's corpse was stripped of papal vestments and cast into the Tiber. The outraged Romans imprisoned Stephen, who was later strangled to death. Sometimes called Stephen VII.

Deposed illicitly by a rival faction, Romanus died within months. His cause of death remains unknown. He had been described as a virtuous pope. He was born in Gallese, in the Papal States.

He was elected during the Cadaver Synod. Born in Rome, Pope Theodore vindicated Formosus' papacy

Oct 891 - 4 Apr 896 (4+ yrs)	#111 Formosus	
4 Apr 896 - 19 Apr 896 (15 days)	#112 Boniface VI	
22 May 896 - Aug 897 (1+ yrs)	#113 Stephen VI (Stephen VII)	
Aug 897 - Nov 897 (3 mos)	#114 Romanus	
Dec 897 (19 days)	#115 Theodore II	

and honorably buried the corpse of Formosus. Due to factional infighting and various intrigues, some believe that Pope Theodore II was murdered.

Pontificate	Name	Notes
Jan 898 - Jan 900 (2 yrs)	**#116** **John IX**	In a synod held in 898, Pope John IX, from Tivoli in the Papal States, nullified Stephen's grisly trial and condemnation of Formosus; and he reaffirmed the validity of ordinations by Formosus. The pope-elect could not be consecrated without the presence of imperial envoys.
Jan 900 - Jul 903 (3+ yrs)	**#117** **Benedict IV**	At this time, the power of the Italian nobles was significantly increasing, and papal authority was threatened. Pope Benedict IV, who was from Rome, excommunicated the Count of Flanders for ordering the murder of the archbishop of Rheims. He crowned Louis III the Blind emperor in 901.

Tenth Century		
Pontificate	Name	Notes
Jul 903 - Sep 903 (1+ mos)	**#118** **Leo V**	Reigned for about a month before being imprisoned by Cardinal Christopher (antipope). Pope Leo V, who was from Ardea in the Papal States, died in captivity; he was believed to have been murdered, either by Christopher or Pope Sergius III.
Sep 903 - Jan 904	**Christopher I** (antipope)	Violently deposed Pope Leo V and made himself pope, until the Romans imprisoned him for his usurpation in January 904.
29 Jan 904 - 14 Apr 911 (7 yrs)	**#119** **Sergius III**	"*Saeculum Obscurum*" begins. Invited by the Romans to replace the antipope, Christopher I, Sergius declared null the ordinations performed by Formosus. Born in Rome, Sergius was considered a valid candidate in 898. However, he proved to be a power-mad miscreant, and it is unclear whether he had Leo and Christopher killed, or if Leo V was imprisoned throughout Sergius's reign. He moved family members and friends to positions of power, allegedly fathered an illegitimate son with his 15-year-old niece, Marozia, and participated in heinous acts of debauchery.
Apr 911 - Jun 913 (2 yrs)	**#120** **Anastasius III**	His papacy overlapped the dominance of Rome by the house of Theophylactus (Counts of Tusculum), and Pope Anastasius III, who was also from Rome,

had little freedom of action. He united some branches of the Church operating in Germany.

Jul/Aug 913 - Feb 914 (6 mos)	#121 Lando	The Roman see was dominated by the relatives of Theophylactus. Born in Sabina in the Papal States, Pope Lando's reputation was that of a humble man with a charitable nature.
Mar 914 - May 928 (14 yrs)	#122 John X	Became pope through the influence of aristocratic relatives. Pope John X, who hailed from Tossignano in the Papal States, gave Marozia the unprecedented title of "senatrix" of Rome. Later, she and her husband, Alberic I, seized power and imprisoned John X in 928; and he died shortly thereafter, strangled in prison.
May 928 - Dec 928 (7 mos)	#123 Leo VI	Born in Rome, Leo VI was a puppet of Marozia. His principal act was the regulation of the jurisdiction of the ruling clergy in Dalmatia.
Feb 929 - Feb 931 (2 yrs)	#124 Stephen VII (Stephen VIII)	Sometimes called Stephen VIII. Like his predecessor, Pope Stephen VII, also of Rome, was a puppet of Marozia. He is remembered for dealing harshly with some clergy. He appears to have been murdered.
Mar 931 - Dec 935 (4+ yrs)	#125 John XI	Elected through the intrigues of Senatrix Marozia from the family of the Counts of Tusculum. Pope John XI of Rome was allegedly the son of Pope Sergius III and Marozia. When she was overthrown and imprisoned by her son, Alberic II (932s), the latter handled the ecclesiastical and temporal affairs; and he confined Pope John XI to the Lateran Palace until his death.
3 Jan 936 - 13 Jul 939 (3+ yrs)	#126 Leo VII	Born in Rome, Pope Leo VII was enthroned by Alberic II, son of Marozia. He encouraged reform of the German clergy and forbade Archbishop Frederick of Mainz from forcing the conversion of Jews to Christianity, but he didn't stop the archbishop from expelling Jews who would not embrace Christianity.
14 Jul 939 - Oct 942 (3+ yrs)	#127 Stephen VIII (Stephen IX)	Sometimes called Pope Stephen IX. He was subject to Alberic II, who was effectively the dictator of Rome. Pope Stephen VIII of Rome had a limited opportunity for independent action, and he had no real power. After displeasing Alberic II, Pope Stephen was deposed, imprisoned, and died.

30 Oct 942 - May 946 (3+ yrs)	**#128 Marinus II**	Enthroned by Alberic II, who gave Pope Marinus II of Rome little room for independent action. He did work on some minor Church reforms and discipline.
10 May 946 - Dec 955 (9+ yrs)	**#129 Agapetus II**	Subject to Alberic II, Roman born Pope Agapetus II was prohibited from issuing new rules, nor could he release any papal bulls that affected Rome. During his papacy, Christianity spread to Denmark. Pope Agapetus mediated multiple disputes among nobility outside of Rome.
16 Dec 955 - 14 May 964 (9 yrs)	**#130 John XII**	In 954, Alberic II forced the Roman nobles to swear they would elect his only son, Octavian, pope upon the death of Pope Agapetus. In 955, Octavian became Pope John XII, a man of corrupt morals. The German king Otto I and John agreed that papal elections should be held canonically, and consecration should take place only after making pledges to the emperor. But in Dec. 963, John was deposed by a synod of fifty bishops, with the emperor's consent. The election of a new pope, Leo, was thoroughly uncanonical. A Roman insurrection expelled the imperial party in 964, enabling John to return to Rome. Leo VIII was excommunicated and declared to be invalidly ordained. Pope John XII died shortly thereafter. Deposed in 964 by Emperor Otto, it ended the "Saeculum Obscurum." John XII has been characterized as an immoral man who drank excessively, murdered frequently, and had many sexual liaisons. The papal residence was described as a brothel. His papacy was renowned for its depravities and unrestrained immorality.
22 May 964 - 23 Jun 964 (<32 days)	**# 131 Benedict V**	Elected after John XII's death by the people of Rome, in opposition to the antipope, Leo VIII, who was appointed by Emperor Otto; Roman born Benedict V was deposed in June 964, leaving Leo as sole pope. He died at Bremen on 4 Jul 966.
Dec 963 - Feb 964; and again Jun 964 - Mar 965 (251 days)	**#132 Leo VIII**	Appointed by Emperor Otto in 963 in opposition to John XII and later Benedict V. He became the 'true pope' after Benedict V was deposed. Pope Leo VIII from Rome was uncanonically ordained. A popular revolt restored Pope John, and upon his death, the Romans elected Benedict as pope. Emperor Otto banished Benedict and again imposed Leo as pope until his death in 965.

1 Oct 965 - 6 Sep 972 (7 yrs)	#133 John XIII	Born in Rome, the papacy of Pope John XIII was caught up in the continuing conflict between the Holy Roman Emperor, Otto I, and the Roman nobility. Pope John XIII was very supportive of Otto's ecclesiastical views. In December 965, he was captured by Roman nobles who were hostile to the emperor, but he escaped from prison. In November 966, the emperor suppressed the Roman conspiracy and restored Pope John XIII.
19 Jan 973 - Jun 974 (1+ yrs)	#134 Benedict VI	The consecration of Pope Benedict VI was delayed several months while waiting for the emperor's ratification. After Otto I's death, Otto II gained control. Roman born Benedict VI was captured by Roman nobles (the Crescentii family) and strangled to death.
Jun-Jul 974; and again Aug 983 - Aug 985	Boniface VII (antipope)	Born Franco Ferrucci, this Roman antipope ordered the execution of the true pope after he was invalidly elected by the Roman faction that imprisoned Benedict VI. A month later, the emperor's envoy took control of Rome, forcing Boniface VII to flee, but not before raiding the papal treasury. Upon the death of Emperor Otto II (Dec. 983), Boniface returned to Rome, and he imprisoned John XIV (Apr 984), who was strangled 4 months later. After Boniface VII was murdered in 985, his body was dragged through the streets by a mob and subjected to public desecration.
Oct 974 - 10 Jul 983 (8+ yrs)	#135 Benedict VII	Under the influence of the imperial envoy who attempted to get Benedict VI released, the Romans elected another Benedict as the Pope (the grandson of Marioza), as the antipope Boniface fled the city.
Dec 983 - 20 Aug 984 (<1 yr)	#136 John XIV	Pietro Campanora was elected with the emperor's consent. He was imprisoned by the antipope, Boniface, in 984. Pope John XIV died 4 months later, allegedly killed on orders from Franco Ferrucci (Boniface VII). John XIV was born in Pavia in the Papal States.
Aug 985 - Apr 996 (10+ yrs)	#137 John XV	Elected after the death of antipope Boniface VII, who had allegedly caused the murders of Popes Benedict VII and John XIV. Pope John XV of Rome was subject to the patrician, John Crescentius, who wielded temporal authority in Rome at the time. Pope John XV's papacy was stained with greed and nepotism.

3 May 996 - 18 Feb 999 (< 3 yrs)	#138 Gregory V	Bruno of Carinthia was the first German Pope. He was born in Carinthia in the Holy Roman Empire (today's Germany). His family were the Counts of Carinthia; and he was nominated by his relative, Emperor Otto III. After Otto III left Rome, Gregory was driven from the city by the noble Crescentius Nomentanus, who established the antipope John XVI (997). Gregory was restored in Rome the following year.
Mar 997 - Feb 998 (< 1 yr)	John XVI (antipope)	John Philagathus was invalidly named pope by the noble, Crescentius Numentanus, who expelled Gregory V from Rome. The emperor's troops captured John a year later, and he was mutilated and degraded, while Crescentius was hanged.
2 Apr 999 - 12 May 1003 (4 yrs)	#139 Sylvester II	Gerbert d 'Aurillac was the first French Pope. He was born in the Auvergne region in France, and he was elected through the imperial influence of Holy Roman Emperor Otto III. Considered an excellent scholar and teacher, he was an avid collector of manuscripts.

Eleventh Century		
Pontificate	Name	Notes
May 1003 - Nov 1003 (5 mos)	#140 John XVII	Roman born Giovanni Sicco was elected through the influence of John Crescentius, son of Crescentius Numentanus. Pope John XVII was viewed as his puppet. Pope John's only accomplishment appears to have been approving missions to evangelize the Slavs.
Jan 1004 - Jul 1009 (5+ yrs)	#141 John XVIII	Giovanni Fasano was elected through Crescentius's influence. Although under Crescentius' thumb, Pope John did push back, and he made most of his ecclesiastical decisions, including the creation of a new diocese. Pope John XVIII eventually abdicated for unknown reasons, returned to a monastery, and died shortly thereafter. John XVIII was born in Rapagnano in the Papal States.
31 Jul 1009 - 12 May 1012 (< 3 yrs)	#142 Sergius IV	Born Pietro Boccadiporco in Rome, Pope Sergius IV labored to keep Emperor Otto III from infringing further on the affairs of Rome. However, his temporal powers were limited by Crescentus.

Sergius was noted for his aid to the poor. There is speculation that Sergius may have been murdered. He died immediately after John Crescentius' death.

Jun - Dec 1012	**Gregory VI** (antipope)	In opposition to Benedict VIII.
18 May 1012 - 9 Apr 1024 (< 12 yrs)	**#143 Benedict VIII**	Pope Benedict VIII was Theophylactus II, Conti di Tusculum (Count of Tusculum). Pope Benedict VIII forcibly acquired his papacy through Tusculan influence (via simony). Due to opposition and threats of Gregory VI (antipope), Benedict VIII did not occupy the papal throne for several months. Henry II of Germany inserted himself in December 1012 to restore Benedict to his position and deposed Gregory VI.
May 1024 - Oct 1032 (8+ yrs)	**#144 John XIX**	Romanus of Tusculum was the brother of Pope Benedict VIII and a layman who was the temporal ruler of Rome. After his family paid for the office, he was recognized by the Byzantine emperor, until John XIX refused to recognize his title of ecumenical patriarch. John XIX was the son of the Count of Tusculum and the uncle of Pope Benedict IX. Born in Rome, Pope John XIX had never been ordained as a priest. In one day, he passed through the necessary clerical stations (priesthood, bishop, and pope). His papacy was marked by controversy, and he was considered an incompetent pope.
Oct 1032 - Dec 1044 (12+ yrs)	**#145 Benedict IX**	*First term.* The family of the Counts of Tusculum gave the papacy to their young, immoral Roman progeny, Theophylactus III, who was the nephew of John XIX and son of Alberic. Elected for the first time at the age of 20. He was renowned for his debauchery and violent conduct, which provoked the Romans to insurrection; so he fled Rome.
Jan 1045 - Mar 1045 (3 mos)	**#146 Sylvester III**	Born Giovanni dei Crescenzi Ottaviani, in Rome, he became the Bishop of Sabina. The validity of his election was questioned (allegations of bribery); he was deposed at the Council of Sutri on 11 Mar 1045. He followed the 1st term of Benedict IX's failed papacy; when Benedict returned to power, Sylvester returned to Sabina as its bishop. He was considered an antipope by many, but the Catholic Church continues to count him as a true pope.

Mar 1045 - May 1045 **(6 wks)**	**#147** **Benedict IX**	*2nd Term.* He was deposed at the Council of Sutri. Benedict IX added to his legacy of thievery, murders, and multiple sexual activities.
Apr/May 1045 - 20 Dec 1046 **(1+ yrs)**	**#148** **Gregory VI**	Born Giovanni Graziano Pierleoni in Rome, he became godfather to Benedict IX. Pope Gregory VI had paid the immoral Pope Benedict IX a large sum to resign, and Gregory VI was recognized as the new pope, despite the apparent taint of simony. Deposed at the Council of Sutri; banished 20 Dec 1046; Gregory VI died the following year.
24 Dec 1046 - 9 Oct 1047 **(289 days)**	**#149** **Clement II**	Born Suidger von Morsleben-Hornburg, from Hornburg, Duchy of Saxony, Clement II was nominated by Henry III to end a schism. He began some reforms, including a strong decree against simony (the buying or selling of a Church office). He also began working with King Henry III of the Holy Roman Empire to bring peace to Italy and Germany. He died shortly thereafter at Pesaro.
Nov 1047 - 17 Jul 1048 **(252 days)**	**#150** **Benedict IX**	*3rd Term: after Pope Clement II died, Benedict IX seized Rome again,* but he was deposed, excommunicated, and expelled. What is amazing is that the RCC not only counts him as a true pope, but it does so three times!
17 Jul 1048 - 9 Aug 1048 **(23 days)**	**#151** **Damasus II**	Upon Pope Clement II's death, the emperor's nominee was installed as Pope Damasus II (whose name was Poppo von Brixen from Pildenau, in the Duchy of Bavaria), while Benedict IX was banished. Reigned 23 days and died at Palestrina.
12 Feb 1049 - 19 Apr 1054 **(5+ yrs)**	**#152** **St. Leo IX**	Bruno von Egisheim-Dagsburg, Count of Dagsbourg (in the Duchy of Swabia), was nominated by the emperor. Leo IX began his papacy with plans for major reforms, including sanctions against simony, concubinage (cohabitation without marriage), and lay investiture. In 1054, Leo IX and Patriarch of Constantinople, Michael I Cerularius, excommunicated each other, beginning the East-West Schism, which had been several centuries in development.
13 Apr1055 - 28 Jul 1057 **(2+ yrs)**	**#153** **Victor II**	Gebhard von Dollnstein-Hirschberg, Count of Calw, Dollenstein, and Hirschberg, took the name Victor II. Also, from the Duchy of Swabia, he was nominated by the emperor, but Pope Victor II accepted only on

condition of the restoration of papal lands. He expanded a program of clerical reform started by Pope Leo IX. He was appointed guardian of Henry IV of the Holy Roman Empire, and he served as adviser to Empress Regent Agnes.

2 Aug 1057 - 29 Mar 1058 **(239 days)**	**#154** **Stephen IX** **(Stephen X)**	Frederic de Lorraine from the Duchy of Lorraine in the Holy Roman Empire (in today's Germany) became Pope Stephen IX; sometimes called Stephen X. He convoked a Roman synod to denounce simony, zealously enforced clerical celibacy, and centralized a number of reforms. He was planning to halt the Norman advances in southern Italy and to negotiate an end to the Schism of 1054 between the Eastern and Western Churches when he died.
5 Apr 1058 - 24 Jan 1059	**Benedict X** (antipope)	Supported by the Counts of Tusculum, Giovanni Mincio di Tuscolo of Rome violently acquired the papacy in defiance of Stephen's request to wait until an election. Expelled in Jan. 1059 and forced to capitulate that autumn.
Jan 1059 - 27 Jul 1061 **(2+ yrs)**	**#155** **Nicholas II**	Gerard de Bourgogne, from Chateau de Chevron in the Kingdom of Arles, became Pope Nicholas II. The coronation ceremony was delayed until January 1059, after Benedict X was expelled from Rome. In 1059, a Lateran synod reformed papal elections. Henceforth, popes were to be elected by cardinals only, while the Roman people could acclaim the pope-elect. The emperor's right of confirmation was recognized, but only as a privilege granted by the papacy. In reaction, a German synod declared these decrees null and deposed Nicholas II, who nonetheless remained Pope in Rome with Norman protection.
30 Sep 1061 - 21 Apr 1073 **(11+ yrs)**	**#156** **Alexander II**	Pope Alexander II was elected by cardinals. The emperor refused to consider confirmation, but Anselmo da Baggio from Milan was enthroned as pope anyway. Roman nobles protested, and German Empress Agnes convoked an assembly that elected antipope Honorius, who forced Pope Alexander II out of Rome briefly in 1062, and again for a year (1063-64), before Alexander's legitimacy was established.
1061-1064	**Honorius II** (antipope)	Appointed by the Imperial Diet of Basle, the bishops and nobles opposed to the cardinalate's control of papal elections chose as pope, Cadalous from

Verona, Italy, who took the name Pope Honorius II. He seized Rome in Apr 1062, but he was expelled the next month. In Oct, Anno of Cologne replaced Empress Agnes as regent, and he determined that Alexander's election was valid. Cadalous was excommunicated in 1063, but he still invaded Rome and occupied it for a year, until he was forced to flee. The Council of Mantua condemned him in 1064.

22 Apr 1073 - 25 May 1085 (12 yrs)	**#157** **St. Gregory VII**	St. Gregory VII was born Ildebrando (Hildebrand) Aldobrandeschi di Soana, from Tuscany, and he was elected canonically in the wake of wide acclamation, even though he was not yet ordained a priest until June 1073. He deferred consecration until the emperor confirmed the election, the last time imperial confirmation was sought. He was a strong advocate of clerical celibacy and repudiation of simony. He banned priests from getting married so the RCC would inherit any property. He banned lay investiture of bishops, infuriating Emperor Henry IV, who Pope Gregory VII later excommunicated. He restricted the use of the title "Papa" to the Bishop of Rome. His *Dictatus papae* (Dictates of a Pope) consisted of 27 declarations that extol papal primacy and include the claim that the pope had the right to depose emperors.
Jun 1080 – Sep 1100 (20 yrs)	**Clement III** (antipope)	Emperor Henry IV convoked a synod at Worms (1076) to depose Gregory, and in 1080, he recognized Guibert, the archbishop of Ravenna in the Papal States, as pope. Henry IV momentarily succeeded in displacing Gregory from Rome (1084), but he was soon forced to retreat, and his pawn, Clement III, was recognized only in parts of Germany. Clement's party was able to briefly expel Pope Victor III (1087) and Urban II (1089). By 1098, he was utterly defeated and retreated to northern Italy.
24 May 1086 - 16 Sep 1087 (1+ yrs)	**#158** **Bd. Victor III**	From the Duchy of Benevento, Dauferio Epifani Del Zotto was elected pope; but he refused to accept the tiara in 1085. In 1086, he was enthroned against his will, and he did not assent to his election until 1087, the year he died. He condemned lay investiture.
12 Mar 1088 - 29 Jul 1099 (11+ yrs)	**#159** **Bd. Urban II**	Previously known as Otho of Lagery (in France), Pope Urban II affirmed Pope Gregory's acts, including the excommunication of the emperor. Fights for power underscored his papacy, especially against the Holy

Roman Emperor, Henry IV. He pushed for hegemony over all monarchies. Pope Urban II called for the First Crusade, using the war against Muslims to unite Christians. He claimed that the Muslims were outside the 'Ark of Salvation,' deeming military action against them as morally acceptable. He also had some wives of priests sold into slavery and their children abandoned. And he was nominated for sainthood? Then again, his canonization as a saint has not moved forward.

Pontificate	Name	Notes
13 Aug 1099 - 21 Jan 1118 (18+ yrs)	#160 Paschal II	Born Raniero Ranieri in Bleda in the Papal States, Pope Paschal II fought with Emperor Henry IV, who maintained his right of investiture, and who died in 1106. The emperor's son, Henry V, imprisoned Paschal II for two months in 1111, and the pope conceded the right of imperial investiture, while the rest of Christendom condemned Henry V.

	Twelfth Century	
Pontificate	**Name**	**Notes**
Sep - Dec 1100	**Theodoric** (antipope)	In opposition to Pascal II.
Feb - Mar 1102	**Adalbert** (antipope)	In opposition to Pascal II.
18 Nov 1105 - 12 Apr 1111	**Sylvester IV** (antipope)	In opposition to Pascal II. His personal name was Maguinulf.
24 Jan 1118 - 28 Jan 1119 (1 yr)	#161 Gelasius II	Pope Gelasius II was born Giovanni Caetani; he was from the Duchy of Gaeta. Despite Henry V's efforts to fix the election through the Roman nobility, the cardinals elected a pope without imperial notification. In response, the imperial faction assaulted the pope-elect and imprisoned him. The Romans liberated the pope and enthroned him as Pope Gelasius II. Little more than a month later, Henry V forced him to flee and established the antipope, Gregory VIII.
Mar 1118 - Apr 1121	**Gregory VIII** (antipope)	Henry V of the Holy Roman Empire declared the election of Gelasius invalid, and he bribed some Romans to acclaim as pope the Archbishop of Braga, Maurice Bourdain from Limousin, France, who had been excommunicated in 1117 for crowning Henry

at Rome. The antipope, Gregory VIII was finally captured by the Romans, deposed, and imprisoned in April 1121 at a monastery until his death. His ordinations were nullified by the First Lateran Council (1123). Gregory VIII was the last antipope supported by the Holy Roman Emperor.

2 Feb 1119 - 13 Dec 1124 (< 6 yrs)	#162 Callixtus II	Elected by the cardinals, yet crowned in exile, while the antipope Gregory VIII occupied Rome. Callixtus II (formerly Guido, Comte de Bourgogne of Quingey, Burgundy in today's France) drove out the usurper and imprisoned him in 1121. The Concordat of Worms (1123) settled the investiture controversy by banning lay investiture; yet it established imperial confirmation of candidates outside the Papal States. This was confirmed by the First Lateran Council in 1123.
Dec 1124	Celestine II (antipope)	Elected pope immediately after Callixtus's death, Cardinal Teobaldo Boccapecci's coronation was interrupted by the aristocrat Roberto Frangipiani, who intimidated the cardinals into changing their selection. Cardinal Teobaldo resigned in order to prevent schism. Celestine II is excluded from many papal lists, though the Celestine-named popes' numbering includes him.
15 Dec 1124 - 13 Feb 1130 (5 yrs)	#163 Honorius II	Lamberto Scannabecchi da Fiagnano (in the Papal States) was elected two days after Pope Callistus's death, due to the intervention of Roberto Frangipiani, who induced the pope-elect to resign and the cardinals to select the Bishop of Ostia. Doubting the legitimacy of his election, Honorius II offered to resign until the cardinals unanimously acclaimed his legitimacy. After the death of Henry V (1125), Honorius helped Lothair get elected king.
14 Feb 1130 – 24 Sep 1143 (13+ yrs)	#164 Innocent II	Roman Gregorio Papareschi was hastily consecrated as Pope Innocent II. In 1130, the antipope Anacletus II forced Pope Innocent II to flee to France. Some archbishops intervened, and the kings of France, England, and Germany sided with Pope Innocent II. Emperor Lothar III of Germany invaded Italy twice to depose Anacletus II, who finally died in January 1138. In his papal bull, *Omne Datum Optimum*, Innocent II endorsed the Knights Templar. Then Innocent II convened the Second Council of the Lateran in 1139.

Feb 1130 - Jan 1138	**Anacletus II** (antipope)	Pietro Pierleoni from Rome was elected by the lower cardinals and some cardinal-bishops three hours after Pope Innocent's election. Since Innocent's election had a canonically sufficient number of cardinals, he was considered a valid pope, and Anacletus's election was invalidated. Nonetheless, Anacletus had greater support in Rome and reigned there until his death in 1138. Had the political lineup differed, Innocent II could have been the antipope, and Anacletus II the legitimate pope.
Jan - Mar, 1138	**Victor IV** (antipope)	Roman Gregorio Conti took the name Pope Victor IV and was a successor of Anacletus. He submitted to Pope Innocent II after two months.
26 Sep 1143 - 8 Mar 1144 **(164 days)**	**#165 Celestine II**	Guido di Castello's principal act as Pope Celestine II was the absolution of Louis VII of France. He also sided with Queen Matilda of England in her quest for the English throne. Pope Celestine was born in Castello in the Papal States.
12 Mar 1144- 15 Feb 1145 **(340 days)**	**#166 Lucius II**	Born Gherardo Caccianemici dal Orso, in Bologna in the Papal States, Pope Lucius II attempted to restore the temporal power of the pope by dissolving the senate established by Pope Innocent II, but he was violently resisted by the Romans. King Roger II of Sicily invaded papal lands and forced Pope Lucius to accept his temporary truce. But the brother of the antipope, Anacletus II, proclaimed a conditional republic, free from papal rule. Pope Lucius II led an unsuccessful assault on the rebel forces and presumably died of his injuries.
15 Feb 1145 - 8 Jul 1153 **(8+ yrs)**	**#167 Bd. Eugene III**	Born in the Republic of Pisa, Pietro dei Paganelli di Montemagno was a non-cardinal, elected unanimously, but Pope Eugene III was forced to stay outside Rome, since the people wanted him to submit to the senate in temporal matters. However, he was recognized as pope throughout Europe. In 1145, through two separate papal bulls, Pope Eugene III called for a Second Crusade, and he allowed the Knights of Templar to take tithes to bury their dead in their own cemeteries. After a brief period of Roman chaos, Eugene agreed to a dual government with the senate, but this failed, and he left Italy for France in 1146. In 1148, he returned to Italy, and he briefly occupied Rome in 1149.

Frederick Barbarossa induced the nobles to submit to the pontiff in 1153.

8 Jul 1153 - 3 Dec 1154 (1+ yrs)	**#168 Anastasius IV**	Born Corrado Demetri della Suburra in Rome, Pope Anastasius IV lavishly restored the Lateran Palace in Rome. Having significant diplomatic skills, he was known for attempts to reconcile conflicts within the Church, particularly regarding the appointment of clergy in England.
4 Dec 1154 - 1 Sep 1159 (< 5 yrs)	**#169 Adrian IV**	Rome was in political revolt, so Nicholas Breakspear, Pope Adrian IV, interdicted the city and returned after it submitted in 1155. He crowned Frederick only after the king did him customary homage, but both pope and emperor were forced to abandon Rome in 1155. Pope Adrian IV returned to the city in 1157. Pope Adrian IV was the first and only English pope (from Hertfordshire); he purportedly granted Ireland to Henry II, King of England.
7 Sep 1159 - 30 Aug 1181 (22 yrs)	**#170 Alexander III**	The election of Rolando Bandinelli from Siena, Italy was opposed by the Holy Roman emperor, who favored the antipope, Victor IV. Pope Alexander III was exiled to France (1162-65), but he ultimately triumphed over the emperor in 1176, when the Lombards defeated the Holy Roman Empire in a decisive battle. Pope Alexander III was a vigorous proponent of papal authority. He was one of the first popes to express concern regarding the Cathar *heresy* in southern France. To remedy past abuses, papal elections were restricted to a two-thirds vote of the cardinals at the Third Council of the Lateran, which Pope Alexander III convened in 1179.
Sep 1159 - Apr 1164	**Victor IV** (antipope)	Ottaviano dei Crescenzi Ottaviani di Monticello from Tivoli in the Papal States was the 2nd Pope Victor IV. Elected by a small minority of cardinals after Alexander III's election. The Emperor Frederick I's favorite, he had only limited recognition in Germany.
Apr 1164 - Sep 1168	**Paschal III** (antipope)	Successor of Victor IV, Guido di Crema, was recognized as Pope Paschal III only in parts of Germany; he was in opposition to Pope Alexander III.
Sep 1168 - Aug 1178	**Callixtus III** (antipope)	Supported by Emperor Frederick I Barbarossa in opposition to Alexander III, Giovanni di Sturma from Arezzo in the Papal States is considered an antipope.

Sep 1179 - Jan 1180	**Innocent III** (antipope)	Lando di Sezze was supported by Emperor Frederick I in opposition to Alexander III.
1 Sep 1181 - 25 Nov 1185 **(4+ yrs)**	**#171** **Lucius III**	Born in Lucca in the Papal States, Ubaldo Allucignoli was driven from Rome for political reasons in 1182. He called a synod which executed the strict decrees of the Third Lateran Council. He founded a medieval inquisition to punish heretics, and he initiated the Catholic Church's attacks on the French Cathars.
25 Nov 1185 - 19 Oct 1187 **(< 2 yrs)**	**#172** **Urban III**	Born Uberto Crivelli in Cuggiono, Milan, Pope Urban III was elected pope on the same day that Pope Lucius III died. Pope Urban III was in continual conflict with the Holy Roman Emperor, Frederick I Barbarossa, a fight that was partially inherited from Pope Lucius III.
21 Oct 1187 - 17 Dec 1187 **(57 days)**	**#173** **Gregory VIII**	Born Alberto di Morra from Benevento in the Papal States, Pope Gregory VIII proposed the Third Crusade via a papal bull, *Audita Tremendi*. He tried to work with the Holy Roman Emperor to improve relations between them. He commissioned the Gregorian calendar to adjust century years with a leap year only every 400 years.
19 Dec 1187 - 20 Mar 1191 **(3+ yrs)**	**#174** **Clement III**	Born Paolo Scolari in Rome, Pope Clement III was an almost unanimous choice. He appointed more than 30 new cardinals. He worked on relationships with other leaders, including Emperor Frederick Barbarossa.
21 Mar 1191 - 8 Jan 1198 **(< 7 yrs)**	**#175** **Celestine III**	Born Giacinto Bobone in Rome, he was the first member of the Orsini family to become pope, when he was 85 years old. Prior to his consecration as pope, he was ordained a priest, and the day after his consecration, he crowned Henry VI of Germany as Holy Roman Emperor. But Henry's ambitious projects and his failure to restore the full extent of the Papal States caused extensive issues for Pope Celestine III.
8 Jan 1198 – 16 Jul 1216 **(18+ yrs)**	**#176** **Innocent III**	Lotario dei Conti di Segni from Gavignano in the Papal States took the name Innocent III, and he restored some temporal powers of the pope lost since 1185. This power-crazed zealot asserted the right of a pope to confirm the election of heads of state and to depose them. In 1213, he convened the 4th Council of the Lateran, and he proclaimed *De*

dignitate patriarcharum, in which he asserted the supremacy of the pope over all Christian nations. He initiated the medieval Inquisition in Spain and Portugal to "exterminate heretics." He convened the Fourth Council of the Lateran. He initiated the Fourth Crusade, but he distanced himself from it when the crusaders sacked the Christian city of Constantinople. He ordered the massacre of the Albigenses. He claimed the title, "Vicar of Christ." He decreed the concept of transubstantiation, confirmed confession to priests, and forbade the reading of the Bible in the vernacular. Pope Innocent III predicted that the world would end 666 years after the rise of Islam. He insisted Jews and Saracens wear distinctive dress within the Papal states.

Thirteenth Century

Pontificate	Name	Notes
18 Jul 1216 - 18 Mar 1227 (< 11 yrs)	**#177 Honorius III**	Born Cencio Savelli in Rome, Pope Honorius III was considered a talented administrator. He tackled Church reform and mediated numerous disputes. He helped organize the Fifth Crusade to restore the Kingdom of Jerusalem by first attacking Egypt. He appointed Frederick II of Sicily as the commander, but Frederick did not embark until after the death of Pope Honorius III, and the crusade was an abysmal failure.
19 Mar 1227- 22 Aug 1241 (14+ yrs)	**#178 Gregory IX**	Born in Anagni in the Papal States, Ugolino dei Conti di Segni, who became Pope Gregory IX, initiated the Papal Inquisition, starting in France and Germany. In 1232, Pope Gregory distributed a papal bull, *Vox in Roma*, declaring that cats bore Satan's spirit, and expressing deep concern about witches in Germany whose rituals (he believed) included cats. There followed a mass extermination of cats throughout Europe, which had an impact on the rat population and the spread of the bubonic plague 100 years later. He introduced the Inquisition in the Papal States. Gregory IX spoke out against the Jewish Talmud and had some texts publicly burned. He endorsed the northern crusades against the 'pagans' in the Baltic states. During his papacy in 1234, the Council of Tarragona prohibited possession of a Christian Bible in any Romance language.

25 Oct 1241 - 10 Nov 1241 **(16 days)**	**#179** **Celestine IV**	Goffredo Castiglioni from Milan became Pope Celestine IV, but he died before his coronation. He was the nephew of Pope Urban III. He was the first pope to be elected in a conclave of the college of cardinals, which was both very long and very contentious.
25 Jun 1243 - 7 Dec 1254 **(11+ yrs)**	**#180** **Innocent IV**	Born Sinibaldo Fieschi in Genoa, Pope Innocent IV clashed with the Holy Roman Emperor, Frederick II, who wanted Pope Innocent to lift his excommunication by Pope Gregory IX for failing to honor his crusading pledge. Pope Innocent summoned the First Council of Lyon to try to resolve the issue with Frederick, but he ended up condemning Frederick and urging an imperial replacement. This pope sold privileges and sanctioned inquisitions.
12 Dec 1254 - 25 May 1261 **(6+ yrs)**	**#181** **Alexander IV**	Born Rinaldo de Conti di Jenne in the Papal States, Pope Alexander IV was the nephew of Pope Gregory IX. Similar to Gregory IX, he was superstitious and cruel. He extended the Inquisition in France, giving his Inquisitor's carte blanche to determine multiple ways to exact torture and punishment. He generally followed the policies of Innocent IV. He tried in vain to organize a crusade against the Tatars.
29 Aug 1261 - 2 Oct 1264 **(3+ yrs)**	**#182** **Urban IV**	Born Jacques Pantaleon in Troyes, France, Urban IV was elected pope without being a cardinal. Pope Urban tried to mediate the conflict between Sicily and the Hohenstaufen dynasty, but he was not successful.
5 Feb 1265 - 29 Nov 1268 **(< 4 yrs)**	**#183** **Clement IV**	Born Gui Faucois in Saint-Gilles in France, Pope Clement IV followed the policies of Pope Urban IV regarding the conflict with the German Hohenstaufen family. He was also known for his interest in literature.
29 Nov 1268 - 1 Sep 1271 **(< 3 yrs)**	*interregnum*	Almost a 3-year period without a valid pope elected. This was due to a deadlock among cardinals voting for the pope.
1 Sep 1271 - 10 Jan 1276 **(4+ yrs)**	**#184** **Bd. Gregory X**	Elected by compromise after a 3-year impasse, Tebaldo Visconti who was born in Piacenza in the Papal States, became Pope Gregory X. His election was quite a surprise as he was engaged in a crusade at Acre with King Edward I of England. He established

the papal conclave system, the rules for which were defined at the Second Council of Lyons, which he convened in 1274. The Council lasted for many years.

21 Jan 1276 - 22 Jun 1276 (5 mos)	**#185 Bd. Innocent V**	Born Pierre de Tarentaise in Savoy (today's France), Pope Innocent V was the first Dominican pontiff. He established the papal look of wearing a white cassock. He unsuccessfully tried to launch another crusade.
11 Jul 1276 - 18 Aug 1276 (38 days)	**#186 Adrian V**	His uncle was Pope Innocent IV. From Genoa, Ottobuono di Fieschi died before he was consecrated or even ordained a priest, but he was recognized as Pope Adrian V at the time by virtue of accepting election. He annulled a papal bull of Pope Gregory X, which called for a committee to elect a new pope. Dante made him a character in his "Divine Comedy."
8 Sep 1276 - 20 May 1277 (8 mos)	**#187 John XXI**	Born Pedro Hispano in Lisbon, Portugal, Pope John XXI unsuccessfully attempted to launch another crusade. He pushed for a union with the Eastern Orthodox Church, and he tried to maintain peace among Christian nations. Due to some confusion over the numbering of popes named John in the 13th century, there was no John XX. Pope John XXI was killed in the collapse of his study.
25 Nov 1277 - 22 Aug 1280 (< 3 yrs)	**#188 Nicholas III**	Giovanni Gaetano Orsini of Rome, as Pope Nicholas III, restored senatorial and municipal power to Roman citizens. Accusations of corruption followed him throughout his time as pope. Nicholas III seems to have accepted that every cardinal was the agent of a political interest, and he exalted his own family. He appears in Hell in Dante's "Divine Comedy" for his practice of nepotism.
22 Feb 1281 - 28 Mar 1285 (4 yrs)	**#189 Martin IV**	Simon de Brion, born in Meinpicien in today's France, was a member of the Council of King Louis IX of France. He assumed the name of Pope Martin IV instead of Martin II due to a clerical error in misreading the names of two previous popes, Marinus II and Marinus III. Pope Martin IV was elected after a 6-month impasse ended with the imprisonment of two Italian cardinals by Charles of Anjou. He could not enter Rome due to his unpopularity as a French pope; he was entirely dependent on Charles of Anjou. Martin IV's political intrigues were disastrous.

2 Apr 1285 - 3 Apr 1287 (2 yrs)	**#190** **Honorius IV**	Born Giacomo Savelli in Rome, Pope Honorius IV was the grand nephew of Pope Honorius III. He pursued the pro-French policies of Pope Martin V. He favored religious orders avowing poverty. He opted for a more diplomatic approach to reconciling the political conflict in Sicily, but he was unable to reach a permanent resolution before his death.
22 Feb 1288 - 4 Apr 1292 (4 yrs)	**#191** **Nicholas IV**	Born Girolamo Masci in Lisciano in the Papal States, he was a Franciscan monk. He relied on the powerful Colonna family, and in return, he increased the number of Colonna cardinals. He mediated the end of the conflict between France and Aragon. In 1291, the loss of Acre ignited new enthusiasm for another crusade, but he died before he could implement his plans.
4 Apr 1292 - 5 Jul 1294 (2 yrs)	*interregnum*	This was a period of more than two years without a valid pope elected. This was due to a political deadlock among the cardinals voting for the pope. Too often in the Catholic Church, politics overshadowed ecclesiastical and spiritual responsibilities.
5 Jul 1294 - 13 Dec 1294 (161 days)	**#192** **St. Celestine V**	At age 79, Pietro da Morrone from Sicily was elected Celestine V to resolve a two-year impasse in what became the last non-conclave papal election. He filled the Roman Curia with supporters of King Charles II of Naples. His resignation after only five months was a canonical controversy, though many previous popes had abdicated. He was a poor choice for pope as he was weak and ineffective. For some reason, the Catholic Church made him a saint. He died in 1296. He is rumored to have been murdered in prison.
24 Dec 1294 - 11 Oct 1303 (< 9 yrs)	**#193** **Boniface VIII**	Elected by conclave after Pope Celestine V's resignation, Benedetto Caetani from Anagni in the Papal States, became Pope Boniface VIII. He imprisoned his predecessor, who nonetheless escaped, although he made no attempt to reclaim the papacy. In 1302, Boniface's bull, "Unam Sanctam," stated that every creature on earth was subject to the Roman pontiff and that there was no salvation outside the Church (*Extra Ecclesiam nulla salus*). This is a man who condoned pedophilia and who destroyed the town of Palestrina over a

331

personal feud. Opposed by Philip the Fair, Boniface VIII was captured in 1303, but he was freed by the Romans. He excommunicated the King of France, who then sent men to abduct and beat him; Pope Boniface VIII died a few weeks later. Dante Alighieri satirized him in his book, <u>The Inferno</u>, putting him in the eighth circle of Hell.'

Fourteenth Century

Pontificate	Name	Notes
22 Oct 1303 - 7 Jul 1304 **(259 days)**	**#194 Bd. Benedict XI**	Born Nicholas Boccasina in Treviso in the Papal States, he was a Dominican friar who was unanimously elected pope, and to restore peace with France, he pardoned Philip the Fair for the beating of Pope Boniface VIII. He worked hard to conciliate his predecessor's enemies. However, he refused to pardon either Sciarra Colonna, who led the attack on Pope Boniface VIII, or Guillaume de Nogaret, Philip's chief adviser, who denounced Boniface VIII at Paris in 1303. Pope Benedict died suddenly in Perugia, and many believed he was poisoned.
5 Jun 1305 – 20 Apr 1314 **(< 9 yrs)**	**#195 Clement V (Avignon)**	Raymond Bertrand de Got from Villandraut, France was Pope Clement V at Avignon, where he moved his Church administration, and he convened the Council of Vienne, 1311-1312. He initiated the persecution of the Knights Templar with the papal bull, *Pastoralis Praeeminentiae,* under pressure from King Philip IV of France. Via four additional papal bulls, Pope Clement established the procedures to prosecute the knights, disbanded them, and gave away their property. By creating a majority of French cardinals, Pope Clement V assured a line of French popes. Philip IV forced Pope Clement V to annul Pope Boniface VIII's bulls forbidding the clergy to pay subsidies to lay authorities. Pope Clement V practiced simony, openly favored his relatives, and appears to have secreted away a large treasure. He was censured in Dante's Inferno XIX.
20 Apr 1314 - 7 Aug 1316	*interregnum*	A 2-year period without a valid pope elected. This was due to a deadlock among cardinals voting for the pope.

7 Aug 1316 - 4 Dec 1334 **(18+ yrs)**	**#196** **John XXII** **(Avignon)**	At the age of 72, Jacques d'Euse from Cahors, France as Pope John XXII became the 2nd Avignon pope. He excommunicated Louis of Bavaria for failing to acknowledge the right of papal adjudication for a disputed imperial election. Louis retaliated by condemning Pope John XXII and establishing an antipope in Rome (1328). His controversial opinion on the Beatific Vision (the afterlife) clashed with the views of most theologians. His papal bull, *Super illius specula* (1326), prescribed that those who engage in witchcraft should be punished. Pope John XXII left a legacy of nepotism and scandalous financial dealings. John XXII involved himself in the politics and religious movements of many European countries in order to advance the interests of the papacy. He would routinely write to non-Catholic heads of state, asserting his authority over them.
May 1328 - Aug 1330	**Nicholas V** (antipope)	Installed by Louis IV (Holy Roman Emperor) in opposition to John XXII, he repented and received Pope John XXII's pardon in 1330.
20 Dec 1334 - 25 Ap 1342 **(7 + yrs)**	**#197** **Benedict XII** **(Avignon)**	Jacques Fournier from Saverdun, France was Pope Benedict XII at Avignon. He was a vigorous opponent of *heresies,* and he condemned *heretical* groups such as the Waldenses and the Cathars. As pope, he reformed monastic orders (he believed that the monks should live in poverty), and he opposed nepotism. He was unable to limit the conflict between England and France (Hundred Years' War), which began in 1337.
7 May 1342 - 6 Dec 1352 **(10+ yrs)**	**#198** **Clement VI** **(Avignon)**	Pierre Roger from Maumont, France was a pope at Avignon. Heavily biased toward France; more of a temporal ruler, with no qualms regarding nepotism. The Countess of Turrenne was his primary mistress. He reigned during the worst period of the Black Death. He dealt with the last of the crusades against the Muslims, the bankruptcies of his Florentine bankers, and the papal possessions in Italy, which were being contested by Italian nobles. He appointed 25 cardinals during his papacy; most were Frenchmen, and nearly half were his relatives.
18 Dec 1352 - 12 Sep 1362 **(< 10 yrs)**	**#199**	Etienne Aubert from Les Monts, France was Pope Innocent VI at Avignon. Elected with prior agreement to share power with the College of Cardinals, a pact he declared null, as he believed it was contrary to

	Innocent VI **(Avignon)**	Church law and papal power. He promoted some clerical and monastic reforms. Although he resided at Avignon, Innocent VI restored authority over the Papal States. Byzantine Emperor John Palaeologus offered to recognize the authority of the RCC and the pope in exchange for help against his rival, John IV Cantacuzenus. Pope Innocent VI declined this offer as he was preoccupied with other political issues closer to home.
28 Sep 1362 - 19 Dec 1370 **(8+ yrs)**	**#200** **Bd. Urban V** **(Avignon)**	Considered an Avignon pope, Guillaume (de) Grimoard from Grizac, France briefly restored the papacy to Rome in 1367, but he returned to Avignon in 1370. He followed the monasterial discipline from his time as a Benedictine monk, and he chose a simplistic lifestyle, instead of a lavish one. He also championed extensive reforms in the Church. He directed the Savoyard crusade in the Balkans.
30 Dec 1370 - 27 Mar 1378 **(7+ yrs)**	**#201** **Gregory XI** **(Avignon)**	Elected at Avignon, Pierre Roger de Beaufort from Maumont, France, the nephew of Pope Clement VI, became Pope Gregory XI. He resisted Milanese and Florentine attempts to acquire the papal states. Pope Gregory XI arrived in Rome in 1377, suppressed riots, but died of natural causes. The Romans demanded an Italian for the next pope. They would regret it.
8 Apr 1378 - 15 Oct 1389 **(11+ yrs)**	**#202** **Urban VI**	**Beginning of the Western Schism.** During the conclave of 1378 a Roman mob demanded an Italian pope. Bartolomeo Prignano from Naples was finally installed as Pope Urban VI, receiving submission of all cardinals, including those in Avignon. Within a few weeks, the 13 French cardinals at Rome left for Anagni; here, they declared the papal election illegitimate, later obtaining the support of the three Italian cardinals. In September, Charles V of France encouraged the cardinals to elect a new pope. They elected Clement VII, beginning the Western Schism. Urban VI was supported in most of Italy and Germany, and all of England, Ireland, and Portugal. Urban excommunicated Clement VII and his supporters. Urban VI drained Church resources in order to fund the War of the Eight Saints (a conflict between the pope and a Florence-led Italian coalition). His ecclesiastical decisions were considered disastrous. By reputation, he was violent, harsh, arrogant, and ill-tempered. Known to have

complained that he did not hear enough screaming when cardinals, whom he felt had conspired against him, were being tortured. He died of injuries sustained from falling from his mule.

Pontificate	Name	Notes
Sep 1378 - Sep 1394	**Clement VII** (antipope)	Born in Annecy, France and elected by the French conclave at Avignon in opposition to Urban VI. He is best known for leading a mercenary army against the city of Cesena in 1377, as a papal legate. After capturing the city, he ordered the massacre of thousands of civilians and earned the nickname, 'the Butcher of Cesena.'
2 Nov 1389 - 1 Oct 1404 **(15 yrs)**	**#203 Boniface IX**	**Western Schism.** Pietro Tomacelli from Naples, as Pope Boniface IX, abolished the municipal independence of Rome. He served as pope contemporaneously with Avignon antipopes, Clement VI and Benedict XIII. Pope Boniface IX viewed the Western Schism as a political problem. He declared himself the true pope, and he refused to step down.
Sep 1394 - May 1423 **(23 yrs)**	**Benedict XIII** (antipope)	Pedro Martínez de Luna from Illueca, Aragon was the successor of the Avignon claimant, Clement VII. He was deposed by the Council of Constance, which he did not recognize, but his following became negligible from that point until his death in 1423. He is known for issuing a number of decrees against the Jewish community.

Fifteenth Century		
Pontificate	**Name**	**Notes**
17 Oct 1404 - 6 Nov 1406 **(2 yrs)**	**#204 Innocent VII**	**Western Schism.** Prior to the election, Cosimo Migliorati from Sulmona in the Kingdom of Naples, who became Pope Innocent VII, and the other cardinals took an oath to end the schism by all possible means, even to the point of abdication. However, after some riots, Pope Innocent VII was forced to flee Rome in 1405 due to popular anger against his nephew, Cardinal Ludovico de Migliorati, who had insurrection leaders murdered. Pope Innocent VII returned the following year, after the Romans realized that Pope Innocent VII was not guilty of the murders.

30 Nov 1406 - 4 Jun 1415 (8+ yrs)	**#205** **Gregory XII**	**Western Schism.** Elected at Rome, Angelo Corraro from Venice became Pope Gregory XII. All candidates swore to abdicate the tiara if a rival pope would do the same, and Angelo Correr, who became Pope Gregory XII, repeated this oath after election. Seven of his cardinals secretly met with the Avignon cardinals and agreed to convene a general council at Pisa in 1409, which deposed both claimants and elected Alexander V as pope. Neither claimant recognized the Council of Pisa. Gregory XII abdicated during the Council of Constance, which had been called by his opponent John XXII.
Jun 1409 - May 1410	**Alexander V** (antipope)	Hoping to end the Western Schism, some Church leaders elected the Archbishop of Milan in a meeting in Pisa. But this was in defiance of both papal claimants in Rome and Avignon. Petros Philargos from Crete (Republic of Venice), as Alexander V, remained in Bologna, though Louis of Anjou occupied Rome in his name in 1410.
May 1410 - May 1415	**John XXIII** (antipope)	Successor of antipope, Alexander V, Baldassarre Cossa from Naples, was elected at Bologna as John XXIII (he was said to have bribed his way into office). He was referred to as the Pirate Pope, and he drove Benedict from Avignon in 1411, acquired the obedience of Naples, and convened a council in Rome in 1412. Driven from Rome by Ladislaus of Naples in 1413, he returned to Rome upon the death of the latter in 1414. Emperor Sigismund had John XXIII convoke the Council of Constance, and John initially presided over the council, which would eventually cause him to abdicate in 1415. John XXIII was a criminal who engaged in the practice of simony to raise money and was known to be a serial rapist. He was considered a legitimate pope until 1958, when the Pisan popes were reclassified as antipopes, and Angelo Roncalli assumed the title of John XXIII.
4 Jul 1415 - 11 Nov 1417	*Interregnum*	A two-year period without a valid pope elected.
11 Nov 1417 - 20 Feb 1431 (13+ yrs)	**#206** **Martin V**	In 1417, the Council of Constance resolved the **Western Schism**, although the antipopes continued their resistance for another two decades. The council secured the abdication of John XXIII and Gregory XII, while Benedict XIII fled to Spain, losing practically all his support. Oddone Colonna of Genazzano in the

Papal States, who became Martin V, was elected pope unanimously by a conclave of representatives of five nations. He did not occupy Rome until 1420. The Council of Constance required general councils every five years, so Martin convened a council at Pavia (moved to Siena) in 1423, only to dissolve it the next year. He promised to convene a new council in Basel within seven years. He convened the Council of Basel in 1431. Additionally, he initiated the Hussite Wars.

Jun 1423 - Jul 1429	**Clement VIII** (antipope)	In opposition to Pope Martin V, Gil Sanchez Munoz of Aragon became Clement VIII. He was a puppet of King Alfonso V of Aragon. When Alphonso and Martin V reconciled, Clement VIII immediately abdicated.
1424 - 1429	**Benedict XIV** (antipope)	In opposition to Pope Martin V, Bernard Garnier of France took the name Benedict XIV. He also countered an already reigning antipope, Clement VIII. Known as the "hidden pope," Benedict XIV conducted his office in secret. He had few followers, and he died in 1429.
1430 - 1437	**Benedict XIV** (antipope)	In opposition to Pope Martin V, a French relative of Bernard, Jean Carrier, also took the name of Benedict XIV in 1430 after the death of Bernard.
3 Mar 1431 - 23 Feb 1447 **(16 yrs)**	**#207 Eugene IV**	Gabriele Condulmer, who became Eugene IV, was born in Venice. He dissolved the Council of Basel, convoked by Pope Martin V, but the Council refused to disperse. Emperor Sigismund persuaded Eugene IV to recognize the Council as ecumenical in 1433. Pope Eugene fled to Florence after the Roman revolution in 1434. He transferred the ecumenical council from Basel to Ferrara, but a minority remained in Basel, eventually electing antipope Felix V. He crowned Sigismund emperor at Rome in 1433. Pope Eugene IV declared the Waldensians to be witches. In 1441, in *Cantate domino*, he stated that there was no salvation outside the RCC.
Nov 1439 - Apr 1449	**Felix V** (antipope)	Amadeus VIII, Duke of Savoy from Chambery, became Felix V. Elected by the Council of Florence in 1439, he accepted in 1440. He received little recognition outside Switzerland. He left Basel in 1442, and in 1449, he submitted to Nicholas V. He is

considered the last antipope. He also ruled as the Count of Savoy.

6 Mar 1447 - 24 Mar 1455 (8 yrs)	**#208 Nicholas V**	From the Republic of Genoa, Tommaso Parentucelli became Pope Nicholas V. He sponsored the Jubilee of 1450, and he crowned Frederick III emperor at Rome in 1452. He sought to make Rome the home of art and literature. Additionally, he strengthened fortifications, restored aqueducts, and rebuilt churches. By 1455, he had restored general peace to the Papal States. In 1453, Pope Nicholas V had ordered a fleet to aid Constantinople against the Turks, but it arrived too late. The city of Constantinople and the Byzantine Empire fell. Via a papal bull, he authorized the King of Portugal to send Muslims and pagans (e.g., African natives) into perpetual slavery. In another bull, *Romanus Pontifex*, he encouraged the enslavement of the New World natives.
8 Apr 1455 - 6 Aug 1458 (3+ yrs)	**#209 Callixtus III**	Born Alfonso de Borgia in the Kingdom of Valencia, Pope Callixtus III appointed two nephews as cardinals, one of whom became Pope Alexander VI. Ironically, Borgia was a compromise candidate chosen in lieu of the feuding noble families, the Orsini and the Colonnae. While the nepotism of Pope Callixtus III was widely resented, he did reopen the trial of Joan D'Arc, proclaiming her innocence.
19 Aug 1458 - 15 Aug 1464 (6 yrs)	**#210 Pius II**	Born Enea Silvio Piccolomini in the Republic of Siena, Pope Pius II tried to unite Europe in a great crusade against the Turks, but he was unsuccessful in garnering the support of the Christian rulers. In Italy, he slowly regained control of the Papal States. He was said to have fathered multiple illegitimate children, and he spoke openly about how he had seduced women.
30 Aug 1464 - 26 Jul 1471 (7 yrs)	**#211 Paul II**	Born in Venice, Pietro Barbo, who became Pope Paul II, was the nephew of Pope Eugene IV. His suppression in 1466 of the College of Abbreviators and the Roman Academy aroused much opposition. It was rumored that he filled the papal residence with his concubines.
9 Aug 1471 - 12 Aug 1484 (13 yrs)	**#212 Sixtus IV**	Born in the Republic of Genoa, Pope Sixtus IV, formerly Francesco della Rovere, did not represent the papacy well. He commissioned the Sistine

Chapel, and he authorized an Inquisition, targeting converted (Jewish) Christians in Spain. Pope Sixtus was known for his cronyism and nepotism to ensure that positions of power were held by his trusted friends and family, including eight nephews whom he appointed as cardinals. He exercised a large sexual appetite while Pope. He had six illegitimate children, allegedly including one with his sister.

Pontificate	Name	Notes
29 Aug 1484 - 25 Jul 1492 (8 yrs)	**#213** **Innocent VIII**	Born Giovanni Battista Cybo in Genoa, Pope Innocent VIII appointed Tomas de Torquemada to lead the Spanish Inquisition. He was the first pope to openly confirm his illegitimate children (he had at least 8). He made a practice of selling Church offices. He was a big supporter of witch hunting, which he blessed in 1484 in his papal bull, *Summis desiderantes,* and then he sent inquisitors to root out the witchcraft in Germany. While there is some debate about it, he appears to have commissioned the *Malleus Maleficarum,* and he clearly supported it once it was published. He was purported to have spent his final days drinking blood from three young boys (who all died) and sucking milk from a nursing young woman.
11 Aug 1492 - 18 Aug 1503 (11 yrs)	**#214** **Alexander VI**	Nephew of Callixtus III, Rodrigo de Lanzol-Borgia from the Kingdom of Valencia became Pope Alexander VI through bribery. He divided the extra-European world between Spain and Portugal in 1493 by the Bull, *Inter Caetera.* Father to Cesare Borgia and Lucrezia Borgia, he was renowned for multiple mistresses and many illegitimate children (estimated at nine). He put his family members in positions of power. He annulled marriages in exchange for alliances. He was famous for hosting a series of orgies and committing incest with his daughter, Lucretia. Considered by some historians to be the most corrupt pope of all. Upon the death of Alexander VI, the troops of his son, Cesare Borgia, seized the Vatican in an attempt to control the conclave electing the next pope.

Sixteenth Century

Pontificate	Name	Notes
22 Sep 1503 - 18 Oct 1503 (26 days)	**#215** **Pius III**	Nephew of Pius II, Francesco Todeschini Piccolomini was born in the Republic of Siena, and he became Pope Pius III. He has been given credit for initiating

some moral reforms combating nepotism. However, that is unlikely given that his uncle, Pope Pius II, appointed him the Archbishop of Siena and then a Cardinal-Deacon before Francesco reached the age of 21.

31 Oct 1503 - 21 Feb 1513 (9+ yrs)	**#216** **Julius II**	Nephew of Sixtus IV, Pope Julius II convened the Fifth Council of the Lateran in 1512. He took effective control of the whole territory of the Papal States for the first time. He commissioned Michelangelo to paint the Sistine Chapel ceiling. And he proposed plans for the rebuilding of St. Peter's Basilica. He was known as a patron of the arts. Born in Albisola, Republic of Genoa, Giuliano della Rovere chose his papal name in honor of Julius Caesar. Julius II was exceptionally wealthy, and he spearheaded the Italian Wars. He had a violent temper, and he was accused of multiple instances of sexual misconduct. He contracted severe syphilis. The Dutch philosopher, Erasmus, wrote a satire called <u>Julius Extended</u>, which was about Julius II's inability to get St. Peter to let him into heaven.
9 Mar 1513 - 1 Dec 1521 (< 9 yrs)	**#217** **Leo X**	Son of Lorenzo the Magnificent, Giovanni di Lorenzo de' Medici of the Republic of Florence extended the Inquisition into Portugal. Pope Leo X was a lavish and reckless spender. He had been made an archbishop as a child and a cardinal as a teenager. He viewed his ecclesiastic office as a source of revenue. Pope Leo led a costly war to secure power, and then he aggressively sold indulgences to fund the reconstruction of St. Peter's Basilica. When Martin Luther spoke out against the practice of selling indulgences and wrote the *Ninety-Five Theses*, Pope Leo excommunicated him, which led to the immediate rise in Lutheranism, and the next great schism - the Protestant Reformation.
9 Jan 1522 - 14 Sep 1523 (< 2 yrs)	**#218** **Adrian VI**	Born in Utrecht in the Holy Roman Empire, Adriaan Florenszoon Boeyens has been the only Dutch pope and was the last non-Italian to be elected pope until John Paul II in 1978. Pope Adrian VI was a compromise candidate when the Spanish and French cardinals were in deadlock. He served as tutor to Emperor Charles V, and he was a cousin of Pope Leo X. During his papacy, Rome was plundered by imperial troops ("Sacco di Roma"). Pope Adrian VI took up the task of reform, but he could accomplish

little with the opposition of the Italian cardinals. He refused to consider compromise with Lutheranism theologically, focusing his efforts on condemning Luther as a *heretic*.

26 Nov 1523 - 25 Sep 1534 (< 11 yrs)

#219 Clement VI

Another member of the de' Medici family, Giulio di Giuliano de' Medici from the Republic of Florence, became Pope Clement VII. He forbade the divorce of Henry VIII and crowned Charles V Emperor at Bologna in 1530. His niece, Catherine de' Medici, was married to the future Henry II of France. While Pope, Great Britain split from the Catholic Church. Clement VII was a cousin of Pope Leo X.

13 Oct 1534 - 10 Nov 1549 (15 yrs)

#220 Paul III

Opened the Council of Trent in 1545. Born Alessandro Farnese in Canino Lazio in the Papal States, or Pope Paul III, similar to his two immediate predecessors, proved not up to the task of containing the Protestant Revolution, much less enabling a rapprochement. In 1545, Paul III repealed an ancient law that enabled slaves to claim their freedom; he then affirmed the rights of Roman citizens to buy and sell slaves publicly. In 1548, Paul III authorized the purchase and possession of Muslim slaves in the Papal States. He offered Charles V his papal army to exterminate the Protestants in the Holy Roman Empire.

7 Feb 1550 - 29 Mar 1555 (5 yrs)

#221 Julius III

Born Giovanni Maria Ciocchi del Monte in Rome, Pope Julius III re-convened the Council of Trent because he wanted to reform the Church. However, political and military concerns led to a second suspension of the Council. He attempted to stop cardinals from receiving too many benefices and to restore monastic discipline. He was accused of homosexual relations with his adoptive nephew, whom he made a cardinal. Given that the lifestyle of Pope Julius III was characterized by banquets, gambling, hunting, masked balls, and other frivolities, he seemed personally ill-suited to fulfilling the ecclesiastical needs of the papacy.

9 Apr 1555 - 30 Apr 1555 (22 days)

#222 Marcellus II

To date, Marcello Cervini degli Spannochi was the last to use his birth name as a regnal name. Born in Montefano Marche in the Papal States, Pope Marcellus II had a reputation for integrity. His strong opposition to nepotism caused him to forbid his nephews from even visiting Rome. His promising papacy only lasted 22 days.

23 May 1555 - 18 Aug 1559 (4 + yrs)	**#223 Paul IV**	Elected due to powerful connections, Giovanni Pietro Carafa from the Kingdom of Naples is believed by many to be the worst pope of the 16th century. He established a Roman ghetto with physical walls to confine the poverty-stricken Jews. When traveling outside the ghetto but within the papal states, the Jewish men had to wear yellow hats, and the Jewish women yellow veils. That is where the Nazis would get their inspiration for the yellow markers. The ghetto walls were not dismantled until 1888. Pope Paul IV was a proponent of the Inquisition, and he expanded the scope of heresy and the number of crimes punishable by death. Additionally, he was such a prude that he ordered Michelangelo to repaint the nudes of the Last Judgment modestly. He did <u>not</u> reconvene the Council of Trent, which had been suspended since 1552.
26 Dec 1559 - 9 Dec 1565 (6 yrs)	**#224 Pius IV**	As so often happened with popes, Giovanni Angelo Medici, from the Duchy of Milan, was the compromise candidate. Because of the rise of Calvinism, Pope Pius IV reopened the Council of Trent in 1562, which concluded its proceedings in 1563. He said he wanted to bring an end to nepotism; yet he appointed his nephew as Cardinal Deacon to help stabilize his base. He reduced some of the power of the Inquisition which had been abused under Pope Paul IV.
7 Jan 1566 - 1 May 1572 (6+ yrs)	**#225 St. Pius V**	Born in the Duchy of Milan, Antonio Ghislieri was a Counter-Reformation pope who had previously served as Inquisitor General. During his papacy, the Inquisition eliminated all known Protestants in Italy. This hypocritical pope declared himself an avowed enemy of nepotism; yet he appointed his nephew a cardinal. He vigorously opposed a modernist interpretation of Catholic doctrine. He seemed to fight *heresies* around every corner. He is known for excommunicating Elizabeth I of England in 1570, in a papal bull, *Regnans in Excelis* (even though she was not nor had ever been a Catholic), and he urged the English Catholics to remove her from her throne. And the Catholic Church proclaimed this guy a saint?

13 May 1572- 10 Apr 1585 (< 13 yrs)	**#226** **Gregory XIII**	Born in Bologna in the Papal States, Pope Gregory VIII, Ugo Boncompagni, was a close friend of King Phillip II of Spain. In 1572, the St. Bartholomew's Day massacre of 4,000 French Protestants (Huguenots) left no hope for reconciliation of the Protestants to Catholicism. Indeed, Gregory XIII is said to have celebrated the Huguenot massacre.
24 Apr 1585 - 27 Aug 1590 (5+ yrs)	**#227** **Sixtus V**	Pope Sixtus V was born as Felice Peretti di Montalto in Grottammare in the Papal States. He limited the College of Cardinals to 70 in number. Prior to his papacy, he served twice as the Inquisitor General. He attempted to root out corruption (lawlessness and banditry) in Rome. He launched a rebuilding program. He wanted a law to execute anyone guilty of adultery, but he couldn't find enough support.
15 Sep 1590 - 27 Sep 1590 (12 days)	**#228** **Urban VII**	Born in Rome, Giovanni Battista Castagna was the shortest-reigning pope; he died before his coronation. He was viewed as a generous and honest pope. He subsidized bakers with his own funds to provide for the poor.
5 Dec 1590 - 15 Oct 1591 (< 1 yr)	**#229** **Gregory XIV**	Born Niccolo Sfondrati in the Duchy of Milan, Pope Gregory XIV made gambling on papal elections punishable by excommunication. However, his nepotism angered the cardinals, and the Roman citizens resented the food shortages and lawlessness that prevailed.
29 Oct 1591 - 30 Dec 1591 (62 days)	**#230** **Innocent IX**	Born Giovanni Antonio Facchinetti in Bologna in the Papal States, Pope Innocent IX supported King Philip of Spain and the Catholic League against King Henry IV of France. He established rules for Church property and prohibited its alienation (the transfer of ownership of ecclesiastical goods).
30 Jan 1592 - 3 Mar 1605 (13 yrs)	**#231** **Clement VIII**	Born Ippolito Aldobrandini in Fano Mare in the Papal States, Pope Clement VIII had a legal background. He initiated an alliance of European states to participate in a war with the Ottoman Empire, known as the Long War (1595). He expanded the Index of Forbidden Books and intensified the activities of the Inquisition, including the burning at the stake of Giordano Bruno for supporting Copernicus' heliocentric theory. He helped settle issues between the Jesuits and the Dominicans.

Seventeenth Century

Pontificate	Name	Notes
1 Apr 1605 - 27 Apr 1605 (26 days)	#232 Leo XI	Born in Florence, he was the last Medici pope and nephew of Pope Leo X; Alessandro Ottaviano de Medici served 26 days as Pope Leo XI. He was a compromise candidate between factions of the College of Cardinals. He was a conservative who wanted to defend Catholicism against the Reformation, but he soon died.
16 May 1605- 28 Jan 1621 (< 16 yrs)	#233 Paul V	Pope Paul V of Rome, also known as Camillo Borghese, was known for building projects, including the facade of St. Peter's Basilica. He restored much of the authority and privileges that had been taken away from the papacy in recent years. During the papacy of Pope Paul V, many theologians took exception to Galileo's scientific contributions. Pope Paul V censured Galileo and placed Copernicus's *Treatise of the Heliocentric Theory* on the Index of Forbidden Books. Paul V was guilty of nepotism and was responsible for his family's gain of inordinate wealth.
9 Feb 1621 - 8 Jul 1623 (2+ yrs)	#234 Gregory XV	Born Alessandro Ludovisi in Bologna in the Papal States. Pope Gregory XV issued a bull in 1621 that imposed secret ballots on conclaves. He also established the first permanent board of control for Roman Catholic foreign missions, the Congregation for the Propagation of the Faith.
6 Aug 1623 - 29 Jul 1644 (21 yrs)	#235 Urban VIII	Born in Florence in the Grand Duchy of Tuscany, Maffeo Vincenzo Barberini became Pope Urban VIII. During his tenure, the imprisonment, inquisition, and trial of Galileo Galilei occurred. He was the last pope to expand papal territory by force of arms. He issued a 1624 communique that declared the use of tobacco in holy places punishable with excommunication. His papacy covered 21 years of the Thirty-Year War. His papal debt substantially ballooned.
15 Sep 164 - 7 Jan 1655 (10+ yrs)	#236 Innocent X	Born Giovanni Battista Pamphilj in Rome, Pope Innocent X was the great-great-great-grandson of Pope Alexander VI. He attacked Pope Urban VIII's relatives, the Barberini, and he confiscated their properties. Pope Innocent X condemned five

doctrines of Jansenism as *heresy*. He increased the temporal power of the pope. He was guilty of nepotism. He supported the Spanish Habsburgs. By the end of this papacy, the prestige of his office had severely declined.

7 Apr 1655 - 22 May 1667 **(12 yrs)**	**#237 Alexander VII**	Born Fabio Chigi in the Republic of Florence, Pope Alexander VII was the great-nephew of Pope Paul V. Pope Alexander VII issued the doctrine of the Immaculate Conception of Mary; it is almost identical to that of Pius IX's two centuries later. His papacy was marked by an array of disputes. He confirmed the condemnation of Jansenism, a theological movement that emphasized the necessity of God's grace for salvation, which seemed too close to Protestantism for most Catholic theologians.
20 Jun 1667 - 9 Dec 1669 **(2+ yrs)**	**#238 Clement IX**	Born Giulio Rospigliosi in the Grand Duchy of Tuscany, Pope Clement IX was a patron of the arts. His papacy saw multiple disputes with France (King Louis XIV) who wanted to restrict papal power. He was unsuccessful in his attempt to safeguard Crete from the Ottomans. He revived the condemnation of Jansenism, which de-emphasized freedom of the will.
29 Apr 1670 - 22 Jul 1676 **(6+ yrs)**	**#239 Clement X**	Born Emilio Altieri Bonaventura in Rome, Pope Clement X promoted good relations among Christian nations. He established a new tax in Rome, which led to conflicts with his cardinals. He organized papal finances and gave Poland considerable aid against the Turkish invasion.
21 Sep 1676 - 11 Aug 1689 **(< 13 yrs)**	**#240 Bd. Innocent XI**	Born Benedetto Odescalchi in Milan, Pope Innocent XI inherited an insolvent papal treasury, but he was able to avert bankruptcy. He opposed Louis XIV's persecution of the Huguenots. He did pass strict rules in relation to the modesty of dress among women. He was somewhat sympathetic toward Jansenists, but he sentenced Miguel de Molinos, the proponent of Quietism (the doctrine of Christian perfection), to life imprisonment.
6 Oct 1689 - 1 Feb 1691 **(1+ yrs)**	**#241 Alexander VIII**	Born Pietro Vito Ottoboni in Venice, he is best known for his condemnation of Gallicanism, a French clerical and political movement that sought to limit papal authority. He opposed Jansenism. He

appointed his nephews to high positions, and he bestowed riches upon his relatives.

Pontificate	Name	Notes
12 Jul 1691 - 27 Sep 1700 (9 yrs)	**#242** **Innocent XII**	In 1692, Antonio Pignatelli from the Kingdom of Naples, as Pope Innocent XII, issued a bull, *Romanum decet Pontificem*, to end nepotism. He banned Cardinal-nephews from having a curial office; decreed that popes could not bestow land, offices, or revenue to their relatives; and no more than one relative could be groomed to become cardinal. He condemned Quietism as a *heretical* doctrine that believed that perfection consists of the passivity (quiet) of the soul, in the suppression of human effort, so that driven action may have full play.
23 Nov 1700 - 19 Mar 1721 (20 yrs)	**#243** **Clement XI**	Born in Urbino in the Papal States, Giovanni Francesco Albani lifted the Inquisition ban on reprinting Galileo's works, but he also issued a papal bull, *Unigenitus*, which condemned Jansenism as well as the reading of the Bible. He addressed the Chinese Rites controversy - a dispute among Catholic missionaries over the religiosity of Confucianism and Chinese rituals (such as ancestor worship). He was a benefactor of the Vatican Library; his interest in archaeology is credited with saving much of Rome's antiquity treasures.

Eighteenth Century		
Pontificate	Name	Notes
8 May 1721 - 7 Mar 1724 (< 3 yrs)	**#244** **Innocent XIII**	Born in Poli in the Papal States, Michelangelo de Conti became Pope Innocent XIII, and he aimed to end nepotism. He named three cardinals of the Church, one of whom was his brother. So much for Pope Innocent XII's efforts to end nepotism! He lent aid to the Venetians and the Maltese to fight the Turks. His papal bull (1484), *Summis desiderantes affectibus*, addressed the malign presence of witches and witchcraft in the Holy Roman Empire, and he authorized an Inquisition to review their activities.
29 May 1724 - 21 Feb 1730 (< 6 yrs)	**#245** **Benedict XIII**	Pope Benedict XIII, who was born in the Kingdom of Naples, Pietro Francesco Orsini, repealed the Church's worldwide tobacco-smoking ban set by Pope Urban VII and Pope Urban VIII. He was said to be fond of asceticism (rigorous self-denial) and religious celebrations. One of his contemporaries

said of him that he "did not have any idea how to rule."

12 Jul 1730 - 6 Feb 1740 (9+ yrs)	**#246 Clement XII**	As Pope Clement XII, Lorenzo Corsini from Florence presided over a growth of surplus in the papal finances. He went blind in 1732. He was the first pope to condemn freemasonry in a papal bull, *In eminenti,* issued on April 1738; and he threatened to excommunicate any Catholic who joined. He collected antiquities for the papal gallery.
17 Aug 1740 - 3 May 1758 (< 18 yrs)	**#247 Benedict XIV**	Born in Bologna in the Papal States, Prospero Lorenzo Lambertini, or Pope Benedict XIV, reformed the education of priests. Additionally, he authorized the publication of an edition of Galileo's complete scientific works.
6 Jul 1758 - 2 Feb 1769 (10+ yrs)	**#248 Clement XIII**	Born in Venice, Carlo della Torre Rezzonico, or Pope Clement XIII, is responsible for covering nude male statues in fig leaves in the Vatican. He pushed back on efforts to suppress the Jesuits, who were ruthlessly expelled from Spain, France, Portugal, Naples, and Sicily.
19 May 1769 - 22 Sep 1774 (5+ yrs)	**#249 Clement XIV**	Born in Sant' Arcangelo di Romagna in the Papal States, Giovanni Vincenzo Antonio Ganganelli was a member of the Conventual Franciscan Order. After a failed attempt to placate the anti-Jesuit secular powers through harsh measures against the Society, Pope Clement XIV issued a brief, *Dominus ac Redemptor*, on July 21, 1773, which formally suppressed the Society of Jesus (Jesuits).
15 Feb 1775 - 29 Aug 1799 24+ yrs	**#250 Pius VI**	A strong mutual dependency between the Catholic Church and the ruling nobility was evidenced when Count Giovanni Angelo Braschi from Cesena in the Papal States, as Pope Pius VI, condemned the French Revolution and the Declaration of the Rights of Man. Later, he was expelled from the Papal States by French troops from 1798 until his death.
29 Aug 1799 - 14 Mar 1800	*Interregnum*	A six-month period without a valid pope elected. This was due to unique logistical problems (the old pope died a prisoner, and the conclave was in Venice), and there was a deadlock among the cardinals voting.

Nineteenth Century

Pontificate	Name	Notes
14 Mar 1800 - 20 Aug 1823 (23+ yrs)	**#251** **SG. Pius VII**	Count Barnaba Niccolo Chiaramonti who was born in Cesena in the Papal States, became Pope Pius VII, and was present at Napoleon's coronation as Emperor of the French. However, Pius VII would soon oppose Napoleon, whom he excommunicated. The Pope was temporarily expelled from the Papal States by the French between 1809 and 1814. He directed all Bibles printed by Bible societies to be placed on the Index of Prohibited Books. Pope Pius excommunicated anyone involved with the Freemasons.
28 Sep 1823 - 10 Feb 1829 (5+ yrs)	**#252** **Leo XII**	Born in Spoleto in the Papal States, Count Annibale Melchiorre Girolamo della Genga, or Pope Leo XII condemned Bible societies and Bible distribution. He pursued a repressive temporal policy in the Papal States. He condemned differentism, a doctrine advocating the equality of all religions. He declared, "Everyone separated from the Catholic Church, however unblameable in other respects, has no part in eternal life."
31 Mar 1829 - 01 Dec 1830 (1+ yrs)	**#253** **Pius VIII**	Born in Cingoli in the Papal States, Francesco Saverio Castiglioni, or Pope Pius VIII, condemned masonic secret societies. He was very critical of new translations of the Christian Bible and denounced Bible societies. He was plagued with ill health throughout his papacy.
2 Feb 1831 - 1 Jun 1846 (15+ yrs)	**#254** **Gregory XVI**	Born in the Republic of Venice, Bartolomeo Alberto Cappellari, or Pope Gregory XVI, was the last non-bishop to be elected pope. He was politically opposed to democratic and modernizing reforms in the Papal States. He condemned the distribution of Christian Bibles. He was an ardent advocate of papal infallibility.
16 Jun 1846 - 7 Feb 1878 (31+ yrs)	**#255** **Bd. Pius IX**	Born in Senigallia in the Papal States, Giovanni Maria Mastai-Ferretti, or Pope Pius IX, was the ninth child of a minor count and a proponent of papal supremacy. Pius IX opened the First Vatican Council and lost the Papal States to Italy. Pope Pius IX led the RCC toward increasing centralization and consolidation of power in Rome and the papacy. He was the longest-serving pope in history. He condemned Bible societies as following in the steps

of "ancient heretics." He was the focus of an international scandal when his Papal Office kidnapped a Jewish boy from his parents, and whom Pius IX kept as his son, and refused to return him. In his papal bull, *Pastor Aeternus*, he defined papal infallibility. He promulgated the "Syllabus of Errors", a document he penned which condemned 80 propositions that the pope considered in error or heresy. He publicly referred to Jews as "dogs [that] we hear barking in all the streets and going around molesting people everywhere." In the 20th Century, Pius IX was nominated for sainthood for political reasons; the RCC soon regretted it.

Pontificate	Name	Notes
20 Feb 1878 - 20 Jul 1903 (25+ yrs)	**#256** **Leo XIII**	Born in Carpineto Romano, Italy, Gioacchino Vincenzo Raffaele Luigi Pecci laid down the seeds of Catholic social teaching through his encyclical, *Rerum Novarum* (On Capital and Labor). He accentuated the centralization of authority in the papacy, rather than in national churches. He claimed that he was appointed to be the Head of all Rulers. He is the third-longest reigning pope. He is renowned for heavily promoting the use of the rosary via eleven encyclicals. He did encourage a more progressive approach to faith and social reform than his four previous ultra-conservative pontiffs. He emphasized papal infallibility, pronounced Protestants as "enemies", and denounced "Americanism."

Twentieth Century

Pontificate	Name	Notes
4 Aug 1903 - 20 Aug 1914 (11 yrs)	**#257** **St. Pius X**	Born in Riese Pio X, Italy, Giuseppe Melchiorre Sarto, or Pope Pius X, expanded the reception of Holy Communion for children who attained the age of reason (about age 7). A staunch conservative, he vigorously condemned the theological movement he termed "modernization," which sought to reinterpret traditional Catholic teaching in light of new modern theories. He instituted a network of papal informants who made multiple accusations of *heresy* based on slim evidence. He opposed Christian democracy, which called for social and economic justice. When the French formally separated church from state, the act was condemned by Pius X.

3 Sep 1914 - 22 Jan 1922 (7+ yrs)	**#258 Benedict XV**	In his papal role, Giacomo Paolo Giovanni Battista Della Chiesa from the Kingdom of Sardina, has been credited with intervening for peace during World War I, while maintaining neutrality. Pope Benedict XV referred to WWI as "the suicide of civilized Europe."
6 Feb 1922 - 10 Feb 1939 (17 yrs)	**#259 Pius XI**	Born in Desio, Lombardy-Venetia, Pope Pius XI, Ambrogio Damiano Achille Ratti, signed the Lateran Treaty with Italy, establishing the Vatican City as a sovereign state. In 1928, he reaffirmed the RCC to be the <u>only</u> Church of Christ. He established Vatican Radio in 1931; and he was the first pope to broadcast over the radio. His papacy saw the rise of the dictator, Benito Mussolini. Indeed, his ties to Mussolini were deep and damaging to his reputation. He was a student of Hebrew, and he appears to have been thwarted in speaking out decisively against antisemitism (which he did not do).
2 Mar 1939 - 9 Oct 1958 (19+ yrs)	**#260 Vn. Pius XII**	Born in Rome, Pope Pius XII, or Eugenio Maria Giuseppe Giovanni Pacelli, has been considered weak and vacillating in his approach to Nazism. In 1951, Pius XII declared that the Big Bang theory didn't conflict with the Catholic concept of creation. He issued a decree that Catholics who professed communist views were to be excommunicated. In 1950, for the first time in Church's history, he invoked papal infallibility with the dogma of the Assumption of Mary, which was not mentioned anywhere in scripture. He instructed theologians that the human body may have evolved from earlier forms.
28 Oct 1958 - 3 Jun 1963 (4+ yrs)	**#261 St. John XXIII**	Born in Sotto il Monte, Bergamo, Italy, and sometimes called "Good Pope John", Angelo Giuseppe Roncalli, or Pope John XXIII, was universally loved. He chose to reuse the number XXIII, citing "twenty-two [Pope] Johns of indisputable legitimacy." [Apparently, he wasn't familiar with papal history.] He did condemn artificial contraception. He opened the Second Vatican Council (1962 - 1965), which saw some significant changes to the practice of Catholicism. John XXIII approved the celebration of mass in a vernacular language; the role of bishop was given more weight; the Roman Catholic Church officially abandoned its

"one true Church" stance; and the RCC formally ended its thousand-year schism with the Greek Orthodox Church (although they remained separate).

Pontificate	Name	Notes
21 Jun 1963 - 6 Aug 1978 (15+ yrs)	#262 St. Paul VI	From Concesio, Italy, Pope Paul VI, Giovanni Battista Enrico Antonio Maria Montini, was the last pope to be crowned with the Papal Tiara. He was the first pope to travel to the United States. He concluded the Second Vatican Council, which he closed in 1965, and then he implemented its decisions. He wrote the encyclical, *Humanae Vitae,* affirming the Church's stance against artificial birth control. He also reaffirmed the celibacy of priests.
26 Aug 1978 - 28 Sep 1978 (33 days)	#263 SG. John Paul I	Born Albino Luciani in Forno di Canale, Belluno, Italy, he was the first pope to use 'the First' in his regnal name. He was the first pope with two names (in memory of his two immediate predecessors). He refused to be crowned, opting for the simple pallium of an archbishop. He died suddenly and early into what had promised a charismatic reign. Due to the discovery of extensive corruption in the Vatican Bank and many discrepancies regarding his death, many conspiracy theories have surfaced. There was no autopsy performed, as the Church considers such action a desecration of the body.
16 Oct 1978 - 2 Apr 2005 (26+ yrs)	#264 St. John Paul II	Born in Wadowice, Poland, Karol Jozef Wojtyla was the first Polish pope and first non-Italian pope in 455 years. He canonized more saints than all his predecessors. He traveled extensively. He was the longest-serving pope since Pius IX (1846-1878). He reached out to other faiths, striving to build bridges. He was globally oriented, and he travelled extensively. He issued an apology on behalf of the Catholic Church for its actions (or lack of actions) in WWII. Tempering a controversial Vatican declaration on salvation, Pope John Paul II said that all who live a just life will be saved, even if they do not believe in Jesus Christ and the Roman Catholic Church.
Twenty-first Century		
Pontificate	Name	Notes
19 Apr 2005 - 31 Dec 2013) (< 8 yrs)	#265 Benedict XVI	From Marktl, Bavaria, Joseph Alois Ratzinger was the first German pope since Stephen IX in 1057. At age

78, Pope Benedict XVI was the oldest to become pope since Clement XII in 1730. Prior to being elected Pope, he was a theologian and the prefect of the Congregation for the Doctrinal Faith (the modern name for the Inquisition). As a cardinal, he was considered an ultra-conservative hard-liner, and he suppressed more liberal theologians. Pope Benedict XVI championed the superiority of the Catholic faith over other religions (in spite of Pope John XXIII having abandoned the "one true Church" position). In 2005, lawyers for Pope Benedict XVI asked President George W Bush for immunity against accusations that he conspired to cover up sexual abuse in the US Catholic parishes. He abdicated his position for health reasons.

3/13/2013 - 4/21/2025 (12 yrs)	**#266 Francis I**	Born Jorge Mario Bergoglio in Buenos Aires, Argentina, Pope Francis is the first pope to be born outside Europe since Gregory III (731–741), and the first from the Americas, as well as the first Jesuit to be elected pope. Considered by many to be a progressive papal reformer. Among many progressive acts, in 2016 Pope Francis declared June 22d as the feast day of Mary Magdalene, effectively declaring her a saint, correcting the misinformation professed by Pope Gregory I in 591.
5/08/2025 - Present	**#267 Leo XIV**	Born Robert Francis Prevost in Chicago, IL (USA), he became the first American pope; however, he is also a citizen of Peru. He is multilingual and belongs to the order of St. Augustine, which he led at one time. He has spent most of his life in Europe and Latin America.

Notes   Antipopes

Bad Popes

Avignon Popes

Sg = Servant of God = Venerable

Bd = Blessed

St = Saint

Appendix 2 – Catholic Heresies

Heresy	Description	Dates
1. **Naassenes** **(Gnostic)**	An early Gnostic sect from circa 100 CE. The Naassenes claimed to have been taught their doctrines by Mariamne. a disciple of James the Just. Declared a heresy by Bishop Hippolytus of Rome.	Early 2nd century
2. **Ophites** **or Ophians** **(Gnostic)**	The belief that the serpent who tempted Adam and Eve was a hero revealer and that the God who forbade Adam and Eve to eat from the tree of knowledge is the enemy. A dualistic theology that opposed a purely spiritual Supreme Being, who was both the origin of the cosmic process and the highest good, to a chaotic and evil material world. Dealt as heresy by Bishop Hippolytus of Rome.	2nd – 3rd centuries
3. **Docetism**	Belief that Jesus' physical body was an illusion, as was his crucifixion; that is, Jesus only seemed to have a physical body and to die physically, but in reality, he was incorporeal, a pure spirit, and hence could not physically die.	2nd – 3rd centuries
4. **Ebionites**	A Jewish-Christian sect that insisted on the necessity of following Jewish law and rites, which they interpreted in light of Jesus' expounding of the Law. They regarded Jesus as the Messiah, but not as divine. It was a form of Adoptionism. The term Ebionites derives from the Hebrew vionim (אביונים), meaning "the Poor Ones."	2nd – 5th centuries
5. **Sethianism** **(Gnostic)**	Has a Judaic foundation. The belief that the snake in the Garden of Eden was an agent of the true God; he brought knowledge of truth to Man. A Syrian sect whose origin goes back to the Ophites. They claimed to have secret knowledge that could unlock transcendent understanding	2nd century
6. **Marcionism**	An early Christian dualist belief system. Marcion affirmed Jesus Christ as the savior sent by God, and Paul as his chief apostle, but he rejected the Hebrew Bible and the Hebrew God. Marcionists believed that the wrathful Hebrew God was a separate and lower entity than the all-forgiving God of the New Testament. Originated in the teachings of Marcion of	Mid-2nd century – early 4th century

Sinope in Rome, circa 144. Marcionites perceived the world as a battleground with opposing forces of good and evil. Many early apologists, such as Tertullian in his *Adversus Marcionem* (year 207), condemned Marcionism.

7. Montanism	This was the belief that the prophecies of the Montanists superseded and fulfilled the doctrines proclaimed by the Apostles.It encompassed the view that Christians who fell from grace could not be redeemed. A stronger emphasis on the avoidance of sin and church discipline, emphasizing chastity, including forbidding remarriage. Montanism taught a radical enthusiasm, the imminent Second Coming of Christ, and a severe perfection, including abstinence from marriage. Named for its founder, Montanus, it originated in Phrygia, Anatolia. Although the orthodox mainstream Christian church prevailed against Montanism within a few generations, labelling it a heresy, the sect persisted in some isolated places into the 8th century.	$2^{nd} - 8^{th}$ centuries
8. Philanthropism	It is a denial of the virgin birth of Jesus. Belief that Jesus is merely human, that he never became divine, and that he never existed prior to his incarnation as a man. Proposed by Theodotus of Byzantium, a leather merchant in Rome, c. 190 CE, and later revived by Paul of Samosata. Rejected by the ecumenical councils, especially in the First Council of Nicaea (325 CE), which was convened to deal directly with the nature of Christ's divinity	$2^{nd} - 4^{th}$ centuries
9. Arabici	Belief that the soul perished with the body, and that both would be revived on Judgment Day. Founder unknown but associated with 3rd-century Christians from Arabia. In 250 CE, the Arabici were reconciled to mainline Christianity through the persuasive mediation of Origen.	Approx 210 - 250
10. Monarchianism	An over-emphasis on the indivisibility of God (the Father) at the expense of the other "persons" of the Trinity, leading to either Sabellianism (Modalism) or to Adoptionism. Monarchianism emphasizes God as one indivisible being, in direct contrast to Trinitarianism, which defines the Godhead as three co-eternal, consubstantial, co-imminent, and equally divine hypostases.	3rd century

11. **Adoptionism**	The belief that Jesus was not the Son of God for eternity, but he was adopted by God at some point. Adoptionism is one of two main forms of *Monarchianism* (the other being Modalism or Sabellianism), which considers God to be one while working through the different "modes" or "manifestations" of God the Father, God the Son, and God the Holy Spirit. In 798, Pope Leo III held a council in Rome that condemned the "Adoptionism" of Felix and anathematized him.	3rd century
12. **Sabellianism/** **Patripassianism**	Sabellianism is the belief that there is only one Person ('hypostasis' in the Greek language of the fourth-century Arian Controversy) in the Godhead. It is the view that the Father, Son, and Holy Spirit are three characterizations of one God, rather than three distinct "persons" in one God. In other words, it maintains that the Father, Son, and Holy Ghost are just different designations of the same subject. First formally stated by Noetus of Smyrna c. 190, refined by Sabellius c. 210, who applied the names merely to different roles of God in the history of salvation. He believed that the Father and Son are not two distinct persons, and thus God the Father suffered on the cross as Jesus. Sabellius was a priest who lived in Rome; he was excommunicated by the Bishop of Rome, Callixtus, in 220 CE.	3rd century
13. **Novatianism**	Held the strict view that refused re-admission to Christianity for baptized Christians who had lapsed in their faith (called *lapsi)* by denying their faith or who had performed a ritual sacrifice to a pagan god. Named after the theologian, Novatian (200 - 258), who opposed the bishop of Rome, Cornelius, because he thought the latter was too lenient in accepting lapsed Christians back into Christianity. Novatian was excommunicated by a synod in 251.	mid-3rd - mid-5th centuries
14. **Manichaeism** **(Gnostic)**	A major dualistic religion that posits that good and evil are equally powerful, with material things being inherently evil. Founded by Manes in the 3rd century CE. Condemned by Emperor Theodosius I and the RCC in 382. It was condemned by Emperor Theodosius in 382.	3rd – 7th centuries
	Denied the divinity of Jesus of Nazareth, but agreed that Jesus was created by the Father and that he had	

15. **Arianism**	a beginning in time, and that the title "Son of God" was just a courtesy. The doctrine is associated with Arius (c. AD 250–336), who lived and taught in Alexandrea, Egypt. Arius was first pronounced a heretic at the First Council of Nicaea; he was later exonerated as a result of imperial pressure and finally declared a heretic after his death. The heresy was officially resolved in 381 by the First Council of Constantinople.	290 CE Thru 7th century
16. **Quartode-** **ciman**	The Quartodeciman controversy in the Church was the question of whether to celebrate Easter on Sunday (the first day of the week) or Passover (the time of sacrifice of the Passover lamb). It involved the disputed chronology of Holy Week. This controversy pitted Christians from Asia Minor against those from Rome. Bishop Victor attempted to excommunicate the Quartodecimanists in 198 CE.	2nd – 4th centuries
17. **Donatism**	A movement that arose in North Africa. They opposed state interference in church affairs. Donatists believed that the Church had become corrupt and that only Donatists were true Christians. They were followers of Donatus who broke with the Catholics in 312 over the election of Caecilian as bishop of Carthage. In 347, Emperor Constantius I exiled Donatus to Gaul. In 411, a Catholic conference enacted severe laws against Donatism.	4th – 6th centuries
18. **Apollinarism**	The belief that Jesus had a human body and a lower soul (the seat of the emotions), but he had a divine mind. Proposed by Bishop Apollinarus of Laodicea who died in 390. Declared to be a heresy in 381 by the First Council of Constantinople. This heresy died out in only a few generations.	late 4th century
19. **Macedoni-** **anism**	While accepting the divinity of Jesus Christ as affirmed at Nicea in 325 CE, they denied that of the Holy Spirit, which they saw as a creation of the Son, and a servant of the Father and the Son. The name originated from the alleged founder, Bishop Macedonius I of Constantinople.	4th century
20. **Priscillianism** **(Gnostic)**	A Gnostic and Manichaean sect. Founded in the 4th century by Priscillian, derived from the gnostic-Manichaean doctrine taught by Marcus. Priscillian was put to death by the emperor Gratian. In the 6th century, Priscillianism declined and died out	4th – 6th centuries

soon after the Synod of Braga in 563. Condemned by the Synod of Zaragoza in 380

21. Pelagianism	The belief that original sin did not taint human nature and that mortal will is still capable of choosing good or evil without divine aid. It also taught that it was unjust to punish one person for the sins of another; therefore, infants are born blameless. Named after Pelagius (c. 355 – c. 420 AD), an ascetic and philosopher from the British Isles. The theology was later developed by Caelestius and Julian of Eclanum into a complete system, but it was refuted by Augustine of Hippo (who had for a time (385–395) held similar opinions, but who became the primary proponent of original sin.	5th century
22. Nestorianism	The belief that Jesus Christ was a natural union between the Flesh and the Word, thus he was not identical to the divine Son of God. Advanced by Nestorius (386–450), Patriarch of Constantinople from 428–431. The doctrine was developed in Nestorius' studies under Theodore of Mopsuestia at the School of Antioch. Condemned at the First Council of Chalcedon in 451, leading to the Nestorian Schism.	5th century
23. Semi-Pelagianism	Semi-Pelagianism flourished in southern Gaul until the mid-sixth century. Unlike the Pelagians, who denied original sin and believed in perfect human free will, the semi-Pelagians believed in the universality of original sin as a corruptive force in humanity. It taught that some come to faith by mercy and grace, but others through free will alone. Meant to be a compromise between Pelagians and Augustinians, this view arose in the East. The label "Semi-pelagianism" dates from the 17th century. Condemned by the Council of Orange in 529.	5th – 6th centuries
24. Monophysitism or Eutychianism	Belief that Christ's divinity dominates and overwhelms his humanity, as opposed to the Chalcedonian position, which holds that Christ has two natures, one divine and one human. Monophysitism teaches that Christ had only one nature after the incarnation. After Nestorianism was rejected at the First Council of Ephesus, Eutyches emerged with diametrically opposite views. Forms of monophysitism include: Apollinarians, Docetists, and Tritheists. Eutyches was excommunicated in 448. Monophysitism and	5th century

Eutyches were rejected at the Council of Chalcedon in 451.

25. Tritheism	Belief that the Father, Son, and Holy Spirit are three independent and distinct divine beings as opposed to three persons of one being and one essence. There have been several heresies that supported tritheism, such as the Monophysites. Tritheism was condemned at a synod in Alexandria in 616, and again at the Council of Constantinople (680–81).	4th – 7th centuries
26. Monothelitism	Belief that Jesus Christ had two natures, but He had only one will. This is contrary to the orthodox interpretation of Christology, which teaches that Jesus Christ has two wills (human and divine) corresponding to his two natures. Originated in Armenia and Syria in AD 633. A theological doctrine in Christianity that was ultimately rejected. Monothelitism was officially condemned at the Third Council of Constantinople (680–681).	7th century
27. Iconoclasm	The belief that icons are idols and should be destroyed. From late in the seventh century onwards, some parts of the Greek Orthodox Church reacted against the veneration of icons. In 726, Emperor Leo III ordered the destruction of all icons and persecuted those who refused. The policy continued under his successors. Condemned by the Council of Nicea II in 787, which regulated the veneration.	Late 7th century – mid-9th century
28. Bogomils (Gnostic)	A Gnostic dualistic sect that was both Adoptionist and Manichaean. Their beliefs were a synthesis of Armenian Paulicianism and the Bulgarian Slavonic Church reform movement. They believed that the visible, material world was created by the devil. Flourished in the Balkans in the mid-10th century, and it spread throughout the Byzantine empire, Serbia, Bosnia, Italy, and France. Named after its priest, Bogomil. Condemned as heresy by the Eastern Orthodox Church.	10th – 15th centuries
29. Catharism	Catharism had a strong dualist influence against the physical world, which was regarded as evil, and they denied that Jesus could become incarnate and still be the son of God. The last known Cathar prefect was Guillaume Bélibaste, who was executed in 1321. It professed a neo-Manichaean dualism (good vs. evil). They sought ways to convert to the spirit world	12th – 14th centuries

through fasting, abstinence, etc. First appeared in the Languedoc region of France in the 11th century and flourished in the 12th and 13th centuries. Condemned by the papal bull, *Ad abolendam*. Persecuted by the RCC and the French king, Louis IX.

30. Henricans

Henry of Lausanne rejected the doctrinal and disciplinary authority of the church; he believed that the gospels were to be freely interpreted as the sole rule of faith; he refused to recognize any form of worship or liturgy; and he condemned the Baptism of infants, the Eucharist, the sacrifice of the Mass, the communion of saints and the prayers for the dead. Henry lived in France in the first half of the 12th century. In 1135, Henry was brought before Pope Innocent II at the Council of Pisa, where he was condemned for heretical views and told to return to a monastery. In 1145, the bishop of Toulouse imprisoned him. He died imprisoned around 1148.

12th century

31. Waldensians (Waldenses or Vaudois)

An ascetic movement within Western Christianity before the Reformation. They rejected some sacraments. The Waldensians held that:
1) relics were no different from any other bones and should not be regarded as special or holy;
2) pilgrimage served only to spend one's money;
3) meat might be eaten any day of the week;
4) holy water was no more efficacious than rainwater; and that prayer was just as effectual if offered in a church or a barn.

By 1215, the Waldensians were not willing to recognize the prerogatives of local bishops over the content of their preaching, nor to recognize standards about who was fit to preach.

12th - 21st centuries

32. Lollardy

Lollards were effectively absorbed into Protestantism during the English Reformation. They rejected transubstantiation, the pope's powers, and many Roman Catholic rituals. Inspired by the teachings of John Wycliffe. England's King Henry IV passed the *De heretico comburendo* in 1401, which prohibited translating or owning the Bible and authorized burning heretics at the stake.

14th – 16th centuries

33. Hussites

The program of the Hussites is contained in the four articles of Prague, which were agreed upon in July 1420. These are often summarized as:
1) Freedom to preach the Word of God.

15th century

2) Celebrate the Lord's Supper with both types of bread (leavened and unleavened)

3) No secular power for the clergy.

4) Punishment for mortal sins.

Centered in Prague, they repelled two crusading attacks. Founded by Czech reformer Jan Hus (c. 1369–1415), who was one of the forerunners of the Protestant Reformation. Jan Hus was condemned by the Council of Constance (1414-1418) and burned at the stake.

34. Quietism

A religious movement within the Catholic Church that held that Christians should do nothing so as not to impede God's active will, and that men ought to remain silent. Quietism is usually identified with the doctrine of Miguel de Molinos, a Spanish priest who became an esteemed spiritual director in Rome during the latter half of the 17th century, and whose teachings were condemned as heretical by the RCC. Molinos's teachings were condemned by Pope Innocent XI in 1687, and he was sentenced to life in prison.

17th century

35. Jansenism

A theological movement within Roman Catholicism, primarily active in France, which arose as an attempt to reconcile the theological concepts of free will and the divine. It emphasized original sin, human depravity, the necessity of divine grace, and predestination. Originating in the writings of the Dutch theologian Cornelius Otto Jansen, Jansenism formed a distinct movement within the Catholic Church. It denied the role of free will in acceptance and application of grace. Condemned by Innocent X's bull, *Cum occasione,* on 31 May 1653, and by Pope Pius VI's *Auctorem fidei.*

17th – 18th century

36. Febronianism

An 18th-century German movement directed towards the nationalizing of Catholicism, the restriction of the power of the papacy in favor of that of the episcopate, and the reunion of the dissident churches with Catholic Christendom. It was a German religio-political doctrine expounded by Bishop Johann Nikolaus von Hontheim (under the pseudonym, Justinus Febronius). The doctrine imposed severe limitations on the pope, making him subject to a general council of bishops. Its practice and ideology were condemned by Pope Pius IX's Syllabus of Errors, Pope Leo XIII's

Late 18th century

encyclical *Immortale Dei*, and the First Vatican Council.

37. Gallicanism	Originating in France in the Middle Ages, this belief sought to regulate the relationship between the RCC and the state. It proclaimed that civil authority over the Catholic Church was comparable to that of the pope's authority. It was condemned by Pope Pius VI's *Auctorem fidei*.	19th century
38. Americanism	A group of related heresies was defined by the endorsement of full freedom of the press, liberalism, individualism, and separation of church and state, as well as an insistence upon individual initiative, which was considered incompatible with the principle of Catholicism, which emphasizes obedience to authority.	Late 19th – early 20th centuries
39. Modernism	Evolution of dogma in time and space. It was the belief that all doctrines are subject to change and that doctrines ought to change depending on the time and location. The heresy of modernism is the belief that there is an evolution in Catholic Church dogma over time and space. Condemned by Popes Leo XIII and Pius X in a series of encyclicals between 1893 and 1910.	Late 19th - early 20th centuries
40. Positive Christianity	It promoted the belief that the racial purity of the German people should be maintained by mixing racialistic Nazi ideology with either fundamental or significant elements of Nicene Christianity. Condemned by Pope Pius XI in his letter, *Mit brennender Sorge* in 1937.	20th century

Appendix 3 - Protestant Christian Sects

Sect	Beliefs	Founder
	Former Protestant Sects	
Huguenots	The Huguenots were followers of John Calvin. Huguenot was frequently used in reference to those of the Reformed Church of France from the time of the Protestant Reformation. By contrast, the Protestant populations of eastern France, in Alsace, Moselle, and Montbéliard, were mainly Lutherans. Today, there are some Reformed communities around the world that still retain their Huguenot identity, including Calvinists in the United Protestant Church of France and some in the Protestant Reformed Church of Alsace and Lorraine.	John Calvin
Puritanism	Puritans believed that it was necessary to be in a covenant relationship with God in order to be redeemed from one's sinful condition, that God had chosen to reveal salvation through preaching, and that the Holy Spirit was the energizing instrument of salvation. The moral and religious earnestness that was characteristic of Puritans was combined with the doctrine of predestination inherited from Calvinism to produce a "covenant theology," a sense of themselves as the elect chosen by God to live godly lives both as individuals and as a community.	It is generally agreed that this specific sect was over by 1740
	Historical Protestantism – 300–600 million	
Anabaptism (4 M)	Anabaptism is a Christian movement that originated during the 16th-century Protestant Reformation. Anabaptists believe that Baptism should be a voluntary choice of adults, not something that happens to infants. They also believe that the church should be separate from the government, and that citizens should be free to choose their own church affiliation. This group includes the Mennonites, German Baptists, Amish, and Hutterites.	Conrad Grebel and George Blaurock
Anglicanism (110 M)	Anglicanism is a Western Christian tradition that developed from the practices, liturgy, and identity of the Church of England following the English Reformation. It is one of the largest branches of Christianity. Anglicanism developed from the practices	Henry VIII

and identity of the Church of England and is a combination of Protestantism and Roman Catholicism. The word "Anglican" means "of England".

Baptist Churches (51 M adults)	Baptists are a denomination of Christianity distinguished by baptizing only professing Christian believers (believer's baptism) and doing so by complete immersion. Baptist churches generally subscribe to the doctrines of soul competency (the responsibility and accountability of every person before God), sola fide (salvation by faith alone), sola scriptura (the Bible is the sole infallible authority, as the rule of faith and practice), and congregationalist church government. Baptists recognize only two ordinances: Baptism and Communion.	Roger Williams and John Clarke
Congrega-tionalism (5 M)	Congregationalism in the USA consists of Protestant churches in the Reformed tradition that have a congregational form of church government and trace their origins mainly to Puritan settlers of colonial New England. In the 20th century, the Congregational tradition in America fragmented into three different denominations: (1) United Church of Christ, which resulted from a 1957 merger with the Evangelical and Reformed Church; (2) the National Association of Congregational Christian Churches, and (3) the Conservative Congregational Christian Conference.	Robert Browne
Continental Reformed (30 M)	Continental Reformed Protestantism is a part of the Reformed tradition within Protestantism that traces its origin in continental Europe. Prominent subgroups are the Dutch Reformed, the German Reformed, the Swiss Reformed, the French Huguenots, the Hungarian Reformed, and the Waldensian Church in Italy.	Ulrich Zwingli
Presbyter-ianism (40 M)	Presbyterian theology typically emphasizes the sovereignty of God, the authority of the Scriptures, and the necessity of grace through faith in Christ. Presbyterianism is based on the idea of a plurality of elders, or presbyters, who are elected by the congregation for fixed terms. The presbyters govern the church in a hierarchy of courts, with the general assembly being the highest legislative body. Predestination is a doctrine in Calvinism dealing with the question of the control that God exercises over the world.	John Calvin /John Knox

Episcopa-lianism (1.6 M)	The Episcopal Church (TEC), officially the Protestant Episcopal Church in the United States of America (PECUSA), is a member church of the worldwide Anglican Communion. It is a mainline Protestant denomination and is divided into nine provinces. The Church was organized after the American Revolution, when it became separate from the Church of England, whose clergy were required to swear allegiance to the British monarch. The Episcopal Church describes itself as "Protestant, yet catholic", and it asserts apostolic succession, tracing its bishops back to the apostles via holy orders.	Henry VIII / US Constitution
Restoration Movement (4M) **Church of Christ (2 M)**	The Church is a loose association of autonomous Christian congregations located around the world. Typically, their distinguishing beliefs are those of the necessity of Baptism for salvation and the prohibition of musical instruments in worship. Many such congregations identify themselves as being non-denominational. The Churches of Christ arose in the United States from the Restoration Movement of the 19th century via Christians who declared independence from denominations and traditional creeds. Churches of Christ generally share the following theological beliefs and practices: 1) Autonomous, congregational church organization without denominational oversight; 2) Refusal to hold to any formal creeds or informal "doctrinal statements" or "statements of faith", stating instead a reliance on the Bible alone for doctrine and practice; 3) Local governance by a plurality of male elders; and 4) Baptism by immersion of consenting believers.	There are multiple founders, including: Barton W. Stone, Thomas Campbell, and Alexander Campbell.
Lutheran-ism (70 - 90 M)	A branch of Protestantism that originated in the 16th century with the teachings of Martin Luther. Lutheranism is based on the idea that salvation comes through faith alone, the authority of Scripture, and the priesthood of all believers. Lutheranism retains many of the liturgical practices and sacramental teachings of the pre-Reformation Western Church, with a particular emphasis on the Eucharist, or Lord's Supper.	Martin Luther
Methodism (60 - 80 M)	Methodists interpret Scripture as teaching that the saving work of Jesus Christ is for all people (unlimited atonement) but effective only to those who respond and believe, in accordance with the Reformation	John Wesley

principles of sola gratia (grace alone) and sola fide (faith alone).

Moravian (Hussites) (1.2 M)	The Moravian Church is one of the oldest Protestant denominations in Christianity. The Bohemian Brethren were held to a strict obedience to the Sermon on the Mount, which included non-swearing of oaths, non-resistance, and not accumulating wealth. The modern Moravian Church, with about 900,000 members worldwide, continues to draw on traditions established during the 18th-century renewal.	Gregory the Patriarch
Plymouth Brethen (The Brethren) (1 M)	The Plymouth Brethren are a conservative, evangelical denomination whose history can be traced to Dublin, Ireland, in the late 1820s, originating from Anglicanism. Brethren generally see themselves not as a denomination, but as a network, or even as a collection of overlapping networks, of like-minded independent churches. Although the group refused for many years to take any denominational name to itself, a stance that some of them still maintain.	John Nelson Darby
The Religious Society of Friends (Quakerism) (.4 M)	The central unifying doctrine of this religious movement is the priesthood of all believers. Many Friends view themselves as members of a Christian denomination. They include those with evangelical, holiness, liberal, and traditional conservative Quaker understandings of Christianity. Unlike many other groups that emerged within Christianity, the Religious Society of Friends has actively tried to avoid creeds and hierarchical structures.	George Fox
Reformed Church in America (RCA) (190,000)	From its beginning in 1628 until 1819, it was the North American branch of the Dutch Reformed Church. The RCA is the oldest Protestant denomination in the United States. The Reformed Church in America (RCA) is a mainline Reformed Protestant denomination in Canada and the United States. It has about 84,957 members. Due to differences related to the adoption of the Belhar Confession, the removal of the conscience clauses related to the ordination of women, and the place of LGBTQ people in the church, a number of congregations have left the RCA to join the Presbyterian Church in America, which is more conservative on these issues.	Jonas Michaelius

Seventh Day Adventists (22.3 M)	Adventism began in the 19th century in the context of the Second Great Awakening revival in the United States. The name refers to belief in the imminent Second Coming (or "Second Advent") of Jesus Christ. The denomination grew out of the Millerite movement in the United States during the mid-19th century, and it was formally established in 1863. The Seventh-day Adventist Church (SDA) is the largest Adventist Protestant Christian denomination, which is distinguished by its observance of Saturday, the seventh day of the week in the Christian (Gregorian) and the Hebrew calendar, as the Sabbath, its emphasis on the imminent Second Coming (advent) of Jesus Christ, and its annihilationist salvation of humanity.	William Miller

Modern Protestantism – 400–500 million

Pentecost-alism (170 - 280 M)	Pentecostalism is a Charismatic Christian movement that emphasizes direct personal experience of God through Baptism with the Holy Spirit. The term Pentecostal is derived from Pentecost, an event that commemorates the descent of the Holy Spirit upon the Apostles and other followers of Jesus Christ while they were in Jerusalem celebrating the Feast of Weeks, like other forms of evangelical Protestantism. Pentecostalism adheres to the inerrancy of the Bible and the necessity of the 'new birth,' an individual repenting of their sin and "accepting Jesus Christ as their personal Lord and Savior. It includes the Assemblies of God, the Apostolic Church, the International Circle of Faith, the Church of God in Christ, and the Church of God.	Charles Fox Parham

Nontrinitarian Restorationism – 43-65 million

Church of the Latter Day Saints (Mormons) (18 M)	Established during the Second Great Awakening, the church is headquartered in Salt Lake City, Utah, and it has established congregations and built temples worldwide. According to the Church, as of 2023, it has over 17.2 million members, of which over 6.8 million live in the U.S. Church theology is restorationist and non-trinitarian; the Church identifies as Christian, in-cluding a belief in the doctrine of salvation through Jesus Christ and his substitutionary atonement on behalf of mankind. It is often included in the lists of larger Christian denominations, though some Catholics, mainline Protestants, and evangelicals have considered	Joseph Smith

the church to be distinct and separate from mainstream Christianity.

Christian Scientist (.4 M)	Christian Science is a set of beliefs and practices which are associated with members of the Church of Christ, Scientist. Adherents are commonly known as Christian Scientists or students of Christian Science, and the Church is sometimes informally known as the Christian Science Church. It was founded in 1879 in New England by Mary Baker Eddy, who wrote the 1875 book Science and Health with Key to the Scriptures, which outlined the theology of Christian Science. The church does not require that Christian Scientists avoid medical care—adherents use dentists, optometrists, obstetricians, physicians for broken bones, and vaccination when required by law—but it maintains that Christian Science prayer is most effective when not combined with medicine.	Mary Baker Eddy
Oneness Pentecostal (Apostolic, Jesus' Name Pentecostalism) (10 - 30 M)	Oneness Pentecostalism is a non-trinitarian religious movement within the Christian family of churches known as Pentecostalism. It derives its name from its teaching on the godhead, a form of modalistic Monarchianism commonly referred to as the Oneness doctrine. The doctrine states that there is one God—a singular divine spirit with no distinction of persons—who manifests himself in many ways, including as Father, Son, and Holy Spirit. This stands in sharp contrast to the mainstream doctrine of three distinct, eternal persons posited by Trinitarian theology. Oneness Pentecostals differ from most other Pentecostals and Evangelicals in their views on the salvation of humanity, believing that true saving faith is demonstrated by repentance, full-submersion water Baptism, and Baptism in the Holy Spirit with the evidence of speaking in tongues.	Frank Ewart and Glenn Cook
Unitarian-ism (800,000)	Unitarianism is a nontrinitarian branch of Christianity that originated in the 16th century in Poland and Transylvania. Unitarians believe in one God, rather than the Trinity of the Father, Son, and Holy Spirit. They believe that Jesus was a man who was inspired by God and saved humanity, but he was not equal to God. Unitarianism was established in order to restore an early version of Christianity. Likewise, Unitarian Christians generally reject the doctrine of original sin. Unitarianism does not constitute one single Christian denomination; rather, it refers to a collection of both	The movement was influenced by many writers, including Ferenc Dávid, Michael Servetus,

existing and extinct Christian groups (whether historically related to each other or not) that share a common theological concept of the unitary nature of God.

Juan de Valdes, and Bernadine Ochino.

www.ingramcontent.com/pod-product-compliance
Lightning Source LLC
Chambersburg PA
CBHW080900120626
46555CB00008B/2889